R. Gupta's®

POPULAR MASTER GUIDE

KVS–PGT

Kendriya Vidyalaya Sangathan – Post Graduate Teachers

SUBJECT

GEOGRAPHY

Recruitment Exam

by

RPH Editorial Board

2026
EDITION

RAMESH PUBLISHING HOUSE, NEW DELHI

Published by
O.P. Gupta *for* Ramesh Publishing House

Admin. Office
12-H, New Daryaganj Road, Opp. Officers' Mess,
New Delhi-110002 ✆ 23275224, 23245124

E-mail: info@rameshpublishinghouse.com
For Online Shopping: www.rameshpublishinghouse.com

Showroom
● Balaji Market, Nai Sarak, Delhi-6 ✆ 23253720, 23282525
● 4457, Nai Sarak, Delhi-6, ✆ 23918938

Book Code: R-1153

ISBN: 978-81-7812-869-6

Price: ₹ 310

Printed at: B.K. Offset Press, Delhi

CONTENTS

❑❑❑

Scheme of Written Examination

<table>
<tr><td>Test Duration</td><td colspan="2">180 Minutes</td></tr>
<tr><td>Total Questions</td><td colspan="2">180 Objective Type Multiple Choice Questions</td></tr>
<tr><td>Total Marks</td><td colspan="2">180 Marks</td></tr>
<tr><td>Section Name</td><td>Marks per Question</td><td>No. of Questions</td></tr>
<tr><td colspan="3">Part-I : Proficiency in Languages (20 marks)</td></tr>
<tr><td>1. General English</td><td rowspan="2">01 mark per question</td><td>10</td></tr>
<tr><td>2. General Hindi</td><td>10</td></tr>
<tr><td colspan="3">Part-II : General Awareness, Reasoning & Proficiency in Computers (20 marks)</td></tr>
<tr><td>1. General Awareness & Current Affairs</td><td rowspan="3">01 mark per question</td><td>10</td></tr>
<tr><td>2. Reasoning Ability</td><td>5</td></tr>
<tr><td>3. Computer Literacy</td><td>5</td></tr>
<tr><td colspan="3">Part-III : Perspectives on Education and Leadership (40 questions & 40 marks)</td></tr>
<tr><td colspan="3">Part-IV : Subject-Specific (Geography) (100 questions & 100 marks)</td></tr>
<tr><td colspan="3">PROFESSIONAL COMPETENCY TEST: 60 MARKS
(Demo Teaching-30 marks and Interview-30 marks)</td></tr>
</table>

Previous Years' Paper

Kendriya Vidyalaya Sangathan (KVS)

PGT–GEOGRAPHY

Recruitment Exam, 2023

(Exam held on 18-02-2023)

1. Eratosthenese, coining the term geography for the first time, belongs to which one of the following groups of scholar?
   A. Arab Scholar
   B. French Scholar
   C. Roman Scholar
   D. Greek Scholar

2. Which one of the following disciplines has interface with Geographical thoughts?
   A. Anthropology B. Economics
   C. Philosophy D. Sociology

3. In which one of the following Epochs, modern man appeared on the earth?
   A. Holocene B. Pleistocene
   C. Pliocene D. Miocene

4. Which one of the earth's layers is in liquid state?
   A. Crust
   B. Outer core
   C. Inner core
   D. Upper most mantle

5. A large body of magmatic material cools in the deeper depth of the crust forming large dome is termed by which one of the followings?
   A. Caldera B. Sills
   C. Batholith D. Dyke

6. Name of the minor plate located between South America and Pacific Plate:
   A. Cocos Plate
   B. Nazca Plate
   C. Arabian Plate
   D. Phillippine Plate

7. Which one of the following is the important characteristic of Mid-Atlantic Ridge?
   A. Divergent boundary
   B. Convergent boundary
   C. Subduction zone
   D. Transform boundary

8. Which one of the following landmasses was NOT the part of Gondwanaland?
   A. Africa B. Madagascar
   C. Australia D. Siberia

9. In which of the following climatic regions, the depth of weathered materials is maximum?
   A. Tundra B. Steppe
   C. Tropical forest D. Desert

10. Which one of the following is NOT involved in exogentic forces?
    A. Erosion B. Metamorphism
    C. Transportation D. Deposition

1. D	2. C	3. A	4. B	5. C	6. B	7. A	8. D	9. C	10. B

11. Which one of the following statements is NOT correct about the process of soil formation?
A. Parent material is passive control factor in soil formation
B. Soils will be thin on steep slopes
C. Humus accumulation in cold climates is fast due to fast bacterial growth
D. Dead plants provide humus to soil

12. Which one of the followings is a characteristic of old stage of landscapes developed by running water?
A. Streams meander freely over vast flood plains
B. Shallow V-shaped valleys
C. Waterfalls and rapids
D. V-shaped deep valleys

13. Which one of the following statements is correct about Point bars?
A. They are low, linear and parallel deposited ridges along the river banks
B. They are loop-like channels
C. They are alluvial fans developed at foothills
D. They are formed on concave side of meanders of large rivers

14. The highest peak Mt. Everest is an example of which landform?
A. Cirque B. Horn
C. Arete D. Col

15. Which one of the following landforms offer the first defence against tsunami?
A. barrier B. beach dune
C. off-shore bars D. mangroves

16. Radio waves transmitted from the earth are reflected back to the earth by which one of the following layers of atmosphere?
A. Stratosphere B. Troposphere
C. Mesosphere D. Ionosphere

17. Which one of the following will be the angle of Sun rays at Tropic of Capricorn when the sun is overhead at Tropic of Cancer?
A. 47° B. 66½°
C. 43° D. 23½°

18. Which one of the following statements is NOT correct about the factors controlling the temperature of air at any place?
A. Compared to sea, land heats up and cools down slowly
B. The places near the sea-level record higher temperature
C. The temperature generally decreases with increasing height
D. Compared to land the sea gets heated slowly and looses heat slowly

19. The highest range of temperature between January and July is recorded over:
A. Central-Africa
B. North-eastern part of Asia
C. Interior part of Australia
D. Coastal part of Canada

20. In which part of the world, temperature inversion is normal throughout the year?
A. Equatorial areas
B. Desert areas
C. Inner areas of continents
D. Polar areas

21. Due to which one of the following reasons, maximum insolation is received over the subtropical deserts?
A. Due to slant sun rays in these regions
B. Here the cloudiness is the least
C. The length of days is shorter here
D. Due to advection process

22. Which one of the followings is the average temperature of the earth at sea-level?
A. 11.2°C B. 13.2°C
C. 15.2°C D. 17.2°C

11. C	**12.** A	**13.** D	**14.** B	**15.** C	**16.** D
17. D	**18.** A	**19.** B	**20.** D	**21.** B	**22.** C

. In which one of the following directions the wind blows at the equator?
A. Perpendicular to the isobars
B. Easterlies
C. Westerlies
D. North-East

. Identify the correctly matched pair of cell and its region of circulation.
A. Hadley cell – Polar region
B. Hadley cell – Temperate region
C. Walker cell – Polar region
D. Ferrel cell – Temperate region

5. Which one of the following fronts of temperate cyclone is associated with rainfall and snowfall?
A. Cold front
B. Stationary front
C. Warm front
D. Occluded front

6. The tropical cyclones originating in the Atlantic ocean are known as:
A. Hurricanes B. Typhoons
C. Willy-willies D. Cyclones

7. Which one of the followings forms on cold surfaces when condensation takes place below freezing point temperature?
A. Dew B. Fog
C. Frost D. Clouds

8. Identify the correct pair of cloud and its description:
A. Stratus – feathery appearance
B. Nimbus – black and dark gray
C. Cirrus – look like cotton wool
D. Cumulus – layered clouds

9. Which one of the followings is the normal lapse rate of temperature in the troposphere?
A. 9.5°C/km B. 8.5°C/km
C. 7.5°C/km D. 6.5°C/km

30. Which one of the followings Koeppen's climate types is characterised by no dry season with warm and cool summer?
A. Cfb B. BSk
C. BWh D. EF

31. Higher salinity is recorded in the North Sea due to which one of the following?
A. Due to high evaporation
B. Due to influx of river waters in large quantity
C. Due to more saline water brought by the North Atlantic Drift
D. Due to influx of melted water from the Arctic ocean

32. Which one of the followings is the general rate of decrease of ocean surface temperature from equator towards poles?
A. 0.3°C/latitude B. 0.5°C/latitude
C. 0.8°C/latitude D. 1.1°C/latitude

33. Which one of the followings is a flat topped submerged seamount?
A. Atoll B. Guyot
C. Seamount D. Submarine Canyon

34. In which one of the followings, the water particles only travel in a small circle?
A. Tides B. Ocean currents
C. Surges D. Waves

35. Identify the country from the following, in which mega diversity centre is NOT located?
A. Netherlands B. Madagascar
C. China D. India

36. The Kobe-Osaka region of Japan is thickly populated. The basic reason of this is:
A. Fertile soils
B. Presence of a number of industries
C. Favourable landscape
D. Government offers incentives

23. A	24. D	25. C	26. A	27. C	28. B	29. D
30. A	31. C	32. B	33. B	34. D	35. A	36. B

37. In the crude birth rate formula, CBR = $\frac{B_i}{P} \times 1000$; 'P' stands for:
A. Population of the area on 31st December
B. Population of the area on 1st January
C. Population of the area on 1st April
D. Mid-year Population of the area

38. The increase of world population from 3 billion to 4 billion took which one of the following durations?
A. 15 years B. 30 years
C. 100 years D. 50 years

39. Which one of the following approaches to human development was initially proposed by the International Labour Organization?
A. Income Approach
B. Welfare Approach
C. Basic Needs Approach
D. Capability Approach

40. The age-sex pyramid of which one of the following countries is bell-shaped?
A. Nigeria B. Japan
C. India D. Australia

41. Which one of the followings is the sub-field of Social Geography?
A. Resource geography
B. Medical geography
C. Agriculture geography
D. Industrial geography

42. Which one of the followings is the characteristics of first stage of demographic transition?
A. High fertility and high mortality
B. High fertility and low mortality
C. Low fertility and low mortality
D. Low fertility and high mortality

43. In high latitude zones, food gathering practised in ....
A. Amazon basin
B. Tropical Africa
C. Northern Canada
D. Papua New Guinea

44. The slash and burn agriculture is know by which one of the followings in Centr America?
A. Jhuming B. Ladang
C. Tamrai D. Milpa

45. Which one of the following regions commercial dairy farming is the largest the world?
A. South-Eastern Australia
B. North-Western Europe
C. New Zealand
D. Canada

46. Mumbai's Dabbawala (tiffin) activities com under which one of the followings?
A. Primary activities
B. Secondary activities
C. Tertiary activities
D. Quaternary activities

47. Which one of the followings is a persona means of communication?
A. Radio
B. Television
C. E-mail
D. Newspaper

48. Which one of the followings is 'Gold colour worker?
A. Consultants
B. Bank officials
C. Insurance service providers
D. Computer operators

37. D	38. A	39. C	40. D	41. B	42. A
43. C	44. D	45. B	46. C	47. C	48. A

. Which one of the followings, does NOT involve quarternary activity?
A. Collection of information
B. Production of i..formation
C. Dissemination of information
D. Dealing in banking services

. Highly mechanised, high per person yield but low per acre yield is associated with which one of the following types of agriculture?
A. Intensive subsistence agriculture
B. Extensive commercial grain cultivation
C. Mixed farming
D. Primitive subsistence agriculture

1. Identify the correct descending sequence (large scale to small scale) of following maps:
A. Topographical map – Atlas map – Wall map – Cadastral map
B. Wall map – Atlas map – Cadastral map – Topographical map
C. Topographical map – Cadastral map – Wall map – Atlas map
D. Cadastral map – Topographical map – Wall map – Atlas map

2. Which one of the following instruments is used to calculate area on a map?
A. Rotameter B. Anemometer
C. Planimeter D. Hygrometer

3. At which one of the following longitudes it will be 6 a.m., when the time at Greenwich is 1 p.m.?
A. 75° W B. 105° W
C. 75° E D. 105° E

4. Which one of the following projections is drawn when the source of light is placed at infinity distance from the globe?
A. Orthographic B. Gnomonic
C. Stereographic D. Mercator

55. Which one of the followings represents the latitudinal and longitudinal coverage of a topographical map on 1 : 50,000 scale?
A. 1° × 1°
B. 15′ × 15′
C. 15′ × 7′30″
D. 30′ × 30′

56. In a standard False Colour Composite (FCC) image, which one of the following colours is assigned to Infrared radiation?
A. Violet B. Green
C. Red D. Blue

57. Which one of the following towns is NOT correctly matched with its functional class?
A. Administrative Town – Chennai
B. Cultural Town – Varanasi
C. Mining Town – Dhanbad
D. Recreation and Health Town – Broken Hill

58. Which one of the following percentages is for present world urban population?
A. 33% B. 45%
C. 56% D. 48%

59. Who applied the term 'megalopolis' for the super-metropolitan region extending as union of conurbations?
A. Patrick Geddes
B. Walter Burley Griffin
C. Le Corbusier
D. Jean Gottaman

60. Which one of the followings is NOT an inland port?
A. Hoogli
B. Athens
C. Manchester
D. Duisburg

49. D	**50.** B	**51.** D	**52.** C	**53.** B	**54.** A
55. B	**56.** C	**57.** D	**58.** C	**59.** D	**60.** B

61. Which one of the following Trans-continental railway routes runs through Uspallata Pass?
A. Trans-Siberian
B. Trans-Canadian
C. Trans-South American
D. Trans-Australian

62. Which one of the following regional bloc is correctly matched with its headquarter?
A. ASEAN – Bangkok
B. CIS – Minsk
C. EU – Vienna
D. OPEC – Brussels

63. Rhine waterway is navigable from Rotterdam to which one of the following places?
A. Basel, Switzerland
B. Stuttgart, Germany
C. Dortmund, Germany
D. Nancy, France

64. Which one of the following statements is NOT correct?
A. Big Inch pipeline is in USA
B. Trans-continental Stuart Highway is in Australia
C. Alaska Highway extends from Los Angeles to Anchorage in Alaska
D. Trans-Canadian Highway links Vancouver and St. John's city

65. Which one of the following sea trade routes is called the 'Big Trunk Route'?
A. The Northern Atlantic sea route
B. Suez canal route
C. Panama canal route
D. The North Pacific sea route

66. Which one of the following is the World's largest land-locked harbour?
A. Vishakhapatnam
B. San Francisco
C. Sao Paulo
D. Maracaibo

67. During which one of the following y General Agreement for Tariffs and T (GATT) was transformed into World T Organization (WTO)?
A. 1948 B. 1987
C. 1995 D. 1998

68. Kochchi port is located on which one the following coasts?
A. Malabar coast B. Coromandel c
C. Andhra coast D. Odisha coast

69. The Tropic of Cancer does not pass thro which one of the following states of In
A. Rajasthan B. Jharkhand
C. Tripura D. Manipur

70. Karewa is found in which one of following parts of the Himalayas?
A. Kashmir Himalaya
B. Himachal Himalaya
C. Uttarakhand Himalaya
D. Sikkim Himalaya

71. Dhaoladhar mountain range is part of wh one of the following mountain ranges?
A. Greater Himalaya
B. Lesser Himalaya
C. Shiwaliks
D. Trans-Himalaya

72. Saddle peak, the highest peak of Andar and Nicobar islands is located in which of the following islands?
A. Great Nicobar
B. North Andaman
C. Middle Andaman
D. South Andaman

73. Gersoppa (Jog) fall is located on which of the following rivers?
A. Juari B. Kalinadi
C. Brahmani D. Sharavati

61. C	62. B	63. A	64. C	65. A	66. B	67. C
68. A	69. D	70. A	71. B	72. B	73. D	

74. According to Koeppen's classification Uttar Pradesh has mainly which type of climate?
A. Cwg B. As
C. Amw D. Dfc

75. The average annual rainfall variability is highest in which one of the following states?
A. Assam B. Rajasthan
C. Meghalaya D. Chhattisgarh

76. The location of which one of the following Biosphere Reserves is NOT correctly matched?
A. Nokrek – Meghalaya
B. Agasthyamalai – Kerala
C. Seshachalam – Karnataka
D. Simlipal – Odisha

77. Silver firs, junipers and rhododendrons trees are common in which one of the following altitudinal ranges in Himalayas?
A. 1000 - 2000 m B. 2000 - 3000 m
C. 3000 - 4000 m D. 4000 - 5000 m

78. Which of the following soils are rich in iron oxide and aluminium compounds due to intense leaching?
A. Laterite soils B. Red soils
C. Black soils D. Alluvial soils

79. Which of the following is commonly added to solve the problem of soil salinity?
A. Gypsum B. Urea
C. Potash D. Phosphate

80. Which one of the following decades represents the International Decade for Natural Disaster Reduction?
A. 1990-2000 B. 2000-2010
C. 2010-2020 D. 1980-1990

81. The Kachchh region of Gujarat falls under which one of the following earthquake damage risk zones?
A. Low Damage Risk zone
B. Moderate Damage Risk zone
C. High Damage Risk zone
D. Very High Damage Risk zone

82. Frequency of cyclonic storms in India is highest during which of the following months?
A. April-May B. May-June
C. July-August D. October-November

83. Trans-Himalayan area of Ladakh and Spiti falls under which one of the following Landslide Vulnerability zones?
A. Very High Vulnerability zone
B. High Vulnerability zone
C. Moderate to Low Vulnerability zone
D. Safe from landslides

84. Which one of the following natural disasters is grouped under atmospheric origin?
A. Flood B. Cyclone
C. Landslide D. Avalanche

85. Which one of the following statements is **correct**?
A. Noise pollution is measured in Dobson units
B. Bronchitis disease is caused by water pollution
C. Urban smog is caused by atmospheric pollution
D. Urban solid waste is collected and disposed efficiently in non-metropolitan cities of India

86. Which one of the following statements is **correct**?
A. Jhabua district is located in Maharashtra
B. Jhabua district has high concentration of Gond tribe
C. In Jhabua administration managed Common Property Resources without people participation
D. Watershed management approach improved livelihoods of people in Jhabua

74. A	75. B	76. C	77. C	78. A	79. A	80. A
81. D	82. D	83. C	84. B	85. C	86. D	

87. National Waterway no. 3 is operational in which one of the following states?
A. Kerala B. Andhra Pradesh
C. Odisha D. Assam

88. In which year the satellite IRS-1A was launched by India?
A. 1975 B. 1983
C. 1988 D. 1992

89. Hill Area Development Programme was initiated in which one of the following Five Year Plans?
A. Third B. Fourth
C. Fifth D. Sixth

90. Dalli-Rajhara iron ore mines are located in which one of the following states?
A. Odisha B. Chhattisgarh
C. Karnataka D. Jharkhand

91. Kakarapura nuclear power project is located in which of the following states?
A. Rajasthan B. Karnataka
C. Gujarat D. Uttar Pradesh

92. Due to topographical, hydrological and other constraints which one of the following percentages represents the available surface water for utilization in India?
A. 60 per cent B. 48 per cent
C. 32 per cent D. 71 per cent

93. About 90 per cent of India's surface and ground water is utilised by which one of the following sectors?
A. Agriculture
B. Urban
C. Power and Industry
D. Domestic

94. Which one of the following river basins is located to the southernmost?
A. Krishna B. Godavari
C. Kaveri D. Tapi

95. The Water Cess Act was introduced during which one of the following years?
A. 1974 B. 1977
C. 1986 D. 1997

96. Which one of the following statements is **correct**?
A. Neeru-Meeru programme is related to Tamil Nadu state
B. Ralegan Siddhi is a small village in Ahmadnagar district of Maharashtra.
C. Jal Kranti Abhiyan for food security was launched in 2017-18
D. Arvary Pani Sansad is active in afforestation in North Bihar

97. Which one of the followings represents Net Sown Area in India during 2014-15?
A. 307.82 million hectare
B. 140.13 million hectare
C. 15.09 million hectare
D. 119.00 million hectare

98. According to FAO Agriculture Statistics India was rank 1 in world production during 2018 in which one of the following crops?
(*a*) Rice (*b*) Wheat
(*c*) Jute (*d*) Sugarcane

Choose the **correct** option:
A. (*a*), (*c*) and (*d*)
B. (*c*) and (*d*)
C. Only (*c*)
D. Only (*d*)

99. Which one of the following Cotton textile industry centres is located in northernmost location?
A. Ujjain B. Kanpur
C. Aurangabad D. Ahmedabad

100. Which one of the following districts is NOT in Telangana state?
A. Warangal B. Nalgonda
C. Medak D. Nellore

87. A	**88.** C	**89.** C	**90.** B	**91.** C	**92.** C	**93.** A
94. C	**95.** B	**96.** B	**97.** B	**98.** C	**99.** B	**100.** D

EXPLANATORY ANSWERS

1. **(D):** Eratosthenes, who coined the term "geography" for the first time, was a Greek scholar. He is also known for calculating the Earth's circumference and for his work in various fields such as mathematics, astronomy, and geography.

2. **(C):** Every discipline has a philosophy that provides roots to a discipline, and in the process of its evolution; it also experiences distinct historical processes. Thus, the history of geographical thought as the mother branch of geography is included in its curricula.

3. **(A):** Humans appeared on the earth around 6 million years ago. The evolutionary path of humans is through Pliocene, Pleistocene and finally finishes in Holocene. The modern human or Homo sapiens arises in the Holocene.

4. **(B):** The Earth's outer core is in a liquid state. This layer is composed mainly of molten iron and nickel, and its movement is responsible for generating Earth's magnetic field.

5. **(C):** A large body of magmatic material that cools at greater depths in the Earth's crust, forming a large dome, is called a Batholith. A batholith is an extensive, deep-seated plutonic intrusion that has solidified from molten magma beneath the Earth's surface. Over time, erosion may expose the batholith at the surface, often forming a large, dome-shaped structure.

6. **(B):** The Nazca Plate is located off the west coast of South America and is bounded by the Pacific Plate to the west and the South American Plate to the east. It is associated with the subduction zone where the Nazca Plate is being pushed beneath the South American Plate, leading to volcanic activity in the Andes mountain range.

7. **(A):** At the Mid-Atlantic Ridge, the tectonic plates are moving away from each other. This is characteristic of a divergent boundary, where new oceanic crust is formed as magma rises from the mantle and solidifies at the ridge, pushing the plates apart.

8. **(D):** Gondwanaland was a supercontinent that included the landmasses that are now Africa, Madagascar, Australia, South America, Antarctica, and the Indian subcontinent. Siberia, however, was not part of Gondwanaland; it was part of the northern landmasses that eventually formed the Laurentia (North America) and Eurasia plates after the break-up of the supercontinent Pangaea.

9. **(C):** In tropical forests, the combination of high temperatures, heavy rainfall, and a dense vegetation cover leads to intense weathering of rocks. The organic acids from plant roots and decaying matter, along with the constant moisture, accelerate the breakdown of rocks and minerals. This results in the formation of deeply weathered soils, often referred to as laterites, which can be quite deep.

10. **(B):** Exogenic forces are external forces that operate at or near the Earth's surface. They include processes like weathering, erosion, transportation, and deposition. These forces generally work to break down and shape the Earth's surface.

    Metamorphism, on the other hand, is a process that occurs deep within the Earth's crust due to high temperature and pressure. It is associated with endogenic forces, which are internal processes that involve the Earth's internal heat and pressure, leading to the formation of new rocks from existing ones.

11. (C): Humus accumulation in cold climates is generally slow, not fast. This is because bacterial and microbial activity, which is responsible for decomposing organic matter and forming humus, slows down significantly in cold temperatures. In colder climates, decomposition is much slower due to lower microbial activity, meaning humus accumulation is not fast.

12. (A): In the old stage of a river's lifecycle (also known as the mature or old-age stage), the landscape is typically characterized by Streams meandering. As rivers mature, they tend to develop meanders, which are large bends in the river. This occurs in flatter, more level areas where the river has less gradient and more energy to flow laterally. The river forms floodplains, which are wide, flat areas adjacent to the river that are periodically inundated during floods.

13. (D): A point bar is a depositional feature found in rivers. It forms on the inside (concave) bend of a meander. As the river water moves in a curved path around a meander, it slows down on the inside bend (the concave side). This decrease in velocity allows the river to deposit sediments, creating a point bar, which is typically made up of sand and gravel.

14. (B): A horn is a sharp, pyramid-shaped peak that is formed by the erosion of glaciers from multiple directions. In the case of Mt. Everest, it is the result of glacial erosion on all sides of the peak, which has created its steep, pointed summit.

15. (C): A ridge of sand and shingle formed in the sea in the off-shore zone (from the position of low tide waterline to seaward) lying approximately parallel to the coast is called an off-shore bar.

An off-shore bar which is exposed due to further addition of sand is termed a barrier bar.

The coastal off-shore bars offer the first buffer or defence against storm or tsunami by absorbing most of their destructive force. Then come the barriers, beaches, beach dunes and mangroves, if any, to absorb the destructive force of storm and tsunami waves. So, if we do anything which disturbs the 'sediment budget' and the mangroves along the coast, these coastal forms will get eroded away leaving human habitations to bear first strike of storm and tsunami waves.

16. (D): The ionosphere is a layer of the Earth's atmosphere that is capable of reflecting or refracting radio waves back to the Earth's surface. This is due to the presence of ionized particles (electrons and ions) in the ionosphere, which interact with electromagnetic waves, such as radio waves, and cause them to be reflected or refracted.

The ionosphere is located roughly between 30 km and 1,000 km above the Earth's surface, spanning parts of the mesosphere and the thermosphere.

17. (D): When the Sun is directly overhead at the Tropic of Cancer (which occurs around the Summer Solstice on June 21st), the angle of the Sun's rays at the Tropic of Capricorn (which is located at 23½°S latitude) will be 23½°.

This is because the Tropic of Cancer is at 23½° North, and during the Summer Solstice, the Sun is directly overhead at this latitude. Conversely, at the same time, the Sun's rays will be 23½° away from being directly overhead at the Tropic of Capricorn, which is on the opposite side of the Earth at 23½° South.

18. (A): The statement that is NOT correct about the factors controlling the temperature of air at any place is Compared to sea, land heats up and cools down slowly. This statement is incorrect because, in fact, land heats up and cools down more quickly than the sea. Water has a higher specific heat capacity than land, meaning it can absorb more heat without a significant change in temperature.

As a result, land areas tend to experience greater temperature fluctuations compared to coastal areas, which are moderated by the presence of water.

19. (B): The highest range of temperature between January and July is recorded over: North-eastern part of Asia. This region experiences extreme continental climate with very hot summers and extremely cold winters, leading to a high range of temperature differences throughout the year.

20. (D): In polar areas (both the Arctic and Antarctic regions), temperature inversion is normal throughout the year. In these regions, the ground cools rapidly during the long polar nights, and since the air above it remains warmer, it leads to a temperature inversion. Normally, in the atmosphere, temperature decreases with altitude. However, during an inversion, the air near the surface is colder than the air above it, which can trap pollutants and create stable weather conditions. This phenomenon is more common in polar regions due to the lack of sunlight during long winters.

21. (B): The subtropical deserts (such as the Sahara, Kalahari, and Arabian deserts) receive maximum insolation due to several factors, but the primary reason is that cloudiness is the least in these regions. Clear skies in subtropical deserts allow the sun's rays to reach the Earth's surface directly, leading to high levels of solar radiation or insolation. The dry air and lack of significant cloud cover mean that little energy is reflected or absorbed by the atmosphere.

22. (C): The average temperature of the Earth at sea level is approximately 15.2°C. This value represents a general estimate of the global average surface temperature, taking into account various factors such as geographic location, altitude, and seasonal variations.

23. (A): At the equator, the Coriolis force is zero and the wind blows perpendicular to the isobars. The low pressure gets filled instead of getting intensified. This explains why tropical cyclones are not formed near the equator.

24. (D): Hadley Cell: This cell is found in the tropical region (between the equator and about 30° latitude) and is not related to the polar or temperate regions. It is characterized by warm air rising at the equator and sinking around 30° latitude.

Ferrel Cell: This cell is located in the temperate regions (between 30° and 60° latitude). It operates between the Hadley Cell and the Polar Cell. Air rises around 60° latitude (near the subpolar low) and sinks around 30° latitude.

Walker Cell: This is a type of atmospheric circulation associated with the tropical Pacific Ocean, not the polar regions. It involves east-to-west flow and is significant in phenomena like El Niño and La Niña.

25. (C): Warm fronts typically bring steady, prolonged precipitation as warm, moist air rises over cooler air. This can lead to widespread rain or snow, depending on the temperature.

However, it's worth noting that other fronts, such as cold fronts and occluded fronts, can also be associated with precipitation, but warm fronts are particularly known for their association with extended periods of rain or snow. Cold fronts can bring more intense but shorter-duration precipitation, while occluded fronts can also lead to complex weather patterns, including precipitation.

26. (A): Tropical cyclones originating in the Atlantic Ocean are known as hurricanes. In the Pacific Ocean, they are called typhoons, and in the Indian Ocean, they are referred to as cyclones. "Willy-willies" is a term used in Australia for a type of small-scale whirlwind, not for tropical cyclones.

27. (C): Frost forms on cold surfaces when condensation occurs below the freezing point of water. It happens when water vapour in the air changes directly into ice crystals without becoming liquid first, typically on surfaces that are below 0°C (32°F).

28. **(B):** Checking options:
   A. **Stratus:** These are low, gray clouds that often cover the entire sky like a blanket, but they do not have a feathery appearance.
   B. **Nimbus:** This term refers to rain-bearing clouds, which can appear dark gray or black, especially when they are thick and heavy with moisture.
   C. **Cirrus:** These clouds are high-altitude clouds that have a wispy, feathery appearance.
   D. **Cumulus:** These clouds are puffy and white, resembling cotton wool, and are not layered.

   Hence, correct option is (B).

29. **(D):** The normal lapse rate refers to the rate at which the temperature decreases as you go higher in the atmosphere, specifically in the troposphere. The troposphere is the lowest layer of Earth's atmosphere, where most weather phenomena, including clouds, storms, and precipitation, occur. The normal lapse rate is about 6.5°C per kilometer. This means that, on average, for every 1 kilometer (1,000 meters) you go up in altitude, the temperature drops by approximately 6.5°C.

   This lapse rate is a general average, and it can vary depending on several factors like weather conditions, geographical location, and time of day. For instance, on particularly sunny or clear days, the lapse rate might be different from cloudy or rainy days due to the distribution of heat and moisture in the atmosphere.

30. **(A):** Köppen's climate type Cfb is characterized by a temperate oceanic climate. This climate type has:
   - No dry season (precipitation is fairly consistent throughout the year).
   - Warm summers and cool winters, with a mild overall temperature range.

   Here's a brief explanation of the other options:
   - **BSk:** This is a semi-arid climate (steppe climate) with dry conditions and more precipitation in the summer.
   - **BWh:** This refers to a hot desert climate (arid), typically very dry with high temperatures.
   - **EF:** This is a polar climate, characterized by permanent ice and snow with temperatures too cold for significant plant growth.

31. **(C):** The North Atlantic Drift is an extension of the Gulf Stream, which originates in the Gulf of Mexico. This current carries warm, saline water north-eastward across the Atlantic Ocean. Influence on North Sea: As the North Atlantic Drift reaches the North Sea, it brings with it warmer and saltier water. This influx of more saline water raises the overall salinity levels of the North Sea.

32. **(B):** At the equator, the sun's rays strike the Earth most directly, leading to higher surface temperatures. This region receives the most solar energy, heating the ocean surface significantly. Average sea surface temperatures can exceed 28°C (82°F) in some equatorial regions.

   As we move from the equator towards the poles, the angle of the sun's rays becomes more oblique. This means the same amount of solar energy is spread over a larger surface area, reducing the intensity of heating. The general rate of decrease is approximately 0.5°C per latitude. This means that for every degree of latitude you move away from the equator, the ocean surface temperature decreases by about 0.5°C (0.9°F).

   In polar regions, the sun's rays are very oblique, and during winter months, there is little to no sunlight. As a result, these areas have much colder ocean surface temperatures.

33. (B): A Guyot is a flat-topped, submerged seamount. It is a type of underwater mountain that has been eroded and flattened by wave action or other environmental forces, typically due to the movement of tectonic plates. Guyots are commonly found in the deep ocean.

34. (D): In waves, the water particles move in a small circular motion. As a wave passes, the water particles move up and down in a circular or elliptical pattern, but they don't travel along with the wave. The particles return to their original position after each wave crest passes.

35. (A): The Netherlands is not considered a mega-diverse country. Mega-diverse countries are those that harbor a large number of species, particularly those found nowhere else on Earth, and are important for biodiversity conservation. The countries that are considered mega-diverse include Madagascar, China, and India, which all have rich and unique ecosystems.

36. (B): The Kobe-Osaka region, also known as the Keihanshin region, is one of the most densely populated areas in Japan. This is primarily due to the presence of a large number of industries, which have driven urbanization, economic development, and job opportunities in the area. The region is home to major industrial hubs, including manufacturing, shipping, and high-tech industries. These industries attract people for employment, leading to thick population settlement in the region.

37. (D): In the crude birth rate (CBR) formula, CBR = (Number of births / Mid-year population) × 1000, the "P" represents the mid-year population of the area. This population figure is typically used to account for the population size at the midpoint of the year, providing a more accurate representation for calculating birth rates over the course of the year.

38. (A): The world population increased from 3 billion to 4 billion between the years 1960 and 1974, which took approximately 14 years. However, the closest available option to this time span is 15 years, making it the best answer among the choices provided.

39. (C): The Basic Needs Approach to human development was initially proposed by the International Labour Organization (ILO) in the 1970s. This approach focuses on ensuring that individuals have access to the basic necessities of life, such as food, shelter, education, and healthcare, to improve their standard of living and overall well-being. It emphasizes meeting the fundamental needs of people for sustainable development and human dignity.

40. (D): A bell-shaped age-sex pyramid typically represents a population with low birth and death rates, often found in more developed countries. Australia has a relatively stable population with lower birth rates and a longer life expectancy, resulting in an age-sex pyramid that appears bell-shaped, with a relatively even distribution across age groups and fewer young dependents compared to countries with high birth rates.

41. (B): Medical geography is a sub-field of social geography that focuses on the spatial distribution of health-related phenomena, diseases, healthcare facilities, and the relationship between environment and health. It examines how geographic factors influence health outcomes and the availability of medical services.

While Resource geography, Agricultural geography, and Industrial geography are all important sub-fields of geography, they are typically considered more focused on physical or economic geography rather than social geography.

42. (A): In the first stage of the demographic transition, both birth rates (fertility) and death rates (mortality) are high. Populations tend to grow slowly because high birth rates are offset by high mortality rates, often due to factors like poor healthcare, high infant mortality, and limited access to resources. This stage is typically associated with pre-industrial societies.

43. (C): In high latitude zones, such as Northern Canada, food gathering (including hunting, fishing, and foraging) is commonly practiced due to the harsh climate and the limited availability of agriculture. In these areas, traditional subsistence activities like hunting game (e.g., caribou, seals) and fishing are essential for survival, as the cold climate makes farming difficult.

44. (D): In Central America, Milpa refers to the traditional system of slash-and-burn agriculture, where farmers clear land by cutting down vegetation and burning it to prepare the soil for planting crops, typically maize (corn) and other staples. This practice is common in regions with tropical climates where soil fertility can be low, and the method helps to temporarily enrich the soil.

45. (B): North-Western Europe is the largest region in the world for commercial dairy farming, particularly countries like the Netherlands, Germany, France, the United Kingdom, and Denmark. This region has a well-developed dairy industry, benefiting from a combination of favourable climate conditions, advanced farming techniques, high levels of mechanization, and significant domestic and international demand for dairy products.

46. (C): Mumbai's Dabbawala (tiffin delivery) system is an example of tertiary activities. Tertiary activities involve the provision of services rather than the production of goods. The dabbawala provide a crucial service by transporting home-cooked meals from people's homes to their workplaces, often in a very efficient and well-organized manner. This service falls under the category of distribution, logistics, and service-oriented activities, which are part of the tertiary sector.

47. (C): Email is a personal means of communication because it allows individuals to send and receive messages directly to and from one another, making it a more personal and direct form of communication compared to the other options listed.

48. (A): The term "Gold Collar" worker generally refers to highly skilled professionals who possess advanced knowledge and expertise, often in advisory or consulting roles. Consultants are often considered "Gold Collar" workers because they provide specialized and valuable insights to organizations.

49. (D): Banking services are generally classified as tertiary activities because they involve the provision of services rather than the creation, management, or dissemination of information. Tertiary activities include services such as finance, retail, education, and healthcare.

On the other hand, quaternary activities are knowledge-based services that involve information processing, research, development, and technology management. These include:

- Collection of information
- Production of information
- Dissemination of information

50. (B): Extensive commercial grain cultivation is characterized by high mechanization and high per person yield, but low per acre yield. This type of agriculture typically involves large-scale farming of crops like wheat, corn, and other grains, often in regions with large tracts of land. The use of advanced machinery and technology increases productivity per person, but the relatively low density of crops on the land leads to lower per-acre yields compared to more intensive farming systems.

51. (D): Descending sequence (large scale to small scale) of maps:

- **Cadastral Maps:** The term 'cadastral' is derived from the French word 'cadastre' meaning 'register of territorial property'. These maps are drawn to show the ownership of landed property by demarcating field boundaries of agricultural land and the plan of individual houses in urban areas. The cadastral maps are prepared by the government agencies to realise revenue and taxes, along with keeping a record of ownership. These maps are drawn on a very large scale, such as the cadastral maps of villages at 1 : 4,000 scale and the city plans at a scale of 1 : 2,000 and larger.

- **Topographical Maps:** These maps are also prepared on a fairly large scale. The topographical maps are based on precise surveys and are prepared in the form of series of maps made by the national mapping agencies of almost all countries of the world. For example, the Survey of India undertakes the topographical mapping of the entire country at 1 : 250,000, 1 : 50,000 and 1 : 25,000 scale. These maps follow uniform colours and symbols to show topographic details such as relief, drainage, agricultural land, forest, settlements, means of communication, location of schools, post offices and other services and facilities.
- **Wall Maps:** These maps are generally drawn on large size paper or on plastic base for use in classrooms or lecture halls. The scale of wall maps is generally smaller than the scale of topographical maps but larger than atlas maps.
- **Atlas Maps:** Atlas maps are very small-scale maps. These maps represent fairly large areas and present highly generalised picture of the physical or cultural features. Even so, an atlas map serves as a graphic encyclopaedia of the geographical information about the world, continents, countries or regions. When consulted properly, these maps provide a wealth of generalised information regarding location, relief, drainage, climate, vegetation, distribution of cities and towns, population, location of industries, transport-network system, tourism and heritage sites, etc

52. (C): A planimeter is an instrument used to calculate the area of a two-dimensional shape on a map or a diagram. It works by tracing the boundary of the shape, and then it calculates the enclosed area based on the traced path.

53. (B): To solve this, we need to understand the relationship between time and longitude. The Earth is divided into 360 degrees of longitude, and the Earth rotates 360° in 24 hours. Therefore, for every 1 hour (which is 15° of rotation), the time changes by 1 hour.

Given:

Time at Greenwich (0° longitude) is 1 p.m. (13:00).

We are asked to find the longitude where it will be 6 a.m. (06:00).

Difference in time: From 1 p.m. to 6 a.m., the time difference is 7 hours earlier (since 6 a.m. is 7 hours behind 1 p.m.).

Longitude difference: A time difference of 7 hours corresponds to a difference of

$$7 \times 15° = 105°$$

Direction of the time difference: Since 6 a.m. is earlier than 1 p.m., we must be looking to the west of Greenwich. So, the required longitude is 105° W.

54. (A): The projection drawn when the source of light is placed at infinity distance from the globe is the Orthographic projection.

In the Orthographic projection, the Earth is depicted as if viewed from an infinite distance, so all projection lines are parallel, creating a perspective similar to what we would see from deep space.

55. (B): The topographical maps of India are prepared on 1 : 10,00,000,

1 : 250,000, 1 : 1,25,000, 1 : 50,000 and 1: 25,000 scale providing a latitudinal and longitudinal coverage of 4° × 4°, 1° × 1°, 30' × 30',

15' × 15' and 5' × 7' 30", respectively.

56. (C): FCC images are a type of image used in remote sensing, where the colours we see are not the true colours of the objects being observed. Instead, they represent different wavelengths of light, including those not visible to the human eye, such as infrared. The primary purpose of FCC images is to highlight specific features or phenomena that are not easily detectable in true-colour images. This helps scientists, researchers, and analysts to study and interpret various environmental and geological data.

In FCC images, infrared radiation is often assigned the colour red to make it easily distinguishable. This helps in emphasizing certain features, such as vegetation, which reflects infrared light strongly. By assigning infrared to red, the vegetation appears red in FCC images, making it stand out clearly.

57. **(D):** Broken Hill, located in New South Wales, Australia, is primarily recognized for its mining activities, particularly silver, lead, and zinc. It is one of the most significant mining centers in Australia and has a long history of mining that dates back to the 1880s.

58. **(C):** Urbanization is one of the leading global trends of the 21st century that has a significant impact on health. Over 55% of the world's population live in urban areas – a proportion that is expected to increase to 68% by 2050.

59. **(D):** The term "megalopolis" refers to a large, densely populated urban area that encompasses multiple cities and their suburbs, forming a continuous metropolitan region. It is characterized by significant economic, social, and infrastructural interconnections among the cities within it. The term highlights the phenomenon of urbanization where cities grow and merge into larger urban agglomerations.

The term "megalopolis" was popularized by Jean Gottmann, a French geographer, in his influential work published in 1961 titled "Megalopolis: The Urbanized Northeastern Seaboard of the United States." In this book, Gottmann analyzed the urban development of the northeastern United States, particularly the corridor stretching from Boston, Massachusetts, through New York City, Philadelphia, and Baltimore, to Washington, D.C.

60. **(B):** Checking options:

A. **Hoogli:** The Hooghly River is an inland waterway in India, and ports along this river, such as Kolkata, are considered inland ports.

B. **Athens:** It is a coastal city and the capital of Greece, located near the Aegean Sea. It has a major seaport, Piraeus, which serves as the main port for Athens and is one of the largest ports in Europe.

C. **Manchester:** Manchester has an inland port that connects to the Manchester Ship Canal, allowing ocean-going vessels to reach the city.

D. **Duisburg:** Duisburg is located in Germany and is known for its inland port on the Rhine River, making it one of the largest inland ports in the world.

61. **(C):** The Trans-South American railway, also known as the Ferrocarril Transandino, connects Argentina and Chile, and Uspallata Pass is one of the key mountain passes in the Andes that facilitates this connection.

The Trans-South American railway is a major rail connection that links Buenos Aires, Argentina, on the eastern coast of South America, to Valparaíso, Chile, on the western coast. This route crosses the Andes Mountains, one of the most significant mountain ranges in the world.

The Uspallata Pass, also known as Paso Internacional Los Libertadores, is a high mountain pass in the Andes, situated at an elevation of approximately 3,200 meters (10,499 feet) above sea level. This pass serves as a critical gateway for transportation between Argentina and Chile, allowing both rail and road traffic to traverse the rugged mountain terrain.

62. (B): Checking options:

A. **ASEAN:** The Association of Southeast Asian Nations (ASEAN) has its Secretariat located in Jakarta, Indonesia, not Bangkok.

B. **CIS:** The Commonwealth of Independent States (CIS) has its headquarters in Minsk, Belarus.

C. **EU:** The European Union (EU) has its main administrative headquarters in Brussels, Belgium. Vienna is the capital of Austria and hosts some UN offices, but it is not the EU headquarters.

D. **OPEC:** The Organization of the Petroleum Exporting Countries (OPEC) has its headquarters in Vienna, Austria, not Brussels.

63. (A): The Rhine River is a major European waterway, and it is navigable from Rotterdam (in the Netherlands) to Basel (in Switzerland). The river flows through several countries, including the Netherlands, Germany, France, and Switzerland, and is an important transportation route for goods.

64. (C): Alaska Highway extends from Los Angeles to Anchorage in Alaska: This statement is incorrect. The Alaska Highway (also known as the Alcan Highway) actually extends from Dawson Creek in British Columbia, Canada, to Delta Junction in Alaska, not from Los Angeles. The highway was built during World War II for military purposes.

65. (A): The Northern Atlantic sea route, often referred to as the "Big Trunk Route," is a major maritime corridor that connects North America and Europe. It is one of the busiest and most important trade routes in the world, facilitating the exchange of goods, raw materials, and commodities between the two continents.

66. (B): The San Francisco Bay is the largest landlocked harbor in the world, covering more than 400 square miles.

67. (C): The General Agreement on Tariffs and Trade (GATT) was transformed into the World Trade Organization (WTO) on January 1, 1995. This transformation marked the establishment of the WTO as a permanent international organization to oversee global trade rules and negotiations, replacing GATT's provisional framework.

The creation of the WTO was the result of the Uruguay Round of trade negotiations (1986–1994), which aimed to address various issues that GATT couldn't fully cover, including services, intellectual property rights, and dispute resolution mechanisms.

68. (A): Kochi (or Cochin) port is located on the Malabar Coast, which is the southwestern coastline of India, in the state of Kerala. The Malabar Coast stretches along the Arabian Sea and is known for its natural harbors, including Kochi, one of India's major ports.

69. (D): The tropic of cancer passes through 8 Indian states. They are Rajasthan, Gujarat, Madhya Pradesh, Chhattisgarh, Jharkhand, West Bengal, Tripura and Mizoram.

70. (A): Karewa refers to the elevated plateaus or terraces found in the Kashmir region, particularly in the Kashmir Valley. These Karewa formations are significant for their fertile soil and are often used for agriculture, especially for the cultivation of saffron and other crops. The term is specifically associated with the geological features of the Kashmir Himalaya.

71. (B): The Dhauladhar mountain range is a part of the Lesser Himalayas. This range is located primarily in the state of Himachal Pradesh, India, and lies to the south of the main Greater Himalayas. The Dhauladhar range is characterized by its rugged terrain and high peaks, with the highest peak being Hanuman Tibba at around 5,800 meters.

72. (B): Saddle Peak is the highest peak in the Andaman and Nicobar Islands, standing at an elevation of about 732 meters (2,400 feet). It is located on the North Andaman Island.

73. **(D):** Gersoppa Falls, also known as Jog Falls, is located on the Sharavati River in the Shimoga district of Karnataka, India. It is one of the highest and most famous waterfalls in India, with a height of about 253 meters (830 feet). The waterfall is formed by the Sharavati River, which plunges down in a spectacular fashion in four distinct cascades.

74. **(A):** According to Köppen's climate classification, the majority of Uttar Pradesh has a "Cwg" climate, which is classified as a "Subtropical highland climate". Cwg indicates a subtropical climate with hot summers and a cool or mild winter, typical of the outer foothills of the Himalayas and parts of northern India. This type of climate is characterized by hot summers with temperatures exceeding 40°C in many areas, followed by cool winters with temperatures dropping to around 5-10°C. The monsoon season brings moderate rainfall, and the winters are generally dry.

75. **(B):** Rajasthan, located in the northwestern part of India, experiences extreme variations in annual rainfall. The state includes both arid and semi-arid regions, which result in significant fluctuations in rainfall from year to year. This high variability is influenced by factors such as the monsoon patterns and the state's geographic characteristics.

76. **(C):** The Seshachalam Biosphere Reserve (SLBR) is located in the Seshachalam Hill ranges of the Eastern Ghats in Southern Andhra Pradesh.

77. **(C):** Silver firs, junipers, and rhododendrons are commonly found at altitudes of 3000 to 4000 meters in the Himalayas due to the suitable climate, soil, and ecological niches available at these elevations. These trees are integral to the biodiversity and ecological health of the region, providing numerous benefits to both the natural environment and human communities.

78. **(A):** Laterite soils are formed in tropical regions with high rainfall, where intense leaching occurs. This leaching process removes soluble minerals and nutrients, leading to the accumulation of iron oxides and aluminum compounds. As a result, laterite soils often have a reddish color due to the high iron content and are typically found in areas with a humid climate. They are commonly used for agriculture after proper treatment and are also used in construction.

79. **(A):** Gypsum (calcium sulfate) is commonly added to soil to mitigate salinity. It works by displacing sodium ions from the soil particles with calcium ions. This process helps to leach the sodium ions out of the root zone, reducing soil salinity and improving soil structure and fertility.

80. **(A):** The United Nations designated the decade from 1990 to 2000 as the International Decade for Natural Disaster Reduction (IDNDR). The main objective of this initiative was to reduce the loss of life, property damage, and social and economic disruption caused by natural disasters through concerted international action.

81. **(D):** The Kachchh region of Gujarat falls under Very High Damage Risk zone. This region is particularly vulnerable to earthquakes due to its location in the seismically active zone where the Indian plate is colliding with the Eurasian plate. The 2001 Gujarat earthquake, which was one of the most devastating in the region's history, highlighted the high seismic risk in this area.

82. **(D):** The frequency of cyclonic storms in India is highest during October-November. This period coincides with the post-monsoon season, when the Bay of Bengal is particularly active in generating cyclones that can affect the eastern coast of India. The months of April-May (pre-monsoon season) also see cyclonic activity, but not as frequently as in October-November.

Previous Paper (Solved)

KVS-PGT Geography Teacher Recruitment Exam-2018*

Subject : Geography

1. According to Land Revenue Records in India, 'crops are sown and harvested' is classified under which one of the following landuse categories?

A. Tree crops and graves
B. Cultivable wasteland
C. Net sown area
D. Fallow lands

2. Which one of the followings is the appropriate distance between Sun and Earth during Perihelion?

A. 146 million km
B. 147 million km
C. 148 million km
D. 150 million km

3. Which one of the following numbers is ***correct*** showing major tectonic plates of the world?

A. 6 B. 7
C. 8 D. 9

4. Which one of the following figures of solar energy (calories per square centimetre per minute) represents ***correctly*** its average received at the top of the earth's atmosphere?

A. 1.94 B. 1.84
C. 2.94 D. 2.84

5. Which one of the following is the second largest body of the Solar System?

A. Sun B. Jupiter
C. Saturn D. Uranus

6. Find out the local time of place 'B' situated at 47° West longitude when the local time of place 'A' situated at 47° East longitude is 8:00 pm.

A. 4:44 pm B. 1:44 pm
C. 4:44 am D. 1:44 am

7. Through which one of the following group of states does the river Chambal flow?

A. Uttar Pradesh, Gujarat, Madhya Pradesh
B. Uttar Pradesh, Madhya Pradesh, Rajasthan
C. Uttar Pradesh, Madhya Pradesh, Chhattisgarh
D. Rajasthan, Madhya Pradesh, Bihar

8. Which one of the following weather elements is shown by the symbol given below as approved by the International Meteorological Organisation?

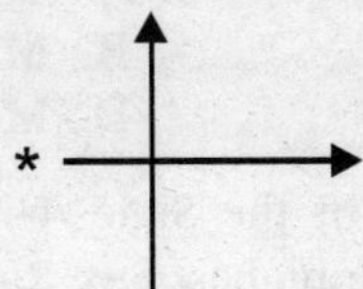

A. Dust storm B. Snow storm
C. Hail D. Sleet

9. Which one of the following slope profiles is ***correct*** when contours are farther to each other at their higher values?

A. Convex slope
B. Concave slope
C. Uniform slope
D. Undulating slope

10. Which one of the following is ***correct*** sequence in increasing order of percentages of atmospheric gases?

A. Helium, Xenon, Carbon dioxide and Argon
B. Xenon, Helium, Carbon dioxide and Argon
C. Helium, Carbon dioxide, Xenon and Argon
D. Xenon, Carbon dioxide, Helium and Argon

11. Lines connecting places of equal air pressure is called :

A. Isohale B. Isohyet
C. Isobar D. Isotherm

* ***Exam held on 23 December, 2018***

12. Mariana trench is situated in which one of the following Oceans?
A. North Atlantic Ocean
B. Indian Ocean
C. South Atlantic Ocean
D. Western Pacific Ocean

13. Which one of the following percentages is ***correct*** for constituting Silicon in the crust?
A. 22.72 B. 27.72
C. 25.72 D. 30.72

14. Which one of the following countries has been important contributor to the SPOT Programme promoted by France?
A. Germany B. U.S.A.
C. Belgium D. Russia

15. Who among the followings proposed the concept of 'sea floor spreading'?
A. Bullard B. McKengie
C. Hess D. Morgan

16. Which one of the States/Union Territory in India has the highest Sex Ratio as per census 2011?
A. Puducherry B. Kerala
C. Tamil Nadu D. Andhra Pradesh

17. Match the List-I with the List-II and select the ***correct*** answer using the codes given below:

List-I ***(Items)***	***List-II*** ***(Definitions)***
(*a*) Absolute distance	(*i*) Location of a person, place or thing in relation to others.
(*b*) Relative distance	(*ii*) Relationship between map and ground distances of two same places.
(*c*) Relative location	(*iii*) Measurement of social, cultural and economic connectivity between two places.
(*d*) Scale	(*iv*) Spatial separating distance between two points on the surface.

Codes:

	(*a*)	(*b*)	(*c*)	(*d*)
A.	(*i*)	(*iii*)	(*iv*)	(*ii*)
B.	(*ii*)	(*i*)	(*iii*)	(*iv*)
C.	(*iii*)	(*iv*)	(*i*)	(*ii*)
D.	(*iv*)	(*iii*)	(*i*)	(*ii*)

18. Match the List-I with the List-II and select the ***correct*** answer using the code given below:

List-I ***(Theory/hypothesis)***	***List-II*** ***(Name)***
(*a*) Tetrahedral Theory	(*i*) Holmes
(*b*) Continental Drift	(*ii*) Kober
(*c*) Convectional Current	(*iii*) Green
(*d*) Mountain Building	(*iv*) Wegener

Codes:

	(*a*)	(*b*)	(*c*)	(*d*)
A.	(*iii*)	(*iv*)	(*i*)	(*ii*)
B.	(*iii*)	(*iv*)	(*ii*)	(*i*)
C.	(*iii*)	(*i*)	(*ii*)	(*iv*)
D.	(*iii*)	(*i*)	(*iv*)	(*ii*)

19. 'Basket of Eggs topography' is created by which one of the following geomorphic processes?
A. River work
B. Glacial work
C. Winds work
D. Sea wave work

20. Under old scheme of road classification, National Highway-1 connects which of the following cities?
A. Ambala–Moradabad
B. Amritsar–Lucknow
C. Amritsar–Delhi
D. Delhi–Hyderabad

21. Narmada-Tapi trough passes through which of the following states?
A. Maharashtra–Madhya Pradesh
B. Maharashtra–Chhattisgarh
C. Madhya Pradesh–Gujarat
D. Madhya Pradesh–Rajasthan

22. Which one of the following landforms provides the clue of multi-cyclic erosional processes?

83. (C): Moderate to Low Vulnerability Zone: Areas that receive less precipitation such as Trans-Himalayan areas of Ladakh and Spiti (Himachal Pradesh), undulated yet stable relief and low precipitation areas in the Aravali, rain shadow areas in the Western and Eastern Ghats and Deccan plateau also experience occasional landslides. Landslides due to mining and subsidence are most common in states like Jharkhand, Odisha, Chhattisgarh, Madhya Pradesh, Maharashtra, Andhra Pradesh, Karnataka, Tamil Nadu, Goa and Kerala.

84. (B): Cyclones are classified as natural disasters of atmospheric origin. They are intense circular storms that originate over warm tropical oceans, characterized by low atmospheric pressure, high winds, and heavy rain. Cyclones are driven by atmospheric processes and are influenced by factors such as sea surface temperatures, atmospheric pressure patterns, and the Earth's rotation.

85. (C): Urban smog is a type of air pollution that results from a combination of smoke, fog, and chemical pollutants in the atmosphere. It is often exacerbated by vehicle emissions, industrial discharges, and other sources of air pollution, leading to poor air quality in urban areas.

86. (D): Watershed management in Jhabua has been implemented to enhance the livelihoods of the local population, particularly in terms of improving agricultural productivity, water conservation, and sustainable resource management.

87. (A): National Waterway No. 3 is operational in the state of Kerala. It stretches from Kollam to Kottapuram and includes a network of waterways running through the picturesque backwaters of Kerala. This waterway plays a vital role in transporting goods and passengers, boosting trade and tourism in the region.

The waterway spans approximately 205 kilometers, connecting several important towns and cities along the way, including Kochi, Alappuzha, and Thrissur. It provides an efficient and eco-friendly means of transportation, reducing the congestion on roads and enhancing connectivity within the state.

88. (C): The Indian Remote Sensing satellite IRS-1A was successfully launched on March 17, 1988, from the Soviet Cosmodrome at Baikonur. This satellite was the first in a series of indigenous remote sensing satellites developed by the Indian Space Research Organisation (ISRO).

89. (C): Hill Area Development Programmes were initiated during the Fifth Five Year Plan covering 15 districts comprising all the hilly districts of Uttar Pradesh (present Uttarakhand), Mikir Hill and North Cachar hills of Assam, Darjeeling district of West Bengal and Nilgiri district of Tamil Nadu.

90. (B): The Dalli-Rajhara iron ore mines are located in the state of Chhattisgarh. These mines are a significant source of iron ore and supply raw materials to the Bhilai Steel Plant, one of the largest steel plants in India.

91. (C): The Kakrapar Atomic Power Station (KAPS), also known as the Kakarapura nuclear power project, is located in the state of Gujarat.

Nuclear Power Plants in India

Power Station	State
Kaiga	Karnataka
Kudankulam	Tamil Nadu
Madras (Kalpakkam)	Tamil Nadu
Narora	Uttar Pradesh
Tarapur	Maharashtra

92. (C): Due to topographical, hydrological, and other constraints, only about 32% of India's surface water is available for utilization. The rest is either lost to evaporation, locked in glaciers, or flows into the sea without being used.

93. (A): Approximately 90% of India's surface and groundwater is utilized by the agricultural sector. This is due to the extensive irrigation needed for crops, which accounts for the majority of water usage in the country. Agriculture remains a crucial part of India's economy and food security, necessitating significant water resources.

95. **(B):** The Water (Prevention and Control of Pollution) Cess Act was enacted in 1977, to provide for the levy and collection of a cess on water consumed by persons operating and carrying on certain types of industrial activities. This cess is collected with a view to augment the resources of the Central Board and the State Boards for the prevention and control of water pollution constituted under the Water (Prevention and Control of Pollution) Act, 1974. The Act was last amended in 2003.

96. **(B):** Checking statements:
   - **Neeru-Meeru programme:** This program is related to water conservation and is actually associated with Andhra Pradesh, not Tamil Nadu.
   - **Ralegan Siddhi:** This village is indeed located in the Ahmadnagar district of Maharashtra. It is well-known for its successful water conservation and rural development efforts, largely attributed to the work of social activist Anna Hazare.
   - **Jal Kranti Abhiyan:** This campaign for water conservation was launched in 2015, not specifically for food security in 2017-18.
   - **Arvary Pani Sansad:** This grassroots water management initiative is active in Rajasthan, not North Bihar.

   Hence, option (B) is correct.

97. **(B):** As per the Land Use Statistics 2014-15, the total geographical area of the country is 328.7 million hectares, of which 140.1 million hectares is the reported net sown area and 198.4 million hectares is the gross cropped area with a cropping intensity of 142%. The net area sown works out to 43% of the total geographical area. The net irrigated area is 68.4 million hectares.

98. **(C):** Jute, the golden fibre, is the 2nd most important fibre after cotton in India. It has bio-degradable and renewal properties, hence it is considered crucial for maintaining the environment and ecological balance. As per Food and Agriculture Organization (FAO) India holds 1st position in jute production with 49.7 percent of world production and 48.4 percent of world's total jute acreage in 2021. West Bengal, Assam and Bihar are major jute growing States in the country. which account for more than 98 percent of the country's jute area and production. Being a natural fibre, it has some inherent properties like silky shine, high tensile strength, considerable heat resistance, long staple length etc., which makes it more suitable than synthetic fibre.

99. **(B):** Kanpur is the northernmost among the listed cotton textile industry centers.

   Kanpur: Located in the state of Uttar Pradesh, it is historically known for its cotton textile industry and is situated furthest north among the options provided.

   Ujjain: Located in Madhya Pradesh, further south than Kanpur.

   Aurangabad: Situated in Maharashtra, even further south.

   Ahmedabad: Found in Gujarat, also further south-west than Kanpur.

100. **(D):** Telangana is a state in southern India, created on June 2, 2014, after being separated from Andhra Pradesh. It consists of 33 districts, including Warangal, Nalgonda, and Medak. Nellore is a district in the southeastern part of Andhra Pradesh, which is south of Telangana.

A. River terraces
B. Gorge
C. Meander
D. Delta

23. Which one of the following terms is used for plant-eating animals?
A. primary consumers
B. secondary consumers
C. decomposers
D. producers

24. Who among the following introduced the concept of 'locational triangle' in space economy?
A. A. Weber
B. T. Plander
C. E.M. Hoover
D. A. Losch

25. Who was the founder of 'Neo-determinism'?
A. C. Darvin
B. F. Ratzel
C. E.C. Semple
D. G. Taylor

26. Which one of the following states recorded the lowest decadal growth of population in India during 2001-2011?
A. Punjab
B. Arunachal Pradesh
C. Nagaland
D. Madhya Pradesh

27. Match List-I with List-II and select the *correct* answer using the codes given below :

List-I *(States)*	**List-II** *(Sex ratio as per census 2011)*
(*a*) Puducherry	(*i*) 995
(*b*) Kerala	(*ii*) 992
(*c*) Tamil Nadu	(*iii*) 1038
(*d*) Andhra Pradesh	(*iv*) 1084

Codes:

	(*a*)	(*b*)	(*c*)	(*d*)
A.	(*i*)	(*iv*)	(*iii*)	(*ii*)
B.	(*iii*)	(*iv*)	(*ii*)	(*i*)
C.	(*iv*)	(*iii*)	(*ii*)	(*i*)
D.	(*iii*)	(*iv*)	(*i*)	(*ii*)

28. Baba Budan Hills are situated in which one of the following states?
A. Maharashtra
B. Karnataka
C. Tamil Nadu
D. Kerala

29. Which one of the following dates is *correct* for launching GSAT-6A under Indian Space Programme?
A. 29 March, 2018
B. 15 April, 2010
C. 2 September, 2007
D. 10 April, 1982

30. Which one of the following reasons is most suited for decrease in velocity of seismic waves in asthenosphere?
A. Decrease in density
B. Increase in density
C. Change in depth
D. Change in the state of matter

31. To calculate the ocean-water salinity by 'principle of constant proportion', which one of the following salts is usually taken into consideration?
A. Chlorine B. Sodium
C. Magnesium D. Sulphate

32. The crystalization is seen in which one of the following rocks?
A. Conglomerate B. Shale
C. Limestone D. Basalt

33. In which one of the following Oceans, the Maldives islands are situated?
A. North Atlantic Ocean
B. Indian Ocean
C. Pacific Ocean
D. South Atlantic Ocean

34. Match the List-I with the List-II and select the *correct* answer from the codes given below :

List-I ***(Books)***	***List-II*** ***(Authors)***
(*a*) Erdkunde	(*i*) Carl Ritter
(*b*) Kosmos	(*ii*) Alexander-von-Humboldt

(*c*) Anthropo-geographie (*iii*) Alfred Hettner

(*d*) Methodology of Geography (*iv*) Friedrich Ratzel

Codes:

	(*a*)	(*b*)	(*c*)	(*d*)
A.	(*i*)	(*ii*)	(*iii*)	(*iv*)
B.	(*iii*)	(*iv*)	(*i*)	(*ii*)
C.	(*i*)	(*ii*)	(*iv*)	(*iii*)
D.	(*iv*)	(*i*)	(*ii*)	(*iii*)

35. Which one of the following states of India touches boundary of three countries?
A. Himachal Pradesh
B. Sikkim
C. Uttrakhand
D. Mizoram

36. Which one of the following states has the highest density of population as per census 2011?
A. Sikkim
B. Arunachal Pradesh
C. Jammu & Kashmir
D. Mizoram

37. Which one of the following regions of the world receive maximum insolation?
A. Equatorial region
B. Subtropical region
C. Temperate region
D. Sub-polar region

38. In Christaller's Central Place Model for organisation of settlements, K = 3 principle denoted by which one of the followings?
A. Market principle
B. Transport principle
C. Administrative principle
D. Economic principle

39. Which one of the following dates is ***correct*** for launching SPOT-1 under Remote Sensing Satellite Program for Europe?
A. June, 2014
B. September, 1993
C. January, 1990
D. February, 1986

40. Sub tropical high pressure belt on the earth is also known as ____.
A. Doldrums
B. Horse latitudes
C. Trade-wind areas
D. Westerly

41. Which one of the followings is in the ***correct*** order of increasing density of bodies in Solar System?
A. Jupiter, Mercury, Earth and Mars
B. Jupiter, Mars, Mercury and Earth
C. Mars, Mercury, Jupiter and Earth
D. Mars, Mercury, Earth and Jupiter

42. Which one of the following processes reduces the rock particle size by erosion?
A. corrasion
B. corrosion
C. attrition
D. suspension

43. If the largest city in a region has a population size of 10,00,000; what might be the population of 5th largest city when cities of this region follow normal rank-size rule?
A. 200,000 B. 400,000
C. 500,000 D. 600,000

44. Which one of the following divisions of the Himalayas has the maximum length from East to West?
A. Kumaon B. Bhutan
C. Nepal D. Punjab

45. Teesta River is the major tributary of which one of the following rivers?
A. Brahamaputra B. Ganga
C. Kosi D. Gandak

46. When two places on the ground are 500 km apart and they are shown on the map by 25 cm, which one of the following Representative Fractions represents the scale of the map?
A. 1 : 2,000
B. 1 : 20,000
C. 1 : 200,000
D. 1 : 2,000,000

47. Who among the followings authored the book "The Study of Landforms"?
A. Arthur Holmes
B. R.J. Small
C. M.J. Selby
D. C.A.M. King

48. Which one of the followings is ***correct*** for Net Photosynthesis?
A. Total photosynthesis plus water in plant
B. Total photosynthesis minus water in plant
C. Total photosynthesis minus respiration
D. Total photosynthesis plus respiration

49. Which one of the following quantities of sea water is taken into account to express normal sea salinity?
A. 10 gram
B. 100 gram
C. 1000 gram
D. 10,000 gram

50. The Krishna River originates near which one of the following places?
A. Nasik
B. Pravara
C. Mahabaleshwar
D. Talakaveri

51. The longest distance between the Sun and Moon is known as ______.
A. Aphelion
B. Perigee
C. Perihelion
D. Apogee

52. Which one of the followings is the capital of Lakshadweep?
A. Silvasa
B. Kavaratti
C. Agartala
D. Aizawl

53. Which one of the following codes represents the category of 'Low class Residential Area' in the given figure of multiple nuclei model of urban land use proposed by Harris and Ullman?

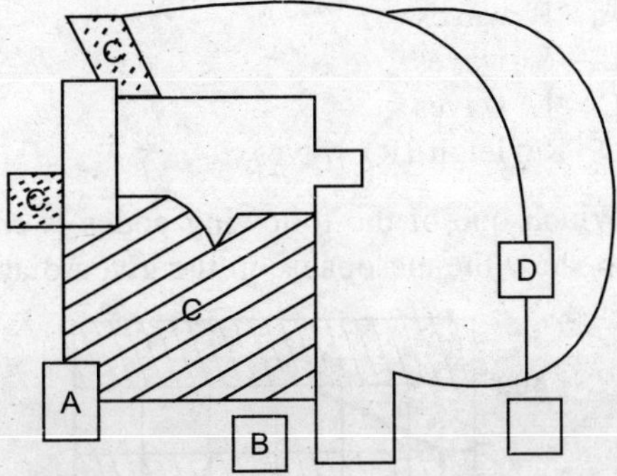

Codes:
A. A
B. B
C. C
D. D

54. Which one of the following states has the highest density of roads as per statistics given by the Ministry of Road Transport and Highways 2012?
A. Tripura
B. West Bengal
C. Kerala
D. Karnataka

55. Who was the propounder of 'stop and go' determinism?
A. E.C. Semple
B. J. Brunches
C. G. Taylor
D. E. Huntington

56. 'The Great Barrier Reef' lies off the coast of which one of the following states of Australia?
A. Queensland
B. South Australia
C. New South wales
D. Victoria

57. Which one of the following ranges shows the shadow zone of 'P' seismic waves?
A. 95° to 150°
B. 100° to 155°
C. 105° to 145°
D. 105° to 155°

58. Back and forth motion of particles of rocks are observed in which one of the following seismic waves?

A. 'P' waves
B. 'S' waves
C. 'L' waves
D. Rayleigh (R) waves

59. Which one of the following codes is ***correct*** to show the mesopause in the given diagram?

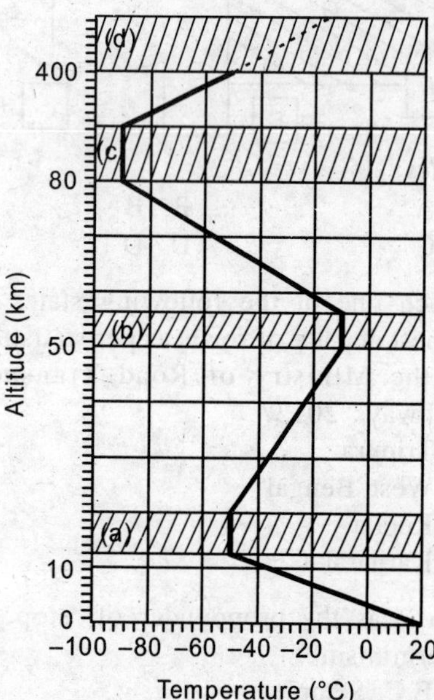

Codes:

A. (*a*) B. (*b*)
C. (*c*) D. (*d*)

60. California Cold current passes through which one of the following coastal areas of the world?
A. Western part of U.S.A.
B. Western part of S. America
C. Eastern part of Canada
D. Western part of Australia

61. Who among the followings put forward the 'Elastic Rebound Theory' of earthquakes?
A. Lowthian Green
B. James Jeans
C. Harry Hess
D. Henry Fielding Reid

62. Match List-I with List-II and select the ***correct*** answer using the codes given below:

List-I (States)	***List-II (Density of population : person/ km² According to census 2011)***
(*a*) Bihar	(*i*) 828
(*b*) Punjab	(*ii*) 550
(*c*) Uttar Pradesh	(*iii*) 1102
(*d*) West Bengal	(*iv*) 1029

Codes:

	(*a*)	(*b*)	(*c*)	(*d*)
A.	(*iii*)	(*ii*)	(*i*)	(*iv*)
B.	(*iii*)	(*i*)	(*iv*)	(*ii*)
C.	(*ii*)	(*iii*)	(*i*)	(*iv*)
D.	(*iv*)	(*ii*)	(*i*)	(*iii*)

63. An important oil bearing Maracaibo Basin is situated in which one of the following countries?
A. Iran
B. Saudi Arabia
C. Venezuela
D. U.S.A.

64. Tsunami disaster occured in which one of the following months caused heavy loss to India?
A. January, 2003
B. December, 2003
C. December, 2004
D. December, 2005

65. Which one of the following soils dominates the larger part of Maharashtra state?
A. Red soil
B. Laterite soil
C. Black soil
D. Grey soil

66. Bomdi-la pass is situated in which one of the following states of India?
A. Sikkim
B. Jammu & Kashmir
C. Arunachal Pradesh
D. Himachal Pradesh

67. Which of the following countries are separated by 'Durand Line'?
A. India and Pakistan
B. India and Afghanistan

C. India and China
D. China and Russia

68. Which one of the followings represents the normal lapse rate of temperature in the troposphere?
A. 6.5°C/km
B. 5.5°C/km
C. 6.0°C/km
D. 5.0°C/km

69. Which one of the following sun-shine hours is applicable for a place at 20° North latitude on December 22?
A. 12 hours 00 minutes
B. 10 hours 48 minutes
C. 9 hours 8 minutes
D. 13 hours 12 minutes

70. The process of lithification is found with which one of the following rocks?
A. Gabbro
B. Limestone
C. Pegmatite
D. Basalt

71. In which one of the following states, Kandla Port is situated?
A. Kerala
B. Maharashtra
C. Gujarat
D. Tamil Nadu

72. In which month, do the equatorial westerlies set in over Indian sub-continent?
A. December
B. February
C. June
D. October

73. 'Sargasso sea' is well developed in which one of the following Oceans?
A. North Pacific Ocean
B. South Pacific Ocean
C. North Atlantic Ocean
D. South Atlantic Ocean

74. The workers engaged is Secondary activities are known by which one of the followings?
A. Blue Coller
B. Red Coller
C. White Coller
D. Golden Coller

75. Which one of the following states in India has the highest rate of literacy as per census 2011?
A. Tamil Nadu
B. Kerala
C. Meghalaya
D. Nagaland

76. Which one of the following crops is the most dominating in Mediterranean Region?
A. Foodgrain crops
B. Commercial crops
C. Industrial crops
D. Fruit crops

77. Which one of the following ratios is ***correct*** to represent 'sea wave velocity'?
A. wave height to wave length
B. wave height to wave period
C. wave length to wave period
D. wave length to wave height

78. A straight line on which one of the following projections represents the shortest distance between two places?
A. Mercator's projection
B. Two-standard parallel projection
C. Gnomonic projection
D. Cylindrical Equal Area projection

79. Which one of the following Union Territories has the lowest literacy rate as per census 2011?
A. Dadra and Nagar Haveli
B. Lakshadweep
C. Puducherry
D. Daman and Diu

80. Which one of the following places has the longest Sun-light on 21st December?
A. Bengaluru
B. Mumbai
C. Jaipur
D. Thiruvananthapuram

Answers

1	2	3	4	5	6	7	8	9	10
C	B	B	A	C	A	B	B	A	B
11	**12**	**13**	**14**	**15**	**16**	**17**	**18**	**19**	**20**
C	D	B	C	C	B	B	A	B	C
21	**22**	**23**	**24**	**25**	**26**	**27**	**28**	**29**	**30**
C	B	A	A	D	C	D	B	A	A
31	**32**	**33**	**34**	**35**	**36**	**37**	**38**	**39**	**40**
B	D	B	C	B	C	A	A	D	B
41	**42**	**43**	**44**	**45**	**46**	**47**	**48**	**49**	**50**
B	C	A	C	A	D	B	C	C	C
51	**52**	**53**	**54**	**55**	**56**	**57**	**58**	**59**	**60**
D	B	C	D	C	A	C	A	C	A
61	**62**	**63**	**64**	**65**	**66**	**67**	**68**	**69**	**70**
D	A	C	C	C	C	B	A	B	B
71	**72**	**73**	**74**	**75**	**76**	**77**	**78**	**79**	**80**
C	A	C	A	B	D	C	C	A	D

Previous Paper (Solved)

KVS-PGT Geography Teacher Recruitment Exam-2017*

Subject : Geography

1. Which one of the following branches of geography was mainly developed by Arab geographers?
A. Oceanography
B. Astronomy
C. Climatology
D. Mathematical Geography

2. The process of receiving and transmitting of messages, ideas and informations is known as ______.
A. Transportation B. Carriage
C. Communication D. Postage

3. The concept of food security was modified by whom in India?
A. Khusro B. Swaminathan
C. Bhatia D. Shafi

4. Wet tropical evergreen forests are found in an area of rainfall?
A. less than 100 cms B. 200 – 300 cms
C. 100 – 200 cms D. More than 300 cms

5. The term 'geography' was first coined by which one of the following?
A. Aristotle B. Ptolemy
C. Eratosthenese D. Herodotus

6. The National Commission on Urbanization, launched a Mega City Scheme in which of the following years?
A. 1991 - 1992 B. 1993 - 1994
C. 1992 - 1993 D. 1994 - 1995

7. 'Mohorovicic discontinuity' is the boundary between:
A. Crust and Mantle
B. Inner Core and Outer Core
C. Mantle and Inner Core
D. Mantle and Outer Core

8. Identify the forests where trees do not shed their leaves in a particular season from the following:
A. Conifereous forests
B. Hot and dry forests
C. Temperate deciduous forests
D. Tropical monsoon forests

9. Who among the following is **not** a supporter of Environmental Determinism?
A. Huntington B. Carl Sauer
C. Mackinder D. A.C. Semple

10. Who made advancement in the theory of Demographic Transition?
A. Thompson and Notestein
B. Zelinskey
C. E. Ravenstein
D. Whittlesey

11. Identify a personal means of communication from the following:
A. Newspaper B. Radio
C. Television D. E-mail

12. The convectional current theory of Arther Holms was propounded in which of the decades?
A. 1920s B. 1940s
C. 1930s D. 1950s

13. Two columns are given below. Match them **correctly.**

(*a*) Food chain	(*i*) Naturally occurring community of flora and fauna
(*b*) Food web	(*ii*) Many hierarchical levels in an ecosystem
(*c*) Trophic level	(*iii*) Many organisms each dependent on the next as source of food
(*d*) Biome	(*iv*) System of interlocking and interdependent food chains

* ***Held on 7 January, 2017***

Codes:

	(a)	(b)	(c)	(d)
A.	(iii)	(iv)	(i)	(ii)
B.	(iii)	(ii)	(i)	(iv)
C.	(iii)	(ii)	(iv)	(i)
D.	(iii)	(iv)	(ii)	(i)

14. Which is normal 'lapse rate' of temperature with height in Troposphere?
A. 10.5 °C/km B. 7.8 °C/km
C. 8.3 °C/km D. 6.4 °C/km

15. Which one of the following disasters is included in a man-made category of disaster?
A. Ecological B. Epidemic
C. Landslide D. Flood

16. Two columns are given below. Match them **correctly.**

Disasters	Precautions
(a) Earthquake	(i) Avoid wastage of water
(b) Flood	(ii) Do not use fire for any purpose
(c) Drought	(iii) Do not take shelter under tall structures
(d) Cyclone	(iv) Stay away from the electrical poles and wires

Codes:

	(a)	(b)	(c)	(d)
A.	(iii)	(iv)	(i)	(ii)
B.	(iii)	(ii)	(iv)	(i)
C.	(iii)	(iv)	(ii)	(i)
D.	(iii)	(ii)	(i)	(iv)

17. Himalayan ranges in Nagaland, Manipur and Mizoram are spread in which one of the following direction?
A. North-South direction
B. East-West direction
C. South-West to North-East direction
D. North-West to South-East direction

18. The doubling period of population was 80 years between ______ .
A. 1960 - 1975 B. 1850 - 1930
C. 1930 - 1960 D. 1650 - 1850

19. Which one of the following islands is **not** the neighbour of India?
A. Maldweep B. Sri Lanka
C. Lakshadweep D. East Timor

20. When the primary tributaries of river flow parallel to each other and secondary tributaries join them at right angles, the drainage pattern is known as ______ .
A. Centripetal B. Trellis
C. Radial D. Dendritic

21. Which one of the following is included in a category of wind made disasters?
A. Flood B. Cyclone
C. Landslide D. Epidemic

22. When the rivers discharge their waters from all directions in a lake or depression, the drainage pattern is known as:
A. Trellis B. Radial
C. Centripetal D. Dendritic

23. Arrange the given layers of atmosphere from earth's surfaces to the top most:
(a) Stratosphere (b) Thermosphere
(c) Troposphere (d) Mesosphere
A. (c), (a), (d) and (b)
B. (c), (d), (v) and (a)
C. (c), (d), (a) and (b)
D. (c), (a), (b) and (d)

24. The book 'Principles of Human Geography' was written by whom ______ .
A. H.J. Mackinder B. A.C. Semple
C. G. Taylor D. E. Huntington

25. 'Stop and go determinism' was presented by whom of the following?
A. Tatham B. G. Taylor
C. Humboldt D. Jean Brunches

26. Which of the following rivers is a tributary of Yamuna?
A. Gomti B. Son
C. Chambal D. Sharda

27. Which is the Nodel Ministry at the centre among the following that coordinates disaster management activities in India?
A. Ministry of Home Affairs
B. Ministry of Civil Aviation
C. Ministry of Agriculture
D. Ministry of Health and Family Welfare

28. 'The environment is essentially neutral, its role being dependent on the stage of technology, type of culture and other characteristics of changing society'. This statement is attributed to whom of the following?
A. Edward Ullman B. Huntington
C. O.H.K. Spate D. G. Taylor

29. In order to show cotton belt of USA and other countries which of the following map projections would be most suitable?
A. Bonne's Projection
B. Cylindrical Equal Area Projection
C. Polyconic Projection
D. Simple Cylindrical Projection

30. If higher value contours are closely spaced and the lower value contours are wider apart then the slope of that area would be ______.
A. Convex slope B. Gentle slope
C. Concave slope D. Undulating slope

31. The data pertaining to five years are given to you for three components. You are supposed to find out the trends for those components. Which one of the following type of illustration is the best to choose for your purpose?
A. Polygraph B. Bar and line graph
C. Line graph D. Pie diagram

32. Match List-I with List-II and select the **correct** answer using the codes given below:

List-I (Sanctuaries)	***List-II (Wild Life)***
(*a*) Bharatpur	(*i*) Indian Elephant
(*b*) Great and Little Rann	(*ii*) Snow Leopard
(*c*) Nilgiri Hills	(*iii*) Birds
(*d*) Great Himalayas	(*iv*) Wild Ass

Codes:

	(*a*)	(*b*)	(*c*)	(*d*)
A.	(*iii*)	(*iv*)	(*i*)	(*ii*)
B.	(*i*)	(*ii*)	(*iii*)	(*iv*)
C.	(*iv*)	(*iii*)	(*ii*)	(*i*)
D.	(*ii*)	(*i*)	(*iv*)	(*iii*)

33. Which one of the following bases is **correct** to identify the 'settlement pattern' of an area?
A. Size of settlement
B. Dispersion of setllement
C. Shape of settlement
D. Intensity of settlement

34. Which one of the following properties is the base for demarcating crust, mantle and core?
A. Temperature B. Pressure
C. Composition D. State of matter

35. Which of the following activities is a quaternary activity?
A. Sericulture B. Business
C. Food processing D. Teaching

36. "The Nature does not drive man along a particular road, but it offers a basket of opportunities from among which man is free to select". This statement is related with:
A. Environmental determinism
B. Neo determinism
C. Possibilism
D. Probabilism

37. Latitudinal and longitudinal extent of the mainland of India is about 30°. Despite of this fact, the east-west extent appears to be smaller than the north-south extent. Find out the **correct** options from the following:
A. The distance between two meridians remain the same throughout
B. The distance between two latitudes remain the same
C. The distance between two meridians decreases towards the pole and the distance between two latitudes remain the same
D. The distance between two latitudes and two meridians remain the same

38. As per Koppen's scheme, the 'Bwh' type of climate is found in which of the following parts of the world?
A. Tundra Region B. Atakama Desert
C. Alps Mountains D. Gobi Desert

39. The variability of rainfall would be more pronounced in which of the following countries?
A. Sri Lanka B. Saudi Arabia
C. Indonesia D. Denmark

40. Which of the following gases is **not** a green house gas?
A. Carbon-di-oxide
B. Carbon-mono-oxide
C. Methane
D. Argon

41. When position of the Sun, the Moon and the Earth is in straight line, this situation for tidal wave is called:
A. Conjunction B. Oppositions
C. Quadrature D. Syzygy

42. Tsunamis belong to which of the category of the following hazards?
A. Water Hazard
B. Environmental Hazard
C. Geological Hazard
D. Climatic Hazard

43. A climograph drawn for Jodhpur would represent a climate of which of the following types?
A. Muggy B. Raw
C. Scorching D. Keen

44. Match List-I with List-II and select the **correct** answer using the codes given below:

List-I (City Zone)	***List-II (Permitted Noise level in dB)***
(*a*) Silent zone	(*i*) 70
(*b*) Residential zone	(*ii*) 65
(*c*) Commercial zone	(*iii*) 55
(*d*) Industrial zone	(*iv*) 50

Codes:

	(*a*)	(*b*)	(*c*)	(*d*)
A.	(*iv*)	(*iii*)	(*ii*)	(*i*)
B.	(*ii*)	(*i*)	(*iv*)	(*iii*)
C.	(*i*)	(*ii*)	(*iii*)	(*iv*)
D.	(*iii*)	(*iv*)	(*i*)	(*ii*)

45. Two columns are given below. Match them **correctly.**

Name of states	***Name given to shifting cultivation***
(*a*) Odisha	(*i*) Kuruwa
(*b*) Jharkhand	(*ii*) Pamadabi
(*c*) Andhra Pradesh	(*iii*) Bewar
(*d*) Madhya Pradesh	(*iv*) Podu

Codes:

	(*a*)	(*b*)	(*c*)	(*d*)
A.	(*ii*)	(*i*)	(*iii*)	(*iv*)
B.	(*i*)	(*ii*)	(*iv*)	(*iii*)
C.	(*ii*)	(*i*)	(*iv*)	(*iii*)
D.	(*iv*)	(*i*)	(*ii*)	(*iii*)

46. The concept of 'areal differentiation' in geography was introduced by ______ .
A. Peter Huggett B. O.H.K. Spate
C. L.C. King D. Hartshorne

47. The 'optimum population theory' was presented by whom ______
A. Thompson B. Malthus
C. Sidgwick D. Notestein

48. The activity of deflation is associated with which of the following agents of denudation?
A. Winds B. Rivers
C. Glaciers D. Under ground water

49. Which of the air pollutants has adverse impact on cardiovascular system of human beings?
A. Sulphur-di-oxide
B. Lead
C. Ozone
D. Carbon-mono-oxide

50. Which one of the following statements is **not** true about the seismic shadow zone?
A. Between 103° to 145° angular distance from the epicentre of an earthquake both 'P' and 'S' waves do not reach.
B. The shadow zone of both 'P' and 'S' waves appear as a band.
C. Beyond 145° angular distance from the epicentre of an earthquake 'S' waves reappear.
D. The shadow zone of 'S' is greater than 'P'.

51. Which one of the following towns does **not** include in the category of Urban settlement?
A. Settlement B. Commercial
C. Administrative D. Cultural

52. What was the name given to Southern supercontinent?
A. Gondwanaland B. Laurasia
C. Pangea D. Panthalass

53. Which one of the following units of heat budget (R) is available on earth surface if heat budget equation, R = Q_s (1 – *a*) – I, has parametalic vaue such as Q_s = solar radiation incoming at the outer limit of atmosphere (100 units), *a* = albedo effect (32 units) and I = outgoing long wave radiation (43 units):

A. 25 B. 35
C. 32 D. 45

54. Which one of the following ocean currents is a warm ocean current?

A. Labrador B. Oyashio
C. Kuroshio D. California

55. Shifting cultivation is prevalent in different names in different countries. Match them appropriately.

Shifting cultivation practices	***Countries***
(*a*) Milpa	(*i*) Venezuela
(*b*) Landing	(*ii*) Brazil
(*c*) Roca	(*iii*) Mexico
(*d*) Conuco	(*iv*) Indonesia

Codes:

	(*a*)	(*b*)	(*c*)	(*d*)
A.	(*iii*)	(*iv*)	(*ii*)	(*i*)
B.	(*i*)	(*ii*)	(*iii*)	(*iv*)
C.	(*i*)	(*iii*)	(*iv*)	(*ii*)
D.	(*i*)	(*iv*)	(*ii*)	(*iii*)

56. On a weather map, sleet is represented by which of the following symbols?

A. ☈ B. ◕
C. ∞ D. ✳

57. Regur soils in India are maximum found in which of the following states?

A. Odisha B. Madhya Pradesh
C. Uttar Pradesh D. Maharashtra

58. Two columns are given below. Match them **correctly.**

Name of Rocks	***Metamorphosed Rocks***
(*a*) Limestone	(*i*) Quartzite
(*b*) Sandstone	(*ii*) Slate
(*c*) Shale	(*iii*) Marble

Codes:

	(*a*)	(*b*)	(*c*)
A.	(*iii*)	(*ii*)	(*i*)
B.	(*ii*)	(*i*)	(*iii*)
C.	(*i*)	(*iii*)	(*ii*)
D.	(*ii*)	(*iii*)	(*i*)

59. Arrange the following Ocean water salts in descending order according to their percentage:

(*a*) Sulphate (*b*) Sodium
(*c*) Chlorine (*d*) Magnesium

A. (*c*), (*a*), (*b*) and (*d*)
B. (*c*), (*b*), (*a*) and (*d*)
C. (*c*), (*d*), (*a*) and (*b*)
D. (*c*), (*d*), (*b*) and (*a*)

60. Arrange different layers of the earth given below from the surface to the centre:

(*a*) Lithosphere (*b*) Inner core
(*c*) Outer core (*d*) Asthenosphere
(*e*) Lower Mantle (*f*) Upper Mantle

A. (*a*), (*d*), (*e*), (*f*), (*b*) and (*c*)
B. (*a*), (*d*), (*f*), (*e*), (*c*) and (*b*)
C. (*a*), (*f*), (*e*), (*d*), (*c*) and (*b*)
D. (*a*), (*f*), (*d*), (*e*), (*b*) and (*c*)

61. On a standard False Colour Composite (FCC), the built up area is represented by which one of the following colours?

A. Magenta B. Black
C. Blue D. Cyan

62. Identify the third most densest planet of the solar system:

A. Mars B. Earth
C. Mercury D. Venus

63. The Nebular Hypothesis about the origin of the Earth was propounded by whom?

A. Sir James Jeans and Harrold Jeffrey
B. Simon Pierre Laplace
C. Immanual Kant
D. Otto Schmidt

64. Which one of the following options is **correct** about the location of India on the globe?

A. Eastern and Northern Hemisphere
B. Northern Hemisphere
C. Northern and Western Hemisphere
D. Eastern Hemisphere

65. When the Kisan call centres were established?
A. 2002 B. 2004
C. 2003 D. 2005

66. When sedimentary rocks come under the contact of very high temperature and pressure conditions, what would be the result?
A. Magma generation
B. Remains sedimentary rock
C. Igneous rock formation
D. Metamorphic rock formation

67. Aircraft, machine tools, telephones and Bharat Electronics are industrial landmarks of which one of the following industrial regions?
A. Vishakhapatnam - Gunture Region
B. Gujarat Industrial Region
C. Gurgaon - Delhi - Meerut Region
D. Bengaluru - Chennai Industrial Region

68. The concept of 'Economic Rent' agriculture landscape was first given by _____ .
A. Von Thunen B. Weber
C. Isard D. Losch

69. As per census of India, how many categories of Urban settlements are classified?
A. 6 B. 4
C. 5 D. 3

70. Two columns are given below. Match them **correctly.**

Demographic Phases	***Population Characteristics***
(*a*) Phase I	(*i*) Population explosion
(*b*) Phase II	(*ii*) Population growth slowing down gradually
(*c*) Phase III	(*iii*) Stationary growth of population
(*d*) Phase IV	(*iv*) Steady population growth rate

Codes:

	(*a*)	(*b*)	(*c*)	(*d*)
A.	(*iii*)	(*i*)	(*ii*)	(*iv*)
B.	(*iii*)	(*iv*)	(*i*)	(*ii*)
C.	(*iii*)	(*i*)	(*iv*)	(*ii*)
D.	(*iii*)	(*iv*)	(*ii*)	(*i*)

71. Which one of the following figures shows the cluster pattern of settlement distribution?
A. 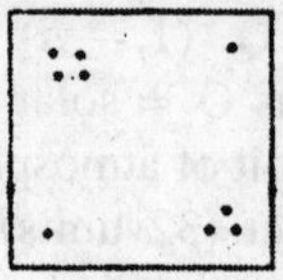 B. 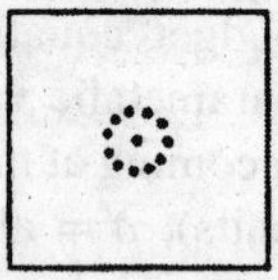
C. 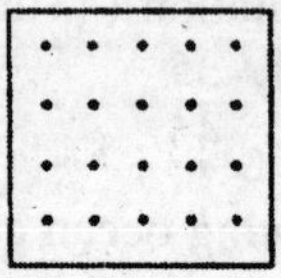 D.

72. Which one of the following is **not** a process of chemical weathering?
A. Solution B. Exfoliation
C. Carbonation D. Hydration

73. Nomadic herding is one of the most important activities of man in which of the following countries?
A. Sudan B. France
C. Japan D. Singapore

74. Which one of the following resources is non-renewable resource?
A. Hydro-electricity B. Forests
C. Minerals D. Fisheries

75. Which one of the following gases is responsible for depletion of ozone layer?
A. Chloro-Fluro-Carbon (CFC)
B. Oxygen
C. Nitrogen Oxide
D. Nitrogen

76. Cyclones are known by the name of Willie-Willie in which of the following countries?
A. Australia B. West Indies
C. Argentina D. U.S.A.

77. What would be the local time of a place situated at 15° E longitude, if its GMT is 10 : 00 A.M.?
A. 10 : 30 A.M. B. 11 : 30 A.M.
C. 10 : 00 A.M. D. 11 : 00 A.M.

78. Which one of the following ports of India is known as the 'Queen of Arabian Sea"?
A. Kandla B. Kochchi
C. Mumbai D. Marmagao

79. Settlements developed along rivers, roads or railway lines are classified as ______ .
A. Linear settlement
B. Economic settlement
C. Zonal settlement
D. Infrastructural settlement

80. In north-western parts of India during winter, the rainfall is caused mainly by _____ .
A. Western disturbances
B. Cyclonic conditions
C. Retreating monsoon
D. ITCZ withdrawal

81. India has the longest international land fronteir with which one of the following countries?
A. Pakistan B. Bangladesh
C. Myanmar D. China

82. What is time lag between two successive tides?
A. 48 minutes and 20 seconds
B. 53 minutes and 42 seconds
C. 48 minutes and 48 seconds
D. 55 minutes and 40 seconds

83. Who among the following explained the geography to be a 'science of spatial distribution'?
A. Ritter B. Varenius
C. Perschel D. Humboldt

84. Incomplete burning of petrol or diesel in vehicles generates ______ .
A. Methane gas
B. Ozone gas
C. Carbon-dioxide gas
D. Carbon-Mono-oxide gas

85. Conservation of environment will lead us to a ______ .
A. Regular development
B. Sustainable development
C. Energy development
D. Improvement in our life

86. Which one of the following rivers presents an example of superimposed drainage?
A. Ganga B. Narmada
C. Brahmaputra D. Cauveri

87. The end feature of the cycle of erosion in a limestone region is which of the following?
A. Doline B. Cavern
C. Polje D. Stalactites

88. 'Kitab-al-Hind' was written by whom of the following?
A. Al Balkhi B. Ibn-e-Batuta
C. Al Baruni D. Iltutmish

89. Northern plains of India can be divided in different parts. Arrange them from North to South direction sequentially:
(*a*) Bhangar (*b*) Khadar
(*c*) Bhabar (*d*) Tarai
A. (*c*), (*a*), (*d*) and (*b*)
B. (*c*), (*b*), (*d*) and (*a*)
C. (*c*), (*d*), (*a*) and (*b*)
D. (*c*), (*d*), (*b*) and (*a*)

90. The Environment Protection Act was implemented by the Government of India in which of the following years?
A. 1976 B. 1996
C. 1986 D. 2006

91. As per Concentric Zone Theory of E. Burgese, the residential zone for middle income group people lies in which of the following zones?
A. 2nd B. 4th
C. 3rd D. 5th

92. Which one of the following cities is the headquarters of World Trade Organisation?
A. Geneva B. New York
C. London D. New Delhi

93. Match the two columns given below appropriately:

Consumers	***Organisms***
(*a*) Primary	(*i*) Omnivores
(*b*) Secondary	(*ii*) Scavengers
(*c*) Tertiary	(*iii*) Herbivorous
(*d*) Decomposers	(*iv*) Carnivores

Codes:

	(*a*)	(*b*)	(*c*)	(*d*)
A.	(*iii*)	(*iv*)	(*ii*)	(*i*)
B.	(*iii*)	(*i*)	(*iv*)	(*ii*)
C.	(*iii*)	(*iv*)	(*i*)	(*ii*)
D.	(*iii*)	(*i*)	(*ii*)	(*iv*)

94. Which one of the following Islands is a coral Island?
A. Tasmania B. Fizi
C. Hawaii D. Bikini

95. The speed of rotation of Earth would be maximum on which of the following parallels of latitudes?
A. Tropic of Cancer
B. Equator
C. Tropic of Capricorn
D. Arctic Circle

96. In a contour map, points A and B are located on 3000 m and 7000 m contours respectively. Which one of the slope gradients is **correct** if horizontal equivalent between them is 4.0 km?
A. 30° B. 40°
C. 35° D. 45°

97. Red Soil is found mainly in ______ .
A. Bihar and Uttar Pradesh
B. Punjab and Himachal Pradesh
C. Tamil Nadu and Andhra Pradesh
D. Rajasthan and Gujarat

98. Which of the following is a type of point source of water pollution?
A. Industrial pollution
B. Acid rains
C. Agricultural run off
D. Urban run off

99. Who established the relationship between 'Regional Geography' and 'Systematic Geography'?
A. Huntington B. Varenius
C. Reclus D. Blache

100. Solfatara is a type of which of the following?
A. A Block Mountain
B. A Folded Mountain
C. A Dissected Plateau
D. A Volcano

ANSWERS

1	2	3	4	5	6	7	8	9	10
B	C	B	C	C	B	A	A	B	A
11	**12**	**13**	**14**	**15**	**16**	**17**	**18**	**19**	**20**
D	C	D	D	A	A	A	B	C	B
21	**22**	**23**	**24**	**25**	**26**	**27**	**28**	**29**	**30**
B	C	A	D	B	C	A	A	B	C
31	**32**	**33**	**34**	**35**	**36**	**37**	**38**	**39**	**40**
A	A	C	C	D	C	C	B	B	D
41	**42**	**43**	**44**	**45**	**46**	**47**	**48**	**49**	**50**
D	C	C	A	C	D	C	A	D	C
51	**52**	**53**	**54**	**55**	**56**	**57**	**58**	**59**	**60**
A	A	A	C	A	D	D	*	B	B
61	**62**	**63**	**64**	**65**	**66**	**67**	**68**	**69**	**70**
D	D	B	A	B	D	D	A	A	B
71	**72**	**73**	**74**	**75**	**76**	**77**	**78**	**79**	**80**
B	B	A	C	A	A	D	B	A	A
81	**82**	**83**	**84**	**85**	**86**	**87**	**88**	**89**	**90**
B	C	D	D	B	B	C	C	C	C
91	**92**	**93**	**94**	**95**	**96**	**97**	**98**	**99**	**100**
B	A	C	D	B	D	C	A	B	D

GEOGRAPHY

NATURE, SCOPE AND BRANCHES OF GEOGRAPHY

DEVELOPMENT OF GEOGRAPHY

The world geography was adopted in the 200 B.C. by the Greek scholar called **Erastosthenes**. It is the combination of two Greek words, ***ge*** meaning "earth" and ***graphein*** meaning "to write". Thus, geography means "to write about the Earth or "earth's description".

The Greeks have played a very important role in the development and study of geography. Some of those who contributed greatly to the development of geography are mentioned period-wise here.

THE CLASSICAL PERIOD

1. **Pythagoras,** a great Greek philosopher and mathematician, was the first to consider that the Earth is spherical in shape and revolves with all the other planets around a central fire.

2. **Herodotus** (484-425 B.C.), a Greek historian, is known as the "father of history". He travelled extensively and provided information about ancient Greece, North Africa and the Middle East. He compiled all his findings and observations in a book entitled *History*, which is the Greek word for "inquiry". The famous epithet "Egypt is the gift of the Nile" was first used by him. He created the term *delta* for the flood plain at the mouth of the Nile. He explained the deposition of silt in the Nile delta.

3. **Aristotle** (384-322 B.C.), a great Greek philosopher explained the eclipses. He demonstrated that earth had a spherical shape. Evidence from this idea came from the observance of lunar eclipses.

4. **Eratosthenes** (276-194 B.C.), a Greek poet, mathematician and geographer measured with great accuracy the circumference of the Earth by observing the angle of the noon day Sun at Syene and at Alexandria.

5. **Hipparchus** (190-120 B.C.), was perhaps the greatest of the Greek astronomers. He devised a method of locating geographical positions by means of latitudes and longitudes.

6. **Strabo** (64 B.C.-20 A.D.). He wrote a 17 volume series called '*Geographia*' He describes the cultural geographies of various societies of people found form Britain to as far as east as India and South to Ethiopia and as far as North as Iceland.

7. **Ptolemy** (90-168 A.D.), was a Greek astronomer and mathematician who lived and worked in Egypt. He wrote two famous books, named *Almagest* and *Geographike* Hyphegesis which charts all the places of the world as known to them at that time. Some of his important contributions include (i) the creation of three different methods for projecting the Earth's surface on a map, (ii) the calculation of coordinate all locations for some eight thousand places on earth, (iii) the development of the concept of geographical latitude and longitude, influenced map-makers for hundreds of years. He was a **cartographer** and he evolved the science of **map-making.**

THE CHRISTIAN ERA

The Christian Era did not contribute much to the development of geography. The Christian Church was the most powerful instrument of education and missionaries spread religious teachings and education. The image of the world was moulded to fit the Bible and the Earth became a disk at the centre of the Universe.

1. **Al Idrisi** (1099-1154 A.D.), was an Arab geographer and scientist who authored one of the greatest geographic works of the medieval world. He compiled a description of the Earth that contains information from his own travels and reports from others. He is best known for his skills at making maps.

   As trade relations between the Arabs and the Asian and European people became widespread, knowledge of the world was much enlarged. Unfortunately none of his work, which was written in Arabic, was translated into Latin or any other western language until the nineteenth century.

2. **Ibn Battuta** (1304-1377 A.D.), was the greatest of all Muslim travellers. Born in Tangier, he spent most of his life travelling or living in distant places. We know about him from the book *Travels* which he wrote.

3. **Macro Polo,** the greatest of all eastern travellers of this period, was the first traveller to trace a route across the entire length of Asia, naming and describing kingdoms he had seen.

THE RENAISSANCE

The Renaissance marked another step towards the making of modern geography. Between the 14th and

16th century, great discoveries and explorations took place and so the knowledge of geography acquired a practical outlook. This era saw the beginning of more accurate maps and map-drawings.

1. **Henry, the Navigator** (1394-1460), was a prince of Portugal. He did not go on any voyage but he set up an observatory and established the first school of navigation. He gave instruction through Arab teachers who did much to spread the knowledge of geography.

2. With the discovery of the New World by the Portuguese, new routes to the east and the west had to be mapped. Germany became a central institution for the development of mathematical and descriptive geography.

3. Newly found coasts, lands and seas had to be named and mapped. All this formed a new phase of geography. This was followed by the capes and bays method of learning which meant memorizing geographical facts. In the 17th century, geography was included in the school curriculum because of its practical utility in navigation.

MODERN GEOGRAPHY

1. **Bernhardus Varenius** (1622-1650), was a German geographer who first recognised the need for organisation of geographical knowledge. He wrote *Geographia Generalis,* the most highly regarded treatise on geography for more than a century. He sub-divided the geography into three distinct branches : (i) dealing with forms and dimensions of earth, (ii) deals with tides, climatic variations over time and space and (iii) distinct regions on the earth.

2. **Immanual Kant** (1724-1804), a German philosopher, is considered by many to be one of the most influential thinkers of modern times. He tried to find a foundation for geography within the framework of other sciences. According to him, all knowledge can be organised into three groups according to the object of study.

The first is the systematic sciences like botany, geology, and sociology. The second is the historical sciences, using relationship through time. Geographical science was the third, that studied things that are associated in space.

3. **Alexander Baron Von Humboldt** (1769-1859), a German naturalist and explorer, moulded the substance of geography into a scientific form. He was interested in all aspects of natural history and has been described by Charles Darwin as "*the greatest scientific traveller that ever lived*".

He wrote a five-volume book *Kosmos* in which he set forth not only his vast scientific knowledge but also his interest in physical and biological features. By presenting explanatory descriptions of areas and by comparing them with other lands, he set the tone for scientific geography.

He invented the **"isotherms"** to compare temperatures.

4. **Carl Ritter** (1779-1859), a German geographer, is considered the founder of modern geographic study. He stressed the importance of using all the sciences in the study of geography.

His most important work Die *Erdkunde* (Earth Science) emphasized the influence of physical environment on human activity. He divided the Earth into natural regions and showed each unit as a whole interrelated complex of elements. His plan of study became the model for regional study and presentation.

5. **Ellsworth Huntington** (1876-1947), an American geographer and explorer, was noted particularly for his study on the effects of climate on human heredity and civilization. Until now teaching of geography consisted of the study of climate, plant and animals and landforms. The human aspect was neglected to a great extent. His approach to geographic study is known as **determinism** in which humans are passive agents while the physical environment is active.

6. **Vidal de la Blanche** advocated the opposite theory of determinism, which is sometimes known as possibilism, in which humans are active agents, at liberty to choose between a wide range in environmental possibilities.

In course of time, geography was no longer considered to be a science of humans on Earth but a science of humans on Earth and the study of their action and inter-action and the inter-relationship between humans and nature.

Today, we have realized that human life is dependent on the environment on one hand, and on the other hand, the environment is modified by human activities and actions. Thus, we cannot conquer nature though we may be able to reduce the effects of harsh environments. The question whether man is a slave of nature or master of nature has no relevance today. If we have to survive on the Earth, we have to live in harmony with nature knowing its secrets, to exploit them wisely for our betterment.

BRANCHES OF GEOGRAPHY

During the 20th century, more attention has been paid to systematic studies of geographical data, while at the same time a strong tradition of field observation and of interest in the natural and human aspects of geographic phenomena have combined to make geography one of the first disciplines to fulfil a bridging function between the natural and social sciences. As a result, the branches of geographical inquiry fall into **three major areas :** (i) studies associated with the regional concept, (ii) the major systematic branches of human geography, and (iii) the major systematic branches of physical geography.

(1) PHYSIOGRAPHY

This is the most important branch of geography. The superstructure of the discipline of geography is built upon it. It studies relief, soil and structure of the Earth.

It is divided into a number of branches making the subject matter of geography more comprehensive.

(i) **Geomorphology** studies the Earth's structure, the rocks that make up the Earth, relief features like mountains and plains and their evolution.

(ii) **Geology** is the science of the study of rocks, and is helpful in the study of geomorphology.

(iii) **Glaciology** is concerned with the study of glaciers.

(iv) **Seismology** is the study of earthquakes and their bearings on the internal structure of the Earth.

(v) **Hydrology** is the study of the characteristics of rivers, lakes, fluvial morphology, floods, fluctuation of water table and underground water resources, development and change of coastal features.

(vi) **Oceanography** is another branch of hydrology. It is the study of the ocean, tides, waves and the ocean floor.

(vii) **Climatology** studies the causes and distribution of temperature and winds, rainfall and runoff, weather and climate.

(viii) **Pedology** is the study of soil science. Soil, which is the result of complex physical and chemical reaction of parent rock material, needs the support of other sciences like chemistry, geology and biology.

(ix) **Biogeography** studies the distribution of flora (plant) and fauna (animal) in different parts of the world. The study of **flora** alongside its environment is known as *Phytogeography* while the study of **fauna** is called *Zoography*.

(x) **Paleography** is the study of physical geography in the past geological ages. It studies the distribution of land and sea through successive geological times.

(2) HUMAN GEOGRAPHY

Human geography, also known as **cultural geography**, as a branch of the modern discipline, deals with the evolution of human beings i.e. changing distribution and spatial organisation of a variety of human characteristics, ranging from great urban centres built by man to the geographical diffusion of specific technical innovations in agriculture. It is accepted that it is not the physical environment alone that determines human ability to make the best use of the natural sources.

It is divided into following sub fields to make the study more comprehensive :

1. **Economic Geography:** Economic geography concerns itself with man's activities in improving his material well-being through economic production, exchange distribution and consumption, of useful goods and services, that human groups and their members need. Economic geography is a very important sub-field of human geography and has developed very fast in the recent past.

2. **Cultural Geography:** This is also called **Social Geography**. It deals with the cultural aspects of different human groups, which include man's habitat, clothing, food, shelter, skills, tools, language, religions, social organisation and his outlook.

3. **Historical Geography:** Historical geography seeks to build up the geographical picture of a region or area, as it has evolved during the years in the past. It gives us important clues in understanding the region as it is at present. Historical geography is considered simply as the geography of the past periods.

4. **Anthrogeography** studies the distribution of human communities on the Earth in relation to their geographical environment.

5. **Demography** is the science that studies the different aspects of population like birth rate, death

rate and age composition. It also studies the socio-economic composition of the population and sex composition.

6. Settlement Geography deals with the size, form and functions of settlement built by human beings, and analyses their historic growth.

7. Agricultural Geography studies how different kinds of farms and farming systems have developed in particular areas and how they are different or similar to the farms and farming systems of other areas.

8. Urban Geography studies the concepts of location, interaction and accessibility as well as distribution and movements of populations. It deals with land use patterns and classification of cities according to their function.

9. Political Geography deals with the government states and countries. It studies human social activities that are related to the location and boundaries of cities, nations and groups of nations.

(3) SYSTEMATIC AND REGIONAL GEOGRAPHY

According to Woolbridge and East, *"Geography may be persued by two methods or upon two levels, which may be distinguished as General (or World) Geography and Special (Regional) Geography."* Thus, geography may be studied either as systematic geography or as regional geography.

Systematic Geography

- In systematic geography, we select one geographical factor and study its distribution for the whole world or a part thereof. Our attention is concentrated on a particular geographical factor.
- Relief, drainage, climate, vegetation, soil, mineral wealth, agriculture, industry, transport, trade and commerce and population are some of the important geographical elements.
- These elements are studied separately with reference to a particular area. This area could be a country, a continent or the whole world.
- This method of studying geography is also known as 'Topical approach' because different topics or element complex is our main concern.
- The best way to study the systematic geography is to consider the variations on the surface of the Earth with reference to a particularly geographical element.
- Some geographers call it General Geography also.
- The main **advantage** of systematic geography is that some elements are selected in their total reality and concentration is focused on the distribution and analysis of these elements.

Regional Geography

- Regional Geography considers the area as a whole first and aims at identifying those geographical factors or components which in their unison create the distinct character of the region.
- The geographical conditions are not the same everywhere. The areal differentiations are so sharp that no two regions are the same.
- Regional geography helps us in identifying the region.
- For intense study, larger regions are further divided into smaller regions. For example, if we take Ganga Plain, Chhotanagpur Plateau, or Assam Valley, rather than taking whole of India, and study their location relief, drainage, climate, soils, vegetation, mineral wealth, agriculture, industry, transport, trade, population, etc. will be termed as *regional geography.*
- Thus, in regional geography, the main emphasis is on the region.
- The process of identifying various regions is known as regionalisation.

Following are the main advantages of regional geography :

1. The study of geography becomes easy and more effective.
2. It examines the man-environment relations. Cause and effect relationship becomes clear.
3. The basic principles of geography are easily understood.
4. We come to know the economic disparities among various regions.
5. The study is intense because the area is limited.

The above discussion makes it clear that both systematic and regional geography are essential to comprehend the geographical knowledge.

Distinction between Systematic and Regional Geography

Systematic Geography	Regional Geography
1. Systematic geography studies a particular element over the earth or a part thereof.region	1. Regional geography, studies a particular with reference to all the geographical elements.
2. It presents an integrated form of the area,	2. It presents isolated form of the arca.
3. It puts more emphasis on the fact that geography should be concerned with the identification of similarities between different areas.	3. It emphasizes that geography should be associated with the identification of differences between different areas.
4. It is based on political units.	4. It is based on geographical units.
5. This study presents the facts.	5. This study examines the man-environment relationship.
6. In the systematic study, types and sub-types are determined on one particular factor, i.e. climate.	6. The boundaries of the regions are identified. This is known as regionalisation.
7. It believes in the formulation of laws and theories in each geographical explanation.	7. It does not believe that no two places are similar on the earth's surface.
8. The approach also, reflects that some similarities always remain in the different areas of the earth's surface.	8. It does not believe in the formulation of laws and theories.

(4) CARTOGRAPHY

It is the science and art of drawing maps and charts. This branch is responsible for geoletic and topographical surveys and the preparation of maps on certain selected scale.

(5) MATHEMATICALGEOGRAPHY

Mathematical Geography is closely related to the making of maps and interpretation and analysis of statistical data.

2 THE EARTH IN SPACE

FACTS ABOUT EARTH

- Earth is the third planet from the Sun and the fifth largest.
- Orbit – 1,49,600,000 km (1.00 *Au*) from sun
- Diametre – 12,756.3 km
- Mass : 5.972e24 Kg
- Earth is the densest major body of solar system
- Earth is the only planet whose English name does not derive from Roman/Greek mythology.
- The interaction of the earth and the moon slows the Earth's rotation by about 2 milli seconds per century.
- Current research indicates that about 900 million years ago there were 48118 hour days in a year

Earth's Satellites

- Earth has only one natural satellite, the *moon*. but
- Asteroids 3753 Cruithne and 2002 AA29 have complicated orbital relationship with the earth.
- Scientists believe the Earth began its life about 4.6 billion years ago.
- The Earth formed as cosmic dust lumped together to from larger and larger particles until 150 million years had passed.
- It gradually contacted under its own gravity and assumed a flattened disc-like shape.
- At about 4.4 billion years, the young earth had a mass similar to the mass it has today.
- The continents probably began forming about 4.2 billion years ago as earth continued to cool.
- The cooling also resulted in the release of gases from the lithosphere, much of which formed the earth's early atmosphere.

THEORIES ON THE ORIGIN OF THE EARTH

Man has propounded many theories of the origin of the Earth. Though there is a lot of difference of opinion among the scientists regarding the age of the Earth, yet most of the scientists agree that the life of the Earth may range from 3 to 5 billion years. Let's know about the Geological history of the Earth.

The following table shows the different theories related to the origin of the earth's surface.

Theory	Geographer	Fact
1) Buffon's Hypothesis	Georges de Baffon	A huge comet came very close to sun and formed planets and sub-planets
2) Gaseous Hypothesis	Kant	Earth originated due to the solidification of the slowly rotating cloud of gas.
3) Nebular Hypothesis	Laplace	Earth is formed by the solidification of a ring that is thrown away by a cooling and rotating nebula.
4) Tidal (collision) Hypothesis	Jeans and Jaffreys	Earth is evolved by the existence of two nebulas instead of a single one.
5) Planetesimal Hypothesis	Chamberlin and Moulton	The earth is originated from two heavenly bodies in the universe.

Most of the Earth's early atmosphere was created in the first one million years after solidification (4.4 billion years ago). Carbon dioxide, nitrogen, and water vapor dominated this early atmosphere. The table below describe the three major stages of development of the atmosphere.

EVOLUTION OF THE EARTH'S ATMOSPHERE

Name of Stage	Duration of Stage (Billions of Years Ago)	Main Constituents of the Atmosphere	Dominant Processes and Features
Early Atmosphere	4.4 to 4.0	H_2O, hydrogen cyanide (HCN), ammonia (NH_3), methane (CH_4), sulfur, iodine, bromine, chlorine, argon	Lighter gases like hydrogen and helium escaped to space. All water was held in the atmosphere as vapor because of high temperatures.

Secondary Atmosphere	4.0 to 3.3	At 4.0 billion H_2O, CO_2, and nitrogen (N) dominant. Cooling of the atmosphere causes precipitation and the development of the oceans. By 3.0 billion CO_2, H_2O, N_2 dominant. O_2 begins to accumulate.	Continued release of gases from the lithosphere. Water vapor clouds common in the lower atmosphere. Chemosynthetic bacteria appear on the Earth at 3.6 billion. Life begins to modify the atmosphere.
Living Atmosphere	3.3 to Present	N_2 - 78%, O_2 - 21%, Argon - 0.9%, CO_2 - 0.036%	Development, evolution and growth of life increases the quantity of oxygen in the atmosphere from <1% to 21%. 500 million years ago concentration of atmospheric oxygen levels off. Humans begin modifying the concentrations of some gases in the atmosphere beginning around the year 1700.

Approximate Origin Time of the Major Plant and Animal Groups

Organism Group	Time of Origin
Marine Plants (algae)	800 Million Years Ago
Marine Invertebrates	570 Million Years Ago
Fish	505 Million Years Ago
Land Plants	438 Million Years Ago
Amphibians	408 Million Years Ago
Reptiles	320 Million Years Ago
Mammals	208 Million Years Ago
Flowering Plants (Angiosperms)	140 Million Years Ago
Home Sapiens	100 Thousand Years Ago

PLACE OF THE EARTH IN THE UNIVERSE

In the ancient times, the earth occupied a central place in the universe. Even Aristotle, the famous Greek philosopher proclaimed that the earth was the centre of the universe. The sun, the moon and the stars were all subservient to the earth. **Ptolemy** declared that the sun, the moon and the stars, revolved round the earth. This belief was called the geocentric views.

HELIOCENTRIC THEORY VS GEOCENTRIC THEORY

In the middle ages it was believed that the earth was located at the center of the universe and all the planets revolved around the earth. This belief was called the ***Geocentric Theory***. The Geocentric theory was believed by the church especially because the church taught that God put the earth as the center of the universe which made earth special and powerful. The Geocentric theory was active for almost 2,000 years and it was not until a man named **Nicolaus Copernicus** that the Geocentric theory was finally proven wrong.

Copernicus was actually the first man to come up with the ***Heliocentric Theory***. Copernicus felt that the Geocentric theory did not accurately explain the movements of the sun, moon, and planets. Copernicus studied the movements of the planets for thirty years and then he figured out that the sun was actually at the center of the universe than that of the earth.

Copernicus was told by many scholars that he should make his new findings accessible to others by publishing it. In 1543 the book called "on the revolutions of the heavenly bodies" was released. Copernicus book had a great impact that angered the Catholic and Protestant Church. The reason why the Church became so angry was because the Geocentric theory made human beings seem closer to God and since earth was in the center that meant humans were more special. The Heliocentric theory changed that perspective completely making humans lose that position in the universe.

But, **Pythagoras and Pilolaus** stated that the Earth was not stationary in the universe but rotates around its axis and makes one rotation in 24 hours. The famous thinker **Aristarchus** believed that the Earth revolves around the sun. Later on. It was an important turning point in the history of thought when on 17 January 1610, **Galileo,** a prominent mathematician of Padua University invented a telescope and proved in a practical way that the earth like any other planet was an ordinary one and revolved around the sun. This belief was know as the Heliocentric views.

Infact, our earth is a very small part of sun for example, from the point of view of size the earth is so small that 1,300,000 earths can be packed into sun which is an ordinary star amongst innumerable star galaxies of the world. **Edington** calculated that the universe might be occupied by 11 billion-billion-billion stars of the size of our sun. Our earth may thus, be considered to be sand particle in the desert of star studded universe.

POSITION, SHAPE AND SIZE

- Lying between Venus and Mars, the Earth is the third and the largest planet of the solar system in distance from Sun. It ranks fifth in size with a mean radius of 6.371 kilometres (3, 960 miles).
- The Earth approximates a sphere in shape but is characterized by a distinct oblateness, that is, a flattening at the poles.
- The definition of the figure of the Earth—that is, its size and shape—usually does not involve the description of mountains and valleys but, rather, the size and shape of the mean sea-level surface and its continuation under the land.
- This hypothetical surface, called a **geoid**, is a reference surface from which topographic heights and ocean depths are measured. Because of the irregular mass distributions in the Earth and the resultant gravity anomalies, the **geoid** is not a suitable reference surface and consequently is not a suitable reference surface for a geometric figure on the earth. As reference figures of the earth, but not for its topography, simple geometric forms are used that approximate the geoid.
- For many purposes an adequate geometrical representation of the earth is a sphere for which only the radius of the sphere must be stated.
- When a more accurate reference figure is required an **ellipsoid** of **revolution** is used as a representation of the shape and the size of the Earth.
- It is a surface generated by rotating an eclipse 360° about its minor exist.

Points to Remember

1. Earth has a circumference of approximately 40,000 km.
2. The equatorial circumference is 40,076.5 km.
3. The polar diameter is 12,714 km.
4. Earth's circumference was first calculated by **Erastosthenes** (200 BC) based on direct observations of the sun's rays. His calculation, that the circumference of the Earth was 43,000 km is very close to modern calculations.

PROOF OF THE EARTH'S SPHERICITY :

Rigorous and convincing proof that the earth is spherical in form is not, however, as evident as it might seem if we limit our observation available to humans before the age of space vehicles.

Pythagoras (572-500 B.C.), Greek philosopher and mathematician, was among the first to suggest that the earth is spherical in shape.

THE EARTH IS NOT FLAT

1. If the earth were a flat disc, then the rising Sun would have been seen at all places at the same time. But, this does not happen. Places in the east see the rising Sun earlier.
2. When a ship approaches land, its funnel or mast is seen first and then the hull. If the Earth had

been flat, the whole ship would have been seen at one time.

THE EARTH IS A SPHERE

1. During a **lunar eclipse,** the shadow of the earth falls on the surface of the Moon. The shadow appears as an arc of a circle. The Earth is rarely oriented in the same position during successive eclipses but it always casts a circular shadow, thus proving that the Earth is a sphere. A sphere is the only solid body that will always cast a circular shadow.

2. At the North Pole, the **Pole Star** can always be observed at 90 degrees in the sky, since the star lies in line with the axis of the Earth.

   1. As one travels southwards, the angle of Pole Star decreases.
   2. At the Equator, the angle becomes zero degrees. This observation proves that the path of travel is an arc of a circle.
   3. The Sun, Moon and all the heavenly bodies appear to be spherical when viewed from different positions. It seems logical to conclude that the Earth is no exception.
   4. The photographs of the Earth taken from space prove beyond any doubt that the Earth is a sphere.
   5. The distant horizon is always and everywhere viewed circular from a cliff of a land or from the deck of a ship.
   6. A ship always appears to sink gradually instead of abruptly. Then, it can be seen again. That time its top is seen before than the hull.

Oblate Spheroid

In 1671, a French astronomer was sent to the island of Cayenne, in French Guiana (South America) to make some astronomical observations. The pendulum of his clock (1m) had been adjusted to beat the same seconds as in Paris (when the pendulum is made shorter, it beats faster, made longer it beats slower). Upon arriving in Cayenne, which is at the Equator, he discovered that his clock was losing two and half minutes per day.

As soon as Newton's laws of gravitation were published (1687), it became possible to explain the slowing down of the clock to the effect of decreased gravity.

This could be accounted by assuming that the equatorial region of the earth lies further away from the Earth's centre than the more northerly regions.

THE EARTH AS AN OBLATE SPHEROID

- Refined measurements of the Earth have proved that the true form of the Earth resembles a sphere that has been **compressed at the poles** and made to **bulge at the Equator.** This form is known as an **oblate spheroid.**
- The diameter measures about **12,756 km** at the Equator which is 42 km more than the polar diameter which is about **12,714 km.** This is because of the centrifugal force caused by the rotation of the earth. (Centrifugal force is the apparent outward force in a rotational body, directed away from the centre.).
- The Equator remains a circle.
- A cross-section through the poles is an ellipse rather than a circle.
- The difference between the polar and equatorial diameter is insignificant when we take the large size of the Earth into account. For practical purposes the Earth can be considered a sphere.

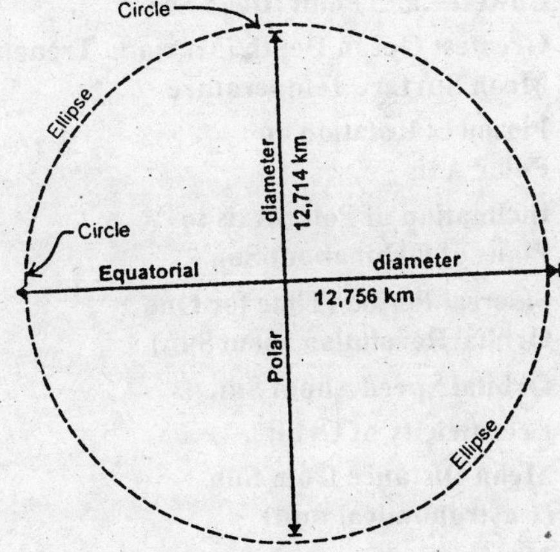

GREAT AND SMALL CIRCLES : When a sphere is divided exactly in half through its centre, the circumference represents the largest circle that can be drawn on the sphere and is known as a **great circle.** For example, the Equator is a great circle and every meridian of longitude is half of a great circle.

STATISTICAL DATA OF THE EARTH

The Earth is the fifth largest planet in the solar system

1. Diameter	
Equatorial Diameter	12,756 km
Polar Diameter	12,714 km
2. Circumference	
Equatorial Circumference	40,077 km
Polar Circumference	40,009 km
3. Total Surface Area	510 million sq. km
29% covered by Continents; 71% covered by Oceans	
4. Volume	1,000,000 million cu.
Once the diameter is known, volume is calculated by using the formula $V=\frac{4}{3}\pi r^3$.	
5. Mass	5.98×10^{21} metric tonnes
Using Newton's law of gravitation, mass of Earth is calculated from the orbit of the Moon.	
6. Density	5.52 g/cm^3
7. Age	4,550 million years
8. Mean Height of Land	29.2% of the total surface area
9. Water Area	756m
10. Mean Ocean Depth	70.8% of total surface area
11. Highest Land Point (Mt Everest)	8850 m
12. Lowest Land Point (Dead Sea)	397 m
13. Greatest Ocean Depth (Mariana Trench)	11,022 m
14. Mean Surface Temperature	14°C
15. Period of Rotation on Polar Axis	23 hr 56 min 4,09 sec.
16. Inclination of Polar Axis to Plane of Orbit about Sun	23°26′ 56″
17. Sidereal Period (Time for One Orbital Revolution about Sun)	365.256 36 days
18. Orbital Speed About Sun	29.8 km/sec
19. Eccentricity of Orbit	0.0167
20. Mean Distance from Sun (1 astronomical unit)	149,598,500 km
21. Maximum distance from Sun (at aphelion- between July 2 and July 5)	about 152 million km
22. Minimum distance from Sun (at Perihelion-between January 2 and January 5)	about 147 million km
23. Temperature	Highest - 58°C at Al-Aziziyah, Libya, Lowest-89.6°C at Antarctica Average 14°C
24. Atmosphere	Oxygen 21%, Nitrogen 78%, Argon and other gases 1%.

The **great circle** route is any line that circles the globe and divides it into two equal halves.

A course of travel along the great circle is known as the **great circle route.** It is the shortest distance between two places on the earth and lies on the arc of a great circle. Thus, the shortest jet route from Moscow to San Fransisco would be over the North Pole.

Circles produced when a sphere is not divided exactly in half (which means that the line of division does not pass through its centre), are always smaller than the great circles and are called **small circles.**

Characteristics of a Great Circle

1. A great circle is the **largest possible circle** that can be drawn on the surface of a sphere.
2. A great circle is always formed when a sphere is **divided exactly in half.**
3. An **infinite number** of great circles can be drawn on a sphere.
4. One and **only one great circle can be drawn that will pass through two given points on a sphere** (unless they are exactly opposite each other, for example the North and the South Pole).
5. An arc of a great circle is the **shortest distance** between two points on a sphere.
6. Intersecting great circles always **bisect each other.**

One important use of great circles is in **navigation.** Since an arc of a great circle is the shortest distance between two points, it is economical in the interest of saving fuel and time, to follow the great circle when travelling between distant places by sea or air, provided there are no obstructions to prevent the use of the great circle. Although more economical in term of time and fuel, it is not always possible to follow the great circle route for many reasons:

1. Air terminals in sparsely populated regions may not have adequate facilities to handle modern air traffic.
2. Airplanes may need to be fuelled if the great circle route involves travel over large expanses of air space.
3. Some countries do not allow use of their air space by others.

Earth Vis-a-Vis the Solar System

Planet	Distance from the sun in million km	Time taken to complete orbit	Temperature in degrees Celsius	Known satellites
Mercury	58	88 days -170 night	350 day	0
Venus	108	225 days	480	0
Earth	150	365 days	22	1
Mars	228	687 days	-23	2
Jupiter	778	11.9 years	-150	80
Saturn	1,427	29.5 years	-180	83
Uranus	2,869	84 years	-210	27
Neptune	4,496	165 years	-220	14

2.4 MOTIONS OF THE EARTH AND THEIR CONSEQUENCES

The Earth has five main motions:

(1) it rotates daily on its axis;

(2) it revolves annually around the Sun;

(3) it precesses, or wobbles, somewhat like a spinning top;

(4) it follows the Sun in the Sun's travels through the Milky Way, and

(5) it moves with the Milky Way as the entire galaxy travels through the universe.

THE EFFECTS OF THE SPEED OF ROTATION

The differences in the speed of rotation at the Equator and at the poles has important consequences.

1. It affects the shape of the Earth.

There is a bulge at the Equator and consequent flattening at the poles.

2. It affects the general circulation of the atmosphere.

a. The moving air is deflected to the right in the Northern Hemisphere and to the left in the Southern Hemisphere.

b. Cyclones and anticyclones are similarly deflected in both hemispheres.

c. The movements of water in the ocean is affected in relation to the rigid crust.

ROTATION

❖ Rotation is the spinning of the Earth on its own axis.

❖ The spinning of the Earth on its polar axis in fact takes 23 hours 56 minutes 4.09 seconds for the rotation through 360°.

❖ The direction of rotation is from west to east and so to a person standing on the Earth the apparent movement of the Sun, Moon and stars across the sky is in the opposite direction—from east to west.

❖ The speed in km/h (mph) at which any point of the Earth's surface is rotating is easily calculated by dividing the length of the relevant parallel of latitude by 24.

❖ Thus at the equator, the rotational velocity is about 1, 667 km/h (1,050 mph) and decreases progressively toward the poles, where it is zero.

❖ People on the Earth's surface are unaware of the movement both because it is a constant motion and because the atmosphere rotates along with the Earth.

Day and Night

Day and night are caused by Earth's rotation. Day is the time required for a celestial body to turn once on its axis; especially the period of the Earth's rotation. The **sidereal day** is the time between two observed passages of a star over the same meridian of longitude. The **apparent solar day** is the time between two successive transits of the Sun over the same meridian. Because the orbital motion of the Earth makes the Sun seem to move slightly east-ward each dav relative to the stars, the **solar day** is about four minutes longer than the sidereal day; i.e., the mean solar day is 24 hours 3 minutes, 56.555 seconds of mean sidereal time; more usually the sidereal day is expressed in terms of solar time, being 23 hours, 56 minutes, 4 seconds of mean solar time long. The **mean solar day** is the average value of the solar day, which, changes slightly in length during the year as Earth's speed in its orbit varies.

REVOLUTION: Revolution is the movement of the Earth in its orbit around the Sun. It completes one circuit in about 365.25 days. This would be an awkward length for calendars and so every fourth year is made a **"leap year"** of 366 days with an extra day in February, the other years being 365 days in length.

Major Differences between Rotation and Revolution

Rotation	Revolution
1. Turning around of the Earth on its own axis.	Movement of the Earth around the Sun.
2. The Earth takes 24 hours to complete one rotation.	The Earth takes 365.25 days to complete revolution.
3. Rotation causes day and night.	Revlution causes change in seasons.

Unequal Days and Seasons. The path of the Earth around the Sun is elliptical. The path is slightly irregular because of the gravitational attraction of the Moon and the other planets. While the Earth is revolving around the Sun and rotating on its axis, a constant angle is maintained between the Earth's axis and its plane of ecliptic. The constant angle is 23.5° away from the perpendicular to the plane of the ecliptic. This is referred to as **'the angle of the inclination of the Earth's axis'**. The inclined axis keeps a constant angle of 66.5° with reference to the plane of the ecliptic.

Not only is the Earth's axis inclined but it remains parallel as well in all the positions of the Earth around the Sun. These two constant factors associated with the Earth's movements cause differences in the lengths of day and night and in the altitude of the Sun above the horizon at different latitudes during the period of revolution.

Since the axis always points toward the same area of space, the North Pole is tilted toward the Sun for half the year and away from it for the other half. This means that the Sun shines more directly on the Northern Hemisphere during one half of the year (Spring and Summer) than during the other half (Autumn and Winter). The tilt of Earth's axis thus changes the amount of heat the land will receive during the day, producing alternate warm and cold seasons.

Seasons are the four divisions of the year, called Spring, Summer, Autumn (or fall), and Winter. North and South of the tropics, Summer is the warmest season, Winter the coolest. Spring and Autumn are transitions between the two extremes. In the tropics, little temperature variation occurs with the seasons.

In the Northern Hemisphere, Spring begins about March 21, Summer about June 21, Autumn about September 23, and Winter about December 22. In the Southern Hemisphere, it is Autumn that begins in March and Spring that begins in September. Winter in the Southern Hemisphere begins about June 21 and Summer about December 22.

Year after year, the seasons form a never-ending cycle. The Sun is farthest south (lowest) in the sky and the period of daylight shortest in the Northern Hemisphere about December 22, the day of the Winter solstice. From then, on each day the Sun reaches a little higher (farther to the north) in the noon sky and each day the period of daylight is a little longer. About March 21, on the date of the vernal equinox, the Sun reaches halfway on its northward journey in the sky; it crosses the Equator. On that day, daylight and darkness are of the same length.

APPARENT MIGRATION OF THE SUN

The Sun does not move, the Earth moves. But to us on the Earth, it appears as if it is the Sun that moves between the Tropic of Cancer and the Tropic of Capricorn. This means that all latitudes between the Tropic of Cancer and the Tropic of Capricorn will have the Sun vertically overheard at least once between June and December and once again between December and June.

Therefore, places between the Tropics will have the Sun overhead twice a year. Places beyond the two tropics will have the Sun directly overhead only once a year.

1. Northward Apparent Migration (*Uttarayan*) : For six months of the year, the Sun appears to be moving north. This northward migration begins after December 22 and is completed on June 21, when the Sun is direcly overhead at 23.5°N of latitude (Tropic of Cancer). This position of the earth (21 June) that is, when Sun shines vertically over the Tropic of Cancer is called the ***Summer Solstice.***

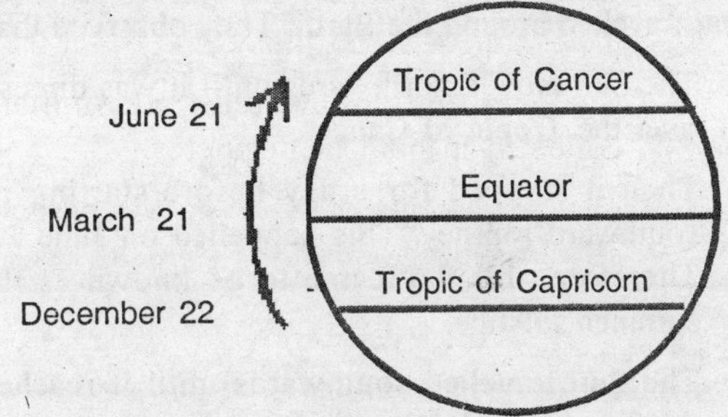

Northward Apparent Migration or Uttarayan

2. Southward Apparent Migration (*Dakshinayan*) : For six months of the year, the Sun appears to be moving south. This southward migration begins after June 21 and is completed on December 22, when the Sun is directly overhead at 23.5°S of latitude (Tropic of Capricorn). This positiojn of the Sun (22 December), that is, when the sun shines vertically over the Tropic of Capricorn is called the ***winter solstice.***

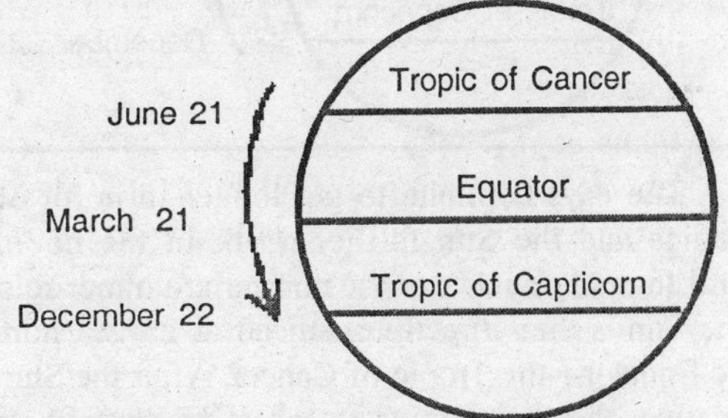

Southward Apparent Migration or Dakshinayan

It is this apparent movement of the Sun, sometimes to the north and sometimes to the south that explains why the exact spot from where the Sun rises shifts a litle every day.

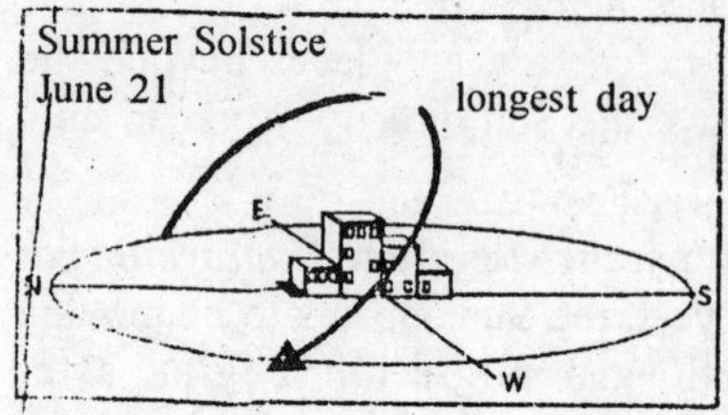

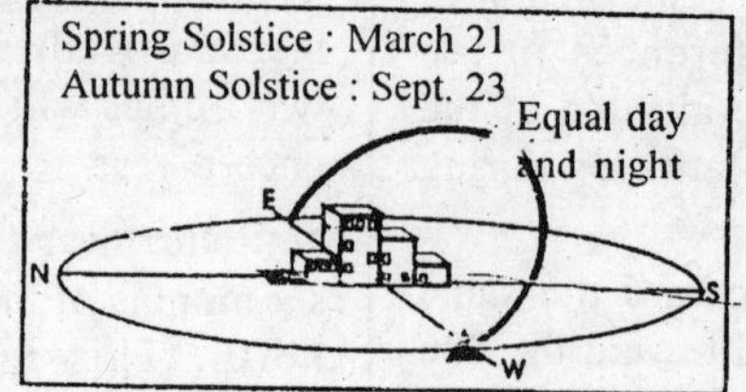

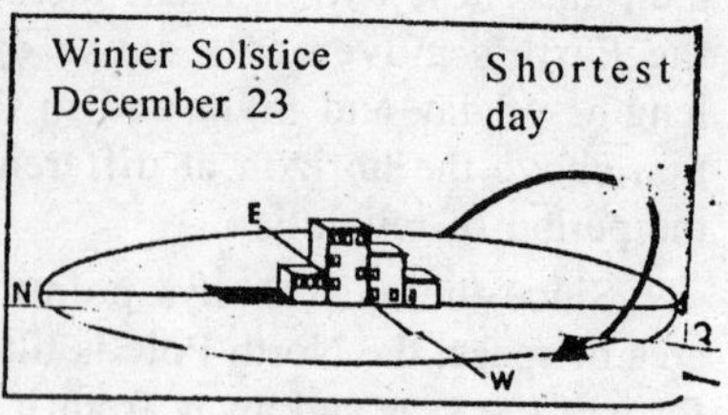

What is a Solstice ?

Solstice means the "standing still of the Sun".

The ancient Greeks believed that it was the Sun that travelled around the Earth. They observed that:

1. The Sun moved northwards until it was directly over the Tropic of Cancer.

   Then it stopped for a day before starting its southward journey. This happened on June 21. Therefore, this day came to be known as the summer solstice.

2. The Sun travelled southwards until it reached the Tropic of Capricorn.

Then the Sun stood still for a day before it began its northward journey. This happened on December 22. Therefore, this day came to be known as the ***winter solstice.***

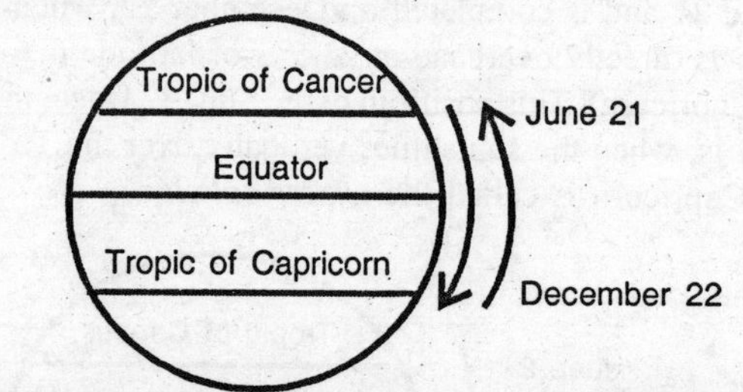

The days continue to get longer in north of the tropics and the Sun farther north in the noon sky until June 21, the date of the northern Summer solstice. The Sun is then directly overhead at 23°27' north of the Equator—the Tropic of Cancer. After the Summer solstice, the Sun begins to move southward again. Each day in the area north of the tropics, the period of daylight is a little shorter and the night is a little longer. Each day the Sun is a little farther south in the sky at noon. In September comes the Autumnal equinox, when day and night are again the same length.

The Sun continues southward until the Winter solstice is reached, when the Sun is directly over the Tropic of Capricorn (23°27') south of the Equator.

If the axis were not tilted, the Sun would always be directly over the Equator and the Northern and Southern hemisphere would both have constant, similar weather the year round.

When the North Pole is directed toward the Sun, the Sun's rays strike most directly on the Northern Hemisphere. The more directly the rays strike, the closer to vertical they are. Vertical rays of sunlight are more effective in producing light and heat than are the slanting rays, for **(1)** the slanting rays must pass through a greater thickness of atmosphere than vertical rays and thus lose more of their heat; and **(2)** slanting rays are spread out over a greater area than vertical rays, and are therefore less concentrated. Thus when the North Pole is directed toward the Sun, Summer is produced in the Northern Hemisphere; the Southern Hemisphere has Winter. When the South Pole is directed toward the Sun, the Southern Hemisphere receives the most heat and has Summer.

Perihelion and Aphelion

The Earth travels 939,886,400 km along its elliptical orbit in a single revolution around the Sun.

The average distance between the Earth and the Sun is 150 million km. Since the orbit is elliptical, the distance of the Sun from the Earth varies about 2.5 million km from the average.

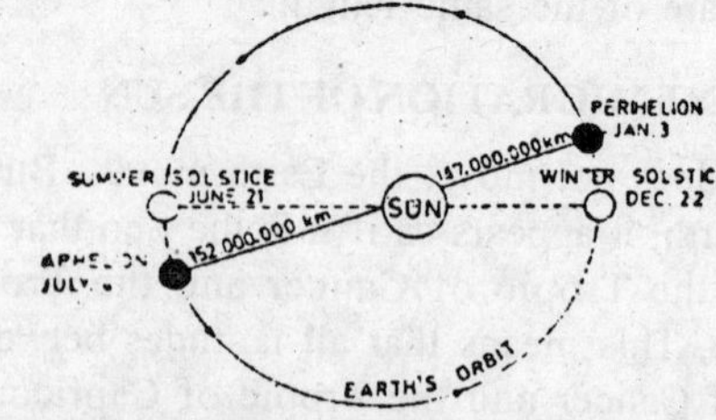

Aphelionand Perihelion. The earth's orbit around the sun is an ellipse. Note that this difference in distance isnot the cause of summer and winter seasons.

1. **Perihelion :** On about January 3rd,the earth is closest to the Sun (147.5 million km). At this time the Earth is said to be in **perihelion.** (This word comes from the Greek word *peri* meaning "near or around" and *helios* meaning "sun").

2. **Aphelion :** On about July 4th, the Earth is farthest from the Sun (152.5 million km). At this time the Earth is said to be in **aphelion.** (This word comes fom the Greek word *ap* meaning "away from" and *helios.*)

These differences in distance is very small when compared to the great distance between the Earth and the Sun and therefore is not the cause for seasons. (It should be noted that the Earth is closest to the Sun in winter and so obviously this is not the cause of seasons).

In accordance with Kepler's laws of planetary motion the Earth moves fastest when it is in perihelion, and slowest in aphelion.

The greater efficiency of the Sun's rays is one reason why the Summer is warmer than Winter. A second reason is that the days are longer. While the Sun is shining, the land and air heat up. When the Sun goes down, they begin to lose heat. From the vernal equinox to the autumnal equinox, each day in the Northern Hemisphere is longer than the night and more heat is gained from the Sun during the day than is lost at night.

The reverse is true as Winter approaches and the northern half of the Earth begins to cool. Not only does the Sun move lower in the sky and become less effective in providing heat, but it shines for a shorter time each day, and heat is lost for a longer time than it is gained.

The Earth's orbit is slightly elliptical, or elongated, so the Earth is farther from the Sun at some times than at other times. The Earth is closest to the Sun and moving most rapidly in January. In early July, when the Earth is farthest from the Sun, it is moving more slowly. The Earth takes 186 days to go from the vernal to the autumnal equinox, but only 179 days to return from the autumnal to the vernal equinox.

There is also a small difference in the amount of heat received by the Earth—less heat in July than in January. The total effect of this variation in time and heat is that the seasons in the Northern Hemisphere are a little milder than those in the Southern Hemisphere. The northern Winter is shorter and warmer than the southern Winter. The northern Summer is longer and cooler than the southern Summer.

Equinox (meanings : equal nights) : Midway between the solstices, are the equinoxes. Equinoxes (March 21 and September 23) indicate the time when the midday Sun crosses over the Equator. Falling midway between the dates of the solstices, on these dates, the earth's axis lies at 90° to the line joining the centres of the earth and the sun and neither the northern nor the southern hemisphere is inclined towards the sun. At the equinoxes, days and nghts are of equal length throughout the world.

A Summary of Daylight Hours in the Northern and Southern Hemisphere		
1. Longest day in the Northern Hemisphere	:	June 21
2. Shortest day in the Northern Hemisphere	:	December 22
3. Equal day and night in the Northern Hemisphere	:	March 21 and September 23
4. Longest day in the Southern Hemisphere	:	December 22
5. Shortest day in the Southern Hemisphere	:	June 21
6. Equal day and night in the Southern Hemisphere	:	March 21 and September 23

On 22nd September and 21st March neither o the poles is inclined towads the sun or away from it. The rays of the sun fall prependicularly on the equator and the circle of illumination passes right through the poles. It is autumn in the northern hemisphere and spring in the southern hemisphere. This position is called to autumn or ***Autumnal Equinox.***

Similarly on 21st March, it is spring in the northern hemisphere and summer in the southern. This position is called the ***spring or vernal equinox.***

On both these days in the year, the days and nights are equal all over the globe.

Equinox
Equinox (*meaning : equal nights*) : Midway between the solstices, are the equinoxes, Equinoxes (**March 21 and September 23**) indicate the time when the midday Sun crosses ove the Equator. At the equinoxes, **days and nights are of equal length throughout the world.**

The Sun, the planets, and other celestial objects in the solar system travel within the **Milky Way**. The solar system is moving toward the constellation Hercules at a speed of about 19.3 km/sec or 69,500 kmph. In addition, the Milky Way is rotating like a giant wheel. In the vicinity of the Sun, the Milky Way rotates at a speed of about 250 km/sec or 898,000 kmph. Moving at this speed, the solar system completes one revolution around the centre of the galaxy in about 200 million years. Finally, the solar system moves with the Milky Way as the entire galaxy travels through the universe.

THE EARTH'S GRID SYSTEM

When **Erathosthenes,** the Greek Philosopher and mathematician, made his calculation of the earth's size, he made another important contribution. He realized that any place of on the Earth could be located with a basic grid of lines called **Longitude** and **Latitude.**

Location of a Place and Time on the Earth's Surface: A spherical surface has normally no reference or starting point, as every point is the same as any other point. But, fortunately for us there are two convenient points of reference on the spherical Earth. They are the North and South poles where the Axis of rotation meets. A system of locating other points between the two poles was first divided by the ancient Greeks, on the basis of which the Earth's grid lines were drawn. Any globe will show that a circle extends around the Earth halfway between the two poles, called the **Equator.**

LATITUDE: Latitude is the angular distance in degrees on the Earth's surface measured north and south of the Equator. The Equator, which divides the Earth into the Northern and Southern hemispheres is designated as latitude 0 degree (0°) . The North Pole is 90 degrees North (90^0N); the South Pole, 90 degrees South (90^0S). Lines of latitude are imaginary lines that circle the Earth in a true east-west direction. They are often called parallels because they run parallel to the Equator and to each other. Viewed on a globe from either pole, the lines form concentric circles, the largest circle being the Equator.

Importance of Latitude
1. Latitude and Temperature. ◆ Latitude is related to temperature. ◆ It tells us about the climate of a place in general terms. 2. Latitude and Location. • It enable us to find the exact location of places on the earth.

Distance : Each degree of latitude spans about 111 kilometres or 69 statute miles (about 60 nautical miles) on the earth's surface. The interntional nautical mile is defined as exactly equivalent to 1852 international metres or 6076.1033 feet. One nautical mile is equal to 1.15077 statute miles.

LATITUDE AND PARALLELS
(i) A latitude is a angular distance of a place north or south of equator. (ii) There are 180 parallels of latitude . (iii) Each parallel of latitude is a circle. (iv) All the parallel of latitude are not of equal length. The circles become smaller towards the poles. (v) Equator, at 0^0 is the most important latitude and is the largest circle that can be drawn on the globe. (vi) The distance between any two parallels of latitude is always equal. (vii) The north pole and the south pole are fixed points and serve as basic points of reference.

The exact distance varies slightly from the equator to the poles because the Earth is an imperfect sphere. From the Equator to 40^0 north and south the span is slightly less than 111 km and from 41^0 to the poles it is slightly more. The length of a degree of longitude is almost the same as the length of 1° of longitude at the equator, i.e. of about 111 km.

The latitude of any point on the Earth is most precisely expressed in degrees, minutes, and seconds. Each degree is divided into 60 minutes (60') and each minute into 60 seconds (60"). At the equator this distance may be computed by dividing the circumference of the earth by 360°; i.e. 40,075 km/360° = 111 km (approximately).

Latitudes and Temperature Zones : The spherical shape of the earth causes different parts of the earth to be heated to different degrees. The region near the equator gets more direct rays of the Sun. The direct rays are concentrated over a smaller area and so it heats up the Earth more. As we go away from the Equator, due to the curvature of the earth, the Sun's rays strike the earth's surface at an angle. The slanting rays spread the heat over a larger areas and so they donot heat to the same extent as the direct rays. Thus the temperature decreases as we go away from the equator.

Three main heat zones are recognised. These are:

1. **Torrid Zone :** The region between the Tropic of Cancer and Tropic of Capricorn receives direct rays of the Sun practically throughout the year. This area receives maximum heat and is called the **Torrid Zone.**
2. **Temperate Zone :** The regions between the Tropic of Cancer and Arctic Circle in the Northern Hemisphere and the Tropic of Capricorn and Antarctic Circle in the Southern Hemisphere are less hot. This is because the angle of the Sun's rays goes on decreasing towards the poles. These areas have **moderate temperatures** and are therefore called Temperatre Zones.
3. **Frigid Zone :** Near the polar regions, the rays of the Sun are very slanted and so it is **very cold.**

The regions/area between the Arctic Circle and the North Pole in the Northern Hemisphere is called the **Frigid Zone.**

There is a similar region in the Southern Hemisphere between the Antarctic Circle and the South Pole, called the Frigid Zone (*frigid = cold*).

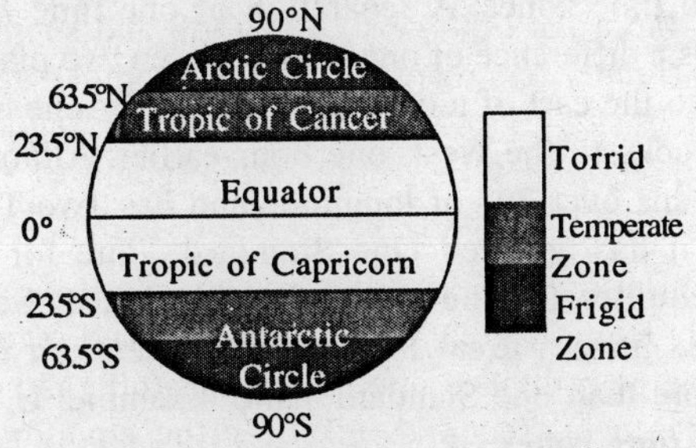

Major Heat Zones of the Earth

LONGITUDE: Longitude is the angular distance on the Earth's surface measured in degrees from a certain meridian. A ***meridian*** is an imaginary line extending from the North Pole to the South Pole at right angles to the Equator. Usually the meridian that passes through Greenwich (a part of London, England) is used in determining longitude. This meridian is called the ***prime meridian***. The longitude of a place reveals how far east or west it is, in degrees, of the prime meridian. The prime meridian marks 0° longitude. Half way around the earth is 180^0 longitude. Thus the earth is longitudinally divided into two hemispheres of 180°—the Eastern Hemisphere, East of Greenwich and the Western Hemisphere, West of Greenwich.

Meridians are spaced farthest apart at the Equator and converge at the poles. At the Equator, 1° of longitude spans about 111 km (69 miles); at 30° North and South, about 97 km (60 miles); at 60° North and South, about 56 km (35 miles) and at the poles, 0 miles. The longitude of a place is generally expressed in whole degrees. More exact longitudes are stated in degrees, minutes and seconds. ***Togther latitude and longitude precisely locate a point on the Earth.***

LONGITUDE
1. Longitude is the angular distance of a place east or west of the Prime Meridian.
2. There are 360 meridians of longitude.
3. The Prime Meridian is a longitude of 0^0.
4. Each Meridian of longitude is a semicircle.
5. All Meridians are of equal length.
6. The distance between only two meridians is not circle. They get closer from equator to the poles.

LONGITUDES AND TIME ZONES : Longitude is also an important factor in determining time-hours, minutes, and seconds—in all parts of the world.

Because the Earth is divided into 360° of longitude and it completes one spin on its axis in a day (24 hours), we can see that time alters by one hour for every 15° of longitude (360 ‸ 24). Each place on Earth has its own local time. This can be measured forwards or backwards from the moment when the Sun reaches its highest point in the sky, which is noon or mid-day. But if every place on Earth could choose its own local time, there would be great confusion. To save this, the Earth is divided into time zones. The simplest time zones would be based on dividing the globe into equal segments of 15° and changing the time by one hour from one zone (segment) to the next. But this is unsatisfactory, because the boundary might pass through a city, giving different times in two sectors of the same city. Time zones, therefore, have irregular boundaries that make allowance for political frontiers. ***Standard time in India is the local time of a place near Allahabad at 82.5°E longitude.***

The prime meridian, or 0° longitude, from which the time zones are measured, passes through Greenwich, England. A person travelling west of Greenwich for 180° of longitude would have to put his clock back by 12 hours. If one were going east of Greenwich for 180°, he would put his clock forward by 12 hours. When they meet on the International Date Line, there would be one day's difference between them. As a result, travellers crossing the International Date Line from east to west lose a day. Travellers crossing from west to east gain a day.

There is a relationship between longitude and time. As the earth rotates, every place has its sunrise, sunset and noon.

When the sun is at its highest point in the sky, it is noon. Noon can be determined by measuring the shadow of a stick in the ground. The shadow is shortest at noon. This highest position of the sun in the sky, which is at noon, is called **Zenith.**

1. LOCAL TIME : *The time of a place reckoned by the mid-day Sun is called the local time.*

All places on the same meridian of longitude have noon at the same time. This is called local time for that particular place. Places located on different meridians have different local times. The Earth takes 24 hours to complete one rotation, i.e., it takes 24 hours to complete 360^0 of its rotation. Therefore, to turn through 1° of the space or 1° of longitude, the time taken is 24 × 60/360 minutes, or 4 minutes, or 360 seconds. Now, the Earth rotates from west to east. Since the Sun does not move, but the earth does, the Earth must be moving in the opposite direction. i.e., from west to east.

MERIDIAN

1. The word meridian is derived from the Latin word meridianus meaning mid-day (*medius = middle dies=day*). Thus, the term meridian signifies sun's position at noon.
2. A.M. stands for ante-meridian (*ante=before*) which means before mid-day or noon.
3. P.M. stands for post-meridian (*post =after* or later) which means after mid-day or noon.

So places in the east see the Sun first. Places in the west see the Sun later. Therefore:

1. For each *1° of longitude towards the east*, a time of four minutes has to be added.
2. For each *1° of longitude towards the west*, a time of four minutes has to be subtracted.

2. STANDARD TIME : When the local time of a central place is taken as the time for the whole country (or a large area), it is called the Standard time of that country or area.

There are about 30 meridians of longitude cutting through India. That means that India has about 30 local times. So, when the railway time-table states that a train will arrive at 8 am., it would be difficult to know exactly when because different places will have 8 a.m. according to their local time There would be confusion. To avoid this confusion, the local time of a central meridian is taken as the time for the whole country. This is called ***Standard Time.***

Indian Standard Time : In India, the longitude of 82.5°E, passing through Allahabad is considered the Standard Meridian. When it is noon on this longitude, the time is taken as noon for the whole the country. This is known as the **Indian Standard Time (IST).**

3. TIME ZONES : A time zone is an area in the world where clocks record the same time. Since it takes 24 hours for the Earth to make one rotation. Standard Fleming, a Canadian, suggested dividing the earth into 24 time zones. In 1884 a group of countries established standard time zones for the whole world. Each zone is almost 15° wide, with adjustments made in some places so that a city or country is not divided into two time zones. A separation of one time zone indicates a difference of one hour between two places. Clocks to the east of a time zone are set for one hour later; clocks to the west, one hour earlier. Although India spans over 30° of longitude and has Two Time Zones, it has adopted One Standard Time for the entire country for the sake of convenience. Some countries have a great longitudinal extent, so they have more than one Standard Time. Example: U.S.A has **five time zones.**

Greenwich Mean Time

The world today has become a global village. People are flying across countries and continents in a matter of hours. It is possible to have dinner in Mumbai, breakfast in London and again dinner in New York.

In order to maintain international uniformity, one uniform time, corresponding to the Prime Meridian is adopted by all countries. This is called the **Greenwich Mean Time or G.M.T.**

For example Indian Standard Time is 5 hours 30 minutes (82.5 × 4 = 330) minutes) ahead of Greenwich time. When it is 5:30 p.m. in India, it is 12:00 noon in Greenwich, England.

Air Time Table of the various airlines follow the Greenwich Mean time.

There is a general understanding among the countries of the world to select the standard meridian of a country or area in multiples of 7.5° of longitude. Every 7.5° of longitude makes a difference of 30 minutes or half-hour. This ensures that the time differences between places is in multiples of half-hour, thus making calculations simple and convenient.

The following table gives the equivalence in distance for the five units of time. These units range from a day to a second.

24 hours of time = 360° of longitude
1 hour of time = 15° of longitude
4 minutes of time = 1° of longitude
1 minute of time = 15' of longitude
1 second of time = 15" of longitude

INTERNATIONAL DATE LINE : Halfway around the world from Greenwich is the International Date Line, at approximately 180°Longitude. 15° of longitude corresponds to one time zone. Therefore each time zone, i.e. 15° makes a difference of 1 hour. It runs down the mid-Pacific Ocean, veering to keep all the islands in a group, such as the Aleutians, together. Although the time is the same on both sides of the line (it is in the centre of a time zone), it is one day earlier on the east side of the line than it is on the west side. Thus when it is Monday just east of the line, it is Tuesday west of the line.

To avoid this confusion of dates the International Date Line was created. The International Date Line follows the longitude of 180° except where it crosses land surfaces. To avoid causing a difference of dates within the same country, the line bends around land regions. Thus, the International Date Line is not a straight line and follows a zig-zag course and passes over only sea or oceans. Ships or planes when they cross the International Date Line, add or subtract a day according to the direction they are travelling in. When crossing the International Date Line from west to east, a day is deducted; when travelling from east to west, a day is added.

MOON AND THE TIDES

The Moon exerts its gravitational pull on the Earth while at the same time the Earth is turning with respect to the Moon. We must understand the movements of the moon.

THE MOON. The moon's average distance from the earth is 3,82,200 km. Its diametre is 3,470 km and weighs about 1/83 of the earth. Its gravitational pull is only 1/6 of the earth. The visible area is 59%. The moon has a low **albedo** (the amount of sunlight which the planets reflect). It reflects only 7 per cent and the rest is absorbed. (The earth reflects 30% and Venus 70%).

Moon's Rotation : The moon rotates on its axis at a constant rate but its path around the earth is not perfectly circular. At some times, it is nearer the earth than at others. **At Perigee** (at its nearest) the distance is 354,330 kms and at **Apogee,** it is about 4,004,320 km. The moon rotates on its axis more or less parallel to the axis of the earth, in the same direction as the earth rotates. The direction of its revolution around the earth is also similar to the earth's revolution around the sun. The orbit of the moon is elliptical, with the earth located at one focus. The moon lacks a large heavy core such as the earth has. There is no atmosphere and without it, there is no sound, no water, no vegetation and no life.

The moon, like all other celestial bodies, seems to rise in the east and set in the west. This movement is not real. It is due to the earth's rotation on its axis from west to east. However each evening the moon rises later than it did on the previous evening and seems to have moved toward the east compared with the background of stars. This progressive movement is due to the moon's actual revolution around the earth. The moon not only revolves around the earth but at the same time, it also moves around itself.

Each day when the earth completes one rotation in 24 hours, the moon has moved about 13 degrees ahead. At the rate of 4 minutes per degree, the earth would take 52 minutes to cover this distance but it cannot do so and therefore the moon rises about 52 minutes later everyday.

Period of Moon's Axial Rotation : The moon's axial rotation period is the same as that of its period of the revolution around the earth, i..e. about 27 days 7.45 hours. The moon rotates on its axis only once during this time, giving it a day and a night each two weeks long. If the moon did not rotate once a month we would be able to see both of its sides. However we are able to see slightly more than one just half of the total surface. This is due to a factor known as the **"Liberation Effect,"** which allows us to peep around the corner as it were.

The Phases of the Moon : The moon has no light of its own. It shines only by reflected sunlight. Therefore, at any one time only one side of the moon can be lighted by the sun's rays. But the moon not only revolves around the earth but also rotates on its axis, facing the earth all the time. Consequently, the angular distance increases every day by about 12° (since it goes around 360° in approximately 30 days). As a result, the lighted portion of the moon we see depends upon its position in the sky in relation to our earth. First we see the thin crescent, then the First Quarter followed by Gibbous and finally the Full Moon. The phases are repeated thereafter in reverse order, namely, the Gibbous, the Last Quarter and the New moon again. These various portions or stages from new Moon to new moon through which the moon appears to go are called the **Phases of the Moon**. As the moon grows from new to full, it is said to be "waxing" and after full, it is said to be **"waning"**.

The phases of the moon have been used since the beginning of history to measure time. This is because the period from New Moon to New Moon is a natural unit to measure lengths of time less than a year.

THE TIDES. The alternate rise and fall in the waters of the ocean twice in about 24 hours are known as Tides.

Every object in the Universe exerts a gravitation pull on every other object. This pull increases or decreases with the distance and the mass of the body. The moon, though small, is very near the earth and exerts a strong gravitational pull on the earth. The Sun is very far from the earth yet it exerts some pull because of its great mass. Its main effect is to modify the lunar tides.

Tides are thus caused by the gravitational pull of the moon and to some extent by the pull of the Sun.

Any one who has lived near a seashore must have noticed that there is some connection between the moon and the tide and that as the moon rises later each day by about 50 minutes than the day before, the high tide occurs late each day.

It is obvious that the water of the earth nearest to the moon will be pulled by the moon's gravitational force. In figure above the moon is directly over A and its attraction causes the water to pile up toward A causing an ordinary **high tide** at that place. As water is drawn toward A from other areas, the water level at C and D is lowered and it is **low tide** (or ebb tide) at those points. At the same time there is a piling up of water on the other side of the earth toward B. The water at A being the nearest is drawn a little away from the solid earth beneath it but at B, on the opposite side, it is the earth that is pulled a little away from the water which, therefore, tends to be left behind. This is why there is a tide on the opposite side as well. These tides travel in a great wave around the earth following the moon except where the land stops them. They hit the sea coast at intervals of about 12 hours and 26 minutes. The tide water rises gradually for about six hours until it reaches high tide. Thereafter there is a fall in the water for about 6 hours until it reaches the low tide. The cycle then begins again.

DIURNAL AND SEMI DIURNAL TIDES. The high tides occur at intervals of about 12 hours and 26 minutes. If there is a high tide at 7 a.m. the next high tide will be at 7.26 p.m. and the next at 7.52 a.m. and so on. This is due to the fact that the moon is revolving around the earth in the same direction as the earth's rotation. If the moon had been stationary each place on the earth's surface would have come exactly under it after 24 hours and the next tide would have occurred after a lapse of 24 hours.

The average difference in water level between high and low tides at any place is called the **Amplitude** (or range) of the tide. The tidal range is generally 1 to 3 metres but it differs from day to day according to the position of the Sun and the moon.

The tides are not so simple as might appear from the figure. We assumed that the earth was surrounded by a uniform shell of water. The seas are of various shapes and depths. In the open oceans such as the Atlantic, tides flow and ebb regularly twice a day. This is called **semi-diurnal** tides. In the enclosed seas or sheltered wates such as those of the Mediterranean and the Baltic, the range is very small but in the Bay of Fundy (in Eastern Canada) the tide may rise 15 to 20 metres. In bodies of water that have restricted access to the open ocean such as the Gulf of Mexico or Caribbean Sea, the tidal pattern may show only one high tide and one low during a day. This type of tide is called **Diurnal.** A third type of tidal pattern can be found along the coasts of Pacific and Indian Oceans. It consists of two high tides of unequal height or two low tides, one much lower than the other. It is **mixed tides** pattern.

Spring and Neap Tides : Spring Tides. These are the tides of the greatest range produced when the earth, moon and the Sun are practically in the same straight line. The Sun is far away so that its tidal pull is only about half of that of the moon.

The Sun alone is therefore incapable of producing tides of the size we see. But the Sun can help the moon in producing a tide. Twice during the lunar month, namely, just after the New Moon and the Full Moon, the earth, moon and the Sun are in the same straight line and the gravitational effects of the moon and the Sun are combined to produce tides which are higher than usual. The high tide is very high and the low tide is very low. When the moon is in perigee the Spring Tides are still higher and if this occurs about Ist January (when the earth is nearest the Sun) the highest Spring Tides are produced.

Neap Tides. At the time of the first and last quarters of the moon, the sun and the moon are at right angles to each other in relation to the earth. The gravitational pull of the Sun opposes that of the moon and the difference between high and low tides levels is the least. The high tide is lower and the low tide is higher than at other times. These are called the Neap Tides.

Effects of Revolution

1. Cycle of Seasons.
2. Apparent migration of the Sun resulting in changes in the altitude of the midday sun at different times of the year.
3. Temperature or Heat Zones.

ECLIPSES

Eclipse is the total or partial obscuration of light from a celestial body as it passes through the shadow of another body. An eclipse of the Sun - a **solar eclipse**—or of the Moon - a **lunar eclipse**—occurs when the Sun, Moon, and Earth lie in or nearly in a straight line. If the plane of the Moon's orbit lay exactly in the plane of the ecliptic, a solar eclipse would take place at each new moon and a lunar eclipse at each full moon. The two planes are however inclined at an angle of about 5°, intersecting at the nodes of the moon's orbit. Eclipses are only observed when the Sun is at or near a node and the Moon is near the same node (solar eclipse) or the opposite one (lunar eclipse). The *ecliptic limits* are the maximum angular distances of the new or full moon from its node for an eclipse to take place.

SOLAR ECLIPSE : Although the Moon is 400 times smaller than the Sun, it is also about 400 times nearer the Earth. As a result, Sun and Moon have almost exactly the same angular size (about 0.5%), so that it is possible for the Moon to obscure the Sun. The Earth and Moon both cast-shadows in sunlight, the shadow having a dark cone-shaped inner region—the ***umbra***—and an outer lighter penumbral region. A solar eclipse occurs, between sunrise and sunset at new Moon, when the Moon passes directly in front of the Sun so that the Earth lies in the Moon's shadow.

When the Moon is sufficiently close to Earth so that its apparent diameter exceeds that of the Sun, then the umbra of the Moon's shadow can just reach the Earth's surface. It moves in a general west to east trend over a very narrow curved zone of the surface, known as the path of totality, which can be up to 250 km wide but averages about 160 km. An observer at a point where only the penumbra will move only past sees a **partial eclipse**, in which only part of the Sun is obscured. An observer in the path of totality will experience a total eclipse, in which the Sun is completely obscured. If the Moon is far enough away to appear smaller than the Sun, a rim (or annulus) of light will be seen around the eclipsed Sun and an annular *eclipse occurs*. The period of annularity never exceeds 12.5 minutes and is normally much less.

In a total Solar Eclipse, ***first contact*** occurs when the Moon just appears to touch the Sun's western limb. As the Moon gradually covers the Sun, the landscape darkens and animals become disturbed.

Totality begins at ***second contact*** when the Sun disappears from sight. The maximum duration of totality is 7m 40s but is usually much less. Totality ends at ***third contact***, just as the crescent sun emerges, and at ***fourth contact*** the whole disc of the sun is once more seen. The time between first and last contact can approach four hours. During totality the chromosphere, corona, and other phenomena can be observed and studied. There are between two and five solar eclipses each year. Total eclipses are however very rare at any particular place.

LUNAR ECLIPSE : A lunar eclipse occurs, at full Moon, when the Moon passes into the shadow cone of the Earth. It can be seen from any place at which the Moon is visible above the horizon. A total eclipse occurs when the Moon enters completely into the umbra of the Earth's shadow. If only part of the Moon enters the umbra the eclipse is partial. When the Moon only enters the penumbral region, a penumbral eclipse takes place in which a slight, usually quite unappreciable darkening of the Moon's surface occurs. The maximum duration of totality is 1 hr. 42m. The Moon can usually be seen throughout totality, being illuminated by sunlight refracted by the Earth's atmosphere into the shadowed area. Since the bluer wavelengths are removed by scattering, the Moon has a coppery-red colour. There are upto either two or three lunar eclipses each year. Upto seven eclipses can occur in one year, either five solar and two lunar or four solar and three lunar.

TERMINOLOGY

Antipodes : Points that are opposite to each other on a diameter of the Earth (180° of longitude apart).

Aphelion : The point in the orbit of a planet, comet, or artificial satellite in solar orbit that is farthest from the Sun. The Earth is at aphelion on July 3.

Apogee : The point in the orbit of the Moon or an artificial Earth satellite that is farthest from the Earth and at which the body's velocity is at a minimum. Strictly the distance to the apogee is taken from the Earth's centre.

Arctic Circle : An imaginary line running parallel to the Equator and circling the Earth at about 66° 33' North latitude. The Arctic Ocean and the northern fringes of Asia, Europe, and North America lie within Arctic Circle. Along the Arctic Circle there is one day each year during which the Sun does not set, about June 21 (Northern Hemisphere's Summer solstice, the first day of Summer). Similarly, the Sun does not rise above the horizon on approximately December 22 (the Winter solstice).

Antarctic Circle : An imaginary line running parallel to the Equator and circling the Earth at about 66°33' South latitude. Except for a few coastal areas, the Continent of Antarctica lies within the circle. Along the Antarctic Circle, there is one day each year during which the Sun does not set, about December 22 (the Summer solstice—first day of Summer in the Southern Hemisphere). Similarly, the Sun does not rise above the horizon on approximately June 21 (the Winter solstice).

Axis : An imaginary line passing through both poles and the centre of the planet.

Ecliptic : The mean plane of the Earth's orbit around the Sun. The ecliptic may be taken as coincident with the Sun's apparent annual path across the sky. The orbits of the Moon and planets, apart from Pluto, lie very near the ecliptic. The planes of the ecliptic and celestial equator are inclined at an angle equal to the tilt of the Earth's axis

Equator : An imaginary line circling the Earth midway between the North and South poles. This great circle divides the Earth into the Northern and Southern hemispheres. It lies 10,002 km or (6,215 miles) or 90° of latitude, from each pole. Degrees of longitude are about 111 km long at the Equator and gradually become smaller, diminishing to zero at the poles.

Equinox : The time and the point on the celestial sphere at which the Sun is directly over the Earth's Equator. This occurs twice a year, on or about March 21 and September 23. The word comes from two Latin words learing "equal night", for on these dates the lengths of day and night are roughly the same everywhere over the Earth.

Geoid : The form of the Earth obtained by taking the average sea level surface and extending it across the continents. The geoid differs from a sphere in that the equatorial diameter is greater than the diameter through the poles. The true geoid is elevated by 17 metres at the North Pole, 81 metres to the north of Australia and by 60 metres south of South Africa and west of the British Isles; in addition: there is a 27 metre depression at the South Pole and 50 metre depressions south of New Zealand and both east and west of the USA. The greatest departure is a 113 metre depression to the south of India.

Great Circle : On a sphere, any circle whose plane passes through the centre of the scheme. Thus, great circles are the largest possible circles that can be drawn on a sphere, and they are of infinite number. A circle whose plane does not pass through the centre of the sphere is called a **small circle**. 'the shortest distance between two points on the Earth's surface is the arc of the great circle passing through them, Consequently, great circles are important in long-distance ocean and air navigation. Such routes are called ***orthodromes***; the art of navigating them is called ***orthodromy***. In navigating short distances, vessels follow compass directions, also called Rhumb lines, or ***loxodromes***. These are not great-circle routes except where they coincide with the Equator or a meridian of longitude, both of which form great circles.

Hemisphere: A half sphere. Any great circle—a circle whose plane passes through a sphere's centre—divides a globe into two equal halves, making possible an infinite number of hemispheres. In relation to the Earth, however, only four hemispheres are normally considered. The Northern and Southern hemispheres are separated by the Equator, 0° latitude. The Western and Eastern hemispheres, in the strictest sense, are separated by the Prime Meridian, 0° longitude, and the meridian of 180° longitude; in common usage, however, Western Hemisphere applies only to the America.

Isopleth: A line drawn on the map along which the value of a particular phenomenon or product is uniform.

Isonomal: Any line representing continuous value on maps.

Isobars: Lines showing the equal pressure.

Isobaths: Lines that joins the equal depth in the sea.

Isobronts: Lines joining places experiencing a thunderstorm at the same time.

Isochrones: Lines joining places that are located at equal travel time from a common centre.

Isogonals: Lines joining places with the same magnetic declination.

Isohalines: Isopleths of salinity.

Isohels: Isopleths of equal amount of sunshine.

Isohyet: Isopleth of rainfall.

Isohypse: (*Or contour lines*) Isopleths of elevation above sea level.

Isonif: Isopleth of amount of snow.

Isophene: Isopleth of seasonal phenomena, e.g. the flowering dates of plants.

Isorymes: Lines of equal frost.

Isoseismals: Lines of equal seismic activity.

Isallobar: Change in atmospheric pressure.

Isobathytherm: Temperature at a given depth.

Isothere: Mean summer temperature.

Isacheim: Mean winter temperature.

Midnight Sun: A name given to the Sun when it can be seen at midnight during the Arctic or Antarctic Summer. From March 21 to September 23, the Sun is visible 24 hours a day at the North Pole. As a person here moves southward toward the midnight sun's limit (just south of the Arctic Circle), the number of days of continuous sunshine decreases. Northern Scandinavia, which extends 480 km into the Arctic zone, is sometimes called "Land of the Midnight Sun". Northern Russia, Alaska, Canada, and Greenland also experience the midnight sun. At the South Pole, the midnight sun is seen from September 23 to March 21.

Solstice: During the course of a year, the Sun appears to move northward for about six months and southward for about six months. The times when it reaches its northernmost point (on or about June 21) and its southern most point (on or about December 22) are called the ***Solstice***.

Tropics of Cancer and Capricorn: Tropics are the regions circling the Earth between the Tropic of Cancer (23° 27'N) and the Tropic of Capricorn (23° 27'S). These two parallels, or imaginary lines of latitude, mark the farthest points reached by the Sun's vertical rays. At all points between the two parallels, the Sun passes directly overhead twice during the year. The usual four seasons of the world's temperate areas do not occur in the tropics. Instead, seasonal variations consist primarily of rainy and dry periods that vary with distance from the Equator. On or near the Equator, even this distinction is missing since rainfall is evenly distributed throughout the year and there is no dry period.

Zenith: The point in the heavens that is directly above the head of the observer. The opposite point, that is directly below the observer's feet, is the nadir.

Zenith also applies to the highest point a heavenly body appears to reach above the horizon. The Sun reaches its zenith at noon.

Zodiac: An imaginary belt of 12 constellations, or groups of stars. The word is from the Greek word for "animal", because most of the constellations of the zodiac are named for animals. The zodiac is about 18° wide, and lies some 9° on either side of the ecliptic, the plane of the Earth's orbit around the Sun. The Sun, Moon, and planets appear to move against the background of these constellations and are said to be "in" a constellation when they pass by its area of sky. The zodiac is divided into 12 areas, or signs, of 30° each. The Sun, in its apparent path, is in each sign for about a month. Because of the precession of the equinoxes, the signs and the constellations no longer coincide.

Zodiacal light: A faint glow that appears along the constellations of the zodiac above the western horizon after sunset and above the eastern horizon before sunrise.

EARTH'S GEOLOGICAL TIME SCALE

It is generally assumed that planets are formed by the accretion of gas and dust in a cosmic cloud, but there is no way of estimating the length of this process. Our Earth acquired its present size, more or less, between 4 billion and 5 billion years ago. Life on Earth originated about 2 billion years ago, but there are no good fossil remains from periods earlier than the Cambrian, which began about 490 million years ago.

The known geological history of Earth since the Precambrian Time is subdivided into three eras, each of which includes a number of periods. They, in turn, are subdivided into epochs and stage ages. In an epoch, a certain section may be especially well known because of rich fossil finds.

NEW GEOLOGICAL PERIOD

In March 2004, geologists added a new time period to Earth's chronology—the Ediacaran Period. The Ediacaran Period lasted about 50 million years, from 600 million years ago to about 542 million years ago. It was the last period of the Precambrian's Neoproterozoic Era. Multicelled organisms first appeared during this time. This period is the first new one added in 120 years.

	ERA	Age/Years before present	Life/Major Events
Origin of Star	5000-13700 million	5000 million	
Supernova		12,000 million	origin of the sun
Big Bang		13,700 million	origin of the universe

PRE-CAMBRIAN TIME

The Precambrian's lower limit is not defined, but ended about 542 million years ago. The Precambrian encompasses about 90% of Earth's history.

Eonothem eon	Duration[1]	Eras	Events
Archaean (Greek *archaios* = ancient) bacteria	2,500?	Eoarchean (Greek *eos* = dawn + *archaios* = ancient) Paleoarchean (Greek *palaios* = old) Mesoarchean (Greek *mesos* = middle) Neoarchean (Greek *neo* = new)	Formation of oceans, atmosphere, and continents;
Proterozoic (Greek *proteros* = earlier + *zoön* = animal)	c. 2,000	Paleoproterozoic (Greek *palaios* = old) Mesoproterozoic (Greek *mesos* = middle) Neoproterozoic (Greek *neo* = new)	Oxygen build-up; multicelled organisms

1. In millions of years.

PALEOZOIC ERA

This era began 542 million years ago and lasted about 291 million years. The name was compounded from Greek *palaios* (old) and *zoön* (animal).

Period	Duration[1]	Epochs	Events
Cambrian (*Cambria*, Latin name for Wales)	54	Lower Cambrian, Middle Cambrian, Upper Cambrian	Invertebrate sea life proliferating during this and the following period
Ordovician (Latin *Ordovices*, people of early Britain)	45	Lower Ordovician Upper Ordovician	Diverse marine life, including vertebrates; vascular plants
Silurian (Latin *Silures*, people of early Wales)	28	Lower Silurian Upper Silurian	Coral reefs; giant scorpions; first jawed fish
Devonian (Devonshire in England)	57	Lower Devonian Upper Devonian	Numerous fishes, other sea life; many plants, first trees; wingless insects
Carboniferous (Latin *carbo* = coal + *fero* = to bear)	60	Upper, Middle, and Lower Mississippian[2]	Upper, Middle, and Lower Pennsylvanian[2] Maximum coal formation in swampy forests; insects, amphibians, reptiles; fishes, clams, crustaceans
Permian (district of Perm in Russia)	48	Lower Permian Upper Permian	Large reptiles, amphibians; most species become extinct

1. In millions of years.
2. Mississippian and Pennsylvanian names are used only in the U.S.

MESOZOIC ERA

This era began 251 million years ago and lasted about 186 million years. The name was compounded from Greek *mesos* (middle) and *zoön* (animal). Popular name: Age of Reptiles.

Period	Duration[1]	Epochs	Events
Triassic (*trias* = triad)	51	Lower Triassic, Middle Triassic, Upper Triassic	Early dinosaurs, crocodiles, turtles; first mammals
Jurassic (Jura Mountains)	54	Lower Jurassic Middle Jurassic Upper Jurassic	Many seagoing reptiles; early large dinosaurs; later, flying reptiles (pterosaurs), earliest known birds
Cretaceous (Latin *creta* = chalk)	80	Lower Cretaceous Upper Cretaceous	Dinosaurs and other reptiles dominate; seed-bearing plants appear

1. In millions of years.

CENOZOIC ERA[1]

This era began 66 million years ago and includes the geological present. The name was compounded from Greek *kainos* (new) and *zoön* (animal). **Popular name: Age of Mammals.**

(Latin *creta* = chalk) **Period**	**Duration[2]**	**Epochs**	**Events**
Paleogene (Greek *palaios* = old + *genes* = born)	42	Paleocene (Greek *palaios* = old + *kainos* = new). Eocene (Greek *eos* = dawn).	Oligocene (Greek *oligos* = few). Rich insect fauna, early bats, increasingly diverse varieties of mammals and birds
Neogene (Greek *neo* = new + *genes* = born)	23	Miocene (Greek *meios* = less + *kainos* = new). Pliocene (Greek *pleios* = more). Pleistocene (Greek *pleistos* = most) (popular name: Ice Age). Holocene (Greek *holos* = entire), the last 10,000 years to the present.	Further development of mammals and birds. Various forms of humans, including *Homo sapiens*

1. This table reflects the divisions used by the International Commission on Stratigraphy. The U.S. Geological Survey divides the Cenezoic Era into the Tertiary Period (with the Paleocene, Eocene, Oligocene, Miocene, and Pliocene Epochs) and the Quaternary Period (with the Pleistocene and Holocene Epochs).

2. In millions of years.

3 INTERIOR OF THE EARTH

Facts about Earth
Composition : Rocks, Metal, Water
Character : Magnetic
The Age of the Earth : 5,000,000,000 years (appx.)
The Dawn of the Life on Earth : 500,000,000 years (appx.)
Appearance of Man on Earth : 50,000 years (appx.)

The Earth is an oblate spheroid. The earth's radius is 6,370 Km with average density being 5.5. It is composed of a number of different layers as determined by deep drilling and seismic evidence. These layers are :

1. CORE : The core is a layer rich in iron and nickel that is composed of two layers: the **inner** and **outer** cores. The inner core is theorized to be solid with a density of about 13 grams per cubic centimeter and a radius of about 1220 kilometers. The outer core is liquid and has a density of about 11 grams per cubic centimeter. It surrounds the inner core and has an average thickness of about 2250 kilometers.

Facts about Core

- Hottest Layer of Earth.

Inner Core

- 1.7% of the earth's mass
- depth of 5,150 – 6,370 km (3219 - 3,981 miles)

Outer Core

- 30.8% of the earth's mass
- depth of 2,890 - 5,150 kms (1806 - 3219 miles)
- 7000 km. Diametre.
- Temperature of outer core is 2200°C
- Temperature of inner core may be as high as 5000°C

2. MANTLE : The mantle is almost 2900 kilometers thick and comprises abort 83% of the Earth's volume. It is composed of several dense layers. The upper mantle exists firms the base of the crust downward to a depth of about 670 kilometers. This region of the Earth's interior is thought to be composed of ***peridotite,*** an ultramafic rock made up of the minerals **olivine** and **pyroxene.** The top layer of the upper mantle, 100 to 200 kilometers below surface, is called the **asthenosphere.** Scientific studies suggest that this layer has physical properties that are different from the rest of the upper mantle. The rocks in this upper portion of the mantle are more rigid and brittle because of cooler temperatures and lower pressures. Below the upper mantle is the lower mantle that extends from 670 to 2900 kilometers below the Earth's surface. This layer is hot and plastic. The higher pressure in this layer causes the formation of minerals that are different from those of the upper mantle.

- **D" :** 3% of Earth's mass; depth of 2700-2,890 kms (1,688 - 1806 miles). This layer is 200 to 300 km (125-188 miles) thick and represents about 4% of the mantle crust mass. Although it is often identified as part of **lower mantle** seismic discontinuties suggest the D" Layer might differ chemically from the lower mantle lying above it.
- **Lower Mantle :** 49.2% of Earth's mass, depth of 650-2,890 kms (406-1,806 miles). The lower mantle contains 72.9% of mantle crust mass and is probably composed mainly of silicon, magnesium and oxygen.
- **Transition Region :** 7.5% Earth's mass; depth of 400-650 km (250-406 miles). The transition region or mesosphere (for middle mantle) sometimes called the **fertile layer,** contains 11.1% of the mantle crust mass and is the source of basaltic magmas.
- **Upper Mantle :** 10.3% of Earth's mass; depth of 10-400 Km (6-250 miles). The upper mantle contains 15.3% of the mantle crust mass. Fragments have been excavated for our observation by eroded mountain belts and volcanic eruptions. Part of the upper mantle called the **asthenosphere** might be partially molten.

3. CRUST : The topmost part of the lithosphere consists of crust. This material is cool, rigid, and brittle. The crust is made up of two layers an upper lighter layer called the **SIAL** (Silicate & Aluminium) and a lower denser layer called **SIMA** (Silicate & Magnesium). Two types of crust can be identified : **oceanic** crust and **continental** crust. Both of these types of crust are less dense than the rock found in the underlying upper mantle layer.

- **Ocean Crust :** 0.099% of the Earth's mass; depth of 0-10 km (0-6 miles). The oceanic crust contains 0.147% of the mantle crust mass. The majority of the earth's crust was made through the volcanic activity. The oceanic ridge system, a 40,000 km (25,000 mile) network of volcanoes, generates new oceanic crust at the rate of 17 km^3 per year, covering the ocean floor with basalt. **Hawaii** and **Iceland** are e.g. of basalt piles.

Mohorovic Discontinuity

The various layers are separated by discontinuities which are evident in seismic data; the best known of these is the Mohorovicic discontinuity between crust and upper mantle. The junction between the mantle and the overlaying crust is referred to as the **Mohorovic Discontinuity** (The Moho) named after the Yugoslav seismologist who first suspected its presence for his analysis of **P** and **S** waves.

- **Continental Crust :** 0.374% of Earth's mass; depth of 0-50 km (0-31 miles). The continental crust contains 0.554% of the mantle crust mass. This is the outer part of the earth composed essentially of crystalline rocks.

The continental crust is 20 to 70 kilometers thick and composed mainly of lighter granite. The density of continental crust is about. 2.7 grams per cubic centimeter. It is thinnest in areas like the Rift Valleys of East Africa and in an area known as the Basin and Range Province in the western United States (centered in Nevada this area is about 1500 kilometers wide and runs about 4000 kilometers North/South). Continental crust is thickest beneath mountain ranges and extends into the mantle. Both of these crust types are composed of numerous tectonic plates that float on top of the mantle. Convection currents within the mantle cause these plates to move slowly across the asthenosphere.

MASS OF THE EARTH

Most of Mass of the earth is in the mantle; most of the rest in the core, the part we inhabit is a tiny fraction of the whole (values below X 10"24 kgms.

❖ Atmosphere - 0.000051
❖ Oceans - 0.0014
❖ Crust - 0.026
❖ Mantle - 4.043
❖ Outer core - 1.835
❖ Inner core - 0.09675

Other important facts about the Interior of the earth

- Temperature inside the earth increases with depth.
- It increases at the rate of 1°C for every 32 metres. In that case, core should be in a moltan state, but it is found in a solid state. This happens mainly due to the high pressure of mantle and crust.
- **Guttenberg** discontinuity separates the core and mantle, while the Mantle and crust are separated by the **Mohorovicic discontinuity. Conard** discontinuity, separates the outer and inner crust.
- The soft plastic layer in the upper mantle is called the **asthenosphere.** It is about 100 km thick.
- Mantle region of the earth's interior is thought to be composed of **Peridotite,** that is made up of two minerals, **olivine** and **pyroxene.**

CHEMICAL ELEMENTS PRESENT IN CRUST

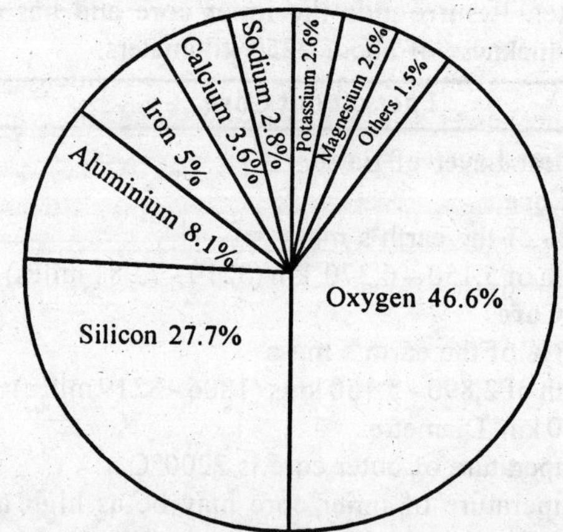

THE LITHOSPHERE

Oceanic Lithosphere : The rigid outermost layer of the Earth Comprising the crust and upper mantle is called the **lithosphere.** New oceanic lithosphere forms through volcanism in the form of fissures at mid-ocean ridges which are cracks that encircle the globe. Heat escapes the interior as this new lithosphere emerges from below. It gradually cools, contracts and moves away from the ridges, travelling across the seafloor to subduction zones in a process called **seafloor spreading.** In time, older lithosphere will thicken and eventually became more dense than the mantle below, causing it to descend (Subduct) cooling the interior. Subduction is the main method of cooling the mantle below 100 km (62.5 miles). If the lithosphere is young and thus hotter at a subduction zone, it will be forced back into the interior at a lesser angle .

Continental lithosphere : Together the crust and upper mantle are called the lithosphere. It is about 150 km (93 miles) thick with a low density crust and upper mantle that are permanently buoyant. Continental drift laterally along the convecting system of the mantle away from hot mantle zones toward cooler ones, a process known as **continental Drift.** Most of the Continents are now sitting on or moving towards cooler parts of the mantle, with the exception of Africa. Africa was once the core of Pangaea, a super continent that eventually broke into today's continent. Several hundred million years, the southern continents– Africa, S. America, Australia, Antarctica and India were assembled together in what is called **Gondwana.**

Asthenosphere (Upper mantle 100-700 km deep): The lithosphere is broken into giant plates that fit around the globe like puzzle pieces. These puzzle pieces move a little bit each year as they slide on top of a somewhat fluid part of the mantle called the asthenosphere. The asthenosphere is ductile and can be pushed and deformed. These rocks actually flow, moving in response to the stresses placed upon them by the churning motion of the deep interior of the Earth. The flowing asthenosphere carries the lithosphere of the Earth, including the continents in its back.

THE LAYERS OF THE EARTH

Name of the Layer	Chemical Composition	Average Thickness	Density	Physical Property
A. (i) *Crust* or outer part of lithosphere immediately below the newer sedimentaries on the surface.	**SIAL** (Sedimentary and the granitic rocks)	8 to 45 km (mainly under Continents)		Solid
(ii) *Inner part of lithosphere* or the substratum of greater strength.	outer silicate layer	45 to 100 km (partly under oceans)	2.75 to 2.90	Partly molten.
B. (i) Inner silicate layer.	**SIMA** (Basic rocks)	100 to 1,700 km. (mainly under oceans).	3.1 to 4.75	Some properties of a solid and some like those of plastic material close to melting point
(ii) Transitional zone of mixed metals and silicates	Wholly SIMA (ultra-basic rocks)	1,700 to 2,900 km.	4.75 to 5.00	
[B (i) and B(ii) together constitute the *mantle*]				
C. (i) Outer metallic *core*.	**NIFE**	2,900 to 4,980 km.	5.1 to 13.00	Liquid or in a plastic state. Solid and rigid because of tremendous overlying pressure.
(ii) Inner metallic *core*.	Barysphere (Heavy metallic rocks).	4,980 to 6,400 km.		

THE THEORY OF CONTINENTAL DRIFT

If sections of the Earth's crust can move up and down in the way posited by isostasy theory, it is not unreasonable to suppose that horizontal movements across the surface of the Earth are also possible. For many years the possibility of such "continental drift" was hotly disputed but in recent decades substantial evidence has been collected that it does indeed take place.

Continental drift refers to the horizontal movement of the continents on a vast scale. **Wegener** was the first to advocate the theory of Continental Drift. According to him, the continents drifted apart from each other in the remote geological periods. There is a geological evidence to show that in the past geological periods equatorial, tropical, and arctic climatic types were located in latitudes far removed from their present-day location.

According to the Theory of Continental Drift, all the sialic layer was concentrated in a large continent called the **Pangea** which meant all earth before the Silurian period (270 million years ago). This block floated in a universal basaltic layer. The basaltic layer is located below the Conrad discontinuity, with a probable depth of more than 17 kms. In the late Palaeozoic period (200 to 500 million years ago), probably during Permian (200 to 235 million years ago) or Mesozoic (70 to 200 million years ago) era, the Pangea broke into pieces under the influence of the tidal force and the force generated by the movements of the Earth's axis of rotation and revolution. The mega ocean was called **Panthalassa.**

EVIDENCE IN SUPPORT OF THE CONTINENTAL DRIFT

1. **Matching of Continents (Jigsawfit) :** The southern parts of the Pangea broke apart during Mesozoic and the northern in the Tertiary periods (2 to 70 million years ago). The Continental Drift was caused by differential gravitational forces which acted upon the protruding block of sial. One force caused the drift towards the equator and the other towards the west. The African block (the Gondwanaland) and the Eurasian block (the Laurasia) moved towards the equator. When the drift towards the equator was taking place, the Americas drifted to the west. Thus, the Atlantic Ocean was created between North and South America in the west and Europe and Africa on the east. Australia was left behind in the beginning. Later, it swung to the east. Only recently in terms of geological time periods did Antarctica separate from South America.

- Before drifting, North and South America formed one unit. They rotated about a point in North America.
- Then they were drawn apart. This produced the narrow land of Central America and the scattered fragments of the West Indies Archipelago. Labrador and New Foundland separated from Europe during Quaternary (about 2 million years ago).
- They swung southwest. Greenland was left behind as a separate block.
- At the same time the Indian part of the Gondwanaland moved north against the mass of the Asian main continent. It separated from Africa. Madagascar was left behind by the compression of the Indian part against the Angara shield, the mountain chains of the Himalayas were created.

2. **Survival of Marsupial Mammals :** Similarly the survival of the marsupial mammals in Australia is all the more readily explicable if Australia separated from the other countinents between 70 and 80 million years ago. Although marsupials had been distributed throughout the world until that time they have been able to survive only in Australia where they have not experienced competition from the placental mammals which have displaced them throughout the rest of the world.

3. **Rock Magnetism :** In the 1950s, evidence began to come to light which was much more favourable to the Continental Drift hypothesis. Of particular significance was the study of rock magnetism. Careful charting of the Earth's fossil magnetic field revealed that the continents had considerably changed their latitudes. Moreover detection of frequent field reversals combined with improved accuracy in the dating of rocks enabled geologists actually to trace in time the widening of the oceans.

4. **Placer Deposits :** The occurrence of rich placer deposits of gold in the Ghana Coast and the absolute absence of source rock in the region is an amazing fact. The gold bearing veins are in Brazil and it is obvious that the gold deposits of the Ghana are

deprived from the Brazil plateau when the two continents lay side by side.

5. Distribution of fossils : When identical species of plants and animals adapted to living on land or in fresh water are found in either side of the marine barriers, a problem arises regarding accounting for such distribution. The observations that Lemurs occur in India, Madagascar and Africa led some consider a contiguous landmass **"Lemuria"** linking three landmasses.

HESS'S CONCEPT OF SEA FLOOR SPREADING

The Post draft studies provided considerable information that was not available at the time Wegener put fourth his concept of Continental Drift. Particularly, the mapping of the ocean floor and paleomagnetic studies of rocks from oceanic regions revealed the following facts :

(i) All along the mid-oceanic ridges, volcanic eruptions are common and they bring huge amounts of lava to the surface in this area.

(ii) The rocks equidistant on either sides of the crest of mid-oceanic ridges show on remarkable similarities in terms of period of formulation, chemical compositions and magnetic properties. Rocks closer to mid-oceanic ridges are normally polarity and are the youngest. The age of the rocks increases as one moves away from the crust.

(iii) The sediments on the ocean floor are unexpectedly very thin. Scientists were expecting, if the ocean floors were as old as continents, to have a complete sequence of sediments for a period of much longer duration. But nowhere the sediment column found to be older than 200 million years.

(iv) The deep trenches have deep seated earthquake occurrences while in mid-oceanic ridge areas, the quake foci have shallow-depths.

These facts led Hess to propose his hypothesis, **known as sea-floor spreading.** Hess argued that

- Constant eruptions at the crust of oceanic ridges cause the rapture of oceanic crust and new lava wedges into it, passing the oceanic crust on either side.
- The ocean floor thus spreads.
- The ocean floor that gets pushed due to volcanic eruptions at the crest, sinks down at the oceanic trenches and gets consumed.

THE THEORY OF PLATE TECTONICS

Today the theory of continental drift is combined with the idea of the seafloor spreading in a theory called plate tectonics.

The Great Plates

The lithospheric plate system consists of 12 major plates. Of these, six - called the great plates - are of enormous extent.

1. **The Pacific Plate:** This occupies much of the Pacific Ocean Basin and consists entirely of oceanic lithosphere. Its relative motion is northwesterly. A bit of continental lithosphere is included, making up the coastal portion of California. The California portion of the plate boundary is the San Andreas Fault, an active transform fault.
2. **The American Plate :** This includes most of the continental lithosphere of North and South America, as well as the entire oceanic lithosphere lying west of the mid-oceanic ridge (Mid-Atlantic Ridge) that divides the Atlantic Ocean Basin down the middle.
3. **The Eurasian Plate :** This is a largely continental lithosphere, but is fringed on the east and north by a belt of oceanic lithosphere.
4. **The African Plate :** This can be visualised as having a central core of continental lithosphere nearly surrounded by oceanic lithosphere.
5. **The Australo Indian Plate :** This takes the form of an elongate rectangle. It is mostly oceanic lithosphere but contains two cores of continental lithosphere - Australia and Peninsular India.
6. **The Antarctica Plate :** This has an elliptical outline and the continent of Antarctica forms a central core of continental lithosphere completely surrounded by oceanic lithosphere.

Some Important Minor Plates are

(i)	**Cocos Plate :**	Between Central America and Pacific Plate
(ii)	**Nazea Plate :**	Between South America and Pacific Plate

(iii) **Arabian Plate :** Mostly the Saudi Arabian landmass.

(iv) **Philippine Plate :** Between the Asiatic and Pacific Plate

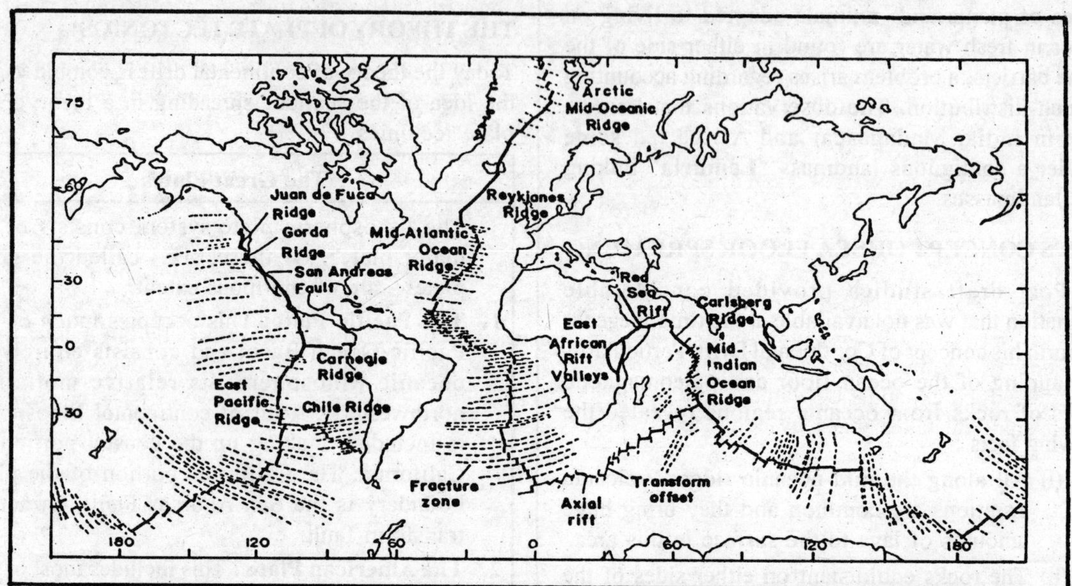

THE MID-OCEANIC RIDGE SYSTEM AND RELATED FRACTURE ZONES

The word "tectonics" comes from the Greek word meaning "builder". The plate tectonics theory states that the outer solid lithosphere is made up of several plates. The high temperature and pressure below the crust produces a trace of melting which allows the plates to move on this layer. About 20 plates of various sizes have been identified so far. Of these the Pacific Plate is the largest and consists of mostly the ocean floor. All the other plates consist of both continents and oceans. The thickness of these plates ranges from 80 to 100 km for oceanic lithosphere, to about 100 to 400 km for continental lithosphere. The plates move as one distinct unit. As the plates move, the distance between places on the same plate, New York and Chicago for example, remains the same, while the distance between New York and London, which are located on different plates, is changing.

All major interaction between plates occur at plate boundaries. Most of the Earth's volcanic activity, earthquakes and mountain-building activities occur along these boundaries.

1. **Plate Boundaries** : Plate boundaries coincide with the region of earthquakes and volcanic activity. There are **three types of plate boundaries** based on the type of movement they exhibit.

(i) **Divergent Boundaries :** Plates move apart, leaving a gap between them which gets filled up with molten rock which oozes from below the crust. e.g. midatlantic ridge.

(ii) **Convergent Boundaries :** Plates move towards each other, causing one to go under the other or causing plates to collide forming mountains.

(iii) **Transform fault boundaries :** Plates slide past each other, scraping and deforming as they pass.

Plate tectonics theory, like the Continental Drift theory', describes the plate movement and the effects of this motion but not what causes it. There are three main theories put forth by scientists.

1. **Convection :** Heat generated deep inside the Earth creates convection currents in the mantle. These currents slowly push the overlying plates around. Rising currents may drive the plates apart and create new crust. This is happening in the middle of the Atlantic Ocean. Sinking currents may drag the plates together and cause mountains to form over the buckled edges.

2. Gravity : The plates are about 2 - 3 km higher at mid-ocean ridges than at ocean rims. It is thought that the plates could simply be sliding slowly downhill under the force of gravity.

3. Weight of Rock : Hot rock rising at mid-ocean ridges cools down as it moves further away from the ridge. As it cools, it becomes heavier and sinks, pulling the rest of the plate with it.

The system of lithospheric plates in motion represents an enormous material-flow system powered by an internal energy-flow system. The energy system that causes plate motions is believed to arise from the radioactive elements in the Earth crust and the upper mantle. The radioactive elements such as uranium and thorium constantly give off energy. As the temperature of the mantle rock rises, the rock expands. Upward motion of the less dense material takes place by convection. As the lithospheric plate is lifted to a higher elevation above the rising mantle it tends to move horizontally away from the spreading axis under the influence of gravity.

VOLCANOES

Volcanic activity is an important process of construction on the Earth's surface; new mountains may be formed as volcanic cones and spreads of new rock material such as lava and ash are laid down. A volcano is basically a vent or fissure in the Earth's crust through which magma consisting of molten rock, solid particles and gas, is expelled. Volcanoes are the most obvious evidence that the interior of the Earth is extremely hot.

Distribution of Volcanoes

Even though volcanoes are some of the striking features of the earth, their distribution is very much restricted to a few areas, and some regions and countries do not have any active or dormant volcanoes. India does not have any volcano, either active or dormant, except in the Andaman and Nicobar Islands.

A large number of volcanoes are concentrated in a narrow belt called the **Circum-Pacific Ring of Fire** which, as the name suggests, is located along the edges of the Pacific Ocean. Most of the volcanoes in this belt are located on the high, young folded mountains, such as the Rockies, the Andes, the Japanese and Indonesian island arcs. Other volcanic areas include the scattered areas in the Pacific, particularly the Hawaiian Islands, around the part of Indian Ocean, a belt that includes Arabia, Madagascar and the Rift Valleys of Africa, the Mediterranean belt, Azores and Canary Islands, the volcanoes of the West Indies, and those of Iceland. Iceland is wholly built of volcanic rocks and it is reckoned that, of all the lava poured out on the Earth in historic times, one third has been "made in Iceland",

TYPES OF VOLCANIC ERUPTION

A useful distinction is made between (a) "**central volcanoes**", which erupt from a point and produce a variety' of cone and crater shapes, and (b) "**fissure eruption**" where fluid lava wells out from a crack to spread out in almost horizontal sheets covering a wide area.

(a) Central Volcanoes

They are divided into several main types according to the viscosity of the laval involved, and degree of explosive activity and the resulting form of the cone.

- In the **Hawaiian type**, named for the forms characteristic of the Hawaiian islands, a low-angle cone or shield volcano is built up by repeated effusions of very mobile lava, which spreads out far from the vent with little or no explosive activity.
- The **Strombolian and Vulcanian types** are both named for volcanoes in the Lipari Islands north of Sicily. In the first, the lava is slightly more viscous than in the Hawaiian type and the gas is liberated in a series of often quite regular thumps or minor explosions, lumps of lava are hurled into the air and fall as congealed "bombs". The **Vulcanian** type is still more explosive; the lava is stiffer and a crust forms over it quite quickly between eruptions. As a result, the gas is sealed in and pressure builds up until the crust of lava is unable to contain it. A violent explosion follows in which great quantities of fragmented material are thrown up, from bombs of redhot lava to fine ash which hangs as a cloud over the volcano.
- A further stage in the intensification of explosive activity is represented by the **Vesuvian type** (named for Vesuvius in southern Italy). Intervals between explosions are longer but outbursts are much more violent. The flanks of the volcano may be breached by the power of the explosions and

lava, highly-charged with accumulated gas, pours out, often emptying the central vent to a considerable depth.

- In the **Pelean type** (named for Mt Pelee in Martinique and its disastrous eruption of 1902), the lava is of high viscosity and the vent is plugged for long intervals. Extreme pressure is generated; bursts of incandescent *nuees ardentes* escape through cracks and roll down the flanks with hurricane velocity and the central plug may be forced bodily upward. Variety is introduced by the fact that some eruptions yield mostly lava, some mostly ash.
- The majority of central volcanoes, however, produce both lava and ash (though perhaps at different phases of an eruption cycle) and are described as composite types. Volcanoes built purely of ash or cinders are much less common. They often form beautifully symmetrical cones, with concave sides rising to a rim around the vent.

Mid-Ocean Ridge Volcanoes : These volcanoes in the oceanic areas. There is a system of mid-ocean ridges more than 70,000 km long that stretches through all ocean basics. The central portion of the ridge experiences frequent eruptions.

(b) Fissure Volcanic Eruptions

- Unlike central volcanoes, fissure eruptions represent magma reaching the surface by way of a long crack and, in nearly every case, the lava spreading out from the crack is very fluid and basaltic.
- The Deccan basalts of India extend over 518, 000 km^2 (200, 000 mi^2), as do the Columbia-Snake River basalt of northwestern USA.
- The Antrim plateau of Ireland represents part of a once-continuous area of early Tertiary flood basalts stretching through the Faeroes to Iceland and Greenland. Large segments of this area have since foundered beneath the sea.

VOLCANIC TOPOGRAPHY

There are two main forms of features of the **volcanic topography**. (i) The high or elevated relief features include hills, mountains, cones, plateaus or upland plains. (ii) The low lying relief features are craters, calderas, and tectonic depressions. Many of these features are related to each other and occur in the same area.

- **Volcanic cones** occur on lava plains, and *craters* are located on the volcanic cones.
- **Basalt domes**, or **shield-volcanoes**, are very high and have a broad base and gentle slopes. Mauna Loa in Hawaii is a typical example. Generally, there is a large depression or volcanic sink on the summit which has inward facing cliffs. After the dome is completely dissected, there remains a volcanic stack or neck or plug as a column. Basalt domes also occur in Iceland, Pacific Islands, and Italy.
- The **ash or cinder cones** have many examples in Mexico, Italy, Philippines, and Alaska.
- **Composite or strato-volcanic cones** reveal rough stratification of alternating sheets of lava and pyroclastic materials. These correspond to the alternate periods of explosive and quiet erections. Volcanoes with such cones arc the highest and the most imposing. They have symmetrical outlines and concave slopes.
- **Craters and calderas** are the depression forms in the volcanic topography.
- **Crater** is a funnel-shaped depression having a circular plan and a neck at the centre. It is rimmed by an infacing scarp. The crater is formed by explosion or subsidence. After, an explosion destroys an existing crater, a new but smaller cone with its own crater is built up. This is termed a **cone-in-cone topography**.
- **Crater Lake :** A crater filled with water is termed a **crater-lake.**
- **Calderas** are very large volcanic depressions. They are also circular in plan, and in diameter they are several times larger than the craters. Calderas are formed by explosion and collapse. A caldera filled with water after the volcano has become extinct is termed a **caldera lake.** The Lunar lake in Maharashtra is claimed to be an example of this category.
- **Composite Cone :** When volcanic material get deposited in the form of a cone, alongwith a series of layers. These volcanoes are characterized by eruptions of cooler and more viscous lava than basalt. Alongwith lava, large

quantities of pyroclastic material and ashes find their way to ground.

EARTHQUAKES

An earthquake is a sudden, temporary motion or a series of motions which originate in a limited region and then spread out from the place of origin in all directions. The point, where earthquakes are generated first, is called focus or hypocentre. while the point where the shock waves reach the surface is known as the **Epicentre.** The duration as well as the direction of motion can be estimated precisely with seismographical methods. The waves generated by an earthquake are measured by seismograph.

DISTRIBUTION OF EARTHQUAKES

- The really destructive earthquakes are concentrated in a ring surrounding the Pacific Ocean. This ring coincides with the Circum-Pacific Ring of Fire.
- The second chain is termed the East Indian. It extends over Indonesia, Andaman and Nicobar Islands, and Burma.
- The third belt extends over Himalayas, Kun Lun, Tien Shan, and Altai Ranges upto the Lake Baikal.
- Another belt extends from the Pamir Knot to Afghanistan, Iran, Turkey, Greece, Rumania, Atlas Mountains, Gibraltar, and the Azores Islands.
- A belt extends from the Gulf of Aden, between Seychelles and Maldive Islands, turns to the west-south of Africa and goes up to the Falkland Islands.
- A belt also runs along the Great Rift Valley of East Africa.
- The earthquakes can also occur away from the circum-Pacific ring of fire.
- They can occur within the plates away from the plate margin. Such plates are popularily known as **in-plate seismicity.** They are also called the weaker zone of the earth's surface. **Narmada-son lineament, Jabalpur earthquake, Latur and Gujarat earthquakes** are the main examples of in-plate seismicity.

Emergence of Shadow Zone
❍ Earthquake waves get recorded in seismographs located at far off locations ❍ However these exist some specific areas where the waves are not reported ❍ Such a zone is called the 'Shadow zone'. ❍ For each earthquake, these exists an altogether different shadow zone. ❍ Seismographs located beyond 145° from epicentre, record the arrived of P-waves but not of S-waves. Thus the zone between 105° and 145° from epicentre was identified as shadow zone for both the types of wave. ❍ The entire zone beyond 105° does not receive S-waves. The shadow zone of S-wave is much larger than that of P-waves. ❍ The shadow zone of P-waves appears as a band around the earth between 105° and 145° away from the epicentre. ❍ The shadow zone of S-waves is not only larger in extent but it is also a little over 40 per cent of the earth's surface.

TYPES OF EARTHQUAKE WAVES

There are four types of earthquake waves, three discovered by *R.D. Oldham* and one later by *A.E.H. Love*. These are :

(i) **P-Waves :** • Also known as primary waves, these waves have the shortest wavelength among the four and are also called **push waves.** • They are compressional or longitudinal and their velocity is 5 to 8 km per second. • They can travel through liquids and solids but travel faster in denser solid materials.

(ii) **S-Waves :** • Also known as secondary waves, these are of medium wavelength and are also called shake or shear waves. • The vibrations are transverse or at right angles to the direction of propagation of waves and can travel only through solid (elastic medium) and not through liquids. • S waves is the main evidence to assume that the earth's core is liquid. Their velocity is 3 to 5 km per second.

(iii) **L-Wave :** Also known as surface waves, these waves travel near the earth's surface, within the depth of 32 km from the surface. These are also called **Rayleigh Waves** after Lord Rayleigh who described these waves. These waves travel like sea waves, with a rotary movement in the vertical plane of the direction of propagation and cause the maximum damage. These are supposed to be produced by a combination of P and S waves.

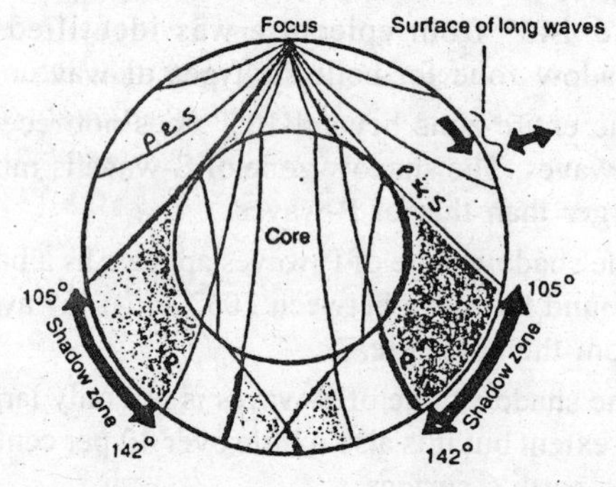

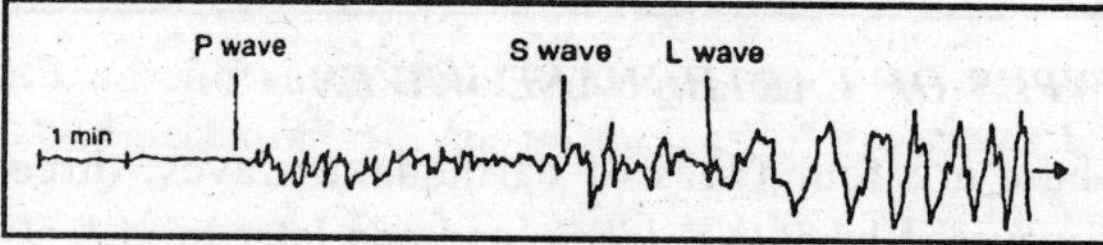

(iv) **Love Waves :** Love waves are also like Rayleigh waves except that they make the ground vibrate at right angles to the direction of waves. Love waves are a variety of S waves where the particles of an elastic medium vibrate transversely to the direction of wave propagation, with no vertical components.

Some earthquake waves (P waves) travel right through the earth's denser core and undergo refraction and reflection (like light waves) at the margin of earth's outer lighter shell and inner denser core. Their total reflection produces a shadow zone where the waves fail to reach. S waves cannot pass through the core because the core, though dense, is not rigid. The surface or long waves cause much damage as they travel along earth's surface.

Types of Earthquakes

❖ **Tectonic Earthquakes :** They are the most common ones. These are generated due to sliding of rocks along a fault.

❖ **Volcanic Earthquakes :** A special class of tectonic earthquake is sometimes called volcanic earthquake. However there are confined to areas of active volcanoes.

❖ **Collapse Earthquakes :** In the areas of intense mining activity, sometimes the roofs of underground mines collapse causing minor tremors. These are called collapse earthquakes.

❖ **Explosion Earthquakes :** Ground shaking may also occur due to the explosion of chemical or nuclear devices. These tremors are called explosion earthquake.

❖ **Reservoir Induced Earthquakes :** The earthquakes that occur in the areas of large reservoirs are referred to as reservoir induced earthquakes.

4 LANDFORMS

LANDFORMS : FORCES AND PROCESSES

The landforms that are found on the surface of the Earth can be grouped into four categories: They are shaped by two types of forces : (1) Endogenic forces (Internal Force) (2) Exogenic Forces (External Force).

ENDOGENIC FORCES OF LANDFORM

A process which the Earth's crust is termed endogenous. Although it originates within, it does affect the earth's surface in a spectacular manner. Mountains, plateaus and volcanoes are some of the striking features produced by endogenous process. The two main endogenous processes are ***volcanism*** and ***diastrophism***. Diastrophism elevates or builds up portions of the earth's surface. Diastrophic processes are classified as ***orogenic*** and ***epeirogenic***. Orogeny refers to mountain-building, with deformation of the crust and the Earth's surface. Epeirogeny refers to regional uplift without marked deformation. Epeirogeny is a vertical and orogeny, a horizontal earth movement. Upwarping and downwarping are the two results of the vertical movement Orogeny is tangential in that the movement is parallel to the Earth's surface.

Warping and **isostasy** cause vertical movements while **folding, faulting,** and **continental drift** constitute horizontal movements.

FOLDING is the bending of rock strata due to compressional forces acting tangentially or horizontally towards a common point or plane from opposite directions is known as folding. It results in crumbling of strata into folds. The compression is usually applied from one direction in mountain-building. Folds occur in a series of troughs and crests alternating with each other. The upfolds are termed *anticlines* and the down-folds, the *synclines*. Thus, anticlines and synclines are the features of structures on which the topography of ridges and valleys is developed. The crests are the upfolds or anticlines, whereas the troughs are the down-folds.

FAULTLINE is a fracture of large magnitude along which the broken crustal blocks have been displaced with reference to each other. Displacement occurs parallel to the plane of the break. Fault is the ultimate result of vast regional tension. Every fault must have two components, the fault plane and the displacement. The **fault plane** or the fault surface is the break along which displacement takes place. The fault plane makes an angle with the horizontal plane which is termed *dip* of the fault. The angle made by the fault plane with the vertical is termed *hade*. The types of features related to faults are scarps of several types, horst, graben block mountain, and rift valleys. Scarp is the most characteristic feature produced by faulting, both normal and reverse. Scraps are also the sites of hanging valleys and strikingly developed waterfalls. Horst or a block mountain is an uplifted landmass located between two adjacent faults. A graben or rift valley is the block lowered between two adjacent faults. The rift valley of East Africa and the Vosges and the Block Mountains of Europe are good examples of rift valleys and block mountains.

In certain faulting the ridges are breached to allow the streams to cut through. The gap is termed as *watergap*.

WARPING is deformation of the Earth's crust but one which does not necessarily involve folding. Warping affects very large areas on the Earth's surface, and thus results in the formation of domes, shields and depressions.

ISOSTASY is a condition of balance. All large land on the Earth's surface rise or sink. After each geologically adequate time period, these land masses tend to get adjusted. This adjustment leads to a hydrostatic equilibrium. Equilibrium is upset in those areas where there are local stresses. Isostasy refers to the state of hydrostatic balance. Isostasy, therefore, is neither a force nor a process. It is a condition of gravitational balance between crustal segments of different thickness. Isostacy also refers to a tendency toward restoration of balance once it has been disturbed by some other force or process. But this isostatic balance is never fully achieved. When the crustal segments are in an isostatic balance the high and lowlying relief features of the Earth's surface are also in a state of balance. This is made possible by the fact that the high relief features have lighter materials in them, while the large, low relief features, such as ocean basins, have heavier materials under them. This enables the maintaining of a condition of mechanical stability on a rotating Earth.

The following graphical model describes the relationship between geomorphic processes and landform types

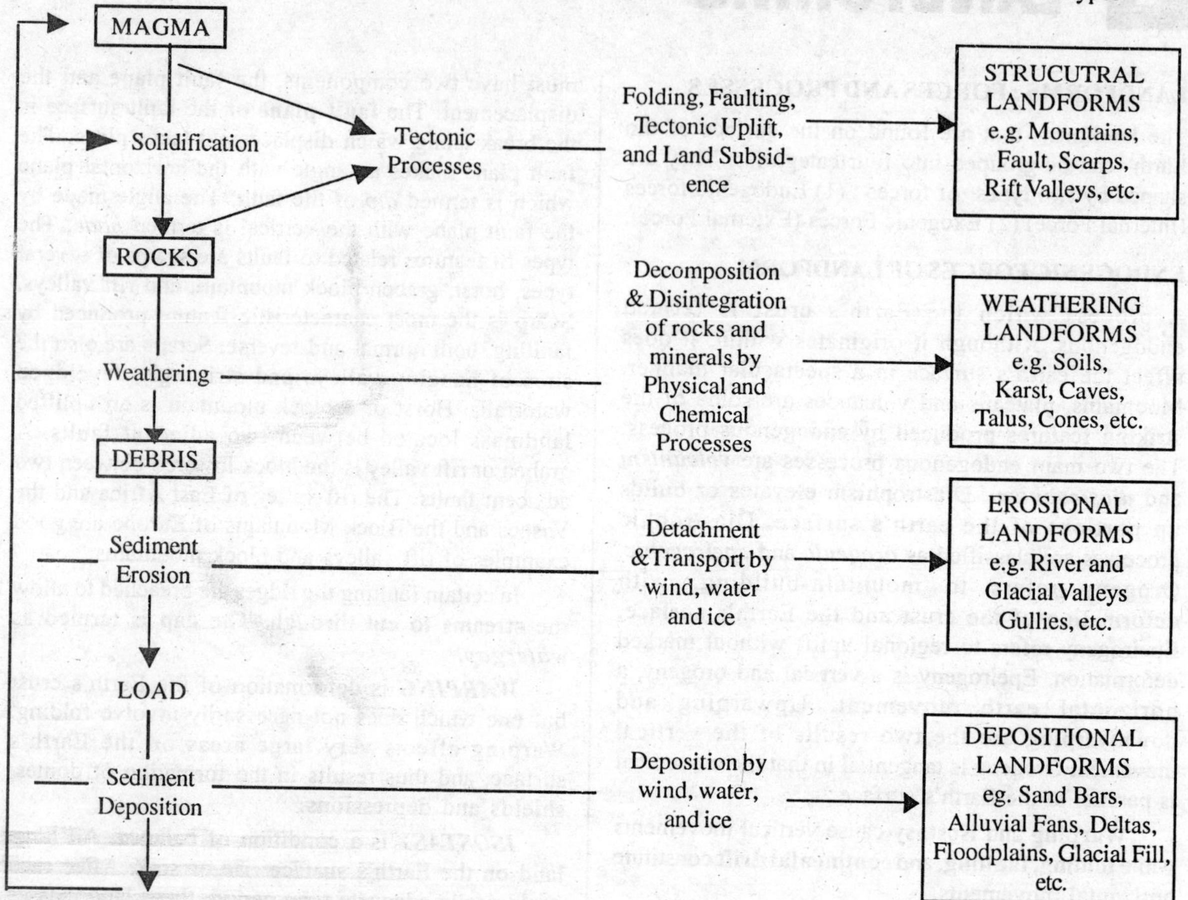

The state of isostasy can be maintained only if there is a continuous compensation at depth. Through erosion, material is being removed from the tops of the mountains which, therefore, are becoming lighter. Material should therefore, move into the roots of the mountains at depth through the interior of the Earth. This movement is termed **compensation.**

Isostatic movements are always vertical. These are related to the processes of erosion and deposition on a large scale and to glaciation on fairly large scale.

EXOGENIC FORCES OF LAND FORMS

Exogenetic processes of landform evolution and landform changes are those which derive their energy from external sources especially from the Sun. These processes are mainly caused by Earth's geomorphic agents, such as river, wind, glacier, and sea-waves. Exogenetic processes include gradation, degradation, aggradation, and weathering.

GRADATION: Due to crustal movement and unequal erosion and deposition the surface of the Earth in its various parts becomes irregular. By and large, these irregularities constitute the surface topography of the Earth. Gradation is the process by which the original irregularities of the Earth's surface are removed and a level surface is created. All gradation processes are also directed by gravity.

DEGRADATION: Degradation constitutes those processes by which material from a high relief feature is removed by exogenetic or external processes and the main geomorphic agents. Degradation is controlled by three factors: the properties of the material on which the processes are operating, the energy available to the geomorphic agents, and the tools used by the agents. **Degradation comprises of three processes: weathering, mass-wasting, and erosion.** *Weathering* is the disintegration or decomposition of rock in *situ.* It is a static proceeds and does not involve in any movement. Mass-wasting involves the bulk transfer of masses of rock debris down slopes under the influence of gravity. Landslides are examples of **mass-wasting.** Weathering helps erosion but is not a part of it. There can be weathering without erosion and erosion without weathering.

WEATHERING*:* There are two main types of weathering: (a) physical (or mechanical) and (b) chemical. Both are affected by rock structure, climate, topography, and vegetation. The minerals control the rate of chemical weathering. The joints in rocks permit water to enter the rock and achieve chemical and physical weathering. Climate determines whether physical or chemical weathering will predominate and the speed with which these processes will operate. Topography directly affects weathering by exposing rocks and indirectly through the amount of precipitation, temperature and vegetation. Topography also determines the aspect or direction which exposes the rocks to the direct attack of rain or wind.

Note: Weathering and Erosion are completely different from each other. No transportation is included in weathering.

A. MECHANICAL WEATHERING

It may be caused by six agents, which are discussed below.

(i) Frost Action : Water expands when being transformed into the solid state, called frost or ice. This expansion exerts enormous pressure so that when water freezes within the cracks of the rock, great strains are caused and fragments may be broken off, or the rocks are shattered to a considerable depth. In the high mountains and even on low ground at high latitudes, melted water from frost and ice enters into cracks during the day and refreezes at night. Repeated freezing and thawing cause the shattering of rocks. Shattered rocks are frequently met with in the higher elevations of the Himalayas.

(ii) Daily Temperature Changes : Weathering due to diurnal temperature changes is essentially a consequence of direct heating of rocks.

(iii) Exfoliation : The breaking or peeling-off of concentric plates from bare rock surfaces is called ***exfoliation***. Plutonic rocks like granites normally get exfoliated. They were formed at a great depth where they had to bear the pressure of the overlying materials, and when they got uplifted and became free from burden, they expanded. The result is peeling-off of scales from their surface and appearing as exfoliation domes as in the Khasi Hills, Kyllang, Meghalaya. Exfoliation on a small scale takes place on the face of a crag which receives and loses the Sun's heat rapidly. Exfoliation produces a large rounded dome shaped hill as in Tiruchirapalli in Tamil Nadu on which stands a fort. ***Spheroidal weathering***, which is very common in granitic hills, is a type of exfoliation.

(iv) Relative Hardness of Rocks : Some rocks like sandstone are hard; and some like shales are soft. Weathering of soft rocks under a capping of hard rocks give rise to 'pedestal rocks'. Such land form features can be seen in the Satpura Hills, Madhya Pradesh. There the softer rocks have been converted into relief the harder rocks as peaks and softer rocks as caves. Dhupgarh peak in the Satpuras is a good example of this type of weathering.

(v) Gravity: Gravity is an indirect cause of mechanical weathering. We may see huge boulders standing on the edge of a cliff about to fall down, and when they actually tumble down the slope, they may break off portions of hill slopes on the way by sheer impact. Such a huge boulder on hill tops is called a balanced rock.

B. BIOLOGICAL WEATHERING

Action of Plants and Animals: The roots of trees on the hillsides penetrate into cracks of rocks and widen them. This facilitates the percolation of water and air, the total effect of which is the breaking down of the rocks. Earthworms bring to the surface vast quantities of finely divided rock materials. Other burrowing animals like rabbits and moles also cause disintegration in this way.

C. CHEMICAL WEATHERING

It is more important than mechanical weathering in almost all the climatic regions. Chemical weathering results in (i) an increase in volume which produces stresses within the rocks; (ii) lower density materials;

(iii) particles of smaller size which produce a large surface for chemical interactions, and (iv) more stable minerals. There are two end products of chemical decomposition and disintegration : (i) residual, such as clay and (ii) soluble, such as calcium bicarbonate which can be removed from the solution.

The chemical weathering of rock follows five major lines of attack:

1. **Hydration**, the absorption of water by some kinds of rock, leads to expansion and disintegrations.
2. **Hydrolysis**, a chemical breakdown of rock caused by rainwater, rots the feldspear in granite, which then decays into a clay, rich in residual mica and quartz.
3. The **oxidation or rusting of iron** can produce a crumbly rock crust and accounts for the reddish colour of many iron-rich rocks in contact with air.
4. **Solution** is the dissolving of minerals (notably augite, hornblende and rock salt) in water.
5. Few rocks are much affected by pure water but rainwater rich in carbon dioxide attacks several rocks in a process called **carbonation**. The carbonate water acts as a weak acid, dissolving the calcium carbonate of which limestone and chalk are largely composed.

EROSION

Erosion is the Earth-sculpting processes by which the rock debris produced by weathering is transported. Agents that move rock fragments include gravity, running water, moving ice, wind and (on the coasts) waves, tides and currents. The two processes by which Earth surfaces are eroded by materials in transit are ***corrasion*** and ***corrosion***.

When gravity acts directly on loose material forming an unstable slope, the resulting slide of rock debris is known as ***mass movement***. Such movement may be slow or rapid. Slow movements include *creep* in which soils, often rendered partly unstable by water, move very slowly down slopes, causing fence posts to lean and trees to bend during growth. In ***talus creep,*** loose rock debris creeps down a steep slope to form scree or talus. In ***solifluction,*** a feature of tundra regions, debris loaded with melted water creeps over a frozen surface, even down slopes as little as 2°. ***Flow*** is a rather faster form of mass movement and involves more water than creep. There are earth flows, involving soil only, mud flows, where the material is fine grained and debris flows where particles vary greatly in size.

Geographers recognize several types of rapid mass movement, notably slipping and subsidence. In *slipping,* tilted beds of firm rock overlying soft or loose rock suddenly sheer away from a steep slope or a cliff; often the slip is triggered by water soaking down through the rocks to add to their weight. In ***subsidence***, a surface surrounded by sound rocks collapses vertically. This often occurs in limestone terrain where subsurface solution undermines rock; it is also induced by the mining of coal and salt.

A river is a sizable stream of fresh water flowing through a natural channel in the land.

RIVER EROSION produces the most obvious results of erosion through its role in carving out valley. Flowing water carries its load of debris in three different ways.

1. Upto 15% of the total load is likely to be in solution. Much of this load is acquired while rainwater percolates down through permeable layers of rock before emerging in springs and seepages to form the headwaters of rivers. The rivers then proceed to dissolve part of their channel beds.
2. Upto 75% of a river's load is fine enough to be borne in suppression.
3. The remaining 10% is bedload dragged along the bed of the stream, wearing away the channel floor and sides. By such methods, rapidly downcutting rivers carve out deep valleys from the sides of hills and wear down the ridges between rivers. Theoretically river erosion can eventually help to reduce entire mountain ranges to imperceptibly sloping plains.
4. River transportation is the movement of eroded particles in chemical solution, in turbulent suspension or by rolling and dragging along the bed.
5. River deposition consists of accumulation of any transported particles on the streambed, on the adjoining floodplain or on the floor of a body of standing water into which the river empties.

The nature of river erosion depends upon the materials of which the channel is composed and the means of erosion available to the river. One simple means of erosion is

6. Hydraulic action, the pressure and drag of flowing water exerted upon grains projecting from the bed and banks. Weak bedrock and various forms of regolith are easily carved out by hydraulic action alone.
7. Mechanical wear, termed abrasion, occurs when rock particles carried in the current strike against the exposed bedrocks of the channel. Small particles are further reduced by crushing and grinding when caught between larger cobbles and boulders.
8. Chemical reactions between ions carried in solution in river water and exposed mineral surfaces result in a form of erosion called solution.

Gentle rain falling on bare surface loosens the soil and muddies the water. The muddy water flows as thin, slow moving surface layer of water called **sheet flow**. As the slope increases, the water scours additional sediments and erodes small channel called **rills**. Headward erosion of rills and their subsequent widening lead to gully formation. Gullies dissect the land into a number of isolated little hills, giving rise to badland topography. **The valley of the Chambal in Madhya Pradesh is an example of badland topography.**

Entering the plains, the running water deposits the transported material laterally called as **lateral accretion.** Point bars formed by meandering rivers on their concave bends are a good example of lateral accretion. Sometimes, when a segment of the meandering river channel is abandoned to straighten its course, the abandoned channel is known as **oxbow lake.**

LANDFORMS CAUSED BY RIVER EROSION

Valley : It starts as small and narrow rills which gradually develop into long and wide gullies. The gullies will further deeper, widen and lengthen to give rise to valleys . This leads to *V-shaped* valley. *U-shaped* valley is generally formed by glacial erosion.

Gorges : When valley sides become so steep that they are almost vertical, they are called Gorges. The Grand Canyon in Arizona, U.S.A. is the largest Gorge in the World.

Canyon : A canyon is characterized by steep step like side slopes. It is wider at the top than at its bottom.

Meander : Meandering rivers are low slope or gradient rivers that are not choked with the sediment and move back and forth over their flood plains in a pattern of loops called meanders. Its serpentine path increases the length of the river channel and it helps it in accommodating the on-coming volume of water.

Incised or Entrenched Meanders : Sometimes a meandering river across a flat landscape becomes reinvigorated by a drop in sea level or a sudden rise of the land. If the drop in sea level is rapid and river cuts down rapidly, the original meanders from the old flat landscape are cut down into steep canyons which are called incised or entrenched meanders.

River Terraces : River terraces are surfaces marking old valley floor or floodplain levels. They may be bedrock surfaces without any alluvial cover or alluvial terraces consisting of stream deposits. River terraces are basically products of erosion as they result due to vertical erosion by the stream into its own depositional floodplain.

Peneplain : When an extensive area has been eroded sufficiently to give the look of almost a plain, it is called a peneplain.

LANDFORMS CAUSED BY RIVER DEPOSITION

Alluvial Fans : When the velocity of running water as it comes out from hills and meets the plain decreases, it dumps the transported material at the foot hills forming **alluvial fans.** By the time a river enters the sea or a large lake, it loses its velocity. The fine material carried down the distance is deposited at this point to form a triangular fan called **delta.**

Delta : Deltas ar of two types :

(i) **Arcuate Delta** : It resembles a fan and convex towards the sea. The Arcuate deltas have been built by the Nile, the Ho, Hwang Po, the Rhone, the Tiber, the Ganga, the Sindh, the Mahanadi, the Mekong and the Irrawady etc.

(ii) **Bird's Foot Delta :** In these deltas, sediment deposited is composed of those fine particles which are received from the limestone rock. Due to these fine particles, the bottoms of the deltas turn non-porous and the seepage of waterdown the bottom steps. The river water flows on the surface in the shape of some distributories. These distributaries appear extended like a foot of a bird e.g. Mississippi Delta.

(iii) **Estuarine Delta :** When a river enters the sea through a single mouth or estuary, then the Estuarine delta is formed. **River Congo and Amazon** form the

Estuaraine delta. While, the Tiber river of Italy forms the cuspate delta. Although all the rivers of India form delta but two rivers, i.e. Narmada and Tapti do not form any delta. They form estuaries.

(iv) **Cuspate Delta :** They are pointed and are shaped by regular opposing, gentle water movement as seen at the **Ebro** and **Tiber** deltas in Italy.

Ox Bow Lakes : They are formed by the depositional and erosional actions taking place simultaneously and they are the result of excessive meandering. They are called ox bow because of their shape resembling the foot of a cow ('C' shape) Ox bow lakes are also known as **billa bongs** in Australia and **Bayous** in Louisiana.

Flood plains : It is a major land forms of river deposition. Large sized materials are deposited first when stream channel breaks into a gentle slope. Also called Alluvial plain, they are formed through deposition of alluvium by the river on its sides where it flows over a relatively level region.

Natural Levees are found along the banks of larger rivers. They are low, linear and parallel ridges of coarse deposits along the banks of rivers, quite often cut into individual mounds. These deposits are called levees and they separate the flood plains from the river valley.

Back Swamp : They are located some distance away from the stream channel on the floodplains. When water spills over onto the flood plains, the heaviest material drops out first and finest material is carried a greater distance. The fine grained alluvium holds much water and drains rather slowly creating wetland areas. Back swamps are important **sponges** that retain water that might cause flooding.

LANDFORMS CAUSED BY RIVER TRANSPORTATION

It takes three different forms. **First,** dissolved solids such as salts travel downstream indefinitely and reach the ocean. They do not affect the mechanical behaviour of the river. **Second,** particles of clay, silt and sometimes, fine sand are carried in suspension.

- **Lower Mantle :** 49.2% of Earth's mass, depth of 650-2,890 kms (406-1,806 miles). The lower mantle contains 72.9% of mantle crust mass and is probably composed mainly of silicon, magnesium and oxygen.
- **Eddies :** Eddies are formed whenever a soft rock obstructs the course of a stream and is eroded and sediments are scattered all around.
- **Potholes :** Sometimes these depressions look like discs and are known as **potholes.**
- **Plunge Pool :** When these potholes grow in size, they are called **plunge pools.** Clay particles, once lifted into suspension, are so readily carried that they travel long distances. As a result, suspension provides a means of separating solid particles of various sizes and carrying each size category to a different location, a process known as **sorting. Third,** rolling or sliding of grains along the stream bed. These dragging motions can be conveniently included in the term traction. Fragments moved in traction are **bed load** of the river.

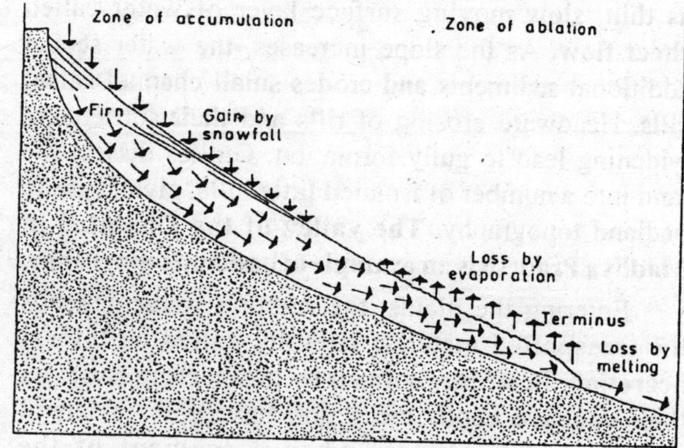

Conditions for Formation of a Glacier
Accumulated ice moves downwards.

GLACIAL EROSION

It acts rather like river erosion. Like water, ice moves downslope under the influence of gravity and transports material which it picks up *en route.* Thus, like a river, a glacier erodes its bed with the material it is transporting. Ice appears to erode in two principal ways.

- The first of them is ***abrasion***—a type of sandpaper action caused as rock fragments stuck in the base and sides of the glacier are dragged over bedrock. Fine-grained rock fragments rubbed across a rock surface by ice produce a high polish; larger boulders gouge out chatter marks and scoop out deep grooves.
- A second form of ice erosion is ***plucking;*** where

ice in the base of a glacier moves away from the ice-rock interface, blocks of rock are dragged out and become incorporated into the basal ice. The scouring action of glaciers has enormously deepened and broadened many mountain valleys throughout the world.

LANDFORMS CAUSED BY GLACIAL EROSION

U-Shaped Valley : A typical glaciated valley has a U-shaped cross-section, and cut-away spurs and side valleys, whose streams now enter the main valley as waterfalls cascading down cliffs. Even more extensive has been the action of ice in the prehistoric ice sheets which helped to bevel huge tracts of arctic and subarctic land as in northern Canada.

Cirque : A cirque is born on the slope in the form of crevasse, due to glacial erosion. **Arete** is when the cirques from the two sides of a mountain are enlarged and extend towards each other, the upper part of the mountain begins to be destroyed. As a result the summit line becomes serrated and thin like a knife. It is known as **steep side ridge.**

Giant Stairway : Many glaciated troughs are formed into a glaciated valley and take the shape of a step and are known as *glaciated steps*. If the glaciated valley is large and long, the glaciated steps become glaciated **staircases**. Every step of a ***glaciated staircase*** forms a lake. If seen from case forms a lake. If seen from a distance these lakes look like a staircase of lakes. They are known as ***Paternoster Lakes.***

A ***Hanging Valley*** is formed where a glacier carves out a deeper U-trough and the tributary valley is left perched on the high wall of the U-trough. The junctions of such valleys are the sites of waterfalls.

LANDFORMS CAUSED BY GLACIAL DEPOSITION

Aretes and Horns : An arete is a narrow crest with a sharp edge. The meeting of three or more aretes creates pointed pyramidal peaks and in extremely steep-sided forms these are called horn.

Moraines : The glaciers bring with it small pebbles, sands etc. All this debris is acquired by the glacier from mountainous slopes, sides, valleys etc. The till which can not be carried by a glacier is deposited at various parts of the glacier. The deposition of this till is known as *Moraines*. Moraines are sufficiently long and their height is usually 30 metres. They cover as much as 8% of the earth's land area.

The high ridges of till which accumulates along the sides of the glaciers are known as ***Lateral moraines***. The till left by the melting of ice of the mouth of the glacier takes the form of a crescent or a horse shoe. This deposit of till is called ***Terminal Moraine***. The mass of till accumulated over the base of the glacier is called ***Ground Moraine***. Whenever two moraines join each other their lateral moraines also joins. These combined moraines are called ***Medial Moraines***.

One of the most conspicuous features of lowlands which have been glaciated by ice sheets is the widespread morainic deposits. Because of the numerous boulders in the clay these are called **boulder clay deposits.**

Drumlins : The deposits are sometimes several hundred metres thick and their surface is marked by long rounded hills, called **Drumlins.**

Erratics : Large blocks of rock of a material, quite different to that of the rocks of the region, often occur in areas which lay under ice sheets. These blocks are known as **erratics.**

Carrie and Tarn : A carrie is an armchair shaped hollow high on a mountain with a steep back and side walls. After glaciation the hollow may be filled by small lake or tarn.

Fjord is a drowned U-shaped valley along the coast. It is deeper toward the coast where it is overlooked by a high, bold cliff.

FLUVIO GRACIAL DEPOSITS

- **Outwash plains** are areas of sorted sand and gravel deposited at the mouth of meltwater rivers which were often braided. **Kettle holes** may be found if a block of 'dead ice' is partially buried by fluvio-glacial deposits. When the ice melts a 'hole' is left which may fill with water to form a kettle-hole lake.
- **Eskers :** Rivers and streams occur inside most glaciers and these are heavily loaded with rock debris. As an ice front retreats, the rivers build up ridge-like deposits called **Eskers.** They develop on top of the boulder clay deposits. Roche mountains are another feature produced by glacial deposition. **Eskers** are similar to

railway embankments. They are formed inside the ice, in tunnels in which meltwater streams flowed.

- **Kame terraces** are gentler slopes of layered sand and gravel at the side of valleys. They were formed at the edge of the glacier and valley side where meltwater forms on the surface.

WIND EROSION

The wind causes erosion in desert areas in three ways:

(i) ***Deflation :*** The particles which are loosened on the rocks due to weathering are blown away by the winds. The action is known as deflation. This action is more prominent on deserts, coasts of seas or lakes and the tilled land in dry season (ii) ***Abrasion***. The dust and sand particles present in the air float in the atmosphere. When the winds blow faster, these particles act as tools of the wind and wear down rocks by scrapping, rubbing, undercutting and scouring. (iii) ***Attrition***. The dust and sand particles strike against one another and get smaller and rounded.

LANDFORMS CAUSED BY AEOLIAN EROSION

(i) **Deflation Hollow :** When the force of wind is concentrated on a particular spot in the landscape, erosion can curve out a pit known as deflation. The broad shallow depressions are called *Pans*.

(ii) **Desert Pavement :** In dry climate areas, persistent winds erode all sediments the size of sand and smaller leaving pebbles and larger particles on the ground surface. Surfaces loaded with such particles are called desert pavement or *reg*.

(iii) **Mushroom/Gara/Gaur :** These are mushrooms-shaped rockmasses formed in the deserts by abrasion action of masses formed in the deserts by abrasion action of wind. If the rockmass comprises layers with carrying resistance to wind erosion, rib like marks may also be produced due to differential erosion which is called mushroom or gara or Gaur.

- **Deflation Basins** i.e. depressions formed by action of wind. ***Dreikanter :*** i.e. the beveled stones. The stones which lie in a certain position and are subjected to abrasion action by wind blowing in the direction, develop one edged stape or sometimes three-edged shape;
- **Inselberg :** meaning island mountain. It is a mountain top rising suddenly from the plains or plateaus. They are common in Kalahari Desert, part of Algeria and western Australia.
- **Zeugen :** The rate of wind erosion is different in areas which have parallel layers of hard and soft rocks. The lower soft portions of rocks are eroded fast and become narrow but the upper portions of hard rocks look like tables of soft rocks. The base of the table of hard rocks is shale or some other rock. They are known as Zengens.
- **Wadis :** Due to cloud bursts, water emerges out of canyons in a fast flowing current and makes a valley 15-20 metre deep and hundred of metres broad. Such valleys are called wadis.
- **Hammada :** Sometimes the sand blown by winds in Sahara exposes the floor of hard rocks. When such floors develop a lot, they are known as hammadas.
- **Reg Serir :** A stony desert called ***Reg*** in Algeria and ***Serir*** in Libya and Egypt has its surface covered with boulders, angular pebbles and gravel which have been produced by diurnal temperature changes.

Sand Dunes : The different types of sand dunes are ***beach dunes***, ***Crag*** and ***Tail dunes*** having a tail like formation.

LANDFORMS CAUSED BY AEOLIAN DEPOSITION

- **Barchan :** Crescent-shaped dune whose long axis is transverse to the dominant wind direction. The points of the dune, called the wings of the barchan, are curved downwind and partially enclosing the slip-face. Barchans usually form where there is a limited supply of sand, reasonably flat ground, and a fairly even flow of wind from one direction. Land forms of Aeolian Deposition Big Barchans are called **Oghurds.**
- **Transverse :** Long asymmetrical dunes that form at right angles to the wind direction. Form when there is an abundant supply of sand and relatively weak winds. These dunes have a single long slip-face.
- **Parabolic** Crescent-shaped dune whose long axis is transverse to the dominant wind direction. The points of this dune curve upwind. Multiple slip-faces. These dunes form when scattered

vegetation stabilizes sediments and a U-shaped blowout forms between clumps of plants.

- **Barchanoid Ridge :** Is a long, asymmetrical dune that runs at right angles to the prevailing wind direction. A barchanoid ridge consists of several joined barchan dunes and looks like a row of connected crescents. Each of the barchan dunes produces a wave in the barchanoid ridge. Occurs when sand supply is greater than in the conditions that create a barchan dune.
- **Longitudinal :** Sinuous dune that can be more than 100 kilometers long and 100 meters high. Created when there are strong winds from at least two directions. The dune ridge is symetrical, aligned parallel to the net direction of the wind, and has slipfaces on either side.
- **Seif :** Sub-type of longitudinal dune that is shorter and has a more sinuous ridge.
- **Star Dune :** Large pyramidal or star-shaped dune with three or more sinuous radiating ridges from a central peak of sand. This dune has 3 or more slipfaces. Produced by variable winds. This dune does not migrate along the ground, but does grow vertically.
- **Dome :** Mound of sand that is circular or elliptical in shape. Has no slip-faces. May be formed by the modification of stationary barchans.
- **Reversing :** Dune that is intermediate between a star and transverse dunes. Ridge is asymmetrical and has two slip-faces.
- **Erg :** It is not proper to say that deserts are nothing but an accumulation of sand dunes. Only one-ninth of Sahara has sand dunes but there are some extensive areas in Sahara where sand dunes extend without a break. They are known as ***Ergs*** in Sahara and ***Koum*** in Asia.
- ***Loess*** is a mixture of feldspar, quartz, mica and calcite. There is no signs of chemical weathering in its particles. These fine particles of sand are deposited at places much away from their sources. The main Leost areas are in Mississippi valley. Palouse hills of East Washington, the plains of Germany and northenly parts of China and Pampas of Argentina.

Wind cannot move large rock fragments. But it piles desert sands into dunes and can carry light dust particles far farther than sand. In the past, such wind-blown dust was borne many hundreds of kilometres from deserts and region of glacial drift, before being dropped to form the thick layers of loess which now blanket large parts of China, Europe and the USA.

WAVE EROSION

It plays a major part in shaping the world's shorelines. The movement of air over water creates waves on the surface of seas and lakes and these disturbances can travel far beyond their point of origin. Waves breaking on the sea shore erode partly through hydraulic force. But abrasion is carried out mainly by the loose shingle and rock that the waves hurl against cliffs, cutting into the land like a saw and eventually reducing the cliffs to a submarine wavecut platform. Besides waves, forces of marine erosion include the chemical action of sea. water upon shore platforms and cliffs slopes, and tidal currents which scour out submarine channels and carry stones, sand and mud along the shore.

While some waves are eroding one part of a coastline, others may be depositing the eroded rock on another part of the shore. This happens when waves breaking obliquely on a beach help to produce the longshore drift or loose sand and shingle which collects at certain points on a coast and builds into ridges as bars and spits. Tides too play a part in marine deposition by dropping fine silt along shallow, sheltered bays and estuaries to build up marshes and mud flats. But the great mass of material worn away from the land is eventually washed out to sea and sinks to the ocean floor. There, it slowly piles up into deep layers of sediment, enriched by the remains of dead sea plants and animals. Over millions of years' compaction transform thick sea-floor layers of sediment into layers of sedimentary rock. Eventually, earth movements may raise such rocks above the ocean surface where the agents of rock weathering and erosion once again start to attack and wear them away.

The waves strikes against coasts. It causes lot of erosion or deposition at the coast. This work is carried on in three manners.

(i) ***By hydraulic pressure*** : water waves exert present on the coast. This pressure breaks sedimentary jointed and faulted rocks. There is air in the rocks. This air so compressed breaks the rocks.

(ii) *By corrasion* : surfs and under tow uproot rocks and transport them from then original places. The surf throws the pebbles against the rocks of the coast. This increases erosion.

(iii) *By Attrition* : It involves breaking up of boulders dashed against the shores into finer particles.

LANDFORMS CAUSED BY WAVE EROSION

- ***Sea cliffs*** i.e. steep or concave shape due to horizontal surfs which acts as a saw. When the notch grows, the upper part of the cliff looks hanging. Gradually this ***overhanging*** part becomes unbalanced and collapses. The surf effects great rock erosion. If there is a soft portion in it, it cuts down and form ***sea caves.***
- ***Headland*** i.e. some narrow land area projects far into the sea. It is known as ***Head land***. When sea caves on either side are joined by head land, the arch over the passage is called **natural bridge.** When the natural bridge collapses, the remains of the natural bridge stands as pillars isolated from one another. Such a pillar is called ***chimney rocks***. *If a hole is developed in the roof of sea cave, it is called* ***Blow Hole.*** ***Spouting*** Hole is the name given because of the noise it makes.
- **Sea caves :** cuts into cliffs at local zones of weakness in the rocks
- **Sea Arches :** Formed by erosion of rock
- **Sea stacks :** Formed by a rock pile seaward from the beach
- **Wave cut platforms :** marks the submerged limits to rapid erosion just offshore

LANDFORMS CAUSED BY WAVE DEPOSTION

(i) ***Beach*** i.e. entire area along the sea extending from the line reached by high tide and the highest storm waves to low tide point

(ii) *Swells* i.e. parallel ridges formed on the coast by the sea

(iii) ***Bars and barriers :*** The deposition made by sea waves have bars and barriers. The bars are submerged under the sea at the time of high tides while the barriers donot submerge.

(iv) ***Spits*** **:** A bar full of pebbles, stones etc. protudes out of an headland. Its one end disappears in the open sea if the bar is submerged in water, it is called spit.

(v) ***Tied Islands and Tombolos*** : Many times islands situated away from the coast are connected by bars. Such an island connected with the coast by a bar is called **tied island** and the bar connecting it to ice coast is called **Tombolo**

(vi) ***Mud Flat and Salt Marshes*** develop behind the sand barriers and bars towards the coast.

Lagoons : At many places bars and barriers enclose the coast and form small lakes. Such lakes are known as lagoons. Lake Chilka is a well-known lagoon.

TYPES OF COASTS

There are many different types of coasts; beaches are just one type.

Coasts are divided into two categories : primary coasts, which were created by non-marine processes, and secondary coasts, which were formed by marine action. Primary coasts happen because of changes in the land, such as river deltas or lava flows. Secondary coasts are caused by changes in the ocean, such as the creation of barrier islands or coral recfs.

PRIMARY COASTS

They are created by erosion (the wearing away of soil or rock), deposition (the buildup of sediment or sand) or tectonic activity (changes in the structure of the rock and soil because of earthquakes). Many of these coastlines were formed as the sea level rose during the last 18,000 years, submerging river and glacial valleys to form bays and fjords (a type of estuary).

River deltas are in example of a primary coast. They form where a river deposits soil and other material as it enters the sea. River deltas are divided into three groups : the river-dominated delta, the tide-dominated delta and the wave-dominated delta. River-dominated deltas, such as the Mississippi or Nile river deltas, are formed when there are large amounts of material in the water, and tidal action is relatively low. Tide-dominated deltas, which are found where the daily tidal range is more than a meter, have many branching channels and long narrow islands formed as the tide and river flow in different directions. Wave-dominated deltas are little more than a bulge on the shoreline since there is so much wave activity that all the sediment is spread evenly along the coast and does not accumulate at the river's end.

Primary coasts are divided into two categories : (i) **submergent** and (ii) **emergent coasts.**

Submergent coastlines result from a general sea-level rise and crustal subsidence (a lot of heavy sediment on top of the bedrock is forcing the bedrock deeper into the earth). Most of the eastern United States has submergent coastlines. One example is the Chesapeake Bay.

Such shorelines are mainly of three types :

(i) **Ria :** When the hills and rivers of high land meet the coast at right angle, ria coasts are formed. It is generally caused by the drowning of the river mouth.Such coasts are found at the Cape Finisterre of north west Spain, south western Ireland and western coast of the Britannia in France.

(ii) **Fjord :** i.e. the valleys of the glaciers which have been submerged. At many places, the glaciers have deepened their valleys to such an extent that the valleys continue to remain submerged even after their snow had melted away. E.g. Sogne Fjord, Trondheim Fjord and Hardanger Fjord.

Difference between Fjord and Ria

Fjord	Ria
1. It is a long, narrow inlet into the seacoast with more or less steep sides.	1. It is long, narrow bay.
2. It is the result of partial sub-mergence of a glaciated area of high relief.	2. It is caused by the subsidence of the earth's surface in a region of ridges and furrows where these are not parallel to the coast.
3. The inlet has very steep sides and U-shaped profile.	3. The inlet has gentle slopes and develop V-shaped profile.
4. It becomes shallow towards the sea because of glacial deposits.	4. It is uniformly deeper towards sea.

(iii) **Dalmatian Shores :** These are the shores where the hills and the highlands of the coast run parallel to the sea coast. E.g. wetern coast of America in Pacific Ocean. If the shores are submerged to a greater extent, the outer hill ranges turn into a series of islands. The parallel valleys between them are called sounds. E.g. east coasts of Yugoslavia.

(iv) **The Haff Shoreline :** It consitss of large sandy strips running parallel to the coast and enclosing between them shallow lagoons known as "Haffs". It does not provide good harbour because it is usually shallow. E.g. the Baltic coast of Germany.

(v) **Submerged Lowlands Shorelines :** When the lowland is submerged, the sea spreads over a vast area because lowland has a gentle slope. The river valley turn into broad and shallow ***estuaries***. As a result of offshore bars spits, lagoons, and marshes continue to form. E.g. Strongford Lough of North Ireland.

(b) **Emergent Coast Lines :** Emergent coastlines result from the land being lifted, either by tectonic activity or rebound from the weight of heavy glaciers, which exposes the former sea bottom bit by bit forming continuously new shoreline. A characteristic feature of emergent coasts are marine terraces, formed as tectonic uplift moves the land upward in short bursts, which are then worn by wave action into relatively flat surfaces, somewhat like a large staircase. Beach ridges can be formed by rebound, and are composed of cobblestones piled at the surfline by storm activity, which is slowly lifted higher over time.

SECONDARY COASTS

They are caused by the action of the sea or by creatures that live in it. Sea cliffs, barrier islands, mud flats, coral reefs, mangrove coasts and salt marshes are all examples of secondary coastlines. While most of the eastern United States is considered submergent, a great deal of the coastline formed between submergent features is secondary, such as marshes, mangroves, sand beaches and islands. Large portions of the US Pacific coast are secondary as well, with eroded headlands and wave terraces.

GROUND WATER EROSION

(i) **Landforms Caused by Ground Water Erosion**

LIMESTONE AND CHALK LANDFORMS

(Karst Regime) Limestone and Chalk are sedimentary rocks of organic origin derived from the accumulation of corals and shells in the sea. In its pure state, limestone is made up of calcite or calcium carbonate, but where magnesium is also present, it is termed **dolomite.** Chalk is a very pure form of limestone, white and rather soft. A region with a large stretch of limestone possesses a very distinct type of topography. It is termed as ***Karst Region, a*** name derived from the Karst district of Ygoslavia where such topography is found.

Karst regions have a bleak landscape and there is a general absence of surface drainage. Limestones are well jointed but progressive widening of joints by rainwater develops an intriguing feature called **Limestone Pavement.** The enlarged joints are called **Grikes** and the isolated, rectangular blocks are termed **Clints.** The small depressions on the surface of limestone are called **Sink Holes** or **Swallow Holes.** When a number of sink holes coalesce a larger hollow is formed and is called a **Doline.** several dolines a may merge as a result of subsidence to form a larger depression called an **Uvala.** In Yugoslavia, some very large depressions are called **Polje** and some are as large as a hundred square miles but these are partly due to **Faulting.**

Caused by Water Depositional

The most spectacular underground features that adorn the limestone caves are stalacites, stalagmites and pillars. **Stalacities** are the sharp slender, downward growing pinnacles that hang from the cave roofs. The water carries calcium in solution and as it trickles down the stalacities and drops to the floor where calcium is deposited to form **Stalagmites.** Over a long period, the stalacities hanging from the roof is eventually joined to stalagmites growning from the floor to form a **Pillar.**

Such features are commonly seen in any well-developed limestone caves. e.g. Batu caves, Kuala Lampur; Mammoth Caves, Kentucky and Carlsbad caves, New Mexico in U.S.A. and Postojna Cave, Yugoslavia.

Main Limestone regions are north-west Yugoslavia, the causses district of southern France, the Pennines of Britain, Yorkshire and Derbyshire in particular, the Kentucky region of U.S.A., the Yucaton Peninsula of Mexico, the cockpit country of Jamacia and the limestone hills of Perlis.

CHALK LANDFORMS are different from limestones. There is little or no surface draiange and valleys which once contained rivers are now dry. These are often called **Coombes.** The chalk forms low rounded hills in southern and south-eastern England where they are called **Downs** and in norhtern France. Because of its friable nature, swallow-holes and underground cave networks do not generally develop.

ORDERS OF EARTH RELIEF : (Megarelief)

1. **First Order Relief :** Continents and Ocean Basins. It has crustal plates.

2. **Second Order Relief :** created by plate tectonics; vertical and lateral motion of plates.

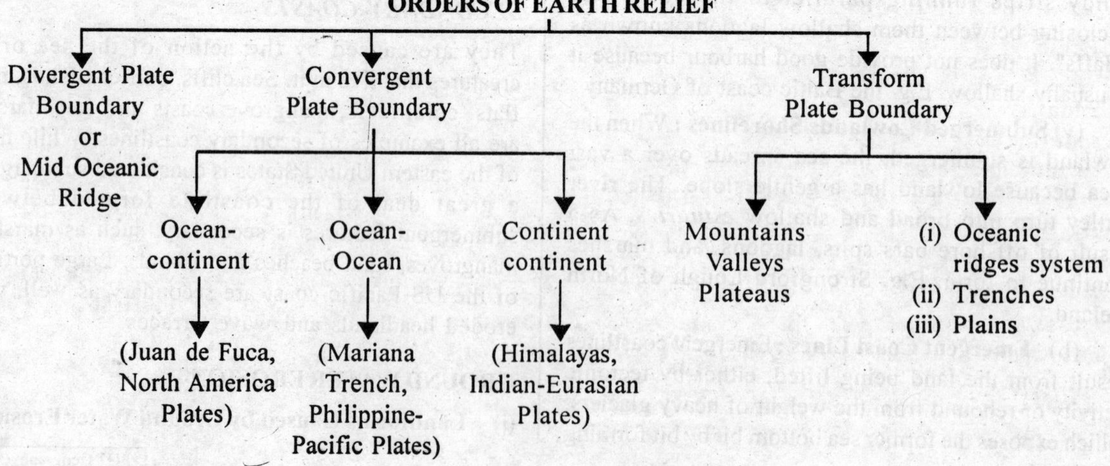

3. **Third Order Relief : (Land Forms):** They are produced by erosion or deposition rather than tectonic movement. e.g. individual mountains, particular valleys, No lower limit in size. (*See Chart on Next Page*)

CONTINENTS AND OCEANS

Continents and ***Oceans*** are two major features of the earth. About 29% of the total surface area of the earth is landmasses and the remaining 71% is covered by water. The highest point on land is Mount Everest (8,848 mt. above sea-level) and the deepest point in the ocean is Challenger Deep in Mariana Trench in the Pacific Ocean (11,022 metres below sea level). Thus, the maximum difference in elevation is about 20 kms which is very insignificant considering the size of the earth.

The continents and ocean are irregularly arranged over the surface of the earth with Northern hemisphere having more land areá than the southern hemisphere. For several million years, large parts of the continents Greenland and Antarctica are still. This period on the earth is known as Ice age. The icesheets melted only few thousand years ago, raising the sea-level in the present position. When the sea level was lower, North America and Asia were connected by the dry land where today exists the Bering Strait.

WORLD LAND AREAS AND ELEVATIONS

How large is the world? What is the largest continent? The continents are listed below size-wise :

Area	Approximate land area sq. km	Approximate land area sq. ml	Percentage of total land area	Elevation, Feet and Height	
				Highest	Lowest
World	148,647,000	57,393,000	100.0%	Mt. Everest, Tibet-Nepal, 29,035 ft.	Dead Sea, Israel-Jordan, 1,349 ft below sea level (8,850 m)1 (-411 m)
Africa	30,065,000	11,608,000	20.2	Mt. Kilimanjaro, Tanzania, 19,340 ft. (5,895 m)	Lake Assal Djibouti, 512 ft below sea level (-156 m)
Antarctica Bentley	13,209,000	5,100,000	8.9	Vinson Massif, Ellsworth Mts., 16,066 ft. (4,897 m)	Lowest land point hidden within subglacial Trench[2]
Asia (includes the Middle East) m)	44,579,000	17,212,000	30.0	Mt. Everest, Tibet-Nepal, 29,035 ft.(8,850 m)	Dead Sea, Israel-Jordan, 1349 ft. below sea level (-411
Australia (includes Oceania)	8,112,000	3,132,000	5.3	Mt. Kosciusko, Australia, 7,310 ft. (2,228 m)	Lake Eyre, Australia below sea level (-12 m)
Europe (the Ural Mountains in Russia form the boundary Between Europe and Asia)	9,938,000	3,837,000	6.7	Mt. Elbrus, Russia/Georgia, 18,510 ft. (5,642 m)	Caspian Sea Russia, Kazakhstan 92 ft. below sea level (-86m)
North America (includes Central America and the Caribbean)	24,474,000	9,449,000	16.5	Mt. McKinley, Alaska, 20,320 ft. (6,194m)	Death Valley, Calif., 282 ft. below sea level (-86 m)
South America	17,819,000	6,879,000	12.0	Mt. Aconcagua, Argentina, 22,834 ft. (6,960 m)	Valdes Peninsula, Argentina 131 ft. below sea level (-40 m)

What's Missing on this Continent ?
We always talk about what each continent has—which is the biggest, which has the longest river, which has the most people. Now let's see what each continent doesn't have. Here are some things that entire continents do without.
Asia and **Europe** are not separate landmasses. They are divided by the Ural Mountains.
Antarctica has no country. The U.S. and other countries have science stations here, but no nation owns the land.
Europe has no desert.
Africa, the world's hottest landmass, has no cold climate.
Australia has no active volcanoes.
Australia has only one country, Australia.

LANDFORMS OF THE SECOND ORDER : PLAINS, PLATEAUS AND MOUNTAINS

The major land forms of the second order on the continent are plains, plateaus, mountains, and lakes and those constituting the ocean beds, are the continental shelf, continental slope, deep sea plain, etc.

1. PLAIN : A plain is an area with gentle sloping land and very low local relief (less than 325 ft). Plains arising continuously inland may attain elevations of high plains over 2000 ft. The main types of plains are:

Peneplains : In due course of weathering and erosion the fold mountains are reduced to an almost level surface not far above sea-level. This surface is called peneplain.

Flood Plains : It is the low-lying land that borders a river and is subjected to periodic flooding. It is composed of deposits of sediment of variable thickness laid down by flood waters e.g. Ganga-Yamuna Doab.

Delta Plains and Alluvial Plains : They are formed by the deposition of eroded material by Rivers. Example of Delta plains is Sunder Bans plains.

Coastal Plain : It is a low lying expanse of land between the coast and higher ground inland. They may be produced by a relative fall in sea level which exposes a stretch of land previously under water or by deposition of alluvium by Rivers.

Lucustrine Plains are the old lakes, beds and are made up of sediments deposited by rivers.

Karst Plains landforms dominated by surface features of limestone solution and underlain by limestone cavern systems.

Pedeplains : Desert land surface of low relief composed in part of pediment surfaces and in part of alluvial fan and plain surfaces.

Abyssal Plains : Large expanse of very smooth, flat ocean floor found at depths of 4,600 to 5500 m.

Glacial Plains are formed through glacial erosion and deposition.

Lava Plains are formed when the lava that flows out of the volume or fissures in the earth spreads over the surrounding lands e.g. Deccan Plateau.

2. PLATEAUS : Upland surface, more or less flat and horizontal, upheld by a resistant bed or formation of sedimentary rock or by lava flows and bounded by a steep cliff. Tibet is the highest plateau in the world.

(a) **Intermontane Plateau** are formed in association with mountains and are enclosed by them e.g. Tibetan Plateau

(b) **Piedmont Plateaus** : They lie between mountains on the one side and the sea or plains on the other e.g. Patagonian plateau in S. America

(c) **Continental Plateaus** : They rise abrubtly from the seas or low lands and are extensive e.g. Indian plateau and Greenland.

3. MOUNTAINS : It is a mass of land considerably higher than a hill (more than 600 m. high) and a fairly steep slopes. They have sharp conical peaks and many of them are formed of a series of ranges.

(a) **Fold Mountains :** They consist of great masses of folded sedimentary rocks whose thickness is often as much as 12 km.

(i) They are caused by rocks being crumpled at plate boundaries. The deformation of layers of rocks is know as folding e.g. Himalayas, the Alps, Rockies and Andes.

(ii) **Anticlines and Synclines :** Horizontal compression results in the formation of upholds called anticlines and downfolds called synclines.

(iii) **Faults :** They are common causes of mountain uplift and faults in turn are due to shrinking of the crust caused by cooling and contraction.

(b) **Block Mountains :** They are formed when a mass of land was pushed up between parallel cracks or faults in the earth's crust or by sinking of the land around them. e.g. Mesta in Spain, Southern uplands of Scotland.

(c) **Volcanic Mountains :** They are the result of the accumulation of volcanic material ejected from the bowels of the earth. They are also called Mountains of Accumulation e.g. Kilimanjaro in Africa, Fuji Yama in Japan, Etna in Italy.

(d) **Residual Mountains :** The agents of denudation such as rain, wind, frost and running water ceaselessly wear away the soft rocks of high mountains leaving behind the harder rocks as remains. These are the residual mountains.

PRINCIPAL DESERTS OF THE WORLD

Deserts are arid regions, generally receiving less than ten inches of precipitation a year, or regions where the potential evaporation rate is twice as great as the precipitation.

The world's deserts are divided into four categories. Sub-tropical deserts are the hottest, with parched terrain and rapid evaporation. Although cool coastal deserts are located within the same latitudes as subtropical deserts, the average temperature is much cooler because of frigid offshore ocean currents. Cold winter deserts are marked by stark temperature differences from season to season, ranging from 100° F (38°C) in the summer to 10° F (–12°) in the winter. Polar regions are also considered to be deserts because nearly all moisture in these areas is locked up on the form of ice.

ROCKS

A rock is any mass of the harder portions of the earth's crust. Rocks are made up of most of the solid materials of the Lithosphere. The substances of which they are made are called minerals. A rock has no definite chemical composition. It is usually a mixture of various materials. Where rocks contain compounds of metals of sufficient value to be mined, they are called Ores.

Rocks, Ores and Minerals
Rocks : Rocks are solid materials which make up the Earth's crust. They include hard and resistant material like granite and marble, and also soft and loose material like silt and sand. They are made up of substances known as minerals. The common minerals found in rocks are **feldspar** and **quartz.** Rocks do not have a definite chemical composition. **Ore :** Some rocks contain metal compounds in large quantities which can be obtained economically. Such rocks are known as ores. **Mineral :** A mineral is a naturally occurring deposit in the Earth's crust consisting of one or more elements. It has definite chemical and physical properties.

The study of the composition of a rock, its strucutre and the fossils it contains is known as ***Stratigraphy*** or historical geology.

CLASSIFICATION OF ROCKS

Petrologists often identify and classify rocks on the basis of three main characteristics; **texture, structure,** and **composition.**

- **Texture** refers to the shape, size and appearance of the individual particles in rock. Smooth-textured rocks may have small, flat particles. Coarse textured rocks may have a variety of large angular particles.
- **Structure** refers to the overall arrangement and appearance of rock in its natural setting. For example, some rock formations occur as massive blocks or columns, while others have a pronounced layered arrangement.
- **Composition** refers to the minerals contained in the rock. By determining the kinds and abundances of minerals in a sample of rock, a scientist can often identify the rock. The colour of a rock sample is often a clue to its mineral composition; red and brown rocks, for example, may owe their colour to the presence of iron rich minerals. Density (weight of a given volume) is another aid in identifying its composition; relatively dense rock may contain minerals that are rich in heavy metals such as lead.

In addition, the rock's original location, especially in relation to nearby rocks that are already known, is of help in identification and classification.

MAJOR TYPES OF ROCKS

There are three major classes of rocks, grouped according to the way in which they are formed; igneous, sedimentary, and metamorphic.

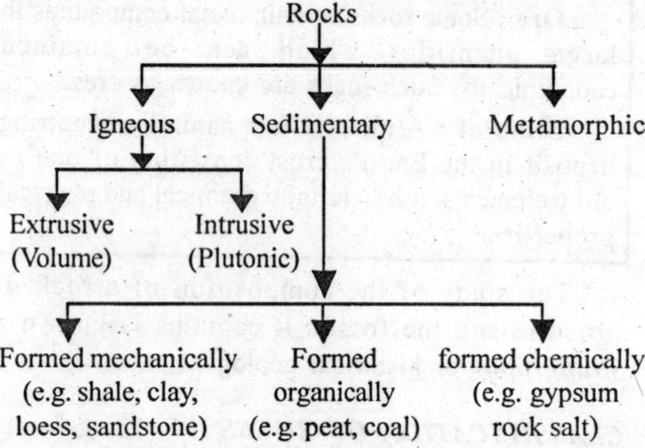

(1) IGNEOUS ROCKS are the most abundant constituents of the Earth's crust. Two origins have been proposed for the formation of igneous rocks (i) solidification of magma and (ii) granitisation. Most of the types of igneous rocks have originated through the former process.

Magma is a complex, very hot solution of silicates containing water and several gases. It originates in the deep interiors of the Earth's body in the upper mantle. Magma moves upward by melting away the overlying rocks and by forcing them aside. This process is termed intrusion. Intrusion cools the magma. Magma that reaches the Earth's surface and then solidifies is called lava. The physical appearance of igneous rock is essentially determined by the rate of cooling of magma. The slow cooling of magma which lies deep in the crust produces large mineral crystals, and thus, results in the formation of a coarse grained or phaneritic texture. Huge masses of coarse-grained igneous rocks formed by the solidifying or magma at a depth below the crust are termed *plutonic rocks.* Granite is a typical coarse-grained plutonic rock.

Igneous Rocks
1. The term "igneous" comes from the Latin word ***ignis*** which means ***fire***.
2. Igneous rocks are the ancestors of all other rocks and make up 85% or more of the Earth's crust.
3. All other types of rocks are formed directly or indirectly from igneous rocks. Hence igneous rocks are also known as **primary rocks.**
4. All igneous rocks are crystalline in nature.
5. **Magma :** When molten material is underground, it is known as magma.
6. **Lava :** When the molten material reaches the surface, it is known as lava.
7. **Dyke :** A thin wall like igneous.
8. **Sill :** A flat, sheet like igneous intrusion.
9. **Batholith :** A large irregularly shaped body of intrusive igneous rock, covering more than 100 sq. metres.
10. **Plutonic :** Igneous rock formed deep beneath the surface of the earth by the consolidation of magma.

Rapid cooling of molten igneous material or magma, either near or on the surface, produces very small crystals which are visible mainly under a microscope. These rocks have a fine-grained or aphanitic texture. On the surface, cooling can be so rapid that the various atoms cannot arrange themselves into the deferred structural arrangements of the silicates. Hence, no crystals are formed and the rock is said to have a glassy texture. Andesite and basalt are examples of aphanitic texture.

Some igneous rocks have been produced through two stages of cooling—slow cooling followed by rapid cooling. The large crystals formed by slow cooling are found embedded in a matrix of very small crystals formed by rapid cooling.

Granitisation is the second process producing the igneous rocks of granitic variety. The minerals found in granitic rock also occur in sedimentary rocks. These minerals, through sufficient heating, are transformed into granite. This process is termed granitisation. In this process the need for having a molten phase is eliminated.

On the basis of the locale of origin the igneous rocks can be classified into ***intrusive*** and ***extrusive*** varieties. The intrusives crystallise beneath the surface and have a coarse texture. In contrast, the extrusive rocks crystallise on the surface and have a finer texture. Many of the intrusive rocks have their extrusive equivalents. Rhyolite and basalt are the extrusive equivalents, respectively of granite and gabbro. Large masses of intrusive rock below the surface of the earth are called ***batholiths***. Some called magma rises vertically to form projections called ***dikes***. Some dikes have been uncovered by erosion and extend above the Earth's surface. Another form of cooled magma, ***sills***, consists of horizontal layers of igneous rock between layers of other kinds of rock.

Igneous rocks can be classified broadly on four bases ; (i) process of origin, (ii) place of origin, (iii) mineral composition and (iv) texture.

Underground Igneous Rocks
❖ **Hypabyssal Rocks :** They form just below the surface of the Earth, usually in dykes and sills. ❖ **Plutonic Rocks :** They form deep beneath the ground in plutons and batholiths.

Composition of Igneous Rocks: There are over 600 types of igneous rock. Each one has its own grain pattern and mineral composition. This is determined by the nature of magma from which the rock forms and how quickly it cools.

Igneous rocks are made mainly of **silicates.** [Silica (SiO_2) often combines with other oxides (of aluminium, potassium, sodium calcium, iron, magnesium etc.) to form silicates.] Silica-rich rocks are acidic and pale in colour. Those containing less silica are dark and basic.

Some of the important igneous rocks are granite, rhyolite, pegmatite, syenite, diorite, andesite gabbro, basalt, dolerite, and periodotite. Granite, rhyolite and pegamatite belong to the acidic group. Quartz, biotite, and feldspar are the essential minerals in all of them. Syenite has a coarsely crystalline texture and the mineral composition of feldspar, mica, amphibole, and pyroxine. It is intermediate between acidic and basic. Diorite and andesite are also intermediate between acidic and basic. Plagioclase, hornblende, biotite and pyroxene are common to both, Gabbro, basalt, and dolerite are common basic rocks. Plagioclase, feldspar and augite are the common minerals. Periodotite, an ultrabasic rock consists chiefly of olivine and also pydoxene, hornblende, and biotite

Volcanic Rocks	Plutonic Rocks
1. They are formed by the cooling and solidification of **lava** on the surface of the Earth.	1. They are formed by the cooling and solidification of magma below the surface of the Earth.
2. They are also known as extrusive rocks.	2. They are also known as intrusive rocks.
3. Volcanic rocks have small crystals.	3. Plutonic rocks have larger crystals.
4. Basalt is an example of such a rock.	4. Granite is an example of such a rock.

(2) SEDIMENTARY ROCKS : Rocks on the surface of the earth are broken up into bits and pieces of all sizes by various agents. These smaller pieces of rock, known as ***sediment***, are usually transported by running water and deposited in layers at the bottom of lakes, seas and oceans. Thus, rock formed from the debris of other rocks and living matter is called sedimentary rock.

Sedimentary rocks are those which are constituted of sediments. Sediment is material from the air and water that settles down. Sedimentary rocks have been formed from sediments which accumulate at the bottom of a lake, in a river bed, or a desert plain and the bottom of the sea. Sedimentary particles vary in size from microscopic to very large fragments. The sediments can be divided into two major groups : ***clastic*** and ***non-clastic***. Clastic sediments are particles broken from a parent rock. Non-clastic sediments are newly created mineral matter precipitated from chemical solution or from organic activity.

Points to Note

1. The word "sedimentary" is derived from the Latin word *sedimentum* which means settling. It is rock formed from the debris of both, other rocks and living matter.
2. About 70% of the rock exposed on the surface of the Earth is sedimentary rock.
3. Sedimentary rocks are found in layers and so they are also known as stratified rocks, (*Strata* means layers in *Latin*).
4. Fossils are found in this layer. A fossil is any part of a once living thing preserved in rock. It may be the entire body, a single bone or a set of footprints.

   Fossils tells us about life in the past and they helps us to date environments. Fossils also show what kinds of animals lived in the past.
5. Sedimentary rock layers hold all reserves of **coal, oil and natural gas.**

LITHIFICATION : The process that turns loose sediment into rock is called lithification. Soft sediment is turned into hard rock over millions of years when the sediments are near the surface, and are under relatively low pressure and temperature (unlike metamorphism). It happens as sediments are buried beneath other layers of sediment and become gradually hardened by **compaction and cementation.**

(i) Compaction : The slow squeezing of sediments to form hard rock is called **compaction.**

As sediments pile up on top of each other they are gradually squeezed and they lose their water. For example, when **mud** is compacted, it changes to **mudstone** and when **sand** is compacted, it forms **sandstone.**

(ii) Cementation : The binding together of compacted sediments is called **cementation.** Certain materials carried by water filter through spaces in the sediment. These natural materials, like calcium compounds, form a cement. This cementing material fills the spaces around the pieces of sediment and glues them together to form rocks. The most common cements are **calcite, silica** (which gives a very hard rock) and **iron** (which gives rock a rusty colour).

Limestone, a chemically precipitated sedimentary rock is formed by the compaction and lithification of the shells from marine organisms. Sandstone, is formed by the compaction of quartz grains.

Almost all sedimentary rocks possess a layered arrangement. Together the layers are called **strata,** each layer is termed a bed or a stratum. The layers have different textural composition and are alternated or inter-layered. The planes of separation between beds are termed **bedding planes.** Most sedimentary rocks are deposited in a nearly horizontal position. After lithification, the earth movements may change the original horizontal position. Some layers are uplifted, some folded, and some faulted. Five factors control the properties of sedimentary rocks : (i) kind of rock in the source area, (provenance), (ii) environment of the source area, (iii) earth movements (a) in the source area and (b) in the depositional area (tectonism), (iv) environment of the depositional area, and (v) post depositional change of the sediment (lithification).

About three-fourth of the earth's surface is covered with sedimentary rock.

Types of Sedimentary Rocks: There are also **three types** of sedimentary rocks, depending on how they have been formed :

1. **Mechanically Formed** Segmentary rocks contain pieces of other rocks. Agents like running water, wind and moving ice break them into smaller pieces and deposit them at new sites where they form new sedimentary rocks.

   Sandstone, shale and **clay** are examples of this type of sedimentary rock. **Sandstone,** a common sedimentary rock, is formed mainly of quartz particles cemented together by silica, lime, or iron oxide. **Shale** is the most abundant of all sedimentary rocks. It is compacted silt and clay. Lamination, paper thin layers, is the chief diagnostic property of the rock. **Kaolin** and **clay** minerals are abundant in it.
2. **Organically formed** sedimentary rocks consist of the remains of animals and plants. **Limestone, chalk** and **coral** are the most common of this type of sedimentary rock. They are formed from the remains of marine life in the past. **Coal** and its other forms like **peat** and **lignite, petroleum** and

natural gas were formed when vast forests in the ancient past were submerged underground and underwent changes.

Chalk is a calcareous rock made up of microscopic skeletal elements from a variety of limesecreting organisms. It is soft and white , and is composed of almost pure calcium carbonate.

Coal and peat represent the accumulation of vegetation which originated in swamps. Peat is the first stage in the transformation of vegetable matter into coal. It contains about 57 percent carbon. Peat is transformed to coal by increase in pressure which expels the moisture and gaseous constituents and increase the proportion of fixed carbon. **Peat, lignite, bituminous,** and **anthractic** are grades of coal which contain, respectively, higher proportions of fixed carbon.

3. **Chemically formed** rocks are formed by the direct precipitation of mineral matter from solution.

Rock-salt is an example of such a rock. It accumulates in salt lakes and lagoons through evaporation. **Gypsum** is also formed in a similar manner. The type of sediment created depends on the temperatures involved and the concentration of mineral salts within water.

Sedimentary Rocks
1. **Organic Sediment :** A sedimentary rock made from the remains of plants and animals.
2. **Chemical Sediment :** a sedimentary rock made from chemicals dissolved in water.
3. **Lithification :** The process that turns loose sediment into rock.
4. **Bedding Plane :** A boundary between one layer of sedimentary rock and another.
5. **Clastic Rock :** Rock made of older rock fragments from weathered and eroded rock.
6. **Clay :** Fine-grained sedimentary rock.
7. **Sandstone :** Medium-grained sedimentary rock.
8. **Limestone :** A sedimentary rock made mainly from calcite ($CaCO_3$).
9. **Chalk :** A white, very pure form of limestone.
10. **Evaporite :** A sediment left behind when salty water evaporates.

(3) METAMORPHIC ROCKS : Metamorphic rocks are formed when Igneous or sedimentary rocks are transformed underground by the altering of sedimentary or igneous rocks. Such altering can be caused by heat, pressure, chemical action volcanic activity or movement of the earth's crust, either separately or in combination. Two broad classes of metamorphic rocks have been recognized, (i) boliated and (ii) non-foliated. Foliated rocks are characterised by parallel arrangement of slaty minerals, such the micas. The foliations are ultimately changed to bonds. The series of shale, slate, schist, and gneiss represent increasing grades of metamorphism. In the non-foliated metamorphic rocks the mineral grains are equi-dimensional, hence there is no specific orientation. **Quartzite** and **marble** are good examples.

Metamorphic Rocks
1. The word ***"metamorphosis"*** comes from two Greek words that mean to change. (In biology, the change from a **caterpillar** to a **butterfly** or from a **tadpole** to a **frog** is known as metamorphosis.)
2. Metamorphic rocks are very hard.
3. Gems are found in metamorphic rocks.
4. **Crystal Metamorphism :** The shape and alignment of crystals are altered, as Schist is changed into Gneiss.
5. **Contact Metamorphism :** The alteration of rocks situated next to Igneous intrusions. Rocks are transformed by coming into contact with the heat of an igneous intrusion.
6. **Regional Metamorphism :** The alteration of rocks on a large scale as continents collide.
7. **Recrystallization :** The growth of new crystals during metamorphosis.

The rock does not melt but it is changed underground by intense heat and pressure. The processes which form metamorphic rocks take place over long periods of time. During mountain-building, especially, intense pressure over millions of years alters the texture and nature of rocks.

Formation of Metamorphic Rocks: In course of time, shale may get changed to **slate** and **schist,** limestone to **marble,** sandstone to **quartzite** and granite to **gneiss** (pronounced *nice*).

1. **Slate** : Shale, after being squeezed and sheared under mountain-building forces, is altered into slate. This gray or brick red rock splits neatly into thin plates and is used as roofing shingles and as flagstones of patios and walks.
2. **Schist** : With continued application of pressure and internal shearing, slate may change into schist, the most advanced grade of metamorphic rock. Schist is set apart from shale by the coarse texture of the mineral grains, abundance of mica, and presence of large crystals of new minerals such as **Garnet**.
3. **Marble** : Limestone after undergoing metamorphism, becomes marble, a rock of sugary texture when freshly broken. Calcite and dolimite are its main rock-forming minerals. During the process of internal shearing, the calcite mineral of the limestone reforms into larger, more uniform crystals than before. Bedding planes are obscured, and masses of mineral impurities are drawn into swirling streaks and bands.
4. **Quartzite** : It is a metamorphosed form of sedimentary rock sandstone. The slow movement of underground waters carry silica into the sandstone and completely fill the spaces between the grains. Pressure and kneading of the rock is not essential in producing a quartzite.
5. **Gneiss** : These are formed either from intrusive igneous rocks or from clastic sedimentary rocks that have been in close contact with intrusive magmas. It is coarser than Schist. Gneisses vary greatly in appearance, mineral composition and structure. One conspicuous variety is strongly banded into light and dark layers. These can be interpreted as relics of sedimentary strata, such as shale or sandstone, to which new mineral has been added from nearby intrusive rocks.
6. **Amphibole** has a green to dark green colour. The rock-forming minerals are hornblende and actionlite.
7. **Serpentine** is generally of a green colour. It is massive and give a soapy feel and has a fibrous or foliated texture. The main rock-forming mineral is an alternative product of olivine.

A COMPARATIVE STUDY OF THE DIFFERENT TYPES OR ROCKS

Igneous Rock	Sedimentary Rock	Metamorphic Rock
1. Formed by the cooling and solidification of magma.	1. Formed by the erosion, transportation, deposition and consolidation of sediment.	1. Formed due to the action of intense heat and pressure.
2. Made up of crystals.	2. Formed in layers, also called stratified rock.	2. These rocks are very hard.
3. Metallic minerals are found in these rocks.	3. Non-metallic minerals are found in these rocks.	3. Gems, precious stones and metallic minerals are found in these rocks.
4. Basalt and granite are examples of Igneous rocks.	4. Limestone and coal are examples of Sedimentary rocks	4. Diamond and marble are examples of Metamorphic rocks.

ECONOMIC MINERALS ASSOCIATED WITH ROCKS: A large number of minerals having a wide variety of uses are associated with Igneous rocks Some, such as iron nickel, copper, lead, zinc and manganese, are used in the metallurgical industries and other, such as diamond, gold and platinum are the measures of wealth. The number of economic minerals associated with sedimentary rock is less than that associated with igneous rocks. Their industrial importance is also less. Some of the common minerals in this group are **rock-salt, gypsum, nitre, pyrite,** and **hematite. Garnet** and **sillimanite** are two of the main minerals associated with metamorphic rocks.

Virtually all rocks are composed of one or more minerals which are natural substances that have characteristic properties and more-or-less specific chemical compositions.

A few minerals are composed of just one element, such as "native" gold, platinum, mercury, or graphite (which is pure carbon), but the overwhelming majority are composed of two or more elements in a compound. Because minerals are as a rule chemically stable, they can, given the right conditions, last for eons. The oldest found on Earth are nearly 4,000 million years old.

Approximately 200 mineral species are known. Of these about 24 minerals are major constituents of the rocks of the earth's crust. These are termed rock forming minerals. All the minerals belong to one or the other chemical group. There are ten chemical groups : oxides, sulphides, sulphates, carbonates, halides, silicates, pyroxene, amphibole, micas, and feldspars. Examples of common minerals belonging to each of these groups respetitively are hematite, pyrite, gypsum, dolomite, fluorite, quartz, augite, hornblende, muscovite, and plagioclase. All these minerals and the chemical groups to which they belong are chemical having fixed chemical composition. For example, Hematite is iron oxide and Augite is pyroxene. The minerals have both very simple and extremely complex compositions.

Some common minerals are called rock forming minerals. The most common mineral of all is Feldspar, an aluminium silicate found in granite. It is usually light in colour. About half of all the rocks in the Earth's crust are made up of Feldspar. The second most common mineral of earth is quartz, which is naturally colourless or white. It is found in granite and as the white grains of sand on a beach. Calcite (calcium carbonate), another common mineral, is found in limestone.

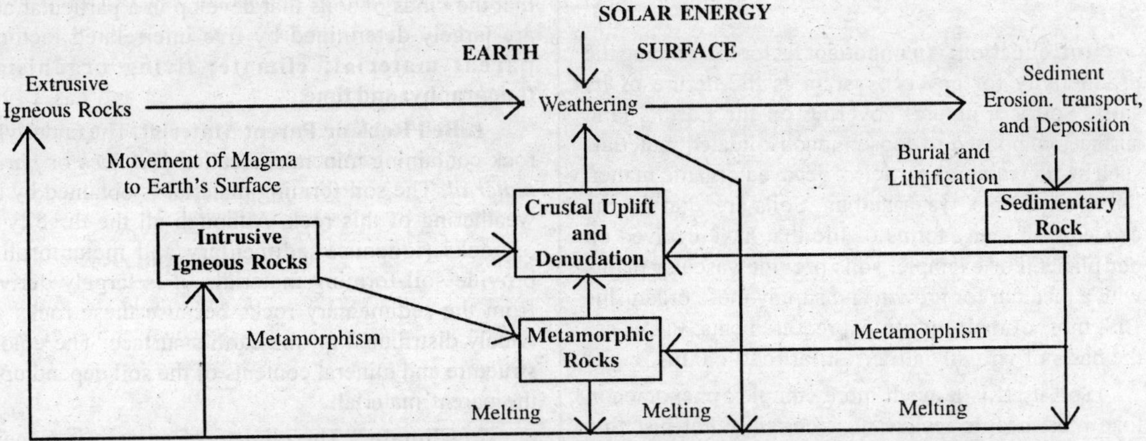

THE ROCK CYCLE: The Rock Cycle is a general model that describes how various geological processes create, modify, and influence rocks. This model suggests that the origin of all rocks can be ultimately traced back to the solidification of molten **magma.** Magma consists of a partially melted mixture of elements and compounds commonly found in rocks. Magma exists just beneath the solid crust of the earth in an interior zone known as the **mantle.**

The Cycle of Rock Transformation : The rock cycle is the relationship between the three types of rock-sedimentary, metamorphic and igneous.

The first part of the rock cycle takes place on the earth's surface. This is the erosion and weathering of older rocks to soil and sand and the transportation of the remaining sediment by rivers down to the sea. Nearly all the sediment produced is eventually transported to deep basins under the sea and areas of great thickness of sediments accumulate.

The loose sediment is changed into hard rock by lithification. Most great thickness of sedimentary rocks accumulate in long, narrow depressions on the sea-floor. These depressions are caused by descending convection currents which, over a period of millions of years, carry the crust of the earth down into the earth's interior, where both the temperature and pressure are high.

The sedimentary rock in the depressions is carried down with the crust. It is folded and squeezed and transformed intc **metamorphic rocks.** The energy to power the rock cycle is derived from the heat of the Sun (which indirectly breaks down existing rocks to sediments), and the heat from the earth's interior which melts existing material to give **igneous rock.**

The rock cycle is a **continuous process** through which old rocks are transformed into new ones. The speed of different parts of the cycle varies. A single layer of sedimentary rock may take thousands of years to build and centuries to wear away. But when magma comes in contact with a rock, changes can occur in days or even minutes.

All of the rock types can be returned to the Earth's interior by **tectonic** forces at areas known as **Subduction Zones.** Once in the Earth's interior, extreme pressures and temperatures melt the rock back into magma to begin the rock cycle again.

SOILS

Introduction: An important factor influencing the productivity for any **ecosystem** is the nature of its **soils.** Soil is a natural covering on the Earth's land surface, composed of loose, unconsolidated materials such as tiny mineral particles, decayed organic matter, living organisms, water and air. Soils are vital for the existence of many forms of life that have evolved on our planet. For example, soils provide vascular plants with a medium for growth and supply these organisms with most of their nutritional requirements. Plants are the basis of virtually all terrestrial **food chains.**

Soil itself is a much more complex phenomenon than most people realize. It is certainly not just fine mineral particles or dirt. A true soil also contains air, water, and organic matter. The formation of a soil is influenced by organisms, climate, topography, parent material, and time. The following items describe some important features of a soil that help to distinguish it from mineral sediments.

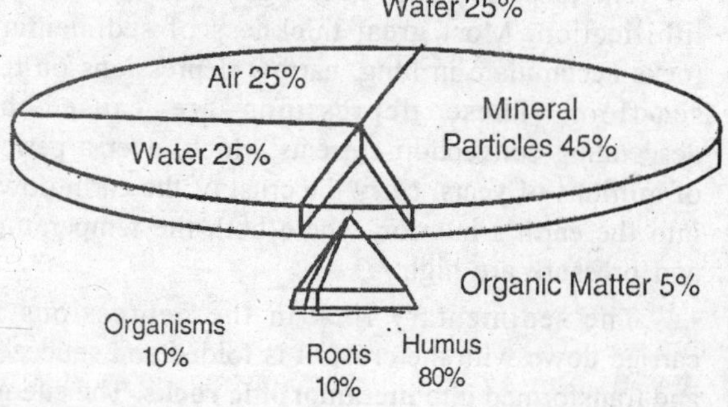

Most soils contain four basic components: mineral particles, water, air, and organic matter. Organic matter can be further sub-divided into humus, roots, and living organisms. The values given above are for an average soil.

SOIL PEDOGENESIS : Pedogenesis can be defined as the process of soil development. Late in the 19th century, two scientists Hilgard in the United States and the Russian Dukuchaev suggested independently that pedosgenesis was principally controlled by climate and vegetation. This idea was based on the observation that comparable soils developed in spatially separate areas when their climate and vegetation were similar. In the 1940s, Hans Jenny extended these ideas based on the observations of many subsequent studies examining the processes involving in the formation of soils. Jenny believed that the kinds of soils that develop in a particular area are largely determined by five interrelated factors : **parent material; climate; living organisms; topography; and time.**

1. Bed Rock or Parent Material. The underlying rock containing minerals is called *bed rock* or *parent material*. The soil forming material is obtained by the weathering of this rock. Although all the three types of rocks (igneous, sedimentary and metamorphic) provide soil-forming materials, it is largely derived from the sedimentary rocks because these rocks are widely distributed on the earth's surface. The colour, structure and mineral contents of the soil depend upon the parent material.

2. Climate : The climate of an area is a major factor of soil formation. Parent material is more important for short period but climate becomes more important during longer duration. Two different parent materials may develop the same soil in one type of climate. For example, sandstone and granite are two different rocks in Rajasthan but they have given birth to same type of sandy soil under arid climatic conditions. Similarly, same parent material may form different types of soil under different climates. For example, the crystalline granite produce laterite soil in moist climate of Rajmahal hill and clayey soil in the dry climate of Andhra Pradesh.

The availability of moisture also has an influence on soil pH and the decomposition of organic matter. At regional and local scales, climate becomes less important in soil formation, instead, pedogenesis is more influenced by other factors.

3. Living Organisms: Living organisms have a role in a number of processes involved in pedogenesis including organic matter accumulation, profile mixing and bio-geochemical nutrient cycling . It includes vegetation, bacteria and animals.

(a) Vegetation: It includes trees, shrubs, grasses and mosses. The decay of leaves and roots of different forms of vegetation provides humus to soil which increases its fertility. This provides life to new plants. It increases chemical action and the rate of soil formation. Humus also quickens the weathering of minerals in the process of soil formation.

(b) Bacteria: Bacteria acts differently in different climates and forms different types of soils. Bacteria lives on humus. In humid tropical climate, bacterial activity is intense. Consumption of humus is so much that soils are left poor in it. In cold climate, bacterial activity is limited and the soils are rich in humus. Bacteria also changes nitrogen from air into a chemical form which is usable by plants. Through litterfall and the process of decomposition, organisms add humus and nutrients, to soil which influences soil structure and fertility. That is why bacteria is termed as *nitrogen-fixing agent.*

(c) Animals: Burrowing animals like ants, rodents, termites and some birds move the surface soil downwards and the sub-soil from it lower horizon upwards. The mixing of two soil layers helps in improving the texture and its aeration. Small organisms like earthworms live in millions in the soil and help in reducing its grains to small size and in mixing the mineral and the organic matter.

4. Topography: Elements of topography (such as altitude, relief and slope) affect the deposition and erosion of soil and the run-off of the water. On steep slopes, there is lot of erosion by river, glacier and wing and only a thin layer of coarse soil is left. This is known as ***residual soil***. This eroded material is deposited in areas of gentle slope and a thick layer of soil is formed. Such soils are very fertile because they are formed from different kinds of rocks from over a wide catchment. But in certain flat areas, the soils are poorly drained and suffer from leaching (downward movement of salts), Thus, the best soils are found in areas of gentle slope with good drainage.

5. Time: Time is an important factor in the formation and development of the soil. The process of formation of soil is very slow. One to two centimetres thick stable soil cover may take thousands of years to form under the most favourable conditions.

The characteristics of soil undergo drastic changes with the passage of time. There are three stages of the development of soil —1. Young stage, 2. Mature stage, and 3. Old stage.

(i) **Young Stage :** The fresh river alluvium or glacial till are soils of the *young stage.* They have a greater control on the parent material and have a poorly developed soil profile.

(ii) **Mature Stage :** *Mature soil* are developed over a long time. The influence of climate and of organic matter is clearly visible on the mature soils. They have well-developed soil profile.

(iii) **Old Stage :** With further lapse of time, humus is properly mixed with soil and its colour changes. The importance of parent material is almost over and the soil attains its old stage. Soils of *old stage* are found in the tropical lands and are one to six million years old.

PHYSICAL AND CHEMICAL PROPERTIES OF SOIL : The physical and chemical properties determine both the fertility and productivity of soils.

(i) The **physical properties** include texture, structure, and colour.

Soil texture refers to the particle sizes composing the soil. These particles are classified as gravel, sand, silt and clay in decreasing order of size. Four textural types are recognised. These are sand, sandy loam, loam and clay. All the textural types are combinations of different sizes of particles. Soil texture determines the water condition of the soil affecting the pore space size. In sand as both the particles and the pore spaces are large, it drains rapidly. The particles and pore spaces are large, it drains rapidly. The particles and pore spaces in clay are small, hence drainage is very slow. Both are poor for plant growth for which loam texture is best.

Soil structure refers to the arrangement in which soil grains are grouped together into larger pieces. Major types of structure are blocky, granular, columnar, prismatic, crumb, and platy. Soil structure influences the absorption of water by the soil, its erodibility, and ploughing

Soil colour is a minor physical attribute but it is the most readily observed. It indicates the origin and composition of the soil. Increasing quantities of humus produce a range from white, through brown, to black. Black and dark brown colours are typical of soils in the cool and humid areas of temperate latitudes. Soil in the steppe lands and deserts are light brown and grey. Red and yellow colours are quite common and both are due to the presence of iron oxides and hydroxides.

(ii) **Chemical Properties** of soil include soil water, chemical composition, soil colloids, humus and soil air.

A soil's chemical composition can be tested only in a laboratory. Some tests for specific purposes, however—such as checking acidity are routinely done in the field.

Acidity and Alkalinity: As soil water absorbs carbon dioxide from the air, a weak solution of carbonic acid is formed. In addition, soil water absorbs acid materials formed by the decomposition of organic and inorganic matter. These weak acid solutions react with soluble bases to form insoluble compounds and water. For example, calcium hydroxide (lime) reacts with the carbonic acid to form calcium carbonate (the chief component of limestone) and water. Thus, acid ground water removes soluble bases from the soil. The removal of soluble materials from the surface soil to lower levels by water is called *leaching*.

Most plants grown best in soils that are neutral—neither acid nor alkaline (basic)—or nearly so. Acidity usually occurs to some degree in soils of humid regions. Where acidity is high enough to cause trouble, lime is usually added to the soil. Alkaline soils—with an abundance of soluble bases—are most common in the drier parts of the world, where little leaching takes place.

Acidity and alkalinity are measured in terms of pH, a numerical value ranging from 0 to 14 soil pH is the most important chemical properties of a soil and is generally related to the concentration of free hydrogen ions in the soil matrix. Soils with a relatively large concentration of hydrogen ions tends to be acidic. Alkaline soils have relatively low concentration of hydrogen ions. A pH of 7 indicates a neutral soil; values slightly below 7 indicate mild acidity and values slightly above 7 mild alkalinity. Maximum soil fertility occurs at the range of 6.0 to 7.2.

PRINCIPAL PEDOGENIC PROCESSES (SOIL FORMING PROCESSES): A large number of processes are responsible for the formation of soils. This fact is evident by the large number of different types of soils that have been classified by soil scientists. However, at the macro-scale we can suggest that there are five main principal pedogenic processes acting on soils. These processes are **laterization, podzolization, calcification, salinization, and gleization.**

Laterization is a pedogenic process common to soil found in tropical and subtropical environments. High temperatures and heavy precipitation result in the rapid **weathering** of rocks and minerals. Movements of large amounts of water through the soil cause **eluviation** and **leaching** to occur. Almost all of the by products of weathering, very simple small compounds or nutrient **ions,** are translocated out of the soil profile by leaching if not taken up by plants for nutrition. The two exceptions to this process are iron and aluminium compounds. Iron oxides give tropical soils their unique reddish colouring. Heavy leaching also causes these soils to have an **acidic pH** because of the net loss of **base cations.**

Podzolization is associated with humid cold mid-latitude climates and **coniferous vegetation.** Decomposition of coniferous litter and heavy summer precipitation create a soil solution that is strongly acidic. This **acidic solid solution** enhances the processes of **eluviation** and **leaching** causing the removal of soluble **basecations** and aluminium and iron compounds from the **A horizon.** This process creates a sub-layer in the A horizon that is white to grey in colour and composed of silica sand.

Calcification occur when evaportranspiration exceeds precipitation causing the upward movement of dissolved alkaline salts from the groundwater. At the same time, the movement of rain water causes a downward movement of the salts. The net result is the deposition of the translocated cations in the **B horizon.** In some cases, these deposits can form a hard layer called **caliche.** The most common substance involved in this process is **calcium carbonate.** Calcificaation is common in the **prairie grasslands.**

Salinization is a process that functions in the similar way to calcification. It differs from calcification in that the salt deposits occur at or vary near the soil surface. Salinization also takes place in much drier climates.

Gleization is a pedogenic process associated with poor drainage. This process involves the accumulations of organic matter in the upper layers of the soil. In lower horizons, mineral layers are stained blue-grey because of the chemical **reduction of** iron.

SOIL CONSERVATION: Soil Conservation is an effort made by man to prevent soil erosion in order to retain the fertility of soil. It may not be possible to stop soil erosion entirely. But much can be done to reduce the rate of certain destructive erosion by taking preventive measures.

Conservation of Soil

Soil can be conserved in many ways :

(i) Afforestation is the planting of trees and other vegetation on previously cleared areas like hill slopes and uncultivated land. The roots of trees and plants anchor and hold the soil together and so it is not easily removed by running water and wind. Trees, plants, shrubs and grasses reduce the speed of flowing water and allow the water to be absorbed by the soil. Trees reduce the force of strong winds and prevent the blowing away of soil particles.

(ii) Restricted Grazing of Animals should be practised. Animals should be moved over different pastures so as avoid the removal of all vegetation from the ground.

(iii) Proper Farming Techniques particularly on hill slopes.

(a) ***Terracing of Hill Slopes*** is effective in controlling soil erosion. Terracing is cutting into the hill slopes in a series of large steps made up of flat fields.

(b) ***Constructing Bunds*** across hill slopes and field boundaries is effective in reducing soil erosion. Bunds are low mud walls or embankments that help to obstruct the flow of water.

(c) ***Contour Ploughing*** should be practised. Contour ploughing is ploughing along the outline of the field in a circular manner. This prevents the soil from being washed away by running water.

(d) ***Strip Cropping*** is another farming technique that helps reduce soil erosion. Strip cropping is planting of alternate rows of different kinds of crops instead of strips of land uncultivated.

(iv) ***Flood Control*** by building dams and multipurpose projects.

Any erosion in gullies already formed should be prevented by construction of **dams** or obstructions. Ploughing and tilling of land should be done along contour levels so that the furrows run across the slope of land. This prevents formation of gullies by the direct flow of water down the slopes. **Bunds** should be constructed according to contours. Finally exclusive grazing should not be allowed. Animals such as the sheep and particularly the goat have proved to be very destructive in the respect.

Trees reduce the force of strong winds and obstruct blowing away of dust particles. Roots of trees, plants and grasses hold soil particles together and strengthen the soil. Plants, grass and shrubs reduce the speed of flowing water. Therefore, such vegetation cover should not be removed indiscriminately, or where it does not exist steps should be taken to plant it.

5 CLIMATE

ATMOSPHERE

The envelope of air that completely surrounds the Earth is known as Atmosphere. It is the presence of the atmosphere with its abundant supply of oxygen that makes the Earth a unique planet in the Universe. The oxygen in the atmosphere has been responsible for the origin and growth of life on the Earth.

Points to Remember

- In 1593, Galileo Galilei made a crude thermometer which was further improved into a mercury thermometre.
- In 1643-47, Evangelista Torricelli invented Barometre.
- In 1623-62 Blaise Pascal showed that air pressure decreases with height as the air gets thinner by taking a barometre up a mountain.

The atmosphere extends to about 1000 km from the surface of the Earth. But 99% of the total mass of the atmosphere is found within 32 km. This is because the atmosphere is held by the gravitational pull of the Earth.

STRUCTURE OF ATMOSPHERE

The atmosphere that surrounds the Earth is essential to life. The lower portion of the atmosphere contains the oxygen required by all land animals and many land plants. The atmosphere acts as an insulator that prevents extreme temperature variations between day and night, such as those that occur on the moon. The atmosphere also absorbs some radiation, such as most ultraviolet rays, that would be harmful to living organisms if it reached the Earth's surface.

The Earth's atmosphere is made up of a series of layers, each of which has a different set of characteristics. The principal regions of the atmosphere, each of which is characterized by the pattern of vertical distribution of temperatures, are the **troposphere**, the **stratosphere**, the **mesosphere**, the **thermosphere**, and **exosphere.** In meteorological research it has long been customary to deal with two regions : the troposphere and the stratosphere. The Main Layers of Atmosphere:

***(i) TROPOSPHERE*:** It is the lowermost part of the atmosphere in which use line. The word troposphere literally means the **zone** of mixing, therefore, it is the realm of the clouds, rain, snow, etc. which extends to a height of 18 km at the equator and 8 km at the poles and is characterized in general by a decrease of temperature with increasing altitude. The upper limit of the troposphere, known as the **tropopause**, which separates the troposphere from the stratosphere. The temperature decreases with the height of this layer, which is called the normal lapse rate. The normal lapse rate of temperature is 1°C for 165 metres.

About 90% of the dust particles and water vapours are concentrated in this layer. All the weather conditions, such as of clouds, precipitation, lightening, thunderstorm, etc. take place in troposphere. Due to the presence of these weather conditions, it is especially avoided by the aviators of jet aeroplanes.

***(ii) STRATOSPHERE* :** It lies above the troposphere. Its height varies from 20 to 50 km. Near tropopause temperature remains low, about 80ºC. But, after this limit, temperature starts to increase, especially due to the presence of Ozone. Ozone is produced by the action of solar radiation on ordinary oxygen atom. It filters sunlight and prevents the harmful ultraviolet rays from reaching the earth's surface. This layer is free from all weather phenomena, therefore it is also called the layer of calm and clear air. This layer is considered best for the high speed jet flights. Strato pause separates the stratosphere and the Mesosphere.

***(iii) MESOSPHERE* :** Above 50 kilometres is the mesosphere, or middle region, characterized by a rapid decrease of temperature to a minimum at about 85 kilometres; this can be below 160 K in the summer at high latitudes. But, like the troposphere, the mesosphere is subject to strong seasonal variations of temperature at high altitudes. The prevailing level of the minimum temperature indicates another division in the atmosphere, known as the **mesopause.**

Vertical air current, unlike the stratosphere, are not strongly inhibited in the mesosphere. Ice crystal clouds, known as *noctilucent clouds* occasionally form in the upper mesosphere.

(iv) THERMOSPHERE AND EXOSPHERE: Above a height of about 85 to 90 kilometre—the mesopause—temperature again increases with height. The layer above this is the thermosphere, where temperatures range from about 500 K during periods when the Sun is inactive to 2,000 K when it becomes active. The **thermospause** can be defined as the level of transition to a more or less isothermal temperature profile at the top of the thermosphere, occurs at heights of about 250 kilometres during quiet Sun periods to almost 500 kilometres when the Sun is active. The **ionosphere**, which extends from about 80 to 300 kilometres in altitude, is an electrically conducting layer from which radio signals can be reflected.

Above about 500 kilometres the motion of ions is strongly constrained by the presence of the Earth's magnetic field. This region of the atmosphere, called the **magnetosphere**, is compressed by the solar wind on the daylight side of the Earth and stretched outward in a long tail on its night side. The colourful auroral displays often seen in polar latitudes are associated with the generation by solar energy outbursts of high-energy particles in the magnetosphere, which are subsequently injected into the lower ionosphere. The layer above 500 kilometres is also referred to as the exosphere. It is the outer most layer of the atmosphere.

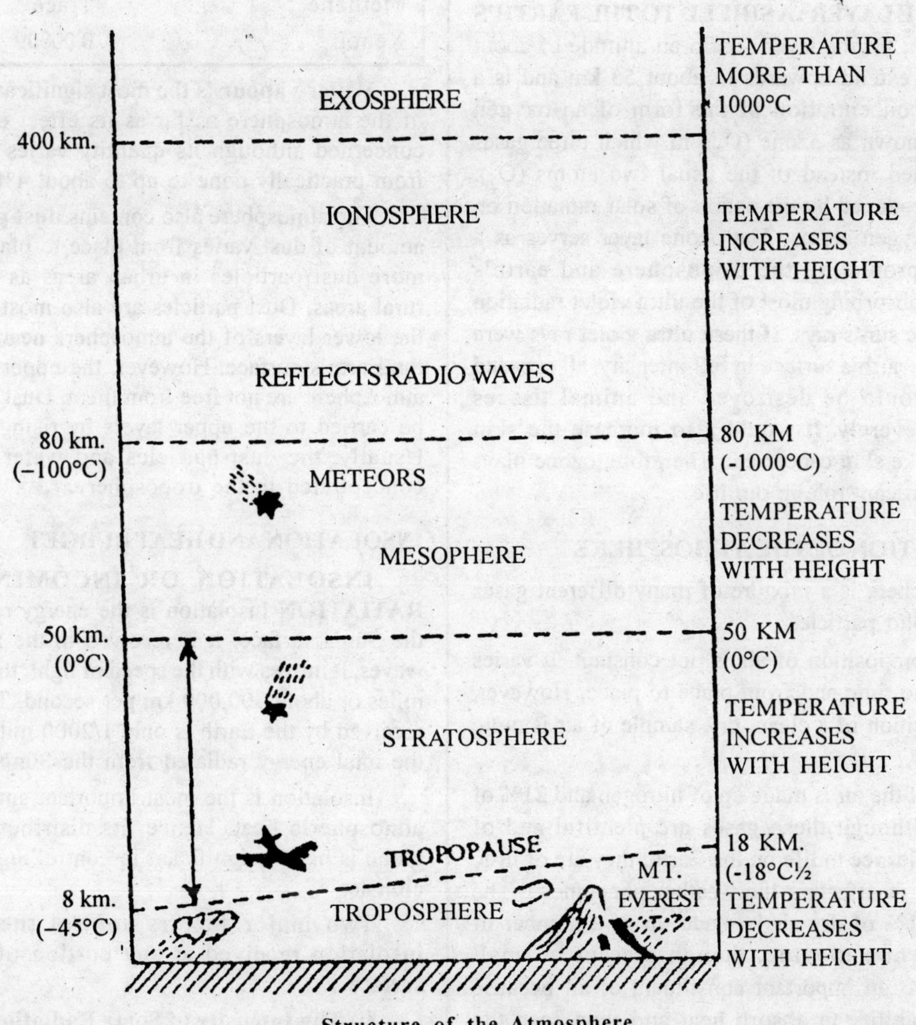

Structure of the Atmosphere

(v) HOMOSPHERE AND HETEROSPHERE: The atmosphere is divided into homosphere and heterosphere mainly on the basis of the composition of various gases. As gases are not evenly distributed in the atmosphere, i.e., heavy gases are concentrated near the earth's surface, while lighter go up. This part of the Atmosphere, where gases are not evenly mixed is called the **heterosphere.** It's height varies from 80 km to 500 km.

Homosphere, on the other hand, refers to the compositional region of the atmosphere, which extends upto an altitude of 80 km. Gases are found nearly uniform almost throughout the homosphere.

OZONE LAYER : A SHIELD TO THE EARTH'S SURFACE : Ozone layer sets in an altitude of about 15 km and extend upwards to about 55 km and is a region of concentration of the form of an oxygen molecule known as ozone (O_3), in which three gases are combined instead of the usual two atoms (O_2). Ozone is produced by the action of solar radiation on ordinary oxygen atoms. The ozone layer serves as a shield of protecting the troposphere and earth's surface by absorbing most of the ultra violet radiation found in the sun's rays. If these ultra violet rays were to reach the earth's surface in full intensity, all exposed bacteria would be destroyed and animal tissues damaged severely. It would also increase the skin problems like skin cancer etc. Therefore, ozone plays a very significant role in our life.

COMPOSITION OF THE ATMOSPHERE

The atmosphere is a mixture of many different gases and tiny solid particles.

The composition of air is not constant. It varies from time to time and from place to place. However, the composition of a clean, dry, sample of air is quite uniform.

78% of the air is made up of nitrogen and 21% of oxygen. Although these gases are plentiful and of great significance to life on the Earth, they are of little importance in affecting the weather phenomena. The remaining 1% of dry air is made up of a number of gases. **Carbon dioxide,** though present in small quantities, is an important constituent of air because it has the ability to absorb heat and thus keep the atmosphere warm.

Average Composition of Dry Air

Constituent Gas	Percentage Volume
Nitrogen	78.08
Oxygen	20.95
Argon	0.93
Carbon dioxide	0.036
Neon	0.002
Helium	0.0005
Ozone	0.00006
Hydrogen	0.00005
Krypton	0.001
Methane	Trace
Xenon	0.00009

Water vapour is the most significant component of the atmosphere as far as its effect on weather is concerned although its quantity varies considerably from practically none to up to about 4% by volume.

The atmosphere also contains **dust particles.** The amount of dust varies from place to place. There are more dust particles in urban areas as compared to rural areas. Dust particles are also most numerous in the lower layers of the atmosphere near their source, the Earth's surface. However, the upper layers of the atmosphere are not free from them. Dust particles may be carried to the upper layers by rising air currents. Usually, the dust particles and water vapours are concentrated in the troposphere.

INSOLATION AND HEAT BUDGET

INSOLATION OR INCOMING SOLAR RATIATION Insolation is the energy radiating from the Sun's surface. It is received in the form of short waves. It moves with the speed of light, that is, 186,000 miles or about 300,000 km per second. The insolation received by the Earth is only 1/2000 millionth part of the total energy radiated from the Sun's surface.

Insolation is the most important single source of atmospheric heat. Hence, its distribution over the globe is highly significant in controlling weather and climate.

Two major factors control the amount of insolation received at any portion of the Earth's surface :

(i) **The Intensity of Solar Radiation** or the angle of incidence of insolation or the Sun's rays, and

(ii) **The Duration of Solar Radiation or the Length of the day.** The angle of solar radiation or the length of the day. The angle of incidence determines the area of the Earth's surface affected by it and also the loss that it suffers through the thickness of the atmospheric path. When the angle of incidence is high, the area affected is small. Insolation is concentrated on a smaller area, hence the heat received per unit area is large and the surface is heated to a higher degree. Also, the high angle of incidence means that the length of the path of the insolation rays through the atmosphere is shorter, and it loses only a small amount of its heat through absorbtion (by water vapours), scattering (by gas particles), and reflection (by clouds). On the other hand, where the angle of incidence is smaller, the area affected is larger and the longer path through the atmosphere results in a larger amount of loss of heat. The duration of solar radiation or the length of the day determines the amount of heat received by the Earth's surface and also contributes to its temperature.

(iii) **Transparency of the Atmosphere :** Both the factors like the angle of incidence and the duration of sunshine are directly affected by the transparency of the atmosphere. It is determined by the thickness of dust particles, water vapours and the amount of cloud cover. If the sky remains free from cloud covers and thick layer of dust & water vapours, then more solar radiation would enter the atmosphere.

Four aspects regarding the amount of insolation produced by this interplay are of interest : (i) the angle of incidence of insolation and the duration of sunlight are directly proportionate to the amount, (ii) on the same parallel of latitude, the values of the two controls *namely, the angle of incidence of insolation and the duration of sunlight)* are the same, and *hence the amount* of insolation on it remains the same, (iii) different parallels receive different amount of insolation, and (iv) insolation decreases from the equator to the poles for the year as a whole.

HEAT BUDGET OR HEAT BALANCE : It has been found that the yearly mean temperature of the earth remains constant. The incoming short-wave solar radiation is balanced by an equal amount of long-wave Earth radiation going back to space. This is termed as *heat balance* or *heat budget* of the Earth. **Heat budget means the balance of heat between the earth and solar radiation.** If we assume that the total heat received at the top of the atmosphere is 100 units, the atmosphere absorbs directly 14 units of this heat and the earth receives 51 units, totalling 65 units. The remaining heat of 35 units is lost to the space, owing to the reflection from the top of the atmosphere (6 units), from the top of the clouds (27 units), and from the snow and ice-covered areas of the Earth's surface (2 units). This total reflection is called the ***albedo*** of the earth. The 65 units received by the Earth gradually escape back into the space in the form of terrestrial radiation. The total radiation returning from the Earth and atmosphere to space is 48+17=65 units which balance the total of 65 units received from the Sun.

TERRESTRIAL RADIATION : The sun's heat energy is absorbed by the Earth and its atmosphere during the day. At night this heat is radiated out by the Earth and its Atmosphere.

The Sun's energy absorbed by the Earth's surface and radiated out into space is called ***Terrestrial Radiation***. It is in the form of long waves. These long waves are more readily absorbed by the molecules of the gases in the atmosphere. Out of the 51 units of Isolation that are absorbed by the Earth (mostly during the day) are radiated out, mostly during the night. Out of the 51 units of terrestrial radiation about 34 units are absorbed by the atmosphere (19% through evaporation, 9% through convection & turbulance, 6% through radiation) and 17 unit is directly reflected by the earth's surface. This means that atmosphere absorbs only 14% of the incoming insolation but absorbs 85% (34 out of 51) of the terrestrial radiation.

Insolation	Terrestrial Radiation
1. It is the incoming solar (51 units) reaching the earth.	1. It is the insolation (51 units) radiated out by the Earth.
2. 14 units out of 100 units of energy coming from the sun are absorbed by gases in the atmosphere i.e. the 14%.	2. 34 units out of 51 units of energy radiating from the Earth are absor-bed by gases in the atmosphere i.e. 85%.

From the above it is clear that the atmosphere is heated more by terrestrial radiation than by the incoming insolation.

During day time, the Earth receives insolation from the Sun. The Earth gets heated gradually after sunrise and reaches the maximum temperature at about 3 p.m.

Unequal Distribution of Insolation on the Surface of the Earth.

There are three main reasons for the variations in distribution of insolation on the surface of the Earth.

(a) Revolution of the Earth around the Sun

(b) The spherical shape of the Earth.

(c) Inclined axis of the Earth.

Points to Remember

Can you tell, how the atmosphere heats and cools? Infact, the atmosphere heats and cools through the processes of **radiation, conduction** and **convection.**

1. **Radiation:** It refers to the direct heating of a body or an object through the transmission of heat waves. The huge amount of energy coming to and leaving the earth's surface is especially due to the radiation.
2. **Conduction:** It can be defined as the transfer of heat through matter by molecular activity. It takes places between the two objects having different temperatures. In it energy flows from warmer to the cooler body/object.
3. **Convection:** It refers to the transfer of heat by the movement of a mass from one place to another. This process can only take place in liquid and gaseous forms.

Some particular conditions i.e., cold winter nights, clear sky, dry air, calm atmosphere etc, are required for the occurance of inversion. All of these conditions help in quick radiation of heat from the earth's surface, which results into the cooling of the air near the surface and heating the air at some heights.

PRESSURE AND WINDS

As we all know that the atmosphere is made up of various gases, water vapours and dust particles. All of these components carry a specific weight, which exerts pressure on the earth's surface. This pressure is popularly known as the **atmospheric pressure.** Hence, **the weight of the column of air at any given place and time, is called the atmospheric pressure.**

Standard Pressure and Temperature at Selected Levels

Level	Pressure in m^6	Temperature °C
Sea level	1,013.25	15.2
1 Km	898.76	8.7
5 Km	540.48	–17.3
10 Km	265.00	–49.7

The atmospheric pressure is measured by an instrument, called the barometer. It is shown on the map by Isobars. Isobars are the lines that join the places having equal atmosphere pressure. Atmospheric pressure is inversely proportionate to temperature, i.e.

high temperature ⇒ low pressure

low temperature ⇒ high pressure

Like temperature, the atmosphere pressure decreases with height. It decreases in an average rate of about 34 mb per every 300 mts of height.

These variations in pressure (high and low) cause a horizontal movement of air called winds.

High and Low Pressure

1. The term 'high pressure' denotes the state of the atmosphere when the Barometre reads about 76 cm (1013mb) or more.
2. The term 'low pressure' denotes the state of the atmosphere when the Barometre reads about 74 cm (986 mb) or less.
3. At sea level, the barometre rarely falls below 71 cm (946 mb) or rises above 79 cm (1050 mb). The average pressure at sea level is about 76 cm (1013.25 mb) or 29.92 inches. One atmospheric pressure (76 cm of mercury) = 1013 mb

EFFECTS OF AIR PRESSURE

1. Winds are caused due to differences in air pressure: Warm air is light. As it rises, it cools. Once it has cooled, the air starts to sink back to the Earth.

1. The region where the air rises, an area of low pressure is created.
2. The region where the air sinks, an area of high pressure is created.

Since the atmosphere constantly works to restore a balance, air moves in from an area of high pressure to an area of low pressure. This movement of air is known as **wind.**

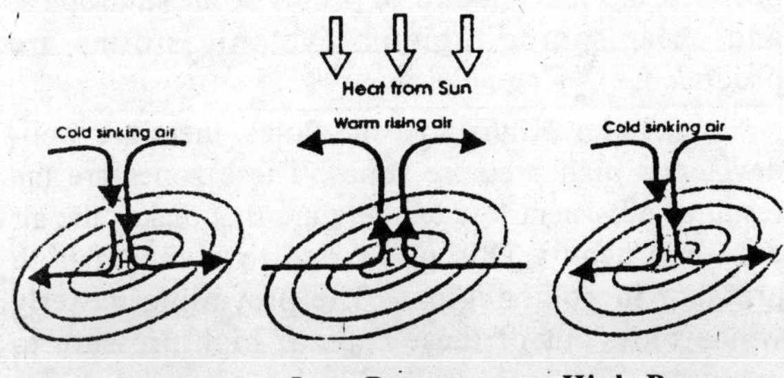

High Pressure Region **Low Pressure Region** **High Pressure Region**

When warm air rises, it creates an area of low pressure. Eventually, the air cools and sinks toward the ground, forming areas of high pressure.

2. Atmospheric pressure influences weather: Upward and downward movement of air creates cloudy or clear skies. As air rises and creates an area of low pressure water vapour in the air condenses and forms clouds. Conversely, sinking air generally means that condensation cannot take place.

1. Low pressure is, therefore, associated with cloudy skies and wet weather.
2. High pressure is normally associated with clear and sunny skies.

3. Weather Forecasting : Fluctuations in air pressure indicate weather changes. For example, rapidly falling pressure indicates that a low pressure system is approaching, which may bring rain.

Seasonal Shifting of the Pressure Belts : Since pressure belts on the Earth are caused mainly due to the differences in temperature on the surface of the Earth, the pressure belts move in response to the apparent migration of the Sun.

When studying the major Pressure Belts of the Earth, we assume that the Sun is directly overhead at the Equator. But this happens only twice a year, on **March 21** and **September 23.**

Between **December and June,** the Sun moves **northwards,** and between **June and December,** the Sun moves **southwards.**

Therefore, the pressure belts follow the annual migration of the Sun towards the north (between December and June) and to the south (between June and December).

Effects of the Shifting of the Pressure Belts
1. Pressure belts affect the direction in which winds blow. Hence, the shifting of the pressure belts causes some places to be in different wind belts during the year. 2. As the wind belts shift with the season, the belts of precipitation (rain and snow) related to the wind belt also changes.

Example : The Mediterranean region (between latitudes of 30° and 45° North and South) come under the influence of the **Trade Winds** when the pressure belts move northwards in summer, and under the influence of the **Westerlies** when the pressure belts move southward in winter.

DISTRIBUTION OF ATMOSPHERIC PRESSURE: Both vertical and horizontal distributions of atmospheric pressure are climatically important.

The lowest layer is the most highly compressed and, hence, has the highest density and pressure. In contrast, the higher layers are less compressed and, hence, have low density and low pressure. The distribution of atmospheric pressure across the latitudes is termed horizontal distribution. The main feature of the distribution of pressure is its zonal or belted character. Each zone or belt comprises several cells of high or low pressures. The cells can be either circular or elongated. The zonal or belted character is strikingly developed in the Southern Hemisphere which has a more homogenous and water-covered surface. In the Northern Hemisphere, the land-water contracts, frictional effects, and mountain barriers produce a series of cells aligned with latitudes.

MAJOR PRESSURE BELTS : On the Earth's surface there are four pressure belts.

(i) Equatorial Trough of Low Pressure : This belt is located on either side of the equator extending between 0° and 5°N and S latitudes. Its outer margin shift north and south of the Tropic of Cancer and the Tropic of Capricorn respectively, due to apparent movement of the Sun. Surface winds are generally absent. It is therefore, a region of extremely calm air and is called **doldrums** or belt of calm.

(ii) Subtropical High Pressure (Horse Latitude) : It is located between 30° and 35° N and S latitudes. This belt is broken into a number of high pressure cells. These regions are often referred to as **horse latitudes** because in the early days the sailing vessels with the cargo of horse found it difficult to sail under such calm conditions. The sailors used to throw horses in the sea to make the vessels lighter for smooth sailing.

(iii) **Sub-Polar Low Pressure Belt :** It is located between 60° and 65° north and south latitudes and the Arctic and Antarctic circles respectively. These low pressure cells are well developed in North Atlantic and north pacific oceans. Due to the great contrast between the temperature of winds from subtropical and polar source regions, cyclonic storms are produced.

(iv) **Polar Highs :** At the Poles, there are well-developed high pressure zones. These zones are the result of persistent low temperature that makes the air cold and heavy. This gives rise to a cap of high pressure in polar regions. The prevailing easterly winds blow out of these caps of high pressure to

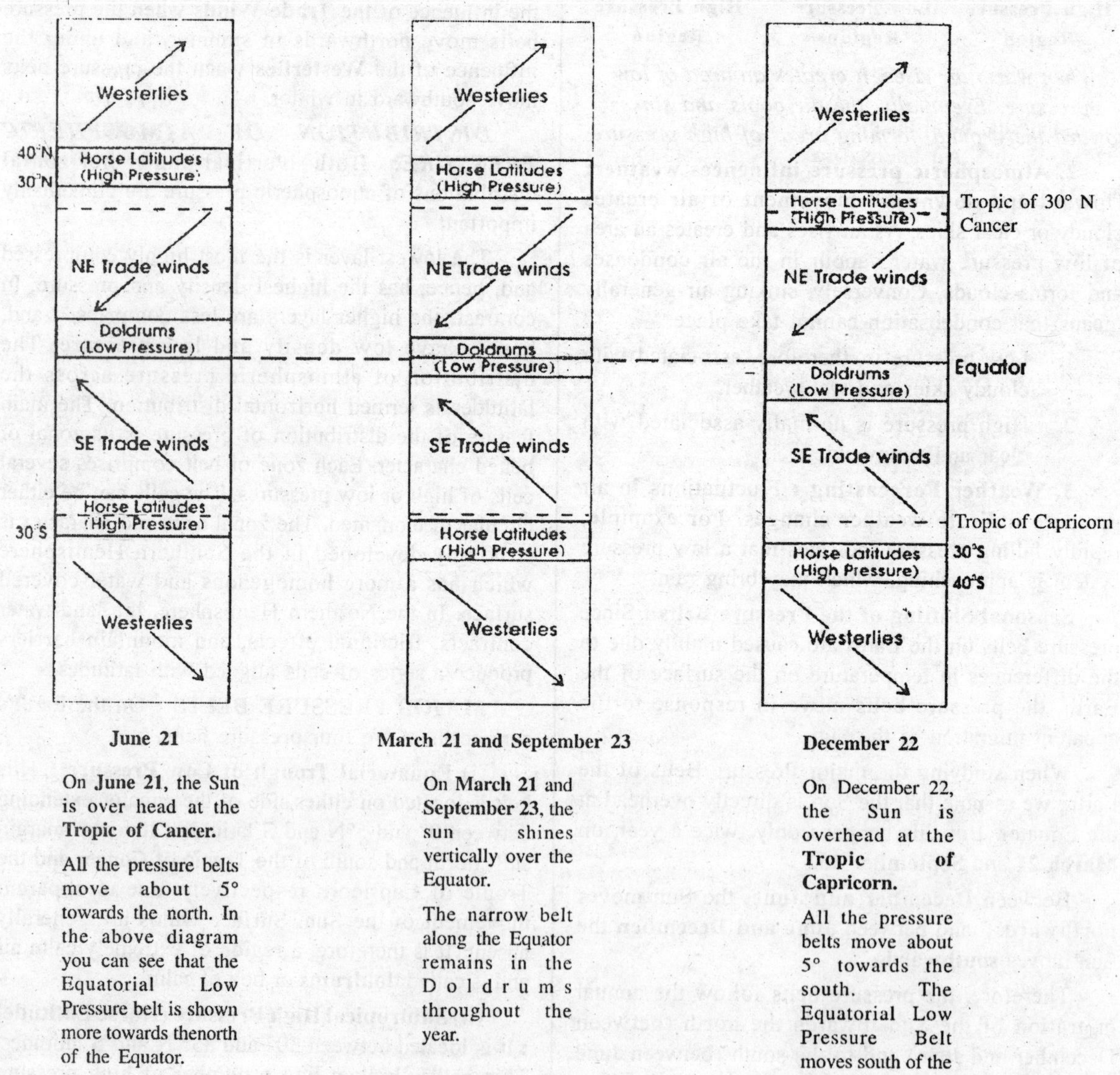

Seasonal Shifting of the Pressure Belts

subpolar low pressure areas.

The location of the belts is based on the annual averages. Following the apparent movements of the sun from one to the other hemisphere, the belts also shifts their location. This is because of the direct relationship between insolation heating, expansion, density, and pressure of air. In the Northern Hemisphere, all the belts shift a little north of their annual average location during the summer and a little south of their location during the winter. Opposite conditions prevail in the Southern Hemisphere.

The belts comprise cells in the Northern Hemisphere and isobaric bands in the Southern Hemisphere. In the belts of high pressure, the air is subsiding and diverging and, hence, stable and dry. On the other hand the air is converging in the belts of low pressure. Air bodies of different properties clash with each other, rise up, become unstable and cause rainfall. Thus, the high pressure belts are dry and the low pressure belts are humid. In both the belts, the winds are light and blow in all the directions.

The main result of the horizontal differences in pressure is the generation of the winds. The winds blow from the high pressure to the low-pressure areas.

WINDS

Wind is the horizontal movement of air caused by the uneven heating of the Earth by the Sun.

You cannot see it or hold it but you can feel its presence. It can be strong enough to carry sailing ships across the oceans and uproot trees from the ground.

1. Wind Direction : A wind is named according to the direction (according to the Campass point) from which it blows. For example, a west wind comes from the west; a north wind comes from the north. However, it must be noted that a wind coming from the west blows towards the east and a north and blows towards the south.

2. Deflection of Winds : If the Earth did not rotate on its axis, all winds would blow straight from high pressure to low pressure and die down when the pressure equalized.

But the Earth rotates, which is why winds curve as they blow. This **curving motion** is called the **Coriolis Effect.**

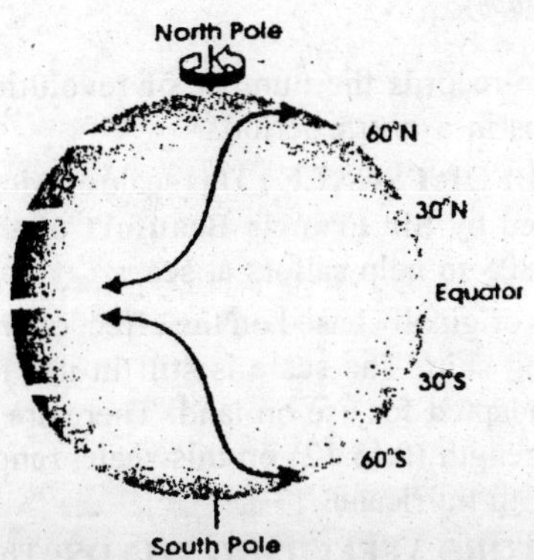

The **direction** of this turning effect is stated in **Ferrel's Law.**

1. Any object or fluid moving horizontally in the **Northern hemisphere** tends to be **deflected to the right of its path of motion.**
2. In the **Southern Hemisphere,** there is a similar **deflection towards the left of the path of motion.**

The Coriolis effect is absent at the Equator but increases in strength towards the poles.

3. Wind Speed : Wind has a great effect on our lives. Sometimes it blows gently, refreshing us. Sometimes, it blows strongly creating storms that cause widespread damage. To give a description of wind, we need measurements of two quantitites : **direction and speed.**

1. Measurement of Wind Direction : Direction is easily determined by a **wind-vane.** It consists of a freely moving arrow-shaped horizontal pointer mounted on top of a pole.

The wind catches the tail of the arrow and swings the pointer to the direction from which the wind blows. Below this is a fixed framework indicating the points of the compass.

A windsock is used to show the strength and direction of the wind. It consist of a conical shape made of cloth open at one end which is attached to a pole.

When strong winds blow, the sock is filled with moving air and it billows out in the direction in which the wind is blowing. A floppy windsock means that the wind is only light.

2. Measurement of Wind Speed : To measure wind speed, an instrument called the **anemometer** is used. This instrument consists of four metal or plastic cups on arms that spin around a vertical pole. A dial at the base records the number of revolutions made by the cups in a given period.

BEAUFORT SCALE : This scale of wind strength was devised by **Sir Francis Beaufort** of the British Navy in 1805 to help sailors at sea.

It was originally based on the effect of wind speed on a sailing ship. The scale is still in use today and has been adapted for use on land. There are **13 levels** of wind strength (0 to 12) on this scale, ranging from dead calm to hurricane.

FACTORS AFFECTING WINDS: The various forces governing the forces of winds are :

(i) **The Pressure Gradient Force** : In order to accelerate anything, there must be unbalanced force in one direction. The force that drives the winds results from horizontal pressure differences. When such a difference occurs, a pressure gradient is formed and air will move from high to low pressures. The pressure gradient is always at right angles to Isobars. It has two attributes (i) direction and (ii) magnitude. The winds always move from high to low pressure area and the more steep is the gradient, the more strong will be the wind. The velocity of wind is indicated by the steepness of Isobars.

(ii) **Coriolis Effect :** The winds blow from high pressure area to low pressure area. But the wind does not cross the Isobars at right angles as the pressure gradient force directs. This deviation is the result of the earth's rotation and has been named the Coriolis Effect.

The Coriolis Effect
In 1835, Gustave-Gaspard de Coriolis explained that air doesn't move in a straight path because the spinning of the earth on its axis causes the air masses to be deflected.

In reality, Coriolis Force is not a real force but only an apparent one. It arises because moving objects like wind tends to keep its original direction fixed with respect to a point in space. By contrast direction on the earth surface are related to a coordinate systems of meridians and parallels which themselves rotate and change absolute direction as the earth turns on its axis.

ISOBARS : The pressure of air is shown on weather maps by means of lines known as Isobars, meaning "equal weight"

— It is an imaginary line, drawn on the map (or a weather chart) joining all places with equal atmospheric pressure.

— Isobars do not take into account variations produced by relief.

— When isobars are far apart, there is little difference of atmospheric pressure and the weather is calm.

— When the isobars are close together, there is a great difference of atmospheric pressure over a small area and the weather is stormy.

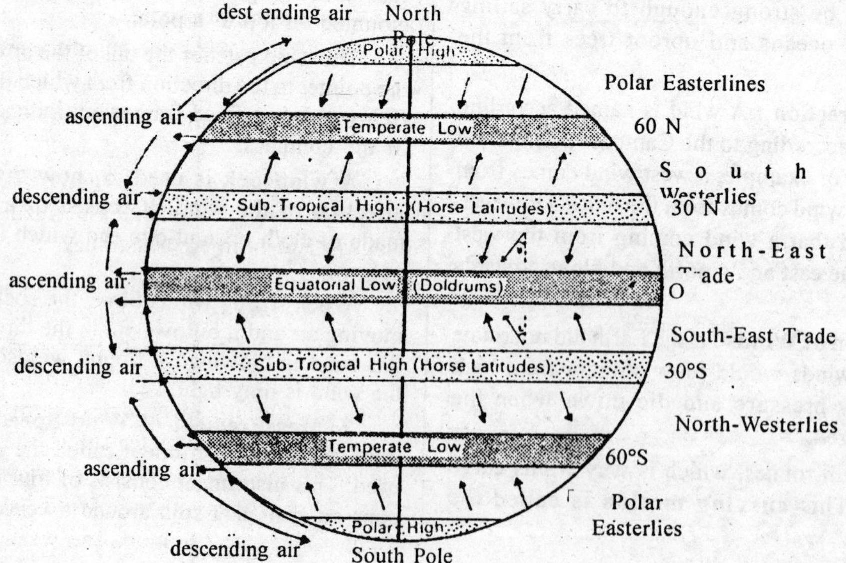

Geostropic Wind : When Isobars are straight and when there is no friction, the pressure gradient force is balanced by Coriolis Force and the resultant wind blows parallel to the isobar, this wind is known as geostropic wind.

Change in the pressure distribution over the earth's surface could be analysed from isobar maps of winter and summer.

TYPE OF WINDS : Normally, three types of winds are recognized :

(i) Planetary winds (which blows all the time in the same areas of world).

(ii) Periodic winds (which blows during a particular period or season).

(iii) Variable winds (which are variable due to different speed and direction).

(i) PLANETARY OR PRIMARY WINDS

The planetary winds are permanent winds which blow throughout the year from one latitude, to the other in response to the latitudinal differences in atmospheric pressure. They blow over the vast areas of the continents and oceans.

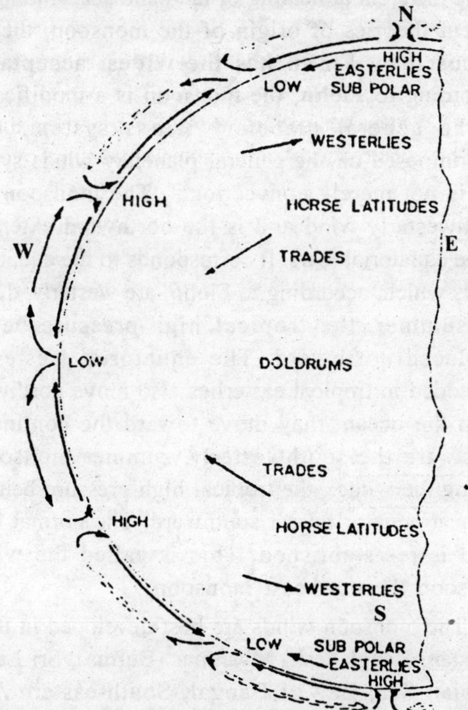

Generalised System of Primary Winds (Planetary Winds)

The planetary winds operate at two levels—at the Earth's surface and in the upper atmosphere. The upper winds generally move from the equator toward the poles. Surface winds, as shown move in different directions at different latitudes.

The circulatory system can be divided into five general zones, called primary wind belts. These zones would exist on the Earth free of such disruptive influences as large land and water masses, ocean currents, and changing seasons. Actually, the zones are not well defined, but are broken and constantly shifting and migrating with the Sun.

(i) The Doldrums lie approximately between 5° north and south of the equator, the area receiving the largest amount of heat from the Sun. This zone has no pressure gradients to induce a persistent flow of wind. Air pressure is generally relatively low, and the air moves chiefly upward from the warm Earth.

(ii) The Trade Winds extend from the doldrums to as much as 30^0 north and south latitudes. The name *Trade* is derived from a nautical expression **"to blow tread"** meaning to blow along a regular path or "tread". The trade winds are constant winds which flow towards the equator. Generally these winds blow from 30°N and 30°S towards the equator, i..e they blow in tropical latitudes. Trade winds blow from the sub-tropical high pressure to the equatorial low pressure belt. Trade winds blows as the north-east trade winds in the northern Hemisphere and in the south-east trade winds in the Southern hemisphere. They are steadiest over oceans. (Trade, in this case, has the old meaning of "steady track or course.") In the northern hemisphere trade winds blow over Florida, West Indies, Central America, East Coast of Mexico, Coast of Venezuela, Guina and in Southern hemisphere, they blow over East Brazil, East Africa, Malagasy and northern Australia.

(iii) The Horse Latitudes, at about 30^0 north and south latitudes, from a belt between the trade winds and the prevailing westerlies. Here part of the high-altitude air flowing poleward accumulates, descends towards the Earth, and becomes warmer because of compression. The barometer shows the air pressure to be high. Some of the world's largest deserts are located here. Horse-latitude winds are weak and shifting. Calms are common. The weather is usually clear and bright. Part of the descending air feeds the trade winds; part flows to the prevailing westerlies.

(iv) The Prevailing Westerlies extend from the horse latitudes to about 60^0 north and south latitudes. Although the wind is highly variable in direction because of travelling high-pressure areas (anti-cyclones) and low-pressure areas (cyclones), the wind comes from the west more often than from other directions. Air flowing toward the poles from the horse latitudes, is here deflected eastward to become a west wind. In the middle latitude of the Southern Hemisphere, where there are few land areas to interfere with the westerlies, wind speeds are greatest. The region from 40^0 to 50^0 south is notorious among seamen as "the roaring forties." These latitudes also called the furious fifties and shrieking sixties.

In the northern hemsiphere, Westerlies blow over British Columbia, N.W. Coast of the U.S.A., Western Europe and in the Southern Hemisphere, they blow over South Chile, S.W. Africa, South Island of New Zealand.

(v) The Polar Easterlies extend from about 60^0 north and south latitude to the poles. Winds blow from the polar High pressure Belt to the sub-Polar low pressure Belt. These are the polar Easterlies. These are north-east in the Northern Hemisphere and south-east in the Southern Hemisphere.

(ii) PERIODIC OR SECONDARY WINDS

(i) Jet Streams : The upper-air westerlies are known as the let streams. It is a high velocity mind, whose velocity is about 250 knots. Some scholars are of view that the origin of the monsoons is closely related to the jet stream found in upper troposphere. Jet streams migrate with the seasons—northward in summer, south ward in winter. The jet stream play an important part in weather changes. For example, jets moving northward tend to pull masses of warm air with them. As they flow south, they pull the cold air from the arctic regions into the temperate zones.

(ii) Monsoon Winds : The word monsoon is derived from the Arabic word ***mausim*** which means season. Monsoon winds are seasonal winds. The term was first applied to the monsoon winds blowing over the Arabian Sea. It is a periodic wind.

Jet Streams

Flying schedules for high-flying planes must take account of jet streams. Jet streams were discovered during World War II, when air force pilots encountered powerful high-level winds, now known as jet streams.

1. Near the tropopause, strong winds develop due to great temperature and pressure differences.
2. The speed Jet stream varies from 250 to 300 Km/hr.
3. Jet streams are stronger in winter due to greater temperature contrasts. They weaken in summer.
4. Jet streams affect the weather considerably. They play a part in moving the major air masses.
5. They may also play role in bringing the summer monsoons to the Indian Ocean.

In earlier times, monsoon was considered a result of the differential heating of land and sea. Among the current theories of origin of the monsoon, the one proposed by **Flohn** has the widest acceptance. According to **Flohn,** the monsoon is a modification of the general planetary winds system. It is superimposed on the general planetary winds system and is not merely convectional. The monsoon is a southwesterly wind and is the northward extension of the equatorial lows. It corresponds to the equatorial winds which, according to Flohn, are westerly, during the summer, the tropical high-pressure belt is displaced northward. The equatorial westerlies embedded in tropical easterlies also move northward. From the ocean, they move toward the continents. These are the southwesterly, summer monsoons. During the winter, the tropical high pressure belt and the heat equator retreat southward. The normal trade wind is re-established. This is called the winter monsoon the northeast monsoon.

The monsoon winds are best developed in India, Pakistan, Bangladesh, Myanmar (Burma), Sri Lanka, Arabian Sea, Bay of Bengal, South-eastern Asia, Northern Australia, China, Japan and South-eastern North America.

Summer Monsoon
Asia lies in the Northern Hemisphere. In June, the rays of the sun fall directly on the **Tropic of Cancer** and the region experiences **summer.** 1. The landmass of Asia gets intensely heated. A **low pressure** develops over the land. The Himalayas separate the Asian Low Pressure area from north Indian Low Pressure areas. 2. On the other hand, the Indian Ocean remains relatively cold during this period. **High pressure** exists over it. Winds blow from an area of high pressure to an area of low pressure. **Moisture-laden winds** blow from the Australian High Pressure over the Indian Ocean to the more intense Asian Low Pressure. 3. Winds blow from the High Pressure Horse Latitude across the Equatorial Low Pressure to the more intense north Indian Low Pressure region.

Winter Monsoon
In December, the rays of the Sun fall directly over **Tropic of Capricorn.** During winters the landmass of Asia cools down rapidly and a **high pressure** exists over it. The Himalayas separate the Asian High Pressure area from the north Indian High Pressure areas. The Indian Ocean, on the other hand remains warm with a low **pressure** over it. (Note : About three-fourths of the Indian Ocean lies in the Southern Hemisphere). Now **dry winds** blow from the land to the sea. They are dry winds as they originate over the landmass of Asia. 1. Winds blow from the Asian High Pressure region across the Equator to the more intense Australian Low Pressure area. They follow the direction of the prevailing Trade winds, which is **N.E.** in the Northern Hemisphere. On crossing the Equator they are deflected and blow as the N.W. Monsoons. 2. Winds blow from the north Indian High Pressure region to the Equatorial Low Pressure area.

Note : Winds that blow out of this region follow the direction of the prevailing Trade Winds in the Southern Hemisphere, which is **S.E.** in direction. On crossing the Equator, they are deflected (Coriolis force), and they blow as the **S.W. Monsoons.**

(iii) LOCAL OR TERTIARY WINDS

Local winds affect only limited areas and blow for short periods of time. Most local winds are developed by temperate depressions (systems with low pressure centres).

Air circulation pattern in :

A. Depression Winds

a. **Hot Winds :** Air is drawn in from **tropical regions** in the **front** of the depression. This gives rise to **hot winds.** Hot winds are usually both hot and dusty. But if they have crossed a sea surface, they become humid.

Example : Sirocco, Leveche, Khamsin, Santa-ana, Zonda

b. **Cold Winds :** Air is drawn in from **polar regions** in the **rear** of the depression. This gives rise to **cold winds.** These winds are very strong and gusty, and bitterly cold.

Example : Mistral, Bora, Pampero, Buran.

B. Descending Winds

These are warm winds which descend mountain slopes onto the lowlands.

Example : Chinook, Fohn, Berg, Nor'wester.

Contrast between Land and Sea Breezes and Monsoon Winds

Land and Sea Breezes	Monsoon Winds
1. Land and sea breezes occur along the coastal region.	Monsoon winds originate in tropical areas where there is a great land and sea contrast.
2. It blows for a few hours daily. At night it blows from the land to the sea and during the day it blows from the sea to the land.	It is a seasonal wind. It blows for months at a time. During summer it blows from the sea to the land, and in winter it blows from the land to the sea.
3. It has a moderating influence on the temperature of the coastal areas.	Its main effect is to bring heavy rain in summer to the areas over which it blows.

Note: Since the Trade Winds blow from the **eastern direction**, these winds **bring rain to the eastern margins** of continents, while the western part gets very little rain. Therefore, all the tropical deserts in the world, are situated on the western margin of the continents.

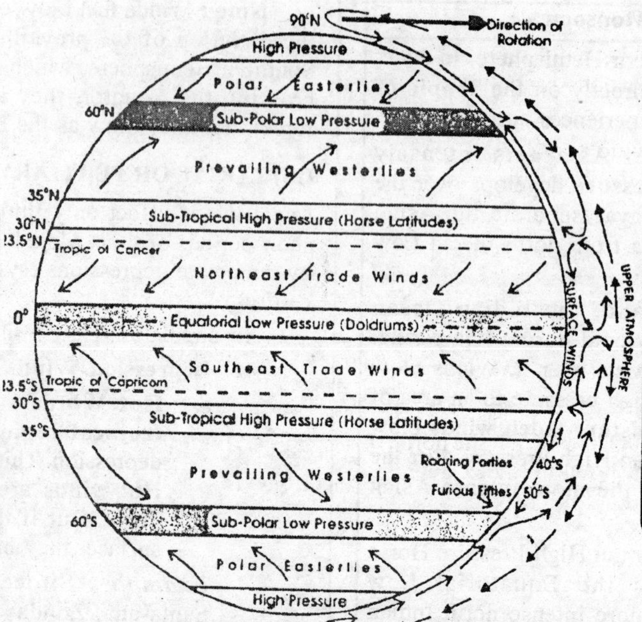

Rains to the West: Since the Westerlies blow from the west, they strike the western margin of continents first giving it plenty of rain. The eastern margins remain quite dry.

Therefore, the temperate deserts is the world, are located on the eastern margin of the continents.

Characteristics of Trade Winds	Characteristics of Westerlies	Characteristics of Polar Winds
1. The name **"Trade"** is derived from a nautical expression "to blow tread" meaning to blow along a regular path or "tread".	1. They blow from the Sub-tropical High Pressure Belt to the Sub-polar Low Pressure Belt in the temperate latitudes between **30° and 60°, on either side of the Equator.**	1. They blow from the Polar High Pressure Belt to the sub-polar Low Pressure Belt between latitudes **60° and the poles in both hemispheres.**
2. They blow from the Sub-tropical High Pressure Belt to the Equatorial Low Pressure Belt in the tropics between **5° to 30° North and South latitudes.**	2. They blow from the **S.W. direction** in the Northern Hemisphere and the N.W. direction in the Southern Hemisphere.	2. These winds **blow from east** to form the Polar Easterlies. They flow **N.E. in direction** in the Northern Hemisphere and in the **S.E. Direction** in the Southern Hemisphere.
3. They blow as the **N.E. Trades** in the Northern Hemisphere and as the S.E. Trades in the Southern Hemisphere.	3. They are not as constant in strength and direction as the Trade Winds. The region of the Westerlies is characterised by frequent **cyclones** and **anticyclones.**	3. The Polar winds are deflected the most. They are deflected as much as 90° from their normal course until they blow directly from the east.
4. They are regular in strength and direction.	4. They are **more constant** and strong in the Southern Hemisphere because there are **no large landmasses** to interrupt them. In places they become so strong that these winds are known as the **Roaring Forties** or the **Brave West Winds,** and the **Furious Fifties.**	4. In the Northern hemisphere these winds take a variety of directions due to local weather disturbances.
5. Trade winds are **permanent winds** but in the Indian Ocean and some parts of the south-west Pacific Ocean, they are reversed in summer by the **Monsoons.**	5. The belts of the Westerlies move north and south following the Sun's movement.	5. They are more regular in the Southern Hemisphere.
6. The belts of the Trade Winds move north and south following the movement of the Sun.		6. Polar winds are extremely cold and dry as they come from the ice-cap regions.

TYPES OF LOCAL WINDS

Austru: A west wind blowing over the lower Danube lands in the winter, usually bringing dry, clear, and cold weather.

Bali: A strong east wind that blows over the eastern end of Java across the Java Sea.

Barber: A term used in some sections of the United States and Canada to describe a strong wind carrying precipitation that freezes on contact with objects, especially the beard and hari.

Berg: Hot, dry, and occasionally dust-laden winds blowing from interior portions of a larger part of the southern African continent.

Blizzard: A term used in Canada and the northern United States to describe a howling, cold, piercing wind, usually of gale force, out of the north or northwest.

Bora: Excessively cold wind that moves rapidly southward from the valleys of the Karst and Dinaric Alps across the Adriatic Sea. Affecting the Dalmation Coast from Trieste to Albania.

Brickfielder or "Brickfelder: A hot, dry, and dustladen wind blowing across the south of Australia from the deserts of the interior during the summer.

Cacimbo: A cooling sea breeze blowing from the southwest to the port of Lobito on the coast of Angola in western Africa.

Chinook: A dry, warm wind blowing from west direction down the east slopes of the Rockies in North America. This fohn-type wind loses its moisture on the windward sides of the Rockies and heats up as it slides down the lee sides. The Chinook sometimes raises the air temperature as much as 25° C in less than a half-hour, causing a rapid melting of snow; thus, the Chinook is sometimes called the **snow eater.**

Elephanta: A strong wind blowing from the Malabar coast to the extreme southwest end of India during September and October.

Fohn: A wind characteristic of many mountainous regions of the world and called by different names in different countries (Chinook, Santa ana, etc.). The term Fohn is more specifically applied in many Alpine valleys, notably in the upper Rhine, the Reuss and upper parts of central Europe. It is a warm dry wind blowing down the lee side of a hill, mountain, or mountain range after it has risen over the windward side where it has lost its moisture.

Gharbi: Occasionally, winds from the Sahara desert blow northward over the northern and eastern Mediterranean.

Haboob: Extremely severe dust storms that occur mostly in the summer in large regional areas of northwest Africa, including Egypt.

Harmattan: This wind is a continental part of the globe-encircling trade winds. It dominates the Sahara Desert and impresses its extremely dry and warm characteristics on a huge area of north and North-west Africa. It is also called the Doctor wind.

Howling Fifties: A term probably originating with whalers and others of the nineteenth century who sailed the oceans of the Southern Hemisphere. These sailors found the winds to be punishing over their routes southward, unhampered by land or mountains.

Karaburan: From early spring to late summer, these gale-force winds form daily in the Gobi Desert and surrounding regions in the heart of Asia. Blowing from the east-northeast, they carry clouds of dust from the desert.

Katabatic Winds : It is a group of local winds, also known as **drainage wind**, in which cold air flows under the influence of gravity from higher to lower regions. Such cold, dense air may accumulate in winter over a high plateau or high interior valley. When general conditions are favourable, some of this cold air spills over low divides through passes to flow out on adjacent low lands as a strong, cold wind. Drainage winds occur in many mountainous regions of the world and go by various names. The **Mistral** of the Rhone valley in southern France is a well-known example; it is a cold, dry local wind. On the ice sheets of Greenland and Antarctica, powerful drainage winds move down the gradient of the ice surface and are funnelled through coastal valleys to produce powerful blizzards lasting for days at a time. Even though the skies are clear, the mistral brings down the temperature below freezing point. Its speed is so great that orchards and gardens have to be protected from it by thick hedges of cypress trees.

Khamsin: In the winter season, Egypt is invaded alternately by outbreaks of cool and hot winds. Khamsin is the name given to a hot wind some times pulled into Egypt from Arabia, the Gulf of Aden and possibly the Arabian Sea far to the south and east. The Khamsin, besides being quite hot, is extremely dry and so hazy with fine dust that lights are sometimes required at midday.

Kharif: A strong, often gale-force wind blowing from the southwest in the Gulf of Aden. It is called the kharif on the Somalil coast on the south shore of the gulf where the wind descends sand-laden and uncomfortably hot from the African interior.

Leveche: One of the many hot and dry winds that originate in the hot deserts of North Africa and Saudi Arabia, affecting areas of the middle and south Mediterranean.

Mistral: This well-known wind, the "masterful" north wind of the Gulf of lions, surges southward in outbreaks from polar regions over north and central Europe to affect a wide area over the northwest coasts of the Mediterranean. It is a cold and dry wind that can cause damage, and is particularly noted in the winter in the lower Rhone Valley.

Kalbaisakhi: It is a warm wind that blows in north India.

EI Norte: An outbreak of polar air, originating in north -central United States or the Canadian basin, which sweeps as far south as the Gulf of Mexico and parts of Central America. The term also refers to cold winds from the north that flow over eastern Spain in the winter.

Northeaster: A wind that blows from moderate to strong force from the northeast over the New England coastal regions. The wind moving in from the North Atlantic, is generally moist and often chilly or cold. The "nor" "easter" usually a portion of a deep migrating low-pressure area, occasionally can have a severe impact on coastal communities.

Northwester: A moderate to strong wind from the northwest bringing cool to cold temperature over broad region of Rockies. The name also is applied to frequent gale winds that batter the Cape region of South Africa from the northwest, attended by overcast skies and heavy rain in the winter.

Ostria: A warm southerly wind on the Bulgarian coast, considered a precursor of bad weather.

Pampero: A violent squall that attends cold fronts as they move from the southwest to the northeast in the pampas of Argentina and Uruguay.

Purga: Another name for the dreaded buran of the tundra regions in northern Siberia in the winter. The purga seeps down from the north with extraordinary violence throughout Siberia and sometimes to south Russia, particularly violent over the open plains sections.

Santa Ana: A fohn-type wind named after a community south east of Los Angeles in the coastal area of southern California. A as a warm wind.

Simmoom or Simoon: A sircoco-type, hot, dry, and dust-laden wind, blowing over the middle and southern portions of the Mediterranean sea. It is called a simmoom when it is abnormally strong over the southeast part of the Mediterranean. The Turkish version of this wind is the Samuel.

Sirocco: A warm wind of the Mediterranean area usually sweeping northward from the hot and dry Sahara deserts.

Sumatra: Strong thunderstorm squalls blowing over the Malacca Straits from the southwest during the southwest monsoon season.

Whirly: A small but violent storm in the Antarctic.

Zonda: A strong and dry west wind blowing over the western region of Argentina.

MEASURING WIND: At the surface of the Earth, the direction of winds is indicated by **wind vanes** and their speed by **anemometers**.

THE BEAUFORT SCALE

Scale Number	Wind Velocity (Kilometers/Hour)	Description of Wind
0	0-1.5	Calm
1	1.6-5	Light air
2	6-11	Slight breeze
3	12-19	Gentle breeze
4	20-29	Moderate breeze
5	30-39	Fresh breeze
6	40-50	Strong breeze
7	51-61	High wind
8	62-74	Gale
9	75-87	Strong gale
10	88-101	Whole gale
11	102-120	Storm
12	over 120	Hurricane

CYCLONES: A cyclone is a small low pressure system with winds blowing anti-clockwise in the northern Hemisphere and clockwise in the Southern Hemispehre. On the basis of the areas of their origin, cyclones are classified into two types: temperate and tropical.

(i) Temperate Cyclones : Cyclones are the low pressure areas which are surrounded by closed, concentric isobars, which indicate the movement of the winds toward the centre from all the quadrant and cardinal directions. Cyclones develop in areas of air-mass conflict and well-developed fronts. Temperate cyclones are concentrated in the middle latitudes between 35°N or S and 65°N or S.

ORIGIN AND DEVELOPMENT

There are two theories of origin of temperate cyclones.

(i) Polar Front Theory : The most accepted hypothesis for the origin of mid latitude cyclone is Polar Front theory, advanced by V. Bjerknes and J. Bjerknes, Norweigian meteorologists, in 1918. According to him, the highs and lows of the Westerly Wind belts result from the interaction and alternations of two contrasting types of air masses, one originating in the polar regions and the other in the subtropics. Cold air from polar highs moves equatorwards and is deflected westwards, forming the northeast and southeast polar winds. Warmer air from subtropical highs moves polewards and by eastward deflection, forms the westerly winds. The contact between these contrasting air masses is the polar front. Eddies or waves develop along this intact and the front becomes highly irregular consisting of interlocking tongues of the two types of air masses. As soon as the cyclone approaches, there is drizzle, followed by heavy downpour. On the approach of warm front, the fall in the pressure stops and the sky becomes clear. This gives us the clue that the centre of the cyclone has reached. Immediately after this, temperature begins to fall and the sky becomes cloudy and rainy again. This indicates the approach of cold front. Sky is clear once again.

(ii) Thermodynamic Theory : This theory was put forward by Lampert and Shaw. According to this theory, in sub-tropical areas, an overcrowding of vertical currents releases the surplus energy upwards, which after meeting the upper cool air, converts into an eddy. This addy lends to settle an inverted V-shaped cyclone.

Cyclones originate as waves in the westerlies and, hence, move from the west to the east. North of the equator, the winds rotate towards the low pressure area in a counterclockwise direction. In the Southern Hemisphere, the rotation is clockwise.

The speed of cyclonic winds may increase if the atmospheric pressure drops rapidly. Middle-latitude cyclones are especially common in late autumn, winter, and spring but are much less common in summer. They usually bring rain storms and cloudy weather.

As the cyclone passes to the east, the barometer drops at first, then rises. After the cyclone has passed, the clouds vanish and the air clears. This signals the approach of the following high-pressure area, of anticyclone, in which colder, drier air from the upper atmosphere circles down to Earth in a clockwise direction.

AREAS PRONE TO TEMPERATE CYCLONES

Most of the temperate cyclones originating in the North Pacific off the eastern coast of Asia move northwards towards the Gulf of Alaska where they merge with the Aleutian low. The winter storms follow a more southerly route in the Pacific and move as far south as southern California. Most of the Pacific weather disturbances dissipate on reaching the windward slopes of the Rockies. The most favourite areas for the rejuvenation of winter storms are Colordo and Alberta. Cyclones forming in Canada move southward toward the Great lakes region and then turn towards northeast and move into Atlantic Ocean. The great lakes in North America are the stormiest region in North America. Baltic sea, middle east countries and Northern India produces winter rainfall by the passage of these storms.

(ii) Tropical Cyclones : Cyclones have their birth in the warm parts of the Atlantic, Pacific, and Indian oceans. They move on a curving course. If these disturbances have a very low atmospheric pressure at their centres, they are given such names as **hurricane** or **typhoon.**

AREAS PRONE TO TROPICAL CYCLONES :

Tropical cyclones occur in the southwestern portion of North Atlantic Ocean, along the west coast of Mexico, south-western part of North Pacific Ocean, including the China Sea, north Indian Ocean, south Indian Ocean and south Pacific Ocean.

In Africa, they are recorded in Ethopia and Kenya. In North America they are prominent in Texas, coastal parts of Mexico, Florida and West Indies, where they are known as hurricanes. In Australia they occur as a willy-willes and in China and Japan as Typhoons.

Characteristics of Temperate and Tropical Cyclones

Temperate Cyclones	Tropical Cyclones
1. They are found both on land and sea.	1. They are produced and develop mainly overseas.
2. Their isobars are usually V-shaped.	2. Their isobars are usually complete Circles.
3. They have a low pressure-gradient.	3. The pressure gradient is steep.
4. The wind speed is low and never very strong.	4. The wind speed is about 100 km. per hour or more.
5. They occupy areas measuring thousands of square km.	5. They have a small area.
6. They travel from west to east.	6. They travel from east to west.
7. Rainfall is slow. Some-times heavy showers take place.	7. Rainfall is heavy.
8. Rainfall continues for many days.	8. Rainfall does ot last beyond a few hours. If cyclone stays at a place, the rainfall may continue for many days.
9. All the sectors of the cyclone have different temperatures.	9. The temperature at the center is almost equally distributed.
10. There are two fronts in energy cyclone.	10. The fronts are usually absent in the cyclones.
11. More cyclones are produced in winter than in summer.	11. These cyclones are produced in summer than in winter.
12. The directions of winds are rapidly changed at the front. Veering and backing of winds take place.	12. Shifting of wind is slow. The winds travel in a cyclic course.
13. There is not a single place where winds and rain are inactive.	13. The center of the cyclone is known as 'eye'. The wind at the eye is calm and there is no rainfall.
14. The energy of the cyclone depends upon the difference of the densities of airmasses.	14. The difference of the densities of airmasses does not contribute to the energy of the cyclone. Its energy is the latent heat of condensation.

DEPRESSION : Cyclones of the temperate latitudes, especially in Europe, are often called depressions since they are systems with low pressure centres. Winds are not very violent and they do not cause any damage. They are mainly associated with rain.

HURRICANES : Tropical cyclones in the Gulf of Mexico, the Caribbean sea and western Pacific Ocean are known as Hurricanes. To qualify as a hurricane, a storm must produce winds over 119 km/hr. It causes severe damages to life and property.

TYPHOONS: Tropical cyclones that originate in the China Sea are known as typhoons. These winds are also very violent and destructive.

TORNADOES : These are storms which form very suddenly on land. The highest windspeeds on Earth occur in tornadoes, sometimes reaching 500 km/hr.

A tornado looks like a twisting funnel of air. As it goes, it sucks up anything in its path including buildings, trees, cows and cars, and drops them when its force decreases. They are most common and most violent in the U.S.A.

If a tornado forms over the sea, it is known as a **waterspout**. When it touches the water of the ocean, water is sucked up. It seems to rise out of the sea like enormous dark grey sea serpents.

Cyclones
1. It is a low pressure system with surrounding high pressure 2. It blows anti-clockwise in the Northern Hemisphere. 3. It blows clockwise in the Southern Hemisphere.

4. It is associated with cloudy skies and very heavy rain usually accompanied by strong winds. 5. It can cause great damage to life and property.

Anti Cyclones
1. It is a high pressure system with surrounding low pressure. 2. It blows clockwise in the Northern Hemisphere.

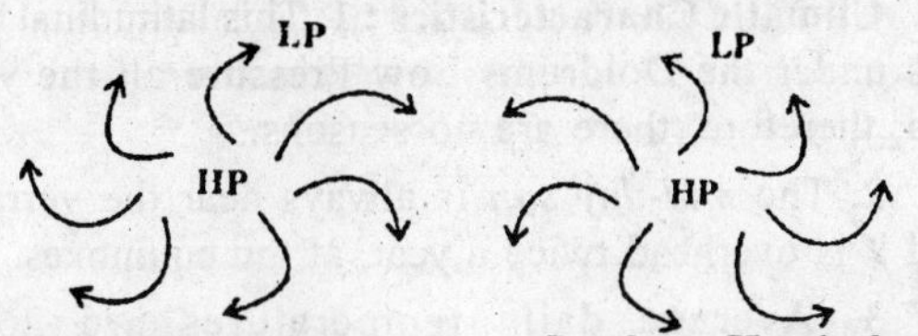

3. It blows anti-clockwise in the Southern Hemisphere. 4. It is associated with clear skies, mild winds and dry conditions. 5. It causes the weather to be settled and pleasant.

WEATHER AND CLIMATE

WEATHER is the state of the atmosphere at a particular place and at particular time. The science that deals with the atmosphere and the weather is called *meteorology*, a branch of physics. The scientists who study the weather and climate are known as meteorologists. The most obvious elements of the weather are the temperature; the amount of moisture present as humidity or precipitation, clouds; the speed and direction of the wind. (The amount of sunshine—another obvious element—is determined by the season, time of day, and degree of cloudiness.) Another element, one that usually cannot be felt but must be measured with an instrument, is the pressure. Each element influences and is in turn influenced by the others.

CLIMATE. Climate is the average condition of the weather in an area for a period of years. Usually, this period refers to 35 years or more. Weather can change daily but the climate of a place is relatively constant. Throughout the world, government and private weather stations measure and record the condition of the atmosphere many times a day. Statistics are compiled on atmospheric temperature, pressure, moisture, wind direction, velocity, and storms. These measurements are averaged for each month and season over a period of years in order to describe the climates of the various regions of the world.

WORLD CLIMATIC ZONES

We have five basis of classification : temperature, rainfall, evaporation evapotranspiration, and water balance. On the basis of temperature the Earth's climates can be classified into three broad groups **the tropical, the temperate** or the middle-latitude, and **the polar.** Rainfall can help in identifying dry, wet, seasonally wet, and seasonally dry climatic types. Evaporation is controlled by temperature. In using evaporation as a basis of identifying climatic types it is matched against rainfall. Evaporation transpiration is the amount of moisture lost by evaporation from the ground and by transpiration from the plants. The relationship of evapotranspiration and rainfall again leads to the identification of humid, seasonally humid, dry, and seasonally dry climatic types. The relationship between water surplus and water deficiency is expressed by water balance. If the former is greater than the later, the climate is humid; if it is less, the climate is dry. There are two well-known types of classification: one suggested by Thornthwaite and other by **Koppen**. We shall describe here the main types of climates based on Koeppen's classification:

KOPPEN'S CLIMATE CLASSIFICATION SYSTEM. The Koppen's Climatic Classification System is the most widely used for classifying the world's climates. Most classification systems used today are based on the one introduced in 1900 by the Russian-German climatologist Wladimir Koppen.

Koppen divided the Earth's surface into climatic regions that generally coincided with world patterns of vegetation and soils.

The Koppen system recognizes five major climate types based on the annual and monthly averages of temperature and precipitation. Each type is designated by a capital letter.

A - Moist Tropical Climates are known for their high temperatures year around and for their large amount of rainfall almost throughout the year.

B - Dry Climates are characterized by little rain and a huge daily temperature range. Two subgroups, S - semiarid or steppe, and **W** - arid or desert, are used with the **B** climates.

C - In Humid Middle Latitude Climates land/ water differences play a large part. These climates have warm,dry summers and cool, wet winters.

D - Continental Climates can be found in the interior regions of large land masses. Total precipitation is not very high and seasonal temperatures vary widely.

E - Cold Climates describe this climate type perfectly. These climates are part of areas where permanent ice and tundra are always present. Only about four months of the year have above freezing temperatures.

Further subgroups are designated by a second, lower case letter which distinguish specific seasonal characteristics of temperature and precipitation.

f - Moist with adequate precipitation in all months and no dry season. This letter usually accompanies the **A, C,** and **D** climates.

m - Rainforest climate in spite of short, dry season in monsoon type cycle. This letter only applies to **A** climates.

s - There is a dry season in the summer of the respective hemisphere.

w - There is a dry season in the winter of the respective hemisphere.

To further denote variations in climate, a third letter was added to the code.

a - Hot summers where the warmest month is over 22°C (72°F). These can be found in **C** and **D** climates.

b - Warm summer with the warmest month below 22°C (72°F). These can also be found in **C** and **D** climates.

c - Cool, short summers with less than four months over 10°C (50°F) in the **C** and **D** climates.

d - Very cold winters with the coldest month below -38°C (-36°F) in the **D** climate only.

h - Dry-hot with a mean annual temperature over 180°C (64°F) in **B** climates only.

k - Dry-cold with a mean annual temperature under 18°C (64°F) in **B** climates only.

1. TROPICAL CLIMATES

(a) EQUATORIAL CLIMATE

Location : 1. The best examples occur in the lowlands between 5°N and 5°S e.g. the Amazon and Zaire Basins.

2. The highlands which occur between these latitudes, e.g. East African highlands, have a much modified equatorial climate. Altitude in these regions 'reduces' temperatures to about 15°C

3. A part of the Guinea coast of West Africa receives low annual rainfall, e.g. Accra, 28 inches. This region really has an equatorial climate which is modified by monsoon winds.

Climatic Characteristics : 1. This latitudinal belt lies under the Doldrums Low Pressure all the year and, therefore, there are no seasons.

2. The *mid-day sun* is always near the vertical and it is overhead twice a year, at the equinoxes.

3. Average daily temperatures are 26°C throughout the year. These are well below the average daily temperatures of other types of climate occurring outside equatorial latitudes. Extensive cloud cover and heavy rainfall prevent temperatures from rising much over 26°C.

4. The ***diurnal temperature range*** is between 6°C and 8°C which is greater than the annual temperature range of about 3°C.

5. Rainfall is heavy and is usually convectional. Rains often come in the *afternoons* and are generally accompanied by lighting and thunder. Annual rainfall is about 80 inches though some regions get higher falls.

Malaysia, Singapore and Indonesia are generally said to have an equatorial climate. Although these countries show some of the characteristics of this climate, e.g. the temperature and humidity patterns, others are not as well developed. This is because they lie under the monsoon winds which sweep across South-East Asia from the N.E. from November to February and from the S.W. from July to September. These winds moderate humidity and give a seasonal pattern to the rainfall regime of many regions.

6. Humidity is always high.

(b) TROPICAL CONTINENTAL (SUDAN) CLIMATE

Location : 1. It occurs between 5°NB and 15°N., and 15°S.

2. It is best developed in Africa and east central South America.

Climatic Characteristics : 1. The latitudinal belt which has this climate comes under the Trade Winds for a part of the year (winter) and lies under the doldrums for the rest of the year (summer).

2. Summers are hot with temperatures around 32°C. Winters are cooler, 21°C. The annual temperature range is therefore about 11°C.

3. *Heavy rains, mainly of convectional type,* fall in summer : winters are usually dry.

4. The Trade Winds in north Africa blow from the Sahara Desert and are dry, hot winds. These are particularly noticeable in West Africa where they are called the **harmattan**. Besides being dry and hot, the harmattan are also dusty. In South Africa and in South America, south of the equator, the Trade Winds blow from the sea and they bring rain to coastal regions.

5. The annual rainfall is often around 30° but it may be more, e.g. for regions near to the equatorial latitudes, or less e.g. regions near the hot deserts.

6. The *highest temperatures* occurs just before the rainy season begins, i.e. April in the Northern Hemisphere and October in the Southern Hemisphere.

7. *Humidity* is high in the summer.

8. The climate can be said to have hot, wet summers and cooler, drier winters, but note the exceptions referred to in (4).

(c) TROPICAL MARINE CLIMATE

Location : 1. It occurs in east coastal areas of regions having a tropical *continental climate,* and in the coastal regions of *Central America.*

2. It is developed best in the lowlands of Central America, the *West Indies, coastal lowlands of Brazil and East Africa,* including *East Malagasy,* north-east Australia and the Philippines.

Climatic Characteristics: 1. On-shore trade winds blow throughout the year and they bring rain almost every day with rather heavier falls in the hot season.

2. Annual rainfall varies from 40 in 80 in depending upon location. Rainfall is both convectional and orographic.

3. Temperatures are similar to those of tropical continental climates. The annual temperature range is about 8°C with hot season temperatures of 29°C and cool season temperatures of 70°F.

(d) TROPICAL MONSOON CLIMATE

Location : In some tropical and temperate latitudes seasonal land and sea winds operate on a huge scale affecting both continents and oceans. These seasonal winds, called monsoon winds, are bes developed over an area extending from south-eastern and eastern Asia to northern Australia. Eastern Asia has a temperate monsoon climate.

Climatic Characteristics : 1. ***Seasonal reversal of winds*** is the chief feature of this climate. For one season the winds blow from the sea to the land bringing heavy rainfall to coastal regions, and for another season the winds blow from the land to the sea and these give little or no rain.

2. Annual rainfall varies greatly, the amount falling depending mainly on ***relief and the angle*** at which the non-shore winds meet this. The south-facing slopes of the Khasi Hills in Meghalaya receives as much as 500 inch annually. In contrast the region around Delhi receives only 25 inch annually.

3. Temperatures range from 32°C in the hot season and about 15°C in the cool season, thus giving an annual range of about 17°C. But these values vary very much.

4. A typical tropical monsoon climate consists of three seasons. For the Indian sub-continent and Burma these are :

(i) Cool, dry season (November to February) when the off-shore north-east monsoon winds blow.

(ii) Hot, dry season (March to May) when temperatures are high because of the near overhead mid-day sun, and when winds are almost absent.

(iii) Hot, wet season (June to October) when the on-shore south-west monsoon winds blow and when rainfall is very heavy in regions receiving the full force and fury of on-shore winds. During this season cloudy skies cause temperatures to fall a little, but humidity rises to its maximum for the year.

(e) TROPICAL DESERT CLIMATE

Location : 1. It occurs on the western sides of land masses in the belt of permanent trade winds. The only exception is the desert belt in north Africa which extends from the west coast right across the continent and into south-west Asia. This is because the trade winds affecting the eastern part of north Africa are blowing in from the land mass of south-west Asia and they are therefore dry winds.

2. The most important regions having this type of climate are the Sahara Desert, the Arabian, Iranian and Thar Deserts, the Australian Desert, the Kalahari and Namib Desert, the Atacama Desert and the Californian and Mexico Deserts.

Climatic Characteristics : 1. Rain rarely falls and the average annual fall is usually below 12 cm (5 in.) Sometimes there are sudden torrential downpours which give rise to temporary flooding.

2. The hot desert occur in the tropical high pressure belts where air is subsiding. Such air absorbs rather than yields moisture. Also, most of the winds blowing into the hot deserts originate in cooler regions. When crossing the desert these winds get hotter and again this prevents condensation. Note also that on-shore winds which sometimes affect the west coasts of desert belts cross cold currents which occur along these coasts. The winds are cooled and condensation takes place giving fog or light showers. The winds are therefore dried and on reaching the warm land surface they are dried still further.

3. Temperatures vary from 29°C in the hot season to 10°C in the cool season.

4. Because there are no cloud, the temperature often go over 38°C and temperatures of over 49°C are not uncommon. At night, again because there is no cloud cover, radiation is rapid and temperature can fall to 15°C in the hot season to 5°C in the cool season. Diurnal temperature ranges are therefore very high.

(2) TEMPERATE CLIMATES

(A) WARM TEMPERATE WESTERN MARGIN CLIMATE—MEDITERRANEAN CLIMATE

Location : (1) This occurs between 30°N and 45°N and 30°S and 40°S, on the western sides of continents.

(2) The climate is best developed around the shores of the Mediterranean Sea, in south-west, Africa, central Chile, central California, and South-west and southern Australia (Adelaide to Melbourne).

Climatic Characteristics : (1) Temperatures range from 21°C in the summer to 10°C or below in the winter.

(2) Off-shore trade winds blow in the summer. These are dry and give no rain. The sky is cloudless and humidity is low.

(3) On-shore westerly winds blow in the winter bringing cyclonic rain. Considerably more rain may fall on steep slopes lying at right angles to the wind. The rain often comes in heavy showers which sometimes cause floods.

(4) The annual rainfall ranges from 20 inches to 30 inches.

(5) Mediterranean climates experience both hot and cold local winds. Some examples are the Sirocco, a hot dusty, dry wind which blow in the summer across the Mediterranean Sea from the Sahara Desert; the mistral, an intensely strong, cold wind, which blows in the winter down the Rhone Valley from the North and often reaching the Mediterranean coast; **the Bora**, another winter wind which develops because of pressure differences between central Europe and the Mediterranean Sea and blowing south across Yugoslavia to the Adriatic.

(6) The climate can be summarised as having bright, sunny, hot and dry summer and mild rainy winters.

(B) WARM TEMPERATE INTERIOR CLIMATE

Location : (1) It occurs in the interior of continents, excluding Asia, between latitudes 20°N and 35°N and 20°S and 35°S. The interior of Asia in these latitudes has very low winter temperatures and very low annual rainfall. *Its climate is therefore better described as Temperate Desert.*

(2) The climate is best developed in the southern continents and is especially well developed in the *Murray Darling Lowland* (Australia) and in

the *High Veldt* (Africa). It also occurs in the USA in *western Oklahoma, Texas* and *northern Mexico.*

Climatic Characteristics : (1) Temperatures range from 26°C in the summer to 10°C in the winter.

(2) The annual rainfall varies from 15 inches to 30 inches depending on location. A good deal of the rain is brought by *South-East Trade Winds* to the southern continental regions in the summer months. This decreases from east to west which means that the western parts of these climatic regions are fairly dry, sometimes semi-arid. There is also convectional rain which is caused by the low pressure systems over these areas in summer. Most of the rain occurs in summer.

(3) Evaporation is high in summer and this often makes irrigation essential for crop cultivation.

(C) WARM TEMPERATE EASTERN MARGIN CLIMATE—CHINA TYPE

Location : (1) It is located on the eastern sides of continents between latitudes 23°N. and 35°N. and 23°S and 35°S.

(2) It is best developed in *central China, south-eastern USA, southern Brazil* and the eastern part of the Pampas (Argentina), *south-eastern Africa and south-eastern Australia.*

Climatic Characteristics : (1) As in the Mediterranean climate, the trades and westerlies are the dominant seasonal winds. But notice the contrasts: In this climate the trades are on-shore winds and they bring rain whilst the Westerlies are off-shore winds. These bring lighter rain.

(2) Summers are hot 26°C and winters are mild 13°C. Temperatures in the winter can be dramatically lowered suddenly when local winds caused by depression develop, e.g. pampero (Argentina) and southerly burster (Australia), and blow strongly.

(3) *Monsoonal winds* tend to develop in both south-eastern USA and in China. In China the development is marked and there is a definite seasonal wind reversal.

(4) Most of the rain falls in summer and it is convectional. The lighter rains of winter are caused by depressions developing in the off-shore westerly winds. Total annual rainfall is about 40 inches.

(5) Typhoons (south China) and hurricanes (south-east USA) are common in summer.

3. COOL TEMPERATE ZONE

(a) COOL TEMPERATE WESTERN MARGIN CLIMATE—THE BRITISH TYPE

Location : (1) It occurs on the western sides of continents between 45°N and 60°N and south of 45°S.

(2) It is best developed in *north-west Europe, western Canada* (British Columbia), coastal southern Chile, Tasmania and South Island of New Zealand.

Climatic Characteristics : (1) Winter temperatures range between 2°C and 7°C, while summer temperatures range from 13°C to 15°C. The annual temperature range is between 8°C and 11°C.

(2) Prevailing winds throughout the year are from the west, but they blow more strongly and persistently in the winter.

(3) The on-shore westerlies, especially in the Northern Hemisphere, cross warm ocean currents (North Atlantic and North Pacific Drifts) which prevent winter temperatures from falling very low. It is the combined effect of ocean currents and winds which results in a small annual temperature range.

(4) Sub-tropical and sub-polar air meet in these latitudes and this gives rise to depressions and anticyclones which move in from the west. These pressure systems produce changeable weather.

(5) *Rain falls* throughout the year, though there is a maximum in inter. *Cyclonic* and *orographic* rains both occur. The total annual rainfall is about 30 inches though in mountainous regions this may be as high as 100 inches.

Westerly winds and the warming influence of the warm ocean currents affects western coastal regions of Alaska and Norway which lie in the cold temperate latitudes. Winter temperatures in these regions are lower, often dropping to just below freezing point. However, these are still much higher than for places in the same latitudes and which are a few hundred miles to the east. Summer temperatures are usually below 15°C

(b) COOL TEMPERATE EASTERN MARGIN CLIMATE—LAURENTIAN TYPE

Location : (1) It occurs on the eastern sides of North America and Asia between 35°N. and 50°N. and on the eastern side of South America, south of 40°S.

(2) It is best developed in the Maritime Princes of

eastern Canada, and the New England states of the USA, northern China, Manchuria, Korea and northern Japan.

Climatic Characteristics : (1) Winter temperatures range from -9°C to -7°C, and summer temperatures 15°C to 24°C. The annual temperature range is therefore high and it averages about 24°C.

(2) Cold winds blow seawards from the interiors of North America and Asia in the winter and this causes the temperatures to be low. In North America these winds pick up moisture from the Great Lakes which gives rise to heavy falls of snow. In Asia the out-blowing winds are dry.

(3) Off-shore currents, the *Labrador current* (N. America) and the *Kurile Current* (Asia) reduce the winter temperatures along the coasts still further. Compare with the warm currents off the western coasts in the same latitude.

(4) Precipitation (as rain and snow in N. America and N. Japan) occurs throughout the year and is fairly evenly distributed. In north-east Asia (except N. Japan and N. Korea) however, rainfall is confined to the summer. The total annual rainfall varies from 25 inches to 1000 mm 40 inches. The rain is both convectional and cyclonic.

(5) *North-east Asia has a typical monsoon wind pattern, i.e. seasonal wind reversal.* Dry cold out-blowing winter winds give no rain to the mainland but heavy snowfalls occur innorthern Japan and northern Korea. Moist, in-blowing summer winds bring rain to all parts.

(c) COOL TEMPERATE INTERIOR CLIMATE

Location : (1) It occurs in the interior of *North America* and *Eurasia* between latitudes 35°N and 60°N

It is best developed in the provinces of Alberta, Saskatchewan and Manitoba, in *Canada,* the *north-central and mid-west of the USA,* in central and western Europe, and western USSR.

Climatic Characteristics : (1) Winter temperatures often fall to as low as—19°C with summer temperature rising to 18°C which gives an annual temperature range of 37°C.

(2) Rainfall occurs mainly in the summer and it is convectional. The annual total rarely exceeds 20.2 inches. Rainfall decreases towards the west in North America and towards the east in Eurasia. Rainfall is so low east of the Caspian Sea that the climate is of the Desert type and it is better described as Interior Desert.

(4) COLD ZONE

(a) TUNDRA CLIMATE

Location : (1) It occurs in the northern continents north of the cold temperate continental climate.

(2) It is best developed in northern Canada, and northern Asia.

Climatic Characteristics : (1) Winter temperatures range from -29°C to -40°C and summer temperatures are about 10°C. The annual range varies from 39°C to 50°C.

(2) Winter nights are long with hardly any daylight and summer days are long with hardly any night.

(3) The total annual precipitation is about 10ches in some of which falls as rain in the summer and some as snow in winter.

(4) *Humidity* is always low because of the low temperatures.

(b) POLAR CLIMATE

Location : This occurs in Greenland, interior Iceland and in Antarctica.

Climatic Characteristics : Temperatures are permanently below 0°C.

(2) Blizzards are frequent.

(3) Winters are really one continuous night and 'summers' one continuous day.

(5) MOUNTAIN CLIMATE

Location : This type of climate is best developed in regions of young fold mountains, e.g. the Rocky Mountains, the Andes, and the Himalayas, and associated mountains.

Climatic Characteristics : (1) In general, pressure and temperature decrease with latitude while precipitation increases. However, if mountains are high enough, there is a height at which maximum precipitation occurs and above which it decreases as the moisture content of the air falls because it becomes rarefied and its temperature falls.

(2) Because the air in high mountain regions is rarefied and relatively dust-free, it cannot absorb much heat. The air is therefore always cool and the daily temperature range is small. In comparison the ground absorbs much more heat in the summer days but loses it rapidly during the night. The daily ground temperature range is much greater.

(3) There is usually a succession of temperature belts, not unlike those extending from the equator to the poles, in very high mountain regions. Such a succession is particularly well developed in the Andes.

THE THORNTHWAITE CLIMATE CLASSIFICATION : Thornthwaite system is like Koppen's in that it attempts to define boundaries quantitatively; it is based on vegetation and employs combinations of symbols to designate the climate types. The chief point of departure from Koeppan's system is in the use of expressions 'temperature efficiency' and 'precipitation effectiveness'. Thornthwaite distinguishes five humidity provinces based which are wet, humid, subhumid, semiarid, and arid.

World Climatic Zones

Climatic Zone	Latitude (approximate)	Climatic Type	Rainfall Regime (with approx. total)	Natural Vegetation
Equatorial Zone	0°—10°N and S.	1. Hot, wet equatorial	Rainfall all year	Equatorial rain forests
Hot Zone	10°—30°N and S	2. (a) Tropical Monsoon	Heavy summer rain : 60 inches	Monsoon forests
		(b) Tropical Marine	Much summer rain: 70 inches	
		3. Sudan Type	Rain mainly in summer: 30 inches	Savanna (tropical grassland)
		4. Desert: (a) Saharan type (b)Mid-latitude type	Little rain : 5 inches	Desert vegetation and scrub
Warm Temperate Zone	30°—45°N and S	5. Western Margin (Mediterranean type)	Winter rain : 35 inches	Mediterranean forests
		6. Central Continental (Steppe type)	Light summer rain : 20 inches	Steppe or temperate grassland
		7. Eastern Margin : (a) China type (b) Gulf type (c) Natal type	Heavier summer rain: 45 inches	Warm, wet forests and bamboo
Cool Temperate Zone	45°—65°N. and S	8. Western Margin (British type)	More rain in autumn and winter : 30 inches	Deciduous forests
		9. Central Continental (Siberian type)	Light summer rain : 25 inches	Evergreen coniferous forests
		10. Eastern Margin (Laurentian type)	Moderate summer rain : 40 inches	Mixed forests (coniferous and deciduous)
Cold Zone	65°—90°N and S	11. Arctic or Polar	Very light summer rain : 10 inches	tundra, mosses, lichens
Alpine Zone		12. Mountain climate	Heavy rainfall (variable)	Alpine pastures,conifers, fern, snow.

GLOBAL CLIMATIC CHANGE

Atmosphere is well structured and fairly dynamic in nature. The dynamism is more complex near the earth's surface where changes take place both spatially and temporally. These changes may be induced internally within the earth's atmospheric system or externally by extra-terrestrial factors. Some of these changes are the results of human intervention and hence, may be slowed down by human efforts. The global warming is one of the changes caused by man's continual and growing introduction of carbon dioxide as well as some other so called green house gases, like methane and chlorofluorocarbon into the atmosphere. It is a cause of concern for the human kind today.

(a) GLOBAL WARMING : The atoms and molecules of atmospheric gases cause absorption and back radiation of sunlight, by the green house gases especially water, carbon dioxide, and methane. The concentration of water in the atmosphere is controlled by evaporation from oceans. Carbon dioxide is introduced in the atmosphere by burning of fuels, traffic, industries, etc. Equivalent amount of carbon dioxide is removed by precipitation as calcium carbonate in oceans. Methane, which is twenty times more effective than carbon dioxide, is produced by metabolisation of bacteria in wood/grass eating animals. The methane rapidly gets oxidised into carbon dioxide.

The carbon dioxide contents of atmosphere play a dominant role in causing worldwide climatic change. The gas is transparent to incoming solar radiation, but absorbs outgoing long-wave terrestrial radiation. The absorbed terrestrial radiation is radiated back to the earth's surface. Thus, it is clear that any appreciable change in carbon dioxide content would bring great changes in the temperature in lower layers of the atmosphere.

Rapid industrialisation and technological changes, revolution in agriculture and transport sectors have resulted in large supplies of carbon dioxide gas, methane and chlorofluorocarbon gases to the atmosphere. Some of these gases are consumed by vegetation and a few part of it is dissolved in ocean. However, about 50 per cent is left over in the atmosphere. During past 100 years the concentration of methane has more than doubled (from 7.0×10^{-7} to 15.5×10^{-7}) and carbon dioxide has increased by 20 per cent (from 2.90×10^{-4} to 3.49×10^{-4}). In 1880-1890 the carbon dioxide content was about 290 parts per million (ppm). It rose to about 315 ppm in 1980, 340 ppm in 1990 and 400 ppm in 2000. This means that proportion of carbon dioxide had increased by 9 per cent by 1950 and nearly 17 per cent by 1990. The rate of increase has become still greater during last one decade.

Of the many climatic parameters, temperature is the most affected due to urbanisation and industrialisation. The thermal characteristics of urban areas are in marked contrast to those of surrounding countryside. The analysis of temperature data for last fifty years reveals that there is an increase of 0.7°C in winter and 1.4°C in summer in India. Many of the scientists have predicted that the concentration of carbondioxide will rise upto 4.5°C by 2050. According to some estimates, rice cultivation in the world is responsible for 20 per cent methane being added to atmosphere, and the coal mining accounts for 6 per cent of methane. The deforestation is responsible for 20 per cent of the carbon dioxide gas being added to the atmosphere. Similarly, industrialisation is adding 25 per cent of chlorofluorocarbon to the aerosol of the atmosphere. Consequently, global temperature increase is by about 1.5°C.

Today, there is much concern that continuing addition of carbon dioxide and methane gases to the atmosphere will increase atmospheric temperature to an extent that it will cause ice to melt in the Arctic Ocean and in Antarctica. As a result, sea level will rise causing drowning of coastal lowlands and islands, altering rainfall and evaporation patterns, creating new plant diseases and pest problems and enlarging the ozone hole.

With a view to get a dependable picture of climatic changes in the past, ice-coring programmes have been undertaken in several countries particularly in Antarctica and Greenland to analyse the trapped gases during the last 1,00,000 years. The results have been fascinating and offer glimpse of the earth's recent history going beyond the phenomena of global warming. During last 10,000 years of the earth's history, climate regime has been exceptionally stable compared to earlier history. Study of oxygen isotope records in Greenland ice core suggests that cooling trend in the northern hemisphere started from 1725 to 1920. These were associated with emissions of volcanic dust at a regular interval of two to three decades but after 1945 there has been increase in temperature globally leading to warming without any major volcanic eruption and increase in level of carbon dioxide concentration in the atmosphere. Scientists predict that by 2020, temperature all over the world, would be higher than ever during the last 1,000 years. As such, it is evident that increasing carbon dioxide content would lead to rise in global temperature.

(b) GREENHOUSE EFFECT : This concept of heating the atmosphere indirectly from the earth's surface is called greenhouse effect or commonly known as atmospheric effect. Obviously the effect of atmosphere is analogous to that of a glass-pane, which lets through most of incoming short wave solar energy but greatly retards the outgoing long-wave earth radiation, thus maintaining surface temperatures considerably higher than they otherwise would be. You can build an instantaneous greenhouse. Park your car in the sun for two hours with the windows closed. Now, observe the interior temperature. It will be more than outside temperature. Growing tomatoes in winter can be accomplished by capitalising on transparency of glass roof in greenhouse to short wave.

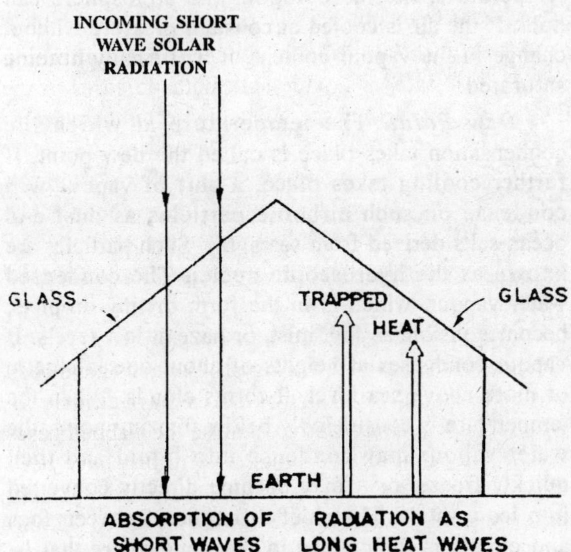

Trapping of Heat in a Glasshouse

The Carbon Cycle and Greenhouse Effect : Three of the principal greenhouse gases—carbon dioxide (CO_2), methane (CH_4) and the chloroflorocarbon (CFC) — contain carbon, 5-20 per cent of current anthropogenic CO_2 emissions. This is usually considered a modern phenomenon, particularly prevalent in the tropical rainforests of South America, southeast Asia, North America, Australia one of the most common elements in the environment, and one which plays a major role in the greenhouse effect. It is present in all organic substances, and is a constituent of a great variety of compounds, ranging from relatively simple gases to very complex derivatives of petroleum hydrocarbons. The carbon in the environment is mobile, readily changing its affiliation with other elements in response to biological, chemical and physical processes. This mobility is controlled through a natural bio-geochemical cycle, which works to maintain a balance between the release of carbon compound from their sources and their absorption in sinks.

The natural carbon cycle is normally, considered to be self regulated, but in a time scale of thousands of years. Over shorter periods, the cycle appears to be unbalanced, but that may be a reflection of an incomplete understanding of the processes involved or perhaps an indication of the presence of sinks or reservoirs still to the discovered. The carbon in the system moves between several major reservoirs. The atmosphere contains more than 750 billion tonnes of carbon at any given time, while 2,000 billion tonnes are stored on land, and close to 4,000 billion tonnes are contained in the oceans. Living terrestrial organic matter is estimated to contain between 450 and 600 billion tonnes, somewhat less than that stored in the atmosphere.

World fossil fuel reserves also constitute an important carbon reservoir of some 5,000 billion tonnes. They contain carbon, which has not been active in the cycle for millions of years, but is now being reintroduced as a result of the growing demand for energy in modern society. The burning of fossil fuel adds more than 5 billion tonnes of CO_2 to the atmosphere every year, with more than 90 per cent originating in North and Central America, Asia, Europe and the Central Asian Republics. The use of fossil fuel remains the primary source of fossil fuel remains the primary source of anthropogenic (human) CO_2. It is augmented by the destruction of natural vegetation, which reduces the amount recycled CO_2 during photosynthesis. Between 1850 and 1950 some 120 billion tonnes of carbon were released into the atmosphere as a result of deforestation and the destruction of other vegetation by fire.

OZONE DEPLETION

The ozone layer plays a very significant role in our life. It is found in the atmosphere between 20-50 km from the earth's surface. It protects from the harmful ultra-violet sun rays that can cause severe skin diseases like skin cancer etc.

But, now-a-days, this layer is depleting due to the increasing pollution, which is undoubtedly a matter of concern. Some ozone depleting substances, especially the chlorofluorocarbons (CFCS), Carbon tetrachloride (CCL_4) and Hydro Chloro-fluorocarbons ($HCFC_3$) are responsible for this depletion. These compounds absorb UV rays, that results in the decomposition of ozone. In this process, chlorine is released. In this way, the ozone concentration within the stratospheric ozone layer can be reduced. This reduction is not only responsible for the global warming, but it also carries great harms for human being.

HUMIDITY AND PRECIPITATION

HUMIDITY: Humidity refers to the amount of water vapour present in air. The amount of water vapour present in air is expressed in four different ways. ***Vapour pressure*** refers to that part of the whole atmospheric pressure which is due to water vapour. ***Absolute humidity*** is defined as the total amount of water vapour present in a given volume of air. The units used to express absolute humidity is 10 gm/cu cm. ***Relative humidity*** is the ratio of the amount of water vapour actually present in air as compared with the maximum that could be contained by the same volume of air at the given temperature and pressure. When the relative humidity is 100 per cent the air is termed fully saturated. The relative humidity changes in accordance with the changes in temperature and amount of water vapour. If the amount of water vapour remains constant but the temperature is increased there is a decrease in the relative humidity. It will increase if the temperature is reduced. In contrast if the temperature remains constant, the increase in the amount of water vapour will increase the relative humidity and a decrease in its amount will decrease the relative humidity. **Specific Humidity** is another way of expressing the amount of water vapour in air.

RELATIVE HUMIDITY is highest at the equator and decreases towards the poles. It is minimum in subtropical anticyclones. It increases from 30°N and S latitudes towards the poles following the decrease in temperature in the same direction. Following the apparent movement of the Sun, the belts of relative humidity experience latitudinal shifting. The seasonal distribution varies with latitudes. The average relative humidity is higher between 30°N and 30°S latitudes in the summer than in the winter. In higher latitudes, it is higher in the winter than in the summer because land is colder in the winter here. Thus, the temperature is low, the specific humidity is the same, hence the relative humidity is higher.

CONDENSATION AND ITS FORMS

CONDENSATION : Condensation is the process in which water vapour convert into water droplets. Condensation can only occur when the air becomes saturated. Water vapour in the atmosphere comes from various sources—evaporation from surface waters, evapo transpiration from plants, volcanic eruptions, etc. A given mass of air can hold only a certain quantity of water vapour. This amount will depend upon the temperature. The higher the temperature, the more vapour the atmosphere can hold. If the air is cooled at constant pressure without change in the vapour content, it will finally become saturated.

Dew Point. The temperature at which the condensation takes place is called the dew point. If further cooling takes place, a part of vapour will condense on such airborne particles as dust and ocean salts derived from sea spray. Such particles are known as the hydroscopic nuclei. The condensed water vapour, which is in the form of tiny droplets, becomes visible as fog, mist, or haze at low levels. If vapour condenses at heights of about one kilometre or more above sea level, it forms clouds. When the temperature is considerably below freezing point, the water vapour may condense into liquid and then quickly freeze, or it may become directly converted into ice crystals. The chief difference, between fogs and clouds is their place in the atmosphere-that is, the height they reach. Fog may arise on sea or land. The different forms of condensation are discussed briefly below:

Dew is the moisture deposited in the form of water droplets on the Earth's surface or on objects near the

Earth's surface, such as blades of grass. The ideal conditions for the formation of dew are a clear sky, little or no wind, high relative humidity, and relatively long nights.

White frost consists of particles of frozen moisture formed on the Earth's surface when condensation takes place at a dew point below 32°F. The ideal conditions for the formation of white frost are the same as those for the formation of dew. The air temperature must be at or below 32°F or 0°C.

Fog comprises a dense mass of small water drops or smoke or dust particles in the lower levels of atmosphere. Fog results from the cooling of air below its dew point. Cooling is caused by radiation, conduction, and mixing of warm and cold air masses.

Drizzle : The lightest form of precipitation.

Snow : Snow is precipitation composed of icy crystals.

Sleet : It is a mixture of snow and rain.

Hail : Hail storms are frozen lumps of ice produced by thunder storms.

Smog : It is a form of fog that occurs in areas where the air contains a large amount of smoke.

Haze : It is formed by water particles that have condensed around nuclei in the atmosphere, but may also be a result of particles of smoke, dust or salt in the air.

Mist is a type of fog in which the visibility is more than 1000 metres but less than 2000 metres. It becomes fog when the visibility is less than 1000 metres.

Cloud is a mass of small water drops or ice crystals formed by the condensation of the water vapour in free air at a considerable height above the Earth's surface. Clouds display infinite varieties of forms. Two main types are recognised according to their shape and mode of formation (i) ***Cumuliform*** or heap clouds which attain great vertical heights, and (ii) ***stratiform*** or layer clouds.

CLASSIFICATION OF CLOUDS

Clouds can be classified on the bases of the height of clouds, sky cover and forms of clouds. The modern international classification is taken into consideration:

(i) Classification on the basis of sky-cover : On this basis, clouds are divided into 8 to 10 types, e.g. partly cloudy, clear sky, scattered, broken overcast etc.

(ii) Classification on the basis of size, shapes of clouds:

Clouds are divided into groups mainly based on the height of the cloud's base above the Earth's surface. The following table provides information about each group and any cloud classes associated with them.

Cloud Group	**Atmospheric Layer in which Cloud is Found**	**Cloud Base Height**	**Cloud Types**
Polar Mesospheric Clouds (PMC's)	Mesosphere	about 85,300m	Also known as noctilucent clouds (NNC's)
Polar Stratospheric Clouds (PSC's)	Stratosphere	19,312m-28,968m	
Clouds with Vertical Growth	Troposphere/Stratosphere	tropics : up to 12000 m mid-latitudes: up to 12000 m polar region : up to 12000m	Cumulus Cumulonimbus
High Clouds	Troposphere/Stratosphere	tropics : 6000-18000m mid-latitudes: 5000-13000m polar region 3000-8000m	Cirrus Cirrostratus Cirrocumulus
Middle Clouds	Troposphere	tropics: 2000-8000m mid-latitudes: 2000-7000m polar region: 2000-4000m	Altostratus Altocumulus
Low Clouds	Troposphere	tropics: Surface-2000m polar region: surface- 2000m	Stratus Stratocumulus

(i) ON THE BASIS OF HEIGHT

(a) **High Clouds** (above 6,000 m) : (i) ***Cirrus Clouds (C):*** They are composed of icy crystals, instead of water droplets and are generally thin. (ii) ***Cirro-cumulus clouds (ci-cum)*** are found in the form of patches of white flakes. They form the "mackerel sky" (iii) ***Cirro-stratus (Ci-st)*** resemble a thin white sheet. Halo around the sun or moon are usually the result of cirro-stratus clouds.

(b) **Middle Clouds** (2,000 to 6,000 m). (i) ***Alto-Cumulus (Alt-Cu)*** clouds are greyish white and they indicate the weather (ii) ***Altrostratus (Alt-st)*** is a sheet of grey clouds and is followed by rain.

(c) **Low Clouds** (From surface to 2,000 m) : (i) ***Strato-Cumulus (St-Cu)*** are large gobular masses (ii) ***Stratus Clouds (St)*** are like dense fog and envelops high ground and can be dangerous for climber (iii) ***Nimbo-stratus (Ni-St)*** : is dense, shapeless and accompanied by rain and snow. The prefix "nimbo" implies a precipitation producing cloud.

(ii) CLOUDS WITH VERTICAL DEVELOPMENT

(a) Cumulus Clouds (CU) : These clouds developing vertically in the form of rising mounds looks like heavy masses of rising mounds but their base is uniform. They look like a mass of wool. It appears as if stream is coming out of steam engines in winters and producing whiteness in sky. These clouds are locally formed where the air rises. These are low clouds, (500-2000m) and the sky in the surrounding areas remains clear. They extent upto 1.9 miles high. They are caused by rising convection currents. They are often seen in the cold sector of a depression after a cold front. When these clouds are sunlit they are brilliantly white and are called wool clouds. Cumulus is generally found in the daytime over land areas. They dissipate at night. They often represent a transition to cumulo-nimbus.

(b) Cumulo-Nimbus (Cb) : From 6,000 to 15,000 feet high, they are large puffy clouds of great vertical extent or flattened tops; frequently anvil-shaped from which showers fall, often with their upper limit turn to ice. The dark base produces rain, hail or snow. They are associated with heavy rainfall, thunder, hail and tornadoes. It appears darker as condensation within it increases and it obstructs the sun. Such thunderstorms are very common during summer afternoons in the middle or low altitudes. This type of cloud is easily recognized by the fall of a real shower and sudden darkening of the sky.

Convection is only one of the ways in which moisture is turned into visible clouds. There are other ways too. When a stream of damp air flows as a wind over the tops of a range (of hills, the temperature at the hill tops may be low enough to cool the air below its dew point. Air that was comparatively dry at sea level may form clouds at these high altitudes. This explains why mountains, on the side from which winds are blowing, are so much cloudier and wetter than the valleys around them. Clouds may be formed in this way even where there are no mountains, Cold heavy air, like that which flows out from the Arctic periodically, makes an excellent "mountain" for this purpose. Any warmer, lighter air mass that happens to meet this cold air over a broad front will ride over it, will become cooler and in time it will condense. The warm and cold air masses behave like oil and water. Instead of mixing, the lighter mass flows over the heavier. Clouds originating in this way are called **frontal**. Clouds can form by the passage of damp air over a colder surface, either land or water. This horizontal atmospheric movement is known as **advection**, to distinguish it from the vertical movement known as **convection.** If the air is moving slowly, this process will be more apt to produce fog than cloud.

(i) Winds blowing over a warm current on to a cooler land surface usually bring heavy rain.
(ii) Winds blowing over a cool current on to a warmer land or surface usually bring little or no rain.
(iii) Winds blowing over a warm current and then over a cold current usually produce fog.

PRECIPITATION

After condensation, precipitation takes place. It can take place in various forms i.e., rainfall, hail, snofall, slect etc. On the basis of its origin three types of rainfall are recognised : (i) **convectional,** (ii) **orographic**, and (iii) **frontal.**

(i) **CONVECTIONAL RAINFALL :** Convectional rain is heavy but highly localised and associated with the minimum amount of cloudiness. Convection currents are normally set up in the atmosphere due to local heating. The rapid rising of warm moist air results in the formation of cumulonimbus clouds. They give heavy rainfall.

Convectional rainfall is common in equatorial regions.

(ii) **OROGRAPHIC PRECIPITATION:** Orographic means related to mountains, since *oros* is a Greek word which means a mountain. Orographic rain occurs where warm, humid air strikes landform barriers, such as mountain ranges, and rises up. The subsequent sequence is similar to that of the convectional rain. Orographic rain is heavy on the windward side of the mountain range, while the leeward side is termed rain shadow region which is arid to semi-arid in nature. Orographic rain occurs in a belt along the mountain range and, hence, decreases in amount as the distance from it increases. Much of the monsoon rainfall in the Western Ghats or in the Himalayas, North America and South America is orographic in nature. Another salient feature of Orographic precipitaion is the inversion of rainfall. An air stream approaching the mountain ranges is given an uplift by the air masses lying close to them. So the amount of precipitation starts increasing some distance away from the mountains. There is a continuous increase in rain on the windward slope upto a certain height. This is called the **Inversion of Rainfall**.

(iii) **FRONTAL OR CYCLONIC** rainfall occurs where a warm and humid air mass slides along the warm front on a cold air mass. Since the warm front is gently sloping, the warm air mass rises slowly and the rainfall is extensive. Since fronts are often found in cyclones, frontal rainfall is also cyclonic in nature and is termed cyclonic rainfall.

Thunderstorms. Thunderstorms are a spectacular example of rapid cloud formation and heavy precipitation in unstable air conditions. A prerequisite is that absolute or conditional instability should extend to great heights. This allows powerful updraughts to develop within towering cumulonimbus clouds, which are always associated with thunderstorms. The largest storms tend to occur in tropical or warm regions where the air can hold considerable amounts of water, and they are rarer in polar regions.

---

6 WATER (OCEAN)

OCEANS

The oceans are the landforms of first order. The Ocean floor is not plain as it generally believed earlier. Floors of various oceans are rugged and complex with world's longest mountain ranges, deepest trenches and largest plains. The relief of the Ocean floor is largely due to the interaction of tectonic, volcanic, erosional and depositional processes.

The ocean floor which are the landforms of second order, can be divided into following four major divisions :

(1) The Continental Shelf
(2) The Continental Slope
(3) The Continental Rise
(4) The Abyssal Plain

In addition, there are many associated features including ridges, hills, seamounts, guyots, trenches, canyons, deeps and fracture zones.

1. Continental Shelf: Continental shelf is slightly inclined, inundated zone which structurally forms the border of a continent. It is generally formed by the drawing of part of a continent with a relative rise in sea-level, marine plantation of land or marine deposition beneath the water. It has a gentle slope which is less than 1° and its maximum depth is normally 200 metres. Its width varies with its slope. The continental shelf of steep slope is narrow while that of gentle slope is quite broad. Its average width is about 70 km. It is almost absent in the eastern Pacific, especially in South America. Along the eastern coast of the USA, it is 120 km. wide. Its maximum width is off the Arctic Coast of Siberia where it is 1,287 km. wide. It covers about 7.5% of the total area of world's ocean.

Sun rays can penetrate upto the depth of the continental shelves which encourages the growth and reproduction of marine organisms and vegetation. Therefore, the continental shelves are of great use to man. Most of the marine food is obtained from the continental shelves. They provide the richest fishing grounds. They are also potential mining sites for economic minerals. About 20% of the world production of petroleum and gas comes from shelves. They are also large stores of sand and gravel.

2. Continental Slope: At the edge of the continental shelf, the seaward slope immediately becomes steep and the angle of slope varies between 2° and 5°. This part with steep slope is known as ***continental slope.*** It extends to a depth of about 3,660 metres. Continental blocks are supposed to end at the site of continental slope. There are five types of continental slopes :

(i) Fairly steep with the surface dissected by canyons;
(ii) Gentle slope with elongated hills and basins;
(iii) Faulted slopes;
(iv) Slopes with terraces; and
(v) Slopes with seamounts.

3. Continental Rise: Beyond the continental slope is the continental rise. It is an area of gentle slope varying from 0.5° to 1°. Its general relief is low. With increasing depth, it virtually becomes flat and merges with the abyssal plain.

4. Abyssal Plains: Where the continental rise ends, the deep sea plain known as abyssal plain or abyssal floor begins. There are almost flat areas with gradient less than 1°. Their depth varies from 3,000 to 6,000 metres. They are extensive areas covering about 40% of the ocean floor. They are present in all the major oceans and several seas of the world.

Apart from the above Four Major Relief Features of the Ocean Floor, there are some Other Important Features also :

1. Submarine Ridges: The mountains that lie under the oceanic water, are called the submarine ridge. They are a few hundred kilometres wide and several thousand kilometres long. They are ridges of high relief and form the longest mountain system on the earth. Mid-Atlantic Ridge is the best example of a submarine ridge. The total length of the submarine ridge system is over 75,000 km. The tectonic forces have played an important role in the formation of the submarine ridges. These ridges are either broad like a plateau, or gently sloping or steep-sided narrow mountains. Their summits may rise above sea-level forming islands. Azores and Cape Verde Islands are of this type.

2. Abyssal Hills: There are thousands of hills on the ocean floor which are submerged under ocean water. A submarine mountain or peak rising more than 1,000 metres above the ocean floor is known as a ***seamount***. Flat topped seamounts are known as ***guyots***. All of these features are of volcanic origin. Pacific ocean has the largest number of seamounts and guyots. It is estimated that there are nearly 10,000 abyssal hills in the Pacific Ocean alone.

3. Submarine Trenches or Deeps: A trench is a long, narrow and steep sided depression on the ocean floor. Trenches are the deepest parts of the ocean bottom with their usual depth of 5,500 metres. The deepest trench of the world is the **Mariana trench** of the Guam Island which is over 11 kilometres deep. If the Mt. Everest were to be submerged in this trench, its peak would still remain two kilometres below the sea-level. Trenches have been formed due to down faulting or down folding of the earth's crust and are, therefore, of tectonic origin. They generally run parallel to the bordering fold mountains or the island chains. Although trenches are found in all major oceans, they are most common in the Pacific Ocean. Trenches form an almost continuous ring along the eastern and western margins of the Pacific. So far 57 trenches have been located out of which 32 are in the Pacific Ocean, 19 in the Atlantic Ocean and the remaining 6 are in the Indian Ocean.

4. Submarine Canyons: A submarine canyon is a steep-sided depression on the seafloor crossing the continental shelf, slope and sometimes continental rise as deep as abyssal waters. Such features may be caused by the erosive activity of turbidity currents, or by the sub-aerial forces of erosion. Sub-marine canyons are of the following three types:

(i) ***Small gorges*** which begin at the edge of the continental shelf and extend down the slope to very great depths, e.g., Oceanographer Canyons near New England.

(ii) ***Canyons*** which begin at the mouth of a river and extend over the shelf, such as the Zaire, the Mississippi, and the Indus Canyons.

(iii) Such *canyons which have a dendritic appearance* and are deeply cut into the edge of the shelf and the slope, like the canyons off the coast of southern California.

The largest canyons in the world occur in the Bering Sea off Alaska. They are the Bering, Pribilof and Zhemchug canyons. Hudson Canyon is the best known canyon in the world. It begins near the mouth of the Hudson river and extends into the Atlantic Ocean.

OCEAN CURRENTS

The ocean current is the general movement of a mass of water in a fairly defined direction over great distances. The most important mechanisms for the great ocean currents are

(i) the drags of winds over the ocean surface and

(ii) unequal forces set up by differences in water density.

CURRENTS OF PACIFIC OCEAN: North Equatorial current from the west coast of Central America reaches the Philippines Island, flowing across from east to west in the North Pacific Ocean. Turning northward, the North Equatorial Current flows along **Taiwan and Japan** to form **Kuroshio Current**. The currents are influenced by the Westerlies from south east coast of Japan and tend to flow from west to east as the North Pacific current. The currents get bifurcated into the northern and the southern branches, called the **Alaska** and the **California** currents. The Oyashio flows in the North of Pacific. The South equatorial currents flows in the South pacific Ocean. Near the south western coast of south America it turns north as the Peru Current.

El-Nino current : This current is also known as Peru or Humboldt current. It is a cold current. It flows northward from the south American coast, near the equator, then it turns westward across the pacific ocean, especially as the south equatorial current.

El Nino occurs after every 3 or 8 years, which in a remarkable disturbance of ocean and surrounding atmosphere. Infact, El-Nino means the "Christ Child" in Spanish. This phenomenon occurs each year around Christman time, similarly the El-Nino also comes around christmas.

La Nina:- It is a warm ocean current. It was recognises during 1988. This current can cause severe drought problems alongs the coast.

CURRENTS OF ATLANTIC OCEAN: To the north and the south of the equator steady trade winds give rise to two streams of surface water that flows coastwards. They are known as the **North and South Equatorial** current. In order to replace the removal of water from eastern side, return currents are generated

Oceans and Seas

Name	Area sq.mi.	Area sq.km	Average depth ft.	Average depth m	Greatest known depth ft.	Greatest known depth m	Place of greatest known depth
Pacific Ocean	60,060,700	155,557,000	13,215	4,028	36,198	11,033	Mariana Trench
Atlantic Ocean	29,637,900	76,762,000	12,880	3,926	30,246	9,219	Puerto Rico Trench
Indian Ocean	26,469,500	68,556,000	13,002	8,963	24,460	7,455	Sunda Trench
Southern Ocean	7,848,300	20,327,000	13,100-	4,000-	23,736	7,235	South Sandwich Trench
Arctic Ocean	5,427,000	14,056,000	3,953	1,205	18,456	5,625	77°45' N; 175°W
Mediterranean Sea	1,144,800	2,965,800	4,688	1,429	15,197	4,632	Off Cape Matapan Greece
Caribbean Sea	1,049,500	2,718,200	8,685	2,647	22,788	6,946	Off Cayman Islands
South China	895,400	2,319,000	5,419	1,652	16,456	5,016	West of Luzon
Bering Sea	884,900	2,291,900	5,075	1,547	15,659	4,773	Off Buldi Island
Gulf of Mexico	615,000	1,592,800	4,874	1,486	12,425	3,787	Sigsbee Deep
Okhotsk Sea	613,800	1,589,700	2,749	838	12,001	3,658	146°10'E 46°50'N
East China Sea	482,300	1,249,200	617	188	9,126	2,782	25°16'N 125°E
Hudson Bay	475,800	1,232,300	420	128	600	183	Near Entrance
Japan Sea	389,100	1,007,800	4,429	1,350	12,276	3,742	Central Basin
Andaman Sea	308,000	797,700	2,854	870	12,392	3,777	Off Car Nicobar Islands
North Sea	222,100	575,200	308	94	2,165	660	Skagerra
Red Sea	169,100	438,000	1,611	491	7,254	2,211	Off Port Sudan
Baltic Sea	163,000	422,200	180	55	1,380	421	Off Gotland

that flows west to east as the **Equatorial Counter Current.** The South Equatorial current bifurcates into two branches near the coast of Brazil. The current that moves along the south eastern coast of United States is **Florida Current.** Beyond Cape Hatteras it is known as **Gulf Stream.** The southerly branch of the drift flow between Spain and Azores as the **Cold Canary Currents.**

CURRENTS OF THE INDIAN OCEAN: The circulation pattern is simple. The south **Equatorial Current** moves westward. Along the coast of Africa it bifurcates. The major part turns to the South as the **Mozambique and Agulhas Currents,** which turn to the east as the **west wind drifts.** Along the west coast of Australia, it flows northwards as the **Australian Current** and then joins the South Equatorial Current.

GREAT ISLANDS OF THE WORLD

The Largest Islands of Various Countries

Islands	Countries
Luzon	Philippines
Borneo	Indonesia
Honshu	Japan
Middle Andaman	India
New Guinea	Oceania
Luba	Carribean

World's Largest Islands in Descending Order of Size

1. Greenland
2. New Guinea
3. Borneo
4. Madagascar
5. Baffin
6. Sumatra

Important Facts about Island

- Great Barrier reef : Largest reef
- Tristan da Cunha : Remotest inhabited island
- Bouvet, S. Atlantic : Remotest island
- Kwajalein (Marshell Island) : Largest atoll
- Java : Most populated island
- Indonesia : Largest Archipelago
- Majuli (Assam) : Largest river island

SALINITY AND COMPOSITION OF OCEAN WATERS

Salinity of Oceans : As water flows in rivers, it picks up small amounts of mineral salts from the rocks and soil of the river beds. This slightly salty water enters into oceans and seas. The water in the oceans only leaves by evaporating but the salt remains dissolved in the ocean. So the remaining water gets saltier and saltier.

Salinity can be expressed as the number of grams of dissolved salts in 1000 grams of sea water. Salinity decreases towards the equator and the poles.

The average salt content is 35 gm per kg of sea water. The salinity of the sea varies from place to place, depending upon two factors :

1. The rate of evaporation.
2. The amount of fresh water added by rivers and rainfall.

Sea Salts	Parts Per Thousand
Chloride	19.3%
Sodium	10.7%
Sulfate	2.7%
Magnesium	1.3%
Calcium	0.4%
Potassium	0.4%
Bicarbonate	0.15%
Bromide	0.07%
Others	0.06%
Total Salinity	**35.08%**

The **Arctic Ocean** has the lowest salinity of **20%.** This is because of the slow rate of evaporation and the several streams and rivers that flow into it. The **Dead Sea** has the maximum salinity of **240%,** especially due to the high rate of evaporation.

COMPOSITION OF OCEAN WATER

About 99.7% of all dissolved materials are the major components of ocean water, but Sodium Chloride (Nacl) is the most abundant constituent of oceans. The table given below shows the major constituents of ocean water:-

Salt	% age	Salt	% age
Sodium chloride (NaCl)	77.8%	Calcium sulphate ($CaSO_4$)	3.6
Magnesium chloride ($MgCl_2$)	10.9%	Potassium sulphate (KSO_4)	2.5
Magnesium Sulphate ($MgSO_4$)	4.7%	Others	0.5

TEMPERATURE OF OCEAN WATER

- **Temperature :** The Sun hits the surface layer of ocean heating it up. Wind and waves mix this layer up from top to bottom so the heat gets mixed downwards too.
- **Latitude :** The temperature of the surface waters varies mainly with latitudes. The polar seas (high latitude) can be as cold as –2°C. While the Persian Gulf (low latitude) can be as warn as 36°C.
- **Unequal Distribution of Land and Water :** The oceans in the northern hemisphere receive more heat due to their contact with larger extent of land than the oceans in the Southern Hemisphere.
- **Prevailing Winds :** The winds blowing from the land towards the ocean drive warm surface water away from the coast resulting in the upwelling of cold water from below. It results in longitudinal variation in the temperature. Contrary to this, the onshore winds pile up warm water near the coast and this raises the temperature.
- **Ocean currents :** Warm ocean currents raises the temperature in cold areas while the cold currents decrease the temperature in warm ocean areas.

SPRINGS AND SEEPS: A spring is a natural discharge with a perceptible current at the land surface or in the bed of a stream, lake, or sea; water that emerges at the surface without a perceptible current is called a seep. Springs and seeps represent water reappearing from the groundwater phase of the hydrologic cycle. Both are widely distributed over the continents and some islands.

Types of Spring
1. **Perennial Spring :** If the water of a spring flows continuously, it is called a perennial spring.
2. **Intermittent Spring :** If the supply of water is not constant and varies from time to time, it is called an intermittent spring.
3. **Hot (Thermal) Spring :** Hot or warm water comes to surface and flows as a hot spring. The water is heated as it seeps down to hot rocks in volcanic regions or deep into the earth.
4. **Mineral or Sulphur Spring :** Springs carry water to the surface which may contain large amounts of dissolved sulphur and other minerals. Such springs are known as sulphur or mineral springs.

In India, springs are found mainly in three regions: the Kumaun Himalaya in Uttranchal; the low granitic hills and uplands of Chotanagpur, Bihar; and the western foot of the Sahyadri in the Konkan region. In the higher mountainous regions sand capping of impervious glacial till, a deposit of heterogeneous mixture of boulders and clays, is found in many places, and wherever the contact zone intersects the hill slope, a spring rises. A step-like pattern of springs occurs on the valley slope where the dip of the bed coincides with the gradient of the slope, and impermeable beds alternate with permeable beds. Each contact point of the permeable and impermeable rocks touching the valley slope provides the site for a spring.

GEYSER: The term 'geyser' is applied to those hot springs which eject columns of hot water and steam at more or less regular intervals to heights varying from a few centimetres to hundreds of metres. The term is derived from an Icelandic proper name Geyser meaning gusher or spouter. Geysers are mostly found in regions of recent volcanic activity, where the lava has not fully cooled down at great depths below the Earth's surface. The ground water coming in contact with these heated rocks is ejected as hot water and steam. There are three regions having a great number of hot springs and geysers; Iceland, Yellowstone National Park (U.S.A.), and the North Island of New Zealand. Some geysers have also been reported from Alaska, Kamchatka, Japan, the Malay Archipelago, Eastern Tibet, and Morocco.

The water of the geysers and hot springs is alkaline, and carries silica in solution which is deposited on the walls of the vent and around the mouth of the vent in the form of a cone.

OASIS : An oasis is an area in a desert made fertile by a source of fresh water. Oasis vary in size from a cluster of date palms around a well, to city at the site of a spring.

Aquifers collect groundwater over thousands of years or longer. The source of this underground water may be hundreds of miles away where the rain originally fell, seeped underground and made its way slowly to the desert along the water table. This underground lake is a precious resource in a desert.

Underground water may come to the surface in the form of springs in some cases but often wells have to be dug down to the water table.

Some of the world's largest supplies of underground water exist beneath the Sahara Desert. It supports over 90 oasis in this desert.

SWAMP : A swamp is an area of land **permanently saturated** with water and sometimes covered by it.

Swamp are dominated by trees. There are two types of swamps :-

1. **Salt water swamps** fringe coastal areas protected from the open sea.

2. **Fresh water swamps** are found around lakes and rivers where the water table is high.

MARSH : A marsh is an area of land where groundwater or surface water saturates or **covers the ground for long periods of time.** Marshes are usually treeless and dominated by grasses. Marshes may be of two types—Tidal and Inland Marshes.

1. **Tidal Marshes** are found near mouths of rivers and along coastlines protected from the open sea, but they are affected by the rise and fall of tides. they have fresh or salty water depending on their location.

2. **Inland Marshes** occur along the fringes of lakes and rivers where the water table is high. The

vast Florida **Everglades** are examples of an inalnd marsh.

Swamp	Marsh
1. Swamps are permanently saturated with water.	A marsh may not be permanently saturated with water.
2. Swamps are found within the tropics.	Marshes are found beyond the tropics.
3. Swamps are dominated by trees.	Marshes are usually treeless and are dominated by grasses.

BOGS : A bog is an area of soft spongy ground consisting of partially decayed plant matter called peat.

Bogs are more common in the cooler climates. Bogs are called **moors** in Europe.

They are formed in **glacial depressions** where the water table is high and are fed by groundwater. The glacial depression gets filled with plant debris. As the lake gets shallower, plants growing along the edge extend into the water. The partially decayed vegetation forms a thick spongy layer called **peat.**

Only certain plants like **mosses, pitcher plants** and **sundew** can grow here.

SINK HOLE : A sink hole is a large hole in the ground that occurs where limestone lies beneath the surface. Sink holes vary from shallow holes about 1 metre deep to deep ones about 50 metres deep.

Sink holes are formed when water flows underground dissolving limestone and widening the cracks and joints. Eventually the cracks and joints cave in forming a sink hole. Sink holes are also formed when the roofs of caves collapse.

RIVERS

A river is a sizable stream of fresh water flowing through a natural channel in the land. Streams too small to be termed rivers are called by such names as brook, branch, and creek. Most rivers flow on the surface, but in some areas they go underground for great distances.

Rivers are among the most powerful natural forces in shaping the Earth's surface. In draining the land of surplus water, rivers wear down mountains, plateaux, and other high landforms. In a never-ending process, eroded material is carried by rivers. Some is deposited to form floodplains in the valleys, some form deltas at the rivers' mouths, and some is deposited in the sea.

Rivers flow in all directions, the only limiting factor being that they follow the slope of the land. Most rivers ultimately flow to the sea, but many rivers lead to land-locked lakes and seas or dry up in arid wastelands. The Volga River is the best example of one flowing to a landlocked sea-the Caspian Sea.

GREAT RIVERS OF THE WORLD: Of all the Continents, South America has the most impressive display of great rivers—the Amazon, the Parana and the Orinoco. Some of the tributaries of the Amazon and the Parana are themselves huge rivers. The drainage basins of the Amazon is the largest, followed by the Congo, the Mississippi—Missouri, the Rio delta Plata, and the Nile.

LONGEST RIVERS OF THE WORLD

Name	Outflow	Length		Rank in world
		miles	kilo-metres	
World				
Nile	Mediterranean Sea	4,132	6,650	1
Amazon	South Atlantic Ocean	4,000	6,400	2
Yangtze	East China Sea	3,915	6,300	3
Mississippi-Missouri	Gulf of Mexico	3,710	5,971	4
Yenisey	Kara Sea	3,442	5,540	5
Hwang Ho (Yellow)	Gulf of Chihli	3,395	5,464	6
Ob	Gulf of Ob	3,362	5,410	7

Parana	Rio de la Plata	3,032	4,880	8
Congo	South Atlantic Ocean	2,900	4,700	9
Amur	Sea of Okhotsk	2,761	4,444	10
Africa				
Nile	Mediterranean Sea	4,132	6,650	1
America, North				
Mississippi Missouri	Gulf of Mexico	3,710	5,971	4
America, South				
Amazon-Ucayali-Apurimac	South Atlantic Ocean	4,000	6,400	2
Asia				
Yangtze	East China Sea	3,915	6,300	3
Europe				
Volga	Caspian Sea	2,193	3,530	23
Oceania				
Darling	Murray River	1,702	2,739	39

LAKES

A lake is a sizable inland body of standing water. Not having a precise meaning, the word lake has been applied to many different bodies of water. It is usually applied to natural inland waters such as Lake Michigan, but it is also used for many man-made reservoirs. Some large bodies of water that are really lakes are commonly called seas. These include the Aral, Caspian, and Dead seas in southwestern Asia and the Salton Sea in California. Large lakes, such as the Great Lakes of North America, have a tempering influence on the local weather. They provide low-cost transportation, supply water for homes and industries, and offer a wide variety of recreational facilities. Lakes provide water for irrigation systems and water power projects. Some lakes support important commercial fisheries.

TYPES OF LAKES : The table given below shows the major **lakes of the world.**

Continent	**Lakes**
(1) Eurasia	Caspian sea
(2) N. America	Superior
(3) Africa	Victoria
(4) Asia	Aral
(5) N. America	Huron
(6) N. America	Michigan
(7) Africa	Tanganyika
Largest in specific terms:-	
(a) Volume of fresh water	Baikal
(b) Freshwater lake	Superior
(c) Highest navigable lake	Titica
(d) Deepest lake	Baikal
(e) Saltiest lake	Van
(f) Lowest lake	Dead sea
(g) Meteoric Crates lake (India)	Lonar (in Maharashtra)

Largest Natural Lakes of the World

Name and Location	**Area* sq km**	**Depth# meters**
Caspian Sea, USSR-Iran	371,000	1,025
Superior, USA-Canada	82,100	406

Name and Location	Area* sq km	Depth# meters
Victoria, Uganda-Kenya-Tanzania	69,400	82
Aral Sea, USSR	64,500	67
Huron, USA-Canada	59,600	229
Michigan, USA	57,800	281
Tanganyika, Burundi-Tanzania-Zambia-Zaire	32,900	1,470
Baykal, USSR	31,500	1,620
Great Bear, Canada	31,200	446
Nyasa, Tanzania-Mozambique-Malawi	28,900	695
Great Slave, Canada	28,500	614
Erie, USA-Canada	25,600	64
Winnipeg, Canada	24,300	18
Ontario, USA-Canada	18,900	244

*All figures are rounded

#Greatest depth

7 LIFE ON THE EARTH

WORLD DISTRIBUTION OF PLANTS AND ANIMALS (DYNAMICS OF VEGETATION)

One of the main themes of plant geography is that vegetation of a particular place evolves with time, usually starting with very simple plant communities than leading gradually to more complex communities and ultimately to the establishment of the relatively stable plant community the climax starting with a newly formed ground surface or one that has been denuded to vegetation, the process of succession takes place in which one plant community invades the area and is followed in turn by other plant communities in an orderly sequence of sere, culminating in the vegetation climax.

A new site for the development of vegetation may have one of several origins a sand dune, a sand beach, the surface of a new lava flow or of a freshly fallen layer of volcanic ash, or the deposits of silt on the inside of a river bend which is gradually shifting. Such a site will not have a true soil with horizons rather it may be a lithosol perhaps little more than a deposit of coarse mineral fragments. In other cases, such as that of the foodplain silt deposits, the surface layer may represent redposited soil endowed with substantial proportions of soil colloids and bases. Ground surface from which vegetation has been destroyed by fire will have the soil profile largely intact.

The first stage of a succession is a pioneer stage consisting of a few plant species unusually well adapted to adverse conditions of rapid water drainage and drying of soil and to excessive exposure to sunlight wind and extreme ground and lower air temperatures. As these plants grow, their roots penetrate the soil, their subsequent decay adds humus to the soil. Fallen leaves and stems add an organic layer to the ground surface. Bacteria and animals begin to live in the soil in large numbers. Soon conditions are favourable for other plant species which invade the area and displace the pioneers. The new arrivals may be larger plant forms, providing more extensive cover of foilage over the ground. In this case, the climate near the ground or microclimate, is considerably altered towards one of less extreme air and soil temperatures higher humidities and less intense insolation. Now still other species can invade and thrive in the modified environment.

When the succession has finally run its course there will exist a stable community consisting of certain definite proportions of the various species, each of which contributes to the total structure of the vegetation. This climax stage represents an ideal model for the so-called natural vegetation of region. Doubt exist as to whether a climax unchanging with time can truly maintained. Some plant geographers consider that the climax must be followed by disturbance leading to a regression or return to one of the earlier stages of the succession, so that a type of self repeating cycle is the rule. There is also the possibility that climatic change prevents the climax from being maintained in one place.

One type of succession is that in which the normal geomorphic processes build new ground continously as on a floodplain, delta, or sandspit. The succession associated with such continuous accretion of ground is described as allogenic. The twelve zones shift gradually to the left as silting by the river raises the level of the ground surface and shifts the water line to the left. Here, we see the hygrophytes, living largely submerged, giving way to plants which thrive under conditions of intense sunlight on ground that is alternately exposed and invandated. Higher upon the bank are successive forest zones, willow elań and finally maple representing the climax of mesophytic trees.

Distribuition of Natural Vegetation : Using principles in combination with our understanding of the climatic types, pedogenic regions and the soil moisture regions, we are now prepared to analyze the worldwide distribution of vegetation and to explain the variations with latitude continental position and altitude.

The great biochores : All natural vegetation of the land falls into four major structural subdivisions the biochores, illustrated schematically in figure given below. First is the forest biochore. We define a forest as a plant formation consisting of trees growing close together and forming a layer of poilage that largely shades the ground. Forests often show stratification, with more than one layer. Shading of the ground gives a distinctly different according than that which would be found over open ground. No single value of precipitation can be stated because the effectiveness of the precipitation depends upon the water loss by evapotranspiration and this in turn depends upon air temperature and humidity. Cousequently, the forest biochore spans a great climatic range from wet equatorial to cold subarctic.

The savanna biochore is a formation consisting of a combinations of tress and grassland in various proportions. The appearance of the vegetation can be described as parklike, with trees spaced singly or in small groups and surrounded by or interspersced with surfaces covered by grasses or by some other plant life form, such as shrubs or annuals in a low layer. The savanna biochere indicates a climate of limited total annual precipitation with an uneven distribution throughout the years. The grassland biochore consists of an upland vegetation largely or entirely of herbs which may include grasses, grasslike plants and ferns (broadleaf herbs). Degree of coverage may range from continuous to discontinuons and there may be stratification. The grassland biochore may include trees in moisture habitats of valley floors and along stream coarses is typical of a climate which has small total annual precipitation, but otherwise the climate may range from one of extreme heat to one of extreme cold.

The desert biochore associated with climates of extreme aridity, has thinly dispersed plants and hence a high percentage of bare ground exposed to direct in isolation and the forces of wind and water erosion or to freeze than action. Although essentially treeless the desert biochore may have scattered woody plants. Typically, however the plants are small, *e.g.* herbs byroids lichens . Because the desert biochore includes climate ranging from extremely not tropical desert to extremely cold arctic desert a great range in plant communities and habitats is spanned by the biochore.

In describing the four great biospheres, emphasis has been placed on the vast range of climate spanned by each. Essentially, the biospheres are determined by the degree to which moisture is available to plants in a scale ranging from abundant (forest biochore) to almost none (desert biochore). But within each biochore condition of temperature are vastly different

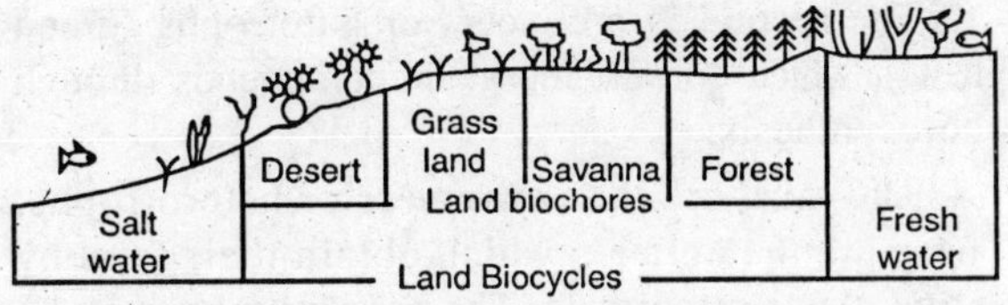

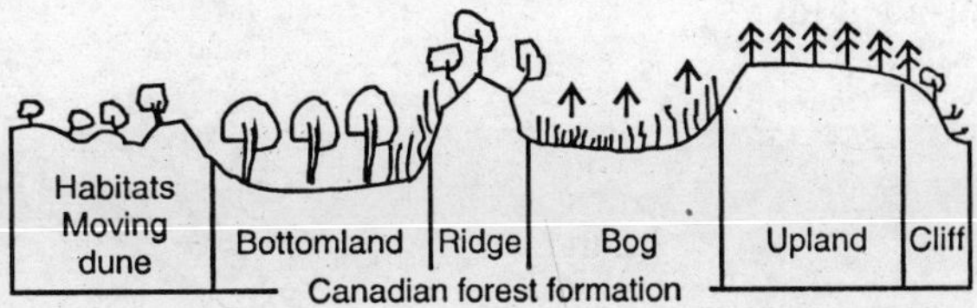

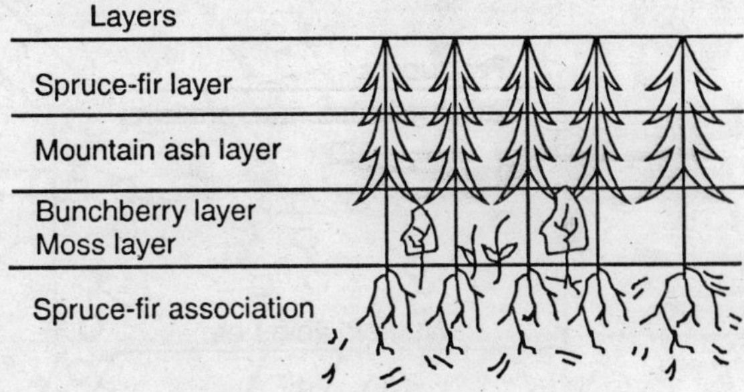

Dimension of the environment

A. The biocycles and biochores.

B. Habitats in the canadian forest formation.

C. Detail of spruce-fir upland association.

from low to high latitude and from low to high altitudes. Consequently, there is need to subdivide each biochore into a number of formation classes.

FORMS AND FUNCTIONS OF ECOSYSTEM

Ecosystem : The complex system of interactions between organisms and the physical environment in any unit of area is referred to as an ecosystem. It could be of any size from a small pond to the Amazon rain forest or the entire world. It can also be said to be a community of plants and animals sharing a given environment together with the nonliving (abiotic) habitat they occupy. Ecosystems characteristically derive their energy from sunlight and receive inputs of nutrients, water, and gases. Heat, oxygen, carbon-dioxide, and organic compounds from the outputs.

There are four basic components of an ecosystem. The first is the abiotic or the non-living environment such as rocks and air. The other components together form the biotic denoting living organisms *i.e.* plants and animals.

The second is producers or autotrophs (green plants), which convert inorganic compounds through photosynthesis.

The third are the consumers or heterotrophs. These are the animals which obtain their food by eating plants or animals. The heterotrophs may be divided into :

Herbivorous : eat only living plant material

Carnivorous : eat other animals

Omnivorous : eat both plant and animal meterials

Detritivorous : eat dead plant and animal materials.

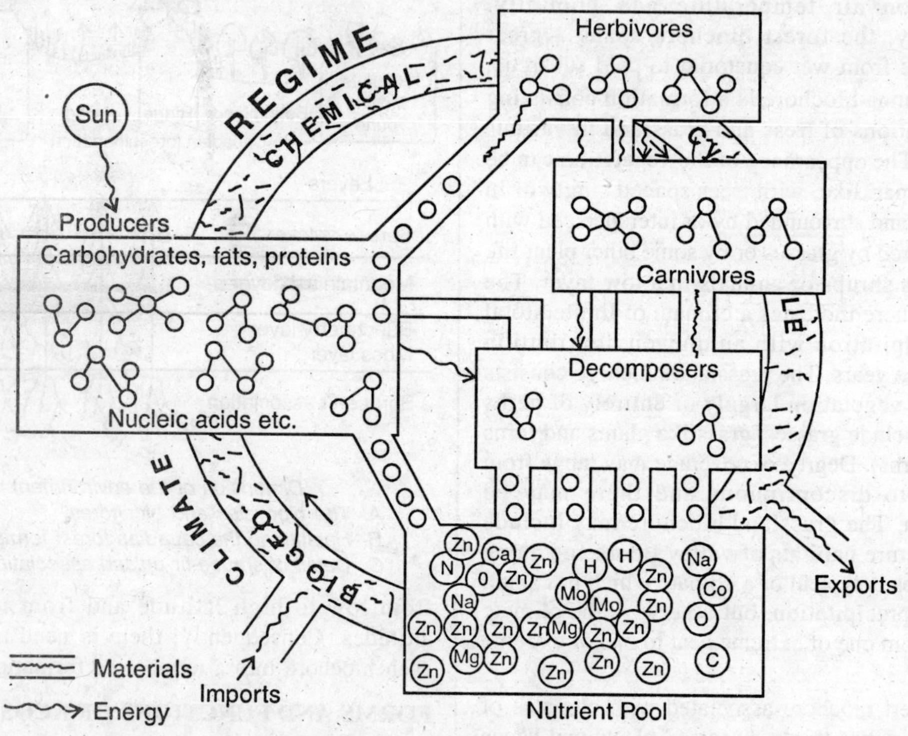

Ecosystem Model Showing its Structure and Function

The fourth component are the decomposers which include the bacteria and the fungi, who promotes the process of decay.

The energy of sunlight fixed in food production by green plants is passed through the ecosystem by food chains or food webs from one tropic level to the next. It helps in the flow of energy.

Example : of a food chain:

Plants → herbivorous → carnivorous decomposes (*e.g.* grass → vole → weasel → becteria)

Example of food web:

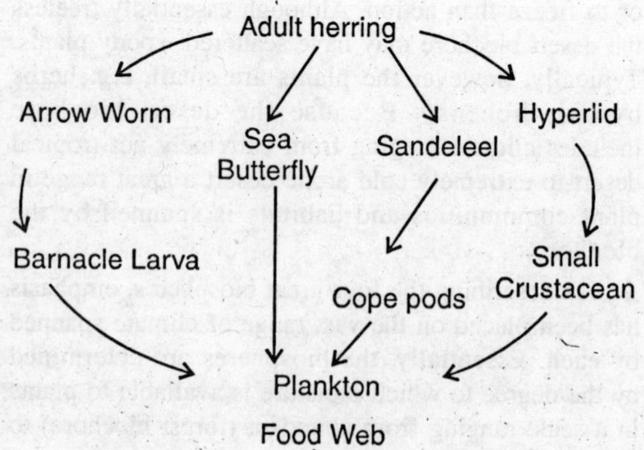

Food Web

All these concepts of energy transfers are based on laws of thermodynamics. The first law of which says energy can neither be created nor destroyed. It can only be transferred from one sort to another for ex: light energy to food energy (as in photosynthesis). Similarly the energy in the food chain and food web is transferred from one source to another and it never get destroyed.

Terrestrial ecosystems : Those which occur on the landmasses forming 29% of the earth's surface. They meet man's needs for food and raw materials. Terrestieal ecosystems are more productive per unit area than aquatic ecosystems. Terrestrial communities are generally recognised as larger units—

The biomes. In a biome, the life form of the climatic vegetation is usually uniform. The major biomes of the world are: *(i)* Tundra Biomes; *(ii)* Northern coniferous forest Biomes; *(iii)* Moist temperate coniferous forest Biomes; *(iv)* Temperate deciduous forest Biomes; *(v)* Broad leaved evergreen Sub-tropical forest Biomes; *(vi)* Temperate grassland Biomes; *(vii)* Tropical Savanna Biomes *(viii)* Desert Biomes; *(ix)* Chaparral Biomes; *(x)* Pinon-Juniper Biomes; *(xi)* Tropical rain forest Biomes.

Ecosystems are classified into :

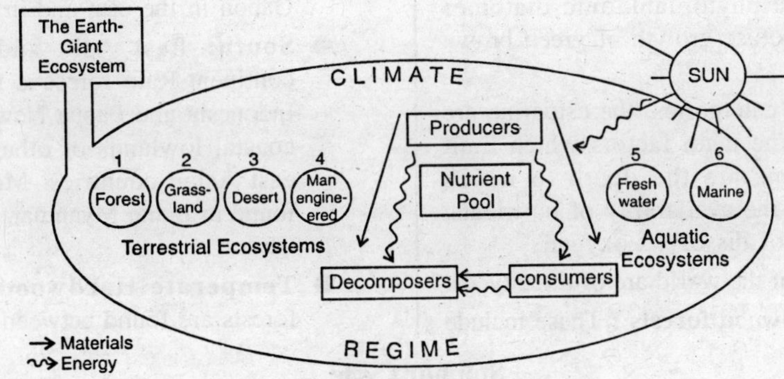

Basic type of Ecosystem

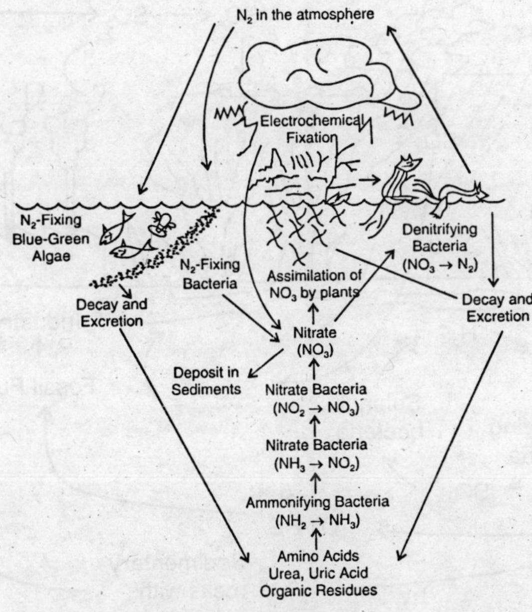

Nitrogen Cycle

Aquatic ecosystems : These systems can be divided into the categories of

(i) **Fresh water ecosystem** —The habitats may be lentic (standing water), such as lake, pond, swamp and bog;

(ii) **Esturarine ecosystems**—They are found in a very interesting type of habitat, *i.e.,* the transition zone between the fresh water and marine habitats under strong influence of tidal currents. The plant communities of such habitats are consituted chiefly by such macrophytes as sea weeds, sea grasses, marsh grasses and some phytoplanktons;

(iii) **Marine ecosystem :** They occur in marine water of seas and oceans. The chief components of plant communities are phytoplanktonic diatomes microflagellates and profuse growth of green brown and red algae.

Out of these three catergories, the estuarine are the most productive. The main factors which limit the aquatic ecosystems are the depth to which sunlight can penetrate, the availability of nurtrients, and the concentration of dissolved oxygen.

The major forests of the world are of three types:

- **Tropical Hardwood forests :** These include the evergreen rain forests of the equatorial latitudes and the tropical monsoon forests. Monsoon forests are less luxuriant than equatorial forests because of the seasonal trough. Tropical forest are found in three main areas.

- **Latin America :** The largest expanse is found in Amazon basin of Brazil extending from the Atlantic coast to the foothills of the Andes and from the guiana Highlands in the north to the Tropic of Carpricon in the south.

- **Africa :** Tropical forests are found in the lowlands bordering the Gulf of guinea from Sierra leone in the West to Rameroun and Gabon in the east and in the Zaire Basin.

- **South:** East Asia and the India Subcontinent-Rain forest is found in Malaysia, Indonesia and Papua New guinea and in the coastal lowlands of other south and south-east Asian countries. Monsoon forests are found in India, Myanmar, Thailand and Indo-China.

- **Temperate Hardwood forests :** These forests are found between opproximately 30°

Sulphur Cycle

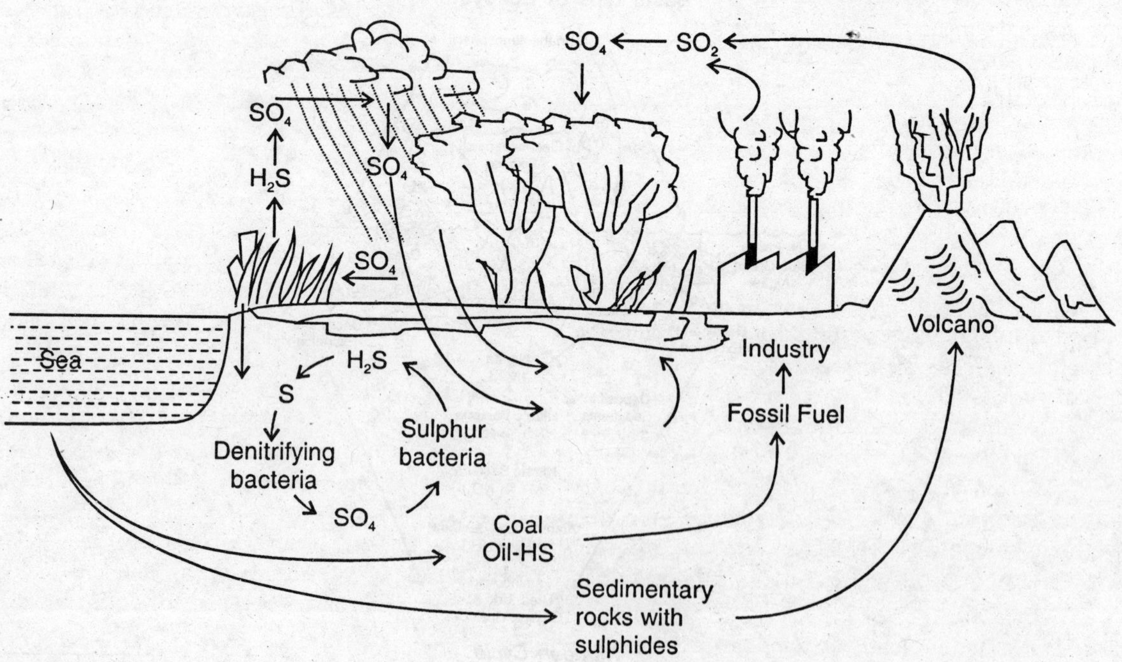

and 50° N and S where temperature and rainfall are moderate. The trees are mostly diciduous shedding their leaves in antumn and remaining leafless throughout the cold winter. They yield a wide variety of hard woods. Temperate hard wood forests are mainly found in northern China and Japan. Some such forests are also found in Southern Australia (Tasmania and swanland), West, South and Central Europe and eastern North America.

- **Coniferous forests :** Conifers are tall, straight evergreen with narrow needle-like leaves. The needles limit transpiration and thus enable conifers to grow in drier areas. They cover a broad belt of land in both North America and Eurasia, to the north of the temperate hardwood belt. Most conifers are softwoods and are light in weight which makes them easier to cut and transport. The major commercial trees are pines, firs, spruces, larch etc. These are the major sources of pulp and paper industry.

Grassland

Grassland is a major world vergetation type that is dominated by extensive grassy plains. Natural grassland occur in both tropical latitudes (*e.g.* savanna) and temperate regions (*e.g.* steppe in Curasia, Prairie in North America and Veld in South Africa). The widespread growth of tress in such areas is prevented to a certain extent by low rainfall, notably during the dry season. The grasses area dopted to these conditions by temporarily dying back and by long roots that effectively trap available soil moisture grasslands merge into forested areas where precipitation is higher and into deserts where it is lower. The temperate grasslands have been largely converted to agriculture, especially grain production. The grassland ecosystem is structurally simpler than that of forests having only a field (herb) layer, in which the tallest grasses are dominant. Though soil drought and precipitation levels are important factors in the maintenance of grassland restriction of forest growth, the grazing by large herbivores and recurrent fire are also contributory factors. Natural grassland is therefore not a truly climatic climax vegetation.

Pampas are the extensive areas of temperate natural grassland in South America that extend across Argentina and parts of Uruguay between the Andes and the Atlantic coast. The E areas are moisture and their original vegetation of pampas grass on rich alluvial soils has been extensively used for grazing beef, cattle or converted to cereal production. In the W, the pampas become desertlike.

Prairie are the gently undulating grassy plains of the interior regions of North America. The main water supply to the prairies tends to be springtime snowmelt from rocky mountains to the W. limited summer rainfall and high temperatures generally restrict tree growth to along the water courses, but provide an ideal environment for cereal production. The prairies are one of main 'granaries' of the world and the equivalent of the Russian steppe and South American pampas.

Savanna is open tropical and subtropical grassland with scattered bushes and trees, which covers extensive parts of Africa, North Australia, and South America (Where it is known as llanos in Venezuela and Colombia and the campos in Brazil). In Africa and Australia it is bordered by rain forest towards the equator and by hot desert on its opposite margin. Within these limits savanna varies considerably from tree-tress plains dominated by grasses up to 3 m in height (*e.g.* elephant grass, especially pennisetum purrpureum) to relatively well-wooded areas. Savanna tree species (*e.g.* baobab and acacia) conserve moisture by shadding leaves at the outset of drought (the cooler season), when grasses also witner fire, grazing by large herbivores and poor soils as well as climatic factors are responsible for the formation and continuation of the savanna vegetation.

Steppe is temperate natural grassland that occupies vast areas of E Europe and Central Asia, including much of the former SSSR. Its total E -W extent is about 5000 km. Steppe grassland is generally drier than the North American prairies and especially in its E parts, becomes semiarid as it approaches the deserts of Central Asia.

Veld is the temperate natural grassland of the plateaus of interior South Africa. The high veld (above 1500m) is cool and dry and is similar to the Eurasian steppe, although for less extensive. The low veld (below 900m) is warmer and has more tree cover. The veld is intensively formed for both animals and crops.

Puszta is an area of natural grassland that forms the westernmost part of Eurasian steppe, mainly in Hungary. More specifically, the term indicates an area of saline soils.

MARINE ECOSYSTEM

It is the most largest and stable ecosystem. Major oceans and their connecters passes about 70% of the earth's surface. Physical factors mainly waves, tides, currents, salinities, temperature, pressures, and light intensities largely determine the life in the ocean. Here the food chain begins with the smallest known autotrophs and end with the largest of animals (like giant fish, squid and whales).

Marine provides largest, thickest and most diverse ecosystem. Marine organisms exhibit an incredible array of adaptations, ranging from floatation devices that keep the tiny plankters within the upper layers of water to the huge mouths and stomachs of deep sea fish that live in a dark, cold water where meals are bulky but few and far between. Continental shelf area is quite productive and seafood produced here is an important source of protein and minerals for men. Here the most productive areas and larest fisheries are those that benefit from nutrients carried up by upwelling currents. For example: Peruvian upwelling region is one of the most productive natural areas in the world. The vast stretches of the deep sea, however are mostly semi desert with considerable total energy flow. The autotrophic layer (photic zone) is so small in comparison with the heterotrophic layer that the nutrient supply in the former is limiting.

BIO-DIVERSITY AND ITS DEPLETION THROUGH NATURAL AND MAN INDUCED CAUSES

Tropical rain forests are found in equatorial Africa, Central America, South America South and South-East Asia. Human occupation of tropical rain forests began in South-East Asia and the pacific 25000-40000 years ago, in the Amazon 10,000 years ago and about 3000 years ago in Africa. These forests now provide millions of people with shelter, food clothing, fuel, medicines, building materials and many other resources. A large number of people reap the economic and environmental benefits of rain forests without living near it.

Timber is the most important economically valuable resources of the forest, althougth other products such as nuts fruits, rattans, medicinal plants and rubber are also other important plants providing economic returns. Rain forest are extremely rich in species. Around 292000 km^2 (0.2% of the earths land surface), area contained 34400 endemic plant species. Tropical forests also contain high concentrations of other endemic species also.

Here the damage caused to bio-diversity of this region by natural means were not so severe. But real damage started when people began to migrate from China to South-East Asia, and from Europe to Africa and South America and started introducing new crops and agricultural methodologies. After the 17th century, forests were cleared to make way for cash crops. For ex: rubber in Indonesia and Malaysia, coffee in Brazil, tea in India and China, sugar in Carribbean Islands and tobacco, Palm oil in Asia.

Most dangerous destruction has taken place within the past 50 years to provide land for agriculture and vital export earning were used from the sale of timber and minerals. Land also cleared to build dams, roads and cities to meet the needs of a growing population. Timber trade has cause maximum damage to the rain forest. Logging has a direct impact on the forests and indirect damage is caused by timber companies opening up large areas of forest to invasion by settlers and shifting cultivators. In some regions poverty, population growth and unequal land owenership, encourage peasants to move out of highly populated areas into less developed, usally forested areas.

Mining and oil companies also leave destruction in their wake. Pollution is a major cause of concern, and the roads built by oil and mining companies attract settlers to the forests, displacing indigenous people destroyed by flooding. The rate of depletion has increased tremendousy in the last 20 years. FAO has estimated that the loss is greatest in central America, South-East Asia and West Africa. Improve-ment in satellite imagery and its interpretation based on ground surveys are helping to increase the accuracy of assessments of forest area and forest loss.

CONSERVATION AND MANAGEMENT OF ECOSYSTEMS

Conservation : Our resources are meant not only for the utilization of the present generation but also for the future generation. Therefore, a balance between the growth of population and the utilization of resources is absolutely necessary. This balance may ensure the continuity of human race. Any imbalance of our economic social and cultural development. The modern awareness about part of preservation and conservation of resources and environment has been created due to the fear of the situation which may arise as a result of large scale destruction of natural resources.

Ecosystem Management : The widespread concern over the status of ecosystem is the result of a movement that has slowly been gathering momentum over the last hundred years or of biological resources of ten arose out of economic necessity. The disappearance of forest and its products prompted the human being to save it for their present and future generation. The conservations movement as such was born in the United States. Currently it has become much wider issue than the maintenance of natural biological systems.

One of the important aspect of ecosystem management is the preservation and protection of wild life or of natural habitats from modification and depletion by man. It may be carried out for a number of reasons such as ethical, scientific, aesthetic etc. For this wild life refuges and sanctuaries have been set up all over the world. But such an experience of east Africa were not good as population of elephant hippo and Buffalo increased to such an extent that caused widespread devastation of their habitat. But one factor that has been over looked in the past is that ecosystem cannot simply be preserved and it is dynamic in nature and also man is an important habitat factor in many cases the ecological niche occupied by man cannot suddenly by left vacant.

One of the newer aspect of ecosystem management is the maintenance of sustained yield from organic, resources. This idea was first applied to the maintenance of the breeding stocks of marine animals and to forestry practice. It is also implicit in the principles of soil conservations, the aim of which is to sustain agricultural fertility. Many people are of the belief that it is the most important aspect of ecosystem management in the face of growing pressure on food resources.

Modern environmental management policies attempt to reconcile preservation and productivity. Multipurpose schemes are now being adopted management of forests which has a variety of use such as for timber, wild life, water supply, recreation, medicinal plants, gum lac etc. are being given top priority. So there clearly is a need to ensure that environmental management permits the maximum use of biological resources consistent with the maintenance of the greatest diversity of organic life.

Management of Environment : In the last decade of the present century environment degradation has emerged as a major global concern for human survival. A large number of international and global organizations with the collective wisdom of scientists economists and planners have come up to settle the environmental issuses confronting the nations and the physical world. The environmental crisis has convinced the world to use technology and resources to repair the damage already done to our environment and also to patent substitutes for certain harmful chemicales in order to protect and preserve nature and natural resoures. The last two decades have witnessed tremendous awareness in the field of environment all over the world. The dictionary of environment is renewed every time with new terminologies like clean technologies environmental auditing environmental friendly products (EFP), etc. Similarly the concept of environmental management has also emerged and accepted as a tool for sustainable development. In fact, proper use of technology, natural resources and human resources can be done through proper management. Many problems related with environment and its degradation can be solved with the help of its proper management. The developed countries of the world has already developed a system of environmental management at all levels, *i.e.*, national, provincial and local as well as domestic. But in developing countries this has to be done both through legislation as well as through people's particiption.

Approaches to Environmental Management : Environmental management has now become a priority throughout the world because of the serious consequences that have either been experienced by mankind or are likely to happen is future. There is a growing urgency of the management of land water minerals soil, grasslands, forests animal life atmosphere etc. in other words, the whole environment, any plan envisaging management of the environment must be based on the fact that each area has certain characteristics and can tolerate a range of physical conditions to a limited extent and every human activity affects the environment favourably or unfavourably, therefore two courses are open to us in using our surroundings :

(a) We adopt our needs and demands to the capabilities of each area, for example some recreations, urban development, waste disposal without over-loading the water or the air.

(b) We modify an area to change its capabilities. To achieve this, we may take up intensive management, controlling the physial features of the environment (*e.g.* agriculture plantation, social forestry, pond fish culture etc). In less intensive management, we modify the environment to favour selected types of living being present in the area (*e.g.*, wildlife management in santuaries, extensive forestry). Regulation of harvest from the available population (*e.g.* plucking or gathering fruits, fire wood in the forest) is also possible.

The best approach to environmental management is an integrated approach in which all the components of the environment have been taken into considera-tion and its proper management as whole is done. While doing so, the following aspects should be taken into consideration :

1. Perception and awareness of environment
   (a) Source of perception and awareness,
   (b) Level of perception and
   (c) Role of perception in environmental planning.
2. Environmental education and training
   (a) At school, college and university levels,
   (b) Environmental education through media and
   (c) Research and training institutes.
3. Resource management
   (a) Classification of natural resources
   (b) Survey and evaluation of ecoresources,
   (c) Conservation of energy, mineral, forest, soil and water resources and
   (d) Proper utilization of human resources.
4. Environmental impact Assessment
   (a) Assessment of present conditions,
   (b) Assessment of the impact of industrial and technological developments,
   (c) Assessment of the efforts done for eco-balance, and
   (d) Development of eco-friendly techniques.
5. Control over environmental degradation and pollution
   (a) Purification of degraded environment
   (b) Pollution control,
   (c) Monitoring and
   (d) Forecasting of natural hazards and to minimize the losses.

There are two approaches of managing the environment, *viz., (i)* Preservative approach and *(ii)* Conservative approach. According to the first approach, man should not disturb the natural system and should adjust according to it. But this is not possible because for all types of developmental activities he will have to use nature and its components resulting in eco-imbalance of varied intensity. The conservative approach is that there should not be overexploitation of nature and conservation of natural resources is essential for sustainable development. In fact, proper utilization and conservation of resources is the prime objective of environmental management. In the world conservation strategy (1980) there main objectives stated were: the maintenance of essential ecological processes the preservation of genetic diversity and the sustainable utilization of natural resources.

The management of environment should be planned and implemented in a hierarchical order, *i.e.*, international, national, regional and local, and priorities should be fixed according to the nature and state of environment and their associated problems. In fact, an integrated and balanced system is necessary similarly implementation of policies be done by trained personel who have a proper perspective and dedication for the maintenance of quality of environment.

Management of Environment Priority sectors: Environment, being so vast and all covering an exhaustive list of issues at the global and national levels, its analysis from the point of view of management needs several volumes. Several environment problems like air, water, land, noise and radioactive pollution and their management and conservation aspects have been discussed in earlier chapters. But there are certain priorities for global and national levels, which need special mention. Mary H. Cooper, in a report on ''setting environmental priorities'' (1988) lists the following as the most important global environment issues :

1. Greenhouse effect and consequent climatic changes,
2. Ozone depletion,
3. Acid rain,
4. Air pollution
5. Indoor air pollution.
6. Municipal and industrial solid wastes,
7. Likely escape of toxic/hazardous chemicals.
8. Nuclear wastes,
9. Arresting pace of deforestation and restoring balanced minimum tree cover areas,
10. Habitat and ecological diversity protection, and
11. Land, water and natural resource management at national level priority.

Some of the important aspects can be deal with very briefly and they are as follows :

(i) **Agriculture :** Nowadays agriculture has evolved beyond ''crop culture'', it has become an environmental technology with its prime focus on the management of air, water, land and biological resources to produce food and fibre and to preserve the natural resources. Through proper management and careful use we can successfully make permanent use of renewable resources (particularly land) improve the quality of the resources to increase our production and income.

There is a need to emphasize on the conservation practices for soil water, effective rotation and cropping practices. Misuse of renewable resources may lead to disasters, droughts and even desertification. Agricultural waste, including manure and crop residue, act as environmental pollutants—recycling of wastes in the farm minimizes the problem. Use of chemicals like pesticides fertilizers, hormones are becoming popular. Farmers should be educated regarding the dangers of indiscriminate use of such chemicals.

(ii) **Forestry :** The importance of forests and their conservation measures have been discussed in earlier chapters. The forest resources of the world are now in danger due to over exploitation for commercial use. It is high time that management practices should be applied not only for the maintenance of minimum forest cover but also for the further growth of trees. It is concerned which the protection, manipulation and use of vegetation. This also involves fuel and timber production, wild life conservation, recreation, protection of sceneric spots, watershed management etc.

Apart from afforestation, the technique of ''cappicing'' be applied in which trees are cut in such a manner that other trees replace them, thus a minimum tree cover can be maintained. Similarly "selective cutting" can also help in supply of timber wood. 'social forestry' is a very successful method for the growth of forests. Similarly more emphasis is given on agricultural forestry in which trees or a beet of trees can be developed along field boundaries. The growth of national parks is another aspect of forest management. Many countries of the world have developed national parks not only to protect bio-diversity but also as tourist centres providing regular income first of all, 'forest survey' be done properly and then proper management system be applied for their conservation and development.

(iii) **Wildlife :** Wildlife management includes both wild animals and their natural habitat or forests. The main objectives of wildlife management include:

(i) The maintenance of non-game species;
(ii) The production and harvest of game species;
(iii) Control of damage to plants, man and animals (domesticated);
(iv) Control of damage by wildlife to crops forests, livestock human beings;
(v) Development and growth of game sanctuaries as tourist spots;
(vi) Restrictions on hunting;
(vii) To conduct census of wildlife is order to provide them protection and
(viii) The protection of wildlife from the adverse affects of pollution and forest fire.

(iv) **Soils :** In order to protect the environment, soil management is also necessary. Soil erosion and loss of fertility are the two main problems. These problems can be solved to a great extent through proper land utilization and by adopting proper farming techniques. Both organic and mechanical methods be applied to control the loss of soil fertility.

(v) **Management for pollution control :** Pollution has become the greatest threat to man and environment throughout the world various types of pollution, *i.e.,* air, water, land, noise, radioactive have already been discussed in detail. Pollution control requires a high degree of management, because it directly affects all us. This can be possible only by adopting following measures :

(i) There is a need to have sizeable technically and scientifically trained personnel capable of handling environmental legislation which demands a specialized integrated knowledge.

(ii) The polluters should also be enlightened and made conscious of their social obligations commensurate to profit mative.

(iii) Public awareness should have a scientific temper devoid of emotional surcharge.

(iv) An enlightened judiciary.

(v) A political will

There is a need to control each type of pollution through proper management. The measures take to control water, air, noise, land and radioactive pollution needs separate management system on the one hand and an integrated system on the other. This can be done from local to regional and national to International levels. The main questions related to pollution management are : What is to be controlled? How much is to be controlled? What will be the pace and phases of control? Where should the control be done *i.e.*, control sites? and how to control? the following steps may be helpful in integrated management :

(i) Strengthening of monitoring network to be able to establish periodically the quality status of water bodies and ambient air along with regulating the compliance of emission norms from the polluting source.

(ii) Generation of base line data along with collection, compilation and simulation of available data. This will help in planning process.

(iii) Environmental information system be established where all types of data related to pollution will be available.

(iv) Both micro and macro level studies of pollution be conducted for each region.

(v) Mass awareness programmes be conducted and full scientific knowledge be given to the people not only regarding, adverse effects of pollution but also for its control.

(vi) Environmental research, including pollution should be encouraged at all levels, for which priority areas should be identified.

(vii) Indigenous methods of pollution control be developed and popularized, wherever possible.

(viii) One of the objectives of the management of pollution is to maximize people's participation in pollution control.

(vi) **Health :** Environment plays a vital role in controlling human health. Society, therefore, should be equally concerned with the environmental health as well as health of the people. Man affects his environment, changes it and in the process transforms himself also. Types and frequency of various diseases are related to environmental conditions. The climate food soil, water, air, etc., effect the health, physical structure and behaviour of the people.

(vii) **Population and urbanization :** The problems associated with population explosion and its impact on environment are varied. Many environmental problems in developing countries are mainly due to rapid growth of population which was resulted in the ever exploitation of existing natural resources. The cities are growing at a fast rate and the rapid growth of urban population is responsible for the lower quality of life growth of slums and other associated problems. The need for houses, tranportation, factories, schools, playgrounds, offices and other infrastructure is growing day by day. Human activities in these places produce lot of wastes and waste disposal, both municipal and other types, is the greatest problem of the modern cities, the waste products act as pollutants thus affecting the environment and man adversely. Therefore, proper waste disposal system, including recycling of waste is an immediate need. Proper use of land, water and air has to be the main concern of the city planners.

(viii) **Management of power and mineral resources :** The power and mineral resources are the building blocks of modern industrial and economic development. On the one hand these are the sources of development but on the other hand generation of

power through coal. Oil and radioactive minerals are also the cause of environmental degradation. Similarly, mining has become a threat to the environment in many parts of the world. Therefore, both these resources require management. In management of power resources the following steps may be helpful:

(i) Limited use of coal and petroleum.

(ii) To plan use of coal and petroleum in such a way that its impact on environment can be checked.

(iii) The sites of hydrodams be selected with full consideration of environmental conditions.

(iv) The establishment of atomic reactor be done at proper sites and strict measures be taken to check leakage of radioactive elements.

(v) Urgent need to develop non-traditional alternative sources of power such as solar energy, wind energy, tidal energy, etc.

(vi) Conservation measures be adopted to control wastage of power.

ENVIRONMENTAL EDUCATION

One of the most important aspects of environmental management is environmental education. This mainly concerns itself with the various aspects of environment and ecology. Its primary objective is to teach the components of environment, ecology and ecosystems, man environment relations, degradation of environment including various forms of pollution and their impact, environment including various forms of pollution and their impact, environment vs. development, population, urbanization and environment, environmental management and contemporary issues related to environment.

In brief, enviornmental education is the need of the hour and the priority should be given to it so that in phases the entire society will become aware of environmental issues. This will be the real successs of environmental management programme. In 1981 Indian environmental institute suggested an outline for environmental education. The main points included in it are:

(i) the pattern of environmental education be such that it should help in formulation of environmental policies and it reflect the relationship between man and environment.

(ii) Environmental education be included in secondary and university level syllabus, so that awareness among students can be developed.

(iii) this should include various principles and concepts of environment.

(iv) At university level knowledge of regional environment be given and a report should be prepared on any aspect of environment of that region by a group of students.

(v) training to the students be provided so that they can educate the public about environment.

(vi) An integrated rural development concept of environment be applied.

(vii) Orientation and reorientation programmes be organized not only for teachers but for doctors, engineers, planners, social workers and politicians to give then complete and up to date knowledge of environment.

Environmental Legislation

The conservation and protection of environment in general as well as of its specific variables like air, water, forests, sea, wild life, etc, is controlled through several international and national laws. Thus, implementation of these laws and to develop public awareness about them is an aspect of management. The laws to protect environment are essential, because with the growth of commercialization and also due to man's greed, over exploitation of environment has become a common feature, this can be checked only through legislation.

Initially, the subject of protection of the environment was deal with in a fragmentary manner under international law through various international conventions and treaties. In 1963, the Nuclear Weapons test ban treaty and in 1968 treaty on the non-proliferation of Nuclear Weapons were signed. Treaties on outer space (1971), Oil pollution in seas (1969) etc., have also been made. A few important international conventions/laws are :

(i) International plant protection convention 1951.

(ii) The International convention for the prevention of the pollution of the sea by oil 1954.

(iii) The African convention on the conservation of natural resources 1968.

(iv) The convention of wetlands of International Importance, 1971.

(v) The convention of the protection of the world cultural and natural heritage 1972.

The year 1972 was a landmark in the field of environment, when united nations conference on the Human Environment was held at Stockholm (Sweden) from 5 to 16 June, in which "Declaration on the Human Environment " was adopted. This may be condsidered as the beginning of environment movement in the world UNO has also adopted a programme known as "UNEP" (United Nations Environmental Programme) and also "Earthwatch" and "Global Environment Monitoring System" and declared 5th June as "World Environment Day" A new international machinery known as "Habitat" was established in Nairobi (Kenya) and in 1982, the tenth anniversary of Stockholm conference was celebrated in Nairobi, followed by the 'Nairobi Declaration'. Fact a number of conventions, treaties and instruments have been concluded or adopted dealing with the problem of the control of environmental pollution in one way or other, which shows that all over the world environment and its protection has become an issue of concern and that all the international bodies have shown their concern over it.

Apart from international laws, every country has enacted laws regarding environment protection pollution control etc., in India there are several acts for environment protection. Even in Indian constitution there clauses, *viz*, 47, 48A and 51 A have been introduced for the protection of the environment. There is no need to elaborate all the acts. The four notable acts of great importance are :

1. The forest conservation Act 1980.
2. The prevention of air and water pollution Act 1974, 1981.
3. The air prevention and control of pollution Act, 1981.
4. The environmental protection Act 1986.

It is duty of the management personnel to have complete knowledge of all the laws and help to develop an awareness among the people about the provisions available under various laws.

Monitoring and mapping of Environment

Monitoring of environment, pollution and its associated aspects are essential for environment management. Monitoring simply means checking of the environment pollution, etc, with special reference to the techniques applied to check its degradation. In other words, quality of environment or quantity of pollutants is to be measured in order to find out the effectiveness of the measures taken for it improvement. Thus monitoring is a continuous process and requires trained personnel the five categories of monitoring are :

1. Instrumental system in which physical characteristics are measured by instruments, such as:

   (i) sound level meter,
   (ii) geiger counter,
   (iii) thermometer,
   (iv) oxygen meter,
   (v) hydrometer, and
   (vi) clorimeter.

2. Chemical analysis through mechanical devices is done by several methods such as :

   (i) atomic absorption spectroscopy,
   (ii) infra-red spectra photometry and
   (iii) gas chromatography.

3. Chemical analysis in which volumetric, gravimetric and colorimetric analysis is done.

4. Biological system of monitoring, which is done by examining the nature of certain plants and other micro organisms.

5. Hybrid system is the combination of any two systems mentioned above.

Nowadays monitoring of environment has become popular even in developing countries because it helps in setting standards and limits of tolerance as well as for examining the effectiveness of the measures taken for improvement.

Environmental mapping is an emerging aspect of management. Since a lot of information regarding environmental variables and pollution is available through GIS and satellite, its mapping is very essential for proper planning and control. Through maps one can get to know the spatial dimensions of the problem. The mapping of environmental aspects has gained impetus and now there is a separate branch of cartography knows as "Environmental Cartography" the landsat imageries received through satellite provide lot of information regarding forest cover water resources. Soil degradation land utilization, etc., which provide a base for computer analysis and interpretation, thus help not only in knowing the existing position but also for its planning.

Biosphere Reserves Environmental Management in Action : A good example of environmental management is the 'biosphere reserve' a concept which is wider than that of a national park. Accroding to Batisse (1985) biosphere reserves, "combine nature conservation with scientific research, environmental monitoring training demonstration and environmental education" Today there are 738 biosphere reserves in a total of 134 countries. The basic idea is that representative areas of ecological importance should be linked together through a network of information. Each reserve would contain at its core a minimally disturbed ecosystem. The preservation of genetic richness in this system would be able to withstand the processes of attrition which have affected protected areas in most parts of the world. The core area is surrounded by buffer zones in which only limited agricultural activities are allowed and research stations are located minimum disturbance of the buffer zones enables the protected areas to survive intact, but an accommodation has to be found with the local human population who habitually use the reserves.

There is need for effective management "on the ground" not simply on paper Goodland (1985) has observed that mere "declaration of intent to protect wildlands or wild life does not ensure effective management unless specific supporting measures are implemented".

In developing countries the pressures on biosphere reserves from "the poverty of the poor and the greed of the rich" (Goodland, 1985 : 12) is much more than in developed countries.

Strategies for the future : The pace of increasing degration in environmental quality has been so great that its management has also become difficult. The enforcement of environmental laws is a very difficult matter even in western countries. The social political and economic factors often become too strong and compliance of policies becomes difficult. Joseph F Dimento (1989) has pointed the following causes :

(i) lack of visible rotionality of the laws regulations and standards;

(ii) Community perceptions of fairness and equitability and compatibility of the regulations with these;

(iii) Continuity and consistency of environment; and

(iv) Popular support and public pressure.

Environmental management is not merely a management of enviornment but it is essentially the management of various activities within tolerable constraints imposed by the environment itself and with full consideration of ecological factors. The future strategy of environment management should aim at :

(i) environmental planning,

(ii) environmental status evaluation and

(iii) environmental legislation and administration.

The primary aim of environmental management is to facilitate economic development without environmental damage. In other words, it should be sustainable development, environmental planing should be directed to control all types of degradation. Separate plans should be prepared at local regional, provincial and national levels for the conservation and protection of the environment. The priorities for each region should be fixed. The assessment of environmental quality be done for which system analysis techniques have already been evolved. Emphasis should be given for the production of ecofriendly products for global environmental problems full international cooperation is necessary. It is the duty of the developed nations to use their resources and knowledge to protect the global environment specially to check problems like green house effect global warming depletion of ozone layer, etc.

Apart from implementation of plans environmental impact assessment should be done regularly well developed monitoring system along with research and training facilities should be developed environment management policy should be prepared keeping in mind the socio-economic structure of the concerned region. Some of the major activities included in environmental management are:

(i) Eco-development activities in fragile ecosystem.

(ii) Natural resources conservation.

(iii) Pollution control.

(iv) Environmental education and awareness.

(v) Creation of environmental data bank.

(vi) Promotion of environmental research on pollution control and nutural resources.

(vii) Energy conservation and promotion of non-conventional sources of energy.

(viii) Supervision and scrutiny of environmental appraisal of development projects and plans.

(ix) Environmental monitoring to assess the quality of physical environment.

(x) Ensuring adequate man power and institutional support.

(xi) Coordination between government and other agencies.

(xii) Formulation of master plan for eco-development.

Although modern environmental management is done by technically trained people with advanced techniques, there is a need to use indigenous methods of environmental management. There are several indigenous methods used by local people in India as well in other Afro-Asian countries for the conservation of natural resources. These methods are still usefull and should be used properly. A proper environmental management system will help in generating a healthy environment, which will lead to a healthy economy for the present as well as for the future generations.

8 INDIA

GENERAL DATA: SIZE AND LOCATION

- The Union of India is the seventh largest country in the world covering an area of 32,87,263 square kilometres and it is an important country of South Asia.
- South Asia has a total area of about 4.488 million sq. km out of which India has the largest area (3.287 million sq.km). It occupies 73.2% of the total area.
- It is 4 times larger than Pakistan which is second largest in South Asia. India is 12 times larger than U.K., 8 times larger than Japan.
- The mainland stretches from latitude 8°4′ north to 37°6′ north and from longitude 68°7′ east to 97°25′ east of Greenwich. The latitudinal and longitudinal extent of the country is almost same in degrees i.e. about 30 degrees.
- Due to vast longitudinal extent, the time difference between the two extreme points in the east and west is of two hours. As such, time along the standard meridian of India (82°30′ E) passing through Allahabad is taken as the Standard Time for whole country.
- The country is of a vast size and measures about 3,214 kilometres from north to south and about 2,933 kilometres from west to east.
- The Tropic of Cancer passes through its middle part.
- India is situated on the northern fringe of the Indian Ocean. South of about 22° north latitude, the country begins to taper and pierces through the Indian Ocean for a distance of about 1,600 kilometres in the form of a wedge, dividing the ocean into two seas, the Bay of Bengal in the east and the Arabian Sea in the west.

OCEAN : India lies midway between the Far East and the Middle East. The trans-Indian Ocean routes connecting the industrially developed countries of Europe in the west and the underdeveloped countries of east Asia pass close by. India being centrally located in South Asia, she enjoys an advantageous position for doing trade with Australia and the countries of Africa, the Middle East and the Far East. Thus, India dominates the Indian Ocean and commands an important strategic position. Her land frontier is 15,200 kilometres long. Her northern borderland, being mountainous, is very difficult to cross and it offers very few transport facilities for trade with the arid, almost barren and very **sparsely** populated regions of Central Asia. India has a coastline of 6,100 kilometres in the main land and she depends on the Indian Ocean for the bulk of her foreign trade. The total length of the coastline of the mainland, Lakshadweep group of Islands and Andaman and Nicobar group of Islands is 7,516.5 km.

MARITIME CLAIMS	
❖ **Territorial Sea**	: 12 nm
❖ **Contiguous Zone**	: 24 nm
❖ **Exclusive economic zone**	: 200 nm
❖ **Continental shelf**	: 200 nm or to the edge of the continental margin.
❖ **Longest River**	: Ganga, Brahmputra
❖ **Longest Lake**	: Vembanad Lake
❖ **Highest Point**	: Kanchan Junga (8,598 m) (28, 209 ft)
❖ **Lowest Point**	: Kuttanad (–2.2 m) (–7.2 ft)

EXTREME POINTS OF INDIA	
❖ **Northenmost Point**	: Siachen Glacier near Karakoram Pass
❖ **Southernmost Point**	: Indira Point, Great Nicobar, Andaman & Nicobar Islands
❖ **Mainland**	: Capa Comorin (Kanya Kumari)
❖ **Westernmost Point**	: West of Ghuar Mota, Gujarat
❖ **Easternmost Point**	: Kibithu, Arunachal Pradesh

PHYSICAL BOUNDARIES: The sub-continent is isolated in a remarkable way from the rest of Asia, making it a geographical unit. For example, barring the plateau of Baluchistan the two great ranges, namely, the Sulaiman and the Kirthar, cut it off from the west. Along the North the great mountain wall formed by the Hindu Kush, Karakoram and the Himalayas, cuts it off the countries that lie beyond as the mountains are very high and difficult to cross. Similarly, the Southward offshoots of the Eastern Himalayas separate it from Burma.

The latitudinal and longitudinal extent of the country is almost the same in degrees i.e. about 30 degrees. But in kilometres, the north-south distance (about 3,200 km) is more than that of the east-west.

The Himalayas and other lofty mountains—Muztagh Ata, Aghil Kunlun mountains to the north of Kashmir and south eastern portion of Zaskar mountains to east of Himachal Pradesh—form India's northern boundary, except in the Nepal region. She is adjoined in the north by China, Nepal and Bhutan. A series of mountain ranges in the east separate India from Burma. Also, in the east, lies Bangladesh bounded by the Indian States of West Bengal, Assam, Meghalaya, Tripura and Mizoram. In the north-west, Afghanistan and Pakistan border on India. The Gulf of Mannar and the Palk Strait separate India from Sri Lanka. The Andaman and Nicobar Islands in the Bay of Bengal and Lakshadweep in the Arabian Sea are parts of the territory of India. Indira Point (earlier called Pygammlion point) in Great Nicobar in the Andaman and Nicobar Islands is the southernmost territory of India.

INDIA AND THE WORLD

India in South Asia : India is a giant among South Asia where other members are Pakistan, Nepal, Bhutan, Bangladesh, Sri Lanka and Maldives, a total of seven countries, encompassing a total area of about 4.488 million sq. km. Out of this, India has the largest area and occupies 73.2% of the total area. It is four times larger than Pakistan which is second largest in South Asia and 11 thousand times larger than the tiniest Maldives. The subcontinent is often referred to as the Indian sub-continent since India occupies major part of it. Pakistan, Afghanistan, China, Nepal, Bhutan and Myanmar and Bangladesh form components of India's land frontiers. The long international boundary is shared in the east with Bangladesh (4096 km), on the north with China (3488 km) and Afghanistan (106 km) and on the northwest with Pakistan (3323 km). It also has border with Nepal (1751 km), Myanmar (1643 km) and Bhutan (699 km).

LAND BOUNDARIES		
Total	:	15,200 km
Border	:	Bangladesh (4,096 km), Bhutan (699 km), Afghanistan (106 km)
Countries		Myanmar (1,643 km), China (3,488 km), Nepal (1,751 km), Pakistan (3323 km).

India in the Eastern World : India lies mid-way between West Asia and East Asia. The transoceanic routes connecting Africa, industrially advanced Europe and petroleum rich West Asia to South east Asian countries, China and industrially developed Japan. Australia and Western Coast of the USA pass through India. Sea has played an important role in India's external relations particularly with its neighbour in Southeast Asia, West Asia and East Africa.

To the West of India are West Asian countries of Oman, Iran, United Arab Emirates, Saudi Arabia and East African countries of Egypt, Sudan, Ethiopia, Somalia, Kenya, Tanzania, Uganda and Mauritius to the north of India bordering with the state of Jammu and Kashmir is the Sinkiang (Xinjiang) region of China. It contains the Tarim basin where once flourished a very rich civilization of K'ashi and Hotan (Khotan). Across the Himalayas lies Tibet, now an autonomous province of China and the Mansarovar lake still attract the Indian pilgrims.

LOCATIONAL ADVANTAGE

India is a unique country as it is easily accessible to other parts of Asia, Africa, Europe and Americas. Its cultural influences have crossed its border from time immemorial and reached far off lands. It acts as a bridge head between developed and developing countries of the world and between the East and the West. India's strength lies in its geography as much as in its culture. Since the opening of the Suez Canal in 1869, distance between India and Europe has been reduced by 7000 kms. India enjoys a favourable situation on the international highway of trade and commerce. The ocean routes from East and South-East Asia and Australia to Africa and Europe pass through Indian Ocean. India is connected with Europe, North America and South America through both the routes-the Cape of Good Hope and the Suez Canal. India can also reach Canada and the U.S.A. through the Strait of Malacca after crossing the Pacific Ocean.

POLITICAL DIVISIONS OF INDIA

A large number of factors like geography, population, local cultures, languages and administrative convenience are the considerations for the political divisions of India.

India is divided into 28 states and 8 union territories.

STATE FACTS : The Union Territories are federally administered territories (Central or Union Government), presided over by the President and the Vice President.

1. **A large area of the State of Rajasthan covers the Great Indian Desert.**
2. **The Coastal States of India:**

   1. Gujarat 2. Maharashtra 3. Goa 4. Karnataka 5. Kerala 6. Tamil Nadu 7. Andhra Pradesh 8. Odisha 9. West Bengal

   Union Territories:

   1. Dadra & Nagar Haveli and Daman & Diu 2. Puducherry
3. **The Union Territories of Andaman and Nicobar Islands and the Lakshadweep are made up of islands.**
4. **The States and Union Territories that form international borders with the neighbouring countries :**

   1. Gujarat 2. Rajasthan 3. Punjab 4. Jammu & Kashmir 5. Himachal Pradesh 6. Bihar 7. Uttar Pradesh 8. West Bengal 9. Sikkim 10. Arunachal Pradesh 11. Nagaland 12. Manipur 13. Mizoram 14. Meghalaya 15. Tripura 16. Uttarakhand 17. Ladakh
5. **The States/UTs that have a Common Border with Pakistan**

   1. Gujarat 2. Rajasthan 3. Punjab 4. Jammu and Kashmir 5. Ladakh
6. **The States that have a common border with Bangladesh**

   1. West Bengal 2. Assam 3. Meghalaya 4. Tripura 5. Mizoram

9 PHYSIOGRAPHY

INDIA'S GEOLOGICAL ERAS

India has its own geological eras and periods. The standard geological eras are :

(i) The Pre-Cambrian (over 570 million years old)

(ii) The Paleozoic (245-570 million yeas old)

(iii) The Mesozoic (66-245 million years old)

(iv) The Cenozoic (66 million years old to the present).

The Indian geological eras are :

(i) The Archean or Early Pre-Cambrian

(ii) The Purana or Late Pre Cambrian

(iii) The Dravidian (400-570 million years old)

(iv) The Aryan (400 million years old to the present)

The Pre-Cambrian derives its name for Wales in the United Kingdom. The periods got their names from places where rock formations of that period were formed. The Pre-Cambrians do not contain fossils of plants and animals. The Paleozoic have the fossils of very early lives, the Mesozoic have middle lives and the Cenozoic recent lives.

MAJOR GEOLOGICAL FORMATIONS OF INDIA

Indian Era	Standard Geological Eras and Periods	Duration of Period (in million years)	Age from beginning (in million years)	Major Formation in Extra Peninsula	Major Formations
	Cenozoic				
	Quaternary (Recent Pleistocene)	Less than 2	2 or 3	Newer Alluvial deserts, laterites	Formation of Ganga Plains
Aryan	**Tertiary** (Pliocene Miocene Eocene	64		Tertiary Coastal Deposits	Formation of Himalayas
	Mesozoic				
	Cretaceous Jurassic Triassic	179	66	Deccan traps, marine Deposits	Volcanic formations, marine sediments
Dravidian	**Paleozoic**		245		
	Permian Carboniferous Devonian Silurian Ordovician	325		Lower Gondwana (coal deposits No deposits	Deposits in Kashmir and Spiti
	Pre-Cambrian		570		
Purana	Late Pre-Cambrian			Vindhayan Cuddaph Dharwar Aravalli Archean systems	Archean Gneiss
Archea					

Eras are in bold letters, periods in normal letters

1. THE PRE-CAMBRIAN ERA

(i) **Archean System :** The Archean of India corresponds to the first half of the Pre-cambrian era. The Archean system contains the first formed rocks of the earth formed at the time of cooling and solidification of the upper crust of the earth's surface in the pre-Cambrian era (about 4,000 million years ago).

The gneisses and schists of the Archaean System form together with the Dharwars the oldest rock systems of India. The schists mostly crystalline include mica, hornblende, talc, chlorite, epidote, sillimanite and graphite schists. Basic trapdykes of dioritic or doleritic or ultrabasic composition cut through the gneisses and schists at a number of places. The Archaeans evince a high degree of metamorphism. They are all azoic, thoroughly crystalline, extremely contorted and faulted, often formed as plutonic intrusions and generally have a well-defined foliated structure.

The crystalline metamorphosed sediments and gneisses of the Archaean System form about two-thirds of the Peninsular surface, and also occur in several localities in the Himalayas. Bengal Gneiss, along with the Khondalites of Orissa, the Closepet, Champion and Peninsular Gneiss of the Peninsula and the gneisses of Jharkhand and Madhya Pradesh, is one of the important groups of the Archaeans. The third important group of the Archaeans is the charnockites which occur widely in Tamil Nadu—forming the Nilgiri, Palni and Shevaroy hills. The bulk of the higher ranges of the Himalayas forming the central zone is formed of crystalline and metamorphic rock like granites, granulites, gneisses, phyllites and schists. The rocks have no marks of fossils.

(ii) The Dharwar System : The Dharwars include some highly metamorphosed rocks of both igneous and sedimentary origin. Hornblende, chlorite and granulite represent the igneous types; whereas the various schists like mica-schist, talc-schist, chlorite-schist, quartzites and ferruginous quartzites are important rocks with sedimentary origin. These rocks are often highly metalliferous containing ores of iron, manganese, copper, lead and gold.

These rocks occur in the Dharwar-Bellary-Mysore belt of Karnataka; in the Aravallis between Jaipur and Palanpur, in Rewa, Balaghat and Jabalpur districts of Madhya Pradesh; Nagpur district of Maharashtra; Ranchi, Hazaribagh and Gaya districts of Jharkhand; Sundargarh and Keonjhar districts of Orissa; and Ladakh and Zaskar Ranges of Jammu and Kashmir and Himachal Pradesh.

2. PURANA OR LATE CAMBRIAN ERA

(i) The Cuddapah System : The Cuddapah System is composed of a number of parallel-series of ancient sedimentary strata of great thickness. They rest with a great unconformity on the Dharwars and Archaean gneisses and schists and underlie the Vindhayan System of Madhya Pradesh.

The most extensive occurrence of the Cuddapah is found in the Cuddapah district of Andhra Pradesh. The Chhattisgarh, Singhbhum district of Jharkhand, Kalahandi and Keonjhar districts of Orissa and the Aravalli Range of Rajasthan show isolated exposure of Cuddapah rocks. These rocks contain ores of iron, manganese, copper, cobalt, nickel and deposits of barytes, asbestos.

(ii) The Vindhayan System : Mainly composed of undisturbed sandstones, shales and limestones reaching a thickness of up to 4,000 metres, the Vindhyan System occupies about one lakh km^2 area, stretching from Sasaram and Rohtas in western Bihar to Chittorgarh in Rajasthan. It covers large areas of Madhya Pradesh, Chhattisgarh, Uttar Pradesh and Rajasthan. The Bundelkhand gneisses mark a gap in this belt while a large area of these rocks is covered by the Deccan Trap.

The Vindhayan system of rocks stand over the Cuddapah rocks. The Vindhayans are divided into Lower and Upper divisions. The Lower Vindhayans comprise the Semri Series and are mostly calcareous in nature. The Upper Vindhayans comprise the Bhander, Rewah and Kaimur Series.

3. DRAVIDIAN OR THE PALAEOZOIC ERA : CAMBRIAN TO CARBONIFEROUS

The Dravidian rocks do not occur in the Peninsular plateau as it was above the sea level at that time, but are found in continuous sequence in the Himalayas. They are well-developed in the extra-Peninsular area, particularly in Kashmir, Himachal Pradesh and Kumaon districts of Uttaranchal.

Cambrian rocks including slates, clays, quartzites and limestones are developed on a large scale in the mountains of Baramula district of Jammu and Kashmir. The 1,600 metre thick Haimanta System of the Spiti Valley in Himachal Pradesh also belongs to the Cambrian period.

The Carboniferous rocks of Spiti referred to as the Kanawar System, comprise limestones, shales and quartzites. In Kashmir they include grey-coloured limestones, quartzites and shales.

Unfossiliferous sedimentary strata of Palaeozoic age occur in the sub-Himalayan region. In Kashmir, they are called the Tanakki Series which contain quartzites, quartz schists and phyllite and are overlain by the Tanakki conglomerate. In the Shimla-Garhwal region the Jaunsar Series including quartzites, phyllites, slates, limestones, lavas and tuffs are possibly of Palaeozoic age. It is overlain by the Blaini boulder-bed.

(i) The Gondwana System : The Peninsula during the upper Carboniferous period experienced crystal movements which led to the formation of basin shaped depressions. These depressions had countless terrestrial plants and animals which were buried to form coal deposits in India known as Gondwana rocks. These contain coal deposits and have marks of climatic changes from arctic cold to tropical and desert conditions. This southern continent incorporated India, Australia, South America, Antarctica, South Africa and Malagasy. These rocks are found mainly in Damodar, Mahanadi and Godavari valley.

The Lower Gondwanas, particularly the Barakar and Raniganj Stages of the Damuda Series, contain most of India's coal reserves. Iron ores occur in the iron-stone shales of the Raniganj Stages of the Damuda Series, contain most of India's coal reserves. Iron ores occur in the iron-stone shales of the Raniganj coal-field.

(ii) The Upper Carboniferous and Permian Systems : The rocks of this system occur only in the western Himalayas from Kashmir to Kumaon and in Mt.Everest. The former, the Permian strata constitute the Kuling System comprising calcareous sandstones and quartzites and shales. In Kashmir, the Panjal volcanics including the agglomeratic slates and the Panjal Trap are formed of Permian rocks. Marine Permian sediments called Zewan beds occur in some parts.

In the Shimla-Garhwal area, the Blaini beds are composed of boulder beds and limestones. They are overlain by slaty shales and quartzites which form the **Infra-Krol Series**. These are succeeded by the **Krol Series** which is well-developed in the Sirmaur area. It contains sandstones, limestones and shales.

The Eastern Himalayas have rocks of the Lower Gondwana System thrust over the Siwaliks. Marine Permian rocks are found in northern Sikkim and in the Subansiri Valley of Arunachal Pradesh.

4. THE MESOZOIC ERA

The duration of the Mesozoic era was 179 million years and it is further sub-divided into following period.

(i) The Triassic System : The Triassic system meaning three fold (180-225 million years) is almost unknown in the Peninsular. The Triassic is one of the best developed sedimentary formations in the Inner Himalayas from Hazara to Nepal. Extensive sections of the system are exposed on the southern flank of the Himadri from Kashmir to Byans in Eastern Kumaon. The topmost beds of the Upper Triassic in all the above areas are the Kioto or Megalodon. Limestones are common in the Middle and Lower systems.

(ii) The Jurassic System : The Jurassic system after Jura mountains on the borders of France and Switzerland (180 milion years) overlies the Triassic covering wide areas in Tibet, South Ladakh, Spiti, Nepal and Bhutan where limestone occurs to a depth of 600-900 m. The marine trangression in the latter part of the Jurassic gave rise to thick series of shallow water deposits in Rajasthan and Kuchchh. Great thicknesses of Jurassic limestones and shales overlie the Triassic rocks in the northern Himalayas. A large part of Rajasthan and Kuchchh have a thick series of shallow water deposits as these areas were inundated by sea during this period. In Kashmir, Jurassic limestone and shales occur in Ladakh and limestones, shales and sandstones in the Pir Panjal Range near Banihal.

Moderately thick elastic strata including limestone occur in the Jurassic beds of Rajasthan. Along the Andhra Coast, between Guntur and Rajahmundry, the Jurassic rocks are interbedded with the Upper Gondwanas.

(iii) The Cretaceous System : The Cretaceous system from Creta, the latin name for chalk (70-135 million years) is one of the best developed marine system of India showing a variety of facies and having a wide distribution.

Cretaceous rocks including sandstones, quartzites, limestones and shales occur in the Spiti area of Himachal Pradesh. Cretaceous limestones occur in Rupshu and Burzil areas of Kashmir. The plateau of Meghalaya has sandstones and shales with carbonaceous layers.

The Cretaceous System is represented by the Ahmednagar Sandstones, Nimar Sandstones, Bagh Beds and the Dhrangandhra Sandstones in Maharashtra, Madhya Pradesh and Gujarat, particularly the Narmada Valley where they underlie the Deccan Trap.

(iv) The Deccan Trap : Towards the end of the Mesozoic era, an intensive volcanic activity took place which flooded with lava vast areas of Maharashtra and other parts of the Deccan. Known as Deccan traps, the volcanic rocks contain some thin fossiliferrous sedimentary layers found between the lava flows. This indicates that the lava flows was not continuous. The volcanic activity led to two great events : (i) breakup of the Gondawana landmasses and (ii) uplift of the Himalayas out of the Tethys sea.

The Deccan Traps have been divided into following groups:

(a) **The Upper Traps :** (about 450 m thick) found in Maharashtra and Saurashtra have numerous intertrapean beds of volcanic ash.

(b) **The Middle Traps (about 1200 m thick) :** are spread over Central India and Malwa. They are totally devoid of intertrapeans and have numerous ash beds.

(c) **The Lower Traps (about 150 m thick) :** are intertrapean beds but rare ash beds. They are found in Central India and Tamil Nadu.

5. THE TERTIARY ERA

The Tertiary age is the most important period in India's geological history as it was during this period that the Himalayas came into existence. Great mountain-building movements during the period led to the folding of the thick massive sediments deposited in the Tethys geosyncline since the Carboniferous age. The compression began as a result of tangential movements of the Tibetan Plateau and the Indian Peninsular Plateau.

The folding proceeded in a series of phases each separated from the other by an interval of comparative quiescence. The most important phase came during the post-Pliocene times when the Himachal and the Siwaliks were folded. There are evidences to prove that the elevatory movement has been continuing even during the recent times.

The early Tertiary rocks are of shallow and deep-water marine origin, whereas the upper strata of subsequent age are of freshwater or even sub-aerial origin. Besides the Himalayas and the Purvanchal, the Tertiary deposits also occur in the Peninsula, particularly in Kutch, Gujarat and along the East and West Coasts.

The tertiary rocks are found mostly in the Himalayas. The teritiary rocks contain brown coal, rock salt, gypsum and Limestone.

(i) The Eocene System : They are about 60 million years old. In India, the Eocene formations have been found in Jammu and Kashmir, Himachal Pradesh, Assam, Rajasthan and Gujarat.

Limestones of Ranikot and Laki Series are overlain by pyritious carbonaceous and ferruginous shales, above which occur variegated shales of the Kirthar Series. Near Riasi and Jammu, pyritious and carbonaceous shales and Nummulitic limestones are underlain by aluminous and ferruginous laterites. The shales contain some coal/graphite seams. The Laki and Kirthar Series are also represented in Kutch. In Gujarat, Eocene rocks, mostly of Ranikot and Kirthar Series, occur in the area between Surat and Broach. Rocks of Lower Eocene age have been discovered in the Pondicherry area along the East Coast.

(ii) The Oligocene and Miocene Systems : They are about 25-40 million years old. The Oligocene system is very poorly developed in India, and is found only in the Barail series of Assam which is overlain by Miocene rocks. These deposits indicate a shallow-water origin, though they are quite thick in places being composed of calcareous sandstones and greenish shales. In Assam, the Surma Series of Lower Miocene age is mainly composed of sandstones. The Nari and Gaj beds are found in Kutch, Saurashtra and parts of Gujarat. The Baripada beds of Mayurbhanj district of Orissa, Durgapur beds of the Raniganj coal-field and the Quilon beds near Quilon in Kerala are of Lower Miocene age.

(iii) The Siwalik System—Middle Miocene to Lower Pleistocene : The Siwaliks strata and their equivalents are found along the foothill zone of the Himalayas. They are called the Dihing Series in Assam. The Siwalik rocks are mostly arenaceous and seem to have been laid down by rivers in lagoons and fresh water lakes. Coarse material predominates in these deposits of 5,000 metre thickness.

The Siwalik System is represented by the Tipam Series of Upper Miocene age and the Dihing Series of Pleistocene age in Assam. The former are predominantly arenaceous and contain lignite.

6. CENOZOIC QUATERNARY OR RECENT PLEISTOCENE ERA

It is a brief period of nearly one million years and it is said to have just begun. The beginning of the Quarternary age was marked in the Northern Hemisphere by a cold climate, large areas being covered by ice-sheets. The evidence of glaciation like faceted boulders, grooved and planed rock surfaces and moraines are found in the Himalayas. The important quaternary formations are : Ice Age deposits in Kashmir, formation of alluvial plains in North India, creation of Rajasthan deserts, Rann of Kachchh, laterite formation in the Peninsula, and the formation of regur soils. Kashmir and the Himalayas experienced deposits of Ice Age.

The Karewa Formation in Kashmir is of Pleistocene age. It forms flat terraces in the Jhelum Valley and on the flanks of the Pir Panjal which are mainly composed of sands, clays, loams and boulder beds of fluviatile or lucustrine origin. River terraces in the upper Sutlej Valley and alluvial deposits in the valleys of the Narmada, Tapti, Godavari, Krishna and Kortalavar are also of the Pleistocene age.

The Older alluvium called *bhangar* in the Ganga Valley is of Middle or Upper Pleistocene age. It is dark in colour and rich in nodules and concretions of calcareous matter called *kankar* and forms relatively higher surface. The Newer alluvium or *khadar* of the Ganga Valley containing lenses of sands and gravel is of the Upper Pleistocene age.

GEOLOGICAL HISTORY OF INDIA

The present day three-fold physiographic divisions of India have evolved through a long geological history. A brief account of each division is given below.

(i) The Peninsular Plateau. The southern part of India consists of an old plateau which is known as the **Southern Plateau** because it is surrounded by sea on three sides. Geologists believe that it is the oldest landform of the Indian sub-continent and is just one of the several plates of the earth's crust. It is known as Indian Plate. During pre-Cambrian era, there was a large depression in which sediment was deposited and a block of crustal rocks known as the Peninsular Plateau came out of this depression and never submerged again. This table land has behaved as a rigid and inflexible block throughout its geological history and is often compared to a **'horst'.**

The first major event in the structural history of the Peninsular block was in Vindhyan or Palaeozoic period. During this period, there was a geosyncline. The strata of this geosyncline was tightly folded with great vigour and the Aravalis were formed. The present Aravalis are much denuded and are much reduced in size. It is a typical example of a residual mountain. Nallamalai range also came into being at the same time. Accumulation of tension in the earth resulted in the faulting and fracturing of the crust associated with vertical movements (uplift and subsidence). With every uplift or subsidence the topography underwent refreshed erosional process. Palani Hills and Nilgiri Hills are the result of uplifting process, while the fault valleys of the Godavari, the mahanadi, the Narmada, the Tapi and the Damodar came into existence due to subsidence process. The Malabar Coast and the Mekran Coast are also the result of subsidence process.

At the time of uplift of the Himalayas, two important events took place. As a result of first event, a volcanic eruption occurred in the north-western part of the plateau leading to the formation of the horizontally arranged beds of the Deccan Lava. In the second event, the western flank of the plateau subsided and the Indian Ocean advanced landwards leading to the formation of the Arabian Sea. The foundering of this flank has given to the Western Ghats a sharp contrast in relief and a prominence of a mountain. It is now commonly accepted view that the Arabian Sea came into being in the Pliocene or late Pleistocene period. The eastern coast and the adjoining continental shelf furnish contrary evidence. There is not much change in the coastline since the upper Palaeozoic Age.

(ii) The Himalayas : The Himalayan mountain ranges are much younger as compared to the Peninsular Plateau and are called young fold mountains

Several scholars have expressed their views regarding the origin of the Himalayas. The prominent among them are O.H.K. Spate, D.N. Wadia, M.S. Krishnan, S. Burrard, E.H. Pasco, G.E. Pilgrim, de Terra,

T.T. Paterson, T. Hagen, Auden, A. Heim and A. Gansser, Wager and a host of others. There is almost a complete unanimity that the Himalayan mountains have come out of a great geosynchine called the *Tethys Sea* and that the uplift has taken place in different phases. But divergent views have been expressed regarding the process and time of uplift as well as the forces responsible for such a vast scale uplift. The consensus which has emerged from the views of different scholars is reproduced as under :

About 120 million years ago, the arrangement of continents and oceans was quite different from what it is today. There used to be a vast shallow sea, known as the *Tethys Sea* lying between the **Angaraland** in the north and the **Gondwanaland** in the south. Sediments were brought by rivers from these land masses and deposited at the bed of the sea. These sediments were subjected to powerful compression, either because of the southward movement of the Angaraland or due to the norhtward movement of the Gondwanaland. Majority of the scientists believe that it is the northward movement of the Gondwanaland which caused compression in the sediments at the floor of the Tethys Sea. In any case, whether Angaraland moved southwards or Gondwanaland moved northwards or both moved towards each other, the net result would be the same; the sediment in the Tethys Sea was squeezed and crushed, and a series of folds were formed one behind the other giving birth to the highest relief features on the earth—the Himalayas. This tertiary mountain building phase is generally known as *Alpine* because Alps mountains of Europe were also formed almost at the same time.

The curved shape of the Himalayas convex to the south, is attributed to the maximum push offered at two ends of the Indian Peninsula during its northward drift. In the norhtwest it was done by the Aravalis and in the north-east by the Assam ranges, both acting as two extended arms pushing out the extremities, while the central area sagged giving the arcuate shape to the Himalayas. The recent studies have shown that India is moving northwards at the rate of about five cms. per year and crashing into rest of the Asia, buckling the Himalayas between Angaraland and Gondwanaland.

The diastrophic movements which helped in the formation of the Himalayas started in the late Cretaceous times and continued through the Eocene, Middle Miocene, Pliocene to the lower Pliocene and finally into the upper Pleistocene to sub-Recent times. There are evidences to show that the process of uplift of the Himalayas is not yet complete and they are still rising. The heights of various places as determined by trigonometrical methods indicate that the Himalayas continue to rise till date. According to the estimates made by Godwin Austen, the average elevation of the Himalayas was 2440 m. above the sea level about a million years ago which has now risen to 3050 m. The Mahabharat range is still in a state of rigorous uplift. Some of the fossil formations found in the Shiwalik hills are also available in the Tibet plateau. It indicates that the past climate of the Tibet plateau was somewhat similar to the climate of the Shiwalik hills and that the elevation of Tibet plateau was almost the same as that of the present Shiwalik hills and the plateau has since risen to its present elevation. The desiccation of the lakes of Tibet within recent or even historical times provides roof of the further uplift of the Himalayas. Surrounding these lakes, the sand and gravel terraces at higher levels, sometimes 60-100 metres above the present water level, are seen which prove that the water stood at a much higher level till recent times. This could be possible only in the event of uplift of the region. The frequent occurrence of earthquakes in the Himalayan region shows that the Himalayas have not yet attained the *isostatic equilibrium* and they still continue to rise further. The Himalayan rivers are still in their youthful stage and have been rejuvenated in recent times. This is another proof of rising trend in the Himalayas. The present rate of uplift of the Himalayas has been calculated at 5 to 10 cm. per year.

(iii) Evolution of Surface Features : The regular extension of the Sunderban Delta indicates that the process of plain formation is still continuing.

UNIFYING ROLE OF GEOLOGICAL PROCESSES

The above description reveals that though the three geomorphological units are quite different from one another, yet they are not mutually exclusive and their similarities are no less important. Following three points will explain it :

It is generally believed that the Himalayas are young and the peninsular plateau represent senile topography. But there is no dearth of senile traits in the Himalayas and youthful features in the peninsular plateau.

The structural evidences show that the peninsular block played an important role in the emergence of the Himalayas in Tertiary Age. The edge of Indian plate and relief features of Shillong (Meghalaya) Plateau, the Aravalis and the Kirana Hills near Chenab played an important role in the formation of north-western and north-eastern extremities of the Himalayas.

The rock strata found in the Himalayan ranges are similar to those found in the Peninsular Plateau. The huge accumulation of sediments in the Great Plains has been derived both from the Himalayan ranges and the Peninsular Plateau.

MAJOR DIVISIONS

The Indian sub-continent is characterised by a great diversity in its physical features. It may be divided following physiographic units :

(i) THE NORTHERN MOUNTAINS

(1) The region extends all along the northern border of the country, from the eastern border of West Pakistan to the frontiers of Burma, for about 2500 km. with an average width of about 240 km; occupied by the Himalayan ranges and its offshoots, it covers an area of about 5,00,000 km^2.

(2) It consists of the *Hindu Kush*, *Karakoram* and the *Himalayas* proper. Almost all the peaks of the world are in Karakoram and the Himalayas.

(3) Three major fold axes represent the *Himadri* (Greater Himalaya), *Himachal* (Lesser Himalaya) and the *Shiwaliks* (Outer Himalaya) extending almost uninterrupted throughout its length. Mighty but older streams like the Indus, the Sutlej, the Kali, the Kosi and the Brahmaputra have cut through steep gorges to escape into the Great Plains and have established their antecedence.

(4) The Himadri, the asymmetrical and the northern most range of the Himalaya owes its scenic beauty to glacier and lofty snowy peaks. Its average elevation is 6000 m. The Gangotri and Jamnotri are found in Himdari. This range has a granitic core, flanked by metamorphosed sediments.

(5) It has the credit of having the world's 14 highest peaks ranging between the Jano (7710m) and the Everest (8848m). Kanchenjunga (8,598m), Dhaulagiri (8,127m), Nanga Parbat (8,126m) and Nanda Devi (7,817m) are the famous peaks.

(6) The Himachal or the Lesser Himalayas forms the central chain composed mainly of highly compressed and altered rocks varying from Algonkian or pre-Cambrian to Eocene in age. In general, the alternating ranges and valleys acquire an elevation of about 5000 m and 1000 m respectively.

(7) Its asymmetrical structures at places provide it a more or less hogback look.

(8) The Shiwaliks in the south, which extend from the Potwar Plateau on the west to the Brahmaputra valley on the east and have an average height of over 1,000 m represent the outermost range of the system with roughly a hogback appearance, a steeply sloping southern and a gently sloping northern face.

(9) These newer and river-borne deposits derived from the rising Himalaya represent the most recent phase of the Himalayan orogeny i.e., from Middle Miocene to the Lower Pleistocene.

(10) The range, bordered on the north by flat-floored structural-longitudinal or erosional valleys called the **Doons** is characterised by fault scarps, anticlinal valleys and synclinal ranges.

REGIONAL DIVISIONS OF HIMALAYAS:

Apart from these longitudinal sub-divisions, the Himalaya exhibit regional characteristics and as such, the following regions have been identified :

(a) Kashmir or Northwestern Himalayas

It comprise a series of ranges such as the Karakoram, Ladakh, Zaskar and Pir Panjal. The northeastern part of the Kashmir Himalayas is a cold desert, which lies between the Greater Himalayas and the Karakoram ranges. Between the Great Himalayas and the Pir Panjal range, lies the world famous valley of Kashmir and the famous Dal Lake.

- **Important Glaciers :** Baltoro and Siachen.
- **Karewas :** Karewas are the thick deposits of glacial clay and other materials embedded with moraines. The Kashmir Himalayas are also famous for Karewas formations, which are useful for the cultivation of *Zafran.*
- **Important Passes :** Zoji La on the Great Himalayas, Banthal on the Pir Panjal, Photu La on the Zaskar and Khardung La on the Ladakh range.
- **Important Fresh Lakes :** Dal and Wular and salt water lakes such as Pangong Tso and Tso Moriri.

- **The river** Indus, and its tributaries such as the Jhelum and the Chenab.
- **Famous Places of Pilgrimage** Vaishno Devi, Amarnath Cave, Charar-e-Sharif.
- **Duns :** The southernmost part of the region consists of longitudinal valleys known as 'duns'. Jammu dun and Pathankot dun are important examples.

(b) The Himachal and Uttarakhand Himalayas

This part lies approximately between the Ravi in the west and the Kali (a tributary of Ghaghara) in the east.

- **Two Major River Systems,** the Indus and the Ganga. Tributaries of the Indus include the river Ravi, the Beas and the Satluj, and the tributaries of Ganga flowing through this region include the Yamuna, the Gomti and the Ghaghara.
- The northernmost part of the Himachal Himalayas is an extension of the Ladakh cold desert, which lies in the Spiti subdivision of district Lahul and Spiti.
- **Three Ranges of Himalayas** are prominent in this section also. (i) Great Himalayan range, (ii) the Lesser Himalayas (which is locally known as Dhaoladhar in Himachal Pradesh and Nagtibha in Uttarakhand) and (iii) the Shiwalik range from the North to the South.
- **Tourism :** In this section of Lesser Himalayas, the altitude between 1,000-2,000 m specially attracted to the British colonial administration, and subsequently, some of the important hill stations such as Dharamshala, Mussoorie, Shimla, Kaosani and the cantonment towns and health resorts such as Shimla, Mussoorie, Kasauli, Almora, Lansdowne and Ranikhet, etc., were developed in this region.
- **'Dun formations' :** Some important duns located in this region are the Chandigarh-Kalka dun. Nalagarh dun, Dehradun, Harike dun and the Kota dun, etc. *Dehradun* is the largest of all the duns with an approximate length of 35-45 km and a width of 22-25 km.
- **Nomadic Groups :** In the Great Himalayan range, the valleys are mostly inhabited by the Bhotia's. These are nomadic groups who migrate to 'Bugyals' (the summer glasslands in the higher reaches) during summer months and return to the valleys during winters. The famous 'Valley of flowers' is also situated in this region.
- **Places of Pilgrimage** such as the Gangotri, Yamunotri, Kedarnath, Badrinath and Hemkund Sahib are also situated in this part. The region is also known to have five famous Prayags (river confluences).

(c) The Darjiling and Sikkim Himalayas

- They are flanked by Nepal Himalayas in the west and Bhutan Himalayas in the east.
- It is relatively small but is a most significant part of the Himalayas.
- **Rivers :** Known for its fast-flowing rivers such as Tista.
- **Mountain Peaks** like Kanchenjunga (Kanchengiri), and deep valleys.
- **Tribes :** The higher reaches of this region are inhabited by Lepcha tribes while the southern part, particularly the Darjiling Himalayas, has a mixed population of Nepalis, Bengalis and tribals from Central India.
- As compared to the other sections of the Himalayas, these along with the Arunachal Himalayas are conspicuous by the absence of the Shiwalik formations.
- **Duar Formation :** In place of the Shiwalik here, the 'duar formation' are important, which have also been used for the development of tea gardens.

(d) The Arunachal Himalayas

- These extend from the east of the Bhutan Himalayas up to the Diphu pass in the east. The general direction of the mountain range is from southwest to northeast.
- **Important Mountain Peaks** Kangtu and Namcha Barwa. These ranges are dissected by fast-flowing rivers from the north to the south, forming deep gorges. Bharamaputra flows through a deep gorge after crossing Namcha Barwa.
- **Important Rivers :** the Kameng, the Subansiri, the Dihang, the Dibang and the Lohit. These are perennial with the high rate of fall, thus, having the highest hydro-electric power potential in the country. An important aspect of the Arunachal Himalayas is the numerous ethnic tribal

community inhabiting in these areas, e.g. the Monpa, Daffla, Abor, Mishmi, Nishi and the Nagas. Most of these communities practise *Jhumming*.

(e) The Eastern Hills and Mountains

- These are part of the Himalayan mountain system having their general alignment from the north to the south direction.
- They are known by different local names. In the north, they are known as Patkali Bum, Naga hills, the Manipur hills and in the south as Mizo or Lushail hills. These are low hills, inhabited by numerous tribal groups practising Jhum cultivation.
- **Rivers & Lakes :** The Barak is an important river in Manipur and Mizoram. 'Loktak' Lake in Manipur at the centre.
- Mizoram which is also known as the 'Molassis basin' which is made up of soft unconsolidated deposits.
- Most of the rivers in Nagaland form the tributary of the Brahmaputra. While two rivers of Mizoram and Manipur are the tributaries of the Barak river, which in turn is the tributary of Meghna; the rivers in the eastern part of Manipur are the tributaries of Chindwin, which in turn in a tributary of the Irrawady of Myanmar.

FOURTEEN MOUNTAIN PEAKS OF THE GREAT HIMALAYAS

(Height in Meters)

1.	Annapurna	8078
2.	Manasulu	8156
3.	Gosainthan (Shisha Pangma)	8018
4.	Cho Oyu	8153
5.	Mt. Everest (Sagarmatha)	8848
6.	Everest South	8754
7.	Lhotse I	8501
8.	Lhotse Intermediate	8410
9.	Lhotse Shar	8384
10.	Makalu I	8481
11.	Makalu South	8010
12.	Kanchenjunga I	8598
13.	Kunchenjunga South	8474
14.	Kanchenjunga West	8320

Eastern and Western Himalayas Compared : In the northwest, the Himalayan ranges coalesce with the diversely arranged mountain chains of the Karakoram, the Hindu Kush, Kun Lun, Tien Shah, Pamir, Alay and the Trans Alay Ranges which converge on the central promontory of Pamir.

Rock Formation in the Himalayas : The four-fold geological division of the Himalayas based on the age of rock formations and their type are : (i) The Tibetan zone, composed of fossil-bearing sedimentary rocks ranging from Palaeozic to Eocene of the Pleistocene era, lies to the north of the Great Himalayas. (ii) The central or the Himalayan zone is mainly composed of crystalline and metamorphic rocks. (iii) The Himalayan Nappe Zone consist of overfolds and thrust faults of a more complex type where large bodies of older rocks have been physically displaced and thrust on the newer ones along the recumbent folds over large areas. (iv) The outer or the sub-Himalayan zones, corresponding to the Shiwaliks, is composed of the sedimentary deposits belonging to upper Tertiary and believed to have been derived from the crowded materials of the main Himalayan ranges themselves.

Passes through the Mountain Wall: Though the mountain wall constitutes a formidable physical barrier between the Sub-continent and the rest of Asia, there are some very important passes. These are (from north to south) : the Khyber Pass, the Kurram Pass, the Tochi Pass, the Gomal Pass and the Bolan Pass.

(i) **The Khybar Pass** (1,000 m) is the most famous of all. It leads from Peshawar to Kabul. Most of the invaders in the past came through this opening in the Northern Mountain Wall.

(ii) **The Gomal Pass:** (1,525 m) South of the Kyber pass there is the Gomal Pass. This pass served as a trade route passing through the districts of Waziristan (now in Pakistan).

(iii) **The Bolan Pass:** (1,800 m) lies between the Sulaiman and the Kirthar Ranges. It leads from Kandahar to Quetta.

(iv) In the very north are two difficult routes via the **Karakoram Pass** and the **Zozila Pass** where there are roads communicating with Srinagar.

(v) **The Shipki Pass** leads from the Punjab to Tibet.

(ii) THE INDUS-GANGA BRAHMAPUTRA PLAIN: The Great Plain of India is formed by the Indus, Ganga and the Brahmaputra rivers. This is the largest alluvial tract of the world extending for 3,200 kilometres between the mouths of the Ganga and the Indus, all along the foot of the mountain rim, with a width varying from 150 to 300 kilometres.

Sub Divisions: Though the northern plain does not exhibit much relief yet there are certain relief features which help us to subdivide it.

(a) The Punjab Plain : This plain means the plain of five rivers or doabs viz., the Satluj, the Beas, the Ravi, the Chenab and the Jhelum. Its Western part is in Pakistan and the eastern part in India. Its tributaries are divided into many doabs. **Bist-Jalandhar Doab** between Beas and Sutlej rivers, **Bari Doab** between Beas and Ravi Rivers, ***Rachna Doab*** between Ravi and Chenab, **Chaj Doab** between Chenab and Jhelum, **Sind Sagar Doab** between Jhelum, Chenab and Indus. It has low flood plains called **Bet** and its border is called **Dhaya.**

(b) The Ganga Plain : It lies in Uttar Pradesh, Bihar and Bengal. It covers 3.57 lakh sq. km. The tributaries of Ganga on its north are the **Gomti, Ghaghra, Gandak, Kosi, Mahanaadi, Kali,** Tista Chambal in the South and in the South are **Son falls, Betwa** and **Ken**. It comprises of **Bhabar, Terai, Khadar** and **Bangar Belts.**

(c) The Deltic Plain of Bengal : It is situated in West Bengal. It is far more extensive and stands 960 kms from the Chenab hills to the Delta. The doab between Ganga and Brahmaputra rivers in the north is also included in it which is called *Para-delta.*

(d) The Assam Plain or Brahmaputra Plain : This plain extends for a distance of about 640 km. from Dhubri to Sadiya. This plain is formed by the sediment brought by the Brahmaputra and its tributaries. Floods are the common feature.

Bhabar	Tarai
1. It lies along the foot of the Shiwaliks from the Indus to the Tista.	1. It lies to the south of the Bhabar and run parallel to it.
2. It is 8 to 16 kms parallel to Shiwalik foot hills at the break up of the slope.	2. It is 20 to 30 kms wide.
3. It comprises of pebble-studded rocks in the shape of porus beds.	3. Most of the streams and rivers re-emerge without any having properly demarcated Channel, thereby creating marshy and swampy conditions known as *Tarai*
4. Due to porosity of the rocks, the streams disappear and flow underground.	4. The underground streams of the bhabar re-emerge on the surface and give birth to marshy area.
5. This region is not much suitable for agriculture.	5. Most parts of the tarai area are reclaimed for agriculture.

(iii) PENINSULAR PLATEAU : This plateau is situated in a triangular form in Southern India. Its southern apex is rising from the height of 150 m above the river plains upto an elevation of 600-900 m Kanyakumari. On its eastern side is Bay of Bengal and on the Western side is the Arabian Sea. Its northern side is concav-spreading from Salt Range (Pakistan), the Aravalis, Bundelkhand, Baghelkhand, Rajmahal Hills, Chotanagpur Plateau to Shillong Plateau. It is the oldest landmass of India whose general elevation is 600-800 metres. Its eastern and western sides are represented by Eastern Ghats and Western Ghats. This vast plateau is 1600 kms. long in north-south direction and 1400 kms. wide in east-west direction. The Narmada Tapi trough divides this great plateau into the ***Malwa Plateau*** and the ***Deccan Plateau***.

(a) The Malwa Plateau: The triangular portion lying north-west of Narmada-Tapi rivers and the Vindhyachal Range is known as the Malwa Plateau. Its normal slope is towards northeast as a result of which the Chambal and the Betwa rivers flowing through this part of the plateau join the Yamuna river. The Chambal river has cut deep ravines and gullies and the area is usually termed as ***badland***. This is not fit for cultivation. The further extension of this plateau are the Bundelkhand, the Ruhelkhand and the Chota Nagpur Plateau.

(b) The Central Highlands : The western and the north-western flank of the plateau is occupied by the Aravallis, relict mountain range much denuded and forming discontinuous ridges. The Aravalis run for a distance of about 800 kms. from Ahmedabad to Delhi. It reaches its maximum height of 1722 at Guru Shikhar in Mt. Abu. Having a north-east-south-west axis, the Aravalis form discontinuous ridges between Gujarat and Delhi. The main hills lie in Rajasthan having an imposing relief south-west of Ajmer. However, they fan out in parallel series of low ridges, north-west of Jaipur towards Haryana. On the periphery of the Vindhayan upland to the west of the Aravali Range lies the sandy waste of the Thar Desert. This is an area of arid topography with a vast expanse of crescent shaped sand dunes called ***Barkhans***. These sand dunes give way to the longitudinal sand ridges in Jaisalmer and beyond the Indo-Pakistan border in Sind.

(c) The Deccan Plateau: This is again a triangular plateau located in the south of River Tapi. Its north-west boundary is demarcated by the Satpura and Vindhyachal ranges while its northern border is flanked by the Mahadev and the Makala ranges. Its western and eastern flanks are represented by the Western Ghats and the Eastern Ghats respectively. Its average altitude is 600 metres although it rises to 1000 metres in the south and slopes down to 500 metres in the north. The general slope of this plateau is from west to east, that is why most of the rivers of the plateau flow from west to east. The Narmada and the Tapi are the two exceptions which flow from east to west.

(d) North Eastern Plateau: In fact it is an extension of the main Peninsular plateau. It is believed that due to the force exerted by the northeastward movement of the Indian plate at the time of the Himalayan origin, a huge fault was created between the Rajmahal hills and the Meghalaya plateau. Later, this depression got filled up by the deposition activity of the numerous rivers. Today, the Meghalaya and Karbi Anglong plateau stand detached from the main Peninsular Block. The Meghalaya plateau is further sub-divided into three : (i) The Garo Hills; (ii) The Khasi Hills; (iii) The Jaintia Hills, named after the tribal groups inhabiting this region. An extension of this is also seen in the Karbi Anglong hills of Assam. Similar to the Chotanagpur plateau, the Meghalaya plateau is also rich in mineral resources like coal, iron ore, sillimanite, limestone and uranium. This area receives maximum rainfall from the south west monsoon. As a result, the Meghalaya plateau has a highly eroded surface. Cherrapunji displays a bare rocky surface devoid of any permanent vegetation cover.

The north-western part of Deccan plateau is known as the ***Deccan Trap***. It has been formed by the flow of lava occurred during volcanic activities. The trap is made up of basalt, and igneous rock. The black soil of the trap is ideal for cotton cultivation. **The Vidharbha** plains, the **Upper Godawari Basin** and the **Bhima Basin** are the three well-defined physical units of Deccan Trap. They are separated from one another by low hills and tabular uplands.

The **Malnad** and the **Maidan** are two subdivisions of the Karnataka Plateau. The Malnad is thickly forested upland having ***Baba Budhan*** as its highest hill. The Maidan is a rolling plateau with low relief.

THE WESTERN GHATS: It extends from the Tapi river in the north to Kanya Kumari in the south and forms the western boundary of the Deccan Plateau. It forms almost a continuous wall and can be crossed only through gaps. These gaps are the Thalghat, Bhorghat, Palghat or the Shencottah gap. These gaps are used by rail routes. The southern part of the Western Ghats is characterised by the presence of the Nilgiri, the Anamalai and the Cardamom Hills. The ***Anai Mudi*** (2695 metres) and the ***Doda Betta*** (2637 metres) are two important peaks of these hills. The **Anaimudi** is the highest peak of peninsular India.

THE EASTERN GHATS: The Eastern Ghats are generally less impressive and form a discontinuous crest on the eastern periphery of the plateau. They do not have any structural unity or a well-defined layout. They are represented by an irregular line of hills, such as the Nallamalais, Velikondas, Palkondas and the Pachmalais. These hills are often referred to as the **Northern hills** in the northern sector, **Cuddapah Ranges** in the middle and the **Tamil Nadu hills** in the south. In terms of altitude they rarely exceed 900 metres but their highly dissected character poses difficulties in cross communication. The Mahanadi, Godavari, Krishna, and the Cauvery rivers cut across the Eastern Ghats to reach the Bay of Bengal.

Comparison Between Western Ghats and Eastern Ghats	
Western Ghats	**Eastern Ghats**
1. They are higher. The highest peak in the Western Ghats is Anaimudi with a height of 2,695 m.	1. They are lower. The highest peak in the Eastern Ghats is Mahendragiri with a height of 1,500 m.
2. They rise steeply. from the West Coast.	2. They rise gently from the east coast.
3. The hills are continuous	3. The hills are discontinuous.
4. All the rivers of the Deccan plateau rise in the Western Ghats.	4. The rivers cut valleys through the Eastern Ghats.

(iv) THE COASTAL PLAINS : The Great Plateau is flanked by narrow coastal strips on both west and east sides along the Arabian Sea and the Bay of Bengal respectively. These are commonly known as the West Coastal plain and the East Coastal plain and are parts of the Great Indian Plains.

POINTS TO REMEMBER

- ❖ Two notable inlets in the western coastal plains are the Gulf of Kachchh and Gulf of Khambhat.
- ❖ Lake Vembanad, about 63 km in length is the longest lake.

(a) The West Coastal Plain: The West Coastal Plain spreads from Gujarat to the Kanya Kumari. Going from north to south it goes on narrowing. It is uneven and has been dissected by numerous fast-flowing rivers—the Narmada and the Tapti are among them. The plain is divided into two parts—the northern and the southern. The northern part from Gujarat to Goa is called ***Konkan coast*** while the southern ***Malabar coast*** from Goa to the Kanniyakumari. Konkan is 50-80 kms. wide and characterised with estuaries while ***Malabar*** is characterised with lagoons, estuaries and back waters (Kayals). *Lagoons* are salt water lakes, separated from the main sea by sands bars and spits.

POINTS TO REMEMBER

- ❖ Lake Chilka in Orissa, Kolleru and Pulicat in Andhra Pradesh are among the large lakes found in eastern coastal plains.

(b) The East Coastal Plain: Along the Bay of Bengal, the extendy a comparatively wide and level plain from Orissa to the Kanniyakumari known as the East Coastal Plain. It also has two parts—the northern and southern. The northern part is ***North Circar plain*** and the southern is ***Coromandel plain.*** The Mahanadi, the Godavari, the Krishna and the Cauvery are major rivers which originate from the great plateau and form deltas at their mouth. A chain of bars is found along the coast that has given birth to numerous lagoons. The Chilka and the Pulicat present good example of lagoons.

West Coast of Peninsular India	East Coast of Peninsular India
1. It lies along the Arabian Sea.	1. It lies along the Bay of Bengal.
2. It is narrow and uneven.	2. It is wider and more level.
3. It has estuaries and lagoons.	3. It has fertile deltas of rivers.
4. Known as the Konkan Coast in Maharashtra, Kanara Coast in Karnataka and Malabar Coast in Kerala.	4. Known as the Northern Circars in the North and Coromandal Coast in the South.

(v) THE GREAT INDIAN DESERT : The Great Indian Desert lies to the west of the Aravali Range. It occupies a major part of the state of Rajasthan and extends into Sind, Pakistan as the Thar Desert.

The land is generally flat and covered with sandy soil. It is a dry region with hardly and rivers. Streams appear during the rainy season, and disappear after that.

The rivers do not have enough water to reach the sea. They dry up or disappear into the sand. This is an area of inland drainage. **Luni** is the only large river in this region.

(vi) THE ISLANDS: The Islands of India are usually divided into two parts (a) Islands close to the coast (b) Islands distant from the coast.

Besides mainland, Indian territory also extends into the Arabian Sea and the Bay of Bengal in the form of the Lakshadweep and the Andaman and Nicobar Islands, respectively. The Lakshadweep meaning a hundred thousand islands is a group of 36 coral islands in the Arabian Sea and none of them is more than a couple of square kilometres in area. The Andamans and Nicobars are a cluster of Islands stretched almost in a line. There are as many as 200 islands in the Andaman groups alone extending for 350 kilometres. There are 19 islands in the Nicobar group. Some of the islands extend from 60 to 100 km, forming a cluster south of the Andaman group. They are fairly large and more numerous than the Lakshadweeps. The Lakshadweeps extend just to the north of the independent country known as the Maldives. The Islands of Andaman and Nicobar are remnants of the sub-merged mountain range, which was an extension of the Arakan mountains of Myanmar and continued through the islands of Java and Sumatra in Indonesia.

These islands, formed of coral deposits are called *atolls* which is originally derived from the Malayalam word '*Atolu*'

- Andaman and Nicobar are separated by a deep sea known as the *Ten Degree Channel* since it coincides with 10°N latitude.
- Lagoons are salt-water lakes which are separated from the sea by the formation of sand bars along the coast.
- Lakshadweep is a coral island.
- On April 10, 1991, India's only volcano erupted in Barren Island in the Andamans after lying dormant for 200 years.

SOME IMPORTANT PEAKS IN ANDAMAN & NICOBAR ISLANDS

☞ Saddle Peak (North Andaman)	-	738 m
☞ Mount Diavolo (North Andaman)	-	515 m
☞ Mount Koyab (South Andaman)	-	460 m
☞ Mount Thuiller (Great Andaman)	-	642 m

INDIA'S DRAINAGE PATTERN

The area drained by a single river system is called a drainage basin or river basin. The rivers in India have been more or less adjusted to its physical conditions. It is largely influenced by the evolution of three fold physiographic divisions.

CLASSIFICATION

Broadly speaking the river systems of the country can be classified on the basis of their origin in two categories (i) **the Himalayan rivers** and (ii) **the peninsular** rivers.

A. THE HIMALAYAN RIVERS

The Himalayan Rivers have very large basins. These rivers aided by the bold features of Himalayan relief, continue to perform intensive erosional activity. They display a meandering tendency. Another striking feature of the Himalayan rivers is seen in their flow pattern which is perennial and is derived from rainfall as well as the snow-melt. **The peninsular rivers**, on the other hand, flow through shallow valleys which are more or less completely graded in most cases. The smooth longitudinal profiles of these rivers indicate that they have very little erosional activity to perform. A large number of them are seasonal as their flow is mainly dependent on rainfall. This immensely reduces their value as a source for irrigation. The hard rocked and the predominantly non-alluvial character of the Plateau surface hardly allows any significant meandering. Many of the peninsular rivers have straight and generally linear courses.

ANNUAL PRECIPITATION IN INDIA

The total volume of annual precipitation in India has been estimated at about 37,00,400 million cubic metres, of which about 45.3% flow through 113 rivers.

The rivers originating in the Himalayan mountain complex consists of 3 systems : (i) the Indus system (ii) the Ganga system and (iii) the Brahmaputra systems

(i) THE INDUS SYSTEM

This system comprises river Indus and its five tributaries-Chenab, Jhelum, Ravi, Beas and Sutlej.

RIVERS OF NORTHERN INDIA

- They are perennial rivers.
- They are fed by the melting of the snow.
- They are prone to floods.
- They are suitable for navigation as they flow slowly in the plains.
- They have large basin and catchment areas.
- They form big deltas at the mouth.

The Indus rises from a glacier near Bokhar Chan in Tibet at an altitude of 4,164 metres near the Mansarovar lake and enters Indian territory in Jammu and Kashmir. It is known as **Singi Kham ban** or Lion's mouth. It flows through Ladakh, Baltistan and Gilgit to finally emerge out of the hills at Attock. The collective flow of its well-known Punjab tributaries—Sutlej, Beas, Ravi, Chenab and Jhelum—goes to make the *Panjnad* which falls into the mainstream a little above Mithankot. The Indus flows south-westwards across Pakistan to reach the Arabian Sea east of Karachi.

The Indus is considered as one of the largest rivers of the world, with the catchment area of 1,165,000 sq. km of which as much as 321,289 sq. km lies in India and with 9 total length of 2,880 km (in India 1,114 km).

(a) The Jhelum : The Jhelum is an important tributary of the Indus. It rises from a spring at Verinag, situated in the south-eastern part of the valley of Kashmir. Its Sanskrit name is ***Vitasta*** and is called ***Veth*** in Kasmir. Its total length is 400 km and drainage area is 28,490 km^2 in India and it flows in India and Pakistan. It joins the Chenab near Jhang in Pakistan.

(b) The Chenab : It is called ***Asikini*** in Sanskrit and is formed by the confluence of ***Chandra*** and ***Bhaga*** in H.P., so is called Chandra Bhaga in H.P. It flows north-westwards and runs parallel to Pir Panjal for some distance. Its length is 1,180 km and its catchment area is 5,967 sq. km in India. The main tributary is Tavi.

(c) The Ravi : It rises west to the Rohtang Pass in the Kullu hills of H.P. and flows between Pir Panjal and Dhauladhar ranges. Its Sanskrit name is ***Iravati.*** It meets Chenab and enters Panchnad. Its length is 725 km and has a catchment area of about 6,000 sq. km.

(d) The Beas : Its Sanskrit name is ***Vipasha*** and it rises from the southern end of Rohtang Pass at the height of 4,000 m. It makes the famous Kullu Valley. It is 470 km long. Its catchment area is about 26,000 sq. km. It meets the Sutlej near Harike.

(e) The Sutlej : Its Sanskrit name is ***Shatdru.*** It originates from Rakas lake at an altitude of 4,555 m in Tibet. It flows for about 1,050 km and drains 24,087 km^2 of area in India. It is very important tributary as it feeds the canal system of Bhakra Nangal Project, Harike and Sirhind.

(f) The Sarswati : It was once an important tributary of the Indus. Now lost in the sands of the Thar, it is believed that flowing under ground, the Sarswati joins the Ganga at her confluence with Yamuna at Prayag in Allahabad. The place where the three rivers meet is known as ***Triveni Sangam.***

(ii) THE GANGA SYSTEM

The Ganga rises in the U.P. Himalayas. The river acquires its name after its headstreams—Alaknanda and Bhagirathi uniting at Devaprayag. The main southern tributary is the Son while, Yamuna is its left bank tributary. Besides the minor streams of the Tons and the Punpun. On its left bank, the Ganga, however, receives a larger number of tributaries, including the Ramganga, Gomati, Ghaghra, Gandak, Kosi and the Mahananda. Beyond Farakka the mainstream of the Ganga flows east-south east wards into Bangladesh and is known as ***Padma.*** In this reach, the river is known as ***Bhagirathi-Hooghly.*** Before falling into the Bay of Bengal below Chandipur in Bangladesh, the Padma receives the Brahmaputra, known here as the **Yamuna**, and the **Meghna**.

The river has a length of 2,525 km. It is shared by Uttranchal (119 km) and Uttar Pradesh (1450 km), Bihar (445 km) and West Bengal (520 km) The Ganga basin covers about 8.6 km^2 in India alone.

FACTS
❖ An ice cave, ***Gaumukh,*** meaning the cow's mouth, in Himalayas is the source of Ganga.
❖ The river forms a delta called *Sunderbans*, near the Bay of Bengal.
❖ After Farakka, the Ganga enters Bangladesh and is called *Padma*.

(a) The Yamuna : is the most important and longest tributary of the Ganga. It has its source in the Yamunotri glacier on the Banderpunch range. Its basin area is 3,66,223 km^2. It joins the river on its right bank at Prayag. The confluence of the Ganga and Yamuna is called *Sangam.* Agra is an important city situated on the banks of Yamuna. Chambal and Betwa are tributaries of Yamuna while Son and Damodar are tributaries of the Ganga. The Yamuna drains the areas of Uttranchal, Delhi and Uttar Pradesh.

(b) The Sharda or Saryu : Known by various names Kali in the Himalayas, the Sharda in Pilibhit and Kheri districts and Chauka before it joins the right bank of Ghaghara. It rises in the Milan glacier in the Nepal Himalayas. It runs along the Indo-Nepal boundary and leaves Himalayas at Baramdeo.

(c) The Ramganga : The river is the left bank tributary of the Ganga. It rises near Nainital and has a length of 690 km. It meets Ganga near Farrukhabad.

(e) The Gomti : This is the only tributary river of the Ganga which rises in the plains and not in the hills. It meets the Ganga down Varanasi.

(f) The Ghaghra : It originates in the glaciers of Map chachungo. This river rises parallel to the Ganga in U.P. and its source is east of the Ganga. The river Sarda (Kali or Kali Ganga) joins it in the plains before it joins the Ganga near Chapra. It is 1,080 km long and its catchment area is 127,500 sq. km.

(g) The Gandak : It rises near Sino-Nepal boundary and drains the central part of Nepal. It is called the **Narayani** in Nepal. It is 425 km long and drains 45,800 sq. km. It comprises two streams namely **Kali Gandak** and **Trishul Ganga.** It meets the Ganga near Bankipur in Bihar.

(h) The Kosi : The Kosi is an anticedent river with its source to the North of Mt. Everest in Tibet where its main stream **Arun** rises. After crossing the Central Himalayas in Nepal it is joined by Son Kosi from the West and the Tamil Kosi from the east. It forms Sapt Kosi after the uniting with River Arun. It drains eastern Nepal and enters Saharsa district of Bihar in numerous channels. The river is notorious for shifting its course, depositing silt and causing floods. It joins the Ganga at Keragola.

(i) The Damodar : It occupies the eastern margins of the Chhotanagpur plateau where it flows through a graben or a rift valley. The Barakar is its main tributary. The Damodar finally joins the Hugli. River Damodar is known as the ***Sorrow of Bengal*** as it causes mass destruction of floods.

(j) The Mahananda : It is another tributary of the Ganga rising in the Darjiling hills. It joins the Ganga as its last left bank tributary in West Bengal.

(k) The Son : It is a large south bank tributary of the Ganga, originating in the Amarkantak plateau. After forming a series of waterfalls at the edge of the plateau, it reaches Arrah, west of Patna to join Ganga.

(iii) THE BRAHMAPUTRA RIVER SYSTEM

It is formed by the Brahmaputra river which is about 2,700 km in length. It has its origin in the Chemayundung glacier of the Kailash range near the Mansarovar Lake. From here it traverses eastward longitudinally for a distance of nearly 1200 km in a dry and flat region of Southern Tibet and is known as ***Tsang-Po*** which means the Purifier. The **Rango Tsangpo** is major right bank tributary of this river in Tibet. It emerges as a turbulent and dynamic river after carving out a deep gorge in the Central Himalayas near Namcha Barwa (7,755 m). The river emerges from the foothill under the name of **Siang** or **Dihang**. It is also known as Brahmaputra as it turns south wards in Arunachal Pradesh and enters Assam.

It has a long mountain stage and therefore, carries a lot of sediment. When it enters the plains, it slow down suddenly, depositing its load causing it to split into 2 to 3 channels forming island in its course. Such a river is called a ***Braided River.***

The Brahmaputra's tributaries are Tista, Subansiri, Barali, Manas, Dhansiri, Buri and Dihing. The world's largest river island, named ***Majauli*** is situated in river Brahmaputra (Assam).

THE BRAHMAPUTRA RIVER

❖ The Brahmaputra, one of the largest rivers in the world is known by different names as :
- Tsang-Po in Tibet.
- Brahmaputra in India.
- Jamuna in Bangladesh.

❖ The Brahmaputra is the only river in India with a male name. It means 'Son of Lord Brahma'.

❖ The Brahmaputra is also called the 'Red River' of India because during floods its water looks reddish in colour after mixing with the red soil of Assam.

RIVER OF PENINSULAR INDIA

- They are non-perennial rivers.
- Water provided by the monsoons.
- They are not prone to floods.
- They are unsuitable for navigation as they are swift-flowing.
- They have small basin and catchment area.
- They have little erosion activities.

MAJOR RIVERS OF THE PENINSULAR PLATEAU

The Narmada (1312 km) rises on the Amarkantak Plateau in the Maikala Range from a spring at a height of 1060 m. It flows west and south-west through a valley between the Vindhya and the Satpura ranges. At Bheraghat, it drops through a height of 15 m forming the famous **Marble Falls.** It then flows through a gorge and forms a large estuary before flowing into the Gulf of Khambhat.

The Tapi (724 km, also known as the Tapti) rises from Multai in the Betul district in the Satpura Hills. It flows westwards, north of Surat and into the Gulf of Khambhat. Nearly 79% of its basin lies in Maharashtra, 15% in M.P. and remaining 6% in Gujarat.

The Purna, Girna and Panjhara are its large tributaries.

The Mahanadi (851 km) has its source in the Maikala Hills in Madhya Pradesh and flows through the state of Orissa. It forms a very large delta before flowing into the Bay of Bengal. 53% of its drainage basin lies in Madhya Pradesh and Chhattisgarh while 47% lies in Orissa.

The Godavari (1465 km) is the largest river of the Deccan Plateau. Its basin covers about 10% of the total area of India. It is called **Vridha Ganga** or Dakhsin Ganga because of its huge size. It rises in the Western Ghats in the Nasik district of Maharashtra. It flows for several kilometres through a gorge before reaching the city of Nasik. After flowing through Maharashtra, the Godavari flows through the Telangana region of Andhra Pradesh. It forms a large delta at its mouth before draining into the Bay of Bengal. 49% of its catchment area (total 3.13 lakh sq. km) lies in Maharashtra, 20% in Madhya Pradesh and Chhattisgarh, and rest in Andhra Pradesh. Its principle tributaries are **Penganga, Indravati Pranhita** and **Manjira**.

The Darna, Pravara, Manjra, Pranhita and Indravati are its important tributaries.

The Krishna (1401) km) is the second largest east-flowing Peninsular river which rises in the Mahabaleshwar Hills and flows eastwards towards the south and into the Bay of Bengal. 27% of its catchment area lies in Maharashtra, 44% in Karnataka and 29% in A.P.

Bhima is its largest tributary. The other large tributaries are ***Koyna, Tungabhadra, Varna, Panchaganga*** and ***Dudhaganga***.

The Kaveri (800 km) (cavery) is known as the "Ganga of the South". It rises in the Coorg district of Karnataka.

About 3% of its basin falls in Kerala, 41% in Karnataka and 56% in Tamil Nadu. Its important tributaries are Kabini, Bhavani and Amravati.

It has several rapids and waterwalls in its course. At Sivasamundram it plunges from a height of 100 m forming the famous **Siva Samundram Falls.** It forms a large delta in Tamil Nadu before flowing into the Bay of Bengal.

The Sharavati in Karnataka is well known for its **Gersoppa (Jog) Falls.** During the Monsoon season these falls can be considered as one of the world's greatest waterfalls. But like all rivers of the Deccan Plateau, the Sharavati has very little water in the dry season.

The Sabarmati and the Brahmani : These two rivers interposed between the Ganga and the Mahanadi deltas and drain an area of 19,300 sq. kms and 39,033 sq. kms. respectively. Jharkhand, Orissa, West Bengal and Madhya Pradesh share the drainage basin of these two rivers. The Brahmani is known as south Koel in its upper reaches in Jharkhand.

The Sabarmati and the Mahi : Sabarmati and Mahi drain from the north-west part of Peninsular India. The Sabarmati originates in the Aravalli hills and flows for a distance of 300 kms. in south-south westward direction for 300 kms to fall in Arabian Sea. The Mahi originates in the east of Udaipur and drains an area of 34,842 sq. kms. and Sabarmati drains an area of 21,674 sq. kms. Mahi falls into the Gulf of Khambhat.

The Chambal : It originates in the Vindhya range and flows towards the north generally in a gorge upto Kota. Below Kota it turns to the north-east direction and after reaching Pinahat it turns to the east and runs nearly parallel to the Yamuna before joining it in the southern part of the Etawah in Uttar Pradesh. It is 1050 kms in length.

The Sone : It rises in the Amarkantak plateau. It flows for some distance to the north and meets the Kaimur range which turns its course towards the north-east. Almost all of its tributaries join it on its right bank and it joins Ganga near Ramnagar after covering a distance of 780 kms.

B. THE PENINSULAR RIVERS

The Western Ghats is the main watershed in the Peninsula. Major rivers of the Peninsula such as the Mahanadi, Godavari, Krishna, Cauvery flow eastwards on the plateau and drain into the Bay of Bengal. These rivers have built huge deltas near their mouths. Rivers which flow westwards from the Western Ghats are generally small. Narmada and Tapi (or Tapti) are the important west flowing streams which occupy structural depressions.

Classification of Peninsular Rivers: These rivers can be divided into three drainage systems.

(i) Towards the Ganga : Chambal, Betwa, Ken, Sind, Son. These rivers rise in the Vindhya range and Join the Yamuna or the Ganga.

(ii) Towards the Arabian Sea : Narmada and Tapi are two large rivers, flowing westwards between the Vindhya and the Satpura ranges and flow into Arabian sea. The Luni, Sabarmati and Mahi are short and swift rivers. Both the west flowing rivers, i.e. Narmada and Tapti do not make delta. Actually, they flow on a steep slopy area which doesn't provide favourable conditions for delta formation. Thus, they make estuaries.

(iii) Towards the Bay of Bengal : The Mahanadi, Godavari, Krishna and Kaveri (cauvery) rise in the Western Ghats and flow into Bay of Bengal.

DIFFERENCE BETWEEN THE HIMALAYAN AND PENINSULAR RIVER SYSTEM

THE HIMALAYAN RIVER SYSTEM	PENINSULAR RIVER SYSTEM
1. These rivers occupy large basins and catchment area	1. These rivers have small basins and catchment areas. The Godavari having basin area of 3.12 lakh sq. kms is less than 1/3rd of Indus (11.65 sq. kms.)
2. The Himalayan rivers flow through deep I-shaped valleys called gorges which have been carved out by downcutting carried on side by side with the uplift of the Himalayas. They signify antecedent drainage.	2. Peninsular rivers flow in more or less graded valley having little erosional activities to perform. They signify consequent drainage.
3. The Himalayan rivers are perennial in nature where water flows throughout the year received from both snow melt and monsoon rain.	3. These rivers receive water only from monsoon rainfall and flows in rainy seasons. Therefore they are seasonal rivers.
4. These rivers flow across the young fold mountain and are still in youthful stage.	4. These rivers have attained maturity because they flow through oldest plateaus of the world.
5. These rivers form meander in plain areas because of huge sediment carried and deposited by them in the plains which obstruct their flow and force them to flow in zig-zag shape (meander).	5. These rivers have been flowing on the oldest plateau having hard rock surface of non-alluvial character forcing them not to flow in zig-zag shape. As such they flow in more or less in straight course.
6. The Himalayan rivers form huge delta at their mouth which is the result of deposition of sediment at mouth.	6. The river like Narmada and Tapti make estuaries whereas other big river forms deltas like Godavari and Cauvery.

C. DRAINAGE OF THE THAR DESERT REGION

The only river rising or flowing through this area which reaches the sea is the Luni which falls into the Arabian Sea after passing through the Rann of Kachchh. The other streams of the inland drainage basin either drain towards the individual basins or salt lakes like the Sambhar or are lost in the sands.

THE RIVER REGIMES

The pattern of the seasonal flow of water in a river is called its **regime**. The main differences in the flow patterns of the Himalayan and the Peninsular rivers are in fact caused by the differences in the two climatic regimes. The Himalayan river regimes are monsoonal as well as glacial. The regimes of the Peninsular rivers, on the other hand, are only monsoonal as they are controlled by rainfall alone. The Ganga has its minimum flow in the period January-June. The maximum is attained in either August or September. The river has thus, a typical monsoonal regime. The Jhelum attains its maximum in June, or even in May, as its flow is mainly derived from the snow-melt from the Himalayas. Two peninsular rivers display interesting differences from the Himalayan rivers in their regimes. The Narmada has a very low volume of discharge from January to July which suddenly rises in August when maximum is attained. The Godavari flows at a low level until May. It has a double maxima—one in May-June and the other in July-August. After August there is a sharp fall in discharge.

The data on water discharge in different rivers in different parts of the year have important implications to their utilization by states. It is on this count that the inter-state disputes arise.

RIVERS AND THEIR TRIBUTARIES

River	Sources	Total Length (Kms)	Area Drained (Kms)	Tributaries
Indus and its Tributaries				
Indus	At an altitude of 5080 mt in Tibet near Mansarover Lake	1114 km (India)	321289	Zanskar, Astar, Dras, Shyok, Skardu, Swat, Kurram, Shigar, Gilgit, Kabul, Jhelum, Chenab, Ravi, Beas and Sutlej
Jhelum	From a mountain spur at Verinage	400 (India)	28490	
Chenab	At an elevation of 4900 mt. At Lahul	1800 (India)	26750	
Ravi	Kulu Hills of H.P.	725	14442	
Beas	Kulu Hills near Rohtang Pass	460	20303	
Sutlej	At 4570 mt. Height near Dharma Pass	1050 (India)	24087	Beas joins at Harike
Ganga and its Tributaries				
Ganga (comprised of two streams)	Alaknanda at an elevation of 7800 mt. at an elevation of 6600 mt.	2525	861452	Yamuna, Ram-Ganga, Gandak, Kosi, Ghaghara, Burhihead, Gandak, Gomti, Bhagirathi-at, an Baghmati, Gomti, Son, Mahanada Kamla, Damodar, Jalangi, Bhairab confluence of Yamuna at Allahabad
Yamuna	from a hot spring at Yamunotri, 6330 mt	1300	359000	Chambal, Betwa, Hindu Ken, Sarda.
Ram Ganga	Near Nainital, 3110 mt. Height	596	32412	Khos, Gangan, Anil-Kosi, Deoha Join Ganga below Farukkhabad
Ghaghara	Near Manearovan Lake	1080	127950	Rapti, Sarda
Gandak	In the central Himalaya Near Tibet, 7620 mt.	425 (India)	9540 (India)	In Nepal called "Narayani, Join Ganga near Patna.
Burhi Gandak	Somesar Hill, 330 mt.	320	10150	Join Ganga at Monghyr.
Kosi	From Tibet/Nepal	730 (India)	11600	Kosi, Arun, Tamur.
Damodar	Chotanagpur Plateau near Tori, 1366 mt.	541	22000	Join Hooghly below Kolkatta Gartus, Konar, Jomunia, Barakar.
Gomti	east of Pilibhit Town	940	30437	Sai, Barma, Saryu, Chuha,
Brahmaputra and Its Tributaries				
Brahmaputra	Chemayungdung glacier, Near Mansarovar Lake	916	194413	Rajo-Tsngpo, Lihotse-Dzong, Ngang chu, Kyi chu, Giamdu-chu, Lohit Dihing, Disang, Dhansiri, Tista, Torsa
West Flowing Peninsular Rivers				
Narmada	from a tank in Amarkantak	1312	98796	Burhner, Baiyar, Sher, Dudhi, Shakkar,

	Plateau, 900 mt.			Tawa, Hiran, Tendoni, Barma, Kolar, Anjal, Machak, Kundi, Goi, Karyan.
Tapi (Tapti)	Near Multai in Betul Districts, 792 mt	724	65145	Puma, Betul, wards Vaghur, Patki, Gangal, Dathranj, Bohad, Bori, Anbhora, Khursi, Kapra, Sipra, Garja, Khokri, Utaols, Bhokar, Subi, Mor, Mautri, Gull, Aner, Annavati, Gomti, Harki, Valer,
Luni	From Annasagar in Ajmer	482	37250	
Sabarmati	in Aravalli Hill	371	21674	Wakal, Jawai, Mitri, Sei, Hamov, Hathmathi, Watrak, Meshwa
East Flowing Peninsular Rivers				
Mahanadi	in Raipur districts, 442 mt.	851	141589	Sheonath, Harde, Mand, Lb, Uny Tel.
Brahmani	in Ranchi, 600 mt.	799	39033	Kuru, Sonhked, Tikra
Baitarni	in Bihar, 600 met.	365	12789	
Subaranrekka	in Bihar	395	19296	Konchi, Karffari
Godavari	from Trambak in Nasik, 1067 mt.	1465	312812	Pravara, Mula, Manjra, Pranhita, Penganga, Maner, Wardha, Wainganga, Sabri, Indaravati, Puma.
Manjra	in Bihar district	724	30821	
Penganga	in Buldhana range	676	23888	
Wardha	in Betul district	483	24087	
Wainganga	in Seonl district	462	61093	
Indravati	in Kalahandi district	531	41663	Narangi, Boardig, Kotri, Bandia.
Sabari	in Sulkaram Hill	418	20427	Silaru.
Krishna	Mahabaleshwar, 1360 mt.	1400	258948	Koyna, Yerla, Muneru, Varma, Panchgango, Dudhganga, Ghatprabha, Malprapha, Bhima, Tunghadra, Musi
Bhima	near Bhimeshwar village	867	69144	Ghad, Nira, Kagna, Sina
Tungbhadra	from Gomantak peak		69562	Runga,Bhadra, Hagari.
Cauvery	in Braham giri hills	800	81155	Hemavati, Harangi, Shimas, Lokpovni, Arkavati, Suvashavathi, Kabbani, Bhavani.

FLOOD-PRONE AREAS

Flood is an annual feature in India. Every year about 6 million ha of land is affected by floods. High floods cause considerable damage to crops, houses, public services, loss of human and animal life, and disruption of means of transport and communication. They disturb normal life of the people of the country's total geographical area of 329 mha, 40 mha is prone to floods, out of which 32 million ha can be provided with reasonable degree of protection.

Areas liable to serious flood in the country are the vast northern plains and coastal tracts of large rivers. The Bihar plain, southern and northern parts of West Bengal, the Assam valley and the Cachar valley are known for frequent floods. Areas which experience occasional and less frequent floods in the country are the Kashmir valley, the Punjab plain, the plains of Uttar Pradesh the Mahanadi, the Godavari, the Krishna delta, the Kaveri delta and lower parts of the Narmada and Tapi rivers. Heavy rainfall, gentle slope of river valleys, heavy deposition of silt in river-beds, and deforested hills in the catchment areas are some of the well-known causes of flood. Construction of roads, railways and canals obstructs the free flow of water in some areas and cause flood. Some of the floods in coastal areas are caused by cyclonic storms.

RIVER BASINS OF INDIA : CATCHMENT AREA AND RUN-OFF

River/Basins	Catchment Area (000 km²)	Run off (000 million cubic metres)
Major River Basins		
Indus	321 (total 1,165)	97,350
Ganga	952	4,93,000
Brahmaputra	240 (total 580)	5,10,000
Sabarmati	55	3,200
Mahi	35	8,500
Narmada	99	40,700
Tapi	65	17,980
Subarnarekha	19	7,940
Brahmani	36	8,310
Mahanadi	142	66,640
Godavari	313	1,05,000
Krishna	259	67,670
Penner	55	3,240
Kaveri	68	20,950
Sub Total	**2,659**	**14,06,000**
Medium River Basins	**240**	**1,12,000**
Minor River and Desert Basins	**300**	**1,27,000**
Grand total	**3,199**	**16,45,000**

Large rivers have great water power potential. The Himalayas in the north, the Vindhyas, the Satpura and the Aravalli in the west, the Maikala and Chhotanagpur in the east, the Meghalaya plateau and Purvanchal the northeast, and the Western and the Eastern Ghats of the Deccan plateaus offer possibility of large scale water power development. Sixty per cent of the total river flow is concentrated in the Himalayan rivers, 16 per cent in the Central Indian rivers (the Narmada, the Tapti, the Mahanadi, etc.), and the rest in the rivers of the Deccan plateaus. Dependable power generation from the peninsular rivers required impounding of water during the monsoon months. The Himalayan rivers do not have such problems as their flow is appreciable ever during the critical winter months. They however, have other kind of problems, namely difficulty in construction of large storage on account of narrow valleys, high seismism of the region and vast alluvial plain has no variation in relief. The country has exploitable power potential of about 41 million kw at 60 per cent load factor from these rivers.

The Ganga and the Brahmaputra in north and north eastern part of the country Mahanadi in Orissa, the Godavari and the Krishna in Andhra, the Narmada and the Tapi in Gujarat, and the lakes and tidal creeks in coastal states possess some of the important and useful water ways of the country. In the past they were of great importance, which suffered with the advent of rail and roads. Withdrawal of large quantities of water for irrigation resulted in dwindling flow of many rivers. The country has a navigable water ways of about 10,600 kms—2480 kms of navigable rivers by steamers and large country boats, 3920 kms of navigable rivers by medium sized country boats, and 4200 kms of canals and back waters navigable by country boats. The most important navigable rivers are the Ganga, the Brahmaputra and the Mahanadi. The Godavari, the Krishna, the Narmada and the Tapi are navigable near their mouths only.

The rivers also supply water to cities, villages and big industrial installations.

LAKES

Lakes in India are mainly found in maintainous or coastal regions. The plains have few lakes. On the basis of their origin, they can be classified as under:

1. **Tectonic Lakes :** Wular lake (Kashmir), Kumayun Lakes.
2. **Lakes formed due to Volcanic Activity :** Lunar Lake (Maharashtra).
3. **Lagoon Lakes :** Chilka (Orissa), Pulicat (Tamil Nadu), Kolleru (Andhra Pradesh)
4. **Glacial Lakes :** Khurpataal, Sambal, Punataal, Malwa Tal, Nainitaal Rakastaal, Saataal, Bhimtaal, Navkuchiataal (all Kumayun Himalayas).
5. **Lakes Formed Due to Aeolean Process :** Sambhar, Panchphidra Luna Kransar, Didwana (Rajasthan).
6. **Others :** Dal lake (Kashmir), Udaisagar, Pichola, Rajasamand, Jaisalmer, Annasagar (Rajasthan), Loktak (Manipur), Vembanad (Kerala,), Hussein Sagar (Andhra Pradesh).

WATERFALLS IN INDIA

Name	Height	State
Barehipani Falls	1,309 feet	Orissa
Barkana Falls	850 feet	Karnataka
Beadon Falls	394 feet	Meghalaya
Bishop Falls	443 feet	Meghalaya
Bundla Falls	328 feet	Himachal Pradesh
Cauvery Falls	320 feet	Mysore
Chachai Falls	427 feet	Madhya Pradesh
Dudhsagar Falls	1,017 feet	Goa
Duduma Falls	516 feet	Orissa
Gatha Falls	300 feet	Madhya Pradesh
Ghaghri Falls	320 feet	Jharkhand
Hebbe Falls	551 feet	West Karnataka
Hundru Falls	320 feet	Jharkand
Jog Falls	829 feet	Karnataka
Joranda Falls	492 feet	Orissa
Kalhatti Falls	400 feet	Karnataka
Keoti Falls	427 feet	Madhya Pradesh
Keppa Falls	380 feet	Karnataka
Khandadhar Falls	800 feet	Orissa
Kiliyur Waterfall	300 feet	Tamil Nadu
Koosalli Falls	380 feet	Karnataka
Kudumari Falls	300 feet	Karnataka
Kunchikal Falls	1,493 feet	Karnataka
Kune Falls	656 feet	Maharashtra
Kynrem Falls	1,000 feet	Meghalaya
Langshiang Falls	1,107 feet	Meghalaya
Lodh Falls	468 feet	Jharkhand
Magod Falls	650 feet	Karnataka
Meenmutty Falls	984 feet	Kerala
Muthyala Maduvu Waterfall	300 feet	Karnataka
Nohkalikai Falls	1,100 feet	Meghalaya
Nohsngithiang Falls	1,035 feet	Meghalaya
Palani Falls	492 feet	Himachal Pradesh
Palaruvi Watefalls	300 feet	
Pandavgad Falls	350 feet	Maharashtra

10 CLIMATE, VEGETATION AND SOIL

INDIA'S CLIMATE

India has 'Monsoon' type of climate. The word monsoon has been derived from the Arabic word *'Mausim'* which means seasonal reversal of the winds during the course of the year.

FACTORS AFFECTING THE CLIMATE OF INDIA

(i) Latitude : India lies between 8°N and 37°N latitudes. The Tropic of Cancer passes through the middle of India, thus making the southern half of India in the **Torrid Zone** and the northern half in the **Temperate Zone.**

(ii) Himalaya Mountains: The Himalayas play an important role in lending a sub -tropical touch to the climate of India. The lofty Himalaya Mountains form a barrier which affects the climate of India. It prevents the cold winds of north Asia from blowing into India, thus protecting it from severely cold winters. It also traps the Monsoon winds. forcing them to shed their moisture within the sub-continent.

(iii) Altitude: Temperature decreases with height. Places in the mountains are cooler than places on the plains. Places on the Deccan Plateau are not very hot in spite of being near the Equator.

(iv) Distance from the Sea: With a long coastline, large coastal areas have an equable climate. Areas in the interior of India are far away from the moderating influence of the sea. Such areas have extremes of climate.

(v) Geographical Limits

(i) Western Disturbances : The low pressure systems that originate over the eastern Mediterranean region in winter and move eastwards towards India passing over Iran, Afghanistan and Pakistan are responsible for the winter rain in northern India.

(ii) Conditions in the Regions Surrounding India: Temperature and pressure conditions in East Africa, Iran, Central Asia and Tibet determine the strength of the monsoons and the occasional dry spells. For example, high temperatures in East Africa may draw the monsoon winds from the Indian Ocean into that region thus, causing a dry spell.

(iii) Conditions Over the Ocean : The weather conditions over the Indian Ocean and the China Sea may be responsible for typhoons which often affect the east coast of India.

(iv) Jet Streams : Air currents in the upper layers of the atmosphere known as jet steams could determine the arrival of the monsoons and departure of the monsoons. The Scientists are studying the jet streams and how it may affect the climate of India but much remains to be learned about this phenomena.

CLIMATE OF INDIA
1. The whole of India has a tropical monsoonal climate, since ○ the greater part of the country lies within the tropics, and ○ the climate is influenced by the S.W. and N.E. Monsoons. 2. The position of the mountain ranges and direction of the rainbearing winds are the two main factors that determine the climate of India. 3. Alternating season is the chief characteristic of India's climate.

CLIMATIC REGIONS OF INDIA

A climatic region is a homogeneous climatic condition which is the result of combined effects of climatic factors. The two important factors of climatic classification are ***temperature*** and ***rainfall.***

KOPPEN'S CLIMATIC CLASSIFICATION

The following five climatic regions have been identified in India according to Koppen's climatic classification : He used letters A, B, C, D and E to denote these climatic types:

A - Tropical climate (with mean monthly temperature over 18°C).

B - Dry climate (If dryness is less, semi desert (S); if it is more, desert (W).

C - Warm climate (with mean temperature between 18°C and 3°C).

D - Snow climate (with mean temperature under – 3°C).

E - Ice Climate (mean temperature under –10°C).

Koppen further sub-divided these types on the basis of seasonal variations e.g. f (sufficient precipitation) m (rain forest despite a dry monsoon season) w (dry winter) h (dry and hot) c (less than 4 months with mean temperature over 10°C) and g (Gangetic plain).

CLIMATIC REGIONS OF INDIA ACCORDING TO KOPPEN'S SCHEME

Type of Climate	Areas
Amw - Monsoon with short dry winter	♦ West Coast of India, South of Goa
As - Monsoon with dry Summer	♦ Coromondal coast of Tamil Nadu
Aw - Tropical Savannah	♦ Most of the Peninsular Plateaus, south of the Tropic of Cancer
BShw - Semi arid steppe climate	♦ North western Gujarat, Same parts of West Rajasthan and Punjab
BWhw - Hot Desert	♦ Extreme Western Rajasthan
Cwg - Monsoon with dry winter	♦ Ganga plain, eastern Rajasthan, northern M.P., most of NE India.
Dfc - Cold humid winter with short summer	♦ Arunachal Pradesh
E - Polar type	♦ Jammu and Kashmir, H.P. and Uttaranchal

MOISTURE INDEX OF THORNTHWAITE

Thornthwaite index is based on the concept of water balance. He found out the water balance for each month for all the places. If the water balance had a water surplus solution, it is called *humid* and if it is water deficient it is called *arid*.

He also used English letters to classify different types of climate

1. Prehumid (A)
2. Humid (B)
3. Moist sub-humid (C_2)
4. Dry sub-humid (C_1)
5. Semi-arid (D)
6. Arid (E)

CLIMATIC REGIONS OF INDIA AS PER THORNTHWAITE'S SCHEME

Types of Climate	Areas
A - pre humid	Mizoram, Tripura, Meghalaya, Lower Assam, Arunachal Pradesh in NE India and Western Coast of India, south of Goa.
B - Humid	Nagaland, Upper Assam, Manipur, North Bengal, Sikkim and West Coast.
C_2 - Moist sub-humid	West Bengal, Orissa and Eastern Bihar, Panchmari, eastern slopes of Western Ghats
C_1 - Dry sub humid	Ganga plain, M.P., Chhattisgarh, Jharkhand, northeastern A.P., Northern Punjab and Haryana, north-eastern Tamil Nadu, Uttaranchal, Himachal Pradesh and J & K.
D - Semi Arid	Tamil Nadu, Andhra Pradesh, Karnataka, E. Maharashtra, N.E. Gujarat, Rajasthan and most of Punjab and Haryana
E - Arid	West Gujarat, West Rajasthan and Southern Punjab,

Dr. Trewartha's Classification : As per Dr. Trewartha's modified form of Koppen's classification, India can be divided into following climatic regions.

(i) *Tropical Rain Forest*

(a) This type of climate is found on the west coastal plain and Sahyadris and in parts of Assam.

(b) The temperatures are high, not falling below 18.2°C even during winter and rising to 29°C in April and May, the hottest months.

(c) Dense forests and plantation agriculture with crops like tea, coffee and spices are the characteristic vegetation in the area.

(ii) *Tropical Savanna*

(a) Most of the peninsula, except the semiarid zone in the leeside of the Sahyadris experiences this type of climate.

(b) A long dry weather lasting through winter and early summer and high temperatures remaining above 18.2°C even during the winter season and rising as high as 32°C in summer are the chief characteristics of this climate.

(c) Nagpur has a mean temperature of 35.4°C for May which is the hottest month and 20.7°C for December the coldest month in the year.

(d) The natural vegetation all over the area is savanna.

(iii) *Tropical Semi-arid Steppe Climate*

(a) The rain-shadow belt, running southward from central Maharashtra to Tamil Nadu, in the leeside of the Sahyadris and Cardamom Hills come under this type of climate of low and uncertain rainfall.

(b) Temperatures varying from 20° to 23.8°C for December and 32.8°C for May. Agriculturally, the climate is suitable only for dry farming and livestock rearing.

(iv) *Tropical and Sub-Tropical Steppe*

(a) This type of climate occurs over a broad crescent from Punjab to Kachchh between the Thar Desert to its west and the more humid climates of the Ganga Plain and the Peninsula to its east and south respectively.

(b) The climate, therefore, is transitional between these two areas. The annual rainfall is not only low but it is also highly erratic.

(v) *Tropical Desert*

(a) The western parts of Barmer, Jaisalmer and Bikaner districts of Rajasthan and most of the part of Kachchh form the sandy wastes of the Thar which experiences a typical desert climate.

(b) Ganganagar has recorded a maximum temperature of 50°C, the highest record.

(vi) *Humid Sub-tropical With Winter*

(a) A large area to the south of the Himalayas, east of the tropical and sub-tropical steppe and north of the tropical savanna running in a long belt from Punjab to Assam with a south-westward extension into Rajasthan east of the Aravalli Range, has this type of climate.

(b) Winters are dry except for a little rain received from the westerly depressions.

(vii) *Mountain Climate*

(a) The Himalayan and Karakoram ranges experience this type of climate with sharp contrasts between the temperatures of the sunny and shady slopes, high diurnal range of temperatures and high variability of rainfall.

(b) The trans-Himalayan region, Ladakh, where the south-west monsoon fails to reach, has a dry and cold climate and a sparse and stunted vegetation.

(viii) *Drought and Floods in India*

(a) The dry areas of Rajasthan and the adjoining parts of Haryana and Gujarat are liable to frequent drought conditions.

(b) Another area liable to frequent drought lies on the leeward side of the western Ghats.

EL NINO AND THE INDIAN MONSOON

El Nino is a cold gean current that flows along the western coast of South America. The system involves oceanic and atmospheric phenomena with the appearance of warm currents off the coast of Peru in the Eastern Pacific and affects weather in many places including India. It is merely an extension of the warm equatorial current which gets replaced temporarily by cold Peruvian current or Humbolt current. This results in : (i) the distortion of equatorial atmosphere circulation; (ii) irregularities in the evaporation of sea water; (iii) reduction in the amount of planktons which further reduces the number of fish in the Sea. It is also called the Peru or Humboldt. It is a complex weather system that appears once every three to seven years, bringing drought, floods and other weather extremes to different parts of the world.

EFFECT OF EL-NINO OVER INDIA

1. Whenever, El Nino appears there is bound to be arid condition in India.
2. In a total of 27 El Nino years since 1875 India experienced at least 10 percent less than normal rainfall 11 times.
3. On 15 other occasions when the Peruvian coast had experienced the appearance of El Nino, rainfall has been normal in India.
4. The interesting thing is that it never rained 10 percent of what its normal for India even once during an El Nino year.
5. In 1979, the monsoon experiment (MONEX), the largest of its kind involving nations, saw the discovery of the dramatic bursts of energy over Indian west coat just before rains. But eight years later they are still to find a satisfactory explanation. They now believe that Tibet holds the clue for many of the unexplained phenomena.

SEASONS IN INDIA

SEASONS BASED ON MONSOON : The climate of India may be described as tropical monsoon. Even northern India, lying beyond the tropical zone, acquires a tropical touch marked by the relatively high temperatures and dry winters. The large size of the country and its varied relief play a crucial role in determining the climatic variations in different parts of India. But the seasonal rhythm of the monsoon is apparent throughout India. It may conveniently form the basis for dividing the year into different seasons. The most characteristic feature of the monsoons is the complete reversal of winds. It eventually leads to the alternation of seasons. Therefore, India is known as the '*land of the endless growing season*'. On the basis of the monsoon variations the year is divided into four seasons:

(i) THE COLD WEATHER SEASON : (N.E. Monsoons) The cold weather season starts in early December, and at the beginning of January the north-east monsoon is fully established over India. The mean January day temperature in Madras and Calicut is about 24°-25°C while in the northern plains it is about 10°-15°C. In December, the sunshines directly over the Tropic of Capricorn. The landmass of Asia, including the sub-continent, cools down very rapidly. There is a high pressure over the continent. The Indian Ocean, being warmer, has a relatively low pressure.

THREE REASONS FOR EXCESSIVE COLD IN NORTH INDIA

(1) States like Punjab, Haryana and Rajasthan being far away from the moderating influence of sea experience continental climate.

(2) The snowfall in the nearby Himalayan ranges create cold wave situation.

(3) Around February, the cold winds coming from Caspean Sea and Turkmenistan bring cold wave along with frost and fog over N. Western parts of India.

N.E. Trade Winds (prevailing winds in the tropical Latitudes), blow, land to sea.

These winds, being off shore do not give rain. They are dry except for the branch that blows over the Bay of Bengal and gives rainfall to the east coast of India.

These winds are also known as the N.E. Monsoons or the Winter Monsoons in India.

The Peninsular region of India, however does not have any well-defined cold weather season. There is hardly any seasonal change in the distribution pattern of the temperature in coastal areas because of moderating influence of sea and the proximity to equator. These western disturbances bring light rainfall, most beneficial to the rabi crop. This rainfall decreases towards the east and the south. The Tamil Nadu coast also receive rainfall during this season. The north-eastern winds absorb fresh moisture while blowing over the Bay of Bengal before crossing the coasts south of Chennai.

(ii) THE HOT WEATHER SEASON: From March to May the Sun moves from over the Equator towards the Tropic of Cancer. By June 21, it is directly overhead the Tropic of Cancer. In March, the highest day temperatures of about 38°C occur in the Deccan Plateau. Therefore :

(a) **Peninsular India,** places south of the Satpuras experience temperatures between 26°C-32°C. Coastal areas, due to the moderating influence of the sea, have lower temperatures (27°-32°).

(b) **Central India,** comprising of Delhi and Madhya Pradesh experience temperatures between 40°-45°C.

(c) **North-west India,** comprising mainly of Rajasthan has very high temperatures (45°C), due also to features like sandy soil, direct insolation and lack of cloud cover.

STORMS DURING THE HOT WEATHER SEASON
(a) Mango Showers (since the rain showers are good for the mango trees) occur along the coast of Kerala. **(b) Norwester/Kalbaisakhi** (meaning the calamity of the month of baisakh) occurs in Assam and West Bengal. These are thunderstorms, accompanied with strong winds and heavy rainfall. This is good for the tea crop in Assam and the jute and rice in West Bengal. In Assam these storms are called **Bardoli Chherha.** **(c) Loo** is the name given to the hot, dry winds that blow in the Northern Plains. It is very common in Punjab. Haryana, Western Uttar Pradesh (called **"aandhi"**) and Bihar. **(d) Blossom Shower** with this shower, coffee flowers blossom in Kerala and its nearby areas.

(iii) *The South-West Monsoon Season* : This season begins in June and lasts until September. The low pressure which existed over the Northern Plain is further intensified. It is strong enough to attract the moisture bearing winds from the Indian Ocean.

FACTS ABOUT S.W. MONSOON
1. The bulk of the rainfall is received during this season in almost every part of India except Tamil Nadu. 2. The amount of rainfall received depends on the relief of the region. 3. The rain is unreliable and there are dry intervals.

The S.E. Trade Winds from the Southern Hemisphere are drawn into India as the S.W. Monsoon Winds after they cross the Equator. Due to the triangular shape of India, the S.W. Monsoon Winds are divided into two branches—the Arabian Sea Branch and the Bay of Bengal Branch.

The Arabian Sea Branch : It gives very heavy rainfall, more than 200 cm, to the windward side of the Western Ghats. The Deccan Plateau, which lies on the leeward side of the Western Ghat, receives less than 150 cm of rainfall. Further east, rainfall decreases for eg, Hyderabad gets less than 100 cm while Chennai gets even less than 40 cm of rainfall. It does not give much rain to Rajasthan because the Aravali Ranges lie parallel to the direction of winds and hence condensation does not occur. Therefore, Rajasthan gets less than 25 cm of rainfall.

These winds advance northwards, attracted to the low pressure in India. Punjab, at the foothills of the Shiwalik, gets Relief Rainfall.

Bay of Bengal Branch : The Bay of Bengal Branch which also blows from the southwest direction, is deflected by the Arakan Mountains of Myanmar and the N.E. Hills of India (Garo, Khasi and Jaintia). They blow into India as the S.E. Monsoons. The delta of the Ganga-Brahmaputra and the windward side of the N.E. Hills of India get heavy rain. For example, Cherrapunji on the windward side gets 2500 cm of rainfall, while Shillong on the leeward slope gets about 250 cm. The rainfall decreases as the winds reach the eastern Himalays and blow westward into the Ganga Plain, attracted by the low pressure in Punjab and Rajasthan. Bikaner, lying in the rainshadow of the Aravali, gets little or no rain. They give the lower Ganga Valley 200 cm of rainfall, the middle 150 cm and the upper 100 cm. Thus, Kolkata (lower Ganga), gets more than 200 cm of rainfall, Patna (middle Ganga) 150 cm and Amritsar (upper Ganga) 100 cm.

(iv) *The Retreating S.W. Monsoon Season* : This season lasts through October and November. The temperature in the Northern Plain begins to decrease as the Sun's rays no longer fall directly at the Tropic of Cancer. In September, the Sun shine directly at the Equator. The low pressure over the Northern Plain is no longer strong enough to attract the Monsoon Winds into the heart of India. By end of September, the Monsoon Winds are drawn only upto Punjab, by mid-October upto the Central India and by early November upto Southern India. Thus, the S.W. Monsoon Winds seem to withdraw in stages during this season. That is why this season is known as the Retreating S.W. Monsoon Season.

This season is marked by cyclones in the Bay of Bengal. They hit the east coast of India and Bangladesh causing widespread damage to life, property and crops.

TRADITIONAL INDIAN SEASONS

Seasons	Indian Calender	Gregerian Calender
Vasanta	Chaitra-Vaisakha	March-April
Grishma	Jyaistha-Asadha	May-June
Varsha	Sravana-Bhadra	July-August
Sharada	Asvina-Kartika	Sept.-Oct.
Hemanta	Margashirsa-Pausa	Nov.-Dec.
Shishira	Magha-Phalguma	Jan.-Feb.

DISTRIBUTION OF RAINFALL IN INDIA

Rainfall is the important element of Indian economy. Although the monsoons affect most part of India, the amount of rainfall varies from very heavy to scanty on different parts. There is great regional and temporal variation in the distribution of rainfall. Over 80% of the annual rainfall is received in the four rainy months of June to September. The average annual rainfall is about 125 cm. but it has great spatial variations.

DIFFERENCE BETWEEN THE RETREATING S.W. MONSOONS AND NORTH EAST MONSOONS

Retreating S.W. Monsoons	North-east Monsoons
1. They blow during the months of October and November.	1. They blow during the months of December, January, February.
2. This is a season of transition between the hot, rainy season and the cold, dry season.	2. This is the cold weather season.
3. Characterised by oppressive heat and humidity known as **'October Heat'.**	3. This is a very pleasant season with low temperatures, low humidity, clear skies.
4. They blow in the S.W. direction but are not strong enough to blow right into the Northern Plain.	4. These winds blow in the N.E. direction from the land to the sea.
5. They withdraw in stages which results in decreasing rain.	5. They do not give rain to any part of India. Only the Bay of Bengal branch gives rain to the east coast.

(a) Areas of Heavy Rainfall (over 200 cm) : The highest rainfall occurs in west coasts, on the western Ghats as well as the Sub-Himalayan areas in N. East and Meghalaya Hills. Assam, West Bengal, West Coast and Southern slopes of eastern Himalayas.

(b) Areas of Moderately Heavy Rainfall (100-200 cm) : This rainfall occurs in Southern Parts of Gujarat, East Tamil Nadu, North-eastern Peninsular. Western Ghats, eastern Maharashtra, Madhya Pradesh, Orissa, the middle Ganga valley.

(c) Areas of Less Rainfall (50-100 cm) : Upper Ganga valley, eastern Rajasthan, Punjab, Southern Plateau of Karnataka, Andhra Pradesh and Tamil Nadu.

(d) Areas of Scanty Rainfall (less than 50 cm) : Northern part of Kashmir, Western Rajasthan, Punjab and Deccan Plateau. The two significant features of India's rainfall is that (a) in the north India, rainfall decreases westwards and (b) in Peninsular India, except Tamil Nadu, it decreases eastward.

SOIL OF INDIA

CLASSIFICATION

Climate and nature of the parent rock are the two most important factors that determine the types of soils found in India. Soils may also be categorized according to their formating:

***(a)* RESIDUAL SOIL :** These are found where they are formed hence called "In Situ". The red, laterite, black, podzolic soils of forests, saline and Alkaline and peaty and other organic soils are residual soils. Of these, the red and laterite soils are zonal soils developed under hot and humid conditions through the laterisation process on a variety of rocks including the archaean granite. The black soil is an intrazonal soil developed on Deccan lavas.

***(b)* TRANSPORTED SOIL :** These are the soils which are carried down by agents of gradations such as rivers, wind.

The Indian Council of Agricultural Research (ICAR) divides the soil found in the country into 8 major groups which are (i) ***Alluvial soils*** including the coastal and deltaic alluvium, (ii) ***Black soils***, of varying types (iii) *Red soils*, including red loams, yellow earths etc. (iv) ***Laterite*** and ***lateritic soils***

(v) *Forest soils* (vi) *Arid* and *Desert soil* (vii) *Saline* and *Alkali soils* and (viii) *Peaty* and *Organic soils.*

INDIAN SOILS WITH PERCENTAGE OF COVERAGE

Soil Types	Percentage to total area
Alluvial soils	22.16
Black soils	29.69
Red and Yellow soils	28.00
Laterite soils	2.62
Arid soils	6.13
Saline soils	1.29
Peaty and Organic soils	2.17
Forest soils	7.94

(i) **ALLUVIAL SOILS :** It is by far the largest and the most important soil group of India contributing the largest share of the country's agricultural production. Alluvial soils cover about 22.1 per cent of the country's total land surface. Composed of sediments deposited by rivers in the interior and sea waves along the coasts, these soils constitute the surface of the Great Plains from Punjab to Assam. They also occur in the valleys of the Narmada and Tapti in Madhya Pradesh and Gujarat, Mahanadi in Madhya Pradesh and Orissa, Godavari in Andhra Pradesh, and Cauvery in Tamil Nadu. Along the coast of Kerala, they are referred to as coastal alluvium and in the deltas of Mahanadi, Godavari, Krishna and Cauvery as deltaic alluvium. Alluvial soils are generally deficient in Nitrogen and humus; this necessitates heavy fertilisation particularly with nitrogenous fertilisers. Phosphorus is also deficient in some areas. These soils are suitable for the cultivation of almost all kinds of cereals, pulses, oil seeds, cotton, sugar-cane and vegetables. Jute can be grown in the eastern areas. In the upper and middle Ganga plain two different types of alluvial soils have developed viz. ***Khadar*** and ***Bhangar***. ***Khadar*** is a newer alluvium developed behind the levees of the numerous streams flowing in this section of the Ganga plain. ***Bhangar*** represents a system of older alluvium developed on the upper reaches of the streams where floods generally do not reach.

(ii) **BLACK COTTON SOILS :** These soils are black in colour and they are eminently suitable for the cultivation of cotton. In some areas they are also called ***regur***. These soils have developed over deccan lavas, gneisses and granites under semi-arid conditions and they occupy many areas of Maharashtra, Gujarat, Madhya Pradesh, Karnataka, Andhra Pradesh, Tamil Nadu, Uttar Pradesh, and Rajasthan. The black colour is variously attributed to the presence of titaniferous magnetite, compounds of iron and aluminium, accumulated humus and colloidal hydrated double iron and aluminium silicate. They are usually deficient in nitrogen, phosphoric acid and organic matter, but rich in potash, lime, aluminium, calcium and magnesium carbonates. They are sticky when wet and develop deep wide cracks on drying which helps in the process of self-aeration and absorption of nitrogen from the atmosphere. An extreme degree of moisture retentiveness is another characteristic of these soils. Black soils are well-known for their fertility. Cotton, cereals and oilseeds, like linseed and safflower, many kinds of vegetables and citrus are some of the crops well suited to black soils. Very good results have also been obtained in crops like sugar-cane and tobacco. On account of their moisture-retentive qualities, the black soils are ideally suited to dry farming.

(iii) **RED SOILS :** These soils comprising red loams and yellow earths and derived from crystalline and metamorphic rocks rich in ferromagnesium minerals occupy much of the Peninsula reaching up to Rajmahal Hills in the East, Jhansi in the North and Kachchh in the west. These soils are generally characterised by light texture with porous and friable strucutre, absence of lime and free carbonates and presence of soluble salts in a small quantity. They are neutral to acid reaction and deficient in nitrogen, humus, phosphoric acid and lime. These soils occupy over two-thirds of the total area of Tamil Nadu. Almost all kinds of crops are grown on red soils, though they seem to be more suitable for the cultivation of rice, ragi, tobacco and vegetables. Groundnut and potato can be grown on coarse soils at higher level and sugar-cane on heavy clays at lower level. Red soils are airy and need irrigation support for cultivation.

***(iv)* LATERITE AND LATERITIC SOILS :** Lateritic soils are formed under conditions of high rainfall and temperature with alternate wet and dry periods. The soil consists of a honeycombed mass of iron oxides which turn black after exposure to rain. Usually laterite soils are poor in nitrogen, phosphoric acid, potash, lime and Magnesia. When they are of low fertility generally, they readily respond to manuring and valley soils are found to be suitable for a variety of crops particularly rice, ragi and sugarcane. Lateritic soils occur especially on the summits of the Sahyadric, Eastern Ghats, Rajmahal Hills and many other hills in the eastern parts of the peninsula, East Godavari districts in Andhra Pradesh, some districts in Orissa and West Bengal also have laterite soils.

(v) **FOREST SOILS :** The forest soils are characterized by the deposition of organic matter derived from forest growth. Humus predominates in all forest soils and it is more raw at higher levels leading to acidic conditions. The Himalayas and the other ranges in the north and the high hill summits in the Sahyadris, Eastern Ghats and the Peninsula have forest soils. Forest soils are deficient in potash, phosphorus and lime and need fertilisation for good yields. Plantations of tea, coffee, spices and tropical fruits are laid out on these soils in Karnataka, Tamil Nadu, Kerala and Manipur. Temperate fruits, Maize, wheat and barley are raised on them in Jammu and Kashmir and Himachal Pradesh.

(vi) **ARID AND DESERT SOILS :** These soils are formed under arid and semiarid conditions in the north-western parts of the country. The entire area west of the Aravalli Range in Rajasthan has desert soils. The soils extend to the southern districts of Haryana and Punjab in the north and the Rann of Kachchh in the south. These soils often have a high soluble salt content and a low to very low humus content. They are quite rich in phosphate but poor in nitrogen. Generally, desert soils improve in fertility towards east.

(vii) **SALINE AND ALKALI SOILS :** Soils of many parts of the arid and semi-arid areas of Rajasthan, Punjab, Haryana, Uttar Pradesh and Bihar have saline and alkaline effervescences mainly of sodium, calcium and magnesium. These soils called ***reh, kallar*** and ***usar*** variously, are infertile. Saline soils contain free sodium and other salts whereas alkali soils contain large quantities of sodium chloride. These salt-impregnated soils can be reclaimed by providing good drainage.

(viii) **PEATY AND OTHER ORGANIC SOILS :** Peaty soils have developed under humid conditions as a result of an accumulation of large amounts of organic matter. In addition, they contain considerable amount of soluble salts. These soils are highly saline, rich in organic matter but deficient in phosphate and potash. Marshy soils with a high quantity of vegetable matter frequently occur in the coastal areas of Orissa, West Bengal and Tamil Nadu, in central and northern Bihar and Almora district of Uttar Pradesh.

PATTERN OF SOIL EROSION

In India, soil erosion is the wearing away of the topsoil cover by natural agencies such as water and wind and also as a result of human and animal interference. ***Sheet erosion*** is common on relatively steeper slopes of the heavy rainfall areas in the Himalayan Foothills, over the north-eastern parts of the Peninsula, in Assam and in the Sahyadris and the Eastern Ghats. ***Rill erosion*** is active over a wide area in Bihar, Uttar Pradesh, Madhya Pradesh, and in the semi-arid parts of the Peninsula in Maharashtra, Karnataka, Andhra Pradesh and Tamil Nadu. The ***chhos*** of northern Haryana and Punjab and the badlands of Madhya Pradesh, Rajasthan and Uttar Pradesh, have resulted due to gully erosion on an extensive scale. ***Gully erosion*** are the most spectacular type of erosion. They have already degraded about 40 lakh hectares of land in the country. This problem affects mainly the states of Uttar Pradesh, Madhya Pradesh, Bihar, Rajasthan, Gujarat. ***Wind erosion*** is active in dry areas devoid of vegetation cover. This type of soil erosion is common all over Rajasthan and Gujarat.

Human and animal interference in a variety of ways leads to soil erosion. Deforestation, overgrazing and shifting cultivation are responsible for soil erosion in large areas. ***The chhos*** of Punjab and Haryana and the ***ravines*** of Madhya Pradesh, Rajasthan and Uttar Pradesh have resulted, to a certain extent, due to reckless cutting of forests in these areas. Erosion due to overgrazing by sheep and goats is very common over the hilly areas of Madhya Pradesh, Rajasthan and the low rainfall areas of Maharashtra, Karnataka and Andhra Pradesh. It is also common in Jammu and Himachal Pradesh. ***Shifting cultivation*** is responsible for soil erosion in many tropical forest areas in the country. This mode of cultivation is a serious menace in Assam, Meghalaya, Tripura, Nagaland, Mizoram, Kerala, Andhra Pradesh, Orissa and parts of Madhya Pradesh. It is estimated that over 80,000 hectares of cultivated land of India have already been lost.

SOIL CONSERVATION

Soil conservation includes all such measures which help in protecting the soil from erosion. contour terracing and bunding, construction of bunds across gullies, levelling of uneven land and raising grass and other vegetation on land are the small measures which are usually taken by farmers to protect soil from erosion. Such methods are quite effective in areas where the degree of erosion is not serious as in the semi-arid tracts of the peninsula and part of Gujarat, Madhya Pradesh, Uttar Pradesh, Haryana and Punjab. Extensive reclamation schemes are under implementation in these states. Construction of bunds across gullies and levelling of surface, control of overgrazing by animals, and afforestation are some of the steps taken under these schemes. In the tropical forest areas, shifting cultivation known as ***jhoom*** in Assam, ***ponam*** in Kerala, ***podu*** in Andhra Pradesh and Orissa, and ***bewar, masham, penda*** and ***beera*** in different parts of Madhya Pradesh is a serious problem. It is necessary to educate the adivasis, who practise it, in better farming techniques. The Central Government created the Central Conservation Board in 1953 to co-ordinate the soil conservation schemes on an all India basis.

Soil conservation is method, especially used by man to prevent the soil erosion which can be done by the following methods :

1. CONTOUR PLOUGHING. If ploughing is done at right angles to the hill slope, following the natural contour of the hill, the ridges and furrows break the flow of the water down the hill. This prevents excessive soil loss, as gullies are less likely to develop and also reduce run-off so that plants receive more water. Row crops and small grains are often planted in contour pattern so that the plants can absorb much of the rain, and erosion is minimized.

2. TERRACING. Slopes may be cut into a series of terraces with sufficient level ground on each terrace for cultivation, and an outer wall at the edge to retain the soil and to slow down the flow of rain-water down the slope. Terracing is widely used in Monsoon Asia for wet paddy cultivation, as the excess water and silt can be retained at each terrace to form flooded paddy-fields. Many tree crops such as rubber are also planted on terraces to combat soil erosion. Terraces are also used in temperate and semi-arid regions where slopes are steep. Terracing enables farmers in mountainous regions to utilize the steep ground on the favoured 'sunny slopes' of valleys for vines or other crops.

3. STRIP CROPPING. Crops may be cultivated in alternate strips, parallel to one another. Some strips may be allowed to lie fallow while others are sown to different kinds of crops, e.g. grains, legumes, small tree crops. The various crops ripen at different times of the year and are harvested at intervals. This ensures that at no time will the entire area be left bare or exposed. The tall-growing crops act as wind-breaks and the strips, which are often parallel to the contours, help to increase water absorption by the soil by slowing down run-off.

4. FALLOWING. Sometimes it is important to allow much used land to rest or lie fallow, so that the natural forces can act on the soil. The decayed natural vegetative matter helps to increase the plant nutrients in the soil. Fallowing also increases the sub-soil moisture and improves the general structure of the soil. Winter fallow is commonly practised in temperate regions after the harvest, but cultivation is resumed in the spring after the snow and frost have weathered the top soil. Long periods of fallow cannot be allowed, however, in intensively run farms as farmers cannot afford it. In semi-arid areas fields may be allowed to lie fallow for several years, though they are often ploughed or mulched, i.e. spread with straw or the stubble of the previous year's harvests. This enables them to build up a sufficient supply of moisture by reducing evaporation, and a crop can be grown every few years. This system of dry farming is practised in western U.S.A. and in parts of Mediterranean Europe.

5. COVER CROPPING. In some cases, as in plantations, where the gestation period of tree crops is long, cover crops may be interplanted between the young trees. Creepers are preferred because they spread around and form a useful cover that protects the top soil from the full force of the tropical downpours. Care must be taken that the cover crop does not compete with the young trees for the essential plant nutrients, and leguminous crops are often used because they add nitrogen to the soil. Cover crops may be grown simply to protect the soil or may consist of other valuable plants such as vegetables which provide an income while the plantation crop matures. Some such catch crops, e.g. cotton, maize or tobacco, should be avoided because they exhaust the soil or promote soil erosion instead of preventing it.

IMPORTANT SOILS OF INDIA

Type of Soil	Origin and Formation	Occurrence	Composition	Characteristics	Crops
1. Alluvial (Transported)	Silt brought by rivers.	River valleys (Ganga, Brahmaputra) Deltas of Godavari, Krishna. Coastal strip of Peninsular India-Punjab, Haryana, U.P, Bihar, W. Bengal.	Rich in potash, lime. Poor in phosphorus and humus. (Ganga delta rich in Humus)	Coarse in upper regions, medium in the middle, fine in the lower region.	Rice wheat, sugarcane, cotton, oilseeds.
2. Black (*In situ*)	Weathering of Volcanic (basalt) rock formed by the Deccan lava.	Deccan trap, valley of Godavari, Krishna, Narmada and Tapi (Tapti). Maharashtra, Gujarat, A.P, M.P, T.N.	Rich in lime, iron, potash, magnesium, alumina, calcium. Lacks nitrogen and humus.	fine grained, moisture retentive, sticky when wet and cracks when dry.	Cotton, sugarcane, tobacco, oil-seeds.
3. Red Soil (*In situ*)	Decomposition of metamorphic rocks	Eastern parts of Deccan plateau, southern states of T.N., Kerala, Karnataka, Chhota Nagpur Plateau.	Rich in iron. Deficient in phosphorous nitrogen, humus and lime.	coarse, porous, crumbly and does not retain moisture.	Wheat, rice, cotton, sugarcane, pulses (with fertilizers).
4. Laterite soil (*In situ*)	Result of leaching.	Hill summits of (eastern, Western ghats) Assam Hills	Rich in iron. Poor in potassium, lime, phosphoric acid, nitrogen, silica.	Acidic, porous, crumbly and coarse.	Coffee, rubber, cashew, tapioca.
5. Desert Soil (*In situ*)	Mechanical weathering of rocks from sand	N. Western parts of India. States of Rajasthan. N. Gujarat and S. Punjab.	Rich in soluble salts. Lacks of organic matter	Loose, porous, coarse and alkaline.	With irrigation—wheat, grams, melon, bajra.

6. CROP ROTATION. It is not advisable to grow the same crop in the same field for more than two years in succession as the crop will tend to exhaust one particular kind of mineral nutrient. For example potatoes require much potash, but wheat requires nitrates. Thus it is best to alternate crops in the fields. Legumes such as peas, beans, clover, vetch and many other plants, add nitrates to the soil by converting free nitrogen in the air into nitrogenous nodules on their roots. Thus if they are included in the crop rotation nitrogenous fertilizers can be dispensed with. By rotating different types of crops in successive years, soil fertility can be naturally maintained. The best known crop rotation is the Norfolk Rotation which involves the growing of four crops in a given field over a period of four years. These crops are wheat (cereal); clover or beans (legume); barley (another cereal); and turnips or sugar-beet (root crops).

7. CROP DIVERSIFICATION : This practice is often like crop rotation in that it helps to maintain soil fertility. Where annually-harvested crops are grown they can be alternated in the field. Where perennial crops like tree crops are grown, however, the chief importance of crop diversification to the farmer is economic. In particular it reduces the danger of depending on a single crop (monoculture) when world commodity prices are falling. All the primary commodities, e.g. rubber, oil palm, cocoa, cotton, are subject to great fluctuation in prices, much depending on the demand of the western world. Over-dependence on one crop can be disastrous to the national economy as well as to the individual farmer, as in the case of Brazil's coffee, Ghana's cocoa, or Malaysia's rubber, when prevailing prices for the major money-earning crop are low. Crop diversification overcomes this difficulty as when one crop is only fetching low prices another may be in good demand. Another great advantage of crop diversification is that all types of land can be used, e.g. rubber can be grown on hill slopes, oil palm on flat plains, coconuts on sandy soils. Thorough crop diversification on a national and local level can lead to the most economic use of land.

8. USE OF FERTILIZERS. Farmers all over the world have found that soils vary in their fertility and crop-bearing capability, because of the different proportions of mineral nutrients they contain. Continuous cultivation will exhaust some or most of the nutrients and soil fertility has to be maintained by the application of manures or fertilizers. Organic manures such as animal dung, compost or decomposed vegetation usually provide a balanced supply of the major soil minerals. Nowadays, however, manufactured chemicals are more commonly used partly because they are easier to apply and partly because of the enormous world demand for fertilizers.

9. WATER MANAGEMENT. One of the major ways in which land can be improved for farming is by water management. By regulating the amount of water in the soil aeration can be improved, activity by useful bacteria can be stimulated and crop yields can be improved. In addition, by draining or irrigating land, areas which are marginal or useless in their natural state, such as deserts or swamps can be brought into agricultural production -

It should be emphasized that drainage and irrigation **are** interdependent. In drained areas, irrigation must be applied to prevent unwanted sea-water from seeping into the drained land. In other words a balance must be carefully maintained.

(a) Irrigation. When a region does not have sufficient natural precipitation to meet the plants' moisture requirements, an artificial supply of water is necessary. This is known as irrigation. The amount of extra water needed depends much on the type of crops grown the prevailing temperature and humidity, the kind of soil and the physical conditions of the surrounding districts. Irrigation is one of the oldest agriculture techniques practised by men, and has many advantages over simple reliance on natural water supplies.

i. The supply of water by irrigation is regular and reliable, whereas rainfall is often seasonal or unpredictable. In desert areas the use of irrigation allows cultivation to take place where it would not otherwise be possible.

ii. Irrigation water supplied by rivers in flood often carries much silt which adds to the soil of the fields, enhancing fertility and thus crop yields.

iii. With irrigation, cultivation can be done all the year round and not only during the rainy season. This allows better use to be made of the land.

iv. In desert areas the constant flow of irrigation water through the soil helps to reduce the salinity of the soil. If, however, the water is allowed to evaporate in the fields this increases the salt content.

v. Modern multi-purpose dams not only provide water for irrigation but also help to control floods, generate hydro-electric power and improve the navigability of the rivers. Water for irrigation may be obtained in a number of ways of varying complexity. The various types of irrigation are described below:

i. ***Lifting Devices.*** Water may be simply lifted from a well, river or canal by a bucket to the fields. Such devices as the *shaduf* the Archimedean Screw and various kinds of water wheel or treadmill have been in use for thousands of years. In modern times diesel steam or electrically operated pumps can be used. They are especially useful where water is obtained from a deep well rather than from canals.

ii. ***Basin Irrigation.*** This method has been practised in Egypt for many centuries but is of less importance today. When the Nile rises in summer, part of the flood-water is allowed to flood basin-like fields on either side of the river. The water is controlled by sluices. Basin irrigation, using canal-water rather than river water is also used to grow paddy in the U.S.A.

iii. ***Tanks.*** Tanks are small reservoirs used for storing water which falls in the rainy season. They are common in southern India and Sri Lanka. The water stored is rarely sufficient for use all the year round but does lengthen the growing season.

iv. ***Canal Irrigation.*** Canals which lead irrigation water from rivers or storage lakes are the most important feature of irrigated lands. Inundation canals lead off water from a river in time of flood. These are simple but do not provide water all the year round. Perennial canals are fed by water stored behind a large dam or barrage and can thus be supplied all the year round. Storage barrages feed canals not only below the dam but also above because, by raising the level of the river behind the dam, water can be led into higher level canals.

v. ***Overhead Irrigation.*** This is a modern system and is now practised in many parts of the world. Sprays and sprinklers are set up in the fields and supplied with water by hoses from public water supplies. The initial cost of the equipment is high and water must be continually pumped. The method is however a common one in the U.S.A., Britain and Europe.

(b) Drainage and Land Reclamation. In wet or low-lying areas it improves the land if drainage work is undertaken to remove excess water. Drainage not only removes unwanted water but also helps to fin-prove soil porosity and aeration, reduces soil acidity or sourness and makes the soil easier to work. Plant roots can penetrate deeper into the soil giving bigger crops and better quality harvests. Nitrification and nitrogen-fixing by leguminous plants and by bacteria are encouraged and at the same time the plants' liability to fungus attack is reduced. Drainage is carried out by a network of pipes open drains and ditches which carry off the unwanted water. Open drains are used in swampy areas or on damp, peaty uplands but pipes are often laid 0.3 to 1 .2 metres (2 to 4 ft) below the ground in temperate farmlands. They are more expensive than open ditches to construct at first but are inexpensive to maintain and do not interfere with farm work. Open ditches are easily and cheaply dug but must be constantly cleared of weeds and unwanted animal or insect life, and they interrupt the fields. hindering ploughing or harvesting.

It is also possible in low-lying areas fringing the sea to reclaim additional land by using drainage techniques. This has been done in the Netherlands, the Fens of Britain and in many other flood-prone coastal areas and river basins all over the world. The land is first ringed with dykes and sea-walls which keep out the water, and then pumped dry by means of windmills (in the past) or diesel pumps. When the land is dry it must be flushed with water to remove salt from the soil and is then used for pasture or arable land. The polders or reclaimed lands form much of the best farmland in the Netherlands, supporting dairying, horticulture and arable farming. Care has to be taken to prevent sea-water seeping in underground and impregnating the soil with salt, and another difficulty is that, as the 'new' land gradually becomes drier over the years, it shrinks and compacts so that it lies well below sea-level. Sea walls and dykes have to be carefully maintained to prevent flooding of such low-lying lands.

(c) Bunding : Contour bunding is the construction of small bunds across the slopes of the land on a contour so that the long slope is cut into a series of small ones and earth contour bunds act as a barrier to the flow of water, thus, making it 'walk' rather than 'run' and at the same time impounding a greater part of water against the bund to increase the soil moisture.

(d) Control of Gully Erosion : Gully control by the diversion of run off proved to be an economical measure. The best method of controlling existing gullies is to re-establish vegetation. Two of the most important types are the sod strip eroded earth till.

(e) Wind Break : The principal method of reducing surface velocity of wind, upon which would depend the abrasive and transportation capacity, are vegetal measures.

NATURAL VEGETATION AND WILD LIFE

INDIA'S NATURAL VEGETATION

Natural vegetation in India is influenced by altitude (in the Himalayan region) and rainfall. On the basis of altitude, the Himalayan region has all the vegetation varieties found in the tropical to tundra region. The rest of the country has mainly three major vegetation regions, namely tropical wet-evergreen and semi-evergreen forests, the tropical deciduous, and the thorn forests. Wild life species are similarly of a great variety.

With about 47,000 per cent species, India is the 10th in the world and 4th in Asia in plant diversity. There are about 15,000 flowing plants which constitue about 6% of the world total.

India's biological diversity is reflected in the heterogeneity of its forest covers. It is one of the 12 'mega-diversity' countries of the world. India is also at meeting zone of three major bio-geographic realms, namely the **Indo-Malayan** (the richest in world) the **Euroasian** and the **Afro tropical.** India also has the two richest bio-diversity areas, one in the north east and other in the western Ghats. India's biological diversity which is estimated to be over 45,000 plant species represents about 7% of the world flora and 6.5% of the world fauna respectively.

The Vegetation in the Himalayan Region: The distribution of vegetation in the Himalayas is mostly along the vertical plane. The *Shiwaliks* or the outer Himalayas are covered with tropical moist deciduous flora of which the ***sal*** is an important species of economic significance. This type of vegetation is followed, at higher elevation, by evergreen oak, chestnut and some ash and beech. This is a typical subtropical wet hill vegetation. This at a higher altitude is replaced by ***chir*** and ***chil*** trees, representative of subtropical moist hill flora. Pine, cedar, silver fir, and spruce are the most important species further up between the altitudes of 1,600 metres and 3,300 metres. These are the well-known conifer trees typical of the dry temperate region found in the inner Himalayan ranges. The conifers give place to the shrubs, scrub and grasses of the Alpine variety at 3,500 metres and above.

FOREST COVER

The country's forest resources are under tremendous pressure. Forests meet 40% of the country's energy needs and 30% of fodder needs. It is estimated that about 270 mt of fuel wood, 280 mt of fodder, over 12 million m^3 (cubic meter) of timber and countless non-wood forest products (NWFPs) are removed from forests annually.

UNEVEN DISTRIBUTION OF FORESTS

The distribution of forests is very uneven. Most of the forests are located in hilly but mainly inaccessible parts of mountaineous areas. The forests area ranges from 86.9% in Andaman and Nicobar islands and 3.8% in Haryana.

In India, Madhya Pradesh is the most densely forested state having 76,429 sq. km. After the formation of Chhatisgarh, the new state has got about 55,998 sq. km forest resources.

The seven North Eastern States together comprise 25.70% of the total forest cover.

INDIA'S FOREST POLICY AND LAW

Forests are a renewable source and contribute substantially to economic development. They play a major role in enhancing the quality of environment.

India is one of the few countries which has a forest policy since 1894. It was revised in 1952 and again in 1988. Main plank of the forest policy of 1988 is protection, conservation and development of forests.

Forest Cover of India in 2021

States/UTs	Geographical Area	VDF	MDF	OF	Total Forest Area	Per cent of Geographical Area
Andhra Pradesh	1,62,968	1,994	13,929	13,861	29,784	18.28
Arunachal Pradesh	83,743	21,058	30,176	15,197	66,431	79.33
Assam	78,438	3,017	9,991	15,304	28,312	36.09
Bihar	94,163	333	3,286	3,762	7,381	7.84
Chhattisgarh	1,35,192	7,068	32,279	16,370	55,717	41.21
Delhi	1,483	6.72	56.60	131.68	195.00	13.15
Goa	3,702	538	576	1,130	2,244	60.62
Gujarat	1,96,244	378	5,032	9,516	14,926	7.61
Haryana	44,212	28	445	1,130	1,603	3.63
Himachal Pradesh	55,673	3,163	7,100	5,180	15,443	27.73
Jharkhand	79,716	2,601	9,689	11,431	23,721	29.76
Karnataka	1,91,791	4,533	20,985	13,212	38,730	20.19
Kerala	38,852	1,944	9,472	9,837	21,253	54.70
Madhya Pradesh	3,08,252	6,665	34,209	36,619	77,493	25.14
Maharashtra	3,07,713	8,734	20,589	21,475	50,798	16.51
Manipur	22,327	905	6,228	9,465	16,598	74.34
Meghalaya	22,429	560	9,160	7,326	17,046	76.00
Mizoram	21,081	157	5,715	11,948	17,820	84.53
Nagaland	16,579	1,272	4,449	6,530	12,251	73.90
Odisha	1,55,707	7,213	20,995	23,948	52,156	33.50
Punjab	50,362	11	793	1,043	1,847	3.67
Rajasthan	3,42,239	78	4,369	12,208	16,655	4.87
Sikkim	7,096	1,102	1,551	688	3,341	47.08
Tamil Nadu	1,30,060	3,593	11,034	11,792	26,419	20.31
Telangana	1,12,077	1,624	9,119	10,471	21,214	18.93
Tripura	10,486	647	5,212	1,863	7,722	73.64
Uttar Pradesh	2,40,928	2,627	4,029	8,162	14,818	6.15

Uttarakhand	53,483	5,055	12,768	6,482	24,305	45.44
West Bengal	88,752	3,037	4,208	9,587	16,832	18.96
A & N Islands	8,249	5,678	683	383	6,744	81.75
Chandigarh	114	1.36	13.51	8.01	22.88	20.07
Dadra & Nagar Haveli and Daman & Diu	602	1.40	85.56	140.79	227.75	37.83
Jammu & Kashmir Shapefile Area* (54,624)	2,22,236	4,155	8,117	9,115	21,387	39.15
Ladakh Shapefile Area* (1,68,055)		2	512	1,758	2,272	1.35
Lakshadweep	30	0.00	16.09	11.01	27.10	90.33
Puducherry	490	0.00	17.53	35.77	53.30	10.88
Total	**32,87,469**	**99,779**	**3,06,890**	**3,07,120**	**7,13,789**	**21.71**

** Area of shapefile provided by Survey of India (August, 2021). Notified geographical areas for individual UTs from SoI are awaited.*

*Includes Jammu and Kashmir areas outside LoC that is under illegal occupation of Pakistan and China.

The programme of preserving and protecting the forests is known as the Programme of Forest Conservation. Under the scheme of forest conservation the following measures have been adopted:

(*i*) Maintenance of environmental stability through preservation and restoration of ecological balance;

(*ii*) Conservation of natural heritage;

(*iii*) Check on soil erosion and denudation in catchment area of rivers, lakes and reservoirs:

(*iv*) Check on extension of sand dunes in desert areas of Rajasthan and along coastal tracts;

(*v*) Substantial increase in forest tree cover through massive afforestation and social forestry programmes;

(*vi*) Steps to meet requirements of fuelwood, fodder, minor forest produce and soil timber of rural and tribal populations;

(*vii*) Increase in productivity of forest to meet the national needs;

(*viii*) Encouragement of efficient utilization of forest produce and optimum substitution of wood and;

(*ix*) Steps to create massive people's movement with involvement of women to achieve the objectives and minimise pressure on existing forests.

Under the provisions of the Forest (Conservation) Act, 1980 prior approval of the Central Government is required for diversion of forest lands for non-forest purposes.

Since the enactment of the Act, the rate of diversion of forest land has come down to around 25,000 hectare per annum from 1.43 lakh hectare per annum, before 1980.

Based on the recommendations of the Ministry of Environment and Forests, the Ministry of Commerce has decided to allow the export of only value added items made out of legally procured Red Sanders Wood.

Sandal wood oil, which was being exported freely till now, has been brought into the restricted list of items for export

FOREST AND TREE RESOURCES

- Forest Cover of the country as per this assessment is 713,789 sq. km which is 21.71 per cent of the geographical area of the country. The tree cover of the country is estimated to be 95,748 sq km which is 2.91 per cent of the geographical area.
- The total Forest and Tree cover of the country as per this assessment is 809,537 sq km which is 24.62 per cent of the geographical area of the country.
- While in the 2019 report, the forest cover in the hill regions had a increased of 544 sq. km, the 2021 report shown a decrease of 902 sq. km.

- The North Eastern-states of India account for one-fourth of the country's forest cover.
- There is a net decline of 1540 sq km in forest cover as compared to the previous assessment.
- Mangrove cover has increased by 17 sq km as compared to the previous assessment.
- Area-wise Madhya Pradesh has the largest forest cover in the country followed by Arunachal Pradesh, Chhattisgarh, Odisha and Maharashtra. In terms of forest cover as percentage of total geographical area, the top five States are Mizoram (84.53%), Arunachal Pradesh (79.33%), Meghalaya (76.00%), Manipur (74.34%) and Nagaland (73.90%).
- Total carbon stock in country's forest is estimated to be 7,204 million tonnes and there an increase of 79.4 million tonnes in the carbon stock of country as compared to the last assessment of 2019. The annual increase in the carbon stock is 39.7 million tonnes.

FOREST COVER IN DIFFERENT DENSITY CLASSES

Forest and Tree cover of India in 2021

Class	Area (sq km)	Per cent of Geographical Area
Forest Cover		
Very Dense Forest	99,779	3.04
Moderate Dense Forest	3,06,890	9.33
Open Forest	3,07,120	9.34
Total Forest Cover	**7,13,789**	**21.71**
Tree Cover	95,748	2.91
Total Forest and Tree Cover	**8,09,537**	**24.62**
Scrub	46,539	1.42
Non Forest	25,27,141	76.87
Total Geographical Area	**32,87,469**	**100.00**

The Chipko Movement

In 1974, the women of Reni in northern India took a simple but effective action to stop tree felling. They threatened to hug the trees if the lumberjacks attempted to fell them. The women's protest saved 12000 sq. km of sensitive watershed.

WILDLIFE IN INDIA

More than 30,377 different species of insects, apart from a great variety of fishes and reptiles are also found. The mammals include elephant, the gaur or Indian bison, Indian buffalo, nilgai, chousingha or four-horned antelope (unique to India), black buck or Indian antelope, ghor-khur or Indian wild ass (restricted to the Rann of Kachchh) and great one-horned rhinoceros (now confined to eastern India). There are also several species of deer, viz., the rare Kashmir stag, swamp deer, spotted deer, musk deer, thamin or brow-antlered deer (found in Manipur) and mouse deer. Among the animals of prey, the Indian lion is remarkable being the only lion to be found in the world outside Africa. Bird life in India is very rich and colourful. Lions are found in the rocky hills and forests of the Gir area of Gujarat, Tigers in the Sunderbans and the Brahmaputra valley. The famous **Project Tiger** is a scheme financed by the government of India to safeguard the tiger in its habitat in nine selected reserves. India Fauna also include the wild ass of Rajasthan, Nilgiri Langur, Lion-tailed macaque, Nilgiri mongoose and Malabar civer of the southern hills and the spotted deer. Leopards are found in many forests, Wolves roam the open country. Cheetahs are found in the Deccan plateau.

FOREST TYPES IN INDIA

The chart below clearly presents the forest types, their characteristics, area and important species of vegetation.

FOREST TYPE AND CHARACTERISTICS	OCCURRENCE	SOME IMPORTANT SPECIES
TROPICAL EVERGREEN (Area: Wet evergreen—4.5m.ha; Semi-evergreen -1.9 m. ha.). **TROPICAL SEMI EVERGREEN** Both are lofty, dense forest with a large number of speciesand numerous epiphytes; climbers heavy in semi-evergreen, though few in wetevergreen forest.	Arunachal Pradesh, Assam, Karnataka, Kerala, Manipur, Nagaland, Tamil Nadu, Andaman and Nicobar Islands and Goa Assam, Gujarat, Karnataka, Kerala, Maharashtra, Nagaland, Orissa, Tamil Nadu, Andaman and Nicobar Island and Goa	Mesua, White Cedar, Hopea and Bamboo occur in both semi and wet evergreen forests. Specific to wet evergreen are Jamun, Canes.Semi-evergreen; Kadam, Irul, Rosewood, Laurel, Haldu, Indian Chestnut, Champa, Mango.
TROPICAL MOIST DECIDOUS: (Area : 23.3.m. ha.) Multi-Layered forest with irregular top storey of predominantly decidous species, a definite second storey of mixed species and shrubby undergrowth fairly complete; climbers heavy.	Andhra Pradesh, Assam, Bihar, Gujarat, Karnataka, Kerala, Madhya Pradesh, Maharashtra, Manipur, Meghalaya, Mizoram, Tripura, Nagaland, Orissa, Tamil Nadu, Uttar Pradesh, West Bengal, Andaman and Nicobar Islands, Goa and Dadra and Nagar Haveli	Padauk, Badam, Kokko, Teak, Laurel, Haldu, Rosewood, Bijasal, Irul, Amla Common Bamboo, Sal, Pula, Jamun, Mahul, Canes.
TROPICAL DRY DECIDUOUS (Area; 29.2 m.ha.) Multi-layered forest, almost entirely deciduous; shrubs and bamboos present, but no luxuriant; climbers, few though some are large and woody.	Andhra Pradesh, Bihar, Gujarat, Haryana, Himachal Pradesh, Karnataka, Kerala, Madhya Pradesh, Maharashtra, Jammu and Kashmir, Orissa, Punjab, Rajasthan, Tamil Nadu, Uttar Pradesh and West Bengal	Teak, Axlewood, Bijasal, Rosewood Aman as, Palas, Haldu, Common Bamboo, Red Sanders, Laurel, Satinwood, Sal
TROPICAL THORN (Area : 5.2 m. ha.) Open low, pronouncedly xerophytic forest, throny, leguminous species predominate; trees have short boles and low branches; ill-defined lower storey of smaller trees and shrubs.	Andhra Pradesh, Gujarat, Haryana, Himachal Pradesh, Karnataka, Madhya Pradesh, Maharashtra, Punjab, Rajasthan, Tamil Nadu and Uttar Pradesh	Khair, Reunjha, Axlewood, Neem, Sandalwood, Nimali, Dhaman, Acacia Senegal Khejra, Kanju, Palas, Ak.
TROPICAL DRY EVERGREEN (Area: 700,000 ha.) complete canopy of evergreen tree, mostly coriaceous leaved, with short boles.	Andhra Pradesh and Tamil Nadu	Khiri, Jamun, Kokko, Ritha, Tamarind, Neem, Machkund, Toddy Palm, Canes.
LITTORAL & SWAMP (TIDAL FORESTS) (Area: 600.000 ha.) Mainly evergreen species of varying density and height, always associated with wetness.	Andhra Pradesh, Gujarat, Maharashtra, Orissa, Tamil Nadu, West Bengal, and Andaman and Nicobar Islands	Sundri, Bruguiera, Sonneratia, Agar, Bhendi, Keora, Nipa.
SUB-TROPICAL BROAD-LEAVED HILL (Area : 300,000ha.) Luxuriant forests, evergreen species predominating.	Assam, Maharashtra, Meghalaya, West Bengal, Tamil Nadu and Kerala	Jamun, Machilus, Melissma, Elaeocarpus, Celtis.
SUB-TROPICAL PINE (Area : 3.7 m. ha.) almost entirely pure chir pine, no under-wood, few shrubs.	Arunachal Pradesh, Himachal Pradesh, Jammu and Kashmir, Manipur, Meghalaya, Nagaland, Sikkim and Uttar Pradesh	Chir, Jamun, Oak, Rhododendron.
SUB-TROPICAL DRY EVERGREEN (Area: 200,000ha.) Low, scrub forest; small, stunted evergreen trees appear, shrubs including thorny species prevalent ; herbs and grasses appear during monsoon.	Himachal Pradesh, Jammu and Kashmir and Mizoram	Olive, Acacia modesta, Pistacia.
MONTANE WET TEMPERATE (Area; 1.6m. ha.) A closed evergreen forest, trees mostly shortboled and branchy attaining wide girth, crowned by dense and rounded leaves, red when young, branmches clothed with mosses.	Arunachal Pradesh, Karnataka, Manipur, Nagaland, Sikkim and Tamil Nadu	Machilus, Cinnamomum, Litsea, Magnolia, Chilauni, Indian Chestnut Birch, Plum.
HIMALAYAN MOIST TEMPERATE (Area; Moist Temperate-2.7m. ha.; **HIMALAYAN DRY TEMPERATE** Dry Temperate -200,000ha.) Predominantly coniferous forests; mosses and ferns grow freely on Birch; trees in the moist temperate forest, while there are hardly any epiphytes and climbers in the dry temperate forests.	Himachal Pradesh, Jammu and Kashmir and Uttar Pradesh Himachal Pradesh and Jammu and Kashmir	Oak, Deodar, Celtis and Maple are common to both Himalayan moist and dry temperate forests. Specific to Himalayan moist Temperate forest are: Chestnut, Kail, Yew, and to the dry temperate forests : Chilgoza, Ash, Parrotia and olive.
ALPINE AND SUB ALPINE (Area : 3,000 ha. total for all) Dense growth of small broad-leaved trees, often crooked; also large shrubs and conifers. ***Moist Alpine Scrub*** : Dense growth of low evergreen alpine shrubs, flowering herbs, mosses and fern. **Dry Alpine Scrub :** xerophytic, dwarf shrubs.	Arunachal Pradesh, Jammu and Kashmir, Nagaland, Sikkim and Uttar Pradesh	Rhododendron and Birch are common to the sub-alpine forest and moist alpine scrub : honeysuckle to both types of alpine scrub. Fir, Kail Spruce, Plum and Yew are specific to sub-alpine; Berberis to moist alpine scrub; and Juniper. Artemesia and Potentilia to dry alpine scrub.

The peacock is the national bird. Several other birds like the pheasants, geese, ducks, mynahs, parakeets, pigeons, cranes, hornbills and sunbirds inhabit the forests and wet lands. The rivers and lakes harbour crocodiles and gharials, the latter being the only representative of a crocodilian order in the world. The salt water crocodile is found along the eastern coast and in the Andaman and Nicobar Islands. A project for breeding crocodiles with United Nations Development Programme assistance, started in 1974, has been instrumental in saving the crocodile from extinction and increasing their population to about 3,000.

The Zoological Survey of India (ZSI), undertakes survey, exploration and research leading to the advancement of our knowledge on the exceptionally rich faunal diversity of the country since its inception in 1916. According to world biogeographic classification, India represent two of the major realms, the Palearctic and Indo-Malayan, and three biomes viz., tropical humid forests, tropical dry deciduous forests and warm deserts/semi deserts. Indian landmass has been classified into 10 biogeographic zones.

ZSI documented the faunal resources in eight biogeographic zones, Himalayas with 30,377 species, Trans-Himalayas with 3,324 species, islands with 11,009 species, northeast with 18,527, desert with 3,346, semi-arid with 7424, coasts with 11,883 species, and Western Ghats with 17,099 species.

ZSI is designated as Forensic Laboratory by Ministry of Home Affairs, Government of India for solving wildlife case materials and supporting the MoEF&CC.

WILDLIFE PROTECTION IN INDIA

India has a great variety of flora and fauna. The mammals include elephant, the gaur or Indian bison, Indian buffalo, nilgai, chousingha or four-horned antelope (unique to India), black buck or Indian antelope, ghor-khur or Indian wild ass (restricted to the Rann of Kachchh) and great one-horned rhinoceros (now confined to eastern India). There are also several species of deer, viz., the rare Kashmir stag, swamp deer, spotted deer, musk deer, thamin or brow-antlered deer (found in Manipur) and mouse deer. Among the animals of prey, the Indian lion is remarkable being the only lion to be found in the world outside Africa. Bird life in India is very rich and colourful. The peacock is the national bird. Several other birds like the pheasants, geese, ducks, mynahs, parakeets, pigeons, cranes, hornbills bills and sunbirds inhabit the forests and wet lands. The rivers and lakes harbour crocodiles and gharials, the latter being the only representative of a crocodilian order in the world. The salt water crocodile is found along the eastern coast and in the Andaman and Nicobar Islands. A project for breeding crocodiles with United Nations Development Programme assistance, started in 1974, has been instrumental in saving the crocodile from extinction and increasing their population to about 3,000. Twelve schemes are in operation in different states for breeding of crocodiles and releasing them in the wild.

THE WILDLIFE (PROTECTION) ACT, 1972 adopted by all the states except Jammu and Kashmir (which has its own Act), governs the wild life conservation and protection of endangered species both inside and outside forest areas. Under this Act, trade in rare and endangered species has been banned, India is a signatory to the Convention on International Trade in Endangered Species of Wild Flora and Fauna. Under this treaty export or import of endangered species of flora and fauna are subject to strict control and commercial exploitation of such species is prohibited.

The Indian Board of Wildlife has listed 36 species which need protection lion, wild ass, pangolin, brow-antlered deer, swamp deer, musk deer, gharial, four-horned antelope, clouded leopard, Nilgiri stag, lesser panda, Kashmir stag, wild buffalo, rhinoceros, Nilgiri langur, golden langur, gazelle, markhor, spotted linsang, pigmy hog, blackbuck, snow leopard, golden cat, marble cat, hunting leopard or cheetah (now considered extinct), dugong, great Indian bustard, Jerdon's courser, mountain quail, pink-headed duck, white-winged wood duck, tragopan, crocodile, leathery turtle, water lizard and python.

Though late, efforts are now being taken by the Department of Environment, Government of India to preserve the ecosystem and biotic life. The 'Man And Biosphere' (MAB) programme launched by the Government aims at conserving as much of the biological diversity of the country as possible and forms part of the international scheme to set up a global network of biosphere reserves. The idea of biosphere reserves was initiated by UNESCO in 1973-74 and the first reserve in the Nilgiris was established in 1986.

BIOSPHERE RESERVE

A biosphere reserve is a multipurpose protected area to preserve the genetic diversity in the representative ecosystem. Its objectives are : (a) to conserve diversity and integrity of plants, animals and micro organisms; (b) to promote research on ecological conservation; (c) and to provide facilities for education, awareness and training.

BIOSPHERE RESERVES IN INDIA

S. No.	Name	Date of Notification	Area (in km²)
1	Nilgiri	01.09.1986	5520
2	Nanda Devi	18.01.1988	5860.69
3	Nokrek	01.09.1988	820
4	Great Nicobar	06.01.1989	885
5	Gulf of Mannar	18.02.1989	10,500
6	Manas	14.03.1989	2837
7	Sunderbans	29.03.1989	9630
8	Simlipal	21.06.1994	4374
9	Dibru-Saikhowa	28.07.1997	765
10	Dehang-Dibang	02.09.1998	5111.50
11	Pachmarhi	03.03.1999	4926
12	Khangchendzonga	07.02.2000	2619.92
13	Agasthyamalai	12.11.2001	1828
14	Achanakamar - Amarkantak	30.3.2005	3835.51
15	Kachchh	29.01.2008	12,454
16	Cold Desert	28.08.2009	7770
17	Seshachalam Hills	20.09.2010	4755.997
18	Panna	25.08.2011	2998.98

Source: *Wildlife Institute of India*

Biosphere Reserves, a concept originated in 1974, are a set of unique ecosystems identified on the basis of their bio diversity, naturalness and effectiveness as a conservation unit.

SPECIAL PROJECTS FOR ENDANGERED SPECIES

PROJECT TIGER : Project Tiger was launched in 1973 for conserving the tiger. From 9 tiger reserves since its formative years, the Project Tiger coverage has increased to 50, spread out in 18 of tiger range states. These reserves are constituted on a core/buffer strategy. "The core areas have the legal status of a national park or a sanctuary, whereas the buffer or peripheral areas are a mix of forest and non-forest land, managed as a multiple use area." The NTCA/ Project Tiger also conducts the country level assessment of the status of tiger, co-predators, prey and habitat once in four years, using the refined methodology, as approved by the Tiger Task Force. "Due to the concerted efforts under the Project, India has the distinction of having the maximum number of tigers in the world 2,967 — to be precise, as per the results of the 4th cycle of the All India Tiger Estimation." The tiger corridors for gene flow have been mapped in the GIS domain.

PROJECT ELEPHANT : Under project Elephant, financial, technical and scientific assistance are provided to states having free-ranging population of wild elephant. The National Wildlife Action Plan adopted in 1983 provides the framework for conservation of wild life. The population of elephants in India has increased from about 25,000 in 1992 to over 29,964 in 2017.

Famous National Parks in India

	State/UT	National Parks
•	Andaman and Nicobar Islands	Campbell Bay, Galathea Bay, Mahatma Gandhi Marine Wandoor, Middle Button Island, Mount Harriett, North Button Island, Rani Jhansi Marine, Saddle Peak, South Button Island
•	Andhra Pradesh	Papikonda, Rajiv Gandhi (Rameswaram), Sri Venkates-wara
•	Arunachal Pradesh	Mouling, Namdapha

	State/UT	National Parks
•	**Assam**	Dibru-Saikhowa, Kaziranga, Manas, Nameri, Rajiv Gandhi Orang
•	**Bihar**	Valmiki
•	**Chhattisgarh**	Guru Ghasidas (Sanjay), Indravati (Kutru), Kanger Valley
•	**Goa**	Mollem
•	**Gujarat**	Vansda, Blackbuck (Velavadar), Gir, Marine (Gulf of Kutch)
•	**Haryana**	Kalesar, Sultanpur
•	**Himachal Pradesh**	Great Himalayan, Inderkillam, Khirganga, Pin Valley, Simbalbara
•	**Jammu & Kashmir**	City Forest (Salim Ali), Dachigam, Hemis, Kishtwar
•	**Jharkhand**	Betla
•	**Karnataka**	Anshi, Bandipur, Bannerghatta, Kudremukh, Nagarahole (Rajiv Gandhi)
•	**Kerala**	Anamudi Shola, Eravikulam, Mathikettan Shola, Pambadum Shola, Periyar, Silent Valley
•	**Madhya Pradesh**	Bandhavgarh, Fossil, Kanha, Madhav, Panna, Indira Priyadarshini Pench, Sanjay, Satpura, Van Vihar
•	**Maharashtra**	Chandoli, Gugamal, Nawegaon, Pench (Jawaharlal Nehru), Sanjay Gandhi (Borivilli), Tadoba.
•	**Manipur**	Keibul-Lamjao
•	**Meghalaya**	Balphakram, Nokrek Ridge
•	**Mizoram**	Murlen, Phawngpui Blue Mountain
•	**Nagaland**	Intanki
•	**Odisha**	Bhitarkanika, Simlipal
•	**Rajasthan**	Mukundra Hills, Desert, Keoladeo Ghana, Ranthambhore, Sariska
•	**Sikkim**	Khangchendzonga
•	**Tamil Nadu**	Guindy, Gulf of Mannar Marine, Indira Gandhi (Annamalai), Mudumalai, Mukurthi
•	**Telangana**	Kasu Brahmananda Reddy, Mahaveer Harina Vanasthali, Mrugavani.
•	**Tripura**	Clouded Leopard, Bison (Rajbari)
•	**Uttar Pradesh**	Dudhwa
•	**Uttarakhand**	Corbett, Gangotri, Govind, Nanda Devi, Rajaji, Valley of Flowers
•	**West Bengal**	Buxa, Gorumara, Jaldapara, Neora Valley, Singalila, Sunderban

Wildlife Sanctuaries in India

	State/UT	Wildlife Sanctuaries
•	**Andhra Pradesh**	Kolleru Lake, Nagarjuna Sagar, Sri Venkateswara, Pulicat
•	**Arunachal Pradesh**	Mehao
•	**Assam**	Sonai, Rupai, Pabha
•	**Bihar**	Kaimur, Bhimbandha
•	**Chhattisgarh**	Sitanadi
•	**Gujarat**	Narayan Sarovar, (Wild Ass) Nal Sarovar
•	**Haryana**	Sultanpur
•	**Himachal Pradesh**	Kugti, Rupi Bhawa, Govind Sagar
•	**Jammu and Kashmir**	Karakoram, Ramnagar
•	**Jharkhand**	Hazaribagh, Dalma
•	**Karnataka**	Ghatprabha, Dandili, Sharavathi, Ranganathittu, Ranebennur
•	**Kerala**	Waynad, Mudimalai, Idukki
•	**Madhya Pradesh**	Pachmarhi, Gandhi Sagar
•	**Maharashtra**	Koyna, Chandoli, Radhanagari, Karnala, Gautalu, Yaval, Melghat
•	**Mizoram**	Murien
•	**Nagaland**	Fakim
•	**Odisha**	Ushakothi, Karlapat, Chilka Lake, Bhittarkanika
•	**Punjab**	Govind Sagar, Abohar, Harike
•	**Rajasthan**	Mount Abu
•	**Tamil Nadu**	Mundanthurai, Kodikkarai, Indira Gandhi, Vedantangal
•	**Telangana**	Kawal, Eturnagram, Papikonda.
•	**Tripura**	Trishna
•	**Uttarakhand**	Kedarnath
•	**Uttar Pradesh**	Katernighat, Sohagbarwa, Ranipur, Chandraprabha
•	**West Bengal**	Jaldapara

11 NATURAL HAZARDS AND DISASTERS

ENVIRONMENTAL HAZARDS AND DISASTERS

Change is the law of nature. It is continuous process that goes on uninterruptedly involving phenomena, big and small, material and non-material that make over physical and socio-cultural environment. It is a process present everywhere with variations in terms of magnitude, intensity and scale. Change can be gradual or slow process like the evolution of land forms and organisms and it can be as sudden and swift as volcanic eruptions, tsunamis, earthquakes and lightening etc. Similarly, it may remain confined to a smaller area occurring within a few seconds like hailstorms, tornadoes and dust storm, and it can also have global dimensions such as global warming and depletion of the ozone layer.

Besides, these changes have different meanings for different people. It depends upon the perspective one takes while trying to understand them. From the perspective of nature, changes are value-neutral. But from the human perspective, these are value-loaded. There are some changes that are desirable and good like the changes of season, ripening of fruits, while there are others like earthquakes, floods and wars that are considered bad and undesirable.

(A) *HAZARDS*

Natural hazards are elements of circumstances in the natural environment that have the potential to cause harm to people or property or both. These are the phenomena that pose a threat to people, structures or economic assests and which may cause a disaster. They can be man made or naturally occurring in our environment.

(a) Types of Hazards : Broadly, hazards can be classified into three categories depending upon the causes.

(i) *Natural Hazards* : These are caused by the forces of nature and man has no role to play in such hazards.

- Earthquakes
- Volcanic eruptions
- Cyclonic storms
- Tsunamis
- Floods
- Drought
- Landslides

(ii) *Man-Made Hazards* : These are caused by the undesirable activities of man. Such hazards include

- Explosion
- Leakage of toxic waste
- Pollution of air
- Dam failures
- War and civil strife
- Terrorism

(ii) *Socio-natural Hazards* : These are caused by the combined effect of natural forces and misdeeds of man.

- Frequency of floods, droughts
- Strom surge hazards due to destruction of mangroves, are some of the examples

(B) *DISASTER*

"Disaster is an undesirable occurrence resulting from forces that are largely outside human control. It strikes quickly with little or no warning, which causes or threatens serious disruption of life and property including death and injury to a large number of people, and requires therefore, mobilization of efforts in excess of that which are normally provided by Statutory Emergency Services."

Hazards and disasters are closely related or sometimes used as synonymous to each other. Hazards is a threat, while disaster is an event. The latter is a calamity or tragedy or a consequence of a hazard.

Classification of Natural Disasters : Broadly natural disasters can be classified under the following four categories.

EARTHQUAKES

Earthquakes are by far the most unpredictable and highly destructive of all the natural disasters. Earthquakes that are of tectonic origin have proved to be the most devastating and their influence is also quite large. These earthquakes results from a series of earth movements brought about by a sudden release of energy during the tectonic activities in the earth's crust. As compared to these the earthquakes associated with volcanic eruption, rock fall, land slides, subsidence particularly in the mining areas, impounding of dams and reservoirs etc. have limited area of influence and the scale of damage. The Indian plate is moving at a speed of one centimeter per year towards the north and north eastern direction and this movement of plates is being constantly obstructed by the Eurasian plate from the north. As a result of this both the plates are said to be locked with each other resulting in accumulation of energy at different points of time. Excessive accumulation of energy results in building up of stress, which ultimately leads to the breaking up of the rock and the sudden release of energy causing earthquakes along the Himalayan arch.

Some of the most vulnerable states are Jammu and Kashmir, Himachal Pradesh, Uttranchal, Sikkim, and the Darjeeling and subdivision of West Bengal and all the Seven States of North-east. Apart from these regions, the Central-Western parts of India, particularly Gujarat and Maharashtra have also experienced some severe earthquakes. Recently, some earth scientists have come up with a theory of emergence of a fault line and energy build-up along the fault line represented by the River Bhima (Krishan) near Latur and Osmanabad (Maharashtra) and the possible breaking down of the Indian plate.

Geological Survey of India has divided India into five zone as show in fig.

(a) Very high damage risk zone
(b) High damage risk zone
(c) Moderate damage risk zone
(d) Low damage risk zone
(e) Very low damage risk zone

TSUANAMI

Earthquakes and volcanic eruptions that cause the sea floor to move abruptly resulting in sudden displacement of ocean water in the form of high vertical wave are called Tsunamis. Tsunami is derived from two Latin words ***'tsu'*** which means harbour and ***'nami'*** means 'wave'.

The speed of the wave in the oceans depends upon the depth of water. It is more in the shallow water than in the ocean deep. As a result of this, the impact of tsunamis is less over the ocean and more near the coast where they cause large-scale devastations. Thus these are also called "Shallow Water Waves". Tsunamis are frequently observed along the pacific ring of fire. Particularly along the coast of Alaska, Japan, Philippines, and other islands of South-east Asia, Indonesia, Malaysia, Myanmar, Sri Lanka, and India.

FLOODS

Flood is the recurring phenomena in some part of India every year. Floods are usually the result of : (i) heavy rainfall (ii) cyclones accompanied by strong winds (iii) spilling of rivers over natural banks and the rising of the river beds. (iv) inadequate drainage arrangement in cultivated areas and changes in river course through the formation and innundation of river meanders. About 60 per cent of the flood damage in the country occurs from river floods while 40 per cent is due to heavy rainfall and cyclones. Damage by Himalayan rivers account for 60 per cent of the total damage in the country.

Floods accounts for about half the destruction wrought by natural hazards every year. The Indian sub-continent has seen world's worst flood related destruction over the years. The Ganga and the Brahmaputra have annually floded vast tracks of land for millennia. Bloated by heavy monsoons, and the Himalayan snowmelt subcontinent rivers, big and small cause much havoc. Their intensity and fury has been increasing mainly due to deforestation. Denuded forests and other vegetative cover no longer absorbs the heavy monsoon rains.

FLOOD CONTROL MEASURES

In the past people constructed protective bunds or drainage channels for the protection of their houses and even cultivated lands from floods. They were, however, constructed only when there was immediate danger of flood. The embankments were not strengthened until people were threatened by another flood. Thus, they were constructed in a haphazard way. Since 1954, concerted efforts on scientific lines have been made at government level to control floods. Multi-purpose projects have provided protection from floods to some areas. The dams across the Satluj, the Mahanadi, the Godavari and the Damodar have reduced the intensity and the frequency of floods along these rivers to some extent. Though multi-purpose projects have gone a long way in reducing the intensity of floods, they do not seem to have completely solved the problem. In West Bengal a large area west of the Hooghly was flooded in 1956 and 1959 soon after the completion of the D.V.C. Project. Similarly coastal districts of Orissa were devastated by unprecedented high floods in 1960 after the completion of Hirakud Dam. The Brahmani, the

Baitarani and the Sulandi flow close to one another and form a common delta contiguous to the northern part of the Mahanadi Delta. Torrential rainfall in the catchment areas of all these streams flooded their deltaic courses simultaneously.

In addition to the storage dams across big rivers, the following flood control measures are adopted in some parts of our country:—

(1) Drainage channels are dug in the areas which suffer from poor drainage and waterlogging. Some of them are well-maintained and connected ultimately with the rivers. It is advisable to keep the drainage channels away from those towns which are situated at a lower level. A large section of Rohtak (Haryana), situated in a saucer-shaped depression suffered from a disastrous flood in 1960 because a drainage channel which flow near by and at relatively a high-level overflowed its banks. Nearly three-fourths of the population left the town to safe places and its important sections remained under water for nearly two months.

(2) Where roads and railways run across the direction of the flow of flood water, adequate number of culverts should be provided. Canals also offer obstruction; they should flow in aqueducts in flood-affected areas.

(3) The catchment areas of the rivers should be afforested. Indiscriminate cutting of trees should be prohibited. The Shivalik Range and the Chhota Nagpur Plateau require immediate afforestation.

(4) Desilting of those reaches of the river courses and drainage channels which obstruct the free flow of flood water should be resorted to. Straightening of the meandering river channels increases gradient and thus permits free flow of water.

(5) Storage dams should be built across those small streams which have devastated large areas in the past.

(6) The high embankments constructed along the river courses have saved some areas. For example, nearly 120 kms. long embankment on each side of the Kosi in Nepal and Bihar was built in the recent past as a measure against floods. These embankments are 5 to 16 kms. apart. The vagaries of the Kosi have been thus confined within embankments and as many as 20,720 square kms. of land has been saved from devastation. Embankments along the Ghaghara, the Rapti, the Burhi Gandak and a number of other small and large rivers are under construction.

(7) Villages built on the raised ground could also minimize misries of people. The fields may be flooded by surging water, but houses built on raised ground may keep food-grains, fodder, life and property safe from devastation.

In the alluvial plains, it is not possible to eliminate completely the danger of floods. Even if it is done at a huge cost, benefit of fertile silt will be lost and the deposition of silt in the river channels would pose constant danger of erosion to the dykes.

FLOOD PRONE AREAS

(1) **The Basin of Himalayan Rivers** (covering a part of the Punjab, Haryana, Himachal Pradesh, Delhi, Rajasthan, U.P., Bihar and West Bengal) gets flooded on account of overflow, erosion and inadequate drainage, steep gradients of the rivers and change in their courses. Kosi and Damodar devastate large areas. The Brahmaputra basin is subject to earthquakes and landslides, which obstruct the free flow of water.

(2) **The North Western River Basin** Comprising Jammu and Kashmir, parts of Haryana, western U.P., Punjab and Himachal Pradesh are flooded by the tributaries of the Indus (Jhelum, Satluj, Beas, Ravi and Chenab). In Kashmir Valley, the Jhelum is unable to carry the flood discharge. In Punjab and Haryana plains, the problem is mainly of inadequate drainage.

(3) **The Central Indian and Peninsular River Basin,** covering Madhya Pradesh, Orissa, Andhra Pradesh and Maharashtra contains the Tapti, Narmada and the Chambal. In their basins, at times rainfall is excessive, causing occasional floods. Heavy floods also occur in the Godavari, Krishna and Cauvery at long intervals. In Andhra Pradesh, the Kolleru lake submerges vast areas along its fringes.

While heavy monsoonal rains cause major floods in the Himalayan regions, the coastal areas suffer from heavy rainfall in association with tropical cyclones and storm surges.

FLOOD CONTROL POLICY AND PROGRAMMES

The national flood control policy comprises three phases :

(i) Immediate phase extends over two years and comprises collection of basic hydrological data, construction of embankments, urgent repairs, improvement of river channels and raising of villages above flood levels.

(ii) Short-term phase concerns the next four to five years. It consists of improving surface drainage, establishing proper flood warning system, shifting or raising of villages over flood level, construction of channel diversions, more embankments and construction of raised platforms for use in times of flood emergency.

(iii) Long-term phase envisages schemes such as construction of dams or storage reservoirs for flood protection and soil conservation in the catchment of various rivers, detention basins, and digging large channel diversions.

Under the National Flood Control Programme, launched in 1954, protection measures have been taken up since second plan. Emphasis has been given to drainage and anti-waterlogging measures. Flood forecasting and warning centres have been established in some of the most flood prone areas. Flood Control Boards and River Commissios have been set up in all states to coordinate and implement the measures. A Central Flood Control Board, at the national level, has been set up to coordinate the work of State Boards and River Commissions.

Multipurpose reservoirs with specific storage for flood control have been constructed on the Mahanadi (at Hirakud), the Damodar (at Konar, Maithon, Panchet and Tilaiya); on the Satluj (at Bhakra), on the Beas (at Pong); and on the Tapti (at Ukai), which have afforded considerable protection to the lower areas of the rivers.

A number of multipurpose reservoirs, like the Bhakra Nangal on Satluj, the Nagarjun Sagar etc., though not having any specific storage for flood moderation, have given incidental benefits of flood moderation in downstream areas. In addition, a number of flood protection works including construction of embankments, drainage channels, town protection works and raising of villages have been carried out. Flood forecasting system have also been set up at various places.

DROUGHTS

Drought can occur in any area regardless of the amount of rainfall the area may receive or irrespective of its scientific and social advancement. it can occur in small pockets or over a large area. Drought can occur at any time and cause scarcity of water for drinking, irrigation, industry and urban needs. Drought causes deficiency in soil moisture and make the land unproductive. This causes damage to the crops. Droughts are caused due to failure of monsoon or when it is delayed or arrives early or withdraws without giving rain. These circumstances have produced a continuing expansion in India's drought prone areas. Drought is no longer a natural disaster; it is a direct consequence of human activity. The resulting human suffering is enormous and growing.

Drought and aridity are closely related and both indicate a shortage of water. Aridity is a permanent condition whereas drought is a temporary situation. Arid and semi arid regions are prone to drought. Droughts based on their cause, nature and character are classified as meteorological, hydrological, agricultural and ecological. Meteorological drought exist when the average annual ranfall is 25 per cent less than the usual. On the other hand, hydrological drought is one when the water level in the surface and ground falls. The agricultural drought occurs when the soil moisture goes below the level needed to sustain plant growth. Ecological drought occurs when the productivity of a natural ecosystem fails and causes environmental damage like the death of a large number of cattle, wild life or trees in the forest.

The main cause of drought is the inadeuqate and uneven distribution of rainfall. West and central India face an uncertainty of rainfall which they receive in the monsoon season; the rainfall is inadequate as well. The scarcity of rainfall triggers off hydrological and agricultural drought. About 19 per cent of the total area of India experiences drought with 12 per cent of the population being affected by it. Drought is a perennial feature in some states of India. About 30 per cent of the country's total area is drought prone, affecting 50 million people and 68 per cent of total sown area annually. The figure shows three types of drought prone areas, namely extreme, severe and moderate.

Droughts lead to scarcity of foodgrains (*akal*), water (*jalkal*), fodder (*tinkal*) and often all of these (*trikal*). The subsequent famine leads to mass migration of humans and livestock. During the famines of 1868-69, in the Thar desert, all the villages between Jodhpur and Pali, spread over 65 square kilometres were abandoned. In the [illegible]ine years between 1812 and 1940, 30 to 80 per cent of the livestock population died. In 1987, a severe drought affected thirteen states, namely Andhra Pradesh, Gujarat, Himachal Pradesh, Karnataka, Kerala, Madhya Pradesh, Maharashtra, Nagaland, Orissa, Punjab, Rajasthan, Tamil Nadu, and Uttar Pradesh and two union territories of Andaman and Nicobar islands and Delhi. It affected 2.6 lakh villages, a cropped area of 45.4 million hectares and a population of 285 millions. The failure of monsoon in 2002 led to the creation of droughts in most of the central, western and southern states of India.

CYCLONES

India's 7,517 kms coastline has been raked by cyclones for centuries. The term 'Cyclone' denote all tropical storms; it is called '*hurricane*' in the Atlantic and the Eastern Pacific, *typhoon*" in the western Pacific, '*willy-willy*' in Australia and *bagius* in the Philippines.

Cyclones are usually located approximately 30 degrees above and below the equator. They vary in diameter from 50 kms to 320 kms, but their effects dominate thousands of sq. kms of ocean surface and the lower atmosphere. The perimeter may measure 1,000 km but the powerhouse is located within the 100 kms radius. Nearer the eye, winds may hit 320 km ph.

Tropical cyclones are intensifying swirls of cloud and rain which then progress into tropical storms. They spin clockwise in the northern Hemisphere and anti-clock wise in the southern hemisphere.

Between five and 20 kms tall when fully formed, they become self-sustaining and bloat until they hit cool land or ocean being of oceanic origin, they generally hit the east coast of the continents.

The Indian subcontinent is the worst cyclone affected part of the world as a result of a low-depth ocean bed topography and coastal configuration. Stretches along the Bay of Bengal Coast-line have the world's shallowest waters. The relatively dense population and poor economic condition completes the picutre. The population density in some of the coastal districts is as high as 670 person per square km compared to the state average of 26 persons per sq km. Cyclone strike here in May-June and October-November, with the monsoon's onset and retreat.

Cyclones of a diameter of 600 kms or more is one of the most destructive and dangerous atmospheric storms on the earth. With about 6 per cent of the world wide cyclones, the Indian sub-continent is the worst cyclone affected areas.

No universally acknowledged theory of occurrence of tropical cyclone is known today. A tropical cyclone can form when the horizontal temperature gradients are exceedingly high around a weakly developed area of low pressure. The cyclone is the heat engine whose heater is the oceanic surface. The released heat after condensation converts it into kinetic energy for the cyclone. The following are the stages in the formation of a cyclone :

(a) Temperature of the oceanic surface over 26°C
(b) Appearance of a closed isobar
(c) Low pressure dropping below 1000 mb
(d) Areas of circular movement, first spreading to a radius of 30-50 kms then increasing gradually to 100-200 kms and even to 1000 kms. and
(e) Vertically the wind speed first rising to a height of 6 km, then much higher.

INDIAN EFFORTS TOWARDS A CYCLONE WARNING SYSTEM

India, according to the World Meteorological Organisation, suffers only six per cent of the total cyclones worldwide. China and Japan face upto 30 per cent (calling them typhoons), and the Americas 23 per cent (hurricanes). But these regions do not suffer such massive devastation. Clearly, there is a way to prevent it. But that needs a comprehensive disaster-management policy.

India has an efficient cyclone warning system. Tropical cyclones are tracked with the help of (i) regular observation from weather network of surface and upper air observation stations, (ii) ships reports, (iii) cyclone detection radars, (iv) satellites, and (v) reports from commercial aircraft.

About 280 ships of merchant fleet have meteorological instruments for taking observations at sea. A network of ten cyclone detection radars have been set up along the coast at Kolkata, Paradip, Visakhapatnam, Machilipatnam, Chennai, Karaikal, Cochin, Goa, Mumbai and Bhuj. The range of coastal radars, its intensity and movement is monitored with weather satellies.

Warnings are issued by the area cyclone warning

centres located at Kolkata, Chennai and Mumbai, and cyclone warning centres at Bhubaneswar, Visakhapatnam and Ahmedabad.

The IMD still largely depends on DoT's telegraph and telecommunication channels for transfer of data to area cyclone centres as well as dissemination of warnings to various users like district collectors, state government officials, etc. As the storm approaches the coasts, many of these channels completely breakdown.

To overcome these difficulties, IMD has developed a system known as Disaster Warning System (DWS) to transmit cyclone warning bulletins through INSAT-DWS to the recipents.

IMD undertakes observations, communications, forecasting and weather services. In collaboration with the Indian Space Research Organisation, the IMD also uses the IRS series and the Indian National Satellite System (INSAT) for weather monitoring of the Indian subcontinent. IMD was first weather bureau of a developing country to develop and maintain its own satellite system.

IMD is one of the six worldwide Regional Specialised Meteorological Centres of the Tropical Cyclone Programme of the World Weather Watch of the World Meteorological Organization.It is regional nodal agency for forecasting, naming and disseminating warnings about tropical cyclone in the Indian Ocean north of the Equator.

The IMD launched System of Aerosol Monitoring and Research (SAMAR) in January 2016 to study the concentration of Black carbon, radiative properties of aerosols, environmental visibility and their climatological impacts. It would contain a network of 16 aethalometers, 12 sky radiometers and 12 nephelometers.

LANDSLIDES

A landslide is the rapid sliding of large masses of bed rocks or regoliths. Whenever mountain slopes are steep there is a possibility of large disastrous landslide. Landslides are triggered by earthquakes or sudden rock failures. They can also result when the base of a slope is over steepened by excavation or river erosion. Severe earthquakes in mountainous regions are a major cause of landslides.

In the Himalayas, the Western Ghats, and along the river valleys landslides are a common feature. Natural removal of soil and rock from slopes is known as mass wasting. Landslide as a hazard has long been recognised by the people living in the mountains. It becomes specially dangerous when there is heavy rainfall or snowfall on the slip and break.

The extent of landslides depends on the steepness of the slope, the bedding plane of rocks, the amount of vegetation cover and the extent of folding and faulting of the rocks. It is the rocks that break and carry with it the soil and debris. A major cause which triggers off the landslide is the weight of the overlying material and the presence of a lubricating material like water, this is known as **solifluction**. Freezing and thawing of the rocks on mountain slopes cause them to break and roll down the slopes. The overbearing weight of snow or ice or water which has seeped into the soft permeable rocks also lead to slipping and breakage of hill slopes.

Other causes of the landslides are the volcanoes and earthquakes. In areas which have sedimentary rock and steep slopes tremors dislodge the rock structures and cause falls. Often near sea coasts as for example the Kanara coast, cliffs are eroded at the base by sea waves and the rocks jutting out on top break off and fall. Landslides occur frequently during the rains. Deforestation as a result of felling of trees for timber and removal of vegetation cover for developmental activities are also responsible for soil erosion and destabilization of slopes. It is estimated that the construction of just one kilometre long road requires removal of 40,000 to 80,000 cubic metres of debris, which slide down the slopes, killing vegetation and choaking mountain streams.

Humans often make changes in the natural slope for construction of roads and buildings. Such changes make hill sides more vulnerable to mass wasting and landslides.

EFFECT OF LANDSLIDES

The landslides cause havoc to man but are the nature's way of getting rid of the excess materials that accumulate on the hill slopes and prevent trees and grasses from finding roots. The formation of new slopes is usually the consequence of landslide and mass wasting. Rivers often get blocked by the debris brought by landslides. The Birahi Tal in Garhwal, for example, was formed in 1893 when 5000 million tonnes of crushed pyrite bearing shale and dolomitic limestone slipped along a 45 degree steep slope filling the valley of the Birahi Ganga and changing the river into a lake. Such lakes are washed out in due course of time.

DISASTER MANAGEMENT

The term disaster management includes all aspects of preventive and protective measures, preparedness, and organisation of relief operations for mitigating the impact of disaster on human beings and socio-economic aspects of the disaster prone areas. The whole process of disaster management can be divided into three phases : impact phase, rehabilitation and reconstruction phase and integrated long term development and preparedness phase.

Impact phase contains three components : forecasting of disaster, close monitoring of agents causing disasters and management activities after the disaster has occurred. Flood forecasting can be done by studying rainfall in the catchment area. Approach of cyclones can be tracked and monitored by satellites; based on these details, early warning and evacuation efforts may be made. Close monitoring of agents responsible for disaster can help deployment of teams to help evacuation and supply of food, clothing and drinking water. Disaster leaves a trail of death and destruction. This will require medical care and help of various kinds to the affected people. Under long term development phase preventive and precautionary measures of various kinds should be chalked out.

In order to draw attention of the people of the world the UNESCO observed International the Decade for Natural Disaster Reduction (IDNDR) during 1990-2000. Along with other nations of the world, India observed World Disaster Reduction Day in October during the decade. Do's and Donot's for the people in areas of earthquakes, floods and cyclones, which were issued by the Government of India on the occasion are useful. The International Day for Disaster Reduction, held each year on 13 October, celebrates how people and communities around the world are reducing their exposure to disasters.

LARGE LANDSLIDES OF INDIA

Year	Location	Effects
1971	Alaknanda (Uttarakhand)	Heavy rainfall and erosion of hill slopes caused damming of river and burst of banks involving loss of life, property and disruption of communication. Village Belakuchi was completely washed away. This is termed as the Alaknanda Tragedy.
1993	Ratighat (Uttarakhand)	Nainital hill area remained cut off for about a week. Five bulldozers worked day and night to clear the debris. Landslide followed heavy rains.
1993	Nilgiri Hills (Tamil Nadu)	Forty people in the landslides, over 600 families shifted to safer places. Road and houses destroyed. Landslide followed heavy rains.

HUMAN IMPACT ON THE NATURAL ENVIRONMENT

The human impact on natural environment is one of the most pressing issues of contemporary times and a subject of discussion. In geographical literature, the ways in which human beings have changed and are changing the face of the earth and the human role in the natural processes and systems have drawn the attention not only of natural scientists but also of social scientists as well as of planners and policy makers.

(A) HUMAN IMPACT ON CLIMATE AND ATMOSPHERE

The increasing human population and the rising level of technology, both have become significant factors in the variation in world climate and are responsible for the various changes in atmospheric conditions as well as of air pollution. The human influence on global climate is due to the Gas Emissions,

(CO_2 Industrial and Agricultural), Chlorofluro Carbons (CFCs) and Nitrous Oxide, Krypton 85, Water Vapour, Deforestation, Overgrazing and extension of irrigation.

(A) *CO_2 EMISSION*

The problem of CO_2 emission has become a major environmental concern. Since the beginning of the Industrial Revolution humans have been taking stored carbon out of the earth in the form of coal, petroleum and natural gas, and burning it to make CO_2, heat, water vapour and small amounts of SO_2 and other gases, which are responsible for air pollution, green house effect, increase in surface temperature, or in other words, global warming. By 2050, it is possible that the increase in global surface temperature ranges between 1.4 and 2.2 degree celsius

The impact of human influence on the atmosphere is more because the atmosphere acts as a major channel for the transfer of pollutants from one place to another. It is in this way that harmful substances have been transferred long distance from their sources of emission. A second example of the possible widespread and ramifying ecological consequences of atmospheric pollution is provided by acid rain.

In recent years, the greatest attention has been focussed on the role of CFCs, the production of which has been rising in last few decades. These gases may diffuse upwards into the stratosphere where solar radiation causes them to become disassociated to yield chlorine atoms which react with and destroy the ozone present there.

(B) *HUMAN IMPACT ON VEGETATION*

The human impact on vegetation is greater than on any of the other components of the environment. The nature of whole landscape has been transformed by human-induced vegetation.

Man has used fire for the clearnance of forest cover, mainly for the use of land for cultivation or for habitation. This practice was common during the early stage of the development of civilizations. But, this practice is still prevalent among many tribals. Uncontrolled and heavy grazing is not only a cause of the disappearence of vegetation cover but is also responsible for desertifications and other environmental problems.

The deliberate removal of forest or deforestation is one of the most long-standing and significant ways in which humans have modified the environment, whether achieved by fire or cutting.

Sometimes forests have been cut down to allow agriculture, at other times to provide fuel for domestic purposes or to provide charcoal or wood for construction etc. The spread of desert like conditions, the arid and semi-arid area is always due to man's influence. Some of the air pollutants, humans have released into the atmosphere, have had detrimental impact on plants. Sulphur dioxide, for example, is toxic to them. Local concentration of Industrial fumes also kill vegetation. Photo-chemical smog is also known to have adverse effect on plants both within cities and also on their outskirts.

(C) *HUMAN IMPACT ON SOIL*

Soil is the most vulnerable of human resource and is one on which humans have had a very major impact, because they lie close to and depend an the soil. Impact on soil can occur with great rapidity in response to land use change by new technologies.

Salinity is a natural characteristicis in semi-arid and arid soils. But humans have increased the extent and degree of salinity in different ways. The extension of irrigation and different techniques used for water abstraction can lead to a build-up of salt levels in the soil through the mechanism of raising ground water level.

Construction of large dams and barrage to control water flow and to give a head of water creates large reservoir from which further evaporation can take place. The seepage of water is responsible for upward movement of ground water. In coastal areas, salinity problems are created by sea water incursion brought by over pumping. Human activities are also responsible for the structural changes in the soil. There are many ways in which humans can alter this, especially by compacting it with agricultural machinery and by changing its chemical character through irrigation. Grazing is another activity that can damage soil structure through trampling and compaction.

The introduction of chemical fertilizers has also changed the chemistry of soils. Some times these create environmental problems such as water pollution, while their substitution for more traditional fertilizers may accelerates structure deterioration and social erosion.

(D) *HUMAN IMPACT ON THE WATERS*

Water is the source of life and right from the origin, human beings are using it for various purposes. The ancient civilizations have developed in river valley. This is also true about medieval townships and other developments, and all modern developments are related directly or indirectly to water. The main concern is that by using waters, humans have influenced both its quantity and quality. Earlier, the influence of human activity on water resources was limited but now this has become a major problem of environmental degradation throughout the world.

The consideration of dams and reservoirs is widespread through out the world for irrigation purpose, to generate power or to provide a reliable source of water. The impact of human activities is especially marked in Africa and North America where about 20% of total run-off is now controlled. The impact of dam-construction is apparent in the form of change in ecosystem and environmental conditions. The recent environment controversy over Tehri and Sardar Sarovar dams show people's awareness against construction of dams and their possible damaging environmental impact.

The environmental consequences of dams include subsidence, earthquake triggering, transmission and expansion in the range of organism, the build-up of soil salinity, changes in ground water levels, waterlogging deforestation, etc.

The process of urbanization has a considerable impact, both in terms of controlling rates of erosion, the delivery of pollutants to rivers and in terms of influencing the nature of run-off and other by hydrological characteristics.

Deforestation gives rises to floods, annual run-off levels and also affects on-stream flow. In many parts of the world, humans obtain water supplies by pumping from ground water, it reduces level of water table and the replacement of coastal areas' fresh water by salt water.

12 HUMAN GEOGRAPHY: NATURE & SCOPE

HUMAN GEOGRAPHY

Human geography, also known as **cultural geography**, as a branch of the modern discipline, deals with the evolution of human beings i.e. changing distribution and spatial organisation of a variety of human characteristics, ranging from great urban centres built by man to the geographical diffusion of specific technical innovations in agriculture. It is accepted that it is not the physical environment alone that determines human ability to make the best use of the natural sources.

It is divided into following sub fields to make the study more comprehensive :

1. Economic Geography: Economic geography concerns itself with man's activities in improving his material well-being through economic production, exchange distribution and consumption, of useful goods and services, that human groups and their members need. Economic geography is a very important sub-field of human geography and has developed very fast in the recent past.

2. Cultural Geography: This is also called **Social Geography**. It deals with the cultural aspects of different human groups, which include man's habitat, clothing, food, shelter, skills, tools, language, religions, social organisation and his outlook.

3. Historical Geography: Historical geography seeks to build up the geographical picture of a region or area, as it has evolved during the years in the past. It gives us important clues in understanding the region as it is at present. Historical geography is considered simply as the geography of the past periods.

4. Anthrogeography studies the distribution of human communities on the Earth in relation to their geographical environment.

5. Demography is the science that studies the different aspects of population like birth rate, death rate and age composition. It also studies the socio-economic composition of the population and sex composition.

6. Settlement Geography deals with the size, form and functions of settlement built by human beings, and analyses their historic growth.

7. Agricultural Geography studies how different kinds of farms and farming systems have developed in particular areas and how they are different or similar to the farms and farming systems of other areas.

8. Urban Geography studies the concepts of location, interaction and accessibility as well as distribution and movements of populations. It deals with land use patterns and classification of cities according to their function.

9. Political Geography deals with the government states and countries. It studies human social activities that are related to the location and boundaries of cities, nations and groups of nations.

CULTURAL GEOGRAPHY

NATURE AND SCOPE OF CULTURAL GEOGRAPHY

Cultural Geography is a systematic branch of geography which deals with the characteristics and identity of communities and societies like language, religion, observing similar manner and customs at local, regional and national level with a central emphasis on people-environment relationships. In other words, the same as similar cultural traits within a particular geographical field or region may be said to form cultural geography.

The cultural geography is synonymous with much narrower geographical traditions concerned with cultural differences. In U.K., it is associated with descriptive regional geography. While in North America it is equated with the human geography.

Cultural geography depends entirely on the direct field observations on the people environment relationship and has its origins in the work of Carl Sauer, who emphasized upon the ways in which the differential impact and succession of culture groups was imprinted in the exploitation, form and personality of the landscape.

Environment and Culture

Environment is the most determining factor of culture. The changing pattern of the culture of a man or a society is directly related with the environmental aspects of the region. For example, in a desert region where hot climate predominate then the culture of the region will be certainly different from the polar region where ice and cold climate predominate.

The culture and traits of these two regions will be entirely different from one-another. Thus, we can say that environment is the most determining factor of culture and plays the most dominant role in the prevalent culture of the region.

CONCEPT OF CULTURE-AREAS AND CULTURAL REGIONS

The characteristics of Cultural Realms fall into two categories:

(a) A unique combination of cultural features should generally pervade the area to be organized as a cultural entity.

(b) The cultural features must be different from the neighbouring area for recognition and demarcation of the boundary.

Various Cultural realms have been identified on the basis of cultural types which includes variations in economic activities, social customs, traditional values, dietary habits, dress patterns, language and physical characteristics.

The major Cultural realms are :

1. The Occidental Realm : It is mainly the culture of European society, influenced mainly by christianity. It has great regional variation according to the levels of industrialization, political and economic thought, colonisation, commercialisation, urbanisation, development of transport system, social, political and economic institutions. The occidental realm is further sub-divided into six sub-regions :

(i) **West European :** It is the most urbanised, industrialised and developed cultural realm.

(ii) **Continental European :** It is influenced by different political and economic thoughts. It is influenced mainly by Christianity.

(iii) **Mediterranean European Culture :** This region is also christian dominated and includes countries lying South of the Alps. The limited economic developement in these countries is due to deep rooted traditional social system.

(iv) **The Anglo American Realm :** The region is endowed with natural resources, hence industrialisation and urbanisation is very high. British influence is quite significant in this region.

(v) **Australian Cultural Realm :** It is an off-shoot of European cultural realm. The region has struck a balance between agriculture and industry. The people of this region are well educated, energenetic and progressive with a high living standard.

(vi) **Latin American Cultural Realm :** Only culture which lies in occidental realm but still backward. The colonial language of spanish and portuguese have become state language. Hence, spanish and portuguese influence is quite prevalent in this realm.

2. The Islamic Cultural Realm : The prominent religious faith in this realm is Islam. This realm lies between the traditional Indian culture in the east and the modernised European culture in the west. This culture is very orthodox and based on traditional beliefs. The level of modernisation is very low here.

3. The Indian Cultural Realm : It is also known as sub-continental realm or paddy culture. It is spread between Himalayas in the north to Indian ocean in the South, Hindukush mountain in the east to Bay of Bengal in the east. This realm has some typical features like joint-family, caste-system, semi-feudal land relations, subsistence agriculture, paddy farming etc.

4. The East Asian Cultural Realm : It is basically a Buddhist Culture with regional modification. The level of industrialisation, modernisation and urbanisation in this realm is high. Japan, South Korea and other countries are part of this realm.

5. The South East Asian Realm : It is generally a traditional culture lying in a region where different culture get inter-mingled.

For example : Dominance of Buddhism can be seen in Myanmar, Thailand and Vietnam, dominance of Christianity in Philippines, impact of Indian culture in Indonesian islands while impact of islamic culture in Malaysia and Indonesian islands can be seen.

6. The Negro African Realm : It is a widely scattered cultural realm characterized by marginalised and relatively isolated communities. It mainly includes tropical African region.

THEORIES OF TRIBAL GROUPS: HUMAN RACES

Race can be defined as "a biological grouping within the human species, distinguished or classified according to genetically transmitted differences".

Thus, race is a large group of people who share a common ancestry and have certain physical characteristics (*e.g.* skin colour, hair colour etc). Races can be scientifically classified on the basis of certain fixed, inherited and identifiable traits such as head shape, facial features, nose shape, eye shape, colour, skin colour, stature etc. These traits represents morphological, biological and genetical aspects. With the inclusion of more traits, the number of combination increases and the analysis becomes more complex.

There are difference among the scholar about the origin of different races. Some argue that the racial differences existed from the very beginning while others argue that different races developed from one single ancestral species. Similarly, there are a lot of differences among scholars on the number of racial groups but seven chief racial groups have been accepted in the world. These are :

1. Negroids : are the people with dark black skin, black woolly hair, dark eyes, broad and flat nose, thick and averted lips, long head, proganthous jaw and stocky body build. They are inhabitants of Africa and Oceania and thus consists of two branches :

(i) **The African Branch :** It includes the sub-groups :

(a) Forest or True Negro in W.Africa.
(b) Sudanese in Central Africa.
(c) Nilotic in East Africa.
(d) The Bantu in S.Africa.
(e) The Bushmen-Hottentot in the Kalahari Desert of S. Africa.
(f) The African Pygmies.

(ii) The oceanic Negroids are commonly called Melanesian of papuan and are found chiefly in Borneo, New Guinea, the Soloman, the Hebrides and Fiji Islands.

2. Mangoloids : They are people with light yellow to brown skin colour, brown eyes, straight and coarse black hair, flat face and nose, broad head, epicanthic eye-fold, high cheekbones and short but stocky build or stature. The Mongoloids are usually divided into following sub-groups :

(i) The Tungus group.
(ii) The palaeo-Asiatic.
(iii) The sinic group.
(iv) The South Mongoloid group.
(v) The Oceanic Mongols.

3. Caucasoids : They are people with fair skin and eyes, light and wavy hair, prominent and narrow nose, thin lips and abundant body hair, medium to tall stature, long to broad-short and medium or high head form. They are further sub-divided into following sub-groups.

(i) The Nordic or North-West European Group.
(ii) The Alpine or central European Group.
(iii) The Mediterranean of S.W. European Group.
(iv) The Baltic or N.E. European Group.
(v) The Dinaric or S.E. European.
(vi) Armenoid in Western Asia minor and North Central Asia.
(vii) The Turanian or Turki Group.
(viii) Indo-Afghans, Dravidians and Pre-Dravidians.
(ix) Nesiot and Polynesian Groups.
(x) The Arabic, Hamitic and berber groups in North Africa.

These three were the major earliest racial groups. But later, other racial groups were also identified. These are :

4. Negritoids : They have yellow to brown skin, black spiral hair, short stature and varying blood groups. Such people are known as Negrillo in Congo Basin and upper Nile region and as Negrito in Andaman Islands, parts of Malaysia and New Guinea. The two display different blood groups.

5. Bushmanoids : They have skin and hair like Negritoids but have flat face, epicanthic eye folds etc. Such groups are found in Southern Africa.

6. Australoids : They have dark skin and eyes, dark wavy hair, broad nose, full lips, long head and A and O blood types. B type is not found among them. Such people include Australian aborigines, Ainu of Hokkaido (Japan), Vedda of Sri Lanka, and Bhil, Kurumba, Gond of Deccan Plateau (India).

7. Papuan-Melanesians : They are much like Australoids but have more frizzly hair. Such racial group is found in New Guinea (Papuans) and Melanesia (salomons).

Dwelling places as cultural expressions

The tribal people constitute about 4% of the world's population. These tribal people differ in their stature, shape of head, blood type, skin colour, hair, eye fold etc. Some of the chief tribes of the world with their food, dress and living ways are as follows:

The Pygmies : They live in tropical Africa. They are further classified into three groups :

(i) Eastern Pygmies of Africa are called Mbuti living in forests of Zaire.

(ii) The central pygmies live in the Congo Republic.

(iii) The Western pygmies live in Gibon and called Bongo.

They vary from 1.33 m to 1.50 m in height. The colour of skin varies from yellowish or reddish brown to dark brown. They have broad flat nose, large eyes and dark woolly hair. They are gatherer and hunter who hunt with bow and poisoned arrow. Their main food items are obtained from trees, plants, nuts, birds and insects. The warm humid and damp climate of the congo-basin allows pygmies to live in a state of complete nakedness.

The Bedouins : They are most numerous tribes of S.W. Asia and North Africa. Usually they are more than 5 feet in height and have a long, narrow face with prominent nose, dark eyes and hair and a pale complexion. They are seasonal migrants. Their main food item is camel milk along with barley, dates and mutton.

The Eskimos : They are found in the Arctic and Antarctic Tundra regions. They are still in the primitive stage of development leading a semi-nomadic life. Hunting, fishing and gathering are their main occupations. They are short in stature, have flat and narrow face, small snub noses, yellow brown skin colour and coarse straight black hair. Their clothes are made up of reindeer and furs. They wear a sack like coat of reindeer which hide them up to knees with long sleeves and tail is attached with it.

The Eskimos construct igloos or snow houses for living. It is made up of snow blocks. They belong to Mongoloid race. They are mainly confined in the regions which include Aleution Islands, Alaska, Northern Canada, Victoria, Baffin, Northern parts of Norway, Sweden, Finland etc.

The Khirgiz : They are located in central Asia, Southern Tien Shan and Pamirs. They are well known for courage, vigilance, wariness, sense of locality and keen powers of observation etc. During winter, they migrate to the valleys with their herds. Barley, Millet, Wheat, and fodder are their agricultural products. Hunting is their occupation also. They wear long, wool-padded clothes to protect themselves from winter.

The Bushmen : They are also called sun. They live in the Kalahari Desert (Namibia) of Africa. They are short in stature and look like Negritos. They eat small animals like Ants, Lizards, Frogs, Beer and locusts. They are basically hunters. The women collect the roots, berries, grubs, insects, Tortoises, Lizards. They wear scanty clothes. Men wear a triangular loin cloth, while women wear cioak.

The Aborigines : The original inhabitants of Australia are known as Aborigines or Aborginals. The term aborigines literally applies to earliest known inhabitants of a land or those found in possession of the land by early colonists. The term may be applied to human inhabitants, animals and plants. They belong to the indigenous Australoid race. Their physical features is like Negroid with the difference that their hair are wavy and never woolly. Their stature varies from short ot medium ranging between 1.6 m to 1.75 m. They have broad and narrow face and colour of eyes varying from brown to brown-black. They indulge in worst evils like cannibalism, human scrifice, slavery and witchcraft. In some cases, the relatives of a deceased person eat portions of his body or the oldmen of trible are killed often at their own request and eaten by their children, relations and friends, who think that it is better to keep their parents in the warmth of their bellies than in the lovely hot or cold of the earth.

The Masai : They belong to East Africa and have a pastoral society. They are well known as cattle-herders of East Africa. They are dark in colour, tall, slim, with long, small limb bones, narrow feet and hands and long fingers. They have thin faces, nose and lips being thinner than those of Negroid people. The older men and girls shave their hair closely to the head.

Livestock is the main source of their food. Ox blood is favourite and important ingredient in the diet. Sheep act as source of milk, blood and meat. The staple food are millets and maize. Root crops and banana are eaten by women and children.

The clothes of Masai are simply made of skin. Women and warrior wear elaborate ornaments. The warrior wear calf's skin garment. Women wear goat skin aprons.

They are mainly concentrated in the interior plateau of the Northern parts of East Africa in Kenya, Northern Tanzania and Eastern Uganda.

Language, Caste and religion: Social Geography

Indian's cultural landscape can be likened to a kaleidoscope revealing the interplay of several religion, sects, creeds, languages, races, and ethnic groups. The diversity and complexity of these culture groups remains virtually unmatched by any other major country. Cultural impact from a variety of sources : Hindu, Buddhist, Greek, Persian, Islamic—and British have left their distinctive imprints and transformed the cultural landscape.

Spatial patterns of Religions :

Of the diverse cultural forces affecting the cultural and political life of most Indians, religion is unquestionably the most dominant. It permeate virtually all aspects of their daily personal and family life.

Geographically, the religious distributions may be studied in several spatial contexts. At the level of the village, religion is a pervasive force. Religious beliefs sanction caste restrictions on types of labour, and prejudice against certain cropping systems and veneration of cows have inhibited technological and agricultural progress. Religious groups and caste divisons have often generated political disharmony in villages. Social stratification based on religion and caste, has been manifested in residential segregation and has restricted cooperative and collective village efforts. In urban centres which are not well-linked among themselves but not well-linked with a vast rural society, there is a greater diversity of religious adherence which has compounded the spatial interactions developing among the various communities. The urban world affords greater opportunities for the various groups to solidify their political forces into political parties. Sharp cleavages along social, linguistic and religious lines fuel inter-community riots, occasionally some of which are masterminded by religion-based political parties. Indian history, during the British occupancy as well contemporaneously, is replete with examples of Hindu-Muslim riots, which were actively supported by political groups.

Another spatial level of geographic enquiry consists of groups of districts (administrative divisions) containing a religious community with a numerical majority. Such compact areas tend to exercise their political influence on state and union administrations.

Religion and the Organization of space

Indian religious beliefs have found direct expression on the landscape in a variety forms like the erection of religious structures, place of worship cemeteries and burial places. Religious adherence has also indirectly affected the land of Hinduism, Islam, Christianity, Jainism and Buddhism have prescribed regulation regarding reproduction, life and death which, in turn, have affected demographic resource relationship. Indian landscape are dotted with sacred places : temples, tombs, Holy rivers and places of piligrimage. Religious injuction have stratified society into caste divisions, which have influenced the whole range of human activites including altitudes to land utilization.

Hinduism is numerically the largest and the oldest of the Indian religions and, its imprint on the cultural landscape is the strongest. Over the centuries, it has grown into a highly complex system, consisting of loosely organised group diverse cults and sects incorporating beliefs ranging from polytheism to monotheism to monism. In its most intellectual form, it emphasizes the pervasiveness of the supreme being, the indestructibility and transmigration of soil, non- violence, reincarnation and preordained birth in a particular caste. Jainism, Buddhism and Sikhism which broke off from it as revolt against its ritual practices, have not escaped. Hindu influence in their social satisfication and in the observance of rituals. These religious groups have, however maintained their distinctive places of worship and their served shrines.

Formal expression of Indian religions on the landscape is manifested in their sacred structures, use of cemeteris and assemblages of plants and animals for religious purposes. Streets, Parks, Bridges, Trees and Rivers are dotted with the statues or abstract figures of Gods, which constantly receive the propitations of the passers by. Scared structures are widely and conspiciously village shrines (or even a small idol embedded in a roadside wall) to large Hindu temples, monumental mosques or ornately designed cathedrals in large metropolitan areas. Whether it is a Hindu temple, or a Sikh Gurdwara, or a Muslim mosque, or a Buddhist monastery, such communal sacred buildings differ in size, form, space use and density, depending on the ideological and organiza-tion requirements of the religious order. All, however, perform a basic religious function.

A distinction between structure, housing a God or those meant for congregation may be made. Hindu temples invariably enshine a statue or a symbol of a deity, whereas mosques, gurdwara, or churches are basically designed for religious congregations. In addition to their basic religious functions, such structures tend to acquire secular attributes as well, and often maintain guest rooms for pilgrims and other visitors. Business and political conventions, folk festivals, and recreational activities are also arranged in areas specially demarcated for such purposes within these religious structures. Although many of the Hindu holy places established at remote places (Badrinath, Kedarnath), most religious structures are located where adherents can regularly attend the services, their spacing and density parallel that of the hierarchy of settlements. Large Hindu temples are maintained by the various caste groups, wealth of Hindu temples is the form of jewelry and property alone is estimated to be in billions of dollars. Hindu temples often house a number of gods, since many Hindus are electric and propiliate not one, but several gods, believing that all gods are merely manifestations of one supreme entity.

A typical Hindu temple is distinctive in layout and architectural style. Unlike a mosque or church, it does not necessarily require a large closed interior space for congregation where prayers are held. The statue of the chief deity is usually sheltered in inner shrine surrounding it are the corridors (pavilions) for ritual circulation (parikrama) by the public. Elaborate temple gateways direct one's entry into the building. Jain and Buddhist temples also adhere to this basic plane. Sikhs do not enshrine a statue, and Sikh temples tend to adopt the congregational aspect of Islam and Christianity; space is allocated for the purpose. Islam and Christianity emphasize the congregational aspect of prayer. The focus of activity in their places of worship is congregational prayer space for which a hall or a compound is specifically allocated within a church or masjid or jami. In Islam community worship is speritually presribed and universally practiced within the precinets of a mosque, an open space, usually rectangular in shape and unclosed by walls, is maintained.

The relative impress of religious structures on the land depends on the frequency of their distribution, the number of clients of the religious order, the wealth and enthusiasm of the religious clientele and the ecclesiastic requirements of the various religions. In Goa, Kerala, parts of Assam and Large Urban centers, Christianity impress of churches, mission houses and Bible centers is pronounced. Areas controlled by Muslim rulers between the thirteenth and eighteenth centuries, especially urban centers like Delhi, Agra, Allahabad, Hyderabad and Lucknow, clearly exemplify the strong Islamic impress on the cultural landscape. Mosques like Jama Masjid in Delhi and Shahi Masjid in Agra (both built by Shahjahan in seventeenth century) are among the noble examples of monumental structures which do most large Indian cities.

Religious functions can also be performed outside temples of worship, often in a home or even in an open space. Virtually every household Hindu, Sikh or Buddhist has a family shrine and place reserved for worship. Many Hindus keep household gods, symbolized by status or paintings, located at a designated place in their homes. Ritual prayers of Muslims (namaz) can be said anywhere at appropriate times, even in a moving train.

Cemeteries, burial places, and cremation grounds constiture other direct expressions of religious affiliation on the land. The Hindu, Buddhist, Jain and Sikh tradition of cremation of the dead is very different from the Muslim and Christian insititution of burial in a community ground and thus leaves a different cultural imprint on the land Burial grounds. For example, impose a squeeze on useful land within cities.

Religions occasionally bestow on certain plants or animals a degree of sanctity or ritual function. Such plants and animals are kept in religions structures or dispersed along pilgrims routes. Tulsi and Pipal tree though of limited economic or decorative value, are sanctified by Hindus and Buddhists. The turmeric plant's sanctity is recognized because its pigments in used in Hindu rituals, sandal wood's dye is considered sacred and is used in the ritual marks on the forehead by religious Hindus. Rice is a sacred plant becuase it is used in most Hindu and Buddhist ceremonies and ritual observances. Coconut and ghee (clarified butter) are also used in ritual ceremonies.

Associations between religions and places are developed in many other ways. The distribution of Holy places and place names honoring thousands of Hindu God Muslim and Christian saints, indicate the direction and history of religious movement. Hundreds of places of pilgrimages express the direct formal expression of religion on the land. The geography of Indian Holy places (Hindu, Jain,

Buddhist, Sikhs and Muslims) is rendered complex by the large pantheon of Hindu gods, Muslim saints, Jain tirthankars and Sikh gurus. River sources such as Mansarovar like (in Tibet) & Badrinath in Himalayas, river confluences (Allahabad) physiographic breaks in the course of rivers (Hardwar, srirangan) mountain peak (Mt. Abu), lakes (Pushkar) caves (Amarnath) have all been sanctified by several religions. Large temple have been established in many of these location, and these in turn, have favoured urbanization. Amritsar located at a spring lake (A holy place of the Sikhs) is another example. Many present day large urban centres originated with a predominantly religious function as sacred places of pilgrimages like Varanasi, Madurai, Tirupati, Allahabad and Mathura. In addition to their normal sanctified character as pilgrimage sites, many of these attract regular periodic assemblages *e.g.* Kumbha Mela every 12 years.

Pilgrimage has been an important mechanism of religious circulation (tirthayatra) involving million of Hindus, Jains, Buddhist, Muslims, Sikhs and to a lesser extent Christians each year, a number increases manifold during Kumbha Mela. These periodic pilgrimages afford a continuing forum for the exchange of religious ideas, often cutting across linguistic and some times religious barriers, Pilgrimages also generate cultural exchange, social mixing and trade and contribute to political integration. Pilgrim circulation, however can also diffuse epidemic diseases. An infromal hierarchy of the distribution of pilgrim centre may be recognizable at the National, regional and local levels, each level maintaining its religious hinterland (Bhardwaj 1989: 225–228)

Religions have prescribing or encouraged taboos on work and food which may interact with the cultural landscape. General taboos against the killing of animals and meat eating among Hindus, Buddhist & Jains has result in a lack of development of the diary & beef industry. The taboo on beef eating by Hindus and extension of the idea of ahinsa (Non-Violence) has resulted in the accumulation of an enormous cattle population, a large part of which is edge, diseased and unproductive. It is a pity that very little attention has been paid to efficient stock breeding in Indias. However, future breeding should be controlled and the stock improved for the extension of a dairy industry within the framework of the ideals of ahinsa (sophes, 1967:40)

Religious mandates largely regulates human occupation. Hindu society is scriptually stratified into caste categories with associated occupation (first expounded in the laws of Manu). Basic nations of ritual purity among high caste Hindus have affected their occupations. Occupations like fishing, leather tenning are downgraded as low caste occupation. Cultivation is a lowly profession and high-caste are reluctant to take up farming, which has traditionally suffered from neglect by castes who possess capital and managerial skills. Non-Hindus also display similar occupational traits. Jainism prohibite any form of agriculture occupations slaved flowing must destroy some insect life. Jains have therefore, taken to trading and banking in large numbers and are concentrated in the cities. Among Hindus different caste display different fruits consumption. Traits as sanctioned by scriptures. Avoidance of meat eating is very strict among Brahmans, the highest caste. Lower castes, lilke the untouchable, who are considered ritually "unclean", do not avoid meat eating. Most upper caste Hindus abstrain from fish and fishing is this occupation is occurded low social status. The fishing industry, in general, has not proposed in India. The development of high class liquor manufacturing industry has also lagged, as most Indian religious forbid or discourage the consumption of alcohol. Religions also mandate food habits. Muslims are forbidden to eaten pork. The Sikh religious proscribes the use of tobacco and thus discourage Sikhs from enterning into any tobacco-related business.

The rhythm of farming activities is regulated by a ritual calendar affecting the quality of production. Religious festivals must be attended even if growing crops need attention. Work in the fields is usually suspended at prayer time (devote Muslims observe prayers five times a day).

Religious mandates has indirectly affected population—resource ratios. High & Middle caste Hindus & Jains forbide widow remarriage, resulting in lower fertility rates. Among them as compared to the higher rates for Sikh & Muslims. The Hindus desire for a child early in life encourages early marriage and high maternity rates among young females. Another spiritually sanctioned desire prevalent among Hindus is to have atleast one male child (who is responsible for most ritual functions for the parents). Religious beliefs also affect social & economic behaviour. Based on the Hindu-Buddhist. Jain values systems in difference to worldly gain has, in General, inhibited the formation of capital investment and labour input. In this respect, Sikhs has proved to be more liberal and successful in farming and parsis in business than have Hindus. The Islamic practice of segregation females deprives them of many economic functions (working in the field in an office or factory).

Religious sentiments often dominate one political behaviour. The partition of the Indian subcontinent into two countries in 1947 was a successful realization of a goal of the Indian Muslim League, a strong political party inspired by religious motives. At several levels local, district and state religion-inspired political parties identified on the basis of their religious affiliation fight elections with the ostensible purpose of winning concessions and privileges for their religious groups.

The Caste system

The caste has been one of the eldest and most distinctive features of Indian society. It is a measure force in the socio-economic and political system of the country. Theoretically, Sikhs, Buddhist, Muslims, Christians are immune to caste distinctions. But most known Hindus in India are the descendants of converts from Hinduism; they interact with the traditional caste-based Hindu society regularly & have maintained the caste traditions of Hindu society. Despite the weakening of caste structures in the cities, the lines over 600 million villages still profoundly shaped by the institutions of caste.

A precise definition of caste is difficult, but the concept includes atleast two levels of comprehension. One is the philosophical and board level comprehend-ing caste as a hierarchical divison of society on the basis of Varna (literally "Color") into Brahmins, Kshatriyas, Vaishyas and Shudras. From the original Varna categories the Hindu society envolved into thousands of castes or jatis. Any visitor to India would soon discover that caste as a functional organic system is more complex than this classification of society into these four broad groups. The second level of caste comprehension is this segmentation of society into thousands or jatis, or castes, each internally bound by marriage lineage, and with characterstic occupational, religious, ritualistic, and social, roles with increasing urbanization, democratization and spatial mobility, the occupational affiliations of the castes have been undergoing social and structural transformation. The functional division of society into castes of jatis is a unique feature of India's human geography, and is of greater socio-economic relevance than the four broad Varna cateogries. Within the broad Varna framework most jatis are traditionally stratified on the basis of their social status, ritual marriage ties and common descent. The most simplistic explanation of the origin of castes may be traced to the Aryan settlement and expansion in India sometime in the second millennium. The Aryans, it is widely believed were pastoral nomads in Central Asia, from where they migrated into North-West India and pressed into the Indo-Ganga plains. In the early days of their settlement, society is thought to have been divided on the basis of race into fair-skinned Aryans and the dark-colored natives, Vedic literature (1500 B.C. to 500 B.C.) suggests such a simple divison of society. Gradually, as Aryans spread to other parts of the country, increasing contact with and assimilation of the natives, and the crystallization of the functional roles of the various groups, society was divided into a hierarchical stage of social classes. First, the four Varna divisions emerged, lates thousands of caste groups of jatis, (distinctive in kinship, lineage, customs and social taboos) grew up with in the Varna framework. The precise procedures of this societal segmentation, and the formalization of ritual, lineage and social codes are not properly understood.

13 PEOPLE (WORLD AND INDIA)

PATTERNS OF WORLD DISTRIBUTION

Human population is an important element of the terrestrial environment. Man is probably the latest occupant of earth, as his evolution took place less than two million years ago. In the early periods, human beings were like other animals at the mercy of the natural environment. He depended on food gathering, hunting and fishing. A large area of land was needed to support a small family. He had to lead a nomadic life. His food habits, clothing and shelter were influenced by the local environment.

The ability to make tools of stone and metals and use them for hunting improved his skill in getting food. The development of shifting cultivation and later settled agricultural in the river valleys improved his food supply. Assumed food supply meant better health and longevity. Population increased gradually. Forests and grassland could be cleared by setting fire to them or by cutting them with his iron axe. With the use of coal, oil and other mechanical sources of energy, productivity increased. Imporvement in sanitation and public health reduced death rates. Thus, man was no longer at the mercy of the environment.

His activities started having an impact on the environment, pressure of population on the land increased. People started immigrating to new continents such as the America, Australia and New Zealand. With increasing population, the activities of man started having adverse impact on the environment.

Development in transport and communication led to greater exchange of commodities between nations. This made possible supply of food grains and raw materials, to tide over shortages in some parts of world.

The role of man in production and consumption of resources is significant. The number of human beings in any area gives as broad idea of the nature and extent of economic activities in that area. The rate at which man utilises his basic resources is also determined by the distribution of human beings on this earth. Human resources are the most precious of all resources.

Developing nations are unable to improve thier standard of living partly because they lack skilled man power for development of their resources. Absolute number of people living in a country have little meaning. The needs and aspirations of people

Trends and Patterns of World

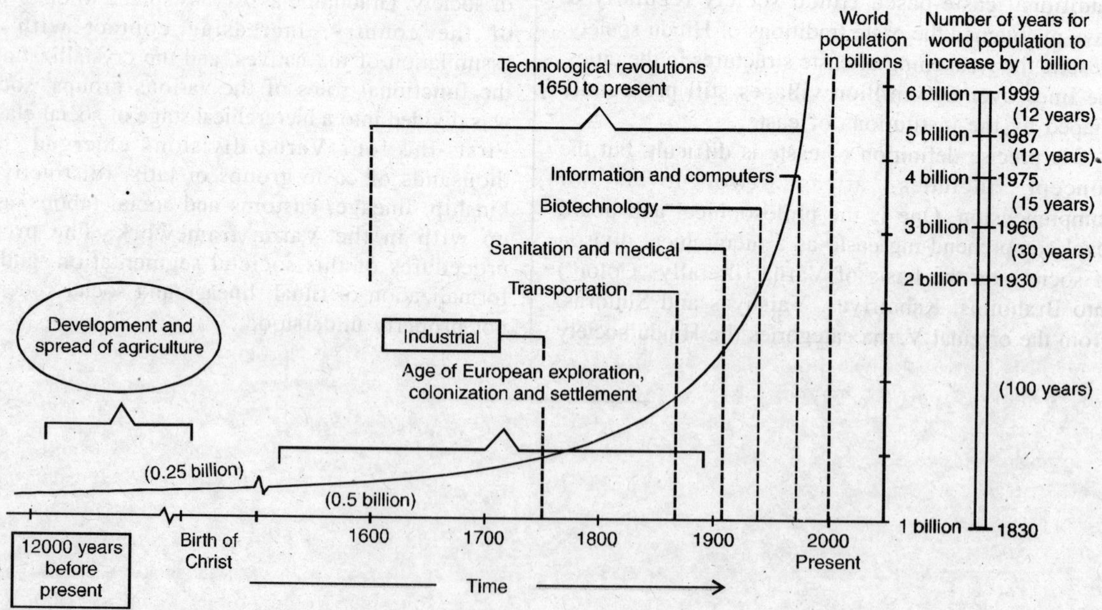

and their consumption levels vary. The per capita consumption of food, fuel, minerals and other products is much greater in countries like the United States than India.

Distribution of population

In terms of continents and countries the world's population is very ill-balanced. More than half of the world's people live in Asia (excluding the USSR) which accounts for only one fifth of the world's land area, while North, Central and South America together, occupying more than a quarter of the land surface, have only one seventh of the population. The African continent also accounts for a quarter of the land surface but has just over one-tenth of the world population. On the other hand Europe, whose area is only one twenty-fifth of the total has about one-ninth of the world's people.

The distribution within the continents is also uneven. In Asia, China alone with about 900 million people, accounts for half the Asian and a quarter of the world population. The Indian subcontinent has a further 850 million people. In Europe too, the population is unevenly distributed. For more people live in Northern and Western European countries. Than in Southern and Eastern Europe. The USSR is the largest country in the world and has 259 million people but only a quarter of them live in the Asian section. In Africa and the America's people are for the most part spread very thinly across the land, leaving large sections such as Northern Canada, South-Western USA the Sahara Desert, and the Amazon forests practically uninhabited.

The distribution of population depends to a large extent on the quality of the land itself, which is very uneven. Where the land is well suited to agricultural or there are natural resources for industrial development the population will naturally be larger than in areas where climatic conditions are hostile or where resources are few.

Thus the distribution of population has all along been quite uneven. More than 90% of population live in the Northern hemisphere. The continent of Asia alone has nearly two thirds of the world's population. The distribution of population even by continents shows considerable variation in growth rates. Africa has a growth rate of 2.6 per cent annually, Asia 2.3 per cent and America 2.1 per cent Europe alone (excluding the USSR) has a rate below 1 per cent (0.8 per cent in recent years). Within each continent there are further difference: larger areas of tropical South America and central America and growing at 3 per cent or more with South-East and South-West Asia not far behind.

This is complex enough, but there are further complexities. Not only is the density of population per square kilometre or per square kilometre of cultivated land uneven, but the urban rural distribution of the world's populations is also strikingly uneven.

FACTORS INFLUENCING THE DISTRIBUTION OF POPULATION

Geographical Factors

(i) *Availability of water:* It is the most important factor for life. So, people prefer to live in areas where fresh water is easily available. Water is used for drinking, bathing and cooking – and also for cattle, crops, industries and navigation. It is because of this that river valleys are among the most densely populated areas of the world.

(ii) *Landforms:* People prefer living on flat plains and gentle slopes. This is because such areas are favourable for the production of crops and to build roads and industries. The mountainous and hilly areas hinder the development of transport network and hence initially do not favour agricultural and industrial development. So, these areas tend to be less populated. The Ganga plains are among the most densely populated areas of the world while the mountains zones in the Himalayas are scarcely populated.

(iii) *Climate:* An extreme climate such as very hot or cold deserts are uncomfortable for human habitation. Areas with a comfortable climate, where there is not much seasonal variation attract more people. Areas with very heavy rainfall or extreme and harsh climates have low population. Mediterranean regions were inhabited from early periods in history due to their pleasant climate.

(iv) *Soils:* Fertile soils are important for agricultural and allied activities. Therefore, areas which have fertile loamy soils have more people living on them as these can support intensive agriculture. Can you name some areas in India which are thinly populated due to poor soils?

Economic Factors

(i) *Minerals:* Areas with mineral deposits attract industries. Mining and industrial activities generate employment. So, skilled and semi-skilled workers move to these areas and make them densely populated. Katanga Zambia copper belt in Africa is one such good example.

(ii) *Urbanisation:* Cities offer better employment opportunities, educational and medical facilities, better means of transport and communication. Good civic amenities and the attraction of city life draw people to the cities. It leads to rural to urban migration and cities grow in size. Mega cities of the world continue to attract large number of migrants every year.

(iii) *Industrialisation:* Industrial belts provide job opportunities and attract large numbers of people. These include not just factory workers but also transport operators, shopkeepers, bank employees, doctors, teachers and other service providers. The Kobe-Osaka region of Japan is thickly populated because of the presence of a number of industries.

Social and Cultural Factors

Some places attract more people because they have religious or cultural significance. In the same way – people tend to move away from places where there is social and political unrest. Many a times governments offer incentives to people to live in sparsely populated areas or move away from overcrowded places.

Region wise Population

	Continent	Population (2018)	Area (Km^2)	Density (P/Km^2)	World Population Share
1	Asia	4,545,133,094	31,033,131	146	59.5%
2	Africa	1,287,920,518	29,648,481	43	16.9%
3	Europe	742,648,010	22,134,900	34	9.7%
4	Lätin America and the Caribbean	652;012,001	20,139,378	32	8.5%
5	North America	363,844,490	18,651,660	20	4.8%
6	Australia/Oceania	41,261,212	8,486,460	5	0.5%
7	Antarctica	0	—	0	0%

PATTERNS AND PROCESSES OF MIGRATION

Migrations have been common since the time immortal. The tendency to leave the original home the outcome of difficulties of life that make life miserable. That is why people beloging to highlands prefer to go towards the lowlands. In the same way people from over populated areas like to settle in sparsely populated areas where competition to lead a better economic life is not tough. People also tend to go to the fertile lands where productivity of crops is many times more than it is found in the infertile lands. Climatical regions have also induced the people to migrate : Mainly there are five aspects of migration which cause permanent or temporary migration. They are : *(i)* Space aspect *(ii)* Time aspect, *(iii)* Cause aspect, *(iv)* Number aspect, *(v)* Stability aspect. We study the main reason of migrations from one place to another in order to know whether the migration is permanent or temporary and whether the number of immigrants has been insignificant or numerically high.

Leaving such reasons aside however there are other clear-cut motives for migration.

1. Availability of land : Agriculturist who cannot make a living in their own country because there is a shortage of land or because their land is too poor, migrate to countries where land is available. This was the motive for many migrations in the past such as that of the Nordemen or Vikings who spread out from their mountainous homeland is Scandinavia, or that of the Magyar pastoralists who moved Westwards and settled on the better land in Hungary. It was also the chief motive behind most nineteenth century migrations. The U.S.A., Australia and South Africa were settled by Europeans who were either landless peasants or farmers who wanted larger areas of land instead of small plots.

2. Availability of Work : Unemployed town-dwellers may migrate to other towns within their own country or to urban centres overseas in order to obtain work. While in the nineteenth century, most migrants to the 'New World' were rural people, in the early twentieth century most were from towns. Workers may also move to countries where they can earn higher wages, for instance Indians or Pakistanis may move to Britain, or Southern European to the industrialized countries of Germany and Switzerland.

3. Hope of Wealth : Most migrants hope to improve their income and living standard but some hope to 'get rich quick'. Mineral strikes, particularly of gold, have drawn people from all over the world. Hopeful miners are prepared to face gruelling conditions in deserts, *e.g.* in central Australia or polar regions, *e.g.* the Yokon. The search for the mythical El Dorado or land of gold led the Spaniards and Portuguese to conquer and later to settle in central and South America in the sixteenth and seventeenth centuries. South Africa, too, gained population partly because of its gold mines. Many of the cities that grow up in new mineral regions are subject to rapid out-migration when the ore has been exhausted, and there are many ghost town in western U.S.A. which bear witness to this.

4. Religious Toleration : Where adherents of a particular religion are persecuted or where sects are not tolerated, people may move to escape repression to places where they may safely practice their religion. The movement of Jews to Israel and the huge transfers of population between India and Pakistan at the time of partition in 1948 are modern examples. The early settlers in the U.S.A., whether catholics in the south or paritans in New England, left England at times when their branch of christianity was not tolerated. Within the U.S.A., the Mormona, whose religion is not widely accepted, moved west to found the remote state of Utah.

5. Political Freedom : People may move to avoid political persecution or may move simply because they are dissatisfied with the form of government in their own country. Thus there has been a steady flow of refugees from communist countries sinth the war, in Europe and Asia. West Germany, South Korea and Hong-Kong have received many of these migrants. Wars cause great numbers of people to migrate. Refuges may flee before an advancing army to avoid subjection to a new regime, to avoid the battle or because their homes and farms have been destroyed.

6. Forced Migration : While most types of migrations are undertaken voluntarily by people who want to improve their living conditions, some major population movements are effected by force, not for the benefit of the migrants but for the benefit of others. Certain groups may be thought undesirable. Racial, religions or political groups may therefore be forced to leave or criminals may be deported. Examples from the past include the 'transported' prisoners who formed the basis of the colony in Australia.

DEMOGRAPHIC TRANSITION

The demographic transition theory was given by W.S. Thompson and F.M.Natestein who based their statements on the trends in fertility and mortality being experienced by Europe. America and Australia.

The theory postulate a particular pattern of demographic change from a high fertility and high mortality to a low fertility and low mortality, when a society progresses from a largely rural agrarian and illiterate society to a dominantly urban, industrial and literate society. The original statements of Thompson and Natestein on the transition theory were subsequently refined and reformulated with the passage of time. Generally a three staged model has been identified with pre-industrial, early western and late western stage. These are called as

(i) High stationary stage with high fertility and high mortality providing very little natural growth.

(ii) Expanding stage with high fertility and decline in mortality providing explosive population increments.

(iii) Low stationary stage with fertility and mortality levelling out each other at low level to re-establish a fairly stationary population.

Stage I : In the first stage, the fertility is over 35 per thousand and is almost stable. The mortality is also high being more than 35 per thousand but its behaviour is erratic due to epidemics and variable food supply. This stage postulates stable and slow growing population. It happens in a country having a predominantly agrarian low-income economy. It is an important feature of underdeveloped countries.

Stage II : It is characterised by a high and gradually declining fertility of over 30 per thousand with a reduced mortality rate of 15 per thousand. The improvements in sanitation and health conditions, general productivity and distribution system result in sharp decline in the mortality rates, but the fertility maintains a high level, at least in the early second stage. As the second stage prolongs, the fertility also shows signs of gradual decline. In this stage, the population as whole expands, firstly at a gradually increasing rate and afterwards at a gradually subsiding rate. Here life expectancy improves process of industrialisation and urban development becomes prominent. Most of the less developed countries of the world are passing through this stage. *e.g.* India, Pakistan and Bangladesh are passing through this stage.

Stage III : This stage is attained when both birth and death rates decline appreciably. The population is either stable or grows slowly. In this stage the population is highly urbanised, and the economic development transforms the agrarian economy to an industrialised one. The technical know—how is abundant, the literacy and education levels are high and the degree of labour specialization is high.

For example, America, Europe, Japan etc. are at this stage.

Although population grow slowly both in the first and last stage, these are the results of different situations. While the slow growth of population in the first stage is the result of approximation of mortality and fertility rates at a fairly high level, the slow population growth of the third and the final stage is the produce of approximation of fertility and mortality rates at the low level.

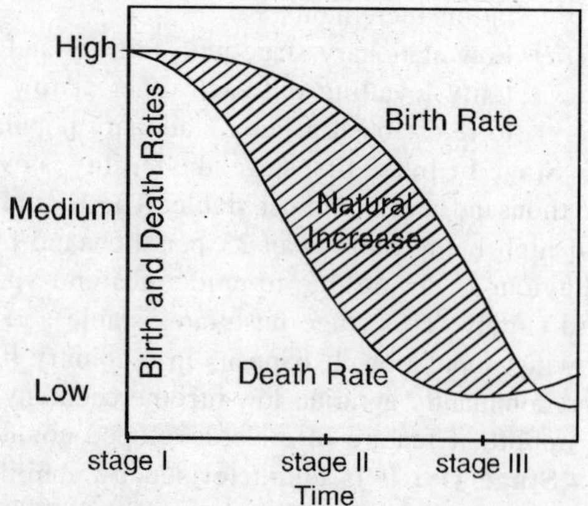

Population-Resources Regions

The geographers have always been concerned with regions and have often examined the problem of resource adequacy and population growth. But a complete lack of attempts and knowledge to regionalised on the basis of population/resource ratio only reinforces the difficulties involved in the quantification of two main factor of population and resources.

The most important effort in this direction was done by Edward A.Ackerman who used three basic criteria for devicing the world's regional scheme of population resource ratio. These included population factor, resource factor and technology factor. Among these the magnitude and quality of available technology is most important. The resources and prosperity are at adequate, where technology is very developed and technically skilled personnel are abundant, for example USA and Europe.

Neither small population nor capious supply of land and potential resources can make for adequate per capita levels of production and consumption. They can only keep over population of a nation under control for few years while the standard of living remains slightly above the distress level. Thus it is in this contex technology factor assumes significance.

Ackerman identified five broad population/ resources regions of the world—

(i) United State type *(ii)* European type
(iii) Brazilian type *(iv)* China or Egypt type
(v) Arctic desert type.

TRIBES IN INDIA		
Abors	:	Assam
Apatamis	:	Arunachal Pradesh
Badagas	:	Nilgiri (TN)
Baiga	:	Madhya Pradesh
Bhils	:	Mostly in Madhya Pradesh and Rajasthan. Also in Gujarat
Bhotias	:	Garhwal and Kumaon regions to U.P.
Chenchus	:	Andhra Pradesh, Odisha
Gaddis	:	Himachal Pradesh
Garos	:	Meghalaya
Gonds	:	Madhya Pradesh. Also in Bihar, Odisha and Andhra Pradesh

Jarawas	:	Little Andamans
Khas	:	Jaunsar-Babar area in U.P.
Khasis	:	Assam, Meghalaya
Khonds	:	Odisha
Kol	:	Madhya Pradesh
Kotas	:	Nilgiri (Tamil Nadu)
Kuki	:	Manipur
Lepchas	:	Sikkim
Lushais	:	Tripura
Murias	:	Bastar region in Madhya Pradesh
Mikirs	:	Assam
Mundas	:	Bihar
Nagas-(Angami, Sema, Ao, Tangkul, Lahora): Nagaland; some in Assam and NEFA region.		
Oarons (also called Kurukh): Bihar, Odisha		
Onges	:	Andaman and Nicobar Islands
Santhals	:	Birbhum region in Bengal, Hazaribagh, Ranchi and Palamau in Jharkhand
Sentinelese	:	Sentinel Island, Andaman and Nicobar
Shompens	:	Andaman and Nicobar
Todas	:	Nilgiri (Tamil Nadu)
Uralis	:	Kerala
Warlis	:	Maharashtra

POPULATION

India in World Population

First results of Census 2011 have been released. India now has a population of 1.21 billion, comprising 624 million males and 587 million females. This is an increase of 181 million people since the Census 2001 which is nearly equivalent to the population of Brazil.

India is a second country in the world after China to cross the one billion mark. It is now estimated that by 2050, India will most likely overtake China and become the most populous country on the earth with 19.4% population living here. The three most populous countries, viz., China, India and USA, together account for four of every ten persons of the world. At present, a little more than one out of every six persons in the world is from India.

Population of Ten countries

S. No.	*Country*	*Population (in millions)*	*Decadal change (in %)*
1.	China	1,341.0	5.43
2.	India	1,210.2	17.64
3.	U.S.A.	308.7	7.26
4.	Indonesia	237.6	15.05
5.	Brazil	190.7	9.39
6.	Pakistan	184.8	24.78
7.	Bangladesh	164.4	16.76
8.	Nigeria	158.3	26.84
9.	Russian Fed.	140.4	–4.29
10.	Japan	128.1	1.1

DISTRIBUTION OF POPULATION

It is clear that India has a highly uneven pattern of population distribution. The percentage shares of population of the States and the Union Territories in the country show that Uttar Pradesh has the highest population followed by Maharashtra, Bihar, West Bengal and Andhra Pradesh.

U.P., Maharashtra, Bihar, West Bengal, Andhra Pradesh along with Tamil Nadu, Madhya Pradesh, Rajasthan, Karnataka and Gujarat, together account for about 76 per cent of the total population of the country. On the other hand, share of population is very small in the states like Jammu & Kashmir 1.04%, Arunachal Pradesh (0.11%) and Uttarakhand (0.83%) in spite of these states having fairly large geographical area.

Such an uneven spatial distribution of population in India suggests a close relationship between population and physical, socio-economic and historical factors. As far as the physical factors are concerned, it is clear that climate along with terrain and availability of water largely determine the pattern of the population distribution. Consequently, we observe that the North Indian Plains, deltas and Coastal Plains have higher proportion of population than the interior districts of southern and central Indian States, Himalayas,

India's Population At A Glance : 2011 (Final Data)

S.l. No.	State/UTs	Population	Sex Ratio	Density	Literacy Rate (%)	(%) Decadal Growth Rate (2001-2011)
1.	Jammu & Kashmir	1,25,41,302	889	124	67.2	23.6
2.	Himachal Pradesh	68,64,602	972	123	82.8	12.9
3.	Punjab	2,77,43,338	895	551	75.8	13.9
4.	Chandigarh	10,55,450	818	9258	86.0	17.2
5.	Uttarakhand	1,00,86,292	963	189	78.8	18.8
6.	Haryana	2,53,51,462	879	573	75.6	19.9
7.	Delhi	1,67,87,941	868	11320	86.2	21.2
8.	Rajasthan	6,85,48,437	928	200	66.1	21.3
9.	Uttar Pradesh	19,98,12,341	912	829	67.7	20.2
10.	Bihar	10,40,99,452	918	1106	61.8	25.4
11.	Sikkim	6,10,577	890	86	81.4	12.5
12.	Arunachal Pradesh	13,83,727	938	17	65.4	26.0
13.	Nagaland	19,78,502	931	119	79.6	–0.6
14.	Manipur	25,70,390	992	115	79.2	–18.6
15.	Mizoram	10,97,206	976	52	91.3	23.5
16.	Tripura	36,73,917	960	350	87.2	14.8
17.	Meghalaya	29,66,889	989	132	74.4	27.9
18.	Assam	3,12,05,576	958	398	72.2	17.1
19.	West Bengal	9,12,76,115	950	1028	76.3	13.8
20.	Jharkhand	3,29,88,134	948	414	66.4	22.4
21.	Odisha	4,19,74,218	979	270	72.9	14.0
22.	Chhattisgarh	2,55,45,198	991	189	70.3	22.6
23.	Madhya Pradesh	7,26,26,809	931	236	69.3	20.3
24.	Gujarat	6,04,39,692	919	308	78.0	19.3
25.	Daman & Diu	2,43,247	618	2191	87.1	53.8
26.	Dadra & Nagar Haveli	3,43,709	774	700	76.2	55.9
27.	Maharashtra	11,23,74,333	929	365	82.3	16.0
28.	Andhra Pradesh	8,45,80,777	993	308	67.0	11.6
29.	Karnataka	6,10,95,297	973	319	75.4	15.6
30.	Goa	14,58,545	973	394	88.7	8.2
31.	Lakshadweep	64,473	947	2149	91.8	6.3
32.	Kerala	3,34,06,061	1084	860	94.0	4.9
33.	Tamil Nadu	7,21,47,030	996	555	80.1	15.6
34.	Telangana	3,50,03,674	999	312	66.54	13.58
35.	Puducherry	12,47,953	1037	2547	85.8	28.1
36.	Andaman & Nicobar Islands	3,80,581	876	46	86.6	6.9
	India	**1,21,08,54,977**	**943**	**382**	**73.0**	**17.7**

Density of Population 2011

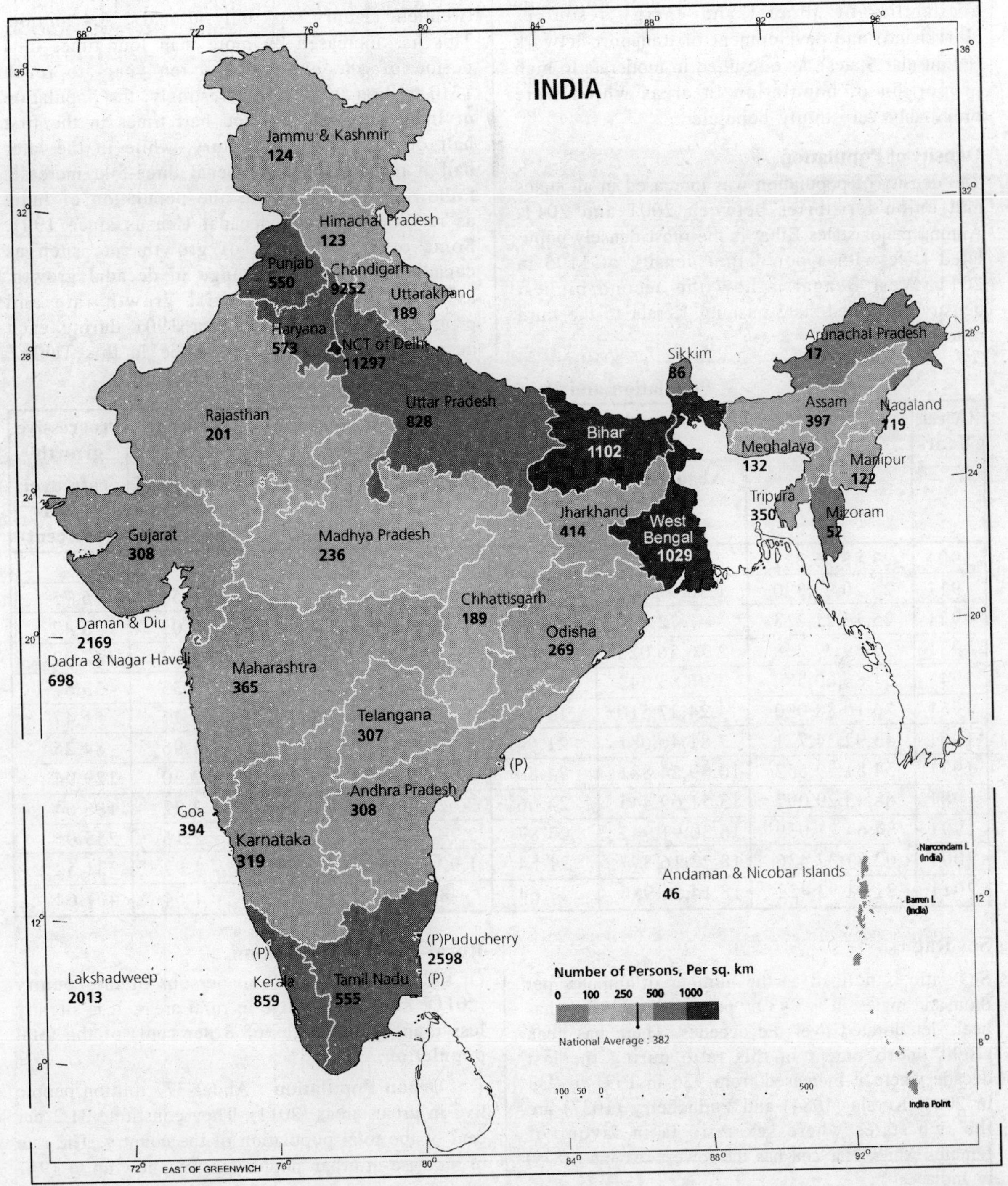

some of the north eastern and the western states. However, development of irrigation (Rajasthan), availability of mineral and energy resources (Jharkhand) and development of transport network (Peninsular States) have resulted in moderate to high proportion of population in areas which were previously very thinly populated.

Density of Population

The density of population was increased in all states and union territories between 2001 and 2011. Among major states Bihar is the most densely populated state with a population density of 1106 in 2011. West Bengal is now the second highest density populated state pushing Kerala to the third place.

Population Growth : India 1901 to 2011

The population of India, at the turn of the twentieth century, was only around 238.4 million. This has increased by more than four times in a period of one hundred and ten years to reach 1210 million in 2011. Interestingly, the population of India grew by one and half times in the first half of the twentieth century, while in the later half it recorded a phenomenal three-fold increase. Following Table presents the population of India as recorded in each decadal Census since 1901. Some other indicators of growth rate such as decadal growth rate, change in decadal growth, average annual exponential growth rate and progressive growth rate over 1901 during each decade have also been presented in this Table.

Population and Its growth, India : 1901-2011

Census Years	Population	Decadal growth		Change in decadal growth		Average annual exponential growth rate (per cent)	Progressive growth rate over 1901 (per cent)
		Absolute	Per cent	Absolute	Per cent		
1901	23,83,96,327	-	-	-	-	-	
1911	25,20,93,390	1,36,97,063	5.75	-	-	0.56	5.75
1921	25,13,21,213	−7,72,177	(0.31)	−1,44,69,240	−6.05	−0.03	5.42
1931	27,89,77,238	2,76,56,025	11.00	2,84,28,202	11.31	1.04	17.02
1941	31,86,60,580	3,96,83,342	14.22	1,20,27,317	3.22	1.33	33.67
1951	36,10,88,090	4,24,27,510	13.31	27,44,168	−0.91	1.25	51.47
1961	43,92,34,771	7,81,46,681	21.64	3,57,19,171	8.33	1.96	84.25
1971	54,81,59,652	10,89,24,881	24.80	3,07,78,200	3.16	2.20	129.94
1981	68,33,29,097	13,51,69,445	24.66	2,62,44,564	−0.14	2.22	186.64
1991	84,64,21,039	16,30,91,942	23.87	2,79,22,497	17.12	2.16	255.05
2001	1,02,87,37,436	18,23,16,397	21.54	1,92,24,455	10.54	1.97	331.52
2011	1,21,01,93,422	18,14,55,986	17.64	−8,60,411	−0.47	1.64	407.64

Sex Ratio

Sex ratio is defined as the number of females per thousand males. It is 943 as per census 2011. It has been deteriorated over the decades. There has been slight improvement in this ratio during the last decade where it increased from 926 in 1991 to 933 in 2001. Kerala (1084) and Puducherry (1037) are the two states where sex ratio is in favour of females while, Haryana has the lowest sex ratio (879) in India.

Rural-Urban Composition

Of the total 1,210 million persons of the country (2011), 833 millions live in rural areas. It is slightly less than three-fourth (68.8 per cent) of the total population.

Urban Population : About 377 million people live in urban areas (2011). They constitute 31.2 per cent of the total population of the country. The rate of increase in urban population was slow up to 1941 when it was 13.9 per cent of total population from

India: Growth of Population 2001-2011

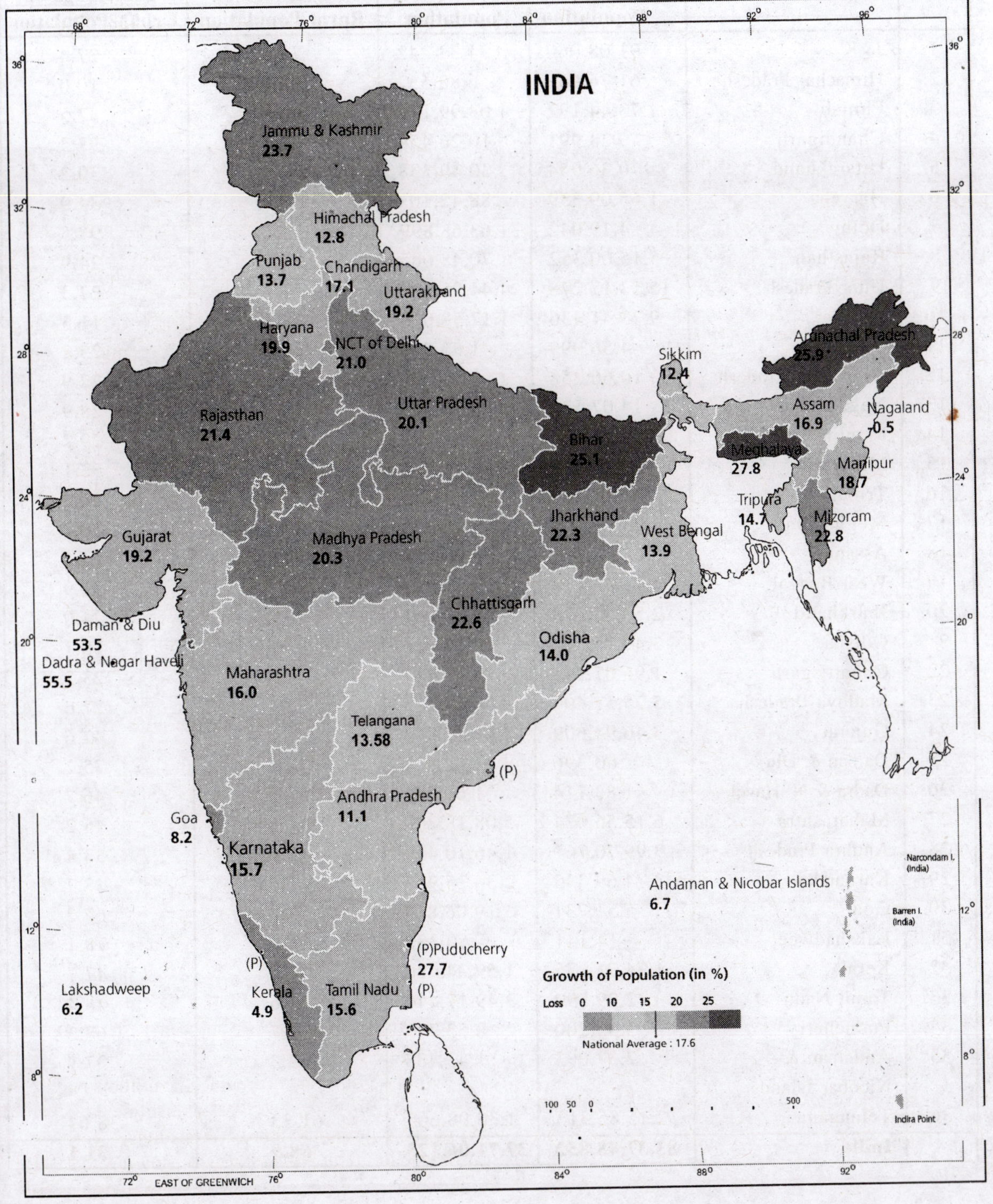

Census-2011: Rural and Urban Population

S. No.	State/UTs	Rural Population	Urban Population	Percentage of Rural Population	Percentage of Urban Population
1.	J&K	91,08,060	34,33,242	72.6	27.4
2.	Himachal Pradesh	61,76,050	6,88,552	90.0	10.0
3.	Punjab	1,73,44,192	1,03,99,146	62.5	37.5
4.	Chandigarh	28,991	10,26,459	2.7	97.3
5.	Uttarakhand	70,36,954	30,49,338	69.8	30.2
6.	Haryana	1,65,09,359	88,42,103	65.1	34.9
7.	Delhi	4,19,042	1,63,68,899	2.5	97.5
8.	Rajasthan	5,15,00,352	1,70,48,085	75.1	24.9
9.	Uttar Pradesh	15,53,17,278	4,44,95,063	77.7	22.3
10.	Bihar	9,23,41,436	1,17,58,016	88.7	11.3
11.	Sikkim	4,56,999	1,53,578	74.8	25.2
12.	Arunachal Pradesh	10,66,358	3,17,369	77.1	22.9
13.	Nagaland	14,07,536	5,70,966	71.1	28.9
14.	Manipur	20,21,640	8,34,154	70.8	29.2
15.	Mizoram	5,25,435	5,71,771	47.9	52.1
16.	Tripura	27,12,464	9,61,453	73.8	26.2
17.	Meghalaya	23,71,439	5,95,450	79.9	20.1
18.	Assam	2,68,07,034	43,98,542	85.9	14.1
19.	West Bengal	6,21,83,113	2,90,93,002	68.1	31.9
20.	Jharkhand	2,50,55,073	79,33,061	76.0	24.0
21.	Odisha	3,49,70,562	70,03,656	83.3	16.7
22.	Chhattisgarh	1,96,07,961	59,37,237	76.8	23.2
23.	Madhya Pradesh	5,25,57,404	2,00,69,405	72.4	27.6
24.	Gujarat	3,46,94,609	2,57,45,083	57.4	42.6
25.	Daman & Diu	60,396	1,82,851	24.8	75.2
26.	Dadra & N. Haveli	1,83,114	1,60,595	53.3	46.7
27.	Maharashtra	6,15,56,074	5,08,18,259	54.8	45.2
28.	Andhra Pradesh	3,99,70,761	1,46,10,410	66.6	33.4
29.	Karnataka	3,74,69,335	2,36,25,962	61.3	38.7
30.	Goa	5,51,731	9,06,814	37.8	62.2
31.	Lakshadweep	14,141	50,332	21.9	78.1
32.	Kerala	1,74,71,135	1,59,34,926	52.3	47.7
33.	Tamil Nadu	3,72,29,590	3,49,17,440	51.6	48.4
34.	Puducherry	3,95,200	8,52,753	31.7	68.3
35.	Andaman & Nicobar Islands	2,37,093	1,43,488	62.3	37.7
36.	Telangana	2,15,85,313	1,36,08,665	61.33	38.64
	India	**83,37,48,852**	**37,71,06,125**	**68.9**	**31.1**

10.8 per cent in 1901. It jumped to 17.3 per cent in 1951 and 27.8 per cent in 2001. Still India is one of the least urbanised countries in the world. Nearly 45 per cent of world population lives in urban centres. The urban population of India record an eleven-fold increase during the last 100 years.

Literacy

Literacy and education are generally taken as indicators of social development. The spread of literacy is associated with the traits of industrialisation, urbanisation, better communication, increased commerce and modernisation. Improved literacy levels help in the growth of awareness and social skills and in the improvement of economic conditions.

As per the 2011 census, literacy rate in the country is 73.0 per cent, 80.9 for males and 64.6 for females. Kerala retained its position by being on top with a 94 per cent literacy rate, closely followed by Mizoram (91.3 per cent).

Socio-Economic & Caste Census 2011

SECC-2011 is a study of socio-economic status of rural and urban households and allows based on predefined parameters. SECC-2011 has three census components which were conducted by three separate authorities but under the overall coordination of Department of Rural Development in the Government of India. Ministry of Rural Development commenced the Socio-Economic Caste Census-2011 on 29th June, 2011.

The Key points of the Census are:

- Out of the country's total 243.95 million households, 179.16 million or nearly three-fourths are in rural areas. However, only 30.1 per cent of rural households depend on cultivation as their 'main' source of income.
- 56.25% of rural households own no agricultural land.
- Only 17.34 million or 9.68 per cent of rural households have members with salaried jobs—and mostly in the government and public sector undertakings (10.95 million). Another 2.89 million (1.61 per cent) households operate non-agricultural own account enterprises. The bulk of rural households have no regular income source, being engaged in cultivation.
- Nearly 40 per cent are landless and work as manual casual labourers.
- 25 per cent rural households have no access to irrigation.
- Only 8.29 per cent of rural households have a member earning over ₹ 10,000 per month.
- 10.69 crore rural families, or 60 per cent, qualify for 'deprivation'.
- Of these over 100 million deprived households, 21.5 per cent belong to scheduled castes or tribes.
- This census takes caste into account for the first time in any such exercise since 1931.

Religion Based Census 2011

The Registar General and Census Commissioner, India has released the data on Population by Religious Communities of Census 2011. The distribution of total population by six major religious communities, viz., Hindu, Muslim, Christian, Sikh, Buddhist and Jain besides 'Other Religions and Persuasions' and 'Religion not stated' has been released by sex and residence up to sub-districts and towns. Total Population in 2011 is 121.09 crores; Hindu 96.63 crores (97.8%); Muslim 17.22 crores (14.2%); Christian 2.78 crores (2.3%); Sikh 2.08 crores (1.7%); Buddhist 0.84 crores (0.7%); Jain 0.45 crores (0.4%), Other Religions & Persuasions (ORP) 0.79 crores (0.7%) and Religion Not Stated 0.29 crores (0.2%).

The proportion of Hindu population to total population in 2011 has declined by 0.7 percentage point (PP); the proportion of Sikh population has declined by 0.2 PP and the Buddhist population has declined by 0.1 PP during the decade 2001-2011. The proportion of Muslim population to total population has increased by 0.8 PP. There has been no significant change in the proportion of Christians & Jains.

The growth rate of population in the decade 2001-2011 was 17.7%. The growth rate of population of the different religious communities in the same period was as Hindus: 16.8%; Muslim: 24.6%; Christions: 15.5%; Sikh: 8.4%; Buddhist: 6.1% and Jain: 5.4%%.

Religion	Population (Crore)	% share in Total Population	Sex Ratio
Hindu	96.63	79.8%	16.8%
Muslim	17.22	14.2%	24.6%
Christian	2.78	2.3%	15.5%
Sikh	2.08	1.7%	8.4%
Buddhist	0.84	0.7%	6.1%
Jain	0.45	0.4%	5.4%
ORP*	0.79	0.7%	-
Religion Not Stated	0.29	0.2%	

* *Other Religions and Persuasions*

The numbers show that the sex ratio among Muslims, already better than among Hindus, has further improved. The sex ratio among Muslims now stands at 951 females for every 1,000 males, substantially better than 936 in 2001, while among Hindus, it is 939 females for every 1,000 males, a slight improvement over the 2001 value of 931. Assam remains the State with the largest Muslim population as a proportion (34.22 per cent) and saw the largest increase in the Muslim proportion between 2001 and 2011, followed by Uttarakhand and Kerala.

Important Highlights at a Glance about the Religious Census 2011

- According to an official statement, the share of Hindus in the population has slipped below 80 per cent for the first time. The population in 2011 was at 121.09 crore—Hindus make up 79.8 per cent of population at 96.63 crore.
- Muslims, with 17.22 crore people, are 14.2 per cent of the population.
- Muslims are the only community to register a growth in their share of the population. The growth rate of Muslims is the highest at 24.6 per cent, the census reveals. Hindus follow with a 16.8 per cent growth rate; Christians come next with 15.5 per cent. The growth rates of Sikhs, Buddhists and Jains are less than 10 per cent.
- Christians are the third largest community with 2.78 crore people, *i.e.*, 2.3 per cent of the population. They are followed by Sikhs (2.08 crore), Buddhists (84 lakh) and Jains (45 lakh).
- Except Madhya Pradesh, the increase in the Muslim population in all big states remained above the national average of 21.6%. In Rajasthan, it increased by 29.81%. Bihar 27.95%, Gujarat 27.3%, Maharashtra 26.3% and Uttar Pradesh by 25.19%. Growth rate in Assam was 29.59% and West Bengal 21.81%.
- Christians are the only community (among major religions) in India that has more women members than men. The sex ratio among Christians was 1023 in 2011 as compared to 1009 in 2001.
- Sikh community has negative population growth in seven states—West Bengal, Uttar Pradesh, Manipur, Assam, Tripura, Mizoram and Jharkhand.
- Buddhists saw negative population growth rate in Jammu & Kashmir, Punjab, Delhi, U.P. and Karnataka.
- The biggest decline was experienced by the Muslims in Gujarat, where their number dropped by 34.5%.

LINGUISTIC COMPOSITION

Language is an Important indicator of ethnic identity. At the same time, it is a strong integrating force in the society. The people of India display a high degree of diversity in their languages and dialects. Because of its unifying power, language was accepted as time basis of state re-organisation after independence. In 1961 census, 1652 languages were listed as mother tongues in India. Out of them, speakers of 23 languages together accounted for 97 per cent of total population of the country. Of these, eighteen languages besides English are specified in the Eighth Schedule of the Constitution of the country.

Classification of Languages and their Distribution: Major languages of the Indian Union belong to two major families, namely, the **Indo-Aryan** and **Dravidian**. The former are spoken and written. In north and central India, while the latter are spoken and written in south India. The Indo-Aryan languages are spoken by about 73 per cent, and the Dravidian languages by about 20 per cent of the total population of the country. Besides these, other languages and dialects spoken belong to the Austric (1.38 per cent) and Sino-Tibetan (0.85 per cent) families. Thus, the Indian languages belong to the following four families:

1. Indo-European (Aryan),
2. Dravidian,
3. Austric, and
4. Sino-Tibetan.

Aryan Languages*:** Nearly three-fourths of the total population speaks one or the other form of the Aryan languages. Languages of this family are concentrated over the northern states including Gujarat and Maharashtra. In terms of the number of speakers, Hindi occupies fourth place in the world. It consists of several dialects; ***Khadi Boli is one of them. ***Urdu*** is very akin to ***Hindi*** and is widely spoken in this belt. Other languages of this group are ***Punjabi***, and ***Gujarati*** concentrated in the states of Punjab and Gujarat, respectively.

Kachchi and ***Sindhi***, belong to this family; they are spoken in Gujarat and Rajasthan. The concentration of Marathi is in Maharashtra. ***Oriya, Bengali*** and ***Assamese*** are languages of the eastern group and are spoken in eastern India, mainly in Odisha, West Bengal and Assam respectively.

Kashmiri, Kohistani, Shina and ***Dardi*** are spoken in different parts of Jammu and Kashmir.

Dravidian Languages: About one-fifth of total population speaks in Dravidian languages. Tamil, Kannada and Malayalam languages are concentrated in Tamil Nadu, Karnataka and Kerala. Telugu is spoken in Andhra Pradesh. The Dravidian languages are less diverse than the other language families of India. The four languages mentioned above account for 96 per cent of the total Dravidian speaking population of India.

Austric Languages : These languages are spoken by the tribal groups of Meghalaya, Jharkhand and western Satpura. There are two branches of this family: ***Munda*** and ***Mon Khmer***. Of the two, ***Mon-Khmer*** (Khasi) is confined to Khasi and Jaintia hills and Nicobarese to the Nicobar Islands. On the other hand, ***Munda*** language is spoken by tribals of Jharkhand and the western Satpura region.

Sino-Tibetan Languages: The languages of this family consist of several branches, groups and sub-groups, and are confined to certain small pockets in the north-eastern states, and in the Himalayan and sub-Himalayan regions of the north and the northwest.

The speakers of the Sino-Tibetan family in India belong to three main branches: ***Tibeto-Himalayan***, ***Arunachal Pradesh*** and *Naga-Myanmari*. The first branch consists of the Bhutia and the Kinnauri groups; the second branch of the Aka, Dafla, Miri and Abor groups; and the third of the Bodo, Naga and Kuka groups.

As the states of India are language-based, the Scheduled languages are spoken by majority of the population in respective states. In Kerala, for instance, 96 per cent of the population speak Malayalam, and in Andhra Pradesh more than 85 per cent of the people speak Telugu.

HUMAN DIVERSITY

Many factors arise from human diversity and sometimes create conflicts. Among these are racial, cultural, linguistic, religious and political differences.

Race: Races are differentiated on the basis of inherited physical characteristics but in fact it is always difficult to draw a hard and fast line between the races. People are differented with the help of various factors *i.e.*, hair, face structure, height, colour, texture etc. The shape of the eyes, the nose and the overall shape of the head are also important, and are used, with skin colour as a minor factor, and also a number of other invisible characteristics such as blood group, to define the three major racial groups—the Caucasoid, Negroid and Mongoloid groups. There is one minor group, the Australoid, whose members combine the facial characteristics of the negroid group with wavy hair.

Caucasoids: This group includes the European peoples, Semitic peoples (Arabs and Jews) and the Indo-Aryan peoples. Skin colour varies from very fair, as in the north European peoples, to brown in

India and south-west Asia. The hair is straight or wavy (or sometimes frizzy) and may be blonde, brown or black. The nose is generally long and narrow. Numerous subtypes are recognized within this group such as the tall fair-haired, blue-eyed Nordic peoples: the stocky, brown-haired, brown-eyed Alpine peoples and the short, slightly built Mediterranean peoples with dark hair and eyes. These three groups, now inextricably inter-mixed, inhabit Europe and the Middle East. Marked differences between sub-groups are found elsewhere, especially in India

Negroids: The negroid peoples live chiefly in Africa, south of the Sahara and include many sub-groups such as the Nilotic and Hamitic peoples of eastern Africa, the Bantus of central and southern Africa and the various groups of West Africa. They also include a number of minor groups such as the Bushmen, the Pygmies and the negrito peoples of India and South East Asia, as well as the Melanesians of the South-West Pacific. All these peoples have crinkly or frizzy hair and broad, rather flat, noses. They are generally long-headed, i.e., their heads are longer than they are broad, and their skin colour varies from black to brown or yellowish. Their stature too is very varied; the Negroes of Sudan and Central Africa are probably the tallest people, on average, in the world, but the Pygmies, also of Central Africa, are the shortest

Mongoloids: The mongoloid peoples inhabit northern, eastern and south-eastern Asia and were the original inhabitants of the America. The eye, with its characteristic fold of skin on the upper lid, and the hair-type, which is lank and straight, are their chief distinguishing characteristics, but there are many minor differences between sub-groups. Short stature is a less reliable factor. The Mongols of Central Asia gave their name to the group, which also includes the Chinese, Japanese, Burmese, Thais, Vietnamese, Kampucheans and Malays. It also includes the Eskimos and similar peoples of northern Siberia such as the Yakuts and Samoyeds, the Red Indians of North America and the Amerindians of South America. Many of the American groups have evolved differently in isolation so that while the people of Tierra del Fuego at the southem tip of South America look almost exactly like Chinese people, the tall, bronze-skinned, hook-nosed Indians of the Great Plains have less in common with Asian groups.

It is clear that racial characteristics were originally linked with climatic factors. It is very important to realize, however, that such links no longer directly affect racial features. It is perfectly possible for all races to live in all parts of the world and facial features or skin colour are merely inherited factors. People who support racial discrimination often think that some races are inferior to others. In fact the differences between races are purely superficial for most apparently intellectual differences stem from cultural and environmental factors.

The table given below shows the major groups of people, their areas and occupations:

Group of people	Areas	Occupations
1. Eskimos Siberia, Greenland	North Canada, Hunters	Collectors,
2. Amerindians central Brazil, Chile	Amazon basin,	Fishers
3. Pygmies, Bushman	Africa	
4. Lapps	North Scandinavia	
5. Alents, Chuchches, Yakut, Tunguses, Koriaks	North Siberia	Pastoralists
6. Gvaicas	Colombia, Ecuador	
7. Karnes, Meos	Myanmar, Thailand, China	Shifting Agriculture

Language: The difficulties caused by language barriers should not be underestimated. Linguists classify languages into three basic types according to their structure. These are (a) ***monosyllabic***, where words have various meanings depending on their position in the sentence, as in Chinese, Vietnamese,

Thai and Tibetan; (b) ***agglutinative***, where words are altered by prefixes and suffixes, as in Malay, Japanese and many African languages; and (c) ***inflexional***, where words are flexible and can be modified to give the required meaning, as in English, French and other Indo-European languages including Arabic, Urdu, Bengali and Hindi. It is naturally difficult for people speaking one type of language to grasp the construction of another and these differences are added to the obvious differences of the words. Vocabulary too is very varied, so that common words in one language may have no equivalent in another. Moreover, language is closely linked with the culture, history and religion of those who speak it and this gives certain words secondary meaning or conjures up specific associations of ideas only for those who know the language really well. All these differences create misunderstanding and confusion.

Religion: Religion originally grew up as a response to the way of life of a group of people. Spirits controlling the weather or the movements of animals had to be propitiated. Many people all over the world still have such ***animistic*** beliefs. More complex ***dogmatic religions*** grew up later which established a correct mode of conduct. The practices and attitudes of the various religions are different and those of one group may be unpleasant to followers of another religion. As a result conflict between religious groups may arise.

The Scheduled Castes (SCs) and Scheduled Tribes (STs) are various officially designated groups of historically disadvantaged people in India. The terms are recognised in the Constitution of India and the various groups are designated in one or other of the categories. For much of the period of British rule in the Indian subcontinent, they were known as the Depressed Classes. The combined percentage of people in scheduled castes and scheduled tribes is essentially the official percentage of people in the lowest part of Indian society.

In modern literature, the *Scheduled Castes/Tribes* are sometimes referred to as *untouchables*; in Tamil Nadu they are referred as *Adi Dravida* or *Paraiyar*; and in other states mostly referred as *Dalits*.

The Scheduled Castes and Scheduled Tribes comprise about 16.6 per cent and 8.6 per cent, respectively, of India's population (according to the 2011 census). The *Constitution (Scheduled Castes) Order, 1950* lists 1,108 castes across 29 states in its First Schedule, and the *Constitution (Scheduled Tribes) Order, 1950* lists 744 tribes across 22 states in its First Schedule.

Since independence, the Scheduled Castes and Scheduled Tribes were given Reservation status, guaranteeing political representation. The Constitution lays down the general principles of positive discrimination for SCs and STs.

SCHEDULED CASTES

People from Scheduled Castes (SCs) – otherwise known as dalits – are socially excluded in India, facing discrimination on the basis of their position at the very bottom of the Indian caste system. As a result, dalits find themselves excluded from many aspects of day-to-day life including health services, economies and educational establishments. SCs make up 16.6% of India's population (Census, 2011) although this percentage is higher if dalits who have converted to other religions, such as Christianity or Islam, are included.

Cultural discrimination

People from Scheduled Castes – otherwise known as dalits – were outside of the Indian Hindu caste system, deemed "untouchable" by the higher castes. Their untouchability status meant that higher caste groups would not touch, speak to or interact with dalits, resulting in their exclusion from community life.

Although the caste system was officially abolished in 1949, dalits are still looked down upon and discriminated against in Indian society due to ingrained cultural norms.

Health discrimination

Under 5 mortality for SCs is substantially above the national average – 88 out of 1000 children from SC groups die before their 5th birthday, whereas the national average is 74 out of 1000. This is due, in part, to the fact that health workers are usually from higher castes and often deny dalits treatment or refuse to touch them. If treatment is provided, quality of care is often poor and unacceptable attitudes are frequently encountered.

Economic discrimination

A person's job was determined by their position in the Hindu caste system. Traditional dalit jobs include street cleaning and removing toilet waste, otherwise known as manual scavenging.

Today, many SCs still find themselves trapped in these caste-based jobs and face discrimination when applying for other jobs. They also tend to get lower wages.

Educational discrimination

Children from SCs face discrimination in schools, often at the hands of higher caste teachers and pupils. Discrimination includes being forced to sit separately from other children, being made to clean toilets and not being given school books and uniforms.

Children from SCs rarely progress beyond the primary level. This is reflected in the gap in literacy between SCs and the rest of the population – only 66.1% of those belonging to SCs can read and write compared with the national average of 73%. Ultimately this leads to lower employment chances and long-term income poverty.

SCHEDULED TRIBES

Article 366 (25) of the Constitution of India refers to Scheduled Tribes as those communities, who are scheduled in accordance with Article 342 of the Constitution. This Article says that only those communities who have been declared as such by the President through an initial public notification or through a subsequent amending Act of Parliament will be considered to be Scheduled Tribes.

Article 342 provides for specification of tribes or tribal communities or parts of or groups within tribes or tribal communities which are deemed to be for the purposes of the Constitution the Scheduled Tribes in relation to that State or Union Territory. In pursuance of these provisions, the list of Scheduled Tribes are notified for each State or Union Territory and are valid only within the jurisdiction of that State or Union Territory and not outside.

The list of Scheduled Tribes is State/UT specific and a community declared as a Scheduled Tribe in a State need not be so in another State. The inclusion of a community as a Scheduled Tribe is an ongoing process. The essential characteristics, first laid down by the Lokur Committee, for a community to be identified as Scheduled Tribes are:

(a) indications of primitive traits;
(b) distinctive culture;
(c) shyness of contact with the community at large;
(d) geographical isolation; and
(e) backwardness.

Tribal communities live, in various ecological and geo-climatic conditions ranging from plains and forests to hills and inaccessible areas. Tribal groups are at different stages of social, economic and educational development. While some tribal communities have adopted a mainstream way of life, at the other end of the spectrum, there are certain Scheduled Tribes, 75 in number known as Particularly Vulnerable Tribal Groups (PVTGs), who are characterised by:

(a) pre-agriculture level of technology;
(b) stagnant or declining population;
(c) extremely low literacy; and
(d) subsistence level of economy.

DISTRIBUTION OF TRIBES

The Scheduled Tribes are notified in 30 States/UTs and the number of individual ethnic groups, etc. notified as Scheduled Tribes is 705.

The tribal population of the country, as per 2011 census, is 10.43 crore, constituting 8.6% of the total population. 89.97% of them live in rural areas and 10.03% in urban areas. The decadal population growth of the tribal's from Census 2001 to 2011 has been 23.66% against the 17.69% of the entire population.

The sex ratio for the overall population is 940 females per 1000 males and that of Scheduled Tribes 990 females per thousand males.

From 30.1 million in 1961, the ST population has increased to 104.3 million in 2011.

Trends in Proportion of Scheduled Tribe Population

Census Year	Total population (in millions)	Scheduled Tribes Population (in millions)	Proportion of STs population
1961	439.2	30.1	6.9
1971	547.9	38.0	6.9
1981#	665.3	51.6	7.8
1991@	838.6	67.8	8.1
2001$	1028.6	84.3	8.2
2011	1210.8	104.3	8.6

Excludes Assam in 1981 @ Excludes Jammu & Kashmir in 1991.

$ The figures exclude Mao-Maram, Paomata and Purul sub-divisions of Senapati district of Manipur, census 2001.

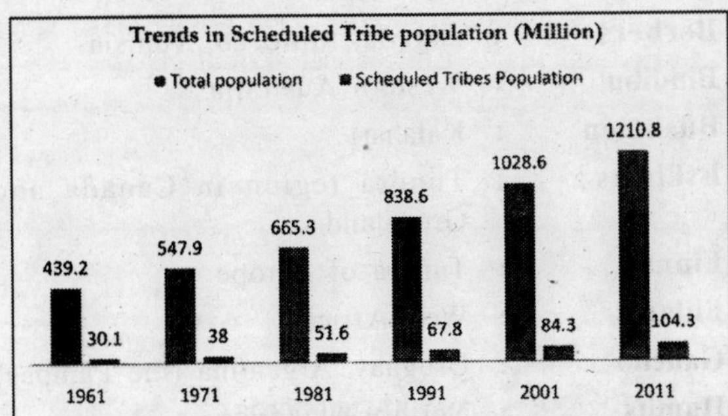

In the detailed section shows a comparative picture of the populations of the Scheduled Castes, Scheduled Tribes and All Categories for Male, Female and Total for Census Years 2001 and 2011. As per 2011 Census Scheduled Caste population in the country is nearly double of the Scheduled Tribe population.

The Changes in percentage of ST to total population and the State-wise Changes in the Scheduled Tribe list between Census 2001 and Census 2011 respectively.

It is important to note that there are some changes in the List of Scheduled Tribes in States/UTs during the last decade. In the detailed section illustrates Modifications made in the List of Scheduled Tribes after Census 2001 in States/UTs, in terms of total number of Modifications, Additions as Synonym/Sub-group in the Existing Entry, Additions as main Entry/Main Entry along with Synonym/Sub-Group, Transfer from SC list, Deletions, Area Restriction Omitted, Area Restriction Imposed/Redefined, Substitution and Modifications in the earlier entry.

In the detailed section shows State-wise Demographic status of Total population & ST population (Census 1991, 2001 & 2011), their decadal growth from 2001 to 2011 & the proportion of STs to the state & to the country's total population.

Broadly the STs inhabit two distinct geographical area – the Central India and the North-Eastern Area. More than half of the Scheduled Tribe population is concentrated in Central India, *i.e.*, Madhya Pradesh (14.69%), Chhattisgarh (7.5%), Jharkhand (8.29%), Andhra Pradesh (5.7%), Maharashtra (10.08%), Odisha (9.2%), Gujarat (8.55%) and Rajasthan (8.86%). The other distinct area is the North East (Assam, Nagaland, Mizoram, Manipur, Meghalaya, Tripura, Sikkim and Arunachal Pradesh). The Graph below shows the states' share of ST population out of India's ST population:

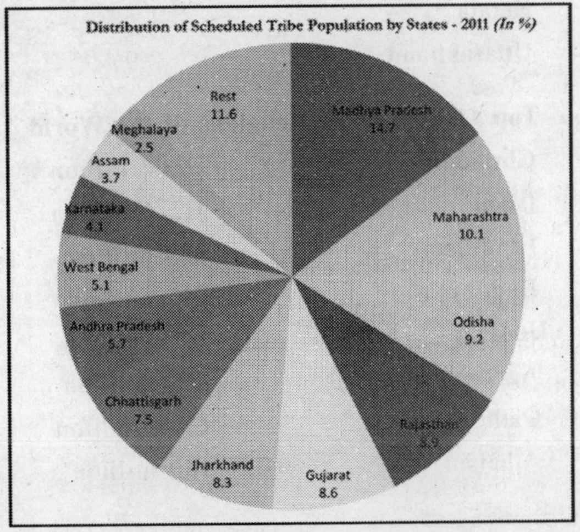

Source: *Presentation "SCHEDULED TRIBES IN INDIA, Census 2011" by Registrar General of India, May 2013*

State/UT Ranked by Proportion of SC-2011

Top 5 States/UTs

Punjab	31.9%
Himachal Pradesh	25.2%
West Bengal	23.5%
Uttar Pradesh	20.7%
Haryana	20.2%

Bottom 5 States/UTs

Mizoram	0.1%
Meghalaya	0.6%
Goa	1.7%
Dadra & Nagar Haveli	1.8%
Daman & Diu	2.5%

State/UTs Ranked by Proportion of STs-2011

Top 5 States/UTs

Lakshadweep	94.8%
Mizoram	94.4%
Nagaland	86.5%
Meghalaya	86.1%
Arunachal Pradesh	68.8%

Bottom 5 States/UTs

Uttar Pradesh	0.6%
Tamil Nadu	1.1%
Bihar	1.3%
Kerala	1.5%
Uttarakhand	2.9%

Top 11 Organized Religions of the World

Christianity	20.04 billion
Islam	1.226 billion
Hinduism	828 million
Buddhism	367 million
Judism	14.5 million
Agnosticism	85.4 million
Catholicism	1.142 billion
Atheism	150 million
Sikhism	23.8 million
Bahai	7 million
Jainism	4.2 million

1. Encompasses multiple dialects, including Hindi and Urdu.

People of Different Regions: Here we give the names of some well-known groups of people and the regions with which they are associated.

Aborigines	: Earliest people in Australia (the term 'aborigine' is actually for original people of any area).
Bantus	: Central and Southern Africa
Bedouins	: Nomadic tribe in Africa and South West Asia
Berbers	: Algeria, Morocco, Tunisia
Bindibu	: Western Australia
Bushmen	: Kalahari
Eskimos	: Tundra region in Canada and Greenland
Finns	: Tundra of Europe
Fulanis	: West Africa
Gaucho	: Uruguay, Argentina (the Pampas)
Hamits	: North-west Africa
Hausas	: Western Africa
Hottenhons	: Kalahari
Ibos	: Nigeria
Kirghiz	: Steppes of Asia
Kikuyus	: Kenya
Lapps	: Tundras of Europe
Maori	: New Zealand
Masai	: East Africa
Papuans	: New Guinea
Pygmies	: Congo (Zaire) Basin
Red Indians	: North America
Samoyeds	: Asiatic Tundra—North U.S.S.R.
Tartars	: Siberia
Tuaregs	: Sahara desert
Veddas	: Sri Lanka
Yakuts	: Tundra region of U.S.S.R.

14 HUMAN ACTIVITIES (WORLD AND INDIA)

WORLD'S FORESTS

FORESTLESS REGIONS: Some form of forests are the natural vegetation of the most parts of the earth surface but some areas, where the climate is too cold or too dry, cannot support forest growth. The two main areas in this category are the polar regions, where the growing season is short, the ground is often frozen or is snow or ice-covered and where rainfall is also very low (often about 225 mm/10 inches); and the deserts where rainfall is too low (below 225 mm/10 inches), atmospheric humidity is also low and where the soils are thin, sandy or saline. The upper slopes of mountains, are often too cold or lacking of fertility in soil to support trees.

Top 10 Countries for Forest area (2020)

Country	Forested area (000 ha)	% of country area
Russia Federation	8,15,312	49.8
Brazil	4,96,620	59.4
Canada	3,46,928	38.7
USA	3,09,795	33.9
China	2,19,978	23.3
Australia	1,34,005	17.4
Republic of Congo	1,26,155	55.6
Indonesia	92,133	49.1
Peru	72,330	56.5
India	72,160	24.3
Total	**4,85,438**	

Top 10 Countries for Average annual net gain in Forest area (2010-2020)

Country	Annual Forest Area Gain	
	Area (000 ha)	% of 2010 forest area
China	1,937	0.93
Australia	446	0.34
India	266	0.38
Chile	149	0.85
Vietnam	126	0.90
Turkey	114	0.53
USA	108	0.03
France	83	0.50
Italy	54	0.58
Romania	41	0.62

Top ten countries for volume of forest growing stock (2020)

Country	Growing Stock (m cum)
Brazil	1,20,358
Russian Federation	81,071
Canada	45,108
USA	41,269
Democratic Republic of the Congo	30,782
China	19,191
Colombia	14,830
Indonesia	12,727
Peru	11,525
Bolivarian Republic of Venezuela	10,254

The temperate and tropical grasslands also support few trees and in most areas this is due to the dryness or seasonal rhythm of the climate. However, it is now thought that the vegetation of many grasslands has been modified by human interference over so long a period that forest cover has been reduced or eliminated. For instance, *savannas* occurring as patches in forests or around the margins of tropical forests may have degenerated from forests as a result of burning by pastoralists or shifting cultivators over many hundreds of years. Similarly, it is thought that the North American *Prairies* have remained as grassland because red Indian tribes periodically burned large areas in order to facilitate hunting. Most grassland areas are capable of supporting tree-growth as is shown by the fact that many Prairie farmers have planted trees as wind breaks or to conserve fallow land. The Asiatic Steppes, however, are probably treeless as a result of aridity.

Largest Forests in the World

Forest	Area (sq. km)	Countries
Amazon rainforest	5,500,000	Brazil, Peru, Colombia, Bolivia, Ecuador, French Guiana, Guyana, Suriname, Venezuela
Congo Rainforest	2,000,000	Angola, Cameroon, Central African Republic, Democratic Republic of the Congo, Republic of the Congo, Equatorial Guinea, Gabon
Atlantic Forest	1,315,460	Brazil, Argentina, Paraguay
Valdivian Temperate Rainforest	248,100	Chile, Argentina
Tongass National Forest	68,000	United States
Rainforest of Xishuangbanna	19,223	China
Sunderbans	10,000	India, Bangladesh
Daintree Rainforest	1,200	Australia

TYPES OF FORESTS: In the more humid temperate and tropical areas of the world there are three main types of forests. These are differentiated not only by climatic factors but also by the dominant types of trees and the types of wood they yield.

(*i*) TROPICAL HARDWOOD FORESTS: These include both the evergreen rain forests of region latitudes and the tropical monsoon forests. In the equatorial forests trees often shed a few leaves or shed their leaves seasonally, but most of the trees retain their leaves for most of the time so that the forest appears evergreen. In monsoon forests the trees are deciduous, shedding their leaves in the dry season and not growing new ones until the rains come. The warm temperatures, around 27°C (80°F) and the heavy rainfall of 2030 mm (80 inches) or more in equatorial regions and of between 1015 and 2030 mm (40 and 80 inches) in the monsoon regions, encourages a prolific growth. The majority of the trees are broadleaved and yield valuable hardwoods. The main commercial species are teak, greenheart, logwood, ebony, mahogany and ironwood.

The tropical forests have several layers of vegetation. The highest layer is of the larger trees which grow to a height of over 46 metres (150 ft) and have huge buttress roots and long straight trunks, ideal for timber. Below these trees are lower layers of smaller trees about 9 to 15 metres (30 to 50 ft) high, palms, shrubs, ferns and grasses. In addition there is a bewildering variety of climbers, creepers and parasitic and epiphytic plants. There is a wide variety of species in any given area and trees do not occur in stands or groups consisting of only one species as do the trees of the coniferous forests.

Monsoon forests are less luxuriant than equatorial forests because of the seasonal drought, but are characterized by a thick undergrowth of shrubs and small trees and by dense thickets of bamboo. Coastal areas in the tropics are often fringed with swampy mangrove forests. The wood of mangrove species has many uses but the many aerial roots of the trees make access difficult.

Tropical forests are found in three main areas:

(a) ***Latin America:*** The largest expanse of tropical forest is found in the Amazon Basin of Brazil, extending from the Atlantic coast of the foothills of the Andes and from the Guiana Highlands in the north to the Tropic of Capricorn in the south. Tropical forest is also found on the Pacific Coast of Colombia and in Central American countries from Panama to Mexico.

(b) ***Africa:*** Tropical forests are found on the lowlands bordering the Gulf of Guinea from Sierra Leone in the west to Cameroon and Gabon in the east, and in the Zaire Basin, especially in the lowlands of the Zaire itself and its major tributaries the Ubangi and the Kasai. They are also found in eastern Malagasy and the coastal plain of tropical East Africa.

(c) ***South-East Asia and the Indian Sub-Continent:*** Rain forest is found in Malaysia, Indonesia and Papua New Guinea and in the coastal lowlands of other South and South-East Asian countries. Monsoon forests are found in India, Myanmar, Thailand and Indo-China. There are some tropical forests, also, in northern Australia.

(ii) TEMPERATE HARDWOOD FORESTS *:* The temperate hardwood forests is found between approximately 30° and 50°N and S latitudes where temperatures and rainfall are moderate, but where the seasonality of the climate, though marked, is not as extreme as in the coniferous forest belt. The trees are mostly deciduous, shedding their leaves in autumn and remaining leafless throughout the cool winter, and they yield a wide variety of hardwoods. Like the tropical forests, the temperate deciduous forests have a variety of species scattered irregularly through the forests, including many shrubs and small plants, but neither the tall trees nor the undergrowth are as luxuriant as those in the tropics. The hardwood, while being very durable and strong, is not usually as heavy or as difficult to work as are tropical hardwoods. On the other hand, it is more difficult to extract than softwoods. The chief commercial species are oak, ash, beech and poplar.

The temperate hardwood forests have greatly suffered from human activities than any other forests. Because of the favourable mid-latitude climate and the rapid expansion of population in these areas, the forests have been extensively cleared to make way for agriculture and industry, and the areas of forest which remain represent only a fraction of the original cover. Temperate hardwoods have also been used for house and ship-building for many generations as well as for fuel, and have thus been greatly depleted. They now occupy only those areas found unsuitable for agriculture or remote from the centres of settlement.

The chief areas of occurrence of temperate hardwood forests are in northern China (including Manchuria) and Japan, where agricultural populations have lived for thousands of years; west, south and central Europe, where the growth of agriculture and industry has made very great inroads into the forests and eastern North America where, though more recently settled, expansion of agriculture and industry has been extremely rapid and where massive exploitation of the accessible eastern forests in the nineteenth and early twentieth centuries has greatly reduced their extent or reduced their value. Some temperate hardwoods are also found in southern Australia, especially in Tasmania and Western Australia.

(iii) CONIFEROUS FORESTS *:* Coniferous (Taiga) forests cover a broad belt of land in both North America and Eurasia, to the north of the temperate hardwood belt. They also grow on uplands and mountains or in areas of sandy or porous soil in the milder temperate areas because they are better adapted to withstand cold and drought than the broadleaved trees. Conifers are tall, straight, evergreen trees with narrow, needle-like leaves, and take their name from the cones in which they bear their seeds. Only a few conifers, such as the larch, are deciduous. The needles limit transpiration and thus enable conifers to grow in drier areas, while the fact that the trees are evergreen means that growth can begin immediately after the long winter and thus the trees can make maximum use of a relatively short growing period. Most coniferous trees are softwoods and are light in weight, which makes them easier to cut and transport. Though they often grow to a height of 30 metres (100 ft) or more, the coniferous trees do not have the wide buttress roots which make tropical trees so difficult to fell. Moreover, although there is a wide variety of species in the spruce, pine, fir and larch families, the trees usually occur in pure stands consisting of one particular species. The major commercial species are the pines, such as the white pine, Scots pine and lodgepole pine; the firs, such as the Douglas fir and the balsam fir; and the spruces, particularly the Norway spruce and the red spruce. The deciduous larch is also of some commercial importance and the Parana or Auracaria pine found in South America, which yields harder wood than many conifers, is also important.

Coniferous forests are only moderately dense and they become appreciably thinner in colder or drier regions. The most dense, luxuriant coniferous forests are found in western North America. The dark shade cast by the uniform tree cover inhabits the growth of an understorey vegetation, especially in areas where there is little sunlight, though where the forest thins on the tundra margins or on mountains, tundra and alpine plants may be interspersed among the trees.

Coniferous forests are located chiefly in the northern hemisphere in a belt between 50° and 70°N latitudes though there are some conifers in the southern hemisphere. The major regions are as follows:

(a) Western North America: The moist, maritime climate of northern California, Washington and Oregon in the U.S.A., British Columbia in Canada and south-western Alaska, gives rise to a very luxuriant coniferous forest cover on the coastal plains and mountain slopes, though the higher and more northerly areas have a poorer vegetation. Some of the largest conifers in the world, such as the Douglas fir, the Sitka spruce, as well as the gigantic Californian redwoods or sequoias are found in this region.

(b) Central and Eastern North America: The drier, more continental climate and the thin soils of the Laurentian Shield support a less luxuriant and often more scattered type of coniferous forest which, however, contains many valuable species such as the red spruce, white pine, jack pine, pitch pine, hemlock and balsam fir. This type of forest extends southwards around the Great Lakes and into the Appalachian mountains.

(c) Southern USA: The dry sandy soils of many parts of the South America support a coniferous rather than a deciduous tree cover despite the warm moist climate. The longleaf, shortleaf, loblolly and slash pines are found from Virginia to Texas.

(d) Northern Europe: The Scandinavian countries-Norway, Sweden and Finland-as well as adjacent areas of northern Russia, support a valuable coniferous forest, the chief trees of which are the Scots pine, Norwegian pine, spruces and larches. Many upland areas farther south, such as northern Britain, the German and Central European uplands and even parts of Italy also support coniferous forests. Many areas in Europe which formerly bore hardwood species have been planted with conifers.

(e) Asiatic USSR: Much of northern Siberia, extending in a broad belt from the Ural to the Pacific coast, is forested with conifers. The forests are thinner on their northern and southern margins where the climate is either too cold or too dry, and in many areas hard birch trees thrive better than conifers. There are also breaks in the forest where huge marshy or swampy areas intervene. These vast forest reserves are remote and, until recently, remained largely unexploited.

(f) Southern Continents: Two major areas of South America have coniferous forests: the western coastlands of southern Chile and the southern part of the Brazilian plateau. The former is remote, rugged and is thus, little exploited but the later is an important forest area and yields the valuable Parana pine.

The North Island of New Zealand is noted for its Kauri pine. South Africa and Australia have only small areas of natural coniferous forests and these are of only local importance.

BIOMES : A biome is a large geographical area of distinctive plants and animal groups which are adapted to that particular environment. Biomes can be defined as a major type of ecological community where the plants occur in distinct groups of communities in areas having similar climatic conditions.

MAJOR BIOMES

Biomes	Subtypes	Regions	Climatic Characteristics	Soil	Flora and Fauna
Forest	A. Tropical 1. Equitorial 2. Deciduous B. Temperate C. Boreal	A1. 10° N-S A2. 10°-25° N-S B. Eastern North America. N.E. Asia, Western and Central Europe C. Broad belt of Eurasia and North America, parts of Siberia, Alaska, Canada and Scandinavia	A1. Temp. 20-25° C evenly distributed A2. Temp. 25-30°C, Rainfall, ave. ann. 1,000 mm, seasonal. B. Temp. 20-30° C. Rainfall evenly distributed 750-1,500 mm. Well-defined seasons and distinct winter C. Short moist moderately warm summers and long cold dry winter; very low temperatures. Precipitation mostly 400-1,000 mm	A1. Acidic, poor in nutrients A2. Rich in nutrients B. Fertile, en-riched with decaying litter C. Acidic and poor poor in nutrients, thin soil cover	A1. Multi-layered canopy tall and large trees A2. Less dense, trees of medium height; many varieties co-exist Insects, bats, birds and mammals are common species in both B. Moderately dense broad leaved trees. With less diversity of of plant species. Oack, Beach, Maple etc. are some common common species. Squirrels, rabbits, skunks, birds, black bears, mountain lions etc. C. Evergreen conifers like pine, fur and spruce etc. Wood peckers, hawks, bears, wolves, deer, hares and bats are common animals
Desert	A. Hot and Dry desert B. Semi arid desert C. Coastal desert D. Cold desert	A. Sahara, Kalahari, Marushthali, Rub-el-Khali B. Marginal areas of hot deserts C. Atacana D. Tundra climatic regions	A. Temp. 20 - 45° C. B. 21 - 38° C. C. 15 - 35° C. A-D Rainfall is less than 50 mm	Rich in nutrients with little or no organic matter	A-C. Scanty vegetation; few large mammals, insects, reptiles and birds. D. Rabitts, rats, antelopes and ground squirrels

ass- ıd	A. Tropical Savannah B. Temperate Steppe	A. Large areas of Africa, Australia, South America and India B. Parts of Eurasia North America	A. Warm hot climates, Rainfall 500-1.250 mm B. Hot summers and cold winter, Rainfall 500-900 mm	A. Porous with thin layer of humus B. Thin flocculated soil, rich in bases	A. Grasses; trees and large shrubs absent; giraffes zebras, buffalos, leopards, hyenas, elephants, mice, moles, snakes and worms etc., are common animals. B. Grasses; occasional trees such as cottonwoods, oaks and willows; gazelles, sebras, rhinoceros, wild horses, lions, varieties of birds, worms, snakes etc., are common animals
uatic	A. Freshwater B. Marine	A. Lakes, streams, rivers and wetlands B. Oceans, coral reefs, lagoons and estuaries	A-B Temperatures vary widely with cooler air temperatures and high humidity	A. Water, swamps and marshes B. Water, tidal swamps and marshes	Algal and other aquatic and marine plant communities with varieties of water dwelling animals
itu- al	—	Slopes of high mountain ranges like the Himalayas, the Andes and the Rockies	Temperature and precipitation vary depending upon latitudinal zone	Regolith over slopes	Deciduous to tundra vegetation varying according to altitude

ASSLANDS

Grasslands are those areas which do not receive cient rainfall to support forests. A large variety asses grow in areas where annual rainfall varies 25 to 75 cm. Grass does not require any special raphical condition and can grow in areas of ty rainfall. This is the reason that grasses can right from equator to the polar areas. About of the earth's surface is covered by grasses. The e and type of grass changes as we move from tor towards the poles. On the basis of location, lands can be divided into following types

(i) Tropical Grasslands

(ii) Temperate Grasslands

(i) Tropical Grasslands: Tropical grasslands nd from 5° to 30° north and south latitudes een the equatorial rain forests and the hot ts. The average annual rainfall of these areas 0 cm occurring mostly in the summer season. e grasslands are known by different names in rent areas. They are called *Savannas* in Sudan, os in Venezuela, *Campos* in Brazil and *Parkland* uth Africa. These grasses are thick, rough and They are 1.8 to 3.0 metres tall. Their height ally decreases as we go from equator towards ot deserts. They are somewhat soft in the rainy n but become extremely rough during the dry n. They also lack in nutrients. Therefore, the cattle which feed these grasses do not provide quality products.

(ii) Temperate Grasslands: These grasslands are found in the temperate belts extending from 30° to 45° north and south latitudes. At some places, they extend upto 50° latitude in the northern hemisphere due to extensive land-masses there. The average rainfall in these areas varies from 25 cm to 75 cm. The rainfall is fairly distributed throughout the year but summers receive more rainfall than winters. Evaporation is less due to low temperature. Hence, even this small amount of rainfall is sufficient enough to support extensive growth of grass. The grass is soft, nutritive and very useful for animals.

The temperate grasslands are of two types *viz* :

(a) Steppes, and (b) Prairies

(a) Steppes: These are short grasses whose height varies from 10 to 20 cm. They grow in semi-arid lands having an annual rainfall of 25 cm to 50 cm. The steppes are less dense than the prairies but cover the land like mats. These are most extensive in the northern hemisphere. They grow over large areas in Eurasia, North America, Australia and South Africa.

(b) Prairies: These grasses grow in comparatively humid regions and are taller than the steppes. They generally grow in areas of 40 to 80 cm. of annual rainfall and provide extensive cover of 40 to 60 cm. tall grass. Prairies mainly grow in the great plain of North America. Some prairies also grow in Argentina, and South Africa.

Temperate grassland are known with different names in different regions. For example. These are called *prairies* in North America, *pampas* in Argentina, *veldt* in South Africa and *downs* in Australia. Livestock rearing is a developed economic activity in the temperate grasslands.

DESERTS

The word desert is used for an area which is not cultivated, unoccupied and is also deserted by the people. Deserts can be defined as an area which receives low rainfall, the temperature is high (in atleast one season) and the ratio of evaporation to rainfall is very high. Deserts occupy about 30% of the surface of the earth. They are found between 15° to 35° north and south latitudes. The deserts of the world can be divided into three classes:—

(a) Low Latitude Desert : These latitudes are found between 15° and 30° north and south latitudes and are under the influence of trade winds. These winds do not generally provide any rainfall to these areas.

Some of the important deserts of the type are Sahara, and Kalahari in Africa, Arab and Thar in Asia and Atacama in South America.

(b) Polar Deserts : In polar areas, the ice is permanent and the weather is dry. Vegetation is very rare. Greenland and Antarctica are examples of these types of deserts.

(c) Deserts of Continental Interior : This type of deserts are found in the interior of continents. Summers are very hot but moisture laden winds do not reach these areas. Cold and dry winds hold sway in these deserts in winter season. The deserts of Central Asia belong to this type.

(d) Deserts in the Lee of Mountains : The parts of mountains which exist opposite to the windward side do not practically receive rain. Moist winds do not reach these areas. The Nevada of U.S.A. and the eastern sides of the Rockies and the Andes belong to this type.

LIVESTOCK

At some stages in history, probably in th Palaeolithic or Old Stone Age, though the exa time is not known, Man began to domestica animals. The first animal to be tamed was probabl the dog. Present domestic species are probabl descended from the wolf.

Cattle: Cattle for beef and dual-purposes mak up the bulk of the world's cattle population. India ha the highest cattle population in the world. The U.S.A is the greatest producer of cattle products. Thoug India has 15 per cent of the world's cattle populatio it has little or no beef production for religious reason Countries like U.S.A., Russia and Brazil, though the possess many cattle have little beef for export becaus of large home consumption.

Many parts of the temperate grasslands of th world, the Steppes, the Prairies, the Pampas, the Vel the Australian Downs and canterbury plains of Ne Zealand, have long been used for cattle ranching.

In terms of the total numbers of cattle man tropical countries are well-endowed, e.g. Indi Bangladesh, Brazil, Ethiopia, Mexico, the norther Andean states and many of the African countrie but they are often kept mainly as draught animals, o for hides. In Central and South America and also i southern Africa, however, they are increasingly kep on the commercial basis.

Dairy Farming: The objective of dairy farmin is to raise cattle to produce milk. The milk may b used in its original form or turned into butter or chees The milk can be processed to make condensed o sweetened milk, or evaporated or ideal milk, whic can then be canned. It can also be dried or powdere and canned, in which case it has to be reconstitute by adding water before it can be used. This is however, an ideal way of preserving milk, especiall for use in tropical countries where the hot climat causes fresh milk to deteriorate rapidly.

Dairy Cattle Breeds: Most of the world's bes known breeds of dairy cows come from Wester Europe, especially Britain, Netherlands an Switzerland. The **Ayrshire breed** is white or red, o mixed in colour and has long, sharp-pointed horn **The Guernsey and Alderney dairy** cows were firs bread on the isles of Guernsey and Alderney in th

Channel Islands, off the coast of north-west France. Their coats have spots and patches of various shades but are dominantly white, especially on the legs. **The Jersey cow** is the smallest of the dairy **breeds**. It yields milk with an extremely high content of butterfat. The **Friesian breed**, with its characteristic black-and-white colour, is the largest of the dairy breeds and is a heavy grazer. It was first breed in the low-lying polders of the northwest Netherlands, but is now used all over the temperate latitudes. Polders are the areas of low lying land reclaimed from a body of water (i.e. ocean, sea etc.). Its milk yield is the highest among dairy cattle. It is also referred to as the Holstein breed because it was traditionally kept in the German province of Holstein adjoining the northern Netherlands.

World Distribution and Production: The greatest dairying areas are in Western Europe, U.S.A. and the temperate parts of the southern continents. Another regions where dairying is important are Japan and South Korea. Russia is the largest producer of milk and butter in the world, followed by the U.S.A. which leads in cheese production. In Europe, France leads in milk, butter and cheese production. Denmark is a leading butter exporter. The Netherlands is the leading exporter of condensed, evaporated and powdered milk. New Zealand is the world's leading butter exporter.

Sheep: Sheep are more widely distributed than any other domesticated animal, but the majority are kept for wool rather than meat especially in the semi-arid regions. Russia, Australia, New Zealand have the largest number of sheep in that order. New Zealand, followed by Australia, is the largest producer and exporter of lamb and mutton.

Goats: They are extensively kept in the drier and more densely populated parts of the world, where the pasturage is too poor or too restricted in area for cattle farming, and where the climate is too warm for largescale sheep production. Goats are kept as a source of milk (often used to make cheese), meat and hides. The main areas in which they are reared are North Africa and the Sahara, the Middle East, Central Asia, India, Pakistan, China, South-East Asia and East Africa.

In addition to milk, meat and hides, certain types of goats, especially those with long silky hair, are valued for their hair which is used in the same way as wool. The most important goats of this type are Angora goats and the Kashmir goats.

Pigs: China is the most important pig-rearing country, accounting for more than a third of the world's swine. Russia, West Germany and Poland are large pig producers but many other countries including the Netherlands, U.K., France, Italy, and East Germany all have large numbers of pigs.

Poultry. The term poultry includes all farm-birds such as chickens, turkeys, ducks, geese and guinea fowls, though chickens alone constitute as much as 95 per cent of all the poultry kept in the world. The largest egg producers are China, U.S.A., Russia, Japan, West Germany and U.K. But now-a-days Chicken's production to the effect of bird-flu.

FISHERIES

Fish are a vital source of food, especially in countries like Norway, Iceland and Japan where the land is bleak or mountainous and agriculture cannot be easily developed. Modern fisheries are not confined to catching fish, but include many other sea harvests such as whales, seals, pearls, crustaceans (i.e., lobsters, crabs, prawns, shrimps), molluscs (i.e. oysters, mussels, cockles, clams), sponges and seaweeds. However, it must not be assumed that fish and other marine animals are an inexhaustible resource. Indeed, there are vast areas of the oceans which have very few fish. Many factors affect the productivity of the seas: the depth of the water, the ocean currents, the temperature and salinity determine the amount of plankton or fish-food present.

Per capita consumption varies for two reasons. **Firstly,** fish is relatively cheaper than meat and is thus, in demand in many underdeveloped or partially-developed countries. **Secondly,** fish is an important source of protei n for countries whose agricultural potential is low. Mountainous Japan and Norway are therefore, large consumers. This pattern may be perpetuated by tradition. Thus, many European nations, e.g. Denmark, Germany, still have relatively high fish consumption figures though fishing is less important in the overall economy than formerly.

FISH SPECIES

Fishes are mainly divided into two main categories i.e., the salt water and fresh water fish. Salt water fish are those fishes which live in the oceans and seas, while the fishes of inland streams, rivers and lakes are known as the fresh water fish. The table given below shows the major types of fish and their locations:-

Types of Fish	Location
(1) **Salt water fish**	
Herring	North Atlantic region, China, Japan
Tuna, Meckerel	Mediaterranean sea, South Scandinavia, Cornwall (Britain), California
Brisling, Pilehards, Sardines, Anchovies, Cod	North sea, Norway coast, iceland sea, Grand Bank of Newfoundland
Haddock	North Atlantic region
Halibut	British Columbia and north-west U.S.A.
Tuna	Japan, Indian Ocean, Eastern Pacific Ocean
(2) **Freshwater Fish**	
Trout, Perch, Pike or Salmon	North America, Europe, East Asia
Sturgeon	Caspian Sea
Carp	In the paddy fields of China and Japan
(3) **Anadromous fish**	
Salmon	North America, espeically along the Pacific coast fro Alaska to Oregon, Canada
Haul	Alaska

AGRICULTURAL PRODUCE AND THEIR PRODUCTS

Sr. No	Type of Agriculture	Crops	Requirements	Fertilizers & Method	World production and Trade
I.	**Cereals:** It is a collective term used mainly for all kinds of grass-like plants, which have starchy edible seeds. It includes, rice, wheat, maize, barley, rye, oats, millet and Sorgham etc.	**Rice** (*Oryza sativa*) probably originated in China or India	• Planty of rainfall, varies between 150 and 200 cm. • It needs temperature between 20°C (68°F) and 27°C (80°F). • Heavy clayey or loamy soil is best for it. • More labourers are required.	• Nitrogen, Phosphorus and Potassium are the main fertilizers. • Transplantation, Drifting and Broad Casting methods are used for rice cultivation.	• 90% of world's rice is grown in east and south Asia. China, India, Vietnam, Brazil, Japan, U.S.A. etc. are the main producers of Rice. • Mainly the crop of monsoon Asia
		Wheat (probably it originated in Asia Minor and middle east)	• It requires 10°C temperature at the time of sowing and 15° to 20°C during ripening time. • 100 frost free days are usually required for its well production. • 50 to 100 cm of rainfall is required. • Light clay or heavy loam soil is best for it. • An open and plain topography is best for wheat cultivation. • Steppes, Downs, Prairies, Pampas etc. are the main regions of wheat production.	• Wheat which is sown in late autumn or early winter and harvested in early summer is called the *winter wheat*, while which is sown in spring and harvested in late summer or autumn is known as *spring wheat*. • Nitrates, animals dung, sulphate amonia, Nitrate of soda, Potash are the main fertilizers which are required for it.	• China, India, Russian, Federation, France, Germany, Canada, Australia, etc. are the leading producers of wheat in the world. • Mainly a crop of the temperate region

		Maize (Indian corn) (originated in Central America)	• It requires temperature varying from 20° and 30°C. • 140 frost free days are its main requirement. • Annual rainfall should be around 1145 mm. • Red soil is best for its cultivation. • The undulating topography is ideal for large-scale cultivation.	• It is an annual of the Gramineae crop (grass family) and grows to a height of between 1 and 5 mts.	U.S.A. is the largest producer of maize in the world. Argentina, Brazil, China etc. are the other main producers of maize in the world.
		Barley (Hordeum Vulgare) Earlier, it was cultivated by the Swiss lake dwellers.	• High latitudes are the best location for barley cultivation. • Also grown in the fringes of the Sahara desert, i.e., Russian Turkestan, Thar desert. • It can grow on dry chalk and limestone uplands in Europe. • It is extensively used for making beer and whisky.		• U.S.S.R. Germany, France, Australia, Canada, U.K. and U.S.A. are the main producers of barley.
		Coffee: Derived from the Kafa highlands of Ehtiopia	• Temperature over 32°C (90°F). • Hot rainy season and dry cool season. • Precipitation around 1016 and 2030 mm. • Well- drained hilly areas. • Volcanic soil like terra roxa is best. • Huge labour • Modern techniques & machines.	• **Arabica:** the most important in world trade and famous for its flavour & taste. • Mocha is the nature of Arabian peninsula. • **Robusta** is a poor quality coffee of west Africa. • **Liberica** is a hard, disease-resistant species of Liberia.	• Brazil produces about 1/5th of world's total coffee production. • Vietnam, Indonesia, Columbia, Mexico, India, Guatemala, Ethopia are also its main producers
		Cocoa: (Theobroma) was first found in lowland central America.	• Annual temperature 23°C 73°F) • Annual rainfall 2030 to 3555 mm. • Can tolerate short dry season. • Heat and direct sunlight • Labour intensive • Deep, well-drained loamy soil.	• Cocao Criollo: from tropical America, gives good beans but with low yield. • Cocao Forastero: from West Africa, poor quality with high yield.	• Ivory coast is the largest producers and exporter of Cocoa. • First exported from Gold Coast of Africa. • Nigeria, Brazil, Cameroon, Ecuador, Columbia, Mexico are other important producers of Cocoa.
		Oats (Avena Saliva) the hardiest cereals.	• Cool humid climate • Found in tropics & sub-tropics of Africa, Asia and South America. • Spring-sown crop. • A wide range of soil types are suitable for it.		• Russian Feederation, Candada, U.S.A., Australia, Sweden, Finland, Germany etc. are its major producers.

		Millet and Sorghum	• Grown in tropical and sub-tropical areas of the world. • 760 mm of rainfall is required. • It can grow in poor soil. • It includes Jowar, Bajra and Ragi.	• In China, great millets are known as *Kaoling*, while they are called *Durra* or *Guinea corn* in Africa	• U.S.A., Southern Europe, Argentina, Russia, India, Nigeria, Nigar, China etc. are its major producers.
II.	Plantation Crops	**Tobacco :** Native plant of tropical America	• A frost-free period of 120 to 180 days is required. • About 18°C of temperature is required. • Fertile soil is required		• India, China, Brazil, U.S.A., Zimbabwe, Turkey, Indonesia, Greece, Argentina, Italy etc are its major producers.
		Tea: It is believed to have originated in the Chang Jiang valley of China	• Temperature around 21°C (70°F). • Warm summer and frequent rainfall. • Required rainfall is 1270 to 6350 mm. • Hill slopes	• Low crown tea-low grade. • Medium crown tea – Intermediate grade. • High crown tea – best grade	• China is the largest producer, consumer and trader in tea. It is famous for green tea India. (Black tea) Taiwan (Oolong tea) Paraguay (Yerba mate), Sri Lanka, Turkey, Japan, Argentina etc. are also the significant producers of tea in the world.
		Wine (Viticulture)	• Best quality grapes • 18°C of temperature • Rainfall 760 – 1016 mm • Fairly deep and well-drained soil, i.e., calcareours, chalk, limestone. • Much manual labour is required.	• Rice wine is made in Japan, China & S.E. Asia. • Cidar is made up of apple juice and famous in France and Britain. • Whisky is made up of barley in Scotland & Scandinavia, U.S.A., Japan • Rum is made up of molasses and is a bi-product of west-Indian sugar industry. • Brandy is made up of grapes, while Vodka originates from potatoes.	• Itlay, France, USA, Australia, Chile etc. are the chief wine producing countries. • Mediterranean countries are the main producers of best quality wine in the world.
III.	Commercial crops	Sugarcane	• Temperature : 21°C to 27°C • Rainfall : 1270 mm • Soil: deep, fertile and well-drained. • Well mechanised • Cheap labour		• Latin America and South-east Asia are its main producers. • Brazil, India, China, Thailand, Pakistan, Mexico etc. are the other large producers.

		Sugarbeet	• Temperature: 16ºC and 23ºC • Well-distributed moderate rain, about 635 mm. • Well-drained deep soil.		• Rusia, France, Germany is the largest producer of sugarbeet, while others are Germany, Turkey, U.S.A., Ukraine etc.
IV.	Industrial Crops	**Rubber :** It is the latex of the tree Hevea brasiliensis	• Temperature 27ºC (80ºF) • Plentiful supply of moisture. • Rainfall 1525 mm • Deep, friable and well-drained soil		• South-east Asia is the biggest producer of Rubber in the world. • Thailand, Indonesia, Malaysia, India, China, Vietnam, Ivory Coast etc. are its main producers.
		Groundnuts: (Arachis hypogoea) originated in Brazil.	• Warm temperature with light to moderate rainfall. • Rich, sandy soil • Labour intensive. • Large mechanised farms		• China, India, Nigeria and U.S.A. are the main producers.
		Soyabeans (glycine max)	• Temperature around 21ºC(70ºF) • Moderate rainfall around 1015 mm • Moisture retentive soil		• Brazil, U.S.A., Argentina, China, India, etc. are its main producers.
		Cotton (Gossypium)	• Temperature 25ºC (77ºF) • Planty of sunshine • About 200 frost free days are required. • Medium loamy soil • Flat or undulating land • Large number of labourer	• Long staple cotton produced in Egypt. • Medium staple cotton: U.S.A., U.S.S.R. • Short staple cotton: Asia	• China, India, U.S.A., Turkey, Uzbekistan, Argentina, Greece etc. are the major cotton producing areas in the world.
		Jute (Corchorus)	• Hot and tropical conditions • Rich alluvial soil. • Plenty of moisture with heavy rainfall. • Labour intensive		• India, Bangladesh, Myanmar, Uzbekistan, Nepal, Vietnam etc, are its major producers.
		Wool	• Warm and dry climate • Tropical regions • Land should be well-drained. • Plenty of nutritious grass.		Main producers of wool are Australia, China, New Zealand, Iran, U.K., South Africa, Germany, Spain, Portugal, India, Pakistan, Morocco etc.
		Silk: It is derived from the cocoon of a moth. It was discovered in China and its production is known as Sericulture	• Low temperature, mainly below 16ºC. • Highly mechanised techniques are required.		China, India, Uzbekistan, Brazil, Iran, Thailand, Vietnam, France, Britain, etc. are its main producers.

CROPS AROUND THE WORLD : HOW THEY BEGAN	
Barley	First grown in Egypt in about 4000 BC. Modern varieties are descended from the strain '*Hordeu* *spontaneum*'. Now grown mostly in Europe, North America and Australia as fodder for catt and as a source of malt used in distilling and brewing.
Beans	Family of plants now very widely grown, and thought to have been first cultivated in about 600 BC. String, kidney and lima beans originated in Central and South America. Mung and soya bear were first cultivated in Asia, broad beans in Europe.
Maize	First cultivated in Mexico in about 5000 BC. Introduced to Europe from the Americas b Christopher Columbus in the late 15th century. Modern varieties are descended from the origin cultivated plant which was crossed with a 15th century hybrid called teosinte. Maize is sometime referred to as Indian corn.
Millet	First cultivated in China in about 2700 BC. Now grown mostly for cattle fodder in the USA an Russia, but because of its resistance to drought conditions it is used as food in tropical Afric
Oats	Probably originated as a weed growing with other cereals such as wheat or barley, and wa domesticated about 2500 years ago in Asia and Europe. The most widely cultivated form i '*Avena sativa*', derived from a western Asian wild grass, '*Avena fatua*'. Predominantly used a cattle food, but also used in breakfast cereals and to make porridge.
Potato	First know to have been cultivated in the Peruvian and Bolivian Andes in about AD 200 Introduced to Europe by the Spaniards in the late 16th century. More than 150 varieties are now grown.
Rice	First known to have been cultivated in India in about 3000 BC, later spreading to China, Japan and Southeast Asia, are now the main producers. About 25 varieties are grown, all descended from an original wild species, '*Oryza sativa*'.
Rye	Originated as a weed growing among other cereals. First cultivated in southwest Asia in abou 1000 BC and is now used as a flour in rye bread or as food for cattle.
Sorghum	Probably originated in Africa in about 3000 BC. It is now grown for human and animal consumption in Africa, India, China and the USA.
Wheat	Probably the earliest domesticated cereal, developing from chance hybridisations of wild grasses more than 10,000 years ago. It was grown by the early civilisations in the Mediterranean and the Middle East, and was being baked into bread in Mesopotamia as early as 8000 BC.

A SURVEY OF IMPORTANT MINERALS (EXCEPT FUEL MINERALS) AND THEIR WORLD DISTRIBUTION

Minerals : Uses and Major Producers

Mineral Resources	Uses	Ore	Major Producing Countries
Aluminium	Electric wires bases of aeroplane	Bauxite	Australia, Guinea, Jamaica, Brazil
Bauxite	Ore of Aluminium		Australia, Brazil, China, Guinea, Guyana and India
Chromium	Alloys, electroplating	Chromite	South Africa, CIS, India, Turkey, Zimbabwe
Copper	Alloys, electric wires	Chalecopyrite, chalcocite	Chile, USA, Canada, CIS
Gold	Jewellery, circuitry in computers, communications equipment, dentistry		South Africa, USA, CIS, Australia,
Magnesite		Magnesite, Dolomite	Australia, Brazil, China, Gabon, Ghana, India

Iron ore	Iron and steel	Limonite, Sedaeite	Russia, Ukraine, China, Australia and Brazil Mauritiania
Lead	Storage batteries, solder, pipes	Galena	CIS, USA, Mexico, Canada, Peru
Manganese	Iron and steel production	Pyrolusite, Psilomelane	CIS, South Africa, Gabon, Australia, Brazil, France.
Nickel	Stainless steel	Pentlaudite	CIS, Canada, New Caledonia, Norway, Dominican Republic
Silver	Jewellery, photogrpahy, dentistry	Argentite	Australia, Mexico, USA, Peru, CIS, Canada
Tin	Coating on metal, tin cans, alloys, solder	Cassiterite	China, Brazil, Indonesia, Malaysia
Titanium	Alloys; white pigment in paint, paper, and plastics	Limenite	Australia, Norway, CIS
Zinc	Iron and steel,alloys rubber products, medicines	Zinc blende and Calamine	Canada, Australia, CIS, China, Peru, Mexico, Spain

COAL

Coal is the major source of power. Its importance increased with the invention of steam engine in 1776. Later on iron and steel industry became the major user of coal. Now the demand for coal is also due to its use as a source of electric energy.

ANTHRACITE OR HARD COAL

(1) It is a black or brown rock, consisting mainly of carbon, which is formed by the compressed vegetative remains of past ages.

(2) Most coal deposits are of Carboniferous age, i.e. about 300 million years old. More recent deposits of Tertiary age are usually composed of lignite or brown coal, and peat which represents an early stage of coal formation is still being formed today.

(3) Coal originated in swampy deltaic areas with a hot, wet climate which encouraged the growth of luxuriant trees and ferns.

(4) New forests grew, died and were covered in the same way so that today we find a series of coal seams interlayered with other sedimentary rocks. The mass of vegetative materials was probably changed into coal by heat and pressure generated not only by the increasing weight of overlying sediments but also by earth movements and contortions.

(5) The heat value of any given coal deposit is governed by such factors as carbon and moisture content, and affects the market value of the coal. It consists of carbon from 60-90%, nitrogen 1-3% and some amount of sulphur and phosphorus.

Classification: The various rocks which contain carbon, such as coal, lignite and peat are ranked according to their composition, characteristics, and stage of development.

The first stage of formation of coal and is a fibrous brownish substance formed by partly decayed organic remains in swamps and bogs. It represents the first stage of coal formation and varies considerably in extent and thickness. It has a high percentage of moisture and volatile matter, and carbon only constitutes about 40-60% of its fuel. In deep peat deposits the carbon content is higher in the more compressed lower layers. Its low heating capacity reduced its value as an industrial fuel.

The world's main deposits of peat 97% occur in the U.S.S.R., Fenno-Scandinavia, parts of the U.S.A. and Canada. It is relatively little developed in the southern hemisphere.

LIGNITE

(1) It is usually regarded as the second stage of coal formation after peat.

(2) It is soft and still retains much of its brownish, woody appearance but is more compact than peat.

(3) Its moisture content is high (over 35 per cent) so that it gives out much smoke but little heat.

(4) It slacks, i.e. breaks up easily when exposed to the air and this renders transhipment difficult. For this reason lignite is seldom used outside its area of production.

(5) The carbon content is 45 to 70%.

(6) About 15 per cent of the world's coal output is from lignite.

(7) It is worked mainly by open-cast methods because it often occurs near the surfaces and seams may be as thick as 15 metres (50 ft) each. It is most extensively used where other more efficient forms of fuel are lacking or to supplement supplies of bituminous coal.

(8) In Eurasia; large lignite deposits occur in the North European Plain (especially in East Germany), the Krasnoyarks region of Siberia, outside Moscow (the Tula lignite field), in Hungary and Czechoslovakia. The huge lignite deposits of the U.S.A. (east of the Rockies and in the Gulf Coast plain) have been little used because of the abundance of bituminous coal and oil in the country.

BITUMINOUS COAL

Bituminous coal is a type of coal containing a tar-like substance called bitumen or asphalt. Its coloration can be black or sometimes dark brown; often there are well-defined bands of bright and dull material within the seams. It is typically hard but friable. Its quality is ranked higher than lignite and sub-bituminous coal, but lesser than anthracite. It is the most abundant rank of coal, with deposits found around the world, often in rocks of Carboniferous age. Bituminous coal is formed from sub-bituminous coal that is buried deeply enough to be heated to 85 °C (185 °F) or higher.

Bituminous coal is used primarily for electrical power generation and in the steel industry. Bituminous coal suitable for smelting iron (coking coal or metallurgical coal) must be low in sulfur and phosphorus. It commands a higher price than other grades of bituminous coal (thermal coal) used for heating and power generation.

Within the coal mining industry, this type of coal is known for releasing the largest amounts of firedamp, a dangerous mixture of gases that can cause underground explosions. Extraction of bituminous coal demands the highest safety procedures involving attentive gas monitoring, good ventilation and vigilant site management.

USES

Coking coal is used in the manufacture of steel. A good coking coal must have excellent agglomeration properties, a high carbon content, and a low content of sulfur, phosphorus, and ash. The best unblended coking coal is high quality medium-volatile bituminous coal. However, since single coals with all the necessary properties are scarce, coking coal is usually a blend of high-volatile bituminous coal with lesser amounts of medium and low-volatile bituminous coal.Coking coal commands a higher price than coal used for energy production.

Smelting coal is bituminous coal of the highest quality, as free of ash and sulfur as possible, used to manufacture coke for use by blacksmiths.

Bituminous coal which lacks the qualities required for use as metallurgical coal is graded as thermal coal. This is used primarily for electrical power generation.The ideal thermal coal is easily ignited but has a high heat content.

Bituminous coal is used for the production of activated carbon. The coal is first coked, removing volatiles, then steam treated to activate it. Chemical processes for activating coke produced from bituminous coal have also been investigated.

ANTHRACITE COAL

Anthracite the most highly metamorphosed form of coal. It contains more fixed carbon (86 per cent or greater on a dry, ash-free basis) than any other form of coal and the least amount of volatilematter (14 per cent or less on a dry, ash-free basis), and it has calorific values near 35 mega joules per kilogram (approximately 15,000 British thermal units per pound), not much different from the calorific values for most bituminous coal. Anthracite is the least plentiful form of coal. In the United States it is found mostly in northeastern Pennsylvania and makes up less than 2 per cent of all coal reserves in the country.

Anthracites are black to steel gray and have a brilliant, almost metallic lustre. They can be polished and used for decorative purposes. Hard and brittle, anthracites break with conchoidal fracture into sharp fragments. Unlike many bituminous coals, they are clean to the touch. Although anthracites are difficult to ignite, they burn with a pale blue flame and require little attention to sustain combustion. In the past they were used for domestic heating because they produce little dust upon handling, burn slowly, and emit relatively little smoke. Anthracite is rarely used for this purpose today because of its limited abundance and relatively high cost and the ready availability of other sources of energy (e.g., natural gas and electricity) for heating purposes.

GRAPHITE

Graphite is a crystalline form of the element carbon. It consists of stacked layers of graphene. Graphite occurs naturally and is the most stable form of carbon under standard conditions. Synthetic and natural graphite are consumed on large scale for uses in pencils, lubricants, and electrodes. Under high pressures and temperatures it converts to diamond. It is a weak conductor of heat and electricity.

The principal types of natural graphite, each occurring in different types of ore deposits, are:

- Crystalline small flakes of graphite (or flake graphite) occurs as isolated, flat, plate-like particles with hexagonal edges if unbroken. When broken the edges can be irregular or angular;
- Amorphous graphite: very fine flake graphite is sometimes called amorphous;
- Lump graphite (or vein graphite) occurs in fissure veins or fractures and appears as massive platy intergrowths of fibrous or acicular crystalline aggregates, and is probably hydrothermal in origin.
- Highly ordered pyrolytic graphite refers to graphite with an angular spread between the graphite sheets of less than 1°.
- The name "graphite fiber" is sometimes used to refer to carbon fibers or carbon fiber-reinforced polymer.

PETROLEUM

The word petroleum is derived from the Latin words, ***petra*** meaning rock, and ***oleum***, meaning oil. It is so called because it is derived from the rocks where it flows freely in either liquid or gaseous state.

Petroleum, the mineral in the greatest demand in modern industry, supplies half of the world's energy requirements. It provides fuel for heat and lighting, lubricants for machinery and raw materials for a number of manufacturing industries. In comparison with other fuels, such as coal, it has several advantages; it occurs in great abundance; it is easily obtained; it can be cheaply distributed; and above all, it has the widest range of domestic as well as industrial uses. It is often, therefore, referred to as 'black gold'.

Since the drilling of first oil, the commodity has emerged as an important part of our life. It has been used as fuel for our transport, a fuel to generate electricity to light our homes, run factories and machines, a raw material to produce fertiliser to increase food production and produce plastic which is used in wide range of things we use in daily life. Since the emergence of oil industry in mid-nineteenth century, the important energy source has also triggered wars, reshaped geo-politics with countries competing to control it. Here is the list of top countries in with proven oil reserves.

The petroleum industry generally classifies crude oil by the geographic location it is produced in (e.g., West Texas Intermediate, Brent, or Oman), its API gravity (an oil industry measure of density), and its sulfur content. Crude oil may be considered light if it has low density, heavy if it has high density, or medium if it has a density between that of light and heavy. Additionally, it may be referred to as sweet if it contains relatively little sulfur or sour if it contains substantial amounts of sulfur.

The geographic location is important because it affects transportation costs to the refinery. Light crude oil is more desirable than heavy oil since it produces a higher yield of gasoline, while sweet oil commands a higher price than sour oil because it has fewer environmental problems and requires less refining to meet sulfur standards imposed on fuels in consuming countries. Each crude oil has unique molecular characteristics which are revealed by the use of Crude oil assay analysis in petroleum laboratories.

Barrels from an area in which the crude oil's molecular characteristics have been determined and the oil has been classified are used as pricing references throughout the world. Some of the common reference crudes are:

- West Texas Intermediate (WTI), a very high-quality, sweet, light oil delivered at Cushing, Oklahoma for North American oil
- Brent Blend, consisting of 15 oils from fields in the Brent and Ninian systems in the East

Shetland Basin of the North Sea. The oil is landed at Sullom Voe terminal in Shetland. Oil production from Europe, Africa and Middle Eastern oil flowing West tends to be priced off this oil, which forms a benchmark

- Dubai-Oman, used as benchmark for Middle East sour crude oil flowing to the Asia-Pacific region
- Tapis (from Malaysia, used as a reference for light Far East oil)
- Minas (from Indonesia, used as a reference for heavy Far East oil)
- The OPEC Reference Basket, a weighted average of oil blends from various OPEC (The Organization of the Petroleum Exporting Countries) countries
- Midway Sunset Heavy, by which heavy oil in California is priced
- Western Canadian Select the benchmark crude oil for emerging heavy, high TAN (acidic) crudes.

There are declining amounts of these benchmark oils being produced each year, so other oils are more commonly what is actually delivered. While the reference price may be for West Texas Intermediate delivered at Cushing, the actual oil being traded may be a discounted Canadian heavy oil—Western Canadian Select—delivered at Hardisty, Alberta, and for a Brent Blend delivered at Shetland, it may be a discounted Russian Export Blend delivered at the port of Primorsk.

Once extracted, oil is refined and separated, most easily by distillation, into numerous products for direct use or use in manufacturing, such as gasoline (petrol), diesel and kerosene to asphalt and chemical reagents(ethylene, propylene, butene,acrylic acid, para-xylene) used to make plastics, pesticides and pharmaceuticals.

NATURAL GAS

Natural gas may occur in association with petroleum, in the uppermost part of an oil trap, or it may occur alone. The larger fields of gas often have no oil. The principal constituents of natural gas are a mixture of gaseous hydrocarbons, of which methane alone may make up 80 to 90 per cent. The other gases include ethane, propane, and butane. Traces of non-hydrocarbon gases may also occur, including helium, nitrogen, carbon dioxide and hydrogen sulphide. Certain natural gas wells contain so much helium that the gas is specially processed to recover this valuable substance. It fulfills 20% of total commercial energy requirements.

Natural gas is sometimes informally referred to simply as "gas", especially when it is being compared to other energy sources, such as oil or coal. However, it is not to be confused with gasoline, which is often shortened in colloquial usage to "gas", especially in North America.

Russia has the largest natural gas reserves in the world and exports more natural gas than any other country, shipping an estimated 238 billion cubic meters of gas in 2020. Iran has the world's second-largest natural gas reserves. Iran is one of the most hydrocarbon-rich areas in the world, with roughly 145 hydrocarbon fields and 297 oil and gas reservoirs discovered so far and the potential for more.

HYDRO ELECTRICITY

Water energy is obtained by harnessing the flowing water. When water falls from sufficient height, it attains a lot of energy which is used to run a power generator.

Electricity is generated in two main ways: by running water which drives hydro-turbines to generate hydro-electric power (H.E.P.); and by burning other fuels such as coal or oil to drive turbines to produce thermal power.

Despite its relatively minor role in satisfying world demands, H.E.P. is often more interesting to geographers than thermal power. There are two reasons for this apparent anomaly. Firstly, whereas thermal electricity generation is really only an extension of the coal, oil and gas industries, the generation of H.E.P. depends on an independent energy source. Secondly, H.E.P. schemes are often spectacular, involving the construction of large dams and other installations, often in remote areas, and at the same time the water stored to generate power may also have other far-reaching geographical effects such as improving river navigation, providing the means of irrigation and preventing floods.

Running water from streams, rivers and melting glaciers has long been utilized by men as a motive power for grinding flour or sawing logs. There important inventions, however, have allowed water power to be used to generate electricity and thus, enhanced the importance of this source of power which had previously been over-shadowed by the use of mineral fuels: (i) the development of the hydro-turbine, a very efficient type of water wheel, which rotates very rapidly when a jet of water is directed against it, so that H.E.P. can be generated; (ii) the invention of the dynamo, which converts the energy of the rapidly turning turbine into electricity; (iii) the development of cement, which allows large dams to be constructed, capable of holding back vast reservoirs.

The ranking of hydro-electric capacity is either by actual annual energy production or by installed capacity power rating. In 2020 hydropower generated 17% of the worlds total electricity and 70% of all renewable electricity. Hydropower is produced in 150 countries, with the Asia-Pacific region generated 32 per cent of global hydropower in 2010. China is the largest hydroelectricity producer, with 721 terawatt-hours of production in 2010, representing around 17 per cent of domestic electricity use. Brazil, Canada, New Zealand, Norway, Paraguay, Austria, Switzerland and Venezuela have a majority of the internal electric energy production from hydroelectric power. Paraguay produces 100% of its electricity from hydroelectric dams, and exports 90% of its production to Brazil and to Argentina. Norway produces 98-99% of its electricity from hydroelectric sources.

A hydro-electric station rarely operates at its full power rating over a full year; the ratio between annual average power and installed capacity rating is the capacity factor. The installed capacity is the sum of all generator nameplate power ratings.

Top Ten largest hydroelectric producers as on 2020.

Country	Annual hydroelectric production (TWh)	Installed capacity (GW)	Capacity factor	% of total production
China	1232	352	0.37	28.5%
Brazil	389	105	0.56	9.0%
Canada	386	81	0.59	8.9%
United States	317	103	0.42	7.3%
Russia	193	51	0.42	4.5%
India	151	49	0.43	3.5%
Norway	140	33	0.49	3.2%
Japan	88	50	0.37	2.0%
Vietnam	84	18	0.67	1.9%
France	71	26	0.46	1.6%

WORLD DISTRIBUTION AND PRODUCTION: In the light of the conditions favouring H.E.P. development, it is clear that certain parts of the world are better suited by relief, climate or other factors to the exploitation of water power. Generally speaking H.E.P. stations are found in the following areas: (i) Mountainous districts, especially those which have been glaciated and have many waterfalls and lakes. (ii) Tropical and temperate areas with a moderate to heavy well-distributed rainfall. (iii) On major rivers with a large volume of water, whether flowing constantly or having seasonal fluctuations which can be minimized by creating reservoirs. (iv) In industrial countries where all power sources, including H.E.P., tend to be well-developed because of the large market. (v) In areas where regional development is promoted by the construction of multipurpose dams.

H.E.P. potential is not equally distributed around the world. Some countries, e.g. the U.S.A., Switzerland, have many more potential sites for H.E.P. stations than others, e.g. Britain, the Netherlands. The developed countries as a whole, North America, Europe and Japan, have about one-third of H.E.P. potential but have developed much of this so that they account for 80 per cent of developed H.E.P. The U.S.A. is the world's leading producer of H.E.P. but so large are the U.S. power requirements that H.E.P. accounts for only about 10 per cent of electricity supplies. In Canada, H.E.P. is much more important, accounting for nearly three-quarters of electricity supplies. In Europe, H.E.P. is most important in Scandinavia and countries bordering on the Alps-Switzerland, France and Italy.

World Distribution and Production: The world distribution of thermal electricity generation shows very similar patterns to the distribution of densely populated industrial areas. The most favoured areas are: (i) the major coalfields of the world (lignite -and even peat are also used in some areas for thermal power generation); (ii) the chief oil and natural gas fields, where these are near markets; (iii) the major oil importing and refining ports; (iv) major industrial regions; (v) highly urbanized regions where there is a large domestic demand.

The greatest concentration of thermal generating plants is in the densely populated and heavily industrialized parts of western Europe and north-eastern North America.

NON-CONVENTIONAL SOURCES OF ELECTRIC POWER

Electricity can be obtained from a variety of sources other than conventional hydro or thermal generators. The most widely used of the new sources of power today is ***geothermal energy***, that is energy derived from hot springs, emissions of dry or wet steam and from hot rocks at depth. Geothermal energy is most used in Iceland. Californian output is about half the world total. Japan, New Zealand, the Philippines, Turkey and the U.S.S.R., all have some interest in exploiting geothermal power from steam or hot water sources associated with volcanic areas.

Alternatives to conventional H.E.P. include **tidal power already** successfully developed on the Rance Estuary in Brittany, France, but there are probably only seven or eight sites in the whole world where it could be developed and initial development costs are enormous. As a result of waves and tides, the sea water rises which is used to generate electricity. Another possible use of the seas is to make use of the heat gradient between surface and deep-sea water (especially in the tropics) or between warm currents such as the Gulf Stream and adjacent colder water. ***Wind power*** has been harnessed for centuries to drive mills and pumps. First successful experiment to harness wind energy with the help of wind mill was conducted in the Netherlands. It is widely used in U.S.A. ***Solar energy*** is probably the most hopeful non-exhaustible prospect for alternative power supplies and is already used on a small scale for domestic heating, but at present the technology for collecting the heat and storing the resultant energy is not sufficiently advanced for large-scale use to be economic.

The most important of the present-day alternatives is ***nuclear power***, which in many industrialized countries already provides as much or more energy than H.E.P.

The first nuclear power station was built in Britain in 1956 at Calder Hall. Britain was rapidly overtaken in this field by the U.S.A. Nuclear power provides 11 per cent of the U.S.A's electricity supplies. Other countries with a significant investment in nuclear power are Japan (11 per cent of total electricity supplies), West Germany (9 per cent), the U.S.S.R., France, Sweden, Canada and Spain. The most recent trend is for a number of developing countries to opt for nuclear power as an alternative to conventional forms of electricity production. Among these countries are Egypt, Brazil, Iran, Iraq and South Korea. India, Pakistan, Taiwan and Argentina already have nuclear plants.

Biogas: Gas obtained from cow's dung is called Biogas. Successful experiments have been done in India to develop Biogas.

Biogas is primarily methane (CH_4) and carbon dioxide (CO_2) and may have small amounts of hydrogen sulfide (H_2S), moisture and siloxanes. The gases methane, hydrogen, and carbon monoxide (CO) can be combusted or oxidized with oxygen. This energy release allows biogas to be used as a fuel; it can be used in fuel cells and for any heating purpose, such as cooking. It can also be used in a gas engine to convert the energy in the gas into electricity and heat.

MANUFACTURING INDUSTRY

HISTORICAL PERSPECTIVE

The first types of industry to be developed were those which transformed raw materials, such as iron, cotton or wool, into manufactured goods. More important now-a-days, however, are industries which bring together partly manufactured items to make complicated equipment such as electrical appliances, automobiles and other means of transportation, watches, and other luxury goods. Some industries, such as textiles or food processing are relatively simple and are now highly mechanized. In the developed countries more people are now employed in more sophisticated electrical and other metal industries, making such things as radios, television sets, computers, specialized machinery, as well as in fields such as printing and publishing, and service industries. However, the later industrialization in underdeveloped countries means that the range of industries in such countries is usually narrower. Most countries begin to industrialize on the basis of food or other raw material processing industries and textiles. They then graduate to metal and engineering industries and electronics.

CLASSIFICATION OF INDUSTRIES

Industries are very diverse but they may be basically divided into three categories known as primary, secondary and tertiary industries.

(*i*) **PRIMARY INDUSTRY** is the simplest form of industry which consists of the first processing of raw materials, for example, the production of metal from mineral ores, the production of power from coal and oil or the processing of agricultural commodities form foodstuffs or industrial raw materials. Such industries include the smelting of bauxite to make aluminium, the processing of latex to make rubber sheets or the pulping of logs to make paper.

(*ii*) **SECONDARY INDUSTRY** covers a very wide range of operations, varying greatly in complexity. They are sometimes subdivided into heavy industries, e.g. engineering, metal goods, heavy chemicals, ship-building, locomotives, and light industries, e.g. electrical equipment, plastics, textiles, cosmetics and toilet articles. Basically they include all re-processing of partially manufactured goods to make more complex products, e.g. the use of cloth in clothing, the use of iron parts in the manufacture of machinery, the use of copper wire in the electronics industry, and the use of paper to make books.

(*iii*) **TERTIARY INDUSTRY** is not a branch of manufacturing at all but consists of service industries, such as trade, transportation, commerce, entertainment, personal tourism, administration and so on.

IRON AND STEEL INDUSTRY

Probably most important amongst the locational factors which led to a shift to the coalfields was the fact that, with the existing techniques, eight times as much coal as iron ore was needed to produce a given quantity of metallic iron. It was therefore, much cheaper to transport ore to coalfields if necessary than to take coal to orefields. By the late nineteenth century techniques had greatly improved so that the proportion of coke to iron in the blast-furnace charge was greatly reduced. Nowadays the ratio has been reversed and only half as much coke is needed as iron ore. The coalfields no longer exert the same tremendous pull on the iron and steel industry. The attractive locations today are of two kinds; (a) ore fields; (b) coastal locations.

METALLURGICAL INDUSTRY

The next most important to the Iron and steel industry as the basis of manufacturing industry are the smelting, refining and processing industries dealing with metals other than Iron.

(i) ENGINEERING: The machine tool industry which produces machinery for other industries is a highly specialized one. Machine-tool plants are generally located in long-established industrial areas with a ready supply of skilled labour. The machine tool industry is basic to modern industrial development because it makes the machines on which other industries depend.

The manufacture of **electrical machinery** and appliances began only after 1880 when large-scale electricity generation was made possible. Since then, electrical engineering has become a very important branch of industry and of modern technological development and has penetrated into every aspect of our daily lives. The **heavy electrical engineering** industry is concerned with the manufacture of equipment for generating and transmitting electricity, *e.g.*, hydro-turbines, thermal generators, transformers, transmitters, switchboards, electric wires, cables and insulators. Such industries are found in established industrial areas or in coastal locations where a wide range of raw materials, including steel, copper, other metals, rubber and so on are available.

Light electrical engineering is concerned with the manufacture of a whole range of electrical apparatus for both industrial and domestic use, *e.g.*, radios, tape-recorders, record-players, refrigerators, washing machines, vacuum cleaners electrical heaters, shavers, dryers, storage batteries, X-ray apparatus, other household and office electrical equipment.

(ii) TRANSPORT EQUIPMENT: The following branches of the transport equipment industry are more important.

(a) The Shipbuilding Industry: In the past, ships and boats were built in countries with a ready supply of timber. Norway is an example. Many such countries have continued to build ships but now the main raw material is steel. Thus shipbuilding, though found all over the world, in major ports, and sheltered, navigable estuaries, is ideally situated in areas noted for the iron and steel industry. Shipbuilding industries are found all round the world. Japan where high wage rates are offset by great efficiency has overtaken Europe and the U.S.A., and countries with even lower costs, such as South Korea, Japan, Singapore, Yugoslavia and Greece, are becoming increasingly important. In Europe, the largest shipyards are sited in the heavily industrialized seaports. Merseyside (Liverpool), Tyneside (Newcastle), Clydeside (Glasgow), Rotterdam, Amsterdam, Antwerp, Dunkirk, Hamburg, Goteborg, Malmo, Marseilles, Genoa, Cadiz, Trieste and Lisbon. In North America the older shipyards of the New England States e.g. at Quincy, Boston, Bath and Portsmouth, are now engaged mainly in the manufacture of smaller coastal vessels, yachts, fishing boats, and motorboats. They have lost ground to the more modern shipyards of New York, Sparrows Point, Newport News (mid-Atlantic region) and those of Montreal, Chicago, Buffalo, Cleveland, Toledo in the Great Lakes, St. Lawrenece region. These yards with deep waters, sheltered docks, and locations more central to the main industrial regions make all sorts of ships. They are within easy reach of the raw materials for shipbuilding; heavy machinery, boilers, engines, cables, ropes and electrical installations. Japan has major shipyards at Yokohama, Tokyo, Kawasaki, Kobe and Nagasaki. Figures of tonnage launched by the U.S.S.R are not released but must be very considerable comprising merchant and fishing vessels of increasing size as well as naval vessels.

Beyond the 2000s, China, South Korea, Japan have dominated world shipbuilding by completed gross tonnage. China State Shipbuilding Corporation, China Shipbuilding Industry Corporation, Hyundai Heavy Industries, Samsung Heavy Industries, Daewoo Shipbuilding & Marine Engineering and Imabari Shipbuilding supply most of the global market for large container, bulk carrier, tanker and Ro-ro ships.

The US is ranked the 10th largest shipbuilder worldwide. The top companies that build large naval vessels, such as aircraft carriers and frigates, include Huntington Ingalls, Bollinger and General Dynamics.

(b) The Automobile Industry: The automobile industry began to develop at the end of the nineteenth century and the hundreds of small firms in the U.S.A., Britain and Europe have merged to form very large corporations with international interests, such as General Motors, **Ford and Chrysler of the U.S.A.; British Leyland in the U.K.; Volkswagen and Mercedes in Germany; Fiat of Italy; Datsun, Toyota and Mazda of Japan, and several others in France**, the U.S.S.R., Sweden and the East European countries. US automakers, "The Big Three" (GM, Ford and Chrysler) have merged with and in same cases established commercial strategic partnership with other European and Japanese automobile manufacturers. Increasing global competition amongst the global manufacturers and positioning within foreign markets has divided the world's automakers into three tiers, the first being GM, Ford, Toyota, Honda and Volkswagen and the two remaining tier manufacturers attempting to Consolidate or merge with other lower tier automakers to compete with the first their companies. The world's major car producers are the U.S.A., Japan, West Germany, France and other European countries, including Belgium where cars are assembled though not actually manufactured. Some of the major car-making centres include Detroit, Chicago, Atlanta (U.S.A.); Coventry, Birmingham, London, Oxford (U.K.); Stuttgart, Dusseldorf, Wolfsburg (VW), Berlin (Germany); as well as Turin, Paris, Norrkoping, Moscow, Tokyo, Sydney, Melbourne and Sao Paulo. Because the industry depends for its raw materials on other industrial concerns, and because these must all be readily available to allow production to continue uninterrupted, the best location for the automobile industry is in established industrial regions with a tradition of manufacturing components.

(c) Railway Equipment: Most railway engineering plants are located either in the heavy engineering districts close to the steel rolling mills or at focal points of the national railway system. The United States is the world's largest locomotive producer. The industry is centred at Detroit, Chicago, New York and Philadelphia. The United Kingdom with production at Doncaster, Derby, Glasgow and Manchester, the U.S.S.R. West Germany and Japan are also important producers.

(d) The Aircraft Industry: Since the Wright brothers first flew in 1903, the world's commercial aircraft industry has experienced periodic booms and slump, and is highly dependent on war, military demands and the volume of commercial airline business. The enormous expenditure on research, design, testing and on constantly modifying and improving aircraft characteristics means that the industry is highly capital-intensive. In normal years, the U.S.A. produces the largest number of planes, of which two-thirds are destined for export around the world. The U.S.S.R is another principal manufacturer and exports mainly to communist countries. Other aircraft makers include the U.K., France, Canada, Italy, Australia, Japan and China, and many other countries assemble imported components.

CHEMICAL INDUSTRY

The major locational factors of the chemical industry are the availability of major raw materials, e.g. coal, petroleum; salt deposits and so on either from nearby deposits or from easy imports, and the existence of a market for the products, e.g. dyestuffs, will tend to be manufactured in or near major textile producing areas. Large supplies of water and power are also essential to the industry. The major raw materials used by the chemicals industry are drawn from a wide variety of sources. They include mineral deposits such as salt, potash, nitrates, sulphur, coal, petroleum and natural gas; vegetable materials from farms and forests such as wood-pulp, vegetable oils, potatoes; industrial by-products such as gas from coke ovens and blast furnaces; petroleum by-products such as carbon black and sulphur. Electro-chemical industries use the atmosphere itself as a raw material from which they extract nitrogen and other chemicals.

The **main heavy chemicals** are sulphuric, hydrochloric, nitric, and acetic acids, and alkalis such as sodium carbonate or salt, caustic soda, lime, chlorine (used as a disinfectant for purifying water and for bleaching purposes), and soda ash (used in the manufacture of soap, glass, paper and detergents). Major producers are the industrialized countries—the U.S.A., west Germany, the U.K. and Japan.

The **main organic chemicals** are explosives, fertilizers, and synthetic fibres. The bulk of the worlds supply of potash fertilizers comes from potassium salt deposits, e.g. from the U.S.A., West Germany, East Germany, France and the U.S.S.R.
Petrochemical products also include paints, adhesives, dyestuffs and detergents. The main petrochemicals manufacturing countries are the U.S.A., the European countries, especially West Germany, Netherlands, Spain and Britain, the U.S.S.R, Japan, and South Korea.

Large international companies specialize in making drugs, and large chemical concerns, such as I.C.I., Du Pont and so on, also have pharmaceutical interests.

TEXTILES INDUSTRY

Modern, mechanized textile manufacture was first developed in Britain, as a result of spinning and weaving machines invented by such people as Hargreaves (spinning jenny, 1765), Crompton (mule), Arkwright (water-frame) and Cartwright (power loom, 1787). Research and development has resulted in the emergence of new and improved fabrics, including synthetic fibres such as rayon and nylon. During the nineteenth century, however, ascendancy in textile production passed to Europe and North America because of the development of mechanization in the industry. Britain, with no local supplies of cotton and only a small proportion of its requirements of raw wool, became the leading textile producer. This position could not be maintained. As the use of mechanization spread and hitherto underdeveloped countries such as Japan, China and India began to industrialize, the traditional producers lost their dominance of the market. Textile manufacture is now one of the most widely distributed industries.

Textile industries are located mainly in relation to power and labour supplies. The lightness and ease of transport of fibres means that raw materials location is of negligible advantage. Coalfields in Britain and Europe, H.E.P. supplies in southern U.S.A. and Japan, are often important locational factors. Cheap labour supplies were an important factor in the establishment of textiles industries in southern U.S.A. and in Japan. Hong Kong, India and other Asian countries where labour is still cheap, still rely to a large extent on this factor for their competitiveness in world markets.

FOOD PROCESSING INDUSTRY

Food has to be processed soon after it is produced to avoid being spoiled, so most food-processing industries are located in towns in the centre of agricultural districts. For example, flour-milling and meat-packing are important industries of such cities as Chicago, Kansas City and Omaha in the Mid-West of the U.S.A. Meat-packing and freezing are important in Argentina, Uruguay,

Australia and New Zealand. Pineapples, peaches, pears and other canned fruits are processed in the immediate area in which they are grown. Wine is made, or grapes are dried for currants and raisins in the Mediterranean regions. Oil is pressed from oil palm fruits in or near the oil palm estates.

MAJOR INDUSTRIAL REGIONS OF THE WORLD

EUROPE: Europe was the home of the Industrial Revolution and was the first to develop heavy industries on a large scale.

The principal manufacturing zone extends from west to east, from Britain through north-eastern France, Belgium, the Rhinelands of West Germany, Saxony-Bohemia to Silesia. Other important industrial areas are found on the Swiss Plateau, northern Italy, in central Sweden and in many large towns and cities throughout Europe such as London, Paris, Berlin, and Milan.

Most of Great Britain's industrial regions are very closely associated with the coalfields. The midlands is the largest British industrial belt centred at Birmingham. Coventry, the heart of the automobile industry, is located on the Warwickshire coalfield. North of Coventry is the Leicestershire coalfield, on which is found Burton-on-Trent, the largest brewery town of Britain. North-east England has heavy engineering and a wide range of metallurgical industries. Britain's woollen and worsted textiles region in the Aire and Calder Valleys is centred around Bradford and Halifax (worsted), Huddersfield and Wakefield (woollens) and Leeds (garments). Sheffield is the world's largest cutlery town. The chief steel and engineering towns, apart from Sheffield, are Rotteram, Doncaster and Chesterfield. The metropolis of London is the capital, a leading seaport, and a financial centre of international importance, and its large population provides both labour and a large and affluent market. The range of manufactures is wide.

The heart of Scottish industrial activity is in the Central Valley and Clydeside, the area around Glasgow, is the most important. The Belfast region is the main industrial area of Ireland and is traditionally noted for shipbuilding and the linen industry.

France has many important industries but as a whole is far less urbanized and industrialized than Britain. The North-East industrial region is the largest single industrial district of France noted for iron and steel, textiles and engineering. The iron and steel towns of Dunkirk, Doual, Denain and Valenciennes also make metal parts and machinery. Lile makes cotton, woollen, linen and synthetic textiles. Roubaix, Tourcoing, Armentieres and Cambral are the other textile towns. Lorraine was traditionally the major French producer of iron and steel. Greater Paris provides a vast labour force and a large market. It makes a very wide range of goods such as jewellery, cosmetics, ornaments, porcelain, wearing aparel, cigaretes, furniture, musical instruments, precise scientific instruments, automobiles, locomotives, aircraft and chemicals. St Etienne makes armaments and bicycles; Clermont Ferrand in the heart of the Central Massif, is the home of Michelin tyres; Limoges is a notable pottery centre; Lyons originally a great silk making city, also produces rayon and nylon and has many other industries. Marseilles has several oil refineries and specializes in the processing of products from the old colonial areas; sugar refining, soap and margarine making, leather tanning, fruit canning and processing. Cities in the south-east of the country especially Grenoble, have developed light industries based on H.E.P. from the Alpine rivers. The West German industrial areas are more concentrated and much greater in extent than those of France. Industries are based mainly on coalfields, though other raw materials such as iron ore in the Ruhr, and timber in the Black Forest have assisted industrial development considerably. The Ruhr-Westphalia Region is Germany's largest industrial region. The factors which contributed to its growth in the nineteenth century were as follows:

(i) Coal outcrops in the Ruhr coalfield;
(ii) local iron ores which were replaced when they were exhausted by ores from nearby Siegerland and later by imported ores;
(iii) an excellent position in relation to transport routes as the region lies not only on the Rhine, which provides a cheap form of transport for heavy goods, both imports and exports, but also on a major east-west land route which linked the region with the rest of Germany.

In response to all these locational advantages a wide range of industries, especially heavy industries including iron and steel (at Duisburg, Essen, Bochum and Dortmund); heavy chemicals (around Dusseldorf and Leverkusen); engineering (Gelsenkirchen,

Oberhausen, Rheinhausen, Essen and Dortmund) including large interests in armaments; and a number of specialized industries such as cutlery (at Solingen and Remscheid), and textiles (at Kiefeld and Wuppertal). In common with other industrial regions located on coalfields, the Ruhr has suffered a decline in the mining industry as such. The Middle Rhine industrial area enjoys the advantages of easy water transport, and convergence of rail and road routes. Frankfurt is a railway engineering centre with electrical, engineering, automobile and engineering industries. Farther south both Mannheim and Ludwigshafen with water-transported raw materials, have developed many industries: chemicals, electrical engineering, agricultural implements, iron and steel. Apart from the large industrial regions there are several large cities which have developed a wide range of industries. West Berlin makes consumer goods, such as furniture and luxury articles, and has important chemicals, engineering and electrical industries, Electrical apparatus and electronic equipment are most important. Hamburg is a major port with important shipbuilding and marine engineering works. Munich makes beer, musical instruments, scientific instruments, photographic equipment. Stuttgart makes automobiles, optical and surgical equipment, car components and watches. Hanover has metal and chemicals industries.

Leipzing is famous for is optical instruments and Jena for Zeiss photographic equipment. Dresden is the centre for Dresden porcelain and Karl Marx Stadt for textiles. The abundant supply of potash salts in Saxony has led to the development of all kinds of chemicals industries in such towns as Magdeburg, Stassfurt and Halle. Other industries in the region include processing of agricultural products from the surrounding region; printing and publishing; and engineering. East Berlin, the capital of East Germany, is another industrial centre with engineering, textiles, electrical industries.

In Belgium, heavy industries, including iron and steel making and the manufacture of armaments, are found on the Sambre-Meuse coalfield, particularly at Liege. The outskirts of Brussels, the capital of Belgium, have many industrial activities, including textiles, chemicals, paper, food processing and metal goods. It is linked to its premier port Antwerp whose ancient specialization in diamond cutting has been completely overshadowed by rapidly-growing port industries including shipbuilding, oil refining and petrochemicals, and mechanical engineering. A textiles manufacturing area is concentrated in the Lys valley with emphasis on linen textiles at Ghent, Courtrai and Tournai. The town of Bruges specializes in lace and embroidery.

The Netherlands has 40 per cent of its population engaged in the industrial sector and many branches of modern industries are well-represented there. Marine engineering and shipbuilding are important in Rotterdam, Schiedam and Dordrecht. Engineering industries are well-developed in Utrecht (light machinery), and Eindhoven (electrical engineering, home of the Philips' electrical company). Groningen is the centre of industries based on the extraction of natural gas from the North Sea. There are a number of towns noted for textiles: Tilburg (woollen textiles), Eindhovcn (linen), Enschede (cotton) Arnhem (rayon) and Breda (synthetic fibres). Amsterdam has long been a centre for diamond cutting and Arnhem for tin smelting.

Amongst the Scandinavian countries, Sweden is the most industrialized. The main industrial region is in central Sweden, the so-called Lake Depression, with its main centre at Stockholm. Sweden has the richest iron ore resources of Europe, has developed much hydroelectric power and has a long history of technological skills. Some of its internationally-known exports include Volvo cars, Bofors guns, Aga beacons, Electrolux refrigerators, Laval cream separators, Ericsson telephones, Nobel dynamites and Johanssons instruments. Orebro makes footwear, Norrkoping makes textiles; and Karlstad, Norrkoping, Orebro and Trollhattan make paper.

Norways leading industries are marine engineering, shipbuilding, fish-canning and the pulp and paper industries.

Denmark's industries are centralized at Copenhagen in Zealand. Dairying and agricultural industries are important chemicals, textiles, fishing vessels, beer, silverware, machinery and electrical equipment are also made. Copenhagen also specializes in diesel engines. The smaller industrial towns such as Odense, Flensburg, Esbjerg and Aarhus are concerned mainly with agricultural industries.

Despite its mountainous nature, Switzerland is highly industrialized. Four main branches of industries are important, namely watch-making, engineering, chemicals and textiles. The engineering industry (machinery, tools, electrical, surgical and optical instruments) is located at Zurich, Basel, and Baden. Textiles have always been a speciality of St. Gallen, Appenzeel and Zurich. Clocks and watches are traditionally a product of the Jure towns, e.g. la Chaux-de-Fonds, Biel and Le Locle.

In Italy, industrial growth has concentrated in the north rather than the south but governmental influence is helping to develop the south. The Lombardy plain is the largest industrial region, and contains the major industrial cities of Milan, Turin, Genoa and Mestre (Venice). The densest industrial zone is that formed by the three cities of Milan, Turin and Genoa within which are located a wide variety of manufactures including iron and steel, chemicals, textiles, automobiles (e.g. Fiat cars, Vespa and Lambretta scooters) machinery (e.g. Olivetti typewriters and sewing machines), tyres (e.g. Pirelli), electrical goods and agricultural machinery. Turin is noted for automobiles, rail coaches and aircraft and Milan for textiles (silk in particular) and engineering works. Genoa has shipbuilding and repairing industries. Venice has long-established craft industries: Venetian glass, lace, silverware, silk brocades and ornaments, and newer mainland towns such as Mestre and Porto Marghera have heavy industries including oil refining, petrochemical and metallurgical industries. In the south, Naples is the most important town, with wine making and food-processing industries. Iron and steel and petrochemicals have been introduced in Taranto, Bari, Naples and Catania (Sicily).

In Poland, there is an important industrial region in the south of the country including the towns of Wroclaw, Czestochowa, Bytom, Katowice, Chorzow, and Krakow, where coal mining, iron and steel and heavy engineering, chemicals, textiles and zinc/lead refining are all important.

NORTH AMERICA: Despite a somewhat later start in industrialization then Europe, North America has achieved greater industrial and technological advances. The reasons for this may be outlined as follows :

(i) North America (USA and Canada) is a vast continent;

(ii) North America is endowed with rich mineral resources,

(iii) the population of North America was originally made up of immigrants from the many advanced European nations;

(iv) location on the opposite side of the Atlantic from Europe has stimulated trade and growing world markets have led to industrial expansion. The U.S.A. is the world's leading industrial nation. There are six major industrial regions.

Southern New England centred at Boston, was the earliest to be developed by settlers from England. The two dominant industries have traditionally been ship-building (at Boston and Quincy) and textiles (including footwear). Two towns, Boston and Beverly, are specialists in footwear machinery and the former is a shoemaking centre. The traditional textile towns are Lowell and Providence for woollen textiles; and New Bedford, Worcester and Fall River for cotton textiles.

The most densely populated part of the United States and also one of the most heavily industrialized is the Mid-Atlantic region, including the cities of New York, Philadelphia and Baltimore. This region has a great diversity of manufactures. The industries of the region include all aspects of iron and steel, engineering, printing, electrical goods, wearing-apparel and consumer goods industries.

The Pittsburgh-Lake Erie Region has an excellent location between the Great Lakes and the metropolis of New York and is the core of the U.S.A.'s heavy industry. Pittsburgh became the 'iron and steel capital of the world'.

The table given below shows the major industrial regions of North America alongwith their specific industries :—

Industrial regions	Industries
Cleveland	Iron and Steel
Toledo	Glass Industry
Chicago	Locomotives, food, processing, machinery, steel and railways.
Akron	Automobile tyres
Detroit	Automobile industries
Hartford (Connecticut)	Aircraft engines

Industrial regions	Industries
Massachusetts	Electronic industry
Rochester, Boston	Photographic equipments
New Oreleans (Baton Rouge)	Oil refining, Petrochemicals
Baltimore, Pittsburgh, Boffalo	Iron & Steel
New York	Garments
Delauare, Wilmington	Chemical industry
New York, Washington D.C.	Printing & Publishing
Winnipeg	Wheat milling
Pittsberg	Iron and steel capital of the world
Canada	Paper & pulp industry
Sudburymines (Canada)	lead, zinc & silver

ASIA: Japan has risen to become one of the most important industrial nations in the world; Hong Kong, Korea and Taiwan have become major exporters of textiles and other goods; China has industrialized rapidly in the last 30 years and will continue to put great stress on industrial development; India and Pakistan already have well-established industries and are striving to increase industrial development to reduce unemployment among their large populations. The South East Asian region, though traditionally agricultural in outlook, is also developing industries such as iron and steel, agriculture-based industries, timber-based industries and oil refining. So far Singapore is the most industrialized of the South-East Asian countries.

Following are the leading producers of minerals in Asia :—

Countries	Minerals
Kazakhstan	Chromite
India	Mica
China	Coal
Malaysia	Tin
Indonesia	Natural gas
Saudi Arabia	Mineral oil
China	Iron ore
India	Lead, Bauxite

AUSTRALIA: In Australia, the main industrial area is the southeast where the concentration of early settlement, the favourable climate, the presence of coalfields around Sydney, and of iron ore resources, led to the establishment of the iron and steel industry especially at Newcastle and Port Kembla. There are also many engineering industries, including the manufacture of cars, locomotives and aircraft, cement works, chemicals and shipbuilding. Melbourne has chemicals, shipbuilding, aircraft engineering, railway equipment and motor vehicles industries. Adelaide has well-developed agricultural industries such as fruit-canning, flour-milling, dairy industries and woollen textiles. It also has iron and steel (at Whyalla) and engineering industries. Brisbane is the major industrial city of Queensland. Locomotives are made at Brisbane, Ipswich, Maryborough and Mackay. Along the coast of Queensland many towns deal with cane-sugar refining, e.g. Cairns, Mackay and Bundaberg. Dairying and tanning industries are well represented. In Western Australia, Perth is the main industrial city dealing with the agricultural products of Swanland and the mineral resources, e.g. iron, aluminium, of the interior.

SOUTH AMERICA: In South America, Argentina and Brazil are probably the best developed. The main industries are ship-building, at Buenos Aires, Rosario, Cordoba and General Pacheco.

Brazil is the most industrialized of Latin American countries. The chief industrial region is the south-east and the city of Sao Paulo has diverse industrial activities. Rio de Janeiro has similar industries with shipbuilding and aircraft engineering in addition. Belo Horizonte is the major metallurgical centre with iron and steel and other metal industries based on H.E.P. and the rich mineral resources of Minas Gerais.

AFRICA: Africa is the least developed of all the southern continents. The main industries are those connected with either mining or agriculture, e.g. smelting and refining of copper in Zambia and Zaire, and processing of rubber, oil palm fruits, etc. in west Africa. Nigeria also has petrochemicals industries. South Africa is, however, an industrially developed country. The main industrial region is the Witwatersrand where there is not only gold but coal, iron and a range of ferrous and non-ferrous metal deposits, as the basis of iron and steel, engineering, locomotives and other industries.

Chemicals, textiles, cement and light industries are also fairly important.

AGRICULTURE IN INDIA

About 54.6% of total work force in India is engaged in agriculture and allied activities. It still provides livelihood to the people in our country. It fulfils the basic need of human beings and animals. It is an important source of raw material for many agrobased industries. India's geographical condition is unique for agriculture because it provides many favourable conditions.

There are plain areas, fertile soil, long growing season and wide variation in climatic condition, etc. Apart from unique geographical conditions,

India has been consistently making innovative efforts using science and technology to increase production.

Depending on environment, different types of cultivation systems in operation in India are given below:

Sedentary Cultivation : Normal practice in most parts of India; method of tillage is somewhat intensive food crops, accounting for over three-fourths of the cropped area, and cash crops like sugarcane, oilseeds, Cotton and Jute receive attention under this system.

Shifting Cultivation : Land is used for a few years until fertility level drops; called Jhoom in Assam, Ponam in Kerala, Podu in Andhra Pradesh and Orissa and Bewar, Masha, Penda and Bera in various parts of Madhya Pradesh; prevalent in the forest areas of Assam, Nagaland, Meghalaya, Manipur, Tripura. Mizoram, Madhya Pradesh, Andhra Pradesh, Orissa.

Terrace Cultivation : Prevalent in mountain areas Cultivation.

Wet or Irrigated Cultivation : Practised with the help of irrigation ; typical crops of this system are rich.

Dry Cultivation : Practised where no irrigation facilities available, crops grown here are resistant to dry conditions.

Crop Rotation : Practice of growing different crops in succession so that the soil remains fertile.

Mixed and Multiple Cropping : A number of crops of different periods of maturity grown together.

Mixed cropping : Growing of two or more crops on a given plot of land in succession (multiple cropping).

AGROCLIMATIC REGIONS

Based on the homogeneity in agrocharacteristics such as rainfall, temperature, soil, topography, cropping and farming systems the country has been divided into 15 agroclimatic regions.

1. Western Himalayan Region

- It includes Jammu and Kashmir, Himachal Pradesh and Kumaun-Garhwal areas of Uttarakhand.
- It shows great variation in relief. The summer season is mild (July average temperature 5°C-30°C) but the winter season experiences severe cold conditions (January temperature 0°C to -4°C).
- The amount of average annual rainfall is 150 cm. Zonal arrangement in vegetation is found with varying heights along the hill slopes.
- Valleys and duns have thick layers of alluvium while hill slopes have thin brown hilly soils.
- The region has perennial streams due to high rainfall and snow-covered mountain peaks of Ganga, Yamuna, Jhelum, Chenab, Ṣatluj and Beas.
- Maize, wheat, potato, barley are important crops.

2. Eastern Himalayan Region

- The Eastern Himalayan region consists of Sikkim, Darjeeling area (West Bengal), Arunachal Pradesh, Assam hills, Nagaland, Meghalaya, Manipur, Mizoram and Tripura.
- It is characterised by rugged topography, thick forest cover and sub-humid climate (rainfall over 200 cm; temperature July 25°C-33°C, January 11°C-24°C).
- The soil is brownish, thick layered and less fertile.
- Shifting cultivation (Jhum) is practised in nearly 1/ 3 of the cultivated area and food crops are raised mainly for sustenance.
- Rice, potato, maize, tea and fruits (orange, pineapple, lime, litchi etc.) are the main crops.

3. Lower Gangetic Plains Region

- This region spreads over eastern Bihar, West Bengal and Assam valley. Here the average amount of annual rainfall lies between 100 cm-200 cm. Temperature for July month varies from 26°C-41°C and for January month 9°C-24°C.
- The region has adequate storage of groundwater with a high water table. Wells and canals are the main sources of irrigation.
- The problem of waterlogging and marshy lands is acute in some parts of the region.
- Rice is the main crop that at times yields three successive crops (Aman, Aus and Boro) in a year.
- Jute, maize, potato, and pulses are other important crops.

4. Middle Gangetic Plains Region

- It incorporates eastern Uttar Pradesh and Bihar (except the Chotanagpur plateau). It is a fertile alluvial plain drained by the Ganga River and its tributaries.
- The average temperature of July month varies from 26°C- 41°C and that of January month 9°C-24°C.
- The amount of annual rainfall lies between 100 cm and 200 cm.
- Rice, maize, millets in Kharif season; wheat, gram, barley, peas, mustard and potato in Rabi season are important crops.

5. Upper Gangetic Plains Region

- This region encompasses the central and western parts of Uttar Pradesh.
- The climate is sub-humid continental with July month's temperature between 26°C – 41°C, January month's temperature between 7°C – 23°C and average annual rainfall between 75 cm- 150 cm.
- The soil is sandy loam. It has 131 per cent irrigation intensity and 144 per cent cropping intensity. Canal, tube wells and wells are the main source of irrigation. This is an intensive agricultural region where wheat, rice, sugarcane, millets, maize, gram, barley, oilseeds, pulses and cotton are the main crops.

6. Trans-Gangetic Plains Region

- The Trans Ganga Plain consists of Punjab, Haryana, Delhi, Chandigarh and Ganganagar district of Rajasthan.
- The climate has semi-arid characteristics with July month's temperature between 26°C and 42°C, January temperature ranging from 7°C to 22°C and average annual rainfall between 70 cm and 125 cm.
- Important crops include wheat, sugarcane, cotton, rice, gram, maize, millets, pulses and oilseeds etc.

7. Eastern Plateau and Hills Region

- It comprises the Chotanagpur plateau, Rajmahal hills, Chhattisgarh plains and Dandakaranya.
- The region enjoys 26°C-34°C of temperature in July, 10°C-27° C in January and 80 cm-150 cm of annual rainfall.
- Soils are red and yellow with occasional patches of laterites and alluviums.
- Rainfed agriculture is practised growing crops like rice, millets, maize, oilseeds, ragi, gram and potato.

8. Central Plateau and Hills Region

- This region spreads over Bundelkhand, Baghelkhand, Bhander plateau, Malwa plateau and Vindhyachal hills.
- The climate is semi-arid in the western part to sub-humid in the eastern part with temperature in July month 26°C-40°C, in January month 7°C-24°C and average annual rainfall from 50 cm- 100 cm.
- Soils are mixed red, yellow and black growing crops like millets, gram, barley, wheat, cotton, sunflower, etc.

9. Western Plateau and Hills Region

- This comprises the southern part of the Malwa plateau and Deccan plateau (Maharashtra).
- This is a region of the respective soil with July temperature between 24°C-41°C, January temperature between 6°C- 23°C and average annual rainfall of 25 cm-75 cm.
- Jowar, cotton, sugarcane, rice, bajra, wheat, gram, pulses, potato, groundnut and oilseeds are the principal crops.

10. Southern Plateau and Hills Region

- It incorporates southern Maharashtra, Karnataka, western Andhra Pradesh and northern Tamil Nadu.
- The temperature of July month lies between 26°C to 42°C, that of January month between 13°C-21°C with annual rainfall between 50 cm-100 cm.
- The climate is semi-arid with only 50 per cent of the area cultivated, 81 per cent of dryland farming, and low cropping intensity of 111 per cent. Low-value cereals and minor millets predominate.
- Coffee, tea, cardamom and spices are grown along the hilly slopes of the Karnataka plateau.

11. East Coast Plains and Hills Region

- This region includes the Coromandel and Northern Circar – the important Coastal plains of India.
- Here the climate is sub-humid maritime with May and January's temperatures ranging from 26°C-32°C and 20°C-29°C respectively and annual rainfall of 75 cm-150 cm.
- Main crops include rice, jute, tobacco, sugarcane, maize, millets, groundnut and oilseeds.

12. West Coast Plains and Ghats Region

- This region extends over the Malabar and Konkan coasts and the Sahyadris and is covered by laterite and coastal alluvials.
- This is a humid region with annual rainfall above 200 cm and average temperatures of 26°C-32°C in July and 19°C-28°C in January.
- Rice, coconut, oilseeds, sugarcane; millets, pulses and cotton are the main crops.

13. Gujarat Plains and Hills Region

- This region includes Kathiawar and fertile valleys of the Mahi and Sabarmati rivers.
- It is an arid and semi-arid region with average annual rainfall between 50 cm-100 cm, and monthly temperature between 26°C-42°C in July and 13°C-29°C in January.
- Groundnut, cotton, rice, millets, oilseeds, wheat and tobacco are the main crops.

14. Western Dry Region

- It comprises western Rajasthan west of the Aravallis.
- It is characterised by hot sandy desert, erratic rainfall (annual average less than 25 cm), high evaporation, contrasting temperature (June 28°C- 45°C, and January 5°C-22°C), absence of perennial rivers, and scanty vegetation.
- Groundwater is very deep and often brackish.
- Famine and drought are common features.
- Bajra, jowar, and moth are the main crops of Kharif and wheat and gram of Rabi.
- Livestock contributes greatly to desert ecology.

15. The Island Region

- The island region includes Andaman-Nicobar and Lakshadweep which have typically equatorial climates.
- The annual rainfall is less than 300 cm, the mean July and January temperatures of Port Blair being 30°C and 25°C respectively.
- The main crops are rice, maize, millets, pulses, arecanut, turmeric and cassava.

MINERAL AND POWER RESOURCES IN INDIA

Mineral resources are the natural means of production which are used in many industries as raw materials. Iron ore, manganese, bauxite, Mica etc., are such minerals. Most of the minerals are exhaustible because they take very long time in their formation. The quality and quantity of minerals is inversely related. Good quality minerals are found in smaller quantity.

Iron Ore : India is rich in Iron ore. Iron ore is an important raw material for our basic Industries. India accounts for about 20% of the total reserves of the world out of this about 68.17% is hematite and the rest is Magnetite.

Manganese : Manganese is an important mineral which is used in making iron and steel and it acts as basic raw material for manufacturing its alloy. The total manganese reserves of India are 495.87 million tonnes. Madhya Pradesh is the leading producing State of manganese ore accounting for 33% of total production during 2019-20 followed by Maharashtra 25% and Odisha 19%.

Mica : The insulating property of mica has made it a valuable mineral in electrical and electronic industry. Three major types of Mica that are found in India are Muscovite, Phlogopite and biotite. Andhra Pradesh leads with 41% share in country's total resources followed by Rajasthan (28%), Odisha (17%), Maharashtra (13%), Bihar (2%) and a small quantity of resources is found in Jharkhand and Telangana.

Bauxite : Bauxite is the raw material for making aluminium. These resources include 656 million tonnes Reserves and 3,240 million tonnes Remaining Resources. By States, Odisha alone accounts for 51% of country's resources of bauxite followed by Andhra Pradesh (16%), Gujarat (9%), Jharkhand (6%), Maharashtra (5%) and Madhya Pradesh & Chhattisgarh (4% each).

Copper-Ore : Cpper is a non-ferrous metal. India is deficient in Copper-ore deposits. India has an estimated reserve of 15115 thousand tonnes of Copper ore. Largest reserves/resources of copper ore to the tune of 813 million tonnes (53.81%) are in the State of Rajasthan followed by Jharkhand with 295 million tonnes (19.54%) and Madhya Pradesh with 283 million tonnes (18.75%).

Common Salt : Common Salt or say Salts are an important Mineral which is used in chemical industry. Sodium Chloride is known as common salt which is edible and consumed as food item.

POWER RESOURCES IN INDIA

Conventional Sources of Energy

Coal : Coal as a source of Power, contributes maximum to industries as fuel. The largest reserve of coal are found in Jharkhand, Orissa and West Bengal. The Jharia and Raniganj Coalfields produce high-grade cooking coal and steam coal respectively. The other major coal field besides these two are East and West Bokaro, Karnapura, Pench-Kanhan, Tawa and valley, Singrauli, Talcher, Chanda-wardha and Godavari valley.

Petroleum : Crude petroleum, also known as crude oil, occurs in the marine sedimentary rocks. Important oil bearing area are Combay basin, upper Assam and Bombay offshore basin Bombay High, Assam, Gujarat and Arunachal Pradesh are also the main contributor.

Natural Gas : The recoverable natural gas which is generally associated with the petroleum is also a dynamic source of Energy. Bombay high, Assam and Gujarat are main regions of gas production. Hazira-Bijaipur-Jagdispur (HBJ) pipeline is a big venture of transporting gas through pipeline. Gas has significantly contributed to the household fuel supply.

Hydroelectricity : The hydroelectric power plants at Darjeeling and Shivanasamudra were established in 1898 and 1902, respectively. They were among the first in Asia and India has been a dominant player in global hydroelectric power development. India also imports surplus hydroelectric power from Bhutan.

In 2022, hydropower capacity of 46,512 MW (megawatts) accounted for roughly 11.7 per cent of total capacity. Roughly 12 per cent of power generation in 2020-21 was from hydropower.

Hydro: It is the cheapest source of electricity. A number of multipurpose river valley projects such as Bhakra Nangal, Damodar Valley, Hirakud, Chambal valley etc., were launched in the first five year plan itself to generate more electricity and other Benefits.

Nuclear Power : The Basic minerals used in generating nuclear energy are uranium and thorium. Uranium is available in the copper belt of Bihar and the rocks of Aravali range in Rajasthan. The monazite sands on the Kerala coasts also contain uranium. It is also obtained from mica mines in Gaya, Nellore and Udaipur district of Rajasthan. It requires great care and huge capital investment. Kalapakkam (near Chennai), Kota (Rajasthan), Narora (Uttar Pradesh), Kaiga (Karnataka) and Kundankulam (Tamil Nadu) are main nuclear power stations of the country.

Non-conventional sources of energy: These are non-exhaustible souce of energy. Sunlight, wind tidal waves and geothermal energies can be considered under this topic.

The renewable energy potential in the country has been assesseed in the medium term at 8,96,602 MW, which includes the potential from solar (7,48,990 MW), wind (1,00,000 MW), small hydro (20,000 MW) and biomass (26,800 MW) power. Apart from grid power requirement, renewable energy sources are also being used for distributed generation, lighting, pumping and motive power requirement in remote and inaccessible areas. India is graduating from Megawatts to Gigawatts in the generation of clean renewable energy. The target from various renewable energy sources has been increased to 175 GW by the year 2022 which includes 100 GW from solar, 60 GW from wind, 10 GW from bio-power and 5 GW from hydro-power.

REGIONAL PLANNING IN INDIA

Regional planning is a specific type of planning, based on a specific planning structure (regional system), for inducing public action aimed at societal well-being. It implies that regional planning is concerned fundamentally with the society in the context of space.

Regional planning may be conceptualized as a geotechnology of re-organising the regional space for its comprehensive development with a view to provide ideal living conditions to all human communities in all regions of human occupance not in isolation from each other but in integration with each other.

NITI Aayog
The planning commission which has a legacy of 65 years has been replaced by the NITI (National Institution for Transforming India) Aayog. The NITI Aayog was formed on January 1, 2015.

The main functions of Planning Commission of India are—

1. To formulate five year/annual plans.
2. To supervise the work of national planning.
3. To consider the national plans formulated by the Planning Commission.
4. To recommend measures for achieving the targets set out by the plans.
5. To review working and monitor the plans from time to time.
6. To encourage people's participation in the planning process.

The scope of regional planning in India is limited due to the fact that states are political entities having their own political machinery. However some schemes have been carried out in this respect. The experience shows that inter-state bodies set up for the purpose of planning can only serve an advisory role.

Inter-State Schemes

1. **Damodar Valley Project :** It involves the states of Jharkhand, West Bengal and the centre and has multipurpose to serve such as irrigations, flood control, power, etc.
2. **South–East Resource Region :** It covers the states of U.P., Bihar, West Bengal, Orissa and Madhya Pradesh.
3. **Bundelkhand :** This region involves M.P. (six districts) and U.P. (five districts). It serve to overcome the problems of scarcity of water, low level of agricultural activity, lack of industries and poor communication.
4. **Western Ghats :** It involves the states of Goa, Gujarat, Maharashtra, Karnataka, Kerala and Tamil Nadu. It serve the purposes of affore- station, plantation agriculture, hydel power development, mineral resources development and wild life protection.
5. **North-Eastern Region :** It involves seven states of Assam, Meghalaya, Arunachal Pradesh, Nagaland, Manipur, Mizoram and Tripura. It is meant ot overcome the prob-lems in this region arising mainly due to inaccessibility, difficult terrain, poor infra-structure, soil erosion, floods, low agricultural yield and low level of industrialization.

In 1972, efforts were made to strengthen the state level planning machinery with special area and target group approach which called for some decentraliza-tion. For example—

1. Planning for Drought prone Areas : These areas are characterized by low productivity which causes regional imbalance. The development programmes was launched by Government in 1973–74 to tackle the special problems faced by these areas. The basic objective of the programme is to minimise the adverse effects of draught on the production of crops, livestocks etc.

2. Desert Development Programme : The programme was started both in the hot desert areas of Rajasthan, Gujarat, Haryana and the cold desert areas of J&K and Himachal Pradesh. The objective of the programme has been—

(i) to mitigate adverse effects of desertification on crops, human and livestock population.

District Level Planning : The decentralized district, level planning has the following benefits—

1. Problems can be properly assessed.
2. Monitoring of the ongoing projects is more effective.
3. Synchronisation among various projects can be properly ensured.
4. Systematic district level planning can well ensure establishment of state level infrastructre.
5. Stimulates economic growth in the hinter-land.

Local Level Planning : This helps to serve the following objectives—

1. Optimum utilization of resources and capacities.

2. Accruing development benefit to the poor.
3. Fulfilling basic needs of the people.
4. Expanding and strengthening of economic and social infrastructure.
5. Higher level of productive employment.

The Dantwala Group identified certain activities which could be planned and implemented at the block level. These included agriculture and allied activities, irrigation, forests, water management etc.

The Regional Planning in India can be divided in to five distinct phases, which are as follows.

Phase	*Time*	*Major Changes*
I	1950–60	Community Development Programme.
II	1960–70	Panchayati Raj Phase
III	1970–80	Block Level Planning
IV	1980–90	District Planning, IRDP & Employment Generation Programme
V	1990–2001	Renaissance of Panchayati Raj System

The sixth plan was the boom which improved the lot of Indians. The sixth plan was heavily oriented to rural development and rural planning. It laid special emphasis on strengthening the levels below the state level. The 73rd and 74th constitutional amendments have paved the way for setting up of a multilevel planning machinery in states on mandatory basis. These amendments identified a large number of economic activities on which planning at local level can be done.

SOME MAJOR IRRIGATION/MULTIPURPOSE PROJECTS

Below is given a list of some of the major projects.

Nagarjuna Sagar (1974) (Andhra Pradesh) is a masonry dam on the Krishna river near Nandikonda village.

Tungabhadra (1958) (a joint project of Andhra Pradesh and Karnataka) is on the Tungabhadra river. It is 2,441 m long.

Poochampad in Andhra Pradesh is a masonry dam across the river Godavari.

Gandak in which Bihar and Uttar Pradesh are the participating states; Nepal, under an agreement signed with India in 1959, also derives irrigation and power benefits from it.

Kosi (Bihar) is a multi-purpose project which envisages irrigation, flood-control and other benefits. The barrage near Hanumannagar in Nepal was inaugurated in 1965.

Kakrapara project in Gujarat is the first phase of the development of the Tapi valley.

Ukai Multipurpose Project in Gujarat consists of a dam across Tapi river near the village, Ukai.

Upper Krishna Project in Karnataka consists of the Narayanpur dam across the Krishna river with a canal taking off from the left bank and the construction of dam at Almatti.

Ghataprabha Valley development scheme envisages harnessing of water of the river Ghataprabha for irrigation in Belgaum and Bijapur district of Karnataka.

Malaprabha (Karnataka): The Malaprabha project, is a masonry dam across the Malaprabha in Belgaum district of Karnataka.

Tawa Project envisages the construction of reservoir across the Tawa river, a tributary of the Narmada in Hoshangabad district (MP).

Chambal Project is being jointly executed by Madhya Pradesh and Rajasthan. In the first stage the Gandhi Sagar Dam and its 112 mw power station and the Kota barrage were completed. The Rana Pratap Sagar dam with a power house of 172 mw capacity was constructed in the second stage. The third stage comprises the construction of the Jawahar Sagar dam and a 99 mw power station.

Bhima Project of Maharashtra envisages construction of two dams, one on the Pawana river near Phagne in Pune district and the other across the Krishna river near Ujjain in Sholapur district. The work on Pawana component of the project is complete. The Ujjain dam is nearing completion.

Hirakud (Orissa) also known as Mahanadi River Project is the world's longest mainstream dam and is on the Mahanadi waters. It is a multipurpose project. The total length of canals is over 880 km and has 10 lakh hectare irrigation capacity.

The Mahanadi delta irrigation scheme, also in Orissa, is being executed to make use of the release from the Hirakud reservoir.

Bhakra Nangal is a joint venture of Punjab, Haryana and Rajasthan. It is India's biggest multipurpose river valley scheme so far. It consists of two dams—the **Bhakra** and the **Nangal**. It consists of a straight gravity dam, across the Sutlej at Bhakra the

29-metre high Nangal dam, the 64 km long Nangal hydle channel, two power houses at Bhakra dam. The Bhakra Dam is 518 m long and 226m high. Behind the Bhakra Dam, a very large reservoir known as Govind Sagar Lake. The Bhakra-Nangal Canal system has about 1,100 km of lands and 3400 km of distributaries and is designed to irrigate an area of 15 lakh hectares of agricultural land of Punjab, Haryana and Rajasthan.

Beas project is the another joint venture of Punjab, Haryana and Rajasthan, consists of (i) Beas Sutluj Link (ii) the Beas Dam at Pong and (iii) Beas Transmission System. The estimated cost of the project including the Transmission Lines is Rs. 715 crores. The Beas Sutlej Link Project is mainly a power project with an installed capacity of 660 mw with a provision for two extension units of 165 mw each. The civil works and conductors system (including Pondoh diversion dam) have been substantially completed. The Beas Dam at Pong, principally an irrigation project is a 133 metre high earth-rockfill dam and has an installed capacity of 240 mw.

Thein Dam Project envisages construction of a 147-metre high earthen dam across the river Ravi in Punjab and a power plant on its left bank.

Rajasthan Canal Project will provide irrigation facilities to the north-western region of Rajasthan which is a part of the Thar desert. The project will use waters from the Pong dam. The first stage of the project consisting of the construction of the feeder canal and part of main canal has been completed. The second stage covers the construction of the remaining of the main canal and the distribution system.

Parambikulani Aliyar is the joint venture of Tamil Nadu and Kerala and envisages the integrated harnessing of eight rivers, six in the Annamalai Hills and two in the plains.

Sarda Sahayak (U.P.) envisages construction of (i) a barrage across the river Ghagra (ii) a link channel (iii) a barrage across the river Sarda. (iv) a feeder channel involving construction of two major adequates over Gomti and Sai and (v) remodelling of 6450 km of distribution system and construction of new channels. The works are being executed in five stages. Stage I and II have been practically completed and commissioned.

Ramganga (U.P.) consists of a 625-metre long and 127.5 metre high earth and rock-fill dam and a 72 metre high saddle dam in the Garhwal district. The project will irrigate 5.91 lakh hectares, have an installed power capacity of 198 mw, supply 200 cusecs of water for the Delhi water supply scheme and reduce the intensity of floods in central and western Uttar Pradesh.

Farakka Project in West Bengal was taken up for the preservation and maintenance of Calcutta port and for improving the navigability of the Hooghly. It consists of a barrage across the Ganga at Farakka, a barrage at Jangipur across the Bhagirathi, a 39 km long feeder canal taking off from the right bank of Ganga at Farakka and falling into the Bhagirathi below the Jangipur barrage and a road-cum-rail bridge over the Farakka Barrage.

Kangsabati Project in West Bengal envisages the construction of earth dams, connected together by intermediate dykes, on the Kangsabati rivers.

Mayurakshi Project in West Bengal comprises the Canada dam and will cater to irrigation and power needs.

Damodar Valley Project was conceived for the unified development of irrigation, flood control and power generation in West Bengal and Jharkhand. The project is administered by the Damodar Valley Corporation (DVC). The DVC has completed multi-purpose dams and hydel power stations at Tilaiya, Konar, Maithon, and Panchet, high barrage at Durgapur and the three thermal power houses at Bokaro, Chandrapur and Durgapur.

Rihand Dam: The Rihand valley project is the most important project in Uttar Pradesh. It is built on Rihand which is the tributary of ***Son River***. Behind the dam, a large reservoir, known as ***Govind Vallabh Pant Sagar Lake*** is created. It is about 468 sq.km making this the largest artificial reservoir in Asia.

Narmada Valley Project : Also known as **Sardar Sarovar project**, the Narmada River Valley Project is one of the largest projects under implementation anywhere in the world. It is sponsored by the States of Gujarat, Madhya Pradesh, Maharashtra and Rajasthan. It is still under construction. It is built on Narmada River. 263 km of canals provided water to the states of Gujarat and Rajasthan.

15 TRANSPORT & TRADE

LAND TRANSPORT

The invention of the wheel was the major step forward in the development of transport. The type of animals used for transport varies from region to region, depending on the climate or the terrain. In the rugged Tibetan highlands, sure-footed, warm-coated yaks are more efficient than horses or cattle, and are very important pack animals in the region. Similarly in the Andes and llama is well-adapted as a pack animal. Camels make ideal desert carriers for men and goods because of their hardiness and ability to subsist on very little water. Buffaloes, oxen and elephants are important in tropical regions. Generally speaking, however, none is as important as the horse, which originated in the rolling temperate grasslands of the Eurasian steppes.

(i) ROADS: Roads and pathways have been stamped out by men since the earliest times. They are the most universal form of communication and also the most varied. It was not until the eigtheenth century that roads were systematically built and surfaced. The pioneers of road building were Telford, Metcalfe and McAdam, in Britain. The need for better roads arose from the rapid increase in traffic, due to the improvement of agriculture, the growth of industry, and the need for moving about large quantities of goods quickly and cheaply. However, it was not until the widespread use of the motor car that the majority of roads were widened, surfaced and improved. Among the first countries to establish a nationwide highway network of this kind was Germany. Hitler was responsible for the initiation of nearly 3,200 km (2,000 miles) of highways in Germany called *autobahns*. The autobahns are straight, cutting directly across country, and have a good surface. The other European nations such as Belgium, France, Italy and Britain have also constructed major highway networks known by various names such as *autoroutes* (French), *autostrade* (Italian) and *motorways* (English) to facilitate modern high-speed motoring, though for economic rather than military reasons. In the United States, even more elaborate highways have been built to cater for the vast numbers of motor vehicles.

ROAD NETWORK SIZE

Rank	Country	Roadways (km)
	World	64,285,009
1.	USA	6,803,479
2.	India	6,371,847
3.	China	5,198,000
4.	Brazil	2,000,000
5.	Russia	1,529,373
6.	France	1,053,215
7.	Canada	1,042,300
8.	Australia	873,573
9.	Mexico	817,596
10.	South Africa	750,000

(ii) RAILWAYS: The first public railway was opened between Stockholm and Darlington in northern England in 1825, and railways became the fastest and most popular form of transport for both passengers and goods during the nineteenth century. The growth of the railways was brought about by two interrelated factors. Firstly, the steam engine was developed and applied not only to industry but also to transport. Secondly, the rapid rise of industry made it necessary to improve existing transport systems. For long journeys railways are still the best form of freight transport, but over relatively short hauls, road transport is faster because of the ability of trucks and lorries to go direct to their destination. Commuter trains are very important in such countries as Britain, the U.S.A. and Japan, and carry thousands of people each day. Where roads are poor, or where the proportion of people owning cars is small, e.g. in the U.S.S.R or in India, rail transport is still vital for passenger transport, but in Europe, Britain and the U.S.A. cars have replaced trains for many passenger journeys.

The **Trans-Siberian Railway (TSR)** connects European Russia to the Russian Far East. Spanning a length of over 9,289 km, it is the longest railway line in the world. It runs from the city of Moscow in the west to the city of Vladivostok in the east.The Trans-Siberian line remains the most important transport link within Russia; around 30% of Russian exports travel on the line. While it attracts many foreign tourists, it gets most of its use from domestic passengers.

The greatest railway densities are found in the industrial regions of Western Europe. Belgium has the greatest density. Underground railways are important in many European capitals, e.g. London, Paris, Moscow, and carry huge numbers of city workers. Transcontinental lines are now of little importance.

RAILWAYS NETWORK SIZE

Rank	Country	Railways (km)
1.	USA	220,480
2.	China	150,000
3.	Russia	85,600
4.	India	68,103
5.	Canada	49,442
6.	Germany	40,625
7.	Argentina	36,966
8.	Australia	33,168
9.	Brazil	29,817
10.	France	29,273
	World	1,370,782

India has the densest network in Asia (about 68,103 route km and more than 7,325 stations).. Japanese railways are mainly electrified and are noted for their speed and efficiency. The Tokyo-Osaka or Tokaido Express is world famous. North America has at present the most extensive network of railways, making up nearly 40 per cent of the World's total.

(iii) Pipelines: Pipes have been used to transport water from place to place for thousands of years, but pipelines are now becoming an increasingly important form of transport. They can be used to carry many liquid commodities, as well as gases, but apart from their use for water, they are in fact almost entirely associated with the petroleum and petrochemicals industries. They carry not only crude oil from the oilfields to the refineries but also petroleum products from refineries to markets. A famous pipeline of the USA known as the **Big Inch** which carries mineral oils from the wells of the Gulf of Mexico to the north-eastern part. About 17 per cent of all freight per tonne-kilometre is carried through pipelines in the U.S.A. In Europe, West Asia, Russia and India, pipelines connect oil wells to refinaries and ports. One of the longest pipeline called COMECON is 4,800 km long. It connects oil wells of Ural and Volga regions of East Europe.

WATER TRANSPORT

The two greatest advantages of water transport are that it uses existing routes, e.g. rivers, seas, and needs no special tracks except in the case of canals; and that it is the cheapest form of transport for large, bulky loads.

WORLD WATERWAYS

Rank	Country	Waterways (km)
1.	Russia	317,505
2.	Brazil	153,348
3.	China	138,357
4.	United States	40,230
5.	Indonesia	21,579
6.	India	20,236
7.	Colombia	18,000
8.	Vietnam	17,702
9.	Democratic Republic Congo	15,000
10.	Myanmar	12,800
	World	**2,293,412**

(i) INLAND WATERWAYS : The largest rivers, such as the Amazon, the Chang Jiang (Yangtze Kiang) and Mississippi are capable of carrying large steam craft over long distances while smaller streams may only be usable by tiny canoes or dugouts. Modern canals such as the St. Lawrence Seaway and the Manchester Ship Canal, however, can carry large craft well inland. Not only is the scale of water transport governed by the nature of the waterways but also by the types of boats used in different parts of the world.

There are basically three types of inland water ways, namely rivers, rivers which have been modified or canalized, and specially constructed canals. In many parts of the tropics as in the Amazon and the Zaire basins and South-East Asia, rivers often play a vital role in the transport of local products where other means of communication, such as railways or roads, are poor or non-existent. In countries such as China, India and Egypt, river basins have been the nuclei of civilization and empire building. Canals are specially constructed channels for either ocean-going or inland vessels. They have been used since ancient times in China and were also built by the Romans in Europe, e.g. the canal between Lincoln and the River Trent in England. Inland waterways are best developed in two continents, Europe and North America.

The major French rivers, e.g. Loire, Garonne, Seine, Rhone, Meuse and Moselle have been modified and improved and are linked by canal systems. It is possible to travel entirely by rivers and canals from the Mediterranean Sea to the English Channel or from the Rhine to the Atlantic Ocean. Generally speaking, the central European waterways fall into three main groups—

(a) The Rhine Waterway: The Rhine flows through Switzerland, West Germany and the Netherlands and forms the eastern border of France. It is navigable as far as Basel and is the most important waterway in Europe.

(b) Waterways of the Germanic-Baltic Lowlands: An extensive network of waterways consisting of east-west canals joining the north-south flowing rivers crosses the North German Plain. The Mittelland Canal, completed in 1938, joins the three major rivers of Ems, Weser and Elbe, and continues eastwards to Berlin and into Poland. Near Hamburg another canal the Kiel Canal, 96 km (60 miles) long and 14 metres (45 ft) deep, links the Elbe estuary to the Baltic Sea, improving access to the Scandinavian countries. The Dortmund-Ems Canal runs north-south and links the Rhine with the ports of Bremen and Emden.

(c) Waterways of Southern Germany: The region is served mainly by the Danube (Europe's second longest river, 2,720 km/l,700 miles) which flows through seven different countries-West Germany, Austria, Czechoslovakia, Hungary, Yugoslavia, Romania and Bulgaria before draining into the Black Sea. The Ludwig Canal links the Main, a tributary of the Rhine, to the Danube and allows water borne traffic from the Black Sea to reach the Mediterranean Sea through the Rhone-Rhine Canal or the Atlantic via the Rhine.

The low-lying Netherlands, at the mouth of the Rhine, is criss-crossed by its distributaries and also has extensive man-made waterways.

The U.S.S.R has an immense system of navigable waterways totalling 144,000 km (90,000 miles), the most important of which are in European Russia. Amongst the more outstanding canals are the Baltic and White Sea Canal, the Moscow-Volga Canal and the Volga-Don Shipping Canal. The vast Volga system links five seas: the Baltic, White, Caspian, Black and the Sea of Azov.

(a) **Great Lakes-St. Lawrence Waterway.** In North America, the most important waterway is the Great Lakes-St. Lawrence Waterway shared by Canada and U.S.A. Its natural barriers such as rapids, waterfalls, gradient differences and shallow stretches of rivers have been overcome by the construction of locks and canals and by constant dredging below Montreal. The St. Lawrence is sufficiently deep for navigation all the way to the Atlantic. Silting is tackled by constant dredging, but in winter from December to March the St. Lawrence is frozen and navigation comes to a standstill. Despite the fact that the Great Lakes-St. Lawrence Waterway is ice-bound for three to four months in a year, the amount of traffic it handles is greater than any other commercial waterway.

In Canada, many of the north-bound rivers are navigable in summer, e.g. the River Mackenzie. These rivers have little commercial importance, however, because of their northerly position.

(b) **The Mississippi Waterways :** In the U.S.A. the most important inland waterway is formed by the Mississippi and its many tributaries. In the deep South the Intra-Coastal Waterway and the Houston Ship Canal also handle much internal and external trade.

(i) Ocean Transport: Ocean transport represents the cheapest means of haulage across water barriers that separate producers from consumers kilometres apart. The use of containers has not only made cargo handling easier but has eased the transfer of goods to land transport by rail or road at the world's major ports.

OCEAN TRADE ROUTES : Although the oceans arc open highways with few natural barriers, the bulk of the world's trade passes along certain well-marked routes. The volume of traffic, the type of shipping and the frequency of services on these routes depend on some of the following factors.

(a) Supply and demand: The greatest traffic is found on routes between regions where economic development is greatest, e.g. on the North Atlantic.

(b) Availability of ocean terminals: The main trade routes thus, link the world's major ports such as London, Rotterdam, Hamburg, New York, Yokohama, Singapore, Colombo, San Francisco and Honolulu, etc.

(c) Absence of physical barrier.

(d) Nature of the cargo: Perishable goods, mail, urgently-needed machinery, or medical supplies, as well as most high-value cargoes are sent by the shortest possible routes.

The major ocean trade routes are as follows:

(a) The North Atlantic Route: On both sides of the North Atlantic are located regions of very dense population and varied industrial activities. Some of the world's largest sea terminals are located in Rotterdam, Antwerp, London, Southampton, Glasgow, Liverpool, Manchester (via the Manchester Ship Canal), Le Havre, Hamburg, Goteborg, Copenhagen, Stockholm and Oslo. These ports fringing the North Sea, the Baltic Sea and the English Channel are the outlets of the rich agricultural, commercial and industrial regions of Europe. Large quantities of manufactured items: textiles, chemicals, machinery, fertilizers, steel, wine, are exported from these ports across the North Atlantic to the United States and Canada.

(b) The Cape of Good Hope Route: This route was once the subsidiary alternative to the Suez Canal route, but because of its long and circuitous journey was avoided by most shipping companies. But with the closure of the Suez Canal in 1967 oil tankers, tramps and liners had no choice but to take this route. Even after the Suez Canal reopened in 1975 much trade continued to follow this route, partly because tankers and other vessels are now-a-days much larger. This route is 6,400 km longer between Liverpool and Colombo. It provides link between Western Europe and West African countries, South Africa, Southeast Asia, Australia and New Zealand

(c) The Mediterranean-Suez-Asiatic Route: The importance of this route linking Europe with the Far East began with the opening of the Suez Canal in 1869. The route was once considered the 'life-line' of Britain because oil supplies from the Middle East and tropical raw materials and food-stuffs from the Asiatic colonies came through Suez. Manufactured products and semi-finished goods went by way of the Suez and the refuelling port of Aden to Bombay, Karachi, Colombo, Singapore, Hong Kong, Fremantle, and other Australian ports. Goods also went to East Africa, Durban and Cape Town via the Suez Canal. Other European nations also made heavy use of this short-cut to their Afro-Asian markets. With the opening of the Panama Canal in 1913, some traffic, especially that destined for New Zealand and the Far East, was diverted, but traffic on the Suez Canal route continued to increase. Although the Suez Canal is now open again and carries a great deal of traffic it can never regain its former strategic or economic importance, partly because of the political insecurity of the Middle East as a whole and partly because of The larger tonnage of today's shipping.

Oil is sent across the Arabian Desert by long distance pipelines from the Persian Gulf oilfields to the Mediterranean terminals at Banias, Tripoli and Saida (Sidon), for shipment to Europe, instead of going by tanker round the Cape of Good Hope. This is not only more economical but the fastest way of transporting the oil to Europe.

(d) The Panama Canal-West Indian-Central American Route: This route, which came into use in 1913 with the completion of the Panama Canal, eliminated the long and hazardous voyage round the stormy Cape Horn. The Panama Canal is 'the gateway to the Pacific'. It has benefited countries on both Atlantic and Pacific seaboards, facilitating the trade in minerals, oil, foodstuffs, raw materials and manufactured products. But the greatest benefits have accrued to traffic between the east and west coasts of the United States.

The Panama route has also greatly facilitated trade in the West Indian islands and the Pacific states of North, Central and South America.

(e) The South Atlantic Route: The ocean traffic in the South Atlantic is far less than that of the North Atlantic, because it connects regions of sparse population and more limited economic development. Only south-eastern Brazil, the Plate estuary and parts of South Africa have large-scale industrial development. There is also very little trade on the east-west route between Rio de Janeiro and Cape Town, since both Africa and South America have similar products and resources. There is some coastal trade amongst the South American republics from Brazil to Argentina round Cape Horn to Chile, Peru and the northern Andean states. A fair volume of traffic also passes between the eastern South American countries and Western Europe and North America. Coffee and cocoa from Brazil; wheat, meat, wool, flax and other products from Argentina are sent to the industrial countries of the North Atlantic in return for manufactured and semifinished commodities.

(f) The Trans-Pacific Route: Trade across the vast North Pacific Ocean goes by several routes which converge at Honolulu, 'the cross-roads of the Pacific', for refuelling and servicing. The direct route further north in a great circle, which links Vancouver and Yokohama without calling at Hawaiian Islands, reduces the travelling distance by half. The ocean terminals that serve the North Pacific trade include Vancouver, Seattle, Portland, San Francisco and Los Angeles on the American side, dealing with wheat, timber, paper and pulp, fish, dairy products and manufactured goods. Their destinations across the 7200 km (4,500 mile) wide Pacific are usually Yokohama, Kobe, Shanghai, Guangzhou (Canton), Hong Kong, Manila and Singapore.

(g) ***The South Pacific Route :*** In the South Pacific, the traffic consists mainly of ships travelling via the Panama Canal between either Western Europe or North America and Australia, New Zealand and the scattered Pacific islands. Goods transported are mostly wheat, meat, wool, fruits, dairy products and manufactured articles.

AIR TRANSPORT

Air transport is relatively independent of physical barriers such as mountain ranges, though, of course, this depends to a large extent on the size and range of the aircraft employed. While the larger jets can fly at great heights, avoiding all barriers, smaller planes have a shorter flight range and must fly at lower altitudes. Commercial airlines came into being after the First World War, the first regular air-service being between London and Paris in 1919. The earliest countries to operate airlines were Britain, France and the U.S.A., where the first planes were developed, but since the Second World War a very large number of airlines have come into operation.

By far the greatest amount of air traffic is found in the U.S.A where both international and internal flights are very numerous. Canada also has a relatively large volume of air traffic. Speed over great distances and the generally high standard of living, which ensures a large potential market for air services, are the main advantages of air travel in North America. The main goods moved by air include printed matter, mail, small machinery, electrical parts, films, optical instruments, personal baggage, drugs, liquor, fresh fruit and vegetables, or, in other words, goods of small size or high value, requiring speedy transport.

United States is served by four large air corporations: the United Air Lines, Trans-World Airlines, Pan-American Airlines and Eastern Air Lines, besides more than 45 domestic air carriers. The busiest airports are those of New York, Chicago, Washington D.C., Los Angeles, San Francisco, Atlanta, Boston and Miami.

In Canada, the largest airline company is the Trans – Canadian Airline, with Montreal, Toronto and Vancouver as the busiest air terminals.

After the United States, the greatest volume of air traffic is found in Europe, especially at London, Paris, Rome, Madrid, Shannon (southern Ireland), Berlin, Warsaw, Vienna, Geneva and Moscow which are linked by international and trans-continental airlines to all parts of the world. European airways probably account for about a fifth of the world's air traffic. London's Heathrow airport is the busiest in the world. Most of the European countries have their own national airlines, the most important of which include British Airways, KLM (the Dutch Airline), Lufthansa (of Germany), Al Italia, Air France, and SAS (jointly operated by the Scandinavian countries—Norway, Sweden and Denmark.

COMMUNICATIONS

Transport involves the physical carriage of goods or people from place to place, while communications only involves the transmission of words and messages.

TELECOMMUNICATIONS: The rise of telecommunications is linked with the rise of electrical technology. The first development in telecommunications was the invention of the telegraph by Samuel Morse in 1844. Telegraph wires soon linked most places and undersea cables were laid across seas and oceans so that within a few decades there were world-wide telegraphic links. England and France were linked in 1851 and the first Trans-Atlantic cable was laid in 1866. The telephone was invented by Alexander Graham Bell in 1875. A close network of telephone wires and undersea cables was soon in existence. Another development was the telex system, by which written messages, typed out in one place, can be transmitted to distant places, where they are typed out by a teleprinter.

The development of radio was the next important step. Television allowed, pictures, as well as sound, to be transmitted. The most recent developments have been the use of satellites for relaying news, pictures, telephone calls and so on all over the world, and from space as well, television pictures of the moon landings were received all over the world as they happened. The use of telephones, television and radio is thus, best developed in the U.S.A. and some European countries but is rapidly increasing in importance in other parts of the world. The U.S.A. and Sweden have over 70 telephones per hundred people and other countries with a high proportion of telephones include Switzerland, Canada, New Zealand, Australia and Britain.

In the late twentieth century, telecommunication steadily merged with computers to form integrated networks through the internet. Today internet is the largest electronic network on the planet, connecting an estimated 100 million people in more than 100 countries.

SATELLITE COMMUNICATION : The United States of America and former Soviet Union have been pioneers in space research. Artificial satellites, successfully placed in the earth's orbit have brought revolutionary changes in the areas of communication. The satellite communication system deployed since the early 1970s have rendered the unit cost and time of communication invariant with respect to distance. It costs the same to communicate over 500 km as it does over 5,000 km via satellite. India, too, has made great strides in space research. Aryabhatta was launched on 19 April, 1975 from the Soviet Union with the help of its Intercosmos rocket. **Bhaskar-1** was sent into the space on 7 June, 1979 and on 18 July, 1980, Rohini was launched from the Indian Cosmodrome at Shriharikota.

On 19 June, 1981, **APPLE** (Arian Passenger Payload **Experiment**) satellite was launched through Arian rocket. BHASKAR-2 was sent into the space on 20 November, 1981, which was also a remote sensing satellite. INSAT 1-A was launched on 10 April, 1982 but in September the same year it stopped working. On 30 August, 1983 INSAT 1-B was sent to space through space shuttle, **Challenger**. INSAT 1-B has made radio, television, and long distance communication very efficient and effective. Now we receive information about the weather on television and forecasting about storm etc., is done effectively.

Remote sensing is the gathering, storing and extracting of geographic information from great distances when the gatherer makes no physical contact with the target. The process usually coves the large areas.

The best known satellite images have come from NASA series of **Landsat satellites**. The first, originally called the Earth Resources Technology Satellite (ERTS) was launched in 1972. The launch of Landsat, which will be operated jointly by NASA and the US Geological Survey, took place in April 1999. The satellites have provided a wealth of information about the earth to scientists as well as to map makers.

As the US and Russian Governments drop security restrictions on data gathered from reconnaissance satellites, private companies are increasingly using this information for non-military applications such as seeking potential energy sources, monitoring pollution, and analysing building sites, besides predicting weather, locating areas of deforestation and mineral deposits, identifying hundreds of other physical patterns and processes. As the technology develops, government, academic and business are continuing to find new applications for these images.

INTERNATIONAL TRADE

In ancient times, transporting goods over long distances was risky, hence trade was restricted to local markets. People then spent most of their resources on basic necessities – food and clothes. Only the rich people bought jewellery, costly dresses and this resulted in trade of luxury items.

The Silk Route is an early example of long distance trade connecting Rome to China – along the 6,000 km route. The traders transported Chinese silk, Roman wool and precious metals and many other high value commodities from intermediate points in India, Persia and Central Asia.

After the disintegration of the Roman Empire, European commerce grew during twelfth and thirteenth century with the development of ocean going warships trade between Europe and Asia grew and the Americas were discovered.

Fifteenth century onwards, the European colonialism began and along with trade of exotic commodities, a new form of trade emerged which was called slave trade. The Portuguese, Dutch, Spaniards, and British captured African natives and forcefully transported them to the newly discovered Americas for their labour in the plantations. Slave trade was a lucrative business for more than two hundred years till it was abolished in Denmark in 1792, Great Britain in 1807 and United States in 1808.

After the Industrial Revolution the demand for raw materials like grains, meat, wool also expanded, but their monetary value declined in relation to the manufactured goods.

The industrialised nations imported primary products as raw materials and exported the value added finished products back to the non-industrialised nations.

In the later half of the nineteenth century, regions producing primary goods were no more important, and industrial nations became each other's principle customers.

During the World Wars I and II, countries imposed trade taxes and quantitative restrictions for the first time. During the post-war period, organisations like General Agreement for Tariffs and Trade (which later became the World Trade Organisation), helped in reducing tariff.

Why Does International Trade Exist?

International trade is the result of specialisation in production. It benefits the world economy if different countries practise specialisation and division of labour in the production of commodities or provision of services. Each kind of specialisation can give rise to trade. Thus, international trade is based on the principle of comparative advantage, complimentarity and transferability of goods and services and in principle, should be mutually beneficial to the trading partners.

In modern times, trade is the basis of the world's economic organisation and is related to the foreign policy of nations. With well-developed transportation and communication systems, no country is willing to forego the benefits derived from participation in international trade.

BASIS OF INTERNATIONAL TRADE

(*i*) **Difference in national resources:** The world's national resources are unevenly distributed because of differences in their physical make up i.e. geology, relief soil and climate.

(*a*) **Geological structure:** It determines the mineral resource base and topographical differences ensure diversity of crops and animals raised. Lowlands have greater agricultural potential. Mountains attract tourists and promote tourism.

(*b*) **Mineral resources:** They are unevenly distributed the world over. The availability of mineral resources provides the basis for industrial development.

(*c*) **Climate:** It influences the type of flora and fauna that can survive in a given region. It also ensures diversity in the range of various products, e.g. wool production can take place in cold regions, bananas, rubber and cocoa can grow in tropical regions.

(*ii*) **Population factors:** The size, distribution and diversity of people between countries affect the type and volume of goods traded.

(*a*) **Cultural factors:** Distinctive forms of art and craft develop in certain cultures which are valued the world over, e.g. China produces the finest porcelains and brocades. Carpets of Iran are famous while North African leather work and Indonesian batik cloth are prized handicrafts.

(*b*) **Size of population:** Densely populated countries have large volume of internal trade but little external trade because most of the agricultural and industrial production is consumed in the local markets. Standard of living of the population determines the demand for better quality imported products because with low standard of living only a few people can afford to buy costly imported goods.

(*iii*) **Stage of economic development:** At different stages of economic development of countries, the nature of items traded undergo changes. In agriculturally important countries, agro products are exchanged for manufactured goods whereas industrialised nations export machinery and finished products and import food grains and other raw materials.

(*iv*) **Extent of foreign investment:** Foreign investment can boost trade in developing countries which lack in capital required for the development of mining, oil drilling, heavy engineering, lumbering and plantation agriculture. By developing such capital intensive industries in developing countries, the industrial nations ensure import of food stuffs, minerals and create markets for their finished products. This entire cycle steps up the volume of trade between nations.

(*v*) **Transport:** In olden times, lack of adequate and efficient means of transport restricted trade to local areas. Only high value items, e.g. gems, silk and spices were traded over long distances. With expansions of rail, ocean and air transport, better means of refrigeration and preservation, trade has experienced spatial expansion.

Important Aspects of International Trade

International trade has three very important aspects. These are:

Volume of Trade

The actual tonnage of goods traded makes up the volume. However, services traded cannot be measured in tonnage. Therefore, the total value of goods and services traded is considered to be the volume of trade.

Composition of Trade

The nature of goods and services imported and exported by countries have undergone changes during the last century.

Trade of primary products was dominant in the beginning of the last century. Later manufactured goods gained prominence and currently, though the manufacturing sector commands the bulk of the global trade, service sector which includes travel, transportation and other commercial services have been showing an upward trend.

Direction of Trade

Historically, the developing countries of the present used to export valuable goods and artefacts, etc., which were exported to European countries. During the nineteenth century there was a reversal in the direction of trade. European countries started exporting manufactured goods for exchange of foodstuffs and raw materials from their colonies. Europe and U.S.A. emerged as major trade partners in the world and were leaders in the trade of manufactured goods. Japan at that time was also the third important trading country. The world trade pattern underwent a drastic change during the second half of the twentieth century. Europe lost its colonies while India, China and other developing countries started competing with developed countries. The nature of the goods traded has also changed.

Balance of Trade

Balance of trade records the volume of goods and services imported as well as exported by a country to other countries. If the value of imports is more than the value of a country's exports, the country has negative or unfavourable balance of trade. If the value of exports is more than the value of imports, then the country has a positive or favourable balance of trade.

Balance of trade and balance of payments have serious implications for a country's economy. A negative balance would mean that the country spends more on buying goods than it can earn by selling its goods. This would ultimately lead to exhaustion of its financial reserves.

Types of International Trade

International trade may be categorised into two types:

(*a*) **Bilateral Trade:** Bilateral trade is done by two countries with each other. They enter into agreement to trade specified commodities amongst them. For example, country X may agree to trade some raw material with agreement to purchase some other specified item to country Y or vice versa.

(*b*) **Multilateral Trade:** As the term suggests multilateral trade is conducted with many trading countries. The same country can trade with a number of other countries. The country may also grant the status of the "Most Favoured Nation" (MFN) on some of the trading partners.

Case for Free Trade

The act of opening up economies for trading is known as free trade or trade liberalisation. This is done by bringing down trade barriers like tariffs. Trade liberalisation allows goods and services from everywhere to compete with domestic products and services.

Globalisation along with free trade can adversely affect the economies of developing countries by not giving equal playing field by imposing conditions which are unfavourable. With the development of transport and communication systems goods and services can travel faster and farther than ever before. But free trade should not only let rich countries enter the markets, but allow the developed countries to keep their own markets protected from foreign products.

Countries also need to be cautious about dumped goods; as along with free trade dumped goods of cheaper prices can harm the domestic producers.

World Trade Organisation

In 1948, to liberalise the world from high customs tariffs and various other types of restrictions, General Agreement for Tariffs and Trade (GATT) was formed by some countries. In 1994, it was decided by the member countries to set up a permanent institution for looking after the promotion of free and fair trade amongst nation and the GATT was transformed into the World Trade Organisation from 1st January, 1995.

WTO is the only international organisation dealing with the global rules of trade between nations. It sets the rules for the global trading system and resolves disputes between its member nations. WTO also covers trade in services, such as telecommunication and banking, and others issues such as intellectual rights.

The WTO has however been criticised and opposed by those who are worried about the effects of free trade and economic globalisation. It is argued that free trade does not make ordinary people's lives more prosperous. It is actually widening the gulf between rich and poor by making rich countries more rich. This is because the influential nations in the WTO focus on their own commercial interests. Moreover, many developed countries have not fully opened their markets to products from developing countries. It is also argued that issues of health, worker's rights, child labour and environment are ignored.

Regional Trade Blocs

Regional Trade Blocs have come up in order to encourage trade between countries with geographical proximity, similarity and complementarities in trading items and to curb restrictions on trade of the developing world. Today, 120 regional trade blocs generate 52 per cent of the world trade. These trading blocs developed as a response to the failure of the global organisations to speed up intra-regional trade.

Though, these regional blocs remove trade tariffs within the member nations and encourage free trade, in the future it could get increasingly difficult for free trade to take place between different trading blocs.

Regional Blocs	Head Quarter	Member nations	Origin	Commodities	Other Areas of Cooperation
ASEAN (Association of South East Asian Nations)	Jakarta, Indonesia	Brunei Darussalam, Cambodia, Indonesia, Laos, Malaysia, Myanmar, Philippines, Singapore, Thailand and Vietnam	August, 1967	Agro products, rubber, palm oil, rice, copra, coffee, coal, nickel and tungsten, Energy petroleum and natural gas and Software products	Accelerate economic growth, development, peace and regional stability
CIS (Commonwealth of Independent States)	Minsk, Belarus	Armenia, Azerbaijan, Belarus, Georgia, Kazakhstan, Kyrgystan, Moldova, Russia, Tajikistan, Turkmenistan, Ukraine and Uzbekistan.	December, 1991	Crude oil, natural gas, gold, cotton, fibre, aluminium	Integration and cooperation on matters of economics, defence and foreign policy
EU (European Union)	Brussels, Belgium	Austria, Belgium, Bulgaria, Croatia, Cyprius, Czech Republic, Denmark,	EEC- March 1957 EU - Feb.	Agro products, minerals, chemicals, wood, paper, transport	Single market with single currency

		Estonia, Finland, France, Germany, Greece, Hungary, Ireland, Italy, Latvia, Lithuania, Luxembourg, Malta, Poland, Portugal, Romania, Slovakia, Slovenia, Spain, Sweden, and Netherlands	1992	vehicles, optical instruments, clocks - works of art, antiques	
LAIA (Latin American Integration Association)	Montevideo, Uruguay	Argentina, Volivia, Brazil, Columbia, Ecuador, Mexico, Paraguay, Peru, Uruguay and Venezuela	1994	—	—
NAFTA (North American Free Trade Association)		U.S.A., Canada and Mexico	1949	agro products, motor vehicles, automotive parts, computers, textiles	—
OPEC (Organisation of Petroleum Exporting Countries)	Vienna, Austria	Algeria, Indonesia, Iran, Iraq, Kuwait, Libya, Nigeria, Qatar, Saudi Arabia, U.A.E., and Venezuela	1960	Crude petroleum	Coordinate and unify petroleum policies.
SAFTA (South Asian Free Trade Agreement)		Bangladesh, Maldives, Bhutan, Nepal, India, Pakistan and Sri Lanka	Jan. 2006	—	Reduce tariffs on inter-regional trade

Concerns Related to International Trade

Undertaking international trade is mutually beneficial to nations if it leads to regional specialisation, higher level of production, better standard of living, worldwide availability of goods and services, equalisation of prices and wages and diffusion of knowledge and culture.

International trade can prove to be detrimental to nations of it leads to dependence on other countries, uneven levels of development, exploitation, and commercial rivalry leading to wars. Global trade affects many aspects of life; it can impact everything from the environment to health and well-being of the people around the world. As countries compete to trade more, production and the use of natural resources spiral up, resources get used up faster than they can be replenished. As a result, marine life is also depleting fast, forests are being cut down and river basins sold off to private drinking water companies. Multinational corporations trading in oil, gas mining, pharmaceuticals and agri-business keep expanding their operations at all costs creating more pollution – their mode of work does not follow the norms of sustainable development. If organisations are geared only towards profit making, and environmental and health concerns are not addressed, then it could lead to serious implications in the future.

GATEWAYS OF INTERNATIONAL TRADE

Ports

The chief gateways of the world of international trade are the harbours and ports. Cargoes and travellers pass from one part of the world to another through these ports.

The ports provide facilities of docking, loading, unloading and the storage facilities for cargo. In order to provide these facilities, the port authorities make arrangements for maintaining navigable channels, arranging tugs and barges, and providing labour and managerial services. The importance of a port is judged by the size of cargo and the number of ships handled. The quantity of cargo handled by a port is an indicator of the level of development of its hinterland.

Types of Port

Generally, ports are classified according to the types of traffic which they handle.

Types of port according to cargo handled:

(i) **Industrial Ports:** These ports specialise in bulk cargo-like grain, sugar, ore, oil, chemicals and similar materials.

(ii) **Commercial Ports:** These ports handle general cargo-packaged products and manufactured good. These ports also handle passenger traffic.

(iii) **Comprehensive Ports:** Such ports handle bulk and general cargo in large volumes. Most of the world's great ports are classified as comprehensive ports.

Types of port on the basis of location:

(i) **Inland Ports:** These ports are located away from the sea coast. They are linked to the sea through a river or a canal. Such ports are accessible to flat bottom ships or barges. For example, Manchester is linked with a canal; Memphis is located on the river Mississippi; Rhine has several ports like Mannheim and Duisburg; and Kolkata is located on the river Hoogli, a branch of the river Ganga.

(ii) **Out Ports:** These are deep water ports built away from the actual ports. These serve the parent ports by receiving those ships which are unable to approach them due to their large size. Classic combination, for example, is Athens and its out port Piraeus in Greece.

Types of port on the basis of specialised functions:

(i) **Oil Ports:** These ports deal in the processing and shipping of oil. Some of these are tanker ports and some are refinery ports. Maracaibo in Venezuela, Esskhira in Tunisia, Tripoli in Lebanon are tanker ports. Abadan on the Gulf of Persia is a refinery port.

(ii) **Ports of Call:** These are the ports which originally developed as calling points on main sea routes where ships used to anchor for refuelling, watering and taking food items. Later on, they developed into commercial ports. For example, Aden, Honolulu and Singapore.

(iii) **Packet Station:** These are also known as ferry ports. These packet stations are exclusively concerned with the transportation of passengers and mail across water bodies covering short distances. These stations occur in pairs located in such a way that they face each other across the water body, e.g. Dover in England and Calais in France across the English Channel.

(iv) **Entrepot Ports:** These are collection centres where the goods are brought from different countries for export. Singapore is an entrepot for Asia. Rotterdam for Europe, and Copenhagen for the Baltic region.

(v) **Naval Ports:** These are ports which have only strategic importance. These ports serve warships and have repair workshops for them. Kochi and Karwar are examples of such ports in India.

TRANSPORT IN INDIA

Railways

The Railways in India provide the principal mode of transportation for freight and passengers. It brings together people from the farthest corners of the country and makes possible the conduct of business, sightseeing, pilgrimage and education. The Indian Railways have been a great integrating force during the last more than 179 years. It has bound the economic life of the country and helped in accelerating the development of industry and agriculture. From a very modest beginning in 1853, when the first train steamed off from Mumbai to Thane, a distance of 34 kms, Indian Railways have grown into a vast network of 7,325 stations spread over a route length of 68,103 km with a fleet of 12,734 locomotives, 79,835 passenger service vehicles and 3,02,624 wagons. The growth of Indian Railways in the 179 years of its existence is thus phenomenal. It has played a vital role in the economic industrial and social development of the country. The network runs broad-gauge operations extending over 64,403 route kilometers.

About 59 per cent (39,900 km) of the route kilolmetres, has been electrified. The network is divided into 18 Zones. Divisions are the basic operating units. The 18 zones and their respective headquarters are given below:

Zonal Railways	Headquarters
Central	Mumbai
Eastern	Kolkata
East Coast	Bhubaneshwar
East Central	Hajipur
Northern	New Delhi
North Central	Allahabad
North Eastern	Gorakhpur
Northeast Frontier	Maligaon (Guwahati)
North Western	Jaipur
Southern	Chennai
South Central	Secunderabad
South Eastern	Kolkata
South East Central Railway	Bilaspur
South Western Railway	Hubli
Western	Mumbai
West Central Railway	Jabalpur
Metro Railway	Kolkata
South Coast Railway	Vishakhapatnam (in Process)

The rolling stock fleet of Indian Railways in services in 2015 comprised 43 steam, 5,714 diesel and 5,016 electric locomotives. Currently, the Railways are in process of inducting new designs of fuel-efficient locomotives of higher horse power, high-speed coaches and modern bogies for freight traffic. Modern signalling like panel inter-locking, route relay inter-locking, centralized traffic control, automatic signalling and multi-aspect colour light signalling, are being progressively introduced. Railways have made impressive progress regarding indigenous production of rolling stock and variety of other equipment over the years and is now self-sufficient in most of the items.

Roads

Road as a mode of transport is a critical infrastructure for economic development of a country. It influences the pace, structure and pattern of development. The Ministry of Road Transport and Highways was formed in 2009 by bifurcating the erstwhile Ministry of Shipping, Road Transport and Highways into two independent ministries. The Ministry of Road Transport and Highways encompasses construction and maintenance of National Highways (NHs), administration of Motor Vehicles Act, 1988 and Central Motor Vehicles Rules 1989, formulation of broad policies relating to road transport, environmental issues, automotive norms, fixation of user fee rate for use of National Highways etc. besides making arrangements for cross-border movement of vehicular traffic with neighbouring countries.

The capacity of national highways in term of handling traffic (passenger and goods) needs to keep pace with industrial growth. India has one of the largest road networks of over 63.71 lakh km. It comprises national highways, expressways, state highways, major district roads, other district roads and village roads with following length distribution:

National Highways/Expressway	1,32,500 km
State Highways	1,79,535 km
Other Roads	6,371,847 km

Development and Maintenance of National Highways

The Government is implementing National Highways Development Project (NHDP), the largest highways project ever undertaken in the country since 2000. The NHDP is mainly being implemented by National Highways Authority of India.

National Highways Authority of India

National Highways Authority of India (NHAI) was constituted to develop, maintain and manage the national highways vested or entrusted to it by the Central Government. It became operational in 1995 with the appointment of the first Chairman. Presently, NHAI is headed by a Chairman with six full time members and four part time (ex-officio) members. The Authority has its field offices in the form of zonal offices, regional offices, project implementation units (PIUs) and corridor management units (CMU) spread all over the country.

The National Highways Development Project is a project to upgrade, rehabilitate and widen major highways in India to a higher standard. The project was implemented in 1998 under the leadership of Atal Behari Vajpayee. "National Highways" account for only about 2.25% of the total length of roads, but carry about 40% of the total traffic across the length and breadth of the country. This project is managed by the National Highways Authority of India (NHAI) under the Ministry of Road, Transport and Highways. The NHDP represents 49,260 km of roads and highways work and construction in order to boost economic development of the country.

The project is composed of the following phases:

Phase I: The Golden Quadrilateral (GQ; 5,846 km) connecting the four major cities of Delhi, Mumbai, Chennai and Kolkata. This project connecting four metro cities, would be 5,846 km. In 2012, India announced the four-lane GQ highway network as complete.

Phase II: North-South and East-West corridors comprising national highways connecting four extreme points of the country. The North-South and East-West Corridor (NS-EW; 7,142 km) connecting Srinagar in the north to Kanyakumari in the south, including spur from Salem to Kanyakumari (Via Coimbatore and Kochi) and Silchar in the east to Porbandar in the west. Total length of the network is 7,142 km. In 2016, 90.99% of the project had been completed, 5.47% of the project work is under Implementation and 3.52% of the total length is left. It also includes Port connectivity and other projects — 435 km.

Phase III: The government recently approved NHDP-III to upgrade 12,109 km of national highways on a Build, Operate and Transfer (BOT) basis, which takes into account high-density traffic, connectivity of state capitals via NHDP Phase I and II, and connectivity to centres of economic importance.

Phase IV: The government is considering widening 20,000 km of highway that were not part of Phase I, II, or III. Phase IV will convert existing single-lane highways into two lanes with paved shoulders.

Phase V: As road traffic increases over time, a number of four-lane highways will need to be upgraded/expanded to six lanes. The current plan calls for upgrade of about 5,000 km of four-lane roads, although the government has not yet identified the stretches.

Phase VI: The government is working on constructing expressways that would connect major commercial and industrial townships. It has already identified 400 km of Vadodara (earlier Baroda)-Mumbai section that would connect to the existing Vadodara (earlier Baroda)-Ahmedabad section. The World Bank is studying this project. The project will be funded on BOT basis. The 334 km Expressway between Chennai-Bangalore and 277 km Expressway between Kolkata-Dhanbad has been identified and feasibility study and DPR contract has been awarded by NHAI.

Phase VII: This phase calls for improvements to city road networks by adding ring roads to enable easier connectivity with national highways to important cities. In addition, improvements will be made to stretches of national highways that require additional flyovers and bypasses given population and housing growth along the highways and increasing traffic. The government has not yet identified a firm investment plan for this phase. The 19 km long Chennai Port—Maduravoyal Elevated Expressway is being executed under this phase.

National Highways Development Project at a glance

NHDP Phase	Particulars	Length
NHDP-I & II	Balance work of GQ and EW-NS corridors	13,000 km
NHDP-III	4-laning	10,000 km
NHDP-IV	2-laning	20,000 km
NHDP-V	6-laning of selected stretches	5,000 km
NHDP-VI	Development of expressways	1,000 km
NHDP-VII	Ring Roads, Bypasses, Grade Separators, Service Roads etc.	700 km
	Total	**45,000 km**

Bharatmala Pariyojana

The Ministry has taken up detailed review of NHs network with a view to develop the road connectivity to border areas, development of coastal roads including road connectivity for non-major ports, improvement in the efficiency of national corridors, development of economic corridors, inter corridors and feeder routes along with integration with Sagarmala, etc., under Bharatmala Pariyojana. The Bharatmala Pariyojana envisages development of about 26,000 km length of economic corridors, which along with Golden Quadrilateral (GQ) and North-South and East-West (NS-EW) Corridors are expected to carry majority of the freight traffic on roads. Further, about 8,000 km of inter corridors and about 7,500 km of feeder routes have been identified for improving effectiveness of economic corridors, GQ and NS-EW Corridors. The programme envisages development of Ring Roads/bypasses and elevated corridors to decongest the traffic passing through cities and enhance logistic efficiency; etc.

Bharatmala Project Components

- **Economic Corridor :** As per the guidelines of the road construction project, the construction of 9000 kms of Economic Corridors will be undertaken by the central government.
- **Feeder Route or Inter Corridor:** The total length of the roads, which fall under the Feeder Route or Inter Corridor category, is a whopping 6000 kms.
- **National Corridor Efficiency Improvement:** 5000 kms of roads, constructed under the scheme will fall in the category of National Corridor for the better connection between roads.
- **Border Road and International Connectivity:** Connecting the cities and remote areas, which are situated in the border regions, the project has kept provision for constructing 2000 kms roads that fall in the Border Road or International Connectivity category.
- **Port Connectivity and Coastal Road :** To connect the areas that are dotted along the shorelines and important ports, the central government has ordered the construction of 2000 km of roads.
- **Green Field Expressway:** The main stress will be given on the construction and development of Green Field Expressway for better management of traffic and freight.
- **Balance NHDP Works:** Under the last segment, the project will see construction and maintenance of about 10,000 kms of new roads.

Green National Highways Corridor Project

The Green National Highways Corridor Project (GNHCP) was launched in 2016. The project includes upgradation of about 781 km of various national highways passing through Rajasthan, Himachal Pradesh, Uttar Pradesh and Andhra Pradesh. It was launched under the Green Highways Policy that was unveiled in 2015 to actualize the vision of developing eco-friendly and green national highways. The greening project has a huge potential to generate jobs and can prove to be a game-changer for agriculture and rural economy. Greening of one km of highway provides employment to ten people. The objectives of the project include: to evolve a policy framework for plantation along national highways; to reduce the impact of air pollution and dust as trees and shrubs are known to be natural sink for air pollutants; to reduce the impact of ever increasing noise pollution caused due to increase in number of vehicles; to arrest soil erosion at the embankment slopes; etc. The project is being run with World Bank aid.

Bhoomi Rashi

The Ministry launched Bhoomi Rashi portal to digitise the land acquisition notification process and avoid parking of public funds with the Competent Authority for Land Acquisition (CALA). The system helps in expediting the process by providing simultaneous Hindi translation and has been made compatible with the e-gazette for expeditious publication of notification. Offline data entry of survey numbers and land parties, interface for appointment of arbitrator and login credentials to arbitrator, module for monitoring court cases and arbitral cases, module for generating cala performance report, module for grievance redressal system have been added to the portal.

Setu Bharatam Programme

The Setu Bharatam programme for building bridges for safe and seamless travel on national highways was launched in 2016. The Setu Bharatam programme is to make all national highways free of railway level crossings by 2019. This is being done to prevent the frequent accidents and loss of lives at level crossings. The Minister informed that 208 railway over bridges (ROB), railway under bridges (RUB) are to be built at the level crossings at a cost 20,800 crore as part of the programme. The details of 208 ROBs are as : Andhra Pradesh-33, Assam-12, Bihar-20, Chattisgarh-5, Gujarat-8, Haryana-10, Himachal Pradesh-5, Jharkhand-11, Karnataka-17, Kerala-4, Madhya Pradesh-6, Maharashtra- 12, Odisha-4, Punjab-10, Rajasthan-9, Tamil Nadu-9, Uttarakhand-2, Uttar Pradesh-9, West Bengal-22.

Maritime Agenda

In the Maritime Agenda 2010-20, a target of 3,130 MT port capacity has been set for the year 2020. More than 50 per cent of this capacity is to be created in the non-major ports as the traffic handling by these ports is expected to increase to 1,280 MT. The objective of the Maritime Agenda is not only creating more capacity but augmenting port performance. This enlarged scale of operation is expected to reduce transaction costs considerably and make Indian ports globally competitive.

Port Sector

During 2015, major and non-major ports in the country handled a total cargo through put of around 786 million tonnes (MT). The traffic grew by 1.4 per cent over the corresponding period of previous year. The 12 major ports handled a traffic of 447.05 MT during April — December 2015, representing an increase of about 3.18 per cent over the corresponding period of previous year.

MAJOR PORTS

Kolkata Port

Kolkata Port officially known as Syama Prasad Mookerjee Port Trust, is the only rivrerine major port of India. It has a vast hinterland comprising the entire Eastern India including West Bengal, Bihar, Jharkhand, U.P., M.P., Assam, North East hill states and the two landlocked neighbouring countries namely, Nepal and Bhutan. The port has twin dock systems viz., Kolkata Dock System (KDS) on the eastern bank and Haldia Dock Complex (HDC) on the western bank of river Hooghly.

Paradip Port

Paradip Port is one of the major ports in the country. Pandit Jawaharlal Nehru, the first Prime Minister of India, laid the foundation stone of the port in 1962 near the confluence of river Mahanadi on the east coast of Bay of Bengal in Odisha. Government of India took over the management of the port from the state government in 1965. The construction of iron ore berth was completed and INS "Investigator" had the privilege of maiden berthing in the port in March, 1966. The Government of India declared Paradip Port Trust (PPT) as the eighth major port in India in 1966 making it the first major port in the east coast commissioned in independent India.

New Mangalore Port

New Mangalore port was declared as the ninth major port in May, 1974 inaugurated in 1975. The provisions of Major Port Trusts Act, 1963 were extended to the new Mangalore port and a Port Trust Board was formed in 1980. Over the years, the port has grown from the level of handling less than a lakh tonnes of cargo to 39.37 million tonnes in 2013-14. The major commodities imported through the port are POL crude for Mangalore Refinery and Petrochemicals Limited (MRPL), coal, iron ore, LPG, fertilizer, edible oil, limestone, wooden logs, cement, liquid chemicals, containerized cargo etc., and the major export cargo are POL products, iron ore pellets, granite stone, maize, wheat, containerized cargo like coffee, cashew kernels, etc.

Cochin Port

The modern port of Cochin was developed during 1920-1940 due to the untiring efforts of Sir Robert Bristow. By 1930-31 it was formally opened for vessels up to 30 feet draught. Cochin was given the status of a major port in 1936. The administration of the port got vested in a Board of Trustees in 1964 under the Major Port Trusts Act, 1963. The port of Cochin is located on the Willington island at latitude 9°58′ north and 76°14′ east on the south-west coast of India about 930 km south of Mumbai and 320 km North of Kanyakumari. With its strategic location on the south-west coast of India and at a commanding position at the cross-roads of the east-west Ocean trade, it is a natural gateway to the vast industrial and agricultural produce markets of the south-west India. The hinterland of the port includes the whole of Kerala and parts of Tamil Nadu and Karnataka. A study carried out on the traffic flow in the hinterland of the port indicates that about 97 per cent of the total volume of traffic is accounted for by Kerala. The hinterland of Cochin port has further spread over to different areas with the growth of containerization in the country and establishment of inland container depots of different load centres in the country. Cochin with its proximity to the international sea route between Europe and the Far East and Australia can attract a large number of container lines offering immense business opportunities. Cochin port has handled 20.89 mt of traffic during 2013-14 compared to 19.85 mt during the previous year.

Jawaharlal Nehru Port

Constructed in the mid 1980's and commissioned in 1989, Jawaharlal Nehru Port has come a long way by becoming a world-class international container handling port. The port is a trendsetter in the matter of port development in India through new initiatives like private sector participation. It is situated in between 18°56′43″ north and 72°56′24″ east along the eastern shore of Mumbai harbour off Elephanta Island. Port handles vessels having draught up to 12.50 metres.

Mumbai Port

Mumbai port is a fully integrated multi-purpose port handling container, dry bulk, liquid bulk and break bulk cargo. The port has extensive wet and dry dock facilities to meet the normal needs of ships using the port. There are three enclosed wet docks namely, Prince, Victoria and Indira Docks, having a total area of 46.30 hectares and quayage of 7,776 meters inside the wet basin and 853 meters along the harbour wall. Oldest of the three was Prince's Dock, a semi-tidal dock, commissioned in 1880. It has 8 berths, each with a designed draft of 6.4 meters. The Victoria dock, commissioned in 1888, was also a semi-tidal dock. It has 14 berths each with a designed draft of 6.7 meters. The Prince's and Victoria Dock basins are now being filled up and will be used as Container Storage Yard under the Offshore Container Terminal Project. The same have been decommissioned for Shipping.

Shipping Corporation of India

The Shipping Corporation of India Ltd. (SCI) was formed in 1961. Presently, the authorised capital of the company is ₹ 450.00 crore and the paid up capital is ₹ 423.45 crore. The status of SCI has been changed from a private limited company to public limited company from 1992. The SCI was conferred the "Navratna" status by the Government of India in August, 2009. Presently, the Government is holding 80.12 per cent of the share capital and the balance is held by financial institutions, public and others (NRIs, corporate bodies etc.)

CIVIL AVIATION IN INDIA

The Ministry of Civil Aviation is responsible for the formulation of national policies and programmes for development and regulation of civil aviation and for devising and implementing schemes for orderly growth and expansion of civil air transport.

The civil aviation sector has three main functional divisions—regulatory, infrastructural and operational. The civil aviation sector in India has seen a phenomenal growth in the operation. The civil aviation sector in India has seen a phenomenal growth in the recent years. As on date there are a large number of companies provide passenger transport and cargo handling services in the country. The Air Transport Companies are both in the public sector and in the private sector. In the public sector, there are Air India Limited and its subsidiaries viz. Alliance Air, Air India Charters Limited (Air India Express) etc.

Apart from Air India, Indian Airlines, Alliance Air and Air India Charters Ltd., there are many private scheduled operators, viz. Spice Jet Ltd., Vistara, Air Asia, Go Airlines (India) Pvt Ltd., and Inter Globe Aviation Ltd. (Indigo) operating on the domestic and global sector providing a wide choice of flights and connectivity to various parts of India. Three cargo airlines viz. Blue Dart Aviation Pvt. Ltd., Deccan Cargo and Express Logistics (Pvt.) Ltd. and M/s Quickjet are operating Scheduled Cargo services in the country.

Airports Authority of India

The Airports Authority of India (AAI) was formed on 1 April 1995 and is responsible for (*i*) providing safe and efficient Air Traffic Services, communication and navigational aids at all the airports, (*ii*) plan, develop, construct and maintain runway, taxiways, apron, terminal building, etc., (*iii*) provide Air Safety Services and (*iv*) arrange search and rescue facilities in co-ordination with other agencies and other functions as per AAI Act. AAI manages 137 airports (As on July, 2020) which include 24 International Airports (including 3 International Civil Enclaves), 10 Customs Airports (Including 4 Customs Civil Enclaves), 80 Domestic Airports and 23 Domestic Civil Enclaves at Defence airfields. Besides these some airforce airports, are also being used as commercial airport to a limited extent.

Policy and Promotion

The Indian aviation sector is an open, liberal and investment-friendly sector. "Entry of low-cost carriers, higher household incomes, strong economic growth, increased FDI inflows, surging tourist inflow, increased cargo movement, sustained business growth and supporting government policies are the major drivers for the growth of the aviation sector in India," according to a Deloitte report on the Indian aviation sector.

The Ministry of Civil Aviation is charged with the responsibility of the formulation of national policies and programmes for the development and regulation of civil aviation in the country; devising and implementing schemes for orderly growth and expansion of civil air transport; and overseeing the provision of airport facilities, air traffic services and carriage of passengers and goods by air.

The responsibility of developing, financing, operating and maintaining all government airports in the country rests with the AAI, which was established in 1994 under the Airports Authority Act. AAI has also entered into operations management and development agreements with Delhi International Airport Ltd for Indira Gandhi International (IGI) Airport in New Delhi, with an objective to develop it into a world-class airport. Phase-1 of the development of IGI airport has been completed with the construction of the new integrated Terminal 3 (T3). It caters to an additional 34 million passengers per annum (mppa) and can operate as a hub.

100% FDI: Under the civil aviation sector's investment policy, 100% FDI is permissible for existing airports, with Government approval required for FDI beyond 74%.

Automatic route: 100% FDI under the automatic route is permissible for Greenfield airports. 49% FDI is permissible in Domestic Scheduled Passenger Airlines, 100% FDI for non-resident Indians (NRIs) under the automatic route.

74% FDI allowed for Non Scheduled Air Transport Service (100% for NRIs) under Automatic route, with Government approval required for FDI beyond 49% and up to 74%.

100% FDI under the automatic route is permissible for Helicopter services/seaplane services requiring DGCA approval.

Other Services under Civil Aviation sector

74% FDI: Under the civil aviation sector's investment policy, 74% FDI is permissible for Ground Handling Services subject to sectoral regulations and security clearance and 100% FDI permissible for NRIs under Automatic route up to 49% with Government approval beyond 49% and up to 74%.

100% FDI: Under the civil aviation sector's investment policy, 100% FDI is permissible for Maintenance and Repair organizations; flying training institutes; and technical training institutions under Automatic route.

Pipeline Networks

Pipeline provide the most convenient mode of transport for petroleum, petroleum products and gas in bulk quantities over a long distance. Nowadays, solid minerals too are transported by pipelines after converting them into slurry. The advantages of pipeline transport are as follows.

(*i*) Pipelines can be laid through rough terrains as well as under water.

(*ii*) The operating and maintenance costs are lower than that for other modes.

(*iii*) Pipelines involve low energy consumption; thus they save the environment from pollution problems.

(*iv*) The industrial regions are well-integrated by pipeline construction. Transport bottlenecks due to poor road conditions or strikes cannot affect the pipeline mode of transport.

The disadvantages are as follows.

(*i*) Construction of pipelines is prohibitively expensive for the developing countries.

(*ii*) The capacity cannot be increased once the pipelines are laid.

(*iii*) Pipelines often face security threats from terrorist organisations which could jeopardise a country's economy; for example, the oil pipelines in the North-East are often blasted by sub-nationalistic elements.

(*iv*) The repair of pipelines is also very difficult, particularly in case of leakages; detection of leakages is quite difficult.

In India, solid minerals are transported through pipelines in two areas: iron ore in the form of slurry is carried from Kudremukh to Mangalore port, and rock phosphate concentrates are taken from Maton mines to Debari smelter plant in Udaipur district of Rajasthan. Mineral oil is carried from Kandla port to Koyali and Mathura refineries through a pipeline. The Hazira-Bijaipur-Jagdishpur (HBJ) pipeline has linked Hazira on the west coast and Jagdishpur in Sultanpur district (Uttar Pradesh). The 1730 km long pipeline carries gas to a number of steel plants, *viz.* Sawai Madhopur in Rajasthan, Auraiya (Etawah), Aonla (Bareilly) and Shahjahanpur (Uttar Pradesh). A new pipeline was laid from Salaya in Gujarat to Mathura via Viramgam which covers a distance of 1220 km. Pipe connection also exists from Barauni to Kanpur and Delhi. Another such line links Mathura and Jalandhar via Delhi and Ambala. Important pipelines also link Naharkatiya oil fields to Guwahati and Siliguri.

Due to the construction of pipeline networks, the petrochemical industries have decentralised from port locations to the interior of the country. This is beneficial: for a developing country like India, a spontaneous industrial development of the periphery regions is important.

Competition and Complementarity in Regional Context

Competition between different modes of transport, *viz.* railways, roadways, airways and waterways can be defined as diversion from one mode to the other at the cost of the former. This is a situation characterised by sub-optimum utilisation of the capacity in any one mode. Complementarity, on the other hand, can be defined as one mode helping the other mode in a reciprocal manner so that optimum utilisation of both the modes is attained. The twin conditions of competition and complementarity are more pronounced in case of the railways and the roadways, while the airways and the waterways play a marginal role. This is because railways and roadways are the two dominant modes of transport in India.

THE PATTERN OF COMPETITION AND COMPLEMENTARITY IN INDIA In general, for long distance transportation of bulk goods like foodgrains, metal ores, cool, fertilisers etc., railways are preferred. On the other hand, transportation of small parcels is preferred through roadways. The long distance road traffic has gained importance mainly after the National Permit Scheme started in the 1970s. As far as long distance goods traffic is concerned railways and roadways are complementary to each other. The road transport carries to and from the railways the bulk goods which have been transported over a long distance by the railways. Similarly, the road transport carries the containers to and from the railways.

In case of passengers, road transport is preferred over railways for short distances. Quantitatively speaking, for distances upto about 250 km, passengers prefer to travel by road. But, here again, the regular commuters prefer railways because of concessional fares on seasonal tickets. Upto this distance of 250 km, there is stiff competition between rail and road transport.

Just like the goods traffic, roadways and railways exhibit complementarity over long distances in case of passenger travel. Night journeys are preferred through railways as in this case, sleeper berths are available. Passengers use road transport to reach the station and from the station at the destination to reach the final point. Between the metropolitan cities of Delhi, Mumbai, Calcutta and Chennai, air transport offers some competition which is limited and costly but efficient and time saving. But, in the Delhi-Mumbai sector, there is greater frequency of flights and the railways are facing stiff competition.

COMPETITION AND COMPLEMENTARITY IN SOME REGIONS OF INDIA

1. Northern Mountainous Regions: Since rail network is underdeveloped or absent in large areas of Jammu and Kashmir, Himachal Pradesh and Uttar Pradesh hills, roads supplement the transportation needs. Thus, rail links are available upto Jammu (J&K), Shimla (Himachal Pradesh) and Kotdwara, Dehradun and Kathgodam (Uttaranchal) and beyond that only road transport is available.

2. Brahmaputra Valley and West Bengal: Here, the roads get real competition from the waterways for freight traffic, especially the traffic in jute as most of the jute mills are situated on the banks of river Hooghly.

3. Backwaters (*kayals*) of Kerala: Along the coast, the canals and roads are in competition for both the goods traffic and the passenger traffic. But for access into the interior areas, roads are the only mode available. For the overall traffic out of Kerala, the road and water transport complement the railways.

4. Nilgiris: The rail link upto Ootacmund faces a successful and effective competition from road transport mainly because of the penetrative capacity, flexibility and speed of the latter.

5. Jharkhand-West Bengal Mineral Belt: In this region, rail and road transport are complementary to each other. The minerals like coal, metal ores etc. are transported from pitheads to the railway station by road and from the railway station, they are moved to different parts of India. Railways dominate in this region because of their capacity to carry large quantities.

THE FISCAL ASPECTS: The competition and complementarity between different modes of transport can be manipulated by adjusting rates for passenger and goods traffic. But inadequate capacities of the railways to absorb the passenger and goods traffic, especially during peak season (summer holidays or harvest season), divert the traffic to road transport. Also, railways have to offer subsidised rates for transport of goods of mass consumption like foodgrains, sugar, edible oil etc. which hurts their economic returns.

Passenger and Commodity Flows

PASSENGER FLOWS: The development of a transport system may have a two-fold impact—development of resources and flow of people. For instance, development of Kudremukh iron ore in Karnataka attracted people to this region. Similarly, in Neyveli (Tamil Nadu), lignite mining and the factories around it based on urea, briquettes and thermal power attracted settlements. And in densely populated regions like Kerala and West Bengal, transport development facilitated out migration to sparsely populated areas like Assam. Thus, there is a continuous sequence:

Transport Development → Transport → Resources Development → Passenger Flow → Settlements

Apart from such permanent movement, there may be seasonal or periodic movement for instance, movement of labour during agricultural harvest season or during lean season for construction and mining activities towards the urban centres. The seasonal movement may also be on account of fairs, festivals, school holidays, marriages; to big cities for court cases, education or medical treatment.

A four-level hierarchy of passenger flows can be identified:

1. village to village—as during harvest or for procuring consumer items.
2. village to the nearest town—to avail of banking, education or health facilities.
3. small town to big city.
4. travel to state capital, metropolitan city or to another state.

Thus, transport development has given a boost to physical mobility.

COMMODITY FLOWS: The commodity flow reflects spatial pattern of our economy. A smooth commodity flow is a must for smooth functioning of our economy. There may broadly be four types of commodity flows.

1. **Transportation of raw materials,** for instance, movement of iron ore, cotton or sugarcane to factories.
2. **Transportation of finished goods,** for instance, movement of petroleum products from refinery or textiles from factories to the consumer centres.
3. **Flow of electricity** which is an important input and cuts down the cost of coal.
4. **Pipeline transport** which involves movement of oil, gas, etc.

For a systematic study of the commodity flow in India, the country was divided into 38 trade blocks. Each state, important major ports and insignificant major ports—all acted as separate blocks. In all, 78 commodities were considered. Only gross weight was taken into account which included the carrier weight also and without any qualitative differentiation. Since no consideration was given to the road transport, an incomplete picture was presented.

Intra- and Inter-regional Trade

For all practical purposes, states can be considered as regional units also, distinguishable on the basis of geographical, economic and administrative features. A sound internal trade (*i.e.*, within the country involving both intra and inter-regional trade) gives boost to both industrial and agricultural sectors which in turn favourably affect a country's trade with other countries. This brings precious foreign exchange into the country, thus accelerating the overall development.

Different regions are endowed with different types of resource development. This diversity may even go to the extent of specialisation by one region in one particular type of economic activity. Because of diverse demands of all states or regions, a mutual give and take becomes inevitable. This situation gives rise to trade. For instance, in Tamil Nadu, the Cauveri delta specialises in rice crop and Coimbatore is an industrial region. Both complement each other in economic terms. Because the intra-regional trade predominantly involves goods of direct consumption, it is larger than inter-regional trade.

The market centres, *i.e.*, the points where trade actually takes place, have their own hierarchy which ranges from small towns which act as collection centres for rural production to metropolitan cities. For instance, Chennai city acts as a trading point for the trade directed within the state as well as for that directed outside Tamil Nadu. Chennai also has an oil refinery from which petroleum products are taken to places within Tamil Nadu and to places in adjoining states like Karnataka and Andhra Pradesh.

The inter-state trade also results from specialisation and localisation. For instance, Assam specialises in tea and oil which are supplied to other states. Similarly, Jharkhand-West Bengal-Odisha belt specialises in metallic minerals and heavy industries, the products of which are supplied to the rest of the country. Those items which do not have a localised production, like bakery, do not generally enter into inter-regional trade.

For a vibrant inter-regional trade, a sound physical infrastructure and financial services are required. Inter-regional trade helps create a unified market in the country which accelerates the process of diversification of the country's economy. These factors help in rationalisation of prices. Inter-regional trade also serves the purpose of removing scarcity in one region and in consumption of surplus from another region.

Role of Rural Market Centres

The rural market centres are at the lowest level of hierarchy of trade centres. In fact, many villages have no contact with the outside world beyond this level. Sometimes, eight to ten villages may combine together to have a rural market centre which could be the headquarters of a block or taluk. Sometimes, a rural market centre is located at the crossing of two or more bus routes or along a bus route. This way, it comes in direct touch with the transport network.

The market could be a daily market, for instance, those for vegetables and fruits and other consumer goods. Weekly markets are popular in West Bengal which are known as *haat, pithia, shandies* etc. In these markets, the vendors may come with their products and the merchants may come to buy the agricultural produce, rural industrial products like metal goods, edible oil, implements etc. With the development of transport, the weekly markets are declining because, now, travelling to nearby towns is possible and the vendors can provide door-to-door service. There is a third variety of rural markets—the seasonal markets which are associated with agricultural harvest season, cattle fairs or festivals. The fourth type of markets are the permanent ones.

TYPES OF COMMODITIES EXCHANGED: The most common item is agri-cultural surplus which is purchased by the whole-sale merchants from the collection centres. This type of trade may be done through a regulated market operation, or, instead of wholesale merchants, some government agency may do the procuring. Agricultural inputs like improved seeds, fertilisers, pesticides, agricultural implements and pumpsets are also quite commonly exchanged. Among small items, which are ubiquitously present, are matches, kerosene, diesel, soap, edible oil, clothings etc. Apart from the goods trade, these market centres may offer services like machine repair, bicycle repair, tyres and tubes, tailoring, medical facilities, cooperative and banking services, agriculture and animal husbandry extension services etc.

CENTRES FOR DIFFUSION OF INNOVATION: In the absence of modern means of communication, the rural market centres act as centres for diffusion of innovation, and help disseminate information regarding new agricultural practices and schemes, new development programmes in the region. Government agencies may even use these centres for demonstrations, training and promotional measures. Rural politics is also discussed at these centres which helps raise the level of political consciousness of the rural populace.

Thus, the rural market centres play an important role in the smooth functioning of the country's economy.

TELECOMMUNICATIONS

Communication has grown to be an essential infrastructure for socio-economic development in an increasingly knowledge intensive world. The reach of telecom services to all parts of country is integral to development of an innovative and technologically driven society. Studies have shown that there is a positive correlation between the penetration of Internet and Mobile Services on the growth of GDP of a country. As a result of the measures taken by the Government over the years, the Indian Telecom Sector has grown exponentially and has become the second largest network in the world, next only to China. At the end of January 2019, there are 117.70 crores telephone connections in the country.

Wire Line vs Wireless

While the wireless telephones continued to grow, the landline telephones kept declining. The number of landline telephones, which was 28.50 million in the beginning of the year 2014 declined to 23.79 million at the end of December 2021. On the other hand the number of wireless telephones increased from 904.52 million to 1154.62 million during this period.

Tele-density

Tele-density, which denotes the number of telephones per 100 population, is an important indicator of telecom penetration. Overall tele-density in the country was 86.89 per cent at the end of November 2021. The rural tele-density was 59.31 per cent while in urban areas it was 138.79 per cent. Amongst the service areas, Himachal Pradesh (142.49 per cent) had the highest tele-density followed by Kerala (127.98 per cent), Punjab (122.97 per cent), Tamil Nadu (107.08 per cent) and

Karnataka (102.89 per cent). On the other hand, it is comparatively low in-service areas such as Bihar (53.54 per cent), Uttar Pradesh (68.73 per cent), West Bengal (70.13 per cent), Madhya Pradesh (69.85 per cent), Assam (69.62 per cent), and Odisha (76.42 per cent). Amongst the metros, Delhi tops in such density with 269.57 per cent, followed by Kolkata (148.23 per cent) and Mumbai (145.26 per cent).

Internet and Broadband Penetration

Government has placed considerable emphasis on the growth of internet and broadband in the country as part its Digital India campaign. The number of internet subscribers (both broadband and narrowband put together) which was 825.30 million at the end of March, 2021 increased to 834.29 million by the end of September 2021. The number of subscribers accessing internet via wireless phones, etc., was 809.82 million at the end of September 2021 while number of wireline internet subscribers was 24.47 million. The number of broadband subscribers was 794.88 million at the end of September 2021.

Software Technology Parks

Software Technology Parks of India (STPI) was set up in 1991 as an autonomous society under the MeitY. Its main objective has been the promotion of software exports from the country. It acts as 'single-window' in providing services to the software exporters. The services rendered by it for the software exporting community have been statutory services, data communications services, incubation facilities, training and value added services. It has played a key developmental role in the promotion of software exports with a special focus on SMEs and start up units.

National Broadband Mission

National Broadband Mission (NBM) was launched in 2019 with a vision to fast-track growth of digital communication infrastructure, bridge the digital divide, facilitate digital empowerment and inclusion, and provide affordable and universal access of broadband for all. Some of the objectives of the Mission which is structured with strong three principles of universality, affordability and quality are: broadband access to all villages by 2022; facilitate universal and equitable access to broadband services for across the country and especially in rural and remote areas; significantly improve quality of services for mobile and internet; develop innovative implementation models for Right of Way (RoW); and to work with states/UTs for having consistent policies pertaining to expansion of digital infrastructure including for RoW approvals required for laying OFC, etc.

16 HUMAN SETTLEMENT

Settlements

A settlement, locality or populated place is a community in which people live. A settlement can range in size from a small number of dwelling grouped together to the largest of cities with surrounding urbanised area. Settlement may include hamlets, villages, towns and cities. A settlement may have known historical properties such as the date or era in which it was first settled or first settled by a particular people. Settlement is a process of grouping of people and acquiring of some territory to build houses as well as for their economic support. Settlements can broadly be divided into two types—rural and urban.

Concepts of Rural and Urban Settlements

Settlement refers to a related set of human dwellings along with associated structures created by man and including the general physical environment, such as roads, railways, ports, water bodies, resorts, etc.

The basic difference between urban and rural settlements is in the chief occupation of the inhabitants. In an urban settlement trade, industry or some secondary or tertiary activity is the dominant occupation. In a rural settlement, on the other hand, agriculture or some primary activity is the dominant occupation. Such villages can be distinguished from the towns with similar activities on the basis of small scale of operation, absence of a commercial centre and absence of mechanised industry. Rural and Urban settlements can be further differentiated, using the following criteria:

1. Site or the actual piece of land on which the settlement is built.
2. Situation or position which implies the location of a town or a village in relation to its surroundings.
3. Functions.

RURAL SETTLEMENTS

Siting Factors: Water is most necessary of human needs. If water and land are available, the site chosen for building of a village will be one where land is dry and not subject to frequent flooding. The availability of building materials, either wood or stone near a settlement is another great advantage. Another aspect of shelter is the choice of sites favoured by climatic conditions. Another important factor is healthy people do not choose to settle in disease-prone areas.

Types of Rural Settlement

(*a*) **Wet Point Settlements:** Such settlements generally tend to cluster around a source of water supply such as stream, lake, etc. Oasis found in deserts have this type of settlements.

(*b*) **Dry Point Settlements:** Such settlements are generally observed in the flood-prone areas and in the regions of excessive dampness. These are generally located at a higher level like a ridge or the house may be lifted up from the ground by using silts. ***For example:*** Settlements in Gangetic Plains.

(*c*) **Market Settlements:** They are located at a site which is easily accessible from other villages and have good transportation links. Markets are the centre around which development of settlements takes place.

(*d*) **Pilgrim Settlements:** Such settlements may come up around a place of worship or any spot with a religious significance.

(*e*) **Strong Point Settlements:** Such settlements are made on hilltop island or on the meander loops due to security concerns. ***For example:*** Durham in England is built on a hill protected on three sides by meanders of a river.

(*f*) **Foothill Settlements:** These are the sites where the hills and plains meet. Such settlements have the advantage of collecting goods from the plains as well as from the hills. ***Example:*** Settlements at Himalayan foothills.

(*g*) **Transplanted Settlements:** When people move from the abondoned village to new place, it forms transplanted settlements.

(*h*) **Transportation Line Settlements:** Such settlements generally come up along rail lines or roadways.

(*i*) **Spring Line Settlements:** Such settlements are found in the hilly areas at the line of contact of permeable and impermeable layers.

Patterns of Rural Settlements

It is the spatial arrangement of settlements in relation to one another. A settlement pattern is a function of relief, climate, water supply and socio-economic factors.

(*i*) **Dispersed Settlement:** These settlements are characterised by widely spaced houses which usually come up in mountains, deserts, semi-arid regions and areas where extensive agriculture using mechanised operations are practised.

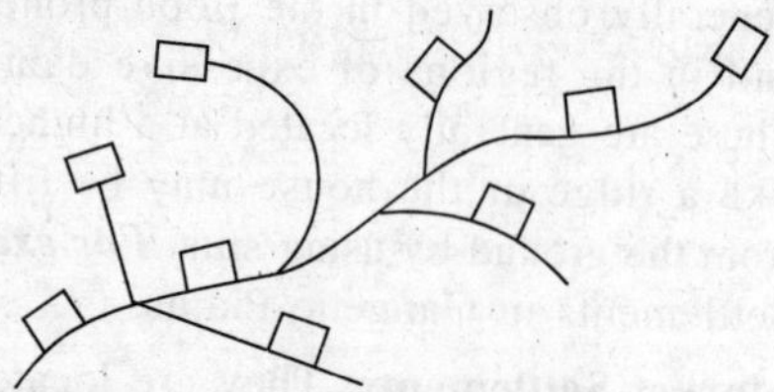

Dispersed settlement

For example: Settlements in West Bengal, Kerala and Himalayan foothill zone.

(*ii*) **Clustered Settlements:** Such settlements are generally found in highly fertile regions where intensive agriculture is practised using more human labour.

For example: North Indian Gangetic Plains.

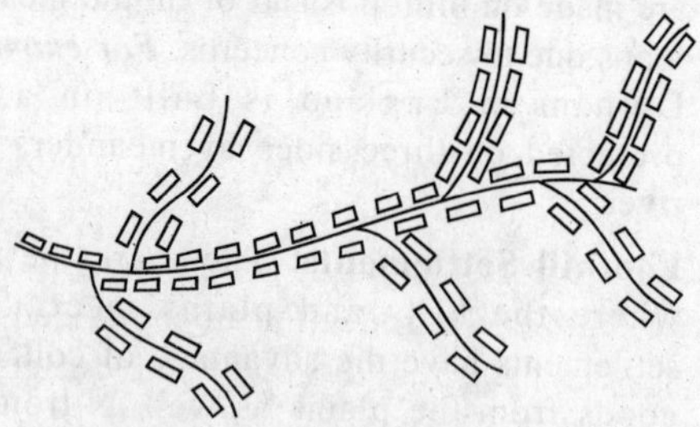

Clustered settlement

(*iii*) ***Linear Pattern:*** These settlements are arranged in a straight line generally along a rail line or a river, a coastline or a highway.

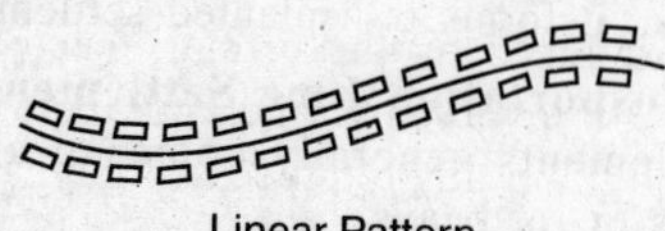

Linear Pattern

(*iv*) **Ring Pattern:** Such type of settlements emerges around a hill in a circular form.

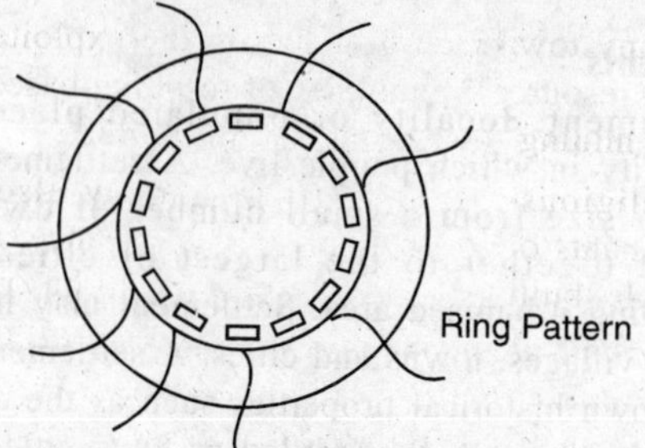

Ring Pattern

(*v*) **T-Shaped Pattern:** When the settlements develop in T-forms, it is called T-shaped pattern of settlements.

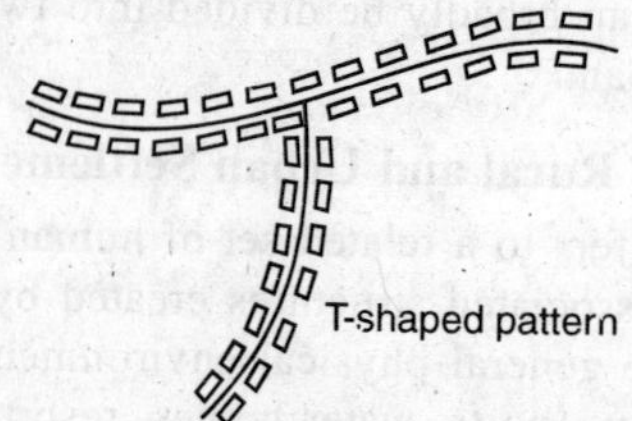

T-shaped pattern

(*vi*) **Cruciform Pattern:** Such settlement of village occurs in a cruciform shape.

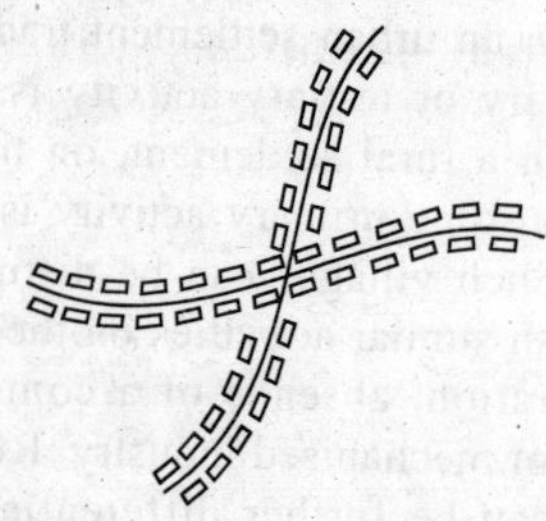

Functions: The functions of rural settlements are:

(*a*) Agriculture, fishing, lumbering, or mining

(*b*) To house the rural population

(*c*) As a shopping centre

(*d*) As a social and religious centre

(*e*) Administrative functions

URBAN SETTLEMENTS

Sites and Situations: Towns, like villagers possess the basic requirements which make settlement possible. These are water and food supplies, shelter and building material and some protection against both natural hazards such as floods and human enemies.

Many towns are founded on the exploitation of specific resources. Examples of resource-based towns are the mining towns and fishing ports.

Religious or cultural factors may also act as determinants of site for towns. For instance, a shrine or temple, built at a certain place which has religious significance may become a centre of pilgrimage. Similarly, the choice of a particular place for an educational or cultural institution may also lead to town development.

The situation of a town is its relationship with the surrounding region. Most town situations can be classified in three classes:

(i) **Linear Situations:** Are usually those whose main advantages are those of trade and transport. Here, towns grow up at specific points along lines of communication.

(ii) **Frontier Situations:** Are those in which a town is situated at the borders of two or more types of land, from which it can draw a variety of goods.

(iii) **Central Situations:** Towns with central situations are those at points which, because of their focal position, are easily reached from all directions and which in turn can exert their influence over a wide radius.

Functions of urban settlements:

(i) Administration (Municipal towns or national capitals)

(ii) Defence (cantonments, air bases, naval dockyards).

(iii) Cultural centres (centres of education, film making like Hollywood, region like Jerusalem, Haridwar)

(iv) Production centres (motor manufacturing towns of Detroit, Toledo and Windsor in the USA)

(v) Transfer and distribution centres

(vi) Residential centres

(vii) Towns of diversified functions (London, New York or Paris are referred to as diversified in function).

Ecology Process of Urban Growth

Economic factors behind Urban Growth: The nature of urbanization depends on the type of economic production going on the region. The nature of economic activities in a town or city relates to production at three levels : primary, secondary and tertiary.

Primary Production and Urbanisation: Agriculture, fishing, forestry and mining come under primary production. Iron ore mining, manganese, bauxite, copper, gold and pertroleum exploration involves the implementation of a high level technology with highly skilled people. People come from remote areas in search of employment and thus help in the process of urbanization.

Agriculture of commercial variety also helps in the urbanization process. For example, Tea plantation of Asom, West Bengal, Tamil Nadu, etc., have led to the development of urban centres.

The green revolution in Punjab has generated a large number of smaller towns which are attracting a large number of agricultural labourers from other backward and poor states. Thus, the process of urbanization through modernization of primary activities is an ongoing and potentially most significant urbanization process. Forest product also led to the development of urban centres. For example, Kagaz Nagar in Andhra Pradesh developed due to the use of forest product. A number of other towns have also developed due to manufacture of plywood, paper and furniture, etc.

Fisheries also lead to the development of a number of coastal towns and cities, along the Western and Eastern coast of India. It attracts traders in this business. With the introduction of motorized boats and modern equipment, these towns and districts have aquired urban character.

Secondary Production and Urbanization: It includes the manufacturing and construction industries. The secondary production included such economic activities which add form of utility to the materials produced by the primary sector. Several stages may be involved in the conversion of basic materials into more finely processed goods and more value is added at each stage.

Due to clustering of industries around cities, urbanization is increasing with rapid rate. Secondary activities around towns like Durgapur, Bokaro, Bhilai, Jamshedpur (steel plants), etc., have led to rapid urbanization in these areas.

Tertiary Production and Urbanization: It includes economic activities which are concerned with the exchange and consumption of goods and services. It includes all those activities associated with commerce and distribution. It also includes personal business, professional services as well as transport and entertainment services.

As the towns expand, the need arose to keep it clean for water supply. All this led to the employment of people in tertiary activities such as transport sector, educational institutions, hospitals, banks, etc. All these led to the growth of urbanization.

CENTRAL PLACE THEORY

The theory was first given by W. Christaller in 1933. His theory derived very largely from a study of central places in southern Germany. This theory is concerned with discovery of order in the spacing of population clusters and settlements in the landscape. The theory recognises some logic in distribution or spacing of settlements of different sizes and functional importance.

Chrirstaller proposed that settlements with the lowest order of specialisation would be equally spaced and surrounded by hexagonal-shaped service areas or hinterlands. For every six of these lower order settlements, he suggested that there would be a larger and more specialised settlement which, in turn, would be situated at an equal distance from the other settlements of the same order and would also be surrounded by a hexagonal service area. Progressively, more specialised towns with even larger hexagonal-shaped hinterlands would be similarly located at an equal distance from each other.

According to Christaller, the smallest centres would lie approximately 7 km apart. Centres of next order were thought to serve three times the area and three times the population. Thus, they would be located ($\sqrt{3} \times 7$) km or 12 km apart. Similarly, the next series of hinterlands would be three times larger than those of the preceding order.

The Main Theory

A *central place* is defined as a settlement serving as a focal point for a number of other settlements which are dependent on it for some services on a regular, lasting basis with daily periodicity. A *complementary service area* is the area for which central place is the focal point.

17 GEOGRAPHICAL PRESPECTIVE ON SELECTED ISSUES AND PROBLEMS

ENVIRONMENTAL POLLUTION

With the increase in population, demand for food grains increased considerably and with the development of newer and newer technologies to exploit more and more to the natural resources. It led to far-reaching effects upon the natural eco-systems.

The modification and destruction of natural ecosystem through human intervention can be demonstrated by keeping the facts in mind that man has cut, burnt and destoryed millions of square miles of forest land, he has allowed overgrazing to his flocks and herds which has led to the destruction of vast areas of natural pastures; he has instigated large soil erosion by his distrubance or removal of the natural vegetative cover, he has hunted many species of wild life to the point of extinction, he has used pesticides, insecticides, weedicides in such away that plants became highly polluted with it, he has polluted water by sewage, factory waste and agricultural chemicals etc.

Air Pollution

Air, which is a mixture of gases, moisture and some inert material, controls life on earth. It is a reservoir of oxygen needed by man and other animals and of carbon dixoide essential for plants. Any contamination in air may disturb the whole atomospheric system which is an insulating blanket around the earth. Without air, there would be no clouds, no winds, no rain, no snow and no fire. In other words, there would be no life on earth. The atomosphere, which shields the earth from ultraviolet radiation, becomes progessively tenuous with increasing distance from the earth. About 75 per cent of earth's atomosphere lies within 16 kilometres from the surface and 99 per cent of it lies below an altitude of 30 kilometers.

The structure of the atmosphere is controlled by various gases persent in the air. The clear, dry air at sea level contains 78 per cent nitrogen, 21 per cent oxygen, 1 per cent argon and 0.03 per cent carbon dioxide and other gases as shown in following table.

All the major as well as minor components of the air/Atmosphere are biologically important and the participation of each in the living processes is in some cases critically sensitive to slight changes in concentration. Whenever the proportion of the components is disturbed by man, that becomes a cause of air pollution, which nowadays has become a major global problem.

Nature of Air Pollution

In an ecosystem, all the elements act and react in an integrated form, therefore, this life supporting system continues in a systematic way. But when any disturbance is created by man even in a micro form, there is a case of pollution. Growing industrialization and transportation and the increasing use of pesticides and unwanted chemicals in the air has rendered the whole atmosphere polluted and its impact is very dangerous not only on man and other living organisms but also on enviroment itself.

Table I

Composition of clear Dry Air at sea Level

Components	*Per cent by volume*
Nitrogen	78.084
Oxygen	20.9476
Argon	0.934
Carbondioxide	0.0314
Neon	0.001818
Helium	0.000524
Methane	0.0002
Krypton	0.000114
Sulphur dioxide	0 to 0.0001
Hydrogen	0.00005
Nitrous oxide	0.00005
Xenon	0.0000087
Ozone	summer 0.000007 winter 0.000002
Nitrogen dioxide	0 to 0.000002
Iodine	0 to 0.000001
Ammonia	0 to trace
Carbon monoxide	0.1 ppm-0.2 ppm

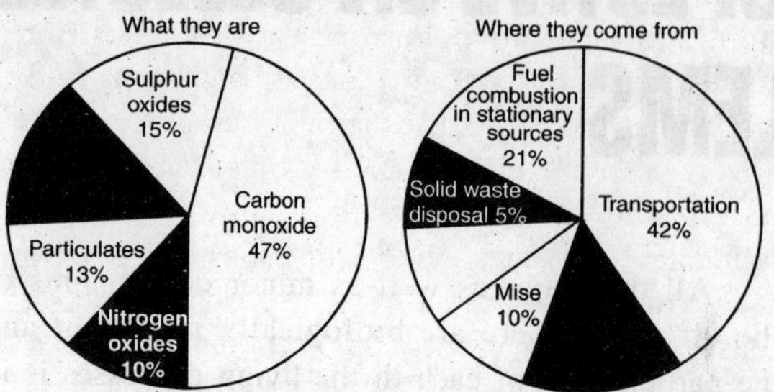

Air pollution may be defined as imbalance in the quality of air so as to cause ill effects. According to Maxwell, "Our enormously accelerated abuse of the atmosphere has become a health hazard and a threat to life, damaging both plants and animals in areas polluted with poisonous fumes, dust and smoke.'' The industrial, automotive and domestic activities have resulted in increasingly outrageous insults to the atmosphere. "In air pollution the pollutants includes gasses and solids and liquid particles of both organic and inorganic chemical classification." The different types of pollutions are continuously introduced into the atmosphere and are removed by natural processes of cleansing. But, when pollution exceeds the atmosphere's self purifying capacity, accumulation of pollutants occurs causing serious hazards for environment and other organisms including humans. The following are the main reasons for the increasing rate of air pollution:

(i) Poisonous gases and other particles emitted from industries without any treatment.
(ii) Heavy increase in the number of automobiles and their emission on (smoke and other dangerous gases).
(iii) Increased use of chemicals and petrochemicals.
(iv) Population concentration in cities.
(v) Fast rate of deforestation.
(vi) Tests of experiments of atomic weapons.
(vii) Tests of chemicals and biochemical weapons.
(viii) Space research and satellite wastes.
(ix) Unorganized mining and traditional practices of the use of fuel wood etc.

Certain natural events such as volcanic eruption, dust storms etc. are also a cause of air pollution. In order to understand the nature of air pollution, it is necessary to know the various sources of pollution.

Sources of Air Pollution

Air pollution is the result of the combined effects of several pollutants. These pollutants are associated with each other and also react with other elements, therefore, it is difficult to categorize them, but for proper understanding they can be divided into the following categories on the basis of their origin, nature, size, impact, etc.

1. According to origin, particulate matter can be divided into two types, *viz.*, natural and man-made. The natural form of particulate matter is the result of volcanic dust and gases, mineral dust, sea-salt, crystals. Another class of natural particulate matter is smoke from forest fires and grass fires. Living plants release pollens and spores into the air, these are organic compounds. From forest trees certain hydrocarbons called terpenes are also released into the atmosphere.

Man-made particulate matter comes from many sources, but the major source is from the combustion of hydrocarbon fuels petroleum products, coal, peat and wood. Combustion of solid wastes is another source. Other kinds of matter introduced into the atomsphere are industrial chemicals, fly ash, refining fossil fuels, mining and smelting ores, as well as pollutants discharged through quarring, farming activities, etc. Use of various types of solvents and also radioactive elements are the cause of air pollution created by man.

2. Another classification according to Origin is *(i)* primary, and *(i)* secondary pollutants. The primary pollutants are those gaseous and other solid micro particles inducted to the atomsphere. These pollutants are emitted and as such are not found in the air. The most important gaseous pollutants are carbon monoxide, oxides of sulphur, hydrogen sulphide, hydrocarbons, oxides of nitrogen, ozone and other oxidants. Secondary pollutants are the result of chemical reactions. Evidences and experiments indicate that exhaust gases of automobiles contribute more in the formation of secondary pollutants. For example, oxides of nitrogen produced in the combustion of petroleum and other rules emitted into the atmosphere, yield ozone in the presence of sunlight. It is to be noted that ozone is not emitted as such into the atomsphere but formed only from primary pollutants.

3. According to chemical composition air pollutants can be divided into organic pollutants and inorganic pollutants. Other have divided them into solid, liquid and gaseous pollutants. The gaseous pollutants are carbon monoxide, sulphurdioxide, hydrogen chloride, oxides of nitrogen, aldehydes and organic acids, etc. Particular pollutants consist of both solid and liquid particles. They vary in size from 0.01 micron to 20 microns. Dust, fume, mist, spray, smoke are included in this category.

4. According to source type, pollutants can be classified as being produced from :

(i) combustion
(ii) transportation emissions
(iii) industrial processes
(iv) use of solvents, and
(v) radioactivity.

Combustion processes yield particulates such as fly ash and smoke and oxides of sulpher and nitrogen. The amount of sulphurdioxide emitted depends upon the contents in the fuel. High temperature processes such as thermal fixation of atmospheric nitrogen yield larger quantities of oxides of nitrogen. Carbon monoxide is also emitted from combustion. The other contaminants that are produced by combustion include acids and aldehydes.

The simplest form of combustion is the use of fuels in domestic use. In India as well as in many developing countries, wood, coal, cow-dung and kerosene oil are commonly used. All these materials yield carbondioxide, carbon monoxide, sulphur dioxide etc.

Automobiles may be considered as the main source of air pollution, specially in urban areas. Automobile exhausts release smoke and to a certain extent lead particles also, smoke contains the gaseous pollutants carbon monoxide, hydro carbons and oxides of nitrogen. The pollutants emitted by petrol and diesel driven vehicles are as follows :

Table II
Pollutants Emitted by petrol and Diesel Driven Vehicles

Emissions	*Petrol Engine*	*Diesel Engine*
Carbon monoxide	3	
Sulphur dioxide	40 ppm	400 ppm
Nitrogen oxides	1100 ppm	300 ppm
Unburnt hydro-carbons	150 ppm	20 ppm
Particulate matter	0.1 g/m³	0.01 g/m³

The rapid rate of industrialization has resulted in more and more air pollution. Various industrial processes release almost all types of pollutants into the air. Some industries like-cement, iron and steel, fertilizer, petrochemical etc., are of great concern because of the difficulty in controlling the emission of pollutants from them. Acid rain has become a great threat to the environment. The use of solvents is increasing with the growing use of paints, 'spray, polish etc. Due to presence of hydrocarbons in these materials, air pollution is caused, which is dangerous for health. Similarly spray of pesticides in agriculture is also responsible for air pollution even in rural areas.

Nuclear material, when released into the air, is hazardous for all living organisms. Nuclear weapon testing nuclear reactors, chemical processing plants, research institutes and hospitals contribute many radionuclides to the atmosphere.

The following table indicates the main sources of air pollution and their impact:

Table III
Main Pollutants of Air and their Impact on Health

Pollutant	*Sources*	*Health Hazards*
1. Carbon mono-xide	Automobiles-due to incom plete combustion burning of carbon in the fuel of internal combus-tion engine.	Displaces oxygen in blood, reduces amo-unt of oxygen to blood tissues. Dulls mental performance causes accident proness. Extra burden on anaemic, heart and lung patients.
2. Particul-ates (soot, smoke, fly ash, etc,)	stationary fuel combustion in industrial process	occurrence of photo-chemical smog which can cause wide spread details in a few days.
3. Oxides of sulphur	mainly industrial processes invol-ving burning of coal and oil as fuel.	temporary or perma-nent injury to the respiratory tract and and lung tissue.
4. Hydro carbons	Automobiles, fuel combustion in electric power	Gaseous hydro-carbon in atmos-phere are not toxic

	plants, industrial process, combustion in solid waste disposal and agricultural-burning	but help in forming photo-chemical smog.
5. Oxides of nitrogen	Burning of fuel at very high temperatures as in transport vehicles, power plants and industrial boilers.	Nitrogen oxides combine with hydrocarbons in the presence of ultra violet rays of the sun to from secondary pollutants called photo-chemical oxidants.
6. Others	photo-chemical oxidants.	photo chemical oxidants feroxy-acetyl, nitrogen, aldehydes and acrolein cause eye irritation and flu, when they combine with particulates to form smog.

Specific Phenomena Related with Air Pollution

Ozone is normally present in the atomosphere at about 0.05 ppm at sea level. It is produced naturally in the atmosphere by the action of electric discharge on oxygen. Ultraviolet radiation in the wavelength of 260 mm is absorbed by oxygen molecules, causing them to react in this manner. Radiation from the sun probably causes high concentrations of ozone in the outer portions of the earth's atmosphere. Ozone is an important component of so-called (smoke-fog). Ozone plays a key role in the photo-chemical formation of atmospheric pollutants as well as being end product in the intricate complex of reactions that take place. The ozone layer provides a cover to the earth's surface and protects the earth from ultraviolet rays.

Until 1974, atomospheric scientists were proceeding in their research on possible impacts of nitrogen oxide Jet engine exhausts on the ozone layer. But later it was found that a new threat to the ozone layer has emerged from synthetic chemicals called chlorofluoro-Carbons. These are simple compounds of the elements chlorine, fluorine and carbon. The chlorine can destroy ozone. Recen scientific studies indicate that if chlorofluorocarbor production continues to grow at the present rate, the compound will enter the stratosphere in quantitie capable of seriously depleting the ozone layer normally termed as 'holes in ozone layer.'

The use of chlorocarbon is increasing becaus of the demand of 'personal care products' such a deodrants, hair sprays, shaving creams and countles other consumer cosmetic products as well as i refrigeration. The ozone layer serves as a shield protecting the troposphere and earth's surface from most of the ultraviolet radiation found in the sun's rays. If these ultraviolet rays reach the earth's surface in fully intensity, all exposed bacteria would be destroyed; plants and animal tissues would be severely damaged. In this protective role, the presence of the ozone layer is an essential factor in man's enviroment.

Greenhouse Effect

The temperature at the surface of the earth is maintained by the energy balance between the sun's rays that strip the planet and the heat that is radiated back into space, some of the heat is absorbed and retained by the earth or objects on the surface. Much of this does not pass through the air envelope to outer space but is absorbed by the carbon dioxide and water vapour in the atmosphere and adds to the heat that is already present. Thus, carbon dioxide acts like the glass of a greenhouse, and on a global scale, tends to warm the air in the low levels of the atmosphere. This is called the greenhouse effect which is also responsible for the increase in temperature over the earth's surface.

Scientists are of the opinion that carbon dioxide will increase global temperature significantly. There is no two opinion about the fact that due to industrial and other forms of air pollution the carbon dioxide content is increasing. Volcanic eruptions are also responsible for the increase of carbon dioxide. Volcanic activity during historical period as well as in present times has thrown out dust and ash which spread throughout the entire atmosphere and last for years.

There is evidence that the temperature of the entire earth has risen slightly during recent decades. Between 1885 and 1940, atmospheric warming was a world-wide phenomenon. There was an increase in mean annual air temperature of about 0.5°C. The greatest increase in mean annual temperature was in the northern hemisphere between 40°N and 70°N, lat and where there was an increase in the average winter temperature of 1.6°C. After 1940, this process of global warming has become much slower, but with the increase in carbon dioxide content of the atmosphere from combustion, the prediction of global warming is there. This will result in the receding of glaciers and melting of snow and increase in the sea level. That may destroy not only the coastal regions but also other parts of the earth.

With the increase in temperature, scientists have predicted that the process of melting of ice caps of Antarctic, Greenland, etc., may lead to a rise in the sea level. Some of them have pointed out that there is a rise of four feet in evey 10 years. There is a crucial relationship between the presence of the polar ice cap and global temperatures and if it happens its impact on climatic conditions of the world will be drastic and change the entire pattern of our ecosystem.

Acid Rain

Acid rain is the outcome of sulphur dioxide gas (SO_2), released into the air by the combustion of fossils fuels. This readily forms sulphuric acid (H_2SO_4) in the minute water films of suspended droplets in the air over cities. The washout of sulphuric acid by precipitation results in rain water with an abnormally high content of the sulphate ion, a condition known as acid rain. Nitric acid, may also contribute to the acidity of rain water.

The degree of acidity is measured in terms of pH value of rainwater. The pH of rain water as measured in the laboratory is 5.65 owing to the dissolution of atmospheric CO_2 in it. Rain, having a pH value of less than 5.65, the value resulting from the equilibrium between atmospheric CO_2 and pure distilled rain water at 25°C, can be termed as acid rain.

In recent years, it has been pointed out by water chemists that pH value of rain in North-Western Europe and USA is going down to 3 and 5, which is an indication of acidity in rain water. The pH numbers are on a logarithmic scale, these values mean that rain in these areas has now often 100 to 1000 times more acid than before. After studying rain water for 20 years US scientists have reported average pH value of about 4. They have also observed values as low as 2.1 in rain water at certain localities. The acid rain is now not only the problem of industrial developed world but is also seen in countries like India. Khemani and his associates (1989), in an article "spread of Acid Rain over India", have summarized the observations as shown in Table.

Some of the adverse environmental effects of acid rain are; excessive leaching of nutrients from plants; foliage and the soil, disturbance of balance of predators and prey in aquatic ecosystem; various metabolic disturbances to organisms; acidification of lakes and streams and the corrosion of structures.

Table IV
Average pH Values of rain water over cities in India

High pH values (> 7.0)	*Medium pH Values (7.0 – 6.0)*	*Low pH Values (6.0-4.5)*	*Very low pH values (<4.5)*
Ahmeda-bad	Agra	Trivendr-um	Chembur (Bombay)
Allahabad	Bhopal	-	-
Amritsar	Kolkata	-	-
Bikaner	Chandigrah	-	-
Jaisalmer	Delhi	-	-
Jodhpur	Nagpur	-	-
Lucknow	Visakhap-atnam	-	-
Srinagar	-	-	-

Smog

'Smog' is the name given for 'smoke + fog'. The term was first used by H.A. Des Voeux in 1911 in a report on smoke fog deaths. During the Autumn of 1909 in Glasgow, Scotland, 1063 deaths were attributed to smoke and fog in 1903, in Meuse valley of Belgium, a large number of people were made ill and many were killed by smog. The 'black fog' that settlled on London in December 1952 caused 3,500 to 4,000 deaths. It was fog accompanied by thermal inversion over most of the British Isles. In Pennsylvania smog killed 20 people and about 40 percent population became ill. The residents of the Konto plains area of Yokohama, Japan were afflicted with an accumulation of smog during winters of 1945 and 1946. Similar type of attack was reported in New Orleans, Louisiana in 1959. In recent years, with the increase in atmospheric pollution, the instances of smog resulting in serious injury or deaths have also become common.

The most irritating and injurious components of smog are the products of reactions in the atmosphere between oxygen, ozone and emission pollutants. The mixture of these products is called photo-chemical smog. These are reactions in which oxygen, ozone, nitrogen oxides and hydrocarbons produce those compounds which are toxic and irritating.

The constituents of smog are quite toxic and are responsible for respiratory and cardiac difficulties. Eye irritation is the most common symptom of smog injury. Similarly, bronchial asthma, chronic bronchitis and pulmonary emphysema are associated with smog. It is also injurious to animal and plants and one of the main causes of environmental degradation.

Pollution by Vehicular Exhaust

The automobile is man's greatest achievement in minimizing distances. The number of automobiles is increasing day by day and has become a cause of air pollution and degradation of the environment. The automobile with its internal combustion engine, emits poisonous gases which are harmful to human health and is the most serious pollution problem of the technical age.

Exhaust emission from diesel engines include carbon monoxide, hydrocarbons, sulphur oxides, organic acids, etc. The two primary pollutants are cabon monoxide and nitrogen dioxide, both of which are extremely poisonous gases and are present in the atmosphere of urban areas, specially in metropolitan areas. A third form of pollutant is constituted by the unburned hydrocarbons of gasoline. Lead is also a very toxic compound and its main source in the environment is believed to be from leaded gasoline used as fuel for internal combustion engines. The lead usually added to gasoline is the organic compound *tetraethyl lead* (TEL), which is extremely poisonous. The presence of lead in the atmosphere is a threat to the environment as well as for all living organisms.

It becomes clear from the above analysis that the problem of air pollution is increasing with the growth and expansion of industries and automobiles. It is high time that all of us should know the harmful effects of air pollution and also evolve technology to control it.

Effects of Air Pollution

Air pollution has now become a widespread problem and every individual in one way or the other is facing problems caused by air pollution. Its impact can be seen locally, at regional level as well as at global level. At local and regional levels its manifestation are in the form of alterations in: *(i)* Visibility *(ii)* intensity of sunshine *(iii)* precipitation amount and *(iv)* acid rain. Its global effects are : *(i)* change in natural climate by rise of temperature, melting of snow *(ii)* increase in carbon dioxide *(iii)* increase in particulates *(iv)* holes in ozone layer etc., several aspects of air pollution, such as effects on the ozone layer, greenhouse effect, smog and acid rain have already been discussed. The effects of air pollution can be grouped under the following heads:

(i) effects on human health,
(ii) effects on animals and plants,
(iii) effects on atmosphere and
(iv) other effects.

Effects on Human health

Some environmental poisons can cause acute illness and even death. Others may be harmful, but the disease may take years or even decades to appear. Air pollution mainly affects the respiratory system. Bronchitis, emphysema, asthma and lung cancer are some of the chronic diseases caused due to exposure to polluted air. It is feared that lung cancer is caused mainly due to polluted air because carcinogens are found in the polluted air. Its mortality rate is higher in urban areas. It shows the various effects of air pollution on the human body. Sulphur dioxide is the most serious and widespread air pollutant. Its lower concentration is a cause of spans in the smooth muscle of bronchioles and its higher concentration induces increased mucus production, sulphur dioxide is also considered to cause cough, shortness of breath, spasm of the larynx and acute irritation to the membranes of the eyes. SO_2 also acts as an allergenic agent. When it reacts with some compounds, sulphuric acid is formed which may damage lungs.

Carbon monoxide often affects the oxygen carrying capacity of blood. Nitric oxide is reported to be a pulmonary irritant and its excess concentration may cause pulmonary haemorrhage. Hydrogen sulphide is also toxic. Lead emitted from automobile exhausts is a cumulative poison and is dangerous particularly to children and may cause brain damage.

The particulate pollutants such as asbestos, silica, carbon, berryllium, lead etc, are capable of exerting a noxious (fibrotic) local action in the interstitial areas of the lungs. Radioactive elements are also harmful to man and other living organisms. As described earlier, smog has a piller effect, which is the result of air pollution. The death toll by smog varies from few persons to thousands. In December 1952, about 4,000 persons died in London itself in 1956, 1957 and 1962 in which the death toll was between 700 and 1,000 persons. In other countries also, smog death have been reported. In fact, the growing air pollution has now become a health hazard for man.

Effects on Animals and Plants

The impacts of air pollution on animals is more or less similar to that of effects on man. Chronic poisoning results from the ingestion of forage contaminated with atmospheric pollutants. Among the metallic contaminants arsenic, lead and molybdenum are important, Fluoride is another pollutant which causes fluorosis among animals. A number of livestock have been poisoned by fluorides and arsenic in North American. Bone lesions in animals due to excessive fluorides have also been reported.

Air pollution has caused widespread damage to trees, fruits, vegetables, flowers and in general, vegetation as a whole. The total annual cost of plant damage caused by air pollution in USA alone has been estimated to be in the range of 1 to 2 billion dollars. The most dramatic early instances of plant damage were seen in the total destruction of vegetation by sulphur dioxide in the areas surrounding smelters. When the absorption of sulphur dioxide exceeds a particular level, the cells become inactive and are killed, resulting in tissue collapse and drying of leaves. Cotton, wheat, barley and apple are more sensitive to this pollutant.

Fluorides are responsible for various types of injuries to plants. The leaves of apple, apricot, fig, peach, prune are more susceptible to air borne fluorides, fluorides seen to interfere with the photosynthesis and respiration of plants, smong also causes injury to plants, similar impact of ozone can be seen in the lesions to plants, Chlorine, ammonia, hydrogen sulphide etc., are also harmful to vegetation.

Effects on Atmosphere

Some of the effects of air pollution on atmospheric conditions have already been discussed such as effect on ozone layer, greenhouse effect etc. There is an increase in the carbon dioxide concentration in the air due to increased combustion of fossil fuels. Carbondioxide absorbs heat strongly and the radiative cooling effect of the earth is thus decreased. The rising of temperatures and ozone holes are some of the problems which have attracted the attention of the scientists of the world. These problems are not related to any region or a country but are the global problems and their impact on world climate may be hazardous to the whole world. The local weather conditions are highly susceptible to air pollution. Its impact on temperature, humidity, rainfall and clouds is apparent. The 'smog dom' on large urban centres are the result of air pollution. Due to air pollution visibility also reduces.

Other Effects

Air pollution can also cause damage to property and materials. The smoke, grit, dust and oxides of sulphur have harmful effects on structures. In 1972, when an oil refinery at Mathura was opened, its impact on Taj Mahal became a major issue. Sulphur dioxide is the most damaging of gaseous pollutants. Aluminium alloys, copper and copper alloys, iron and steel are corroded when exposed to contaminated air. Hydrogen sulphide reacts with lead paints to form lead sulphide theory producing a brown to black discolouration. The damage caused by air pollution to structures is not serious but form an aesthetic point of view it is not desirable.

Measures for controlling Air pollution

World-wide efforts are going on to control air pollution. Scientists and technologists have developed certain measures but still progress in this field is not satisfactory. For the control of air pollution there is a need to deal this problem from two angles : *(i)* to check the present prevalent air pollution in such a way that their harmful effects can be minimized and *(ii)* to develop such methods and technology so that air pollution can be controlled in future, some of the measures to control air pollution are as follows:

1. The forest cover should be protected by restricting deforestation and through adoption of afforestation programmes. Trees are the best controllers of air pollution. It is an accepted fact that

33 percent of the land area should remain under forest tree cover. It will help in controlling air pollution and also help in maintaining the ecological balance.

2. There must be a 'green belt' around every township and village. Similarly, industrial areas, should be surrounded by green belts.

3. The main source of air pollution is the automobiles, therefore, their engines should be redesigned in such a way that their emission cause minimum pollution. Several steps have been taken and some technology has also been developed, but still it is in a very preliminary stage. Apart from techno-logical changes, some steps on individual level should be taken by auto owners, such as :

(i) regular service of the vehicle,
(ii) change or replacement of old engines,
(iii) use of filters and after burner,
(iv) the engine should be well tuned and
(v) mixing of anti tibs in diesel and petrol etc.

4. The use of steam engine by the railways should be stopped or minimized. As far as possible, electrically operated rail engines should be used, which are pollution free.

5. In countries like India traditional use of fuelwood, coal etc., should be checked and newly devised smoke free furnaces be used.

6. The industrial areas should be located at a certain distance from residential areas. The selection of the site should be done with consideration of air direction.

7. Steps should be taken for immediate check on forest fires. For this purpose proper arrangement and sound infrastructure is necessary.

8. In industries, arrangements for pollution control should be done. Only after full arrangements of effluent treatment is done, permission for production should be given.

9. With the help of chemical reactions, harmful effects of pollution can be controlled. Measures for such methods should be taken and the methodology and material should be available to the concerned presons.

10. Some methods of controlling air pollution are filtering, settling, dissolving, absorption etc. For these methods cheap devices should be developed.

Actual prevention of air pollution is not so simple as explained above. However, much of the pollution could be minimized or controlled without undue cost by careful planning. For this, the following steps will be helpful.

1. Control of Gaseous Pollutants : The equipments which can be used to control gaseous pollutants are classified as combustion, absorption and adsorption equipments. *Combustion* is applicable to pollutant gases which are oxidizable. In petro-chemical, fertilizer, paint and varnish industries combustion control equipments are useful. *Absorption* is a diffusional process in which the transfer of gas molecules into a liquid phase takes place. Such equipments include spray chambers, packed towers and sieve plate contractors. Absorption is the means of controlling air pollution which occurs due to some gases and vapours and inflammable compounds which cannot be treated by other means.

2. Control of Emission from Motor Vehicles: The emission control techniques include tune-ups, catalytic reactors and engine modifications. A high air-fuel ratio will reduce the concentration of both carbon monoxide and hydrocarbons. The modified engines have an efficient system of burning of the fuel. At present, there is no system of reduction of sulphur dioxide although, researches in this direction are in progress throughout the world.

3. Control of Aerosol Emissions: This can be controlled by arresters and serubbers. Arresters include inertial separators, filters and precipitators. The electrostatic precipitators is considered to be the most effective device for preventing the emission of dust from fuel gases and is the standard equipment for large power stations.

4. Control by fuel selection and Utilization: Coal and oil are the primary fuels in which smoke, grit and sulphur dioxide are the major pollutants. Coal pollutes more because it releases more smoke and carbon in the air. Instead of coal, oil can be used but in oil, the amount of sulfur dioxide emission is higher. Therefore, fuel selection should be done properly and the harmful impact be restricted by inducing other chemicals. In order to control smoke, the coal is pulverized before being used. When oil is used for fuel, it is essential that the ratio of air should be maintained constant in order to prevent smoke emissions.

5. Control of Air Pollution by site selection and Zoning: Selection of an industrial site is the most important factor through which impact of air pollution can be minimized. The industrial site should be selected considering *(i)* residential areas

ii) nature of industries and (iii) climatic conditions, specially the direction of winds.

The UNO and WHO have issued guidelines to its members for the formulation of laws regarding prevention of air pollution, in India, the prevention of Air and water pollution Act, 1974, 1981, the Air prevention and control of pollution Act, 1981 and the environmental protection Act, 1986, have been enacted for air pollution control it can be checked only through the combined efforts of the government, NGOs and the public.

Noise Pollution, land pollution and pollution by radioactivity

Sound Pollution

Sound is a normal feature of our life and a medium through which communication is possible, it may be pleasant, like the sound of running water of a stream or the sweet sound of the birds in the forest or the pleasant sound produced by music instruments. On the other hand, it may be the noisy and harsh sound of lighting and thunder or noise produced by machines, automobiles, railways, aeroplanes or even the blaring sound of loud speakers or some musical instruments. But all sounds are not noise"Noise is any sound that is not wanted. It is one of the more common forms of atmospheric pollution". Sound is caused by the vibration of molecules, while noise radiates from vibrating surfaces. More and more noise is the creation of modern civilization and has now become a major envornmental pollutant specially in urban areas. In 1972, the UN environment conference at Stockholm, noise problem has been accepted as a problem, which needs proper control.

Noise pollution is an environmental problem that has only recently received much attention, yet it has been decades in the making. The perception of noise as a problem is different for diffrent people.

Noise at certain levels might be an aggravation or nuisance for some, while at higher levels, noise might become a more widespread or general aggravation. At still, higher levels, noise, noise might fall within discomfort rangen and at even higher levels, it may lead to physical and psychological damage.

Measurement of sound/noise and its intensity

The most popular measure of noise level is the decibel measured by an instrument known as decibel metre. A sound between 0 and 1, decibel is about the weakest that the average human can hear. For testing purposes, 0 decibel is considered to be the threshold of hearing. A whisper is about 20 decibels and an average speaking voice is about 60 decibels. The loudest sound that a person can stand without discomforts is about 90 decibels.

Automobiles horns may reach 90 decibels and a Jet airplane may have an intensity of about 140 decibels. The levels of common noise is give in the table.

In most of the countries, maximum limit fixed for noise is 75 to 85 decibels. According to scientists noise above 90 decibels for long time may result in deaftness. In the most of the cities in India, the noise level is 75 to 90 decibels put is more in industrial areas, near aerodromes, railway stations and highways, etc. but since noise pollution is increasing day by day, planning for its control should be done, Actually loudness alone is not the role cause of noise problem. Pitch of the noise also influences the degree of annoyance, higher the pitch the greater the annoyance duration of noise also determines how annoying or irritating noise will be. The degree of noise in closed space or indoors is different from the level of outdoor noise.

Source of Pollution

The sources of noise can be divided into two categories, *viz,* natural and artificial.

Natural sources are associated with natural phenomena like lighting, volcanic eruption, earthquakes, sound of the ocean waves, etc. These reasons are local or regional and generally their impact is very limited and not very harmful. On the contrary, noise produced by man is much greater and harmful.

Artificial sources are responsible for noise pollution. The sources of noise pollution in an industrial society are manifold. The main sources in cities and other highly developed countries are noise associated with transportation, automobiles, motorcycles, rail engines, buses, fire brigade, police cars, ambulances, air planes, industries, high Pitched musical instruments etc. During religious or domestic functions and in political meetings during elections noise pollution often increases due to use of electronic medium of sound.

The main source of noise, however, comes from transport. The number of road vehicles, particularly, diesel engine vehicles, has increased the level of noise enormously. This problem is more in metropolitan cities where number of vehicles ply simultaneously and their noise is unbearable, the horns and sirens used by these vehicles, specially, the pressure horns are very noisy. The value of horns and sirens except in emergencies is questionable. The whistle of rail engines is very harmful to the ears. Busy traffic streets, highways, bus stands and railway stations have problems of noise pollution. Lager and faster jet aircrafts have been built over the years and have become one of the most troublesome sources of noise pollution.

TABLE V

Intensity of various sounds

Sound source	*Intensity*	*Response criteria*
	0-10	audible
Broad casting Studio	20	-
Soft whisper (15 feet)	30	very quiet
Library bedroom Slow radio	30-50	quiet
Light audio traffic, air Conditioning unit freeway	50-70	Intrusive
Traffic fright team	70-80	annoying
Motor cycle, heavy traffic	80-100	very annoying hearing damage
Rail noise	110-130	intolerable
Lighting thunder	120	„
Career deckjet operation	140	painfully loud.

For example, international airport in Chicago, the busiest airport in the world, has more than a thousand operational Jet flights on average day. This means a flight in or out every 40 seconds. The residents within 20 km radius from the airport are facing great problems not only in their conversations, television viewing, sleep and relaxation but it has also begin to tell on their health. The air traffic has increased to an extent that nobody likes a new air field in this neighbourhood.

Noise associated with manufacturing, building, constructions, mining, road, building, etc, are sound in intensity to transportation noises. But their impact is felt more by factory and other workers. It is reported that noise inside factories can become a health hazard causing deafness. Industrial noise particularly from mechanical saws and preumatic drills, is unbearable and nuisance to the ears.

The impact of noise in a factory varies with age groups. For workers below 30 years of age, the 95 decibel noise is not harmful, put for 40 to 50 years age group this limit is 84 decibels and for 50 to 60 years age the bearable limit is 80 decibels.

In mining, noise produced by blasting and digging is also an uncomfortable noise.

Now a days, music has also become noisy and the electronic medium and the instruments have further developed its intensity. In a closed space, high volume music is harmful and is responsbile for noise pollution. Similarly, during social and religious functions, marriages and other gathering including political meetings, the use of high volume loudspeakers has become a common feature and an irritating cause of noise pollution. The popular 'pop music' may be entertaining but its ultimate impact is not healthy for man.

Effects of noise pollution

The most notable of noise pollution is on hearing. Violent noise can cause temporary or permanent impairment of hearing, thus of a cause of deafness. Continual noise can lead for gradual decline auditory activity and eventual deafness. Acute damage occurs to the eardrum when exposed to very loud sudden noises.

Noise causes several undesirable effects also. Damage and loss of sleep are only two of the obvious results. Noises produce irritability and a feeling of fatigue and may reduce a worker's efficiency. There is evidence that noise is of the major cause of stress and anxiety. It also has its impact an blood pressure and is a cause of other cardiovascular diseases. The rate of heart beat may be affected may be noise. A recent report indicates that blood is also thickened by excessive noises. Eosinophill hyperglycemia, hypokalemia, and hypoglycemia also caused by a change in blood and other body fluids else to noise. Noise also causes headaches and irritability. The effects of noise on the foetus are not fully known, medical scientists have noted that an urban child will move and kick when there is a level noise. Some of studies indicate that children born in areas of high noise have some defects in comparison, to the children born, in peaceful areas.

Control of noise pollution

Since noise pollution is created by man. It can be controlled by adopting certain measures. Some of measures are as follows :

(i) Noise producing industries should be located away from residential areas.

(ii) Inside industries proper arrangements to minimize noise be done by constructing sound proof walls and also to provide such instruments to workers which can protect their ears from noise.

(iii) old machines often create more noise, therefore, all the machines should be well maintained and replaced if necessary.

(iv) the automobile horn should be designed in such a way that the noise it produces may not be harmful.

(v) use of horn should be minimum and pressure horn should be baned as has been done in many countries.

(vi) the noise created by musical instruments and other in door equipments can be checked by individuals in their own interest.

(vii) The noise created by railway can be checked by construction of ballastless rail tracks.

(viii) special arrangements done to check noise near air bases. Control of aircraft noise requires several changes, which should be done.

(ix) Dense tree plantations around or nearby areas of noise can also reduce its intensity.

(x) Every Govt. has enacted certain laws to control noise population. The basic need is the proper implementation of these laws and regular supervision in countries like India the problem of noise pollution is still in its many stage, therefore, measures to control this problem are necessary.

Soil and land Pollution : The problem of solid wastes disposal.

Although ¼ of the surface of the earth is land surface, half of this surface is not useful to man due to permanent snow cover, deserts, mountains, etc, and only about 448 lakh sq./kms of land can be used by man for his multifarious activities. Any misuse or wastage of land may create problems not only for the present generation, but for the future ones as well. The problem of land and soil pollution is growing day by day with the rapid growth of population, urbanization, industrialization, agricultural and other developmental activities.

Land pollution is the result not only of man's misuse of land but more due to solid waste disposal. The disposal of solid waste is more problem of developed nations but now it has also become a grow problem of all the countries of the world, solid wastes are dumped in the ocean or open grounds; mining wastes are produced at the rate of millions of tons a day; stag heaps and miltilings accumulate near processing operations; and industrial refuse contaminates streams and lakes. Only in U.S.A. solid waste produced annually includes 30 million tons of paper and paper products, 4 million tons of plastics, 30 billion bottles, 60 billion cans, 100 million tyres, 8 million junked and abandoned automobiles and millions of major appliances of innumerable makes, sizes and kinds. No one knows the total amount of world's waste, but is certain that the problem of solid waste disposal now has become a threat to our environment, specially the enviornment of our cities.

Land pollution can be defined as the changes in physical, chemical and biological conditions of the soil through man's intervention or misuse of land resulted into degradatory in quality and productivity of the soil. The problem of land pollution differs from water and air pollutions in the respect that the pollutions remain in place for relatively longer periods, rapid urbanization with the consequent increase in buildings has resulted in the reduction of lands for the wastes to be disposed. Dumping of industrial and municipal wastes causes leaching by toxic materials which seep in to the soil and affect the ground course.

Agricultural practices introduce pesticides, fertilizers and manures to the land resulting in both biological and chemical contamination.

Thus, land and soil pollution increasing day by day hazards materials and micro-organisms enter the food chain or water and are consequently ingested by man.

Therefore, there is an urgent need not only to control the soil of the pollution but also for its proper management.

Sources of land pollution

The soil and land pollution is the result of several sources, which can be categorized under following heads :

A. Domestic and musical wastes
B. Industrial and mining wastes,
C. Agricultural wastes
D. Rodioactive materials
E. and biological agents. *(i)* Domestic and municipal wastes

One of the main cause of land and soil pollution is the growing quantity of domestic and municipal wastes.

Household garbage includes food scraps, old newspapers, a variety of plastic items, bottles, discarded papers, wood, lawn trimmings, glass, canes old appliances, tyres, worn out furniture, broken toy and a host of other items. The total quantity of solid waste is large and increasing. In United States, municipal solid waste averaged 1.2 kg per person per day in 1920. The quantity rose to 2.3 kg in 1970 and 3.6 kg in 1980 and now its quantity is more than 4.5 kg. Urban wastes comprise both commercial and domestic wastes including dried sludge of sewage. In general, all the urban solid wastes are referred to as 'refuse'.

The amount of solid wastes generated is directly related with prosperity.

In contrast to the 3.6 kg. per person per day in the United States, residents of Australia produce 0.8 kg per person per day. The everage person in India produces only about 0.2 kg per day. The general composition of municipal wastes is as follows :

Table VI
Average composition of municipal refuse in developed countries (% by weight)

Paper wastes	H_2	
Wood and bar	-	2.4
Grass	-	4.0
brush		1.5
Cutting green		1.5
Leaves dry	-	5.0
Leather goods	-	0.3
Rubber	-	0.6
Plastic	-	0.7
Oil paint's		0.6
Linoleum	-	0.1
Rags	-	0.6
Street refuse	-	3.0
Household dirt	-	1.0
unclassified	-	0.5
Total rubbish		34.0
Garbage	-	9.6
Fats	-	2.0
Total food wastes	-	1.2
Metals	-	8.0
Glass and Ceramics	-	5.0
Ashes	-	10.0
Total non-Combustibles	-	8.4
Grand total	-	100

It has been estimated that in 45 major cities of India, the quantity of average per day muncipal waste is about 50,000 tonnes. The National Environmental Engineering Institute (NEERI) Nagpur, has given details of the muncipal waste in Indian towns as follows :

Table VII
(Nature of solid waste in Indian towns)

Material Composition	*Towns according to Population size*			
	up to 2 lakh	*2 to 5 lakh*	*5 to 20 lakh*	*above*
Paper	3.09	4.74	3.80	7.7
Plastic	0.57	0.59	0.81	0.86
Metals	0.57	0.39	0.64	1.03
Glass	0.29	0.34	0.44	0.76
Ash and dust	46.60	39.97	41.81	34.79
Mixed material	34.41	39.76	40.05	41.74
Carbon	12.36	12.51	11.95	15.92
Nitrogen	0.61	0.61	0.50	0.57
Phosphorus (Phosphate)	0.70	0.71	0.67	0.59
Pottassium	0.70	0.73	0.72	0.67

It becomes clear from the above table that in our cities, 90 per cent wastes includes ash, dust, mixed material and carbon, while in developed countries paper, plastic glass, metal, etc.

The dumping of domestic and municipal wastes is a serious problem in cities because of its impact on environment and public health. Solid wastes may or may not cause diseases in many but are hazardous to health. Diseases such as dysentry, diarrhoea, plague, malaria and numerous others are the result of the indiscriminate dumping of wastes.

Industrial and mining wastes

The disposal of industrial solid wastes is the major source of soil pollution by toxic chemicals. The industrial wastes are mainly discharged from coal and mineral mining industries metal processing industries and engineering industries. They contain toxic metals such as lead, copper and chemicals having acids are responsible for soil pollution. It has been reported that about 50 percent of raw materials ultimately become waste products in industry and about 15 per cent of it are toxic. The chemicals discharged from the industries often enter the surface or groundwater or poison the soil or crops.

The production of consumer goods also involved in environmental problems uncluding lands and soil pollution. The following table lists some of the effects of production of consumer goods.

NOISE POLLUTION AND POLLUTION BY RADIOACTIVITY

Table VIII
Production of Consumer Goods and its Effects on Land/Soil

Process	*Activity*	*Effects*
Extraction	Mining and oil driling	Surface land disruption, acid mine drainage, mine failing, sludge ponds, oil spills.
	Agriculture	Disruption of natural habitats, soil erosion, fertilizer run-off, poisonous pesticides.
	Forestry	Habit disruption, Soil erosion, pesticides
Processing	Manufacturing	Soil and underground water pollution, loss of soil productivity, air and water pollution.
Energy	Energy Conversion and transmission	Deplection of resources, thermal and radio-active pollution, disruption of land for transmission rights of way hitter, land use disruption, release of hazardous wastes, dust, etc

The expansion of mining activities in many countries of the world has now become a main cause of land pollution due to loss of soil and destruction of land.

Agricultural Wastes : Agricultural practices also pollute the soil. According to an estimate agricultural activities produce more than 1.8 billion tonnes of waste each year. Much of this manure is piled in dumps where it pollutes streams and waterways, yet at the same time, farmers across the continent are suffering from worm-out and depleted soils.

Soil Pollution by Radioactive Material: The redioactive wastes produced by nuclear testing laboratories and industries, reach the soil and accumulate there. Wastefrom nuclear reactors contain ruthenium –106 and rhodium – 106, iodine – 131, barium – 140, Lanthanum – 140, cerium – 144 etc.

Soil pollution by Biological Agents : The excreta of humans, animals and birds is also a source of soil pollution by biological agent.

Faulty sanitation, waste water and wrong method of agriculture also include soil pollution.

Harmful Effects of Land/Soil Pollution

The following are the harmful effects of the land and soil pollution :

(i) Land and soil pollution is responsible for loss of fertility and productivity of soil.

(ii) The decomposition of the various types of waste material causes harmful gases and bad smell, which not only polute environment but is also harmful if mixed with chemical.

(iii) The municipal and domestic waste is often discharged in water bodies, thus responsible for water pollution.

(iv) The dumping of waste in oceans is a common practice and a main cause of imbalance of the marine ecosystem.

(v) Industrial and chemical wastes are also responsible for the pollution of underground water.

(vi) Those bacteria which are transmitted from man to soil infect man causing dysentery, cholera, tuberculosis, typhoid, paratyphoid fever, etc.

CONTROL OF LAND AND SOIL POLLUTION

Methods of the disposal of wastes

Land and soil pollution can be controlled by adopting measures for the disposal of solid wastes, which unfortunately involves large finances and tech-nology. Prior to disposal, the watste have to be collec-ted from the places by trucks to the disposal area.

Organic matter rots or is consumed by insects, rates or hogs.

Sanitary landfill is commonly used for final disposal of solid wastes. This is cheaper than other disposal methods and have the advantage of avoiding acute pollution problems associated with discharging wastes into waterways or polluting air from incineration.

Ocean dumping of wastes is practised by many coastal cities. It was considered to be the favourite disposal method under the prevalent notion that the ocean is an infinite capacity for covering, holding, absorbing or decomposing materials, not the capacity for anywhere near the load of pollution that would result if the rate of ocean disposal continues, as in the past.

Incineration is a method through which the volume of waste can be reduced by 60 per cent and it also reduces the public health problems.

Chemical processing of solid wastes is also applied but it is costly and technically not feasible for poor countries. The reclamation of non-ferrous scrapmetals has long been an established industry.

Composting municipal refuse to convert it into a fertilizer and soil conditioner is appealing not only because it appears to be a good way to recycle the resources in solid wastes, but also because of the beneficial nature of the compost.

New methods of waste disposal that are under trial in various parts of the world are :

- The transformation of the organic content into sugar or proteins
- The heating of organic refuse under anaerobic conditions to convert it into useful gases such as methane which is usable as fuel, or into a liquid product.
- The compression of refuse into briquettes that can be used a fill. A mixture of fly ash, dried sewage sludge, incinerator residue and river and lake dredgings is under study.
- The transport of refuse as a liquid slurry in pipelines, a method now under study.

Energy from Refuse

In many metropolitan areas of developed countries, the garbage is burnt in a well-engineered furnance.

Inspite of these difficulties, incineration may become profitable in the future because:

1. Increasingly large quantities of dry paper and cardboard have appeared in refuse, thereby increasing the fuel content of the trash.
2. The price of fuel has skyrocketed and therefore the value of steam has also gone up. Thus it will be more economical day by day.

Recycling of waste material

Most refuse contains a wealth of raw materials that can be easily reused or recycled. The following table indicates the possibilities of recycling the various waste materials :

Table IX

Various Recycling Routes for some common wastes

Waste	*Recycling Possibilities.*
Paper	use the backs of business letters for scrap paper or personal stationery level magazines and newspapers to friends. Repulp to reclaim fibre compost incinerate heat
Glass	Purchase drinks in deposit bottles and return them, use other bottles as storage being in the home Crush and remelt for glass manufacture crush and use as aggregate for building material or antiskid additive for road surface
Tyre	Recape usable casing use of swings, crash guards, boat bumpers, etc. Shred and use of manufacture of new tyres. Grind and use as additive in road construction
Manure	Compost or spread directly on fields. Ferment to yield methane; use residue as compost convert to oil by chemical treatment. Treat chemically and reuse as animal feed
Food Scraps	Save for meals of leftovers sterlize and use as hog food compost Use as culture for yeast for food production
Slaughter house and butcher	Sterlize and use as animal feed.
Shop-wastes	Render compost

It becomes clear from the above table that if the recycling process is adopted properly, not only, can the problem of waste disposal be minimized but it will save financial resources also.

Radioactive Pollution

Nature and sources

Radioactive substances are among the most toxic materials known. Naturally occuring, radioactive elements are present in the rocks, water and air and in all living organisms

Environmental radiation may be divided into two types :

(i) Natural and *(ii)* man-made radiation

Naturally occurring radiations are

(i) cosmic radiations form the outer space reaching the earth's surface and *(ii)* terrestrial radiation from natural radio-isotopes present in the earth's crust. The following table indicates the half-life and radiation of the important radioactive elements

Table X
Commonly used Radionuclides

Material	*Half-life*	*Radionuclides*
Carbon-14	5,568 Yrs.	beta
Cobalt-60	5.24 Yrs.	beta, gamma
Hydrogen-3 (tritium)	12.26 Yrs.	beta
Iodine-131	8.08 days	beta, gamma
Phosphorus-32	14.3 days	beta
Plutonium-239	24,360 Yrs.	alpha, beta, gamma
Strontium-90	27.7 Yrs.	beta
Uranium-235	710 million Yrs.	alpha, gamma
Uranium-238	4.51 billion Yrs.	alpha, beta, gamma

Man-made radiations originate from the activities of man involving the use of radioactive materials. They are used for the production of nuclear weapons, nuclear fuel and for the production of electric power.

Nuclear fuels used in operation of reactors also contribute to pollution.

Effects of Radioactive Pollution

In spite of certain harmful effects of radioactivity, nuclear power and other uses of radioactive elements have become an integral part of modern development.

Monitoring of radiation is very necessary for the control of radiation. The samples of air, water and oil have to be collected regularly and their analysis both manual and instrumental be done, not only to know the actual level of radioactive pollution but also for its control.

There is a need for regular monitoring and clean-up of surface, careful washing is necessary, apart from this proper kit to protect from radiation effects and health care of workers is also necessary.

Water

Water is an essential resources for life on the earth we drink it, bathe in it, relax in it, fish in it, keep cool with it, irrigate the plants, produce energy with it and also use it for transportation and recreation. Many ancient civilizations have developed in river valleys of the Nile, Indus, Tigris and Euphrates etc. Even now also water resources provide a base for social cultural and economic development. It seems that water is abundant, but uscable water is very limited and creates a serious conservation problem in many places where it is needed. Apart from scarcity of water, we are also facing a problem of water. Pollution not of rivers and lakes but also of underground water. The into rable burden of chemical and human waste products have become a threat to aquatic life as well as to human health.

Therefore, much attention has been given to study the various facets of water pollution, not only to understand the nature and effects of water pollution but also for its control.

Sources of water and quality

The planet earth has 71 per cent of its area as ocean and the ocean contain 97% of all water in the form not suitable for human consumption, much of the remainder is frozen in the ice caps and glaciers. The water in rivers and lakes is very small. Less than 1 per cent in the form of ice free fresh water yet this negligible portion of the planet's water is crucially important to all forms of terrestrial and acquatic life. Apart from surface water available in rivers and lakes, under ground water resources are important.

The per cent of land water distribution over earth's surface other than ocean's is as follows :

Rivers and streams	0.14%
Fresh water lakes	01.4%
Salt lakes and inland Sea	01.2%
Soil moisture and seepage	0.7%
Ground water (one km deep)	48.3%
Ground water (below 1 km deep)	, 48.3%

Fresh water is a scarce commodity with greatest amount locked in glaciers and ice caps. But it is constantly replenished in a cyclicway known as hydrological cycle. The hydrological cycle is a simplified description of water movement from place to place.

The cycle begins with evaporation by solar energy. The formation of clouds(condensation) leads to sub-sequent precipitation which results in the conversion of salt water to fresh water. The precipitation on the surface may own off as rivers or may infiltrate into the soil and rock and form ground water. Surface and sub-surface water retruns to the water of ocean unless evaporation interrupts the cycle.

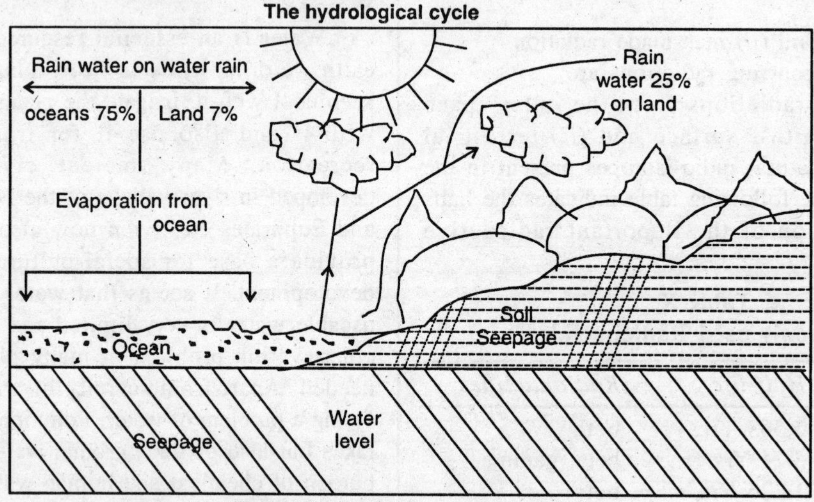

(Permissible limits of impurities in water)

The quality of water is the most important fact or from chemical point of view water is the monoxide of hydrogen (H_2O) in which two parts of hydrogen and one part oxygen are present. But this form of pure water is not available in nature. As soon as water vapour enters into the atmosphere after condensation, impurities like dust, particles, gases etc, are mixed in it and when it reaches the surface several mineral and chemicals are also mixed in it. The quality of drinking water depends on the quantity of harmful elements present in its. Drinking water should be clear, odourless and tasteless and its value should be between 7 and 8.5. In 1971, WHO has given the following limits of various impurities in drinking water.

Table XI

Impurities	*Max. Permissible Limit (mg/litre)*
1. Total solid matters	500
2. Hardness	2.8 eg/litre
3. Calcium (Ca)	75.00
4. Magnesium (Mg)	30.00
5. Sulfate (SO_4)	200.00
6. Iron (Fe)	0.10
7. Manganese (Mn)	0.05
8. Copper (Cu)	0.05
9. Zinc (Zn)	0.05
10. Arsenic (As)	0.05
11. Cadmium (Cd)	0.005
12. Cyanide (Cn)	0.05
13. Lead (Pb)	0.05
14. Mercury (Hg)	0.001
15. Phenolic elements	0.001

The permissible organic impurities include bacillus calinot more than one in 100 m/litre and other coli bacteria not more than 10. In natural water impurities are found in three forms.

(i) Suspended inpurities

(ii) Colloidal impurities, and

(iii) Dissolved impurities.

Supended impurities float on the water surface as dust particles, particles of minerals, paper cloth, foam, leaves and floating vegetation as well as other organic and inorganic materials colloidal impurities are those which are mixed with water and difficult to separate, such as silica glass, oxides of various minerals, micro bacteria, etc., on the other hand dissolved impurities become part of the water during its flow.

These include carbon dioxide (CO_2), sulfur dioxide (SO_2) methane (CH_4), sodium (Na^+), (Fe^{++} = iron) ammonium (NH_4^+), etc.

Apart from these, man has induced several impurities in the water, which are responsible for water pollution

Water pollution

Water pollution simply means contamination of water due to any external material, or in other words, introduction of something to natural water which makes unsuitable for human comsumption. WHO has defined water pollution as any foreign material either from natural or other sources that may contaminate the water supply and makes it harmful to life, cause of their toxicity leads to reduction of normal oxygen level of water, causes aesthetically unpollutable effects and spread of epidemic diseases, "Owen has defined it as many unreasonable contamination of water which lessens its value to man". In general water, "water pollution may be defined as the adverse change in composition or reduction of the water such that it becomes less suitable for the purposes for which it would be suitable in its natural state". The changes include, physical changes, chemical changes and biological changes. 2. According to Gilpil, "the deterioration in chemical, physical and biological properties of water brought about mainly by human activities". 3 is the water pollution. Whatever additions are done to the water either by natural processes or by human activities invariably, they change the natural qualities. The problem of water pollution was recognized by hippocrates (450 BC), who suggested filtration and boiling as remedial measures. With the fast increase in our industrial civilization, the demand for water is also increasing day by day. At the same time, population increase urbanization, improper sewage disposal, unsafe, industrial wastes, readioactives wastes oil etc., have polluted our water resources so much so that 70%, rivers and streams not only of India but of all the countries contain the polluted water.

Sources of Water Pollution

Water pollution is caused by several sources which are not independent in nature but interact with one another. Generally one or two factors are prominent and may be considered the primary source of water pollution. The various sources of water pollution can be classified as follow

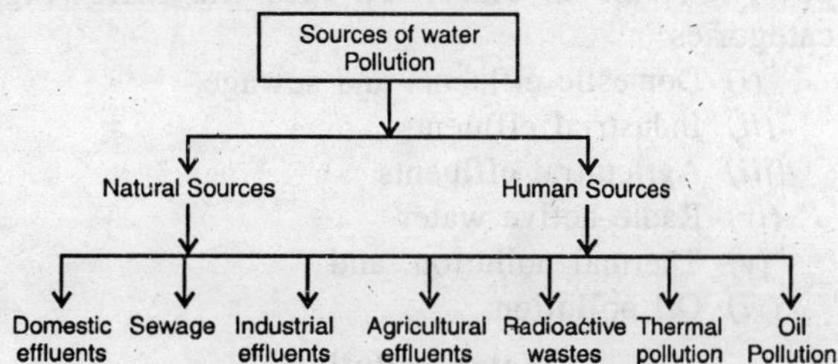

Natural Sources: There are some natural elements which create water pollution. These are gases, soil, minerals, humus material, waste created by animals and other living organisms present in water.

During rains, one can see the direct impact of soil on the water of rivers tanks and other water bodies.

The brown and dirty water is the result of mud mixed in the water, which becomes clear after sometime. Similarly, several types of natural suspended and coloidal impurities are also there in the water. Those elements may be organic or inorganic and may even the harmful. The minerals like sodium, potassium calcium, magnesium, iron etc.are also present in the water, and if there quantity is more than the permissible limit, these are harmful. Some poisonous minerals as nickel, beryllium, cobalt, lead, mercury, cadmium, etc. are very harmful and are responsible for water pollutions. Sometimes water borne vegetation also becomes a cause of pollution.

Human Sources: There is no doubt that water pollution is the result of the human activities. The rapid growth of population, urbanization, industrialization and increasing use of chemicals have resulted in water polution and this problem is increasing day by day inspite of several measures taken in this direction. This is not only a problem of developed countries and urban areas but has also become an uncontrollable problem of developing countries as well as several areas. A misconcept developed right from the down of human civilization is that water bodies can be used as dumping grounds for all types of wastes and this is responsible for water pollution throughout the world. This is not hazardous to human health and other organisms but also disturbs the delicate ecosystem sources or type of contaminate responsible for water pollution and their impact.

For detailed analysis, the human sources of water pollution can be classified into the following categories

(i) Domestic effluents and sewage,
(ii) Industrial effluents
(iii) Agricultral effluents
(iv) Radio-active water
(v) Thermal pollution, and
(vi) Oil pollution.

Water pollution

Contaminates and their impact

Source or type of contaminates	*Impact*
1. Degradable wastes Domestic and municipal sewage and other O_2 demanding industrial wastes, they are acted upon by the bacteria and OX_2 dissolved in water and reduced to inorganic form as also in quantity	Depletion of dissolved oxygen in water harmful for fish and other acquatic life.
2. Plant nutrients phosphatic and nitrogenous compounds dissolved in water from industrial wastes, or due to washing away of fertilizers due to heavy rains from fields	Stimulate growth of algae/ plankton and other plants resulting in clogging of waterways and rendering the water on fit for human use
3. Infectious agents polluted, stagnant water breeding grounds for parties, bacteria, viruses of all kinds.	Cause water borne diseases and out breaks of epidemics such as amoebiasis dysentry, cholera typhoid etc.
4. Synthetic organic compounds Such as pesticides, agricultural chemicals, detergents industrial wastes, DDT, etc.	Instance of cadmium, lead and mercury poisoning in human beings. cause neurological impairement and even death.
5 Inorganic minerals and other chemicals asbestos and acids etc.	Asbestos produces lung cancer. Acids cause aillergies-ulcers, skin diseases, also have catastrophic impact on fish and acquatic life.
6 Radio active elements wastes from nuclear power plants and nuclear fuel processing plants are packaged and burried under water/oceans.	potential hazardous in the event of leakage and induce radiation related illness
7. Sediments Soil and mineral particles washed into streams or water.	Reduce amounted sunlight available for marine plants, cause clogging of filter plants.
8. Thermal pollution water used for cooling in electric, thermal nuclear power plant when recirculated in water bodies.	Can raise lake water temperature 70°/80° C. Aggravate dimenition of dissolved oxygen, kills marine fish and plant life.

***(i)* Domestic effluents sewage**

Man for his various domestic purposes such as drinking, preparation of food, bathing, for cleaning the house, cooling etc. Uses on averages 135 litres of water per day. About 70 to 80 per cent of this is discharged and drained out which although municipal drains poured into, in many cases, a river tank or lake.

This water is known as domestic waste water in which when other waste material such as paper, plastic, detergents, cloth, other waste materials are mixed, is known as municipal waste or sewage. The domestic waste water and sewage is the main source of the water pollution. This is the inevitable and unfortunate fall out of urbanization. As it decays, this organic waste depletes the oxygen from water and upsets the natural balance of the aquatic ecosystem.

Municipal sewage is considered to be the main polluted water. Most of the sewage receives no treatment before discharge, especially in developing countries like India in Delhi alone, 120 crore litres of water is consumed per day out of which 96 crore litres waste water is drained in to the Yamuna river through 17 big drains. All the 47 towns located on the bank of river Ganga drain their sewage into it. With the growth of populaiton the quantity of waste water is also increasing sewage contains decomposable organic mattter and exert on oxygen demand on receiving waters. The common organic materials found in a sewage are soaps, synthetic detergents, fatty acids, proteinaceous matters such as amines, amino acids, amides and amino sugars. In addition to the above components it also contains numerous micro-organisms. Sewage also contains pathegenic bacteria and viruses derived from human faces. Untreated waste water is often the carrier of viruses and bacteria and along with household sanitation practices.

Sewage supports the growth of other forms of life that consume oxygen.

It is measured in terms of Biochemical Oxygen Demand (BOD). It is the lack of oxygen that kills fish and aquatic life.

In recent years, there has been considerable growth in the use of detergents, which causes the severe water pollution, many component of agricultural fertilizers. When phosphate detergents are discharged into water ways, they supply nutrients and promote rapid growth of algae. This enrichment process is known as Eutrophication in many areas of world, aquatic weeds have multiplied explosively. They have interfered with fishing, navigation, irrigation and even production of hydroelectrocity. In developing countries, human population and settlements are growing fast, often faster than waste water treatment facilities can be provided. Thus much of the untreated waste water and sewage is discharged into rivers and other water bodies, making the water unsuitable for drinking and is a main cause of water pollution.

(ii) **Industrial Effluents**

Industrial activities generate a wide variety of waste products which are generally discharged into water caurses. Major contributors are the pulp and paper, chemicals, petro-chemicals and refining, metal working, food processing, textile, distillery, etc.

The wastes, broadly categorized as heavy metals or synthetic organic compounds reach bodies of water either through direct discharge or by leaching from waste dumps. Indeveloped countries of the world, many industrial discharges are strictly controlled. Yet, water pollution continues from accumulations of wastes discharged over the past 100 years. But, in developing countries, industrial discharges are largely uncontrolled, thus a main cause of water pollution.

All the Indian rivers have been polluted by industrial effluents. The holy river Ganga has become a highly polluted river due to various types of industrial discharges. Along the Ganga, several chemical, textile tanning, pulp and paper petrochemicals, rubber, fertilizers and other heavy industries are located and all of them discharge their waste waster and other effluent, directly or indirectly, into the river, resulting in the pollution to such an extent that even the Ganga action plan, to control water pollution, has failed. From Delhi industrial alone more than 8 lakh tonnes of industrial waste is discharged into the river Yamuna.

Damodar river of Bihar is a highly polluted river due to industrial wastes discharged from Bokaro, Rourkela, Tata Iron and Steel Company. Bengal paper mills, Sindhri fertilizer factory, etc. A study reveals that from Durgapur plant 1800 cu/m washed coal has been discharged into the river. Similarly, from ISCO 15,000 cu/m and from Bengal paper mills 12,000 culm per day industrial waste is discharged into river water.

The story of the Hooghly river of West Bengal is also similar. Its water has been polluted to such an extent that even fish fertilization becomes difficult.

Chambal, Narmada, Kaveri, Godavari, Mahanadi and other small rivers have been polluted and more pollutants have been discharged, resulting in greater water pollution.

Pulp and paper industries effluents from paper and pulp destroy include wood chips, bits of park, cellulose fibres dissolved liginin, in addition to a mixture of chemicals.

All these produce sludge which blankets fish spawning grounds and destroies certain types of aquatic life.

Textile industries, effluents are alkaline in nature and have a higher demand for oxygen food processing industries include dairies.

Textile industries, effluents are alkaline in nature and a higher demand from oxygen.

Food processing industries include dairies, breweries, distilleries meat packing etc., where the waste products include fats, proteins and organics coastes. These industries, discharge wastes containing nitrogen, sugar, proteins etc. All these coastes have a higher BOD and responsible for water pollution.

Chemical industries include acid manufacturing, alkali manufacturing, fertilizers, pesticides and several other industries. The effluents from these industries contain acids which have corrossive effects. The effluents from fertilizer industries contain phosphorus, fluorine, silica and large amounts of suspended solids.

Metal industries usually discharge effluents containing, copper, lead, chronuim, cadmium, zinc, etc., which are toxic to man as well as to acquatic life.

These wastes also contain acids, oils, greases and cleansing agents.

Petroleum industries include oil refinery and petro-chemical plants. The effluented include hydro carbons, phonolic compounds and other organic and inorganic sulphur compounds.

Other industries which pollute water are tanneries, soaps and detergents industries, glass, electroplating, bleaching, atomic plants, explosive factories, etc.

Mining operations can result in metals leaching into the acid effluents, the adding to the metal load in rivers, lakes and ground water. Discharge of the mercury from gold mining of activities has polluted some streams in Brazil and Ecuador and created serious health problems, with the reference to the water pollution through mercury, mention of minimata gulf incident must be made. In 1950 near the Japanese coast, in minimata gulf fishermen suffered form blindness, weakness, mental illness, paralysis etc. It was found that effluents discharged from a plastic factory contained mercury which entered the fish and eating those fish, all the fishermen suffered from effects of mercury poisoning. The problem of water pollution through industrial effluents has become a major environmental problem and sufficient measures should be taken to control it.

(iii) **Agricultural Effluents :** Agricultural water pollution is caused by fertilizers, insecticides and pesticides, from animal wastes and sediments. In recent years, use of chemical fertilizers has increased manifold. The green revolution of India is a reflection of the increased use of fertilizers. The chemicals used in fertilizers enter the ground water by leaching and the surfaces by run off. The nitrates, when mixed with waters may cause naethemoglobinemia in infants.

Incidences of nitrates poisoning are also there in live stock. The plants nutrients, nitrogen and phosphorus are reported to stimulate the growth of algae and other aquatic plants.

The use of various types of pesticides and insecticides in agriculture is also one of the causes of the water pollution. There presence in water is highly toxic to man and animals, because all these have a high persistance capacity, *i.e.,* their reduces remain for long periods.

The farm animal wastes often pose serious problems of odour and water pollution.

These wastes also contain pathogenic organisms which get transmitted to humans. Sediments of soil and mineral particles washed out, from fields also cause water pollution. They fill stream channels and reservoirs and reduce the sunlight available to acquatic plants.

(iv) **Radioactive wastes:** Radio active elements such as uranium and radium possess highly unstable atomic nuclei. This disintegration results in radiation emission which may be highly injurious. During nuclear tests, radio active dusts may encircle the globe at altitudes of 3,000 metres or more, the same of ten comes down to the earth as rain. Eventually, some of

radio active material, such as strontium 90 (which can cause bone cancer), percolated down through the soil into groundwater reservoirs or its carried out into streams and rivers. In both cases, public water supplies may be contaminated. The construction of more nuclear reactors and the increasing of radioactive materials in medical research represent other potential contamination sources.

(v) **Thermal pollution:** Most of the thermal and electric power plants also discharge considerable quantities (about 66%) of hot effluent/water into nearby streams or rivers. This has resulted in thermal pollution of our water courses. Thermal pollution is undesirable for several reasons. Warm water does not have the same oxygen hloding capacity as cold water. Therefore, fishes like black bass, trout and walleyes, etc, which require a minimal oxygen concentrate of about 4 ppm would either have to emigrate from the polluted area or die in large numbers. When the temperature of the receiving water is raised, the dissolved O_2 level decreases and demand for O_2 increases hence anaerobic conditions will set in resulting in the release of soul gases.

Thermal pollution is considered hazardous for the whole aquatic ecosystem.

Several industries have installed cooling towers where the heated water is cooled. But even so, thermal pollution has become a serious problem for water bodies located near thermal plants.

Oil Pollution

The spread of oil in the sea has become a common feature nowadays. Oil is transported across oceans through tankers and either due to some accident or leakage oil spills into the water and causes the degradation of aquatic and marine environment between 1968 and 1983, there were more than 500 tanker accident that involved oil spills.

Altogether, more than one million tons of oil was released. A dramatic incident was that of the tanks 'Torry Canyon, when it struck of the southern tip of the British isles in March 1967. The Torry Canyon was the largest oil spill up to that time.

The pollution caused wide spread destruction on of many forms of marine life despite strenous efforts to clean up the spill. Similarly, on March 16, 1978, the oil tanks Amoco cadiz, lost its steering of the coast of britanny in France and the total spilling of oil was 1.6 million barrels. Such accidents have very common due to technical problems or heavy marine traffic.

During the 1991 gulf war, there was heavy bombing on oil tanks which resulted in the spilling of oil.

The impact of this oil spill on the marine ecosystem in this area has not yet been remedied off shore drilling operations also contribute their share of oil to the sea. The total quantity of oil that finds its way into sea each year is very large. It has been estimated that about one million terms of oil spills into the ocean each ear from tankers and oil drilling operations.

Harmful effects of water pollution

Since use of water is universal to all living organisms, the impact of its pollution is also wide spread. The effects of water pollution become severe because water is the controlling factor in the food 'chain', therefore, its impact is not only wide spread but intensive also. The harmful effects of water pollution can be divided into three groups, *viz.*, *(i)* effect on man, *(ii)* effect on aquatic life, and *(iii)* other effects.

The effect of water pollution on man

On a worldwide scale, the pollution of water supplies is probably responsible for more human illness than any other environmental influence. The diseases so transmitted are chiefly caused by micro organisms and parasites. Sewage and polluted water are responsible for several water borne diseases, some of the diseases caused by polluted water are cholera, typhoid, infantile diarrhoea, dysentry, infectious hepatitis, polio, giardisis-amoebic dysentry, infectious Jaundice zondic, etc. Cholerais, an illness coused by ingstion of the bacterium vibreocholeral, results reapidly in massive fluid deption and death in a very large percentage of patients. It is transmitted by drinking water contaminated with the faces of infected of individuals. In developing countries, deaths by Cholera are still common. Guineaworm is another disease caused by polluted drinking water.

In India alone about 18 lakh people suffer from this disease.

Schistoshomi is a group of diseases caused by infection through worms in water. There are certain chemicals present in polluted water which may cause diseases like nepurities, writ drop, foot drop, etc. In spite of full measures taken for the supply of purified drinking water in U.S.A., there are incidents of diseases caused by water contamination in one way or other. The developing countries of Africa, Asia and Latin America, where arrangements of water treatment are limited or negligible a large section of the population is susceptible to water borne diseases.

(ii) Effects of water pollution on animals, marine life, and vegetation.

The effect of water pollution is more on aquatic life because their existence depends on water and when there is any disturbance in their ecosystem, the impact is maximum on them in the polluted, due to abandant growth of algae the oxygen content becomes lesser, causing the death of fishes and other organisms. It is estimated that during the last 20 years, there is a decrease of about 40% in aquatic life. Algae are responsible for imparting a peculiar taste and colour to many of the water supplies and also are a cause of gastroentritis. A report by wheler indicates that algae poisson usually act on the central nervous system and skin is reported to be capable of producing cirrhosis of the liver.

There are many cases on record of the destruction of marine life by polluted waters.

(iii) Other effects

Due to water pollution, the physical and physiological nature of water has also changed. The colour of water changes due to pollutants mainly due to organic dyes. The colour in itself is not harmful, however, aesthetic considerations make coloured water unsuitable for any purpose. The turbidity.

Foam is the product of water mixed with soaps and detergents. It consists of a suspension of air bubbles in water medium. Industrial effluents containing chemical substances as iron, chlorine, phenols, etc, affect the taste of the water. The decomposition of organic matter and algae, fungi and filanentous bacteria also imparts peculiar tastes. Similarly the odourly, the odour of water also changes due to the presence of pollutants.

In fact, the effects of water pollution are multi dimensional in nature.

Apart from above mentioned direct effects there are several indirect effects also.

In general, water pollution has now become a threat to the ecosystem and an important cause of environmental degradation

Measures for controlling water pollution

As earlier described, water pollution now has become a world wide problem. Not any developing countries but developed countries are also facin[g] this problem.

However developed countries has initiate[d] several methods not any to control water pollutio[n] but also for the purification of polluted water.

Apart from technological methods. There a[re] other measures which are useful in minimizing wat[er] pollution.

Ozone Depletion

We know that increase in the concentration o[f] greenhouse gases and acidification have alread[y] initiated the process of environmental change, huma[n] activities have caused changes in the ozone layer i[n] the stratosphere and increasing concentrations o[f] atmospheric pollution causing real damage to it ha[s] caused acid rain in the 1960's in Northern Europe the United States and Canada leading to large scal[e] destruction of forests and lakes. These hav[e] singnificant implications on human health as wel[l] as on the entire ecosystems.

The presence of ozone in the stratosphere is ver[y] important because it filters out the incoming ultraviole[t] (UV) radiation and thus acts as a screen agains[t] ultraviolet B (UV – B) which can cause some forms o[f] skin cancer, catracts and other eyes diseases. It als[o] suppress body defence mechanism which increase[s] valunerability to a variety of infectious diseases.

The problem of ozone depletion was firs[t] identified in 1970's due to the advent of supersoni[c] aircraft which fly in the lower stratosphere and whic[h] emit nitrogen oxides. But it was latter known tha[t] major cause of ozone depletion is the freons o[r] chlorofluorocarbons (CFCs). These are non-toxic non-flammable and chemically inert gases. These properties make them useful in a large no. of applications including aerosol propellants, refrigerant Cleansers for electronic components fine retardent, solvents and in the production of foamed plastics. The CFC gases do not rapidly degrade and after passing through troposphere they come into contact with stratosphere (due to depleted ozone layer) where they are subjected to intense ultraviolet radiation. This radiation is absorbed by ozone. Chlorine destroys ozone and oxygen from ozone also get destroyed each chlorine atoms released can over time destroys upward of 10,000 ozone molecules.

The first significant data about the depletion of ozone layer was presented by Farman (1985), the der of the British Antarctic survey, who said that ozone hole has occurred in the stratospheric ozone er over Antarctica since 1977. About 90% of the tarctica is covered by the ozone hole which has panded also over ocean areas for the period 1977- the concentration of ozone has decreased by 40% sequently Kerr in 1988 also reported the decline ozone layer over Arctic atmosphere. But it is more nificant than Antarctic ozone hole phenomena ce any destruction in the northern hemisphere one hole would be more destructive as density of pulation is more there.

The enhanced greenhouse effect, acidification l ozone depletion are all examples of atmospheric llution that have occurred mainly after lustrialisation, urbanisation and deforestation. so some metals like zinc, cadmium, mercury, and enic released by burning of fuels and as industrial stes are creating serious problems of vironmental pollution.

How do CFCs *(i)* Damage the Ozone Layer?

Most of us do not think about how our everyday ivities might influence the global environment. example in our use of chloroflurocarbons or CFCs. mpounds are useful as propellants in aerosol ays, refrigerants, coolants, cleaning agents, ulants and plastic foam are the main eaters of one present in the ozonosphere. Ozonosphere is general stratum of the upper atmosphere in which re is an appreciable ozone concentration and in ich ozone plays on important part in the radiative ance of the atmosphere.

It lies roughly between 10 and 50 kilometres, h maximum ozone concentration at about 20 to kilometres ozone; O_3, a blue gas is unstable otropic form of the oxygen. It is scarce even in the atosphere (12-50 km from the earth's surface) where s most concentrated. But each molecule counts.

Highly unstable, an ozone molecule readily ts up when hit by ultraviolet radiation. The energy life-damaging UV rays is thus converted into mless heat and never reaches the earth. The akup leave a free oxygen atom (O) and an oxygen lecule (O_2), the stuff we breathe. The O and O_2, in an ongoing cycle, recombine to form new ozone molecules.

The chloroflurocarbons (tradenamed freons) released by us are stable and can live up to 100 years. They are non-toxic and harmless to life. But when they drift slowly upward to reach the stratosphere by convection, they are struck by the high energy short wavelength rediations such as ultra voilet rays and this initiates a ozone clearing process.

When a CFC molecule is exposed to strong UV radiation in the stratosphere, it is broken apart. This releases a chlorine atom; which attacks on ozone molecule pulls away one of the three oxygen atoms and forms a chlorine monoxide molecule thus destroying the ozone molecule. The destructive process continues further.

The oxygen atoms from the new chlorine monoxide molecule is pulled away by free oxygen atoms freeing the chlorine atom to restart the cycle. Thus progressively more ozone molecules are decomposed.

It has been estimated that one chlorine atom can eat up to 1,00,000 moleculs of ozone.

A severe depletion in the ozone layer will result in an increase in the case of skin cancer, eye cataract and suppression of the immune system in humans and other species, food crops sensitive to UV rays could also be affected.

In 1984 a hole in the ozone layer was discovered over Antarctica and more recently a similar hole was discovered which extends over the Arctic, scandinavia and North America.

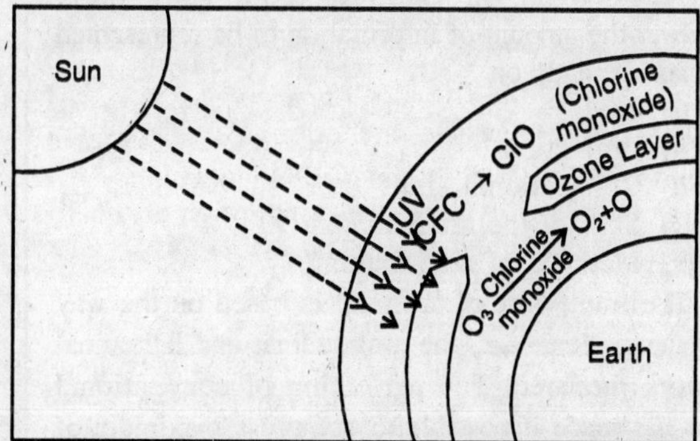

18 GENERAL CARTOGRAPHY (PRACTICALS)

CARTOGRAPHY

Cartography is the science and art of designing, constructing and producing maps. It is concerned with the measurement and representation of the shape, size and other broad details of the earth's surface in the past.

According to Smith the cartography is the science of constructing maps and charts which includes the making of original surveys, the selection of suitable map projections and the decisions on colours, layer tinting and other visual representations.

According to Rao Cartography refers to the whole series of processes of map-making from an actual survey of the ground to the printing of the map.

1. Map as a Tool in Geographical Studies

A map is the representation of the earth's pattern as a whole or a part of it, or the heavens on a plane surface, with conventional signs, drawn to a scale and projection so that each and every point on it corresponds to the actual terrestrial or celestial position.

Map representation is very essential for the understanding of geograph as it is more concerned about earth, its variations and inequalities surrounding it. The theoretical knowledge and explanation, without proper representation gives only the partial information about geography. However the amount of information to be represented on map depends on

(i) Scale
(ii) Projection
(iii) Conventional signs
(iv) Skill of the droughtsman
(v) Methods of map-making

The framework of the map is based on the way how the graticule *i.e.,* the longitudinal and latitudinal network prepared. The perfection of conventional signs has made it possible to compress maximum of information in the minimum of space without losing legibility. Every symbol, sign represents a definite meaning. Earth can be mapped by a number of ways:

(i) by actual survey with the help of instruments like chain, prismatic compass, planetable, theodolite etc.
(ii) by photographs
(iii) by freehand sketches and diagram
(iv) by computer
(v) by satellite and remote sensing methods.

Photographs are the representative of a small portion of the earth. The remote sensing images give very detailed account of a region without much of distortion and are more accurate. On a topographical survey map every point on the map bears a true relationship with the corresponding point on the ground.

TYPES OF MAPS

A map is the representation of the earth surface, or a part of it or some other celestial body such as Sun, Moon, Stars or planets on a flat surface *i.e.,* a plane surface. The representation is drawn to a specific scale and map projection and shows distinctive aspects of the surface such as relief features, routes, settlements etc.

Maps may be classified with respect to :

(i) Scale
(ii) Purpose or content

Maps based on scale

(a) **Cadastral Maps :** are drawn to register the ownership of landed property by demarcating the boundaries of fields and buildings etc. They are prepared specially by government to realize revenue and tax.

For example-Village maps, city plan maps etc.

(b) **Topographical Maps :** They are prepared on a large scale. They show general surface features in detail comprising both natural landscape and cultural landscape. They do not show plot or boundaries of the buildings but topographic forms like relief and drainage, swamps and forests, villages and towns and means of communication are generally depicted on them. In India 1:50,000 scale maps are generally prepared.

(c) **Wall Maps :** They are used in classrooms. In these maps the world as a whole or in hemisphere is distinctly represented. They may also be prepared for a continent or country, large or small, according to need. Their scale is smaller than that of topographical maps but larger than that of atlas maps

(d) **Chorographical or Atlas Maps :** These maps are drawn on a very small scale and gives more or less highly generalised picture regarding the physical, climatic and economic conditions of diffrent region of the earth. These maps show only important peaks, important rivers, chief towns, railway lines etc.

Based on purpose or contents

(a) **Astronomical Maps :** These maps show heavenly body or heavenly feature.

(b) **Geological Maps :** They show the rocks that form the crust of the earth and their mode of occurrence and their deposition. A corelation of these maps with the corresponding relief maps reveals the causes and evolution of landforms.

(c) **Orographic or Relief Maps :** Maps showing the surface forms is termed as orographic or relief maps. They show the bulges and depressions found over the surface. The level of land, its slope and drainage are well marked on it.

(d) **Weather and Climatic Maps :** They show the average condition of temperature, pressure, wind and precipitation over a short period, which range from a day to a season. Maps showing daily weather conditions are termed as daily weather maps, while those showing the average of weather conditions over 10 years or more are called climatic maps.

Cultural maps are those which represents the cultural patterns designed over the surface of the earth. These are :

(e) **Political Maps :** Show boundaries between different states or boundaries between different political units within a country.

(f) **Historical Maps :** Maps showing historical events are called Historical maps.

(g) **Social Maps :** Social organism-tribes and races, their languages, religions etc. are depicted on social maps.

(h) **Population Maps :** It denotes distribution of man over an area.

(i) **Economic Maps :** Maps displaying the distribution of important centres of agricultural, mineral and industrial products and its linkages with various means of communication may be termed as Economic map.

(j) **Military Maps :** These maps records strategic points, routes, battle plans etc.

(k) **Land Utilisation Maps :** They exhibit the nature and character of land use.

Similarly, these may be other types of maps such as distribution maps, Location or physiographic maps etc.

3. Techniques for the Study of Spatial Patterns of Distribution

CHOROPLETH

The most suitable method to show economic and geographical phenomenon is the Choropleth—a map that uses colours or shading to show area density patterns.

Suppose we have to show the population density of a region. Then using cartography we can show which portion or district has high density and which district has a low density. **For example-** Bundelkhand is consist of Datia, Tikamgarh, Chhatarpur and Panna districts of M.P. and Lalitpur, Jhansi, Jalaun, Banda and Hamirpur districts of U.P. The density of each district is taken from the population census abstract 2001.

Datia	-	194	Person/km^2
Tikamgarh	-	186	Person/km^2
Chhatarpur	-	133	Person/km^2
Panna	-	96	Person/km^2
Jhansi	-	285	Person/km^2
Jalaun	-	267	Person/km^2
Banda	-	244	Person/km^2
Hamirpur	-	205	Person/km^2

Here we take highest and lowest value and then categorise the population density values into five different categories. Darkest shade is choosen for the densest districts, which decreases with decrease in the value of density figure. Since Jhanshi has the densest population it has got most concentrated shades (darkest) and Panna has got the least concentrated shade (as it has the lowest value of population density).

While drawing choropleth maps shading and colours must be carefully choosen to give the desired visual effect. A choropleth map represents effectively and with a good visual appeal the average values per unit area, *e.g.*, density of population per sequare kilometre, yield of wheat per hectare, etc. These maps also show percentages, as for example, percentage of area under wheat to the total cropped area.

ISOPLETH MAPS

Isopleths are lines of equal value in the form of quantity, intensity and density. This is the collective term for the various types of lines representating specific values that are drawn on a map. They are generally drawn as contour lines at some selected intervals. The spacing of the lines expresses the rate of variation. If the lines appear much apart, variation is gentle and if the lines are closely set, variation is sharp.

To draw an isopleth maps, we require:–

(a) Data of a large number of stations of the area of which the isopleth map is to be prepared and.

(b) An outline map of the area on which the stations are marked.

When the data in details are not available, the isopleth cannot be drawn and even if they are drawn, they give an erroneous picture of facts. But in cases where great variations is observed say in case of population distribution, it loses its significance and become irrelevent. Hence, this method is commonly used for isotherm, isobar maps because these elements are uniformly distributed over wide areas. The isopleth map is also used in ratio or percentage maps.

Types of Isopleth Maps

A line on a map joining points having the same amount of rainfall is called Isohyet. An isopleth map connecting places of the same temperature is called Isotherm. Similarly, there are several other isopleths namely isohaline (salinity), isobar (pressure) isobath (depth), isoseismal line (earthquake intensity), isohel (sun-shine), isoneph (cloudiness) etc.

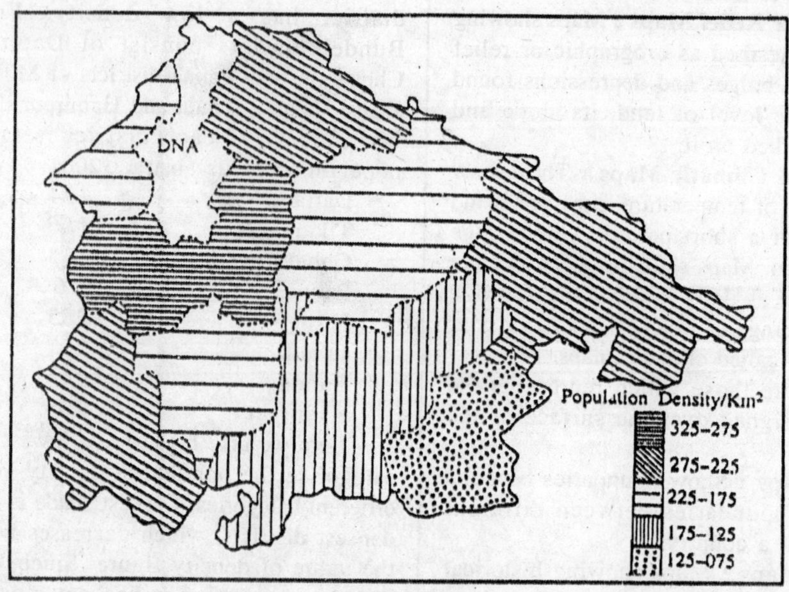

Choropleth Map

CHOROCHROMATIC MAPS

Maps showing non-quantitative areal distribution by shading and tinting the areas are called charochromatic maps. They are also called colour of tint method. The method generally uses different colours to show the distribution of different features in the map. *For example*—in a vegetation map forests may be shown by green colour, grassland by yellow and desert by brown. A colour index is also shown in a corner of the map. The distribution of various types of forests may be shown with different colours. This method may also be called layering method which is commonly used in relief maps to show different elevation.

Non-quantitative areal distributions are also shown by symbols such as dots, circles, traingles etc, index letters (such as T for tea, R for rice etc.) and drawings or pictures of the objects. Since these symbols are qualitative and do not represent quantities, these maps are termed as Non-Quantitative. The maps showing non-quantitative

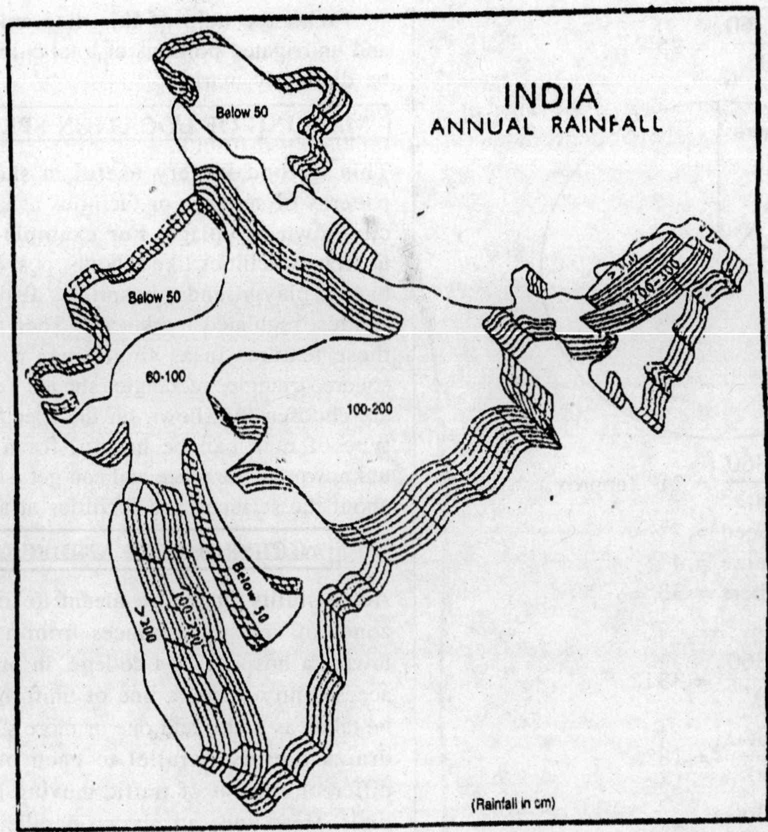

India : Annual Rainfall Isopleth

areal distribution by symbols, index letters are called Choroschematic maps. These maps are generally prepared when it is desired to convey regional variations effectively.

Industrial Centres :

Location of Town ⊙

Biscuits □

Dairy Product D

Water-Pipe W

Pharmaceuticals ■

Tractors ☼

A non-quantitative areal distribution map showing industrial centres.

Pie Diagrams : It is a graph in the form of a circle divided into sectors. Each sector represents a certain proportion or percentage of the total, with each 1% being represented by an angle of 3.6% on the circle. They are used widely in Human geography, **for example**—to show energy consumption in the country by type of energy used.

Such a map is extremely helpful for showing the share of the crop of the total cultivated land.

For example : During 1989-92 period three years average of % of Gross cropped area in Ranchi and Dhanbad district are as follows :

Ranchi	Dhanbad
Rice = 75%	Rice = 92%
Ragi = 7%	Maize = 5%
Pulses = 6%	Pulses = 2%
N. Seed = 2%	Others = 1%
Maize = 1%	
Others = 9%	

With the help of pie diagram these crops can be easily shown over Ranchi and Dhanbad. The angles that has to be shown inside a circle areas follows Ranchi—

$$\text{Rice } \frac{75 \times 360}{100} = 270°$$

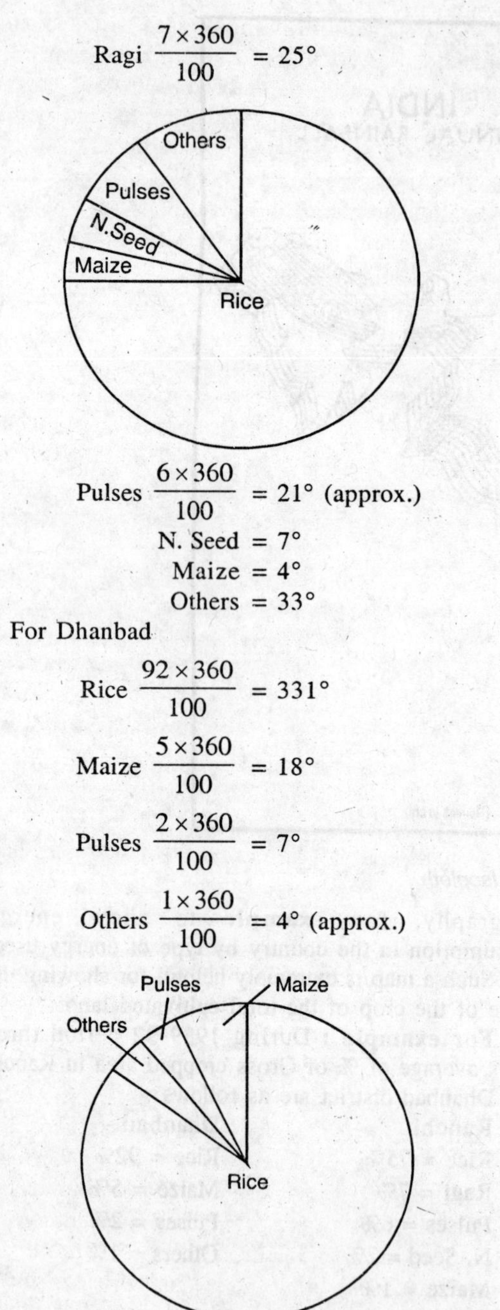

Ragi $\dfrac{7 \times 360}{100} = 25°$

Pulses $\dfrac{6 \times 360}{100} = 21°$ (approx.)

N. Seed = 7°

Maize = 4°

Others = 33°

For Dhanbad

Rice $\dfrac{92 \times 360}{100} = 331°$

Maize $\dfrac{5 \times 360}{100} = 18°$

Pulses $\dfrac{2 \times 360}{100} = 7°$

Others $\dfrac{1 \times 360}{100} = 4°$ (approx.)

Thus these can be easily plotted on a circle and different shades or colours can be used to show different crops of the district. It can be used in both cases where there is lesser number of crops or where there is higher number of crops.

With the help of this diagram, even irrigated and unirrigated portions of total cultivated areas may be distinctly marked.

MAPPING OF LOCATION SPECIFIC DATA

This method is very useful in showing different patterns of services or facilities available in a given city, town or village. **For example**—if a particular town has facilities like schools, post offices, colleges, banks, playgrounds, hospitals, dispensaries, health centres, regulated market etc. Then to show each of these features in as single map a symbol such as square, triangle, rectangle, shaded square, circle etc, are choosen the shown on the specific location such type of map can be helpful for a person who is unknown for the place and can get a lot of knowledge about the services and facilities at a glance.

ACCESSIBILITY AND FLOW MAPS

Accessibility maps are meant to identify different zones of varying distances from a road or from a towns, a hospital or a college. In order to make the accessibility maps, a line of uniform thickness may be taken as a unit and one or more such lines may be drawn closely parallel to each other to express different amount of traffic moving along respective lines. Here lines are drawn parallel to the road on both the sides, while taking into account the scale of the map. **For example**—a distance of 5 km, 10 km and so on depending upon the scale of the map. The different zones thus obtained are shaded differently. **For example**—the zone within 5 km from the road is left blank, the next *i.e.,* between 5 and 10 km from the road, is shaded with oblique lines, the zone away from this is shaded with check.

Thus, the zone shaded check is distantly located from the road. If a new road is required to constructed, the zone shaded with check will, get the priority.

In the same manner, zones of varying distances can be marked around a central point such as district headquarters, a hospital or a college. In this case, concentric circles with varying radii representing the distances, which are considered appropriate are drawn. In no case should distance zones parallel to railway lines be drawn. Here concentric zones will have to the drawn around railway stations as in case of a town.

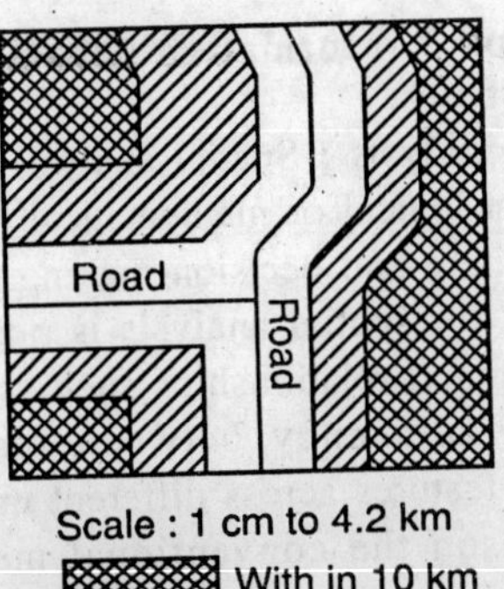

REMOTE SENSING AND COMPUTER APPLICATION IN MAPPING

Remote Sensing : It is defined as the science and art of acquiring information about objects from measurements made from a distance without any physical contact with the object. Using various sectors, we can collect data, process and analyse it to obtain information about the earth. Remote sensing uses the visual, infrared and microwave portions of electromagnetic spectrum. It is generally conducted by means of remote sensors installed in aircraft and satellite.

Advantages of Remote Sensing

1. We can easily identify and detect the geological rocks and structures.

2. With the help of satellite imageries we can know the actual amount of dip and dip direction of rocks easily.

3. Continuation of Beds, layers, complexes, truncations, turns, plunges and interuption of features can be detected with the help of this techniques. These can help in the detection of mineral oil, natural gases or ground water.

4. Topographic cuts are generally detected with the help of remote sensing techniques, here more vegetations are observed due to presence of more amount of moisture in the soil. These are the points from where one can get groundwater at relatively lower costs.

5. Faults and unconfornities can easily be detected. These can help in the detection of ground water, petroleum, diamonds etc.

6. Delineation of well drained, imperfectly drained and water logged areas can easily be done with the help of this techniques.

7. Location of side hill sepage, springs, potential old and active landslide areas and areas of high salinity can easily be detected with this tecnniques.

8. Remote sensing helps us to find out about crop area, stage and stage in the field.

9. It also helps to know the forest resource potential, problems and manage of forest.

10. Land degradation of various kinds like salinity, alkalinity, shifting cultivation, erosion, ravines, desertification etc. can be detected with the help of this technique.

Remote sensing Techniques

1. Photography : It is the most useful remote sensing system. This technique allows selection of the significant bandwidths in which a given area of terrain displays maximum tonal contrast and hence increases the effective spectural resolution of the system over conventional black and white or colour system. Because of its spectral selectivity capabilities, the multispectral approach provides a means of collecting a great amount of specific information.

Multispectral Imagery : Multispectral scanning system record the spectral reflectance by photoelectric means simultaneously in several individual wavelengths within the visual and infrared portions of the electromagnetic spectrum.

Infrared : Thermal infrared radiation is mapped by means of infrared scanners. The imagery provided by an infrared scanning system gives information that is not available from ordinary photography or from multispectral scanners.

Thermal infrared mapping (thermography) from satellite altitude is proving to be useful for a number of purposes like mapping of thermal currents in the ocean. Thermal infrared mapping from aircraft and satellite altitudes has many other uses like the mapping of volcanic activity and geothermal sites, location of ground water discharge into surface and marine waters, and region pollution monitoring.

Microwave Radar : This remote sensing technique used both active and passive sensors are used. The active sensors such as radar supply their own illumination and record the reflected energy while passive microwave sensors record the natural radiation. A variety of sensor types are used in it such as imaging radars etc. These instruments, can be used in all-weather conditions both during day and night.

Computer Application in Mapping

With the growing use of computers, geographers are handling the more complex mapping procedures, spatial, patterns, regional taxonomy and data computation, which are for beyond the capacity of human manipulation or analytical abilities. Computers help to solve special distributional problems in ferential statistics.

In geography, map is the basic and fundamental device, but the construction of a map is often extremely time consuming and sophisticated analytical uses are frequently ignored because of long duration of time needed to conduct the computations and transfer them to the map as a clear summary expression. For such purposes, many effective programmes have been advanced *e.g.,* CONTOUR, CONTUR, POPMAP, SYMAP etc.

GEOGRAPHIC INFORMATION SYSTEM (GIS)

GIS is computerised information storage processing and retrieval system that has both hardware and software specially designed to cope with geographically referenced spatial data and the corresponding attribute information (tables, charts statistics etc). The system permits capturing as well as storage of both spatial and non-spatial data sets from variety of sources including maps, aerial photographs, another analog and digital remote sensing data sources, ground surveys, GPS, and conventional sources. The greatest advantage of GIS is that it has the capability to relate the two types of data sets and look through or wide range of integrater queries, searches and permit manipulation.

GIS full functions combines three basic types of capabilities :

1. Presentation of mapping : In includes the ability to show geographic features on a map, to assign data values and ranges to those features to zoom in and zoom out to indicate various levels of details. Presentation mapping starts where spread sheet and presentation graphics programmes (*e.g.,* Microsoft Excel, lotus 1-2-3 and Harvard graphic) leaves off. Presentation mapping programmes help viewers recognise spatial pattern of information.

2. Using maps as an organising tool for large data basis : Its becomes a mechanism by which users can query data bases. It can reorganise data into different spatial units. It can keep records of spatial data and compare information across different features or databases.

3. Spatial analysis : Spatial analysis is the use of spatial data in logical or mathematical models for purpose of planning and decision making. The ideal GIS technology for spatial analysis is one that can operationalise spatial relationships such as distance, proximity and adjacency between features or compare spatial features across different map layers.

In comparison the conventional methods of surveying and portraying, the new technologies of remote sensing, global positioning system, geographic information system etc., have emerged as most useful tools for the planners is recent decades. Such modern technologies have facilitated an easy access to the diverse databases, which have very high level of accuracy and reliability.

Thematic Maps

Maps that include information or attributes are usually referred to as Thematic maps. This map can be used to show the locations of different features and activities, or they can be used to show somethings about the attributes of those activities.

Thematic maps are of three basic forces: Polygon maps, Line maps and Point maps.

Polygon thematic maps consist of polygon features that are crosshatched or coloured according to the value of some attribute. A real estate market analyst, **for example**—might produce a polygon thematic map showing household income by census tract or polygon.

Line thematic maps consist of line segments of varying width or colour according to an attribute value. A Railroad company, for example, might produce a line thematic map showing tonnes of coal carried by a rail route.

Point thematic maps consists of point symbols sized or coloured according to the value of a particular attribute. A national retailer for example, night produce a national point thematic map showing quaterly sales volume by metropolitan area.

Thematic maps usually involve only a few map layers and limited amounts of detail. As a result, the various GIS packages designed around thematic mapping applications typically emphasise ease of use over computational power.

STATISTICAL METHODS

DATA SOURCES AND TYPES OF DATA

Statistics refers to the statistical principles and methods used in collecting, analysing and interpretation of the data.

Statistical Methods are the techniques used for collection, summarisation, classification, analysis, comparison and interpretation of the huge and complex numerical data. By their use, useful deductions and inferences are drawn, and statistical laws are formulated. Though such laws are not perfect and completely exact, they are true only on the average or in the long run.

The collection of data is the basis or foundation of statistical investigation. It is, therefore, necessary to collect data very carefully.

There are two types of statistical data :

(i) Primary data *(ii)* Secondary data.

The data which are collected for the first time by the collector or investigator for his own purpose or statistical enquiry from the sources of information is called Primary data.

The data which are collected by some one else and used by the investigator for his own purpose from published or unpublished sources is known as Secondary data.

So the data which are primary in the hands of one become secondary in the hands of the other.

For example: The data collected by Election office are primary for the office but secondary when used by others.

Sources of Data

1. Primary Data Sources : Among the primary sources of the demographic data are the census, the surveys, the registrations etc.

(a) **Census :** The population census is the most important source of data for demographers. In India first complete census of population was conducted in 1881. Since then it is being conducted at a regular interval of 10 years. Under this census, the informations are collected on population numbers, their rural and urban distributions their sex, age composition, literacy, religion, occupation, etc.

(b) **Surveys :** Surveys are conducted for supplementing the census data as for investigating the determinants of a particular demographic attribute. They are generally conducted to collect a veriety of informations regarding fertility, mortality, morbidity, mobility, unemployment, health, education etc.

(c) **The Registration :** Under this category data birth, death, marriage and divorce statistics are generally registered.

2. The Secondary Data Sources : The main sources of secondary data are :

(a) **Published Statistics :** These include official publications of governments, reports of enquiry committees and commissions, publications of trade associations, banks, publication of technical journals etc.

(b) **Unpublished Statistics :** This include large amount of data collected by government institutions or others which remain unpublished. This collected data can be put to use, if available.

STUDY OF FREQUENCY DISTRIBUTION AND CUMULATIVE FREQUENCY

Study of frequency distribution : The summary table which arranges a large amount of information in a compact, systematic form is known as Frequency distribution.

After collecting relevant statistical data, the process of classification is adopted and the data are presented in the form of frequency distribution. Thus frequency distribution is simply a table in which data are grouped into different classes and the number of cases which fall in each class are recorded.

For example : The districts of Karnataka have following percentages of employees to total population :

	Districts	*% of employees to total population*
1.	Bangalore	32.20
2.	Bidar	48.15
3.	Chitradurga	42.20
4.	Gulburga	36.10
5.	Kolar	33.20
6.	Raichur	39.70
7.	U. Kannada	46.70
8.	Belgaun	43.05
9.	Bijapur	42.10
10.	D. Kannada	40.10
11.	Hassan	36.70
12.	Mandya	42.40

13.	Shimoga	48.70
14.	Bellary	41.10
15.	Chikmangalur	32.90
16.	Dharwar	39.90
17.	Kodagu	40.10
18.	Mysore	39.70
19.	Tumkur	42.50

Here the highest value is 48.70 and lowest value is 32.10%.

Taking a class interval of 2 the lengthy table can be tabulated in a much simples way where frequency can be shown—

% of Workers to total population	*Tally mark*	*Frequency*
32-34	III	3
34-36	-	-
36-38	II	2
38-40	III	3
40-42	III	3
42-44	IIII	5
44-46	-	-
46-48	I	1
48-50	II	2
		19

Cumulative Frequency : It is total number of observations less than or equal to a given vlue of the different classes.

Whereas in the frequency distribution the frequencies shown against each class are those of the class only in cumulative frequency distribution the frequency of a particular class is obtained by adding to the frequency of that class all the frequencies of the previous classes. So the cumulative frequency table is obtained from the ordinary frequency table by successively adding the several frequencies. Obviously the cumulative frequency of the last class is the sum of the frequencies of all the classes.

For example :

% of workers to total population	*Tally mark*	*Frequency*	*Cumulative frequency*
32-34	III	3	3
34-36	-	-	3
36-38	II	2	5
38-40	III	3	8
40-42	III	3	11
42-44	IIII	5	16
44-46	-	-	16
46-48	I	1	17
48-50	II	2	19
		19	

Statistical Diagrams

Statistical diagram may be defined as the representation of statistical data, or a geographic element in a highly abstract and conventionalised form by laying emphasis on one selected element. They are the most convincing and appealing ways for presenting statistical results.

Statistical diagrams may be daily, monthly, or annual production of each and every commodity.

They enable us to compare the data relating to different periods of time, different regions, etc. quickly and make accurate comparison of the data. They also help us in a analytical thinking and investigation.

The statistical diagrams can be grouped into three groups :

1. One Dimensional : These include :

(*a*) Line diagram.

(*b*) Bar diagram (simple, compound, multiple bar diagram)

(*c*) Pyramid diagram (Simple Pyramid, Super–imposed and Compound pyramid)

(*d*) Water budget or rainfall dispersion diagram

2. Two Dimensional : These include :

(*a*) Unit square diagram

(*b*) Square block diagram

(*c*) Rectangular Diagram (simple and divided rectangular diagram)

(*d*) Pie Diagram

3. Three Dimensional : These include :

(*a*) Spherical Diagram

(*b*) Cube Diagram

(*c*) Block Pole Diagram

Besides these star diagram, triangular diagram, scatter diagram are the other diagrams through which the cartographic representation can be made.

The statistical diagrams, however depends on the nature of data how they can be most suitably represented any one of the above methods.

For example:

The percentage of coal produced by different states in India can be most suitably shown in a bar diagram, while landuse patterns can be represented in a wheel or pie diagram. Similarly production of different food grains of a particular year can be shown in a rectangular block diagram in a more suitable way.

MEASURES OF CENTRAL TENDENCY

Any statistical measure which gives an idea about the position of the point round which other observations cluster, is called a Measure of Central Tendency.

The commonly used measures of central tendency are :

1. Arithmatic mean or simple mean
2. Medium
3. Mode

Arithmetic Mean : It is the sum of the values divided by their total number *i.e.,* we obtain its value by adding together the sizes of all items and dividing this total by the number of items.

$$\overline{X} = \frac{X_1 + X_2 + X_3 + \ldots X_n}{n} \text{ or } \overline{X} = \frac{\Sigma X}{N}$$

where $\overline{X}$ is the arithmetic mean and ΣX the sum of the values of all the variables and n is the number of observations.

Arithmetic Mean of a frequency distribution :

If the numbers X_1, X_2, X_3, ... occur with frequencies f_1, f_2, f_3 ... etc., the arithmetic mean is given by :

$$\overline{X} = \frac{f_1X_1 + f_2X_2 + f_3X_3 \ldots + f_nX_n}{f_1 + f_2 + \ldots f_n}$$

$$= \frac{\Sigma fX}{\Sigma f} = \frac{\Sigma fX}{N}$$

where $N = \Sigma f$ is the total frequency and $\overline{X}$ = arithmetic mean of distribution.

Short Cut Method : In this method, an arbitrary origin A is taken, the deviation of sizes of the variable X from A are noted as d, these deviations are multiplied by the corresponding frequencies and the total Σfd found out. Divide Σfd by N and add this to A. Thus, if A is the arbitrary origin and $d = \frac{X-A}{c}$, the deviation of the sizes X from A in terms of the class interval C, then $\overline{X} = A + \frac{\Sigma fd}{N} \times C$ gives the Arithmetic Mean.

Calculation of Arithmetic Mean from a Frequency Distribution-Discrete Series

Direct Method : If-algebraically, X_1, X_2 ... X_n are quantities with frequencies f_1, f_2, ... f_n then the mean is :

$$\overline{X} = \frac{X_1f_1 + X_2f_2 + \ldots + X_nf_n}{f_1 + f_2 + \ldots + f_n} = \frac{\Sigma f_n}{\Sigma f}$$

Short-cut Method :

$$\overline{X} = a + \frac{\Sigma f\,dx}{\Sigma f}$$

where $\Sigma f\,dx$ = total of the products of the deviations from the assumed average and the corresponding frequencies.

Calculation of Arithmetic Mean—Continuous Series

Direct Method, $\overline{X} = \frac{\Sigma fX}{N}$

where X is the mid-value of various classes, f the frequency of each class and N the total frequency.

Short Cut Method : $\overline{X} = A + \frac{\Sigma fd}{N} \times C$

where A is the arbitrary mean, f is the frequency, d the deviation of the mid-values from the arbitrary origin in terms of the class interval C.

Median

The median is that value of the variable which divides the group in two equal parts, one part comprising all values greater and the other all values less than median.

Example : Find the median of 88, 72, 33, 29, 80, 86, 48, 75, 69

Solution : Arranging the given numbers in accending order we get 29, 33, 48, 69, 72, 75, 80, 86, 88

The median is the middle term *i.e.,* 72.

Simple Frequency Distribution : First of all, calculate the cumulative frequency corresponding to each value of the variable. The value of the variable corresponding to the cumulative frequency $\frac{N+1}{2}$, if N is odd and $\frac{N}{2}$, if N is even is the median where N is the total frequency.

Grouped Frequency Distribution : The cumulative frequency corresponding to each class boundary is first calculated. The median is given by the formula.

$$\text{Median} = I_1 + \frac{\frac{N}{2} - m}{f} \times C \text{ if N is even and}$$

$$= I_1 + \frac{\frac{N+1}{2} - m}{f} \times C \text{ if N is odd}$$

where I_1 is the lower boundary of the median class, N the total frequency, m cumulative frequency below I_1, f the frequency of the median class and C width of the median all intervals.

Mode

Mode is that value of the variable which occurs most frequently and so with the maximum frequency.

(i) **Individual Series :** When the series or observations are of individual nature, the mode can be located merely by inspection. The frequency which occurs maximum times, is the mode.

For example : 5, 7, 7, 7, 9, 8, 4, 7, 6, 10, 8, 6, 8 when re-arranged-4, 5, 6, 6, 7, 7, 7, 7, 8, 8, 8, 9, 10

M = 7 because it occurs for or maximum number of times.

(ii) **Discrete Series :** Mode is located by using the method of grouping and thus is found out at the point of maximum concentration. The aim of grouping is to eliminate irregularities. Items are arranged in ascending order and the frequencies against each item are written down and then groups are formed to determine the model class.

(iii) **Continuous Series :** Two steps are followed in this case. First, the process of grouping is followed and by analysis table, the class group is located in which mode is located. Then, the method of interpolation is applied to know the exact value of mode.

Formula for interpolation (Model) is :

$$Z = L_1 + \frac{(f_m - f_1)}{(f_m - f_1) + (f_m - f_2)} \times i$$

where Z = Mode,

f_m = Frequency of modal group

f_1 = Frequency of the group preceding modal group.

f_2 = Frequency of the group succeeding modal group

L_1 = Lower limit of the modal group.

i = Class interval

It is to be noted that while calculating differences between $(f_m - f_1)$ and $f_m - f_2)$, algebraic signs are to be neglected. All differences are to be taken as positive.

SELECTION OF CLASS INTERVALS FOR MAPPING

We know that :

Class Interval : Upper class limit—Lower class limit

In a given data the value of the variable may increased (or decrease) steadily or by leaps. The methods used for selecting class intervals would differ from the one in case of steadily increasing variable to that increasing by leaps. Some of the methods used for selecting class intervals are :

Arithmetic Progression : It is a sequence of numbers which increase or decrease by the same amount *e.g.* 50, 100, 200 or 25, 20, 15, 10. Then according to this method, every class has the same class-interval. This method is quite appropriate when the values of the items increase steadily and the number of items is small.

For example : A state has 23 districts. The highest net irrigated area as percentage of net sown area for a given area is 85.10 and the lower value is 6.38. The range is :

85.10 – 6.38 = 78.72. Following six groups can be easily formed.

	Net irrigated area as percentage of net sown area
Low irrigation	5-20
Low medium irrigation	20-35
Medium irrigation	35-50
High medium irrigation	50-65
High irrigation	65-80
Very high irrigation	80-95

Geometric Progression

It is a sequence of numbers in which the ratio of each number to proceedding one does not alter.

For example : In a sequence showing the geometric progression as 25, 50, 100, 200, 400.

This method is used when the range is very high. As per 1991 census the density of population is Jaisalmer and Calcutta distric was 9 and 23,699 persons per sq. km. respectively. In view of the wide range, geometric progression method was used for preparing the density of population map of India. The following division points were used.

Quantile Method : When items of extreme values are present, we make use of median instead of arithmetic mean or and standard deviation for determining groups. Quantile method is preferred when the items are less than 50 and extreme values are present in the data.

It should be noted that-

(a) Quantiles are the values which divide the ranked data into a number of groups, each group having the same number of items.

(b) Quantiles are the values of three points which divide the ranked data into 4 groups, each group having the same number of items,.

(c) Quintiles are the values of four points which divide the ranked data into 5 groups each group having the same number of items.

Other terms are sextiles (6 groups), septils (7 groups), octiles (8 groups), Noniles (9 groups) and Deciles (10 groups).

MEASURES OF DISPERSION AND CONCENTRATION

The degree to which numerical data tend to spread about an average value is called the Variation or Dispersion of data. With the help of these values the distances of the varieties from the central value are assessed generally there are two types of measures of dispersion :

(i) **Absolute :** Which assumes the units of the distribution.

(ii) **Relative :** Which is numerical expression having no-unit.

(i) Absolute Measures of Variation or Dispersion :

(a) **Range :** This is the simplest measure of dispersion. It is the difference between the biggest value and the smallest value of the items of the distribution.

Range = $X_{max} - X_{min}$

$$\text{Coefficient of Range} = \frac{X_{max} - X_{min}}{X_{max} + X_{min}}$$

(b) **Mean deviation :** It is the mean of the departures of varients from the central value taking all positive value. It can be expressed as :

Mean deviation

$$MD = \frac{(X_1 - \overline{X}) + (X_2 - \overline{X}) + (X_i - \overline{X}) + ... + (X_n - \overline{X})}{N}$$

$$= \frac{\sum_{i=1}^{N} \left|(X_i - \overline{X})\right|}{N}$$

where,

$\overline{X}$ is the mean value

X_i is the ith value

X_n is the nth value

N is total number of observations

(c) **Quartile Deviation :**

It is given by

$$Q = \frac{Q_3 - Q_1}{2}$$

where Q = Quartile deviation

Q_1 and Q_3 have their usual meanings.

(ii) **Relative Measures of Dispersion :** These are the measures expressed in terms of ratio, % and co-efficients and are widely used in geographic studies. It can be used in the cases where percentage departure from rainfall or say percentage variations in production etc, are required.

The relative measure of dispersion of coefficient of quartile deviation is computed by dividing the absolute measure by the average of two quartiles. In other words, in order to obtain coefficient, the difference of two quartiles is divided by the sum of the two quartiles.

$$\text{Co-efficient of Q.D.} = \frac{Q_2 - Q_1}{2} \times \frac{2}{Q_3 + Q_1}$$

$$= \frac{Q_3 - Q_1}{Q_3 + Q_1}$$

Average Deviation or Mean Deviation :

It is also called the first moment of dispersion and is based on all items of series. It is the arithmetic average of the deviations of the group (all taken as positive from mean, median or mode), their sum divided by their number.

The releative measure of average deviation is known as Coefficient of Mean Deviation and is obtained by dividing the mean deviation by a particular average used to compute the mean deviation. It is given by coefficient of mean.

deviation : based on $\overline{X}$, M and Z

$\frac{\delta x}{X}, \frac{\delta m}{M}$ and $\frac{\delta z}{Z}$ respectively.

It is important to note that in a normal distribution mean deviation covers nearly 57.5% of the items *i.e.*, M ± δ covers nearly 57.5% of the items.

For example in the series given below

21, 23, 25, 28, 30, 32, 38, 39, 46, 48,

$$\text{Mean} = \frac{330}{10} = 33$$

$|dx|$ (33) : 12, 10, 8, 5, 3, 1, 5, 6, 13, 15 = 78

$$\text{Arithmetic mean} = \frac{330}{10} = 33$$

$$\text{Mean deviation} = \frac{\Sigma|dx|}{n} = \frac{78}{10} = 7.8$$

STANDARD DEVIATION

Standard deviation is the sequence root of the arithmetic average of the square of the deviations measured from the actual arithmetic mean. In other words, standard deviation is the root mean square of the deviations from the arithmetic mean.

The standard deviation is an absolute measure of dispersion. For the purpose of comparison, a relative measure is obtained by dividing the standard deviation by the arithmetic average. This is known as "Standard Coefficient of Dispersion" or "Coefficient of Standard Deviation."

Coefficient of standard deviation = $\sigma + \bar{x}$

The computation of standard deviation can be done by two different methods *i.e.,* by *(i)* Direct method (by taking deviation from the actual mean); and *(ii)* Short-cut method (by taking deviations from the assumed mean).

Individual series :

(i) Direct Method, $\sigma = \sqrt{\frac{\Sigma dx^2}{n}}$

(ii) Short-cut Method $\sigma = \sqrt{\frac{\Sigma dx^2}{n} - \left[\frac{\Sigma dx}{n}\right]^2}$

where σ = standard deviation; n = number of items

Σdx^2 = sum of the squares of deviations measured from the actual mean

Σdx^2 = sum of the squares of deviations measured from the assumed mean.

For example : To fixed standard deviation of X = 9, 4, 11, 10, 6

x	dx (8)	dx^2
9	1	1
4	– 4	16
11	3	9
10	2	4
6	– 2	4
40		34

$$\bar{x} = \frac{40}{5} = 8$$

$$\sigma = \frac{\Sigma dx^2}{n} = \sqrt{\frac{34}{5}} = \sqrt{6.8} = 2.607$$

Discrete series : Here the square of the deviations is multiplied by the respective frequencies of these items.

(i) Direct Method, $\sigma = \sqrt{\frac{\Sigma f dx^2}{\Sigma f}}$

(ii) Short-cut method, $\sigma = \sqrt{\frac{\Sigma f dx^2}{\Sigma f} - \left[\frac{\Sigma fdx}{\Sigma f}\right]^2}$

Continuous series

$$\sigma = \sqrt{\frac{\Sigma fd'x^2}{\Sigma f} - \left[\frac{\Sigma fd'x}{\Sigma f}\right]^2} \times i$$

where i = common factor

Coefficient of variation

It can be defined as the standard deviation expressed as the percentage of arithmetic mean.

$$\text{C.V.} = \frac{\sigma}{x} \times 100 \text{ or } \frac{\text{Standard deviation}}{\text{Arithmetic mean}} \times 100$$

Variance : It is also known as the second moment about the mean and is infact the square of the standard deviation.

Variance = (S.D)^2

or, $\sigma = \sqrt{\text{Variance}}$

LORENZ CURVE

Lorenz Curve is a graphical method of studying dispersion. This curve is used to study the distribution of profits, wages, turnover, etc. The most common use of this curve is in the study of the degree of inequality in the distribution of income or wealth between two periods of time. This is a cumulative percentage curve in which the cumulative percentage of sizes is associated with the cumulative percentage of other things such as wealth, profits, turn over, etc.

The technique of drawing the curve is as follow :

(i) The size of the item (Variable value) and the frequencies are both cumulated. Taking

grand total for the variable and the frequencies as percentage of their corresponding grand totals.

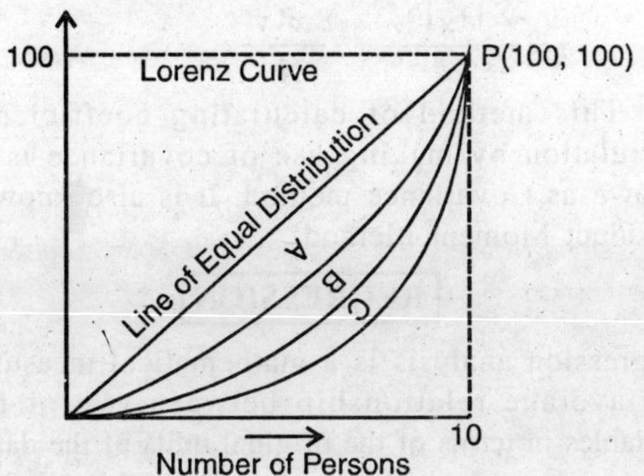

(ii) A long the x-axis, represent the percentages of the cumulated frequencies (x) and along the y-axis represent the percentages of the cumulated values of the variable (y). Both X and Y take the values from 0 to 100.

(iii) Draw the diagonal line $y = x$ joining the origin 0 (0, 0) with the point P (100, 100) as shown in the figure. The line OP makes an angle of 45° with the x-axis and is called the line of equal distribution.

(iv) Plot the percentages of the cumulated values of the variable (y) against the percentages of the corresponding cumulated frequencies (x) for the given distribution and join these points with a smooth free hand curve. For any given distribution the curve will never cross the line of equal distribution OP. It will always lie below OP unless the distribution is uniform (equal) in which case it will concide with OP.

Thus when the distribution of items is not proportionately equal, the variability (dispersion) is indicated and the curve is further from the line of equal distribution OP. The greater the variability the greater is the distance of the curve from OP.

METHODS OF MEASURING ASSOCIATION AMONG DIFFERENT ATTRIBUTES

Very frequently in experimental work we deal with some characteristics or attributes that are not susceptible of accurate measurement, although it is possible to divide the population into two or more categories with reference to these attributes. Association of attributes deals with such situations.

Classification according to Attributes

Classification acording to attributes is of two types—simple and manifold. In simple classification, a given population, is divided into two parts, one part showing presence and the other showing absence of the attribute. In Manifold classification there are a number of attributes or more than two classes and subclasses, *e.g.*, profession teaching, business, service, agriculture.

The presence of the attribute is generally written is Roman capital letter such as A, B, C, D etc. and is termed positive attribute and the greek letters α (alpha), β (beta), γ (gamma) etc. are used to represent absence of the attributes and termed negative attribute.

Class Frequencies : The number of observations assigned to any class is termed the frequency of the class.

Order of Classes : Order of classes is defined as the number of attributes involved in classification.

Number of Frequencies : The total number of class frequencies in a study of n attributes is given by 3^n.

From the following nine square table, the frequencies of the positive, negative and ultimate classes can be known.

Attributes	A	α	Total
B	(AB)	(αB)	(B)
β	(Aβ)	(αβ)	(β)
Total	A	(α)	N

In this way, the frequency (A) can be expressed as the sum of two frequencies in which the letter A is present. From the above table, certain relationships can be described

$A = (AB) + (A\beta); (\alpha) = (\alpha B) + (\alpha\beta)$

$B = (AB) + (\alpha B); (\beta) = (A\beta) + (\alpha\beta)$

$N = (A) + (\alpha)$ or $(B) + (\beta)$

or $(AB) + (A\beta) + (\alpha B) + (\alpha\beta)$

Types of Association

There can be three kinds of association between attributes—positive association, negative association and independence.

If the actual observation is equal to the expectation, the attributes are said to be independent; if actual observation is more than the expectation, the attributes are said to be positively associated and if the actual observation is less than the expectation, the attributes are said to be negatively associated.

SIMPLE AND MULTIPLE CORRELATION

The correlation is a statistical tool which studies the relationship between two variables and the correlation analysis involves methods and techniques used for studying and measuring the extent of the relationship between the two variables.

Simple Correlation : The problem in which only two variables are considered to be influencing each other is one of simple correlation.

Multiple Correlation : The problem in which more than two variables are considered is one of multiple correlation.

Measurement of Correlation : It means the expression of degree of correlation that exists between two or more variables by following certain statistical methods. The methods used are :

(a) Graphic methods :

(i) Scatter diagram;

(ii) Correlation graph

(b) Mathematical Methods

(i) Product moment or covariance method;

(ii) Rank method;

(iii) Method of concurrent deviations :

Coefficient of Correlation : Coefficient of correlation of two variables is calculated by dividing the sum of the products of the corresponding deviations of the various items of two series from their respective arithmetic means by the product of their standard deviations and the number of items. It is thus a mathematical method of studying coefficient of correlation.

$$r = \frac{\Sigma x'y'}{n.\sigma x \sigma y} = \frac{\Sigma XY}{n\sigma X \sigma Y} = \frac{\Sigma D_X D_Y}{n \sigma x \sigma y} = \frac{\Sigma xy/N}{\sigma x\ \sigma y}$$

$$= \frac{\text{Covariance}}{\sigma x\ \sigma y}$$

where $x = (x - \bar{x}) = DX = x'$

$y = (y - \bar{y}) = DY = y'$

where $\Sigma\, xy$ or $\Sigma\, D_x D_Y$ refers to the sum of the product of deviations of X and Y series from the pairs of observations. σ_x and σ_y refers to standard deviation of X and Y series.

$$\text{Cov. }(x, y) = \frac{\Sigma(x-\bar{x})(y-\bar{y})}{N} = \frac{\Sigma xy}{N}$$

$$= \frac{\Sigma D_X D_y}{N} = \frac{\Sigma x'y'}{N}$$

This method of calculating coefficient of correlation by making use of covariance is also known as Covariance method. It is also known as 'Product Moment Method'.

REGRESSION

Regression analysis is a mathematical measure of the average relationship between two or more variables in terms of the original units of the data. In regression there are two types of variables.

(i) **Dependent variable or Regressed variable:** The variable whose value is influenced or is to predicted.

(ii) **Independent or Regressor or Predictor variable :** The variable which influences the values or is used for prediction.

Lines of Regressions : Line of regression of y on x is the line which gives the best estimate for the value of y for any specified values of x.

Similarly, line of regression of x on y is the line which gives the best estimate for the value of x for any specified value of y.

Regression Equations : are the algebraic expression of regression lines. They help in estimating from a given value of one variable the average corresponding value of the other. There are two regression lines and there will be two regression equations x on y and y on x.

Regression Equation of X on Y :

$$x = a + by$$

$$\Sigma X = Na + b\Sigma y$$

$$\Sigma XY = a\Sigma Y + b\Sigma y^2$$

From above, we find

$$b = \frac{N\Sigma XY - (\Sigma X)(\Sigma Y)}{N\Sigma Y^2 - (\Sigma Y)^2}$$

and $$a = \frac{\Sigma X}{N} - \frac{b\Sigma Y}{N}$$

or, $$a = \overline{X} - b.\overline{Y}$$

or, $$a = \frac{\Sigma X.\Sigma Y^2 - \Sigma XY.\Sigma Y}{N.\Sigma Y^2 - (\Sigma Y)^2}$$

Fitting a straight line becomes quite easy if arithmetic mean $\left(\Sigma\overline{X},\overline{Y}\right)$ is taken as the point of origin. The reason is that in such a situation.

$$\Sigma\, Dx = \Sigma\left(X-\overline{X}\right) = 0 \text{ and } \Sigma\, Dy = \Sigma\left(Y-\overline{Y}\right) = 0.$$

The two normal equations shall be

(i) $\Sigma x = Na$, and $\Sigma xy = b\Sigma y^2$

Here 'b' is known as 'regression coefficient and the above expression refers to regression coefficient of X on Y and is denoted by b_{xy}

$$b_{xy} = \frac{\Sigma\, xy}{\Sigma\, y^2} = \frac{\Sigma\, xy}{N.\sigma_y^2} = \frac{\Sigma\, xy}{N.\sigma_x\sigma_y} \times \frac{\sigma_x}{\sigma_y} = r\frac{\sigma_x}{\sigma_y}$$

or, $$b_{xy} = \frac{\text{Cov}(x,y)}{\sigma^2 y} = \frac{\Sigma(x-\bar{x})(y-\bar{y})}{\Sigma(y-\bar{y})^2}$$

For example, to obtain x/y regression line when :

x = 6, 2, 10, 4, 8
y = 9, 11, 5, 8, 7

Regression line 'X' on 'Y' or X/Y

X	Y	X²	Y²	XY
6	9	36	81	54
2	11	4	121	22
10	5	100	25	50
4	8	16	64	32
8	7	64	49	56
30	40	220	340	214

Regression line $\frac{X}{Y}$: $x = a + by$

$$b = \frac{N(\Sigma XY)-(\Sigma X)(\Sigma Y)}{N\Sigma Y^2-(\Sigma Y)^2}$$

$$= \frac{5\times 214-30\times 40}{5\times 340-(40)^2}$$

$$a = \frac{\Sigma X}{N} - b\frac{\Sigma Y}{N} = \frac{30}{5} - (-1.3)\frac{40}{5} = 16.4$$

$$x = 16.4 - 1.3y$$

MEASUREMENT OF SPATIAL PATTERNS OF DISTRIBUTION NEAREST-NEIGHBOUR ANALYSIS:

It is most popular statistical analysis concerning spatial association and distribution. It was formerly introduceu in mathematics by P. Hertz but its systematic used was initiated by Clark and Evans two American plant ecologist.

It is a technique that enables geographers to make simple objective comparisons between distributions ex-distribution of settlements. The analysis in values a comparison between the observed spacing of a set of points and the spacing that might be expected in a random distribution pattern. The formula is.

$$RN = 2\, d_o \sqrt{n/4}$$

where RN is the nearest neighbour value, d_o is the observed mean distance (measured distance between each point and its nearest neighbour), n is the total number of points in the pattern and A is the area over which the points are distributed.

Values for RN can range in theory from of 0 (maximum clustering) to 2.15 which would be produced by a perfectly uniform distribution of points in an area. A value of 1 indicates a random ditribution.

Among the statistical indices compared to the varying RN value, variance Index (V) and standard variate of the normal curve (C_s) are very important variance index is calculated with the formula

$$V = \frac{(4-\pi)}{4d\pi}$$

$$= \frac{0.0683086}{d}$$

where d is the density of points. The interpretation of V can be done with the help of the following :

(i) rE > V, uniform distribution

(ii) V > rE, clustered

(iii) rE/V = 1, random distribution

RN value	Nature of clustering
0.00 – 0.30	High clustering
0.30 – 0.59	Moderate clustering
0.60 – 0.89	Least clustering
0.90 – 1.10	Random
1.11– 1.45	Least uniformity
1.46 – 1.80	Moderate uniformity
1.81– 2.15	High uniformity.

SCALING TECHNIQUES

It has been observed that no single variable is sufficient enough to reflect all the complex characteristics. So a composite picture from a large number of choosen variables has to be worked out, which is called a Composite Index. But in such case the composite index are highly sensitive to the units of measurement of the original variables.

For example : To show the statewise transport development by a weighted index of :

(i) The number of railway stations per 100 sq. km.

(ii) The average capacity of the transaction in tonnes for a certain year.

In this case the number of stations would be very small in comparison to the yearly tonnage per station. The variations in tonnage are also expected to be much higher than the number of stations. If the two variables are added together, the state having a highest level of tonnage but mainly concentrated in fewer numbers of huge transport junctions, may rank higher than the state having fairly balanced distributions of railway stations, but may not have a tonnage turnover comparable with the first state. The planners may not agree with this kind of ranking. But the problem with this type weightage is that the two variables have different scales of measurement. So it is necessary to eliminate the biasness of scale before evolving any system of weightage.

There are a number of methods for scaling, which are :

RANKING METHOD OR RANK SCORE

In this method we rank the observations and their ranks become new variables. But in this method some points which can affect the result are as follows :

(i) The rank variable is discrete and has no dimension.

(ii) The value of two consecutive ranks do not have an equal amount of difference in their original values.

(iii) Mean, standard deviation and coefficient of variation of all the variables after ranking become equal.

(iv) The larger the number of variables, the smaller will be the distortion in composite index due to ranking.

For example : Suppose there is a state having ten districts and we have to find out the level of development with the help of composite index by ranking different variables.

Here the most developed district would be E followed by D and least developed district would be I. From the composite index column we can comment on the levels of development of districts

District	*Literacy % Ranks*	*Urbanisation Ranks*	*Per Capita Income Rank*	*Composite Index*
A	40 (3)	35 (3)	6234 (6)	12
B	30 (6)	31 (4)	7218 (3)	13
C	32 (5)	29 (5)	6310 (5)	15
D	72 (2)	44 (1)	9888 (2)	5
E	78 (1)	42 (2)	10242 (1)	4
F	21 (8)	22 (6)	6620 (4)	18
G	22 (7)	20 (7.5)	5672 (7)	21.5
H	19 (9)	16 (10)	5200 (8)	27
I	16 (10)	17 (9)	5176 (9)	28
J	36 (4)	20 (7.5)	3720 (10)	21.5

WEIGHTED SCORE

When the biasness of scale is eliminated the main problem remains infront of planners is to assign weights to them.

The weights are generally of two types :

(i) **Subjective Weightage System :** is purely arbitrary and depends upon the ability of the person to determine the weights. But this is not considered good in the absence of strong favourable arguments relating the weights with the objective of the study. Here there are greaters scope of manipulation of the results. The advantage of this method is that it being the simple saves labour and expedits the work.

(ii) **Mathematical Weightage System :** It minimizes the subjectivity. Here a system is evolved through theoretical framework of the problem and its mathematical logic.

SAMPLING TECHNIQUES FOR GEOGRAPHICAL ANALYSIS

Samples are devices for learning about large masses by observing a few individuals. The methods by which a sample is drawn out of a given population are called Techniques of Sampling.

The different methods of sampling which ensure better representation of the population under different situations are given as below.

Simple Random Sampling : It is a method of drawing the sample in which every member of the population has equal chance of being selected in the sample. This method is useful only when the members of the population are fairly Homogeneous.

Areal Random Sampling : The procedure of areal random sampling is slightly different from the ordinary random sampling. By using a random numbers table, a set of points may be selected as random sample of all the points. The areas around the sample points may be considered as sample areas.

Systematic Sampling : Many times a random sample does not have the good coverage of the area of study. A systematic sampling selects the population at regular intervals. For example, every 7th name of an electoral list, every 10th household, every alternate grid intersect etc. will yield the systematic sample. It also gives a more uniform coverage of the population. But if there are regularities in the population distribution, a systematic sample may be biased.

Ex. - Exit polls are done by this method.

Stratified Sampling : When the population is composed of highly varied observations, random sample may not work. For example, for a family planning survey one has to select urban as well as rural households. So a balanced representation may be ensured by dividing the population into two sets of urban and rural households and then drawing a random sample of appropriate size from each set. This type of sampling is called Stratified Sampling.

MULTIPLE CHOICE QUESTIONS

1. Who amongst the following was the first to state that the earth was spherical?
   (a) Copernicus (b) Aristotle
   (c) Ptolemy (d) Strabo
2. Name the Geographer who tried to show a meridian on the world map.
   (a) Erastosthenes (b) Ptolemy
   (c) Herodotus (d) Aristotle
3. Who wrote *the Almagest* ?
   (a) Henry (b) Marco polo
   (c) Ptolemy (d) Al Idrisi
4. Match the following:

(a) Almagest	1. Bernhard Varenium
(b) Isotherms	2. Homboldt
(c) Geographia Generalis	3. Ibn Battuta
(d) Travels	4. Ptolemy

Codes:

	A	B	C	D
(a)	4	2	1	3
(b)	3	4	2	1
(c)	4	1	3	2
(d)	1	3	4	2

5. Who wrote the book "Erdkunde".?
   (a) Carl Ritter (b) Vidal de la Blanche
   (c) Varenius (d) Immanaul Kant
6. "Geography may be persued by two methods or upon two levels which may be distinguished as General geography and specific geography". Who said this?
   (a) Carl Ritter (b) Woolbridge and East
   (c) Humboldt (d) Huntington
7. The study of physical geography in the past geological ages is included in
   (a) Bio geography (b) Historical geography
   (c) Paleography (d) All of these
8. "Geography of development" is a branch of which geography.
   (a) Regional geography
   (b) Economic geography
   (c) Demography
   (d) Political geography
9. Who was the **father of History?**
   (a) Pythagoras (b) Marco Polo
   (c) Herodotus (d) Henry
10. Who had observed the angle of the noon sun at Syene and at Alexandria?
    (a) Hipparchus (b) Erastosthenes
    (c) Ibn Battuta (d) Al Idrisi
11. That the earth is spherical in shape is not proved by which of the following statements-
    I. If the earth were flat there would be some sharp edges to be found by travellers.
    II. Solar eclipses show the shadow of earth as circular.
    III. Sunrise is not visible from all places on earth's surface at the same time.
    IV. The altitude of stars seen from different places on earth's surface vary.
    (a) I and II (b) III
    (c) II (d) I and IV
12. Which of the following gives the constitution of the earth in the correct descending order of layers?
    (a) Atmosphere, hydrosphere, lithosphere, barysphere
    (b) Barysphere, hydrosphere, lithosphere, atmosphere
    (c) Hydrosphere, atmosphere, lithosphere, barysphere
    (d) None of the above
13. Which of the following is matched wrongly?
    I. 23 1/2° N latitude-Tropic of Cancer
    II. 66 1/2° S latitude-Tropic of Capricorn
    III. 23 1/2° S latitude-Arctic Circle
    IV. 66 1/2° N latitude--Antarctic Circle
    (a) I (b) II, III and IV
    (c) II and IV (d) All of them
14. Which of the following is incorrect?
    (a) Within the Arctic and Antarctic Circles there is at least one day in the year during which the sun does not set and at least one day on which it never rises.
    (b) At the North Pole there is darkness for half the year.
    (c) At the summer solstice, the sun shines vertically over the Tropic of Capricorn.
    (d) The sun shines vertically over the Equator twice in the year.
15. The North Pole is always in the light
    (a) from September 23 to March 21
    (b) from March 21 to September 23
    (c) from June 21 to December 22
    (d) on June 21

Direction: (For Q. No. 16):

(a) A and R are true and R explains A
(b) A and R are true but R does not explain A
(c) A is true but R is untrue
(d) A is false but R is true

16. ***Assertion (A) :*** Days and nights all over the globe except the equator and the poles are of varying lengths at different times of the year.
Reason (R) : The earth's axis is oblique and it points in the same direction throughout the year.
(a) A is true but R is false.
(b) A and R are true and R correctly explains A.
(c) Both A and R are false.
(d) A is true but R is not the correct explanation of A.

17. The inequality between day and night becomes greater, or more marked as one travels from .... to ....
(a) poles, equator
(b) equator, poles
(c) Tropic of Cancer, Tropic of Capricorn
(d) Tropic of Capricorn, Tropic of Cancer

18. London and St. Louis (in America) are 90° of longitude apart. Therefore
(a) sunrise at London will be 3 hours earlier than at St. Louis.
(b) sunrise at London will be 3 hours later than at St. Louis.
(c) sunset at London will be 6 hours later than at St. Louis.
(d) sunset at London will be 6 hours earlier than at St. Louis.

19. If the earth's axis were perpendicular to the plane of its orbit and the circle of illumination would pass right through the poles, which of the following would not happen?
(a) Days and nights would be equal throughout the year.
(b) No change of seasons will take place.
(c) The North Pole will always be in the dark.
(d) Nights are longer than days.

20. Which of the statements as regards the consequences of the movement of the earth is not correct?
(a) Revolution of the earth is the cause of the change of seasons.
(b) Rotation of the earth is the cause of days and nights.
(c) Rotation of the earth causes variation in the duration of days and nights.
(d) Rotation of the earth affects the movement of winds and ocean currents.

21. The longitudinal, transverse and surface waves in an earthquake originate from
(a) the focus within the body of the earth
(b) the epicentre on the surface of the earth
(c) the focus on the surface of the earth
(d) the epicentre within the body of the earth

22. The temperature at the core of the earth is about
(a) 20,000°C (b) 2000°C
(c) 2,00,000°C (d) 26,000°C

23. Which of the following gives the correct descending order by volume of the three basic layers of the earth?
I. Core, crust, mantle
II. Crust, core, mantle
III. Core, mantle, crust
(a) I (b) II
(c) III (d) None of these

24. There are two types of crusts—the continental and the oceanic. The continental crust is
(a) thicker below the plains than below mountains
(b) thicker below the mountains than below the plains
(c) almost same all over
(d) thicker under the oceans than under the seas

25. The most abundant constituents of earth's crust are
(a) Igneous rocks (b) Sedimentary rocks
(c) Metamorphic rocks (d) Granite

26. Magma that reaches earth's surface and then solidifies is called
(a) granite (b) lava
(c) quartz (d) silicates

27. Put in descending order of content of fixed carbon
I. Peat II. Lignite
III. Bituminous coal IV. Anthracite
(a) IV, II, III, I (b) I, II, III, IV
(c) III, IV, II, I (d) IV, III, II, I

28. The formation of metamorphic rocks takes place
(a) always in the liquid state
(b) always in the solid state
(c) sometimes in the solid and sometimes in the liquid state
(d) always by chemical recombination process

29. The number of economic minerals associated with sedimentary rocks is

(a) more than that associated with igneous rocks
(b) less than that associated with igneous rocks
(c) same as that in igneous rocks
(d) unknown

30. Gypsum, Saltpetre, Pyrite and Haěmatite all can be found in
(a) sedimentary rocks
(b) igneous rocks
(c) matamorphic rocks
(d) sedimentary and igneous rocks

31. Which of the following has the minimum humus?
(a) Grey-desert soil (b) Red-desert soil
(c) Chestnut soil (d) Chernozem

Direction: (For Q. No. 32):
(a) A and R are true and R explains A
(b) A and R are true but R does not explain A
(c) A is true but R is untrue
(d) A is false but R is true

32. ***Assertion (A) :*** Assam has tertiary coal and oil deposits.
Reason (R) : In the neozoic era the silting up of a gulf created the Assam region.
(a) A and R are true and R explains A
(b) A is true but R is not true
(c) A and R are true but R does not explain A
(d) A and R are false

33. Carbonaceous rocks which produce coal and oil belong to the category of rocks called
(a) metamorphic (b) igneous
(c) sedimentary (d) inorganic

34. Sedimentary rocks are finally and ultimately derived from the
(a) weathering of igneous rocks
(b) weathering of metamorphic rocks
(c) marine deposits
(d) action of earth movements

35. Which one of the following statement is untrue?
(a) The sea-floor is older than the land.
(b) The first rocks were formed as a result of the cooling of molten matter.
(c) Sedimentary rocks are also called aqueous rocks because they were formed by the agency of water.
(d) Stalactites and Stalagmites are deposits of lime found in caves.

36. In which of the following periods were South India, Australia, South and Central Africa part of one compact landmass known as Gondwanaland?
(a) Triassic period of the Mesozoic Era
(b) Neozoic or Tertiary Era
(c) Great Ice Age
(d) None of the above

37. Formation of potholes in river beds is an example of
(a) corrosion (b) corrasion
(c) hydration (d) erosion

38. Fractures in rocks can be caused by
I. Removal of pressure leading to expansion of rocks.
II. Crystal growth and frost heaving.
III. Repeated thermal expansion and contraction.
IV. Penetration of plant roots into rocks.
(a) I and III (b) I, II, III
(c) II, III, IV (d) I, II, III, IV

39. Match the following columns of landforms and their agents of formation

List-I	**List-II**
A. Fault and fold mountains	1. Earth movements
B. Deltas and flood plains	2. Fluvial effect
C. Moraines	3. Glacial activity
D. Coral reefs	4. Organic activity

	A	B	C	D
(a)	1	2	3	4
(b)	4	3	2	1
(c)	3	4	2	1
(d)	2	1	4	3

40. Which of the following is not correct?
(a) Destructional activity of waves produce sea cliffs.
(b) Depositional activity of wind produces loess plains and sand dunes.
(c) Constructional activity of soil movement produces landslide accumulation.
(d) Destructional activity of volcano eruption leads to lava plains and crater lakes.

41. Which one of the following statements is true about glaciers ?
(a) Glaciers occur in areas having a permanent cover of snow and ice
(b) The height above which there is permanent cover of snow and ice is called the snowline
(c) Glaciers are the moving masses of ice and snow
(d) All the above

42. Malaspine Glacier is in

(a) Karakoram Range (b) Alps
(c) Alaska (d) Hindukush4

43. What is the usual altitude of the plains?
(a) Sea levei
(b) Less than 500 metres above sea level
(c) Less than 600 metres above sea level
(d) Less than 800 metres above sea level

44. Which one of the following types of plains is not formed by the action of the rivers?
(a) Loess plains
(b) Alluvial plains
(c) Flood plain deposits
(d) Deltas

45. Changing of colour of a rock into yellow or red is due to
(a) hydration (b) oxidation
(c) carbonation (d) exfoliation

46. Climate of a place is dependent on several factors. Which one of the following is the most significant?
(a) Distance from sea
(b) Direction of winds
(c) Latitude
(d) Ocean currents

47. Seasonal contrasts are maximum in
(a) low latitudes (b) high latitudes
(c) mid latitudes (d) subtropics

48. A line drawn on a weather map connecting points that receive equal amounts of sunshine is
(a) Isohel (b) Isobar
(c) Isothere (d) Isotherm

49. Most of the weather phenomena take place in the
(a) Ionosphere (b) Stratosphere
(c) Troposphere (d) Mesosphere

50. Shimla is cooler than Amritsar although both are on the same latitude. This is because
(a) Shimla is further north.
(b) Shimla is at a greater height above sea level than Amritsar.
(c) Shimla is farther from the equator.
(d) Their longitudes differ.

51. Excess carbon dioxide in the atmosphere due to pollution will cause
(a) earth's temperature to rise
(b) earth's temperature to fall
(c) no change in earth's temperature
(d) increase in ultra-violet radiation reaching the earth

52. The radiation that heats earth's atmosphere comes from the
(a) sun (b) earth
(c) ionosphere (d) sun and earth

53. Match the following:

List-I	**List-II**
A. Chinook	1. Local hot wind in mid latitudes
B. Mistral	2. Cold dry wind in winter
C. Simoon	3. Whirlwind in the Sahara

	A	B	C
(a)	1	2	3
(b)	2	1	3
(c)	3	2	1
(d)	1	3	2

54. Hurricanes or typhoons (tropical cyclones) develop and mature
(a) over land bodies only.
(b) in a belt 35°-65°N and S Latitudes.
(c) anywhere in the tropical zone
(d) over water bodies only

55. Relative humidity
(a) is lowest at the equator increasing towards the poles
(b) is maximum in sub-tropical anticyclones
(c) varies with latitudes seasonally
(d) is lower in winter than in higher latitudes

56. The fog that commonly occurs along the sea coasts is of the....type.
(a) radiation (b) advection
(c) frontal (d) convection

57. Which of the following is wrong?
(a) Stratocumulus, cumulus, cumulonimbus upto 2000 metres
(b) Altocumulus and altostratus upto 6000 mts
(c) Cirrus upto 10,000 metres
(d) Nimbostratus above 10,000 metres

58. Match the following

List-I (Timber)	**List-II (Country)**
A. Cedar	1. Myanmar
B. Doughals fir	2. Canada
C. Mahogany	3. Mexico
D. Teak	4. Honduras

Codes

	A	B	C	D
(a)	3	2	1	4
(b)	3	2	4	1
(c)	2	3	4	1
(d)	2	3	1	4

59. Which one of the following is an area of evergreen forests?
(a) Amazon basin
(b) Zaire basin
(c) South-eastern Asia
(d) All of these
60. Which one of the following is an example of "desert vegetation"?
(a) Temperate grassland
(b) Coniferous forests
(c) Acacia and Cactus
(d) Mosses and lichens
61. Which one of these forests is mostly used for gathering?
(a) Tundra (b) Wet tropical
(c) Dry tropical (d) Temperate
62. Which is the most common areas of nomadic herding?
(a) Cool humid region (b) Rainy area
(c) Dry areas (d) Hot humid regions
63. How much of the world area is under forests?
(a) more than 25%
(b) 15 to 20 percent
(c) less than 15 percent
(d) 20 to 25 percent
64. Which of the following are the chief sources of hard wood timber?
(1) Needle leaf deciduous forests
(2) Broad leaved evergreen forests
(3) Evergreen coniferous forests
(4) Broad leaved deciduous forest
Which of the above statements is/are correct?
(a) 1 and 3 (b) 1 and 2
(c) 1, 2 and 3 (d) All of these
65. It is an example of temperate hardwood
(a) Pine (b) Fir
(c) Cidar (d) Oak
66. Temperate hardwoods are found between
(a) Polewards of 50°N and S
(b) 30° to 50°N and S
(c) 30° to 50°N
(d) 30° to 50°S
67. Which product is formed by Coca leaves?
(a) Cocoa beverage (b) Cocaine
(c) Quinine (d) Camphor
68. Which factor affects the choice of crops in an area?
(i) Market demand and soil conditions
(ii) Climatic conditions
(iii) Economic development
Which of the above statements is/are correct?
(a) (i) and (iii) (b) (ii) and (iii)
(c) (i) and (ii) (d) (i), (ii) and (iii)
69. Which one of the following is not a medicinal plant?
(a) Chinchona (b) Palm
(c) Cocoa shrub (d) Camphor
70. The plant yielding quinine flourishes in
(a) dry subtropics
(b) Tropical highlands
(c) Mediterranean regions
(d) Equatorial forests
71. Match the following:

List-I (Tribes)	**List-II (Regions)**
A. Karen	1. East Africa
B. Ainu	2. Myanmar, Thailand
C. Kikuyu	3. Japan
D. Bushman	4. Kalahari desert

Code:

	A	B	C	D
(a)	2	3	1	4
(b)	4	1	2	3
(c)	3	2	1	4
(d)	1	2	3	4

72. Which one is the tiniest species of human being?
(a) Lapps (b) Pygmies
(c) Dayak (d) Vedda
73. Which one of the following is the most densely populated country of the world?
(a) China (b) India
(c) Monaco (d) Canada
74. Which one is wrongly matched?
(a) Veddas - Nepal
(b) Papuans - New Guinea
(c) Kikuyu - Kenya
(d) Pygmies - Zaire
75. Consider the following statements:
1. The "Masai", is a tribe of settled cultivators, who once wondered with their herds of cattle in the central highlands of East Africa.
2. The cattle kept by the Masai are the "Zebu" cattle with humps and long horns.
Which of the above statements is/are correct?
(a) Only 1 (b) Neither 1 nor 2
(c) Both 1 and 2 (d) Only 2
76. Which of the following is incorrect?
(a) Eskimos live in tents called 'tupics' in summer
(b) Eskimos and the yakuts hunt reindeer for food

(c) In winter Eskimos live in dwellings called igloo

(d) In winter the Eskimo fishes for the subsistence and in summer hunts for the fur trade.

77. Match the following

List-I	List-II
A. Bushmen	1. Malaysia
B. Pygmies	2. Kalahari Desert
C. Semang	3. Congo Basin
D. Lapps	4. Central Asia
E. Kirghiz	5. Norway

	A	B	C	D	E
(a)	2	3	1	5	4
(b)	1	2	3	4	5
(c)	5	4	2	1	2
(d)	2	3	5	1	4

78. Which of the following are not pastoral nomads?
(a) Pygmies (b) Kazaks
(c) Masai (d) Lapps

79. The urban population of the world is growing faster than its rural population. This is mainly because of
(a) high birth rate in towns
(b) rural-urban migration
(c) high death rate in rural areas
(d) low death rate in towns

80. 'Principles of Geology' was written by:
(a) Charles Lyell (b) Play Fair
(c) Cvijic (d) Brukner

81. Submarine form is studied in:
(a) Oceanography (b) Coral reefs
(c) Geomorphology (d) Geology

82. 'Morphology of the Earth' was written by:
(a) Penk (b) L.C. king
(c) Brown E.H. (d) Wooldride

83. Deep weathering theory was propounded by:
(a) Schumn (b) Marie Morisawa
(c) Linton (d) None of these

84. What is the death rate in Australia?
(a) High (b) Extremely high
(c) Low (d) Moderate

85. Name the cultural region which is characterised by the highest urbanisation.
(a) Asia (b) Africa
(c) North America (d) None of these

86. The density of population is mainly influenced by the factor namely :
(a) Transport (b) Pollution
(c) Climate (d) Religion

87. Which type of settlements are found in the areas of low water table?
(a) Widely spaced large settlements
(b) close spaced small settlements
(c) Widely spaced small settlements
(d) None of the above.

88. Which country has a less than 1% population growth rate?
(a) Iraq (b) Libya
(c) Pakistan (d) Japan

89. A higher density of population is favourable to
(a) Capital formation (b) Agricultural growth
(c) Industrial growth (d) Labour supply

90. Most of the people of Europe belong to
(a) Mongoloid (b) Dinaric
(c) Caucasoid (d) Alpnoid

91. In U.S.A. rice is grown
(a) in Texas (b) in the West
(c) in Colorado (d) nowhere

92. Most of the world wheat producing regions have
(a) more than 1500 mm of rainfall
(b) less than 300 mm of rainfall
(c) very high rainfall
(d) less than 1000 mm of rainfall.

93. The leading producer of coffee in the world is
(a) Turkey (b) Brazil
(c) Venezuela (d) Cuba

94. Historical geology was founded by:
(a) Jovan Cvijic
(b) Charles Lyell
(c) A.F. Bernhardi
(d) Walter Penk

95. The Ruhr-Complex is a major industrial centre in
(a) North America (b) Germany
(c) Europe (d) Russia

96. Collective farm of Ukraine is also known as
(a) Kolkhoz (b) Dom
(c) Ryckay Eczik (d) Sovkhoz

97. Match the following countries and commodities in whose production they lead

List-I	List-II
A. Argentina	1. Wool
B. Australia	2. Meat
C. U.S.A.	3. Cotton

D. South Africa 4. Nickel
E. Canada 5. Gold

	A	B	C	D	E
(a)	1	2	3	4	5
(b)	2	1	3	5	4
(c)	2	1	4	5	3
(d)	1	2	3	5	4

98. Oyster-fishing is practised in
(a) Peru and Chile (b) North America
(c) Japan (d) China

99. Fish farming in paddy fields is practised in
(a) Africa (b) South Africa
(c) China (d) Peru and Brazil

100. Today Malaysia has become the home of rubber which was originally brought from
(a) Penang (b) Amazon basin
(c) Congo basin (d) Nile delta

101. Which among the following states is the major producers of Bauxite in India?
(a) Karnataka
(b) Goa
(c) Madhya Pradesh
(d) Odisha

102. Which one is the easiest and cheapest metl.od of mining?
(a) Open-cast mining
(b) Alluvial mining
(c) Underground mining
(d) All of these

103. Name the major ore of Uranium.
(a) Cinnabar (b) Pitchblend
(c) Argentite (d) Bauxite

104. Match the following:

Minerals	**Ore**
(a) Lead	1. Cinnabar
(b) Tungsten	2. Galena
(c) Mercury	3. Pentlaudite
(d) Nickel	4. Wolframite

Codes:

	A	B	C	D
(a)	2	4	1	3
(b)	2	1	4	3
(c)	4	2	3	1
(d)	3	2	4	1

105. The Sullivan mines of British Columbia (Canada); are famous for which mineral resource?
(a) Lead (b) Zinc
(c) Aluminium (d) Tin

106. Which one of the following is thé world's largest producer of Bauxite?
(a) Mexico (b) Atacama desert
(c) Australia (d) Finland

107. The Witwatersrand of South Africa is famous for
(a) Pearls (b) Gold
(c) Diamond (d) Asbestos

108. The largest copper deposits are to be found in
(a) Chile and Arizona
(b) Chile and the Congo
(c) Russia and the Congo
(d) Mexico and Zaire

109. Newcastle, Pennsylvania, Inner Mongolia and Damodar Valley are mining centres of
(a) diamond (b) copper
(e) iron (d) coal

110. Match the following

List-I	**List-II**
A. Zaire	1. Veldt
B. South Africa	2. Diamond
C. Iran	3. Iron ore
D. Ukraine	4. Petroleum

	A	B	C	D
(a)	1	2	3	4
(b)	2	3	1	4
(c)	2	1	4	3
(d)	1	2	4	3

111. Which of the following is wrongly matched:

List I	**List II**
(a) Zinc	Calamine
(b) Magnesium	Dolomite
(c) Sodium	Borax
(d) Manganese	Galena

112. Cassiterite is an ore of
(a) Lead (b) Iron
(c) Tin (d) Silver

113. Diastrophic forces are:
(a) The forces that were generated due to widening of valley
(b) Endogenetic forces
(c) The forces that were generated due to deepening of the valley.
(d) Exogenetic forces

114. Name the most important source of Thorium.
(a) Monazile (b) Pitchblande
(c) Argentite (d) All of these

115. Arrange the following countries according to their coal reserves:
(a) U.S.A., China, Germany, India

(b) India, U.S.A., China, Germany
(c) U.S.A., Russia, Australia, China, India
(d) Russia, China, Germany, U.S.A.

116. Name the Uranium producing centre of Japan :
(a) Tobo (b) Tokyo
(c) Yakohama (d) Osaka

117. Ruhr region (Germany) is famous for
(a) Iron-ore (b) Coal
(c) Aluminium (d) Natural gas

118. The most important uranium ore deposits occur in
(a) Canada (b) Zaire
(c) Pakistan (d) China

119. "White coal" is
(a) uranium (b) hydro-electricity
(c) ice (d) diamond

120. Scandinavia is a suitable country for exploiting hydroclectricity because of the presence of
(a) lakes (b) steep slopes
(c) great rivers (d) waterfalls

121. Which one is the major industrial city of Queensland (Australia)?
(a) Adelaide (b) Brisbane
(c) Perth (d) Hobert

122. Match the following:

Countries	Major textile industrial centres
(a) Britain	1. Osoka, Yakohama
(b) India	2. Manchester, Birmingham
(c) Japan	3. Mumbai
(d) U.S.A.	4. Boston

Codes :

	A	B	C	D
(a)	1	2	3	4
(b)	1	3	4	2
(c)	3	2	4	1
(d)	2	3	1	4

123. Match the following regions and industries

List-I	List-II
A. Switzerland	1. Textiles
B. New England	2. Watches
C. Detroit	3. Steel
D. Pittsburg	4. Automobiles

	A	B	C	D
(a)	2	1	3	4
(b)	2	1	4	3
(c)	3	1	2	4
(d)	2	3	4	1

124. Which of the following is an important occupation of New Zealand?
(a) Mining (b) Industrial activity
(c) Fishing (d) Animal rearing

125. The Fuji is famous for
(a) Automobiles (b) Paper
(c) Silk (d) Pottery

126. The Ichinomiya (Japan) is known for
(a) Petroleum industry
(b) Silk industry
(c) Atomic power plant
(d) Woollen industry

127. Hiroshima - Kobe region of Japan is an important region for
(a) Large iron and steel mills
(b) Ship building
(c) Lumbering
(d) None of these

128. Match the following:

Industrial Significance	**Location**
(a) Automobile capital	1. Pittsburg
(b) Coal and Steel city	2. Detroit
(c) Iron-ore deposits	3. Mesabi range
(d) Naval station on Pacific Coast	4. Pearl Harbour

Codes:

	A	B	C	D
(a)	2	1	3	4
(b)	1	2	3	4
(c)	4	3	2	1
(d)	1	4	3	2

129. Name the highly industrial region of Europe.
(a) Ruhr (b) Rhine
(c) Lorraine (d) Alsace

130. Which country is known for its highly developed dairy industry?
(a) New Zealand (b) Denmark
(c) Tusmania (d) Italy

131. Which one is wrongly matched?

List I	**List II**
(a) Baku	Petroleum
(b) Glasglow	Ship building
(c) Windsor	Meat
(d) Osaka	Cotton textile

132. Name the meat city of the world?
(a) New York (b) Adeleide
(c) Chicago (d) Detroit

133. Where is the Silicon Valley situated?
(a) Near San Francisco
(b) Detroit
(c) Mexico
(d) Florida

134. What do you mean by "APPLE"?
(a) Air passengers experiment
(b) Arial passengers payload experiment
(c) Arian passenger payload experiment
(d) None of these

135. The railroad that originates in the interior and moves towards the coast is found in Africa, and is part of what is known as intragressive railways. It generally reflects the socio-economic situation of
(a) high industrialisation
(b) low industrialisation
(c) being an exporter of raw materials
(d) being backward

136. A short cut sea route between the European and Asian countries was provided by
(a) Cape of Good Hope route
(b) Suez Canal
(c) Panama Canal
(d) North Atlantic route

137. The construction of Panama Canal in 1914 eliminated the long and hazardous voyage
(a) round the stormy Cape Horn
(b) round the Cape of Good Hope
(c) between North and South America
(d) in the stormy Atlantic Ocean

138. Which of the following is the busiest of ocean trade routes?
(a) Suez Canal (b) Cape of Good Hope
(c) North Atlantic (d) Panama Canal

139. Suez Canal links
(a) Mediterranean Sea and Caribbean Sea
(b) Black Sea and Baltic Sea
(c) Red Sea and Mediterranean Sea
(d) Arabian Sea and Red Sea

140. If I wanted to reach the South Atlantic from the South Pacific while touching South America, I would have to use
(a) Florida Straits (b) Dardanelles
(c) Magellan Straits (d) Bosporus

141. Trans-Siberian railway joins the
(a) Halifax to Vancover
(b) Sydney to Perth
(c) Cairo to Capetown
(d) St. Petersburg to Vladivostok

142. Name the largest railways junction in the world
(a) New York (b) Boston
(c) Chicago (d) Philadelphia

Direction: (For Q. No. 143):
(a) A and R are true and R explains A
(b) A and R are true but R does not explain A
(c) A is true but R is untrue
(d) A is false but R is true

143. **Assertion (A):** The Canadian national railways connect Halifax to Prince Rupert in British Columbia.
Reason (R): It is a trans-continental railway.

144. Which one of the rivers is the most navigable river in the world?
(a) Denube (b) Rhine
(c) Mississippi (d) Nile

145. Name the country which has the most dense railway networks?
(a) China (b) U.S.A.
(c) Russia (d) India

146. The Australian trans-continental railway joins
(a) Perth to Darwin (b) Hobart to Perth
(c) Sydney to Perth (d) Adelaide to Perth

147. When was the Panama canal started?
(a) 1914 (b) 1915
(c) 1918 (d) 1869

148. Name the two oceans which are joined by the canal Panama.
(a) Indian Ocean to Atlantic
(b) Atlantic to Pacific
(c) Pacific to Arctic
(d) Indian to Antarctic

149. Why is the Panama Canal famous?
1. It joins two major oceans
2. It lies in Central Africa
3. It is a big canal
4. It reduces the distance between the eastern and western coasts of U.S.A.

(a) 1 only (b) 1 and 2 only
(c) 1,2,3,4 (d) 1, 3, 4 only

150. Kiel canal joins
(a) Baltic sea to Mediterranean sea
(b) Red sea to Mediterranean sea
(c) North sea to Black sea
(d) None of these

151. Which of the following lies on the Nile river?
(a) Nairobi (b) Addis Ababa
(c) Khartoum (d) Kinhasa

152. Match the following

List-I	List-II
A. Budapest	1. Arakawa
B. Lisbon	2. Irrawady
C. Tokyo	3. Tigris
D. Baghdad	4. Danube

E. Ryngoon 5. Tagus

	A	B	C	D	E
(a)	1	2	4	5	3
(b)	5	4	2	3	1
(c)	5	4	1	2	3
(d)	4	5	1	3	2

153. The Radcliffe Line demarcates the boundary between
(a) India and China
(b) India and Pakistan
(c) Pakistan and Afghanistan
(d) India and Afghanistan

154. Which one of the following countries has common borders with the largest number of countries ?
(a) India (b) France
(c) Russia (d) Zimbabwe

155. The world's largest river is
(a) Amazon (b) Nile
(c) Mississippi (b) Brahmaputra

156. Which of the following gives the three largest countries of Europe in correct descending order?
(a) Russia, Turkey, France
(b) Russia, Turkey, Spain
(c) France, Turkey, Spain
(d) France, Spain, Sweden

157. Match the following:

Town	River
(a) Bonn	1. Rhine
(b) Washington	2. Potomac
(c) Cairo	3. Nile
(d) Lahore	4. Ravi

Codes :

	A	B	C	D
(a)	1	2	3	4
(b)	4	3	2	1
(c)	1	2	4	3
(d)	2	1	3	4

158. Where is Gate of Tears?
(a) Egypt
(b) Strait of Beb-el-Mandeb
(c) Ireland
(d) Korea

159. Which one of the following is known as the land of white elephants?
(a) India (b) China
(c) Indonesia (d) Thailand

160. Which is wrongly matched?
(a) Windy city Chicago
(b) Eternal city Rome
(c) Herring Pond Korea
(d) Island of cloves Zanzibar

161. Palk Strait separates India from
(a) Pakistan (b) China
(c) Andaman Island (d) Sri Lanka

162. Lakshadweep Islands are situated in
(a) Arabian Sea (b) Palk Strait
(c) Indian Ocean (d) Bay of Bengal

163. India's latitudinal and longitudinal extent, measured in degrees, are almost the same, but its east-west extent, measured in km, is greater than its north-south extent. This is due to the fact that
(a) longitudes are not parallel lines
(b) the distance between latitudes remains the same but the distance between longitudes is greatest at the equator and nil at the poles where all longitudes join
(c) all longitudes, with their opposites, form great circles
(d) the earth is not a perfect sphere

164. The longest shore-line is along the state of
(a) Gujarat (b) Maharashtra
(c) Orissa (d) Kerala

165. The territorial waters of India extends up to
(a) 5 nautical miles
(b) 12 nautical miles
(c) 15 nautical miles
(d) 2 nautical miles

166. Which of the following States of India do not lie entirely in the Tropical Zone of the earth ?
(a) Kerala and Tamil Nadu
(b) Gujarat
(c) Karnataka
(d) Maharashtra and Andhra Pradesh

167. The Indian States which have common borders with Pakistan are:
(a) Gujarat, Himachal Pradesh, Haryana and Jammu and Kashmir
(b) Gujarat, Jammu and Kashmir, Ladakh, Punjab and Rajasthan
(c) Jammu and Kashmir, Haryana, Rajasthan and Punjab
(d) Jammu and Kashmir, Himachal Pradesh, Punjab and Rajasthan

168. Which of the following Indian islands lies between India and Sri Lanka ?
(a) Elephanta (b) Nicobar
(c) Rameshwaram (d) Salsette

169. The sun rises in Arunachal Pradesh two hours before it does in Dwaraka in Gujarat. This is because the former is
(a) higher in elevation than Dwaraka
(b) situated further north than Dwaraka
(c) situated further east (about 300 longitude) than Dwaraka
(d) situated about 300 east of Dwaraka and the earth rotates from west to east

170. Which of the Indian States has the maximum number of common borders with other Indian States?
(a) West Bengal (b) Uttar Pradesh
(c) Madhya Pradesh (d) Karnataka

171. The vigorous glacial action of the Himalayan rivers in the past is proved by
(a) the awe-inspiring gorges
(b) the sedimentary beds of the Kashmir valley
(c) the hanging valleys at lower altitudes
(d) the frequent shifts in the courses of the rivers

172. What is the most important characteristic of the islands (Indian) located in the Arabian Sea ?
(a) They are all very small in size
(b) They are all of coral origin
(c) They have a very dry climate
(d) They are extended parts of the mainland

173. What do the basalt layers of the Deccan indicate?
(a) The influence of weathering
(b) The immense erosional activity of the rivers
(c) Huge volcanic eruptions in the distant past
(d) All the above

174. The main difference between the Eastern Ghats and the Western Ghats is in the matter of
(a) continuity
(b) proximity to coast
(c) ending in Nilgiris
(d) height

175. The region on the southern side of the Shiwaliks is called the
(a) Dunes (b) Bhabhar
(c) Terai (d) Khadar

176. The Nilgiris are part of the
(a) Eastern Ghats
(b) Western Ghats
(c) Vindhyachal
(d) Tamil Nadu Hills

177. Which of the following is characterised by excessive dampness with a thick growth forest and a variety of wild life?
(a) Bhabhar (b) Bhangar
(c) Terai (d) Khadar

178. Match the following

List-I	List-II
A. Kumaon Himalayas	1. Between the Indus and the Sutlej
B. Nepal Himalayas	2. Between the Kali and the Teesta
C. Punjab Himalayas	3. Between the Teesta and the Brahmaputra
D. Assam Himalayas	4. Between the Sutlej and the Kali

	A	B	C	D
(a)	1	2	3	4
(b)	2	3	1	4
(c)	4	2	3	1
(d)	4	2	1	3

179. Consider the following statements:
1. Longitudes of Jabalpur's location is between those of Indore and Bhopal.
2. Latitude of Aurangabad's location is between those of Vadodara and Pune.
3. Bangalore is situated more southward than Chennai.

Which of three statements is/are correct?
(a) 1 and 3 (b) Only 2
(c) 2 and 3 (d) 1, 2 and 3

180. The Cudappah range lie between
(a) Godavari and Palkonda range
(b) Godavari and Jamshedpur
(c) Palar and Cauveri
(d) Satpura and Mohadeo-Maikal range

181. Which of the following have almost the same point of beginning ?
(a) Ganga and Indus
(b) Ganga and Brahmaputra
(c) Beas and Tapti
(d) Indus and Brahmaputra

182. Which of the following river makes an estuary?
(a) Cauvery (b) Krishna
(c) Narmada (d) Ganga

183. The river Damodar ends in
(a) river Ganga (b) river Hooghly
(c) the Bay of Bengal (d) salt lake

184. River Tapti rises from
(a) Vindhyas (b) Aravalis
(c) Satpura range (d) Amarkantak plateau

185. The youngest rivers in India originate from
   (a) Eastern Ghats (b) Western Ghats
   (c) Himalayas (d) Deccan Plateau
186. The source of the Brahmaputra is
   (a) Pindari glacier
   (b) a glacier near the Mansarovar lake
   (c) somewhere near Tibet
   (d) Punjab
187. Which of the following rivers divides the Deccan Tableland from Northern India ?
   (a) Chambal (b) Krishna
   (c) Godavari (d) Narmada
188. Which of the following is not a characteristic of Peninsular rivers ?
   (a) Seasonal flow
   (b) Meandering tendency, often shifting their beds
   (c) Flow through shallow valleys
   (d) Little erosional activity
189. Tochi, Gilgit and Hunza are tributaries of
   (a) Ganga (b) Indus
   (c) Brahmaputra (d) Yamuna
190. The right Ganga tributaries of the Plain do not include
   (a) Alaknanda (b) Yamuna
   (c) Son (d) Tons
191. The weather office predicts 'depression" over a certain area. It means:
   (a) cloudy skies
   (b) atmospheric pressure in that area is lower than that in the surrounding areas
   (c) heavy weather causing a feeling of depression
   (d) low atmospheric pressure over a large area
192. Where would you experience a dry winter?
   (a) The Ganga plain
   (b) North-eastern India
   (c) Kashmir
   (d) Coromandal Coast
193. Which of the following is not one of the traditional Indian seasons?
   (a) Shisira (b) Grishma
   (c) Varsha (d) Margashirsha
194. Consider the following:
   1. Chilka lake
   2. Pulicat lake
   3. Vembanad lake
   Which of the above is/are lagoon (S)
   (a) 1 and 2 (b) 2 only
   (c) 1 and 3 (d) 1, 2 and 3
195. The retreating monsoon withdraws itself from
   (a) the west coast to the east coast
   (b) North-East India to the west coast
   (c) the north to the south
   (d) North-West India to Bengal and then to Kerala
196. How do dust storms in summer affect the temperature?
   (a) Increase it (b) Decrease it
   (c) No effect (d) Cannot say
197. At which place will you find maximum sunlight in December?
   (a) Kanniyakumari (b) Pune
   (c) Kolkata (d) Leh
198. The irregularity in the amount of rain in different parts of the north-Indian plains, during different years, is mainly due to
   (a) irregular intensity of low pressure in the north-western part of India
   (b) difference in frequency of cyclones
   (c) variations in the location of the axis of the low pressure trough
   (d) the amount of moisture carried by the winds not being the same every year
199. There is heavy rainfall on the western coast of India but very little in the Deccan because
   (a) the Deccan plateau is situated in the rain shadow of the Western Ghats
   (b) the region is bypassed by the south-west monsoons
   (c) lack of high mountains in the Deccan
   (d) of some unknown reason
200. Which of the following does not have influence over the climate in India?
   (a) Nearness to equator
   (b) Presence of Indian Ocean
   (c) Monsoons
   (d) Ocean currents
201. Rajasthan receives very little rain because.
   (a) it is too hot
   (b) there is no water available and thus the winds remain dry
   (c) the monsoons fail to reach this area
   (d) the winds do not come across any barrier to cause the necessary uplift to cool the winds
202. Which of the following indicates the types of soil erosion in decreasing order of damage caused in India
   (a) Ravine erosion and gullies, alkalinity and salinity, weeds and water-logging

(b) Alkalinity and water-logging, ravine erosion and weeds
(c) Water-logging, weeds, salinity and ravine erosion
(d) All are equally damaging

203. Which of the following States has very little alluvial soil?
(a) Bihar (b) Madhya Pradesh
(c) Tamil Nadu (d) Punjab

204. The soils of the Plains have not been derived
(a) from the Himalayan rocks
(b) from the Peninsular rocks
(e) only from the rocks existing locally
(d) from material brought by the rivers

205. Match the following types of soil and regions where they are found in India

List-I	List-II
A. Alluvial soils	1. Highland areas of the Plateau
B. Black soils	2. Periphery of the Plateau
C. Red soils	3. Deccan lava tracts
D. Laterite soils	4. River basins and coastal plains

	A	B	C	D
(a)	4	3	1	2
(b)	4	2	3	1
(c)	1	2	3	4
(d)	4	3	2	1

206. Which of the following soils is formed under typical monsoonal conditions?
(a) Black soils (b) Red soils
(c) Laterite soils (d) None

207. Which of the following is incorrect?
(a) Red soils are rich in iron
(b) Black soils are rich in phosphorus, nitrogen and organic matter
(c) Alluvial soils are rich in potash but poor in phosphorus
(d) Red soils are suitable for cultivation of pulses and coarse grains

208. Which is the chief characteristic of the soil of the Indo-Gangetic plain?
(a) It is derived from Himalayan rocks
(b) It is rich in humus
(c) It is formed of peninsular rocks
(d) It is derived from local rocks

209. Where in India would you find endemic flora?
I. Gangetic Plains II. Peninsular areas
III. Himalayas IV. Thar desert
(a) II and III (b) I only
(c) III only (d) II and IV

210. ***Assertion (A):*** Most of the 'exotics' or plants that have come to India from outside are troublesome weeds which thrive here.
Reason (R): They have no 'natural' enemies of their home land to curb them in their new habitat.
(a) A and R are true but R is not a correct explanation of A
(b) A and R are true and R correctly explains A
(c) A is true but R is untrue
(d) A and R are both incorrect

211. "Reserved forests" are forests:
(a) reserved for hunting
(b) reserved for commercial exploitation and prohibited for grazing
(c) reserved for local use
(d) reserved for growing medicinal herbs

212. Black soils is ideal for cultivation of cotton as
(a) it colour is black
(b) it can retain moisture
(c) it is made up of lava
(d) it is found on plateau regions

213. Which state in India has the largest area under forests?
(a) Himachal Pradesh (b) Madhya Pradesh
(c) Karnataka (d) Assam

214. Which of the following is/are correct?
1. Black soils are also called Bangar.
2. In some parts of Gujarat and Tamil Nadu the origin of black cotton soils is ascribed to old lagoons in which the river deposited the materials brought down from the interior of Peninsula covered with lava.
3. Geographically black soils are spread over 24.6% of the total geographical area of the country
4. The black colour is due to presence of hematite ores in the soil.
(a) only 2 (b) 1, 2 and 3
(c) 1 and 4 (d) 1, 3 and 4

215. The soils which have supported agriculture for centuries without much manuring or fallowing are
(a) alluvial and laterite soils
(b) red and laterite soils
(c) black and alluvial soils
(d) laterite and black soils

216. The minimum forest cover necessary to maintain ecological balance is
(a) 50% of the total land area
(b) 40% of the total land area
(c) 33% of the total land area
(d) 25% of the total land area

217. The tropical deciduous plants special to the Deccan are
(a) teak (b) shisam
(c) sandalwood (d) sal

218. The Periyar Game Sanctuary in Kerala is renowned for
(a) tiger (c) wild elephant
(b) lion (d) spotted deer

219. Which sanctuary has been selected as an alternative home for the Indian lion?
(a) Bandipur Sanctuary (Karnataka)
(b) Ghana Sanctuary (Rajasthan)
(c) Periyar Sanctuary (Kerala)
(d) Chandra Prabha Sanctuary (U.P.)

220. Mudumalai sanctuary, famous for elephants and deer, is situated in
(a) Assam (b) Gujarat
(c) Tamil Nadu (d) Karnataka

221. What is the number of females per thousand males as per the 2001 census?
(a) 967 (b) 937
(c) 936 (d) 933

222. Bengali, Hindi, Gujarati, and Marathi belong to the linguistic family
(a) Aryan (b) Dravidian
(c) Austric (d) Sino-Tibetan

223. Tamil, Telugu and Malayalam belong to the linguistic family
(a) Aryan (b) Dravidian
(c) Austric (d) None of the above

224. Where is the sex ratio lowest?
(a) Punjab
(b) Andaman and Nicobar Islands
(c) Rajasthan
(d) Sikkim

225. Which among the following States supports the maximum percentage of tribal population?
(a) Madhya Pradesh (b) Andhra Pradesh
(c) Sikkim (d) Nagaland

226. The scheduled tribes population is around of the total population in India.
(a) 13% (b) 12%
(c) 8% (d) 4%

227. The maximum percentage of the tribal population in India consists of
(a) Santhals (b) Bhils
(c) Mundas (d) Nagas

228. The Bhils and the Kols live
(a) along the Vindhya ranges
(b) in the Nilgiris
(c) in the North-East frontiers of India
(d) all over India

229. In the Andaman Islands live the:
(a) Todas (b) Onge
(c) Gonda (d) Lepcha

230. Where are the Lepchas mainly to be found staying?
(a) Meghalaya (b) Mizoram
(c) Sikkim (d) Arunachal Pradesh

231. Which of the following is wrongly matched?
(a) Shompens - Andaman & Nicober
(b) Minicoy - Lakshadweep
(c) Khasi - Mizoram
(d) Garo - Madhya Pradesh

232. In which of the following states would you not find Bhils?
(a) Gujarat (b) Karnataka
(c) Madhya Pradesh (d) Uttar Pradesh

233. Lambadis are concentrated in
(a) Kerala (b) Andhra Pradesh
(c) Karnataka (d) All these

234. Where would you find Oraon, Munda, Santhal, Gonds and Asurs?
(a) Madhya Pradesh (b) Gujarat
(c) Maharashtra (d) Bihar

235. Match the following:

List-I	List-II
A. Jarawas	1. Tamil Nadu
B. Abor	2. Himachal Pradesh
C. Kotas	3. Bihar
D. Gaddi	4. Arunachal Pradesh
E. Banjara	5. Andaman & Nicobar

	A	B	C	D	E
(a)	5	4	2	1	3
(b)	4	1	2	3	5
(c)	5	4	1	2	3
(d)	4	5	2	1	3

236. In which state women outnumber men?
(a) Tamil Nadu (b) Kerala
(c) Himachal Pradesh (d) Karnataka

237. Put the following in correct descending order of density of population as per the 2001 census

I. Tamil Nadu I. West Bengal
III. Kerala IV. Uttar Pradesh
(a) III, II, IV, I (b) II, III, IV, I
(c) III, II, IV, I (d) II, III, I, IV

238. Which of the following sequences is correct with respect to the descending order of population?
(a) U.P.-Maharashtra-Bihar-West Bengal
(b) U.P.-Maharashtra-Bihar-West Bengal
(c) U.P.-West Bengal-Bihar-Maharashtra
(d) U.P.-Bihar-West Bengal-Maharashtra

239. Jarawas are tribes living in
(a) Madhya Pradesh
(b) Nagaland
(c) Arunachal Pradesh
(d) Andaman and Nicobar

240. One of the chief effects of urbanization in India is
(a) overcrowding in cities
(b) more jobs available
(c) lower standard of living
(d) stagnant agriculture

241. States which have gained population through in migration to their industrial centres, are
(a) Maharashtra and West Bengal
(b) Gujarat and Tamil Nadu
(c) Punjab and Rajasthan
(d) Assam and Tripura

242. Which amongst the following States has the highest population density as per Census 2011?
(a) Kerala (b) Madhya Pradesh
(b) Uttar Pradesh (d) Bihar

243. The Dravidian language family
(a) has its members throughout the Peninsular Plateau
(b) accounts for nearly 40% of the Indian population
(c) is the least dispersed among the four major language families of India
(d) is an offshoot of Sanskrit

244. In which of the following areas is Konkani spoken as the local language?
(a) Kerala and Karnataka
(b) Maharashtra and Goa
(c) Orissa and West Bengal
(d) Andhra Pradesh

245. In a country like India, the rate of human capital formation will increase
(a) through purposeful and work-oriented education
(b) if there are more births
(c) if all the unemployed take to self-employment
(d) through labour-intensive development programmes

246. What is the reason for the higher percentage of female workers in rural areas compared to the towns and cities in India?
(a) Rural females are uneducated
(b) There are more employment opportunities for females in rural areas than in towns
(c) Rural women are more educated and job-oriented
(d) Subsistence agriculture forces women to take to work

247. Where do Birhors live?
(a) Madhya Pradesh (b) Assam
(c) Nagaland (d) Tamil Nadu

248. How many towns have been listed according to the 2011 census?
(a) About 7935 (b) About 3700
(c) About 3500 (d) About 4500

249 The present stage of demographic transition in India marked by high birth rate and low death rate indicates
(a) undeveloped primitive economy
(b) partially industrialized economy
(c) agrarian economy with some development impulses
(d) low income agrarian economy

250. In general, it is observed that the rate of population growth has been in the densely populated areas compared to sparsely populated areas.
(a) low (b) high
(c) negligible (d) almost the same

251. The main hydroelectric power potential of the Indus river system lies in India and not in Pakistan because
(a) the need for hydroelectric power is greater in India than the Pakistan
(b) India has superior technology to develop hydroelectric power
(c) India has a greater labour force to develop hydroelectric power
(d) the mountain stages of these rivers lie in India

252. Which multipurpose project was taken up first of all after independence?
(a) Bhakra Nangal project
(b) Damodar Valley project

(c) Kosi project
(d) None of these

253. Which of the following factors is/are responsible for **West-Bengal** being the largest producer of jute in India?
1. It experiences high temperature and receives high rainfall.
2. Annual flood-silts provide natural fertilizer.
3. It has the highest concentration of jute mills.
4. It is located at the seaboard.

(a) 1 only (b) 1 and 2
(c) 1, 2 and 3 (d) 1, 2, 3 and 4

254. Match List I (produce) with List II (Major producer state) and select the correct answer using the codes given below the lists.

List-I (Produce)	**List-II** (Major Producer)
A. Sun Flower	1. Gujarat
B. Soyabean	2. Tamil Nadu
C. Groundnut	3. Maharashtra
D. Wheat	4. Karnataka
	5. Uttar Pradesh

Codes:

	A	B	C	D
(a)	4	1	2	5
(b)	5	3	1	4
(c)	4	3	1	5
(d)	5	1	2	4

255. The world's longest masonary dam is:
(a) Hirakud (b) Bhakra Nangal
(c) Nagarjuna Sagar (d) Aswan

256. The Kosi project is aimed towards
(a) irrigation
(b) drainage and power generation
(c) power generation and flood control
(d) irrigation, flood control and power generation

257. The Farakka project is mainly aimed towards
(a) irrigating more land in West Bengal
(b) utilizing maximum of Ganga water
(c) preserving the port of Kolkata
(d) production of electricity

258. Irrigation facilities are difficult to create in the Himalayan regions, because of
(a) the difficulty in digging channels from the nearby rivers
(b) non-availability of sub-soil water
(c) the inclined surface of mountain slopes not retaining water
(d) there being no rivers near the cultivable land

259. Many parts of India face difficulty in producing multiple crops because
(a) temperature fluctuates in extreme
(b) monsoons are unpredictable
(c) water is not easily available
(d) it is not economically satisfactory

260. The Central Frozen Semen Bank at Bangalore was set up in order to help in
(a) producing high quality bulls
(b) producing quality sheep
(c) doing research in family planning and eugenics
(d) all the above

261. The States involved in the Dandakaranya Project are
(a) Uttar Pradesh, Maharashtra and Karnataka
(b) Karnataka, Andhra Pradesh and Tamil Nadu
(c) Orissa, Madhya Pradesh, and Andhra Pradesh
(d) Kerala, Tamil Nadu, Andhra Pradesh

262. Match the columns

List-I	**List-II**
A. Beas Project	1. Krishna
B. Nagarjunasagar Dam	2. Godavari
C. Ukai Project	3. Bhagirathi
D. Poochampad Project	4. Tapi
E. Tehri Project	5. Pong dam.

	A	B	C	D	E
(a)	4	1	5	2	3
(b)	5	1	4	2	3
(c)	5	1	2	4	3
(d)	1	4	3	2	5

263. Which of the following hydro-electric stations is situated in Uttar Pradesh?
(a) Mayurakshi (b) Rihand
(e) Kangsabati (d) Hirakud

264. Hidkal Dam is on the river
(a) Krishna (b) Cauvery
(c) Pennar (d) Ghataprabha

265. Which of the following crops will be beneficial in Rajasthan if adequate water supply through rivers and wells is provided?
(a) Wheat (b) Rice
(c) Cotton (d) Maize

266. Which of the following is not a project in Gujarat?
(a) Panam (b) Salal
(c) Mahi (d) Tawa

267. Marine fisheries in India face an important limitation of development in

(a) coastal ocean currents
(b) lack of enterprise in fishermen
(c) coastlines being straight, thus making it difficult to build protected ports
(d) none of the above

268. The multipurpose project irrigating maximum area in India is
(a) Beas (b) Bhakra Nangal
(c) Damodar Valley (d) Hirakud

269. The areas of high crop intensity do not include
(a) Western Assam Valley
(b) Eastern coastal plains
(c) the north Indian plains
(d) dry Deccan areas

270. The Green Revolution involved the use of high yielding varieties of seeds which require
(a) less fertilizer and less water
(b) more fertilizer and less water
(c) less fertilizer and more water
(d) more fertilizer and more water

271. Where in India is mica mined?
(a) Nasirabad (Rajasthan)
(b) Gaya (Bihar)
(c) Nellore (Andhra Pradesh)
(d) All the above

272. Which of the following is associated with the recent discovery of tungsten by the Geological Survey of India?
(a) Agucha in Rajasthan
(b) Thar Desert in Rajasthan
(c) Tuensang in Nagaland
(d) Sirohi in Rajasthan

273. Niobium will be produced for the first time in India at the plant in the Sung Valley in the Jaintia Hills district in Meghalaya. Niobium occurs in the mineral called
(a) Pyrochlore (b) Dolomite
(c) Rock salt (d) Ilmenite

274. What is Bailadila famous for?
(a) Bauxite (b) Iron ore
(c) Copper (d) Coal

275. In which State is chromite abundantly found?
(a) Orissa (b) Maharashtra
(c) Madhya Pradesh (d) Karnataka

276. India has eight coastal states, but more than half the sea salt is made along the Gujarat coast because
(a) Gandhiji started the salt movement in Gujarat
(b) low rainfall and relative humidity are ideal for the production of salt through evaporation of sea water
(c) Kandla port exports salt
(d) the salinity of sea water is very high near the Gujarat coast

277. Gondwana coalfields are found in
(a) Assam (b) Madhya Pradcsh
(c) Meghalaya (d) Jammu & Kashmir

278. In terms of total value of production in India, the mineral group next to iron ore is
(a) bauxite (b) phosphorite
(c) minor minerals (d) None of the above

279. Which of the following states has oil resource based on geographical location?
(a) Maharashtra (b) Meghalaya
(c) Assam (d) Kerala

280. Which of the following States can boast, of important deposits of copper, lead, and zinc ores together?
(a) Bihar (b) Madhya Pradesh
(c) Rajasthan (d) Karnataka

281. The India city famous for glass bangle industry, is
(a) Lucknow (b) Sikandrabad
(b) Ferozabad (d) Agra

282. The first machine-made paper was manufactured
(a) in 1870 near Kolkata
(b) in 1903 in Mumbai
(c) in 1910 at Delhi
(d) after independence

283. Newsprint in India is not produced in
(a) Nepanagar (M.P.) (b) Mysore
(c) Velboor (Kerala) (d) Nelloor (A.P.)

284. The first cotton mill was set up at Fort Gloster in Kolkata in
(a) 1919 (b) 1926
(c) 1818 (d) 1854

285. Mathura Refinery gets its crude oil from
(a) crude imported through Kandla
(b) Kalol
(c) Naharkatiya
(d) Bombay High

286. H.M.T, industries are set up at
(a) Kalamassery
(b) Hyderabad and Bangalore
(c) Pinjore and Ajmer
(d) All of these

287. The nuclear power plant in India, which will provide power mainly for agriculture, is located at

(a) Kalpakkam (b) Narora
(c) Kota (d) Tarapur

288. Which one of the following statements is false?
(a) The biggest steel plant in India is the Bokaro steel plant
(b) The only private-sector steel plant is situated in Jamshedpur
(c) Soyabean leads in productivity of sugar
(d) The coir industry is chiefly found in the State of Kerala

289. The first fertilizer plant was set up at
(a) Nangal (Punjab)
(b) Sindri (Bihar)
(c) Alwaye (Kerala)
(d) Trombay (Maharashtra)

290. Penicillin is produced at
(a) Bangalore (b) Alwaye
(c) Poona (d) Pimpri

291. Tanks are manufactured at
(a) Kanpur (b) Chittaranjan
(c) Perambur (d) Avadi

292. Passenger and merchant ships are constructed at
(a) Mazagon Docks
(b) Hindustan Shipyard at Vishakhapatnam
(c) no place; the Indian docks only make navy ships
(d) Goa Shipyard

293. Railway passenger coaches are manufactured at
(a) Varanasi (b) Chittaranjan
(c) Perambur (d) Kolkata

294. The Bokaro steel plant has been set up with the assistance of
(a) Russia (b) U.K.
(c) U.S.A. (d) Germany

295. The first Alumina plant in India is situated at
(a) Kiriburu (Jharkhand)
(b) Ratnagiri (Maharashtra)
(c) Sirpur (A.P.)
(d) Korba (M.P.)

296. At which of the following places is a fertilizer plant is not located?
(a) Churk (b) Alwaye
(c) Namrup (d) Baroda

297. The major thermal power station fed on natural gas is at
(a) Lunej (b) Trombay
(c) Naharkatiya (d) Digboi

298. Where is the Ambassador car manufactured?
(a) Mahindra & Mahindra (Pune)
(b) Premier Automobiles (Mumbai)
(c) Standard Motor (Chennai)
(d) Hind Motors (Kolkata)

299. Which of the following is not an important reason for the suitablility of the Mumbai for textile industry?
(a) Moist climate
(b) Availability of cheap labour
(c) great demand for textile goes in Mumbai
(d) Availability of raw material

300. Which of the following is not an important industry in Kanpur?
(a) Cement
(b) Leather
(c) Cotton and woollen textiles
(d) Sugar

301. Which one of the following mountains is formed due to convergence of one oceanic and one continental plate?
(a) Urals (b) Alps
(c) Andes (d) Appalachians

302. Which one of the following processes is responsible for the weathering of rocks in a Karst region?
(a) Hydrolysis (b) Carbonation
(c) Oxidation (d) Scree formation

303. Match List-I with List-II and select the correct answer from the codes given below:

List-I (River)	***List-II (Type of Delta)***
A. Nile	1. Estuarine
B. Mississippi	2. Arcuate
C. Ganga	3. Bird foot
D. Tiber	4. Cuspate

Codes:

	A	B	C	D
(a)	2	4	3	1
(b)	4	2	1	3
(c)	1	4	2	3
(d)	2	3	1	4

304. The term panplane refers to:
(a) A level surface formed by wind erosion.
(b) A plane formed by joining of flood-plains.
(c) A level surface formed by the fluvial cycle at the old age.
(d) A level plain formed by human intervention.

305. The statement "The present is the key to the past" was made by:
(a) Walther Penck (b) W.M. Davis
(c) Huntington (d) James Hutton

306. A band of wind called 'Jet Stream' is found in:
(a) Lower Troposphere
(b) Middle Troposphere
(c) Upper Troposphere
(d) Whole Troposphere

307. 'Negative Southern Oscillation Index' refers to which of the following?
(a) Favourable condition for El Niño
(b) Favourable condition for La Nina
(c) Favourable conditions both for El Niño and La Nina
(d) Unfavourable conditions both for El Niño and La Nina

308. In which of the following areas, the main centre of 'Hurricane Mathew' that occurred in Caribbean Sea in the 1st week of October, 2016 was located?
(a) Florida (b) Georgia
(c) South Carolina (d) South-West Haitti

309. In Indian Ocean between 0°–10° N and 0°–10° S latitudinal zones, the temperature variations is of about:
(a) 3°C (b) 2°C
(c) 1°C (d) 0°C

310. The general depth of abyssal plains varies between:
(a) 1000 – 6000 metres
(b) 2000 – 6000 metres
(c) 3000 – 6000 metres
(d) 4000 – 6000 metres

311. Match List-I with List-II and select the correct answer from the codes given below:

List-I (Ocean Deeps)	*List-II (Location)*
A. Challenger	1. South Pacific
B. Aldrich	2. North Atlantic
C. Romanche	3. North Pacific
D. Nares	4. South Atlantic

Codes:

	A	B	C	D
(a)	3	1	4	2
(b)	4	3	2	1
(c)	1	2	3	4
(d)	2	4	1	3

312. Tropical Evergreen Forests are found in the areas of rainfall ranging between:
(a) less than 100 cms
(b) 100–200 cms
(c) 200–300 cms
(d) more than 300 cms

313. India has how many major bio-geographic regions?
(a) 7 (b) 8
(c) 9 (d) 10

314. Which one of the following countries is devoid of Glossopteris flora?
(a) India (b) Australia
(c) Norway (d) South Africa

315. Given below are two statements, one labelled as Assertion (A) and other labelled as Reason (R). Select your answer from the codes given below:

Assertion (A) : In the altitudinal range between 3400 metre and 4500 metre in the Himalayas Alpine forest is found.

Reason (R) : Alpine forest like no human interference.

Codes:
(a) Both (A) and (R) are true and (R) is the correct explanation of (A).
(b) Both (A) and (R) are true, but (R) is not the correct explanation of (A).
(c) (A) is true, but (R) is false.
(d) (A) is false, but (R) is true.

316. In describing the process of spatial interaction, geographers are most concerned with:
(a) Density and Dispersion
(b) Diffusion and Pattern
(c) Accessibility and Connectivity
(d) Pedestrian Cities

317. Who among the following formalised the concept that there exists relationship between the spatial organization and national development?
(a) Luten (b) Dickens
(c) Kuklinski (d) Friedman

318. The concept of 'paradigm' was propounded by:
(a) Peet (b) Haggett
(c) Kant (d) Kuhn

319. Who defined Geography as human ecology?
(a) Schaefer (b) Barrows
(c) Hartshorne (d) Ellen Semple

320. The approach that some geographical facts according to Ritter, cannot be explained scientifically, is termed as:
(a) Locational (b) Ecological
(c) Teleological (d) Regional

321. How much of the liquid precipitation is equivalent to ten inches of snowfall at deep/near freezing temperature?
(a) About 3 inches
(b) About 2 inches
(c) About 1 inch
(d) At times about one inch and at times about two inches

322. Which one of the following letters represent the total number of settlements of a certain order served by a central place of the next higher order?
(a) K (b) J
(c) L (d) F

323. Who developed the theory of demographic transition?
(a) Zelinskey (b) Whittlesey
(c) Warren Thompson (d) Ravenstein

324. Match List-I with List-II and select the correct answer from the codes given below:

List-I *(General Terms)*	*List-II* *(Definitions)*
A. Crude birth rate	1. Births over deaths per thousand of population
B. General fertility rate	2. Number of deaths per thousand of population
C. Natural increase of population	3. Ratio between number of births and number of females in productive age
D. Death rate	4. Ratio between the number of births and total population

Codes:

	A	B	C	D
(a)	4	3	1	2
(b)	1	2	3	4
(c)	3	4	2	1
(d)	2	1	4	3

325. The rule "size of population of *n*th ranking town in a region will be 1/*n*th of the largest city in terms of population" was given by:
(a) M. Jafferson
(b) J. Gattman
(c) G.K. Ziph
(d) C.D. Harris and E.L. Ullman

326. When 0-14 and 15-44 age groups population of a country is almost identical, the growth of population would be called:
(a) Rapid growth (b) Slow growth
(c) Zero growth (d) Negative growth

327. Who modified the crop-combination method propounded by J.C. Weaver?
(a) S.M. Rafiullah (b) Jasbir Singh
(c) Doi (d) S.S. Bhatia

328. Which among the following countries has the world's largest reserves of Uranium?
(a) Australia (b) Chile
(c) Zaire (d) Nigeria

329. Which one of the following deserts is famous for the deposits of Nitrates?
(a) Sahara (b) Gobi
(c) Kalahari (d) Atacama

330. Who among the following is credited with incorporation of concept of geographical space in the Growth Pole Theory?
(a) Myrdal (b) Haggerstand
(c) Boudeville (d) Friedman

331. What are the three basic aspects for spatial interaction as described in Edward Ullman's model?
(a) Human behaviour, Transferability, Convenience
(b) Surplus-deficit relationship, Community specific relationship, Complementarity
(c) Complementarity, Intervening opportunity, Transferability
(d) Residential neighbourhood, Complementary, Convenience

332. The concept of Cultural landscape was promoted by:
(a) Ratzel (b) Carl Sauer
(c) Wilber Zelinsky (d) Aune Bultimer

333. Which one of the followings is the largest entity in areal location?

(a) Cultural Region (b) Cultural Landscape
(c) Cultural Realm (d) Cultural Point

334. Match List-I with List-II and select the correct answer from the codes given below:

List-I (Scholar)	List-II (Definition)
A. O.H.K. Spate	1. Role of relief features in the horizontal expansion and segregation of cultures.
B. Terre and Peterson	2. Late stone age must be associated with people much like the modern tribal groups in more remote regions.
C. Richards and Subbarao	3. Values of the mountain wall are determined by as much as what lies beyond as by its own topography.
D. Allchin	4. Direct relationship between the climatic changes and the rise of early human cultures.

Codes:

	A	B	C	D
(a)	3	4	1	2
(b)	3	2	1	4
(c)	2	4	3	1
(d)	4	1	3	2

335. Match List-I with List-II and select the correct answer using the codes given below:

List-I (Macro Economic regions by Bhatt)	List-II (Group of States)
A. Southern	1. Maharashtra and Gujarat
B. North-Central	2. Bihar, Odisha, West Bengal and Assam
C. Eastern	3. Mysore, Tamil Nadu and Andhra Pradesh
D. Western	4. Uttar Pradesh and Madhya Pradesh

Codes:

	A	B	C	D
(a)	2	4	3	1
(b)	3	2	4	1
(c)	4	3	1	2
(d)	3	4	2	1

336. Which one of the following regions separates the Great Plains of North India from the plateaus and coastal plains of the Deccan?
(a) Central Highlands (b) Western Himalayas
(c) Eastern Himalayas (d) Western Arid Plains

337. For which one of the following regions, the flow analysis technique is used for delineation of regions?
(a) Political (b) Formal
(c) Functional (d) Physiographic

338. Which one of the following authors used 1961 Census of India date to group the seven industrial categories of workers (excluding the first two categories representing the agricultural sector) into the functional types of manufacturing town, trade and transport town and service towns?
(a) Amrit Lal (b) Qazi Ahmed
(c) Ashok Mitra (d) S.M. Rafiullah

339. Who wrote the book 'Elements of Regional Economics'?
(a) Harvey S. Perloff
(b) Jean Forbes
(c) Anotoni Kuklinski
(d) Harry W. Richardson

340. Which one of the following authors presented model that formed the basis of the planning strategy in the second plan in India?
(a) Harrod (b) Mahalanobis
(c) Domer (d) Dandeker

341. The Planning Commission of India was set up in which year?
(a) 1950 (b) 1952
(c) 1960 (d) 1965

342. Which one of the following regions has been classified as the 'Western Dry Region' by the Planning Commission?
(a) North Bihar Dry Region
(b) Rajasthan Dry Region
(c) NEFA Region
(d) West Bengal Duars

343. Whose portrayals epitomized the relationship of political Geography to foreign policy?
(a) Adolf Hitler (b) Winston Churchill
(c) Karl Haushofer (d) Isaiah Bowman

344. Given below are two statements, one labelled as Assertion (A) and other labelled as Reason (R). Select your answer from the codes given below:

Assertion (A) : The Tarai region represents a marsh like landscape.

Reason (R) : The Tarai region is a zone of seepage where the fine sand, silt and clay are deposited by the emerging streams.

Codes:

(a) Both (A) and (R) are true and (R) is the correct explanation of (A).
(b) Both (A) and (R) are true, but (R) is not the correct explanation of (A).
(c) (A) is true, but (R) is false.
(d) (A) is false, but (R) is true.

345. Which one of the following statements is correct?

(a) One Himalayas were formed due to faulting of the earth's crust.
(b) Himalayas are the oldest mountains.
(c) Himalayas belong to the Caledonian mountain system.
(d) Himalayas have risen from the Tethys Sea when the sea got compressed.

346. Cumulative frequency distribution is shown by:

(a) Histogram (b) Frequency Curve
(c) Pie diagram (d) Ogive

347. In linear regression equation, Y = a + bX, if mean of X and Y series are 23 and 94.5 respectively and slope gradient is 1.5, then what is the value of intercept, a, in the distribution of (X, Y) series?

(a) 50 (b) 55
(c) 60 (d) 65

348. Given below are two statements, one labelled as Assertion (A) and other labelled as Reason (R). Select your answer from the codes given below:

Assertion (A) : Maps that are usually referring various attributes' information are called Complex Thematic Maps.

Reason (R) : Complex Thematic Maps are used to show locations of earth's different features and activities.

Codes:

(a) Both (A) and (R) are true and (R) is the correct explanation of (A).
(b) Both (A) and (R) are true, but (R) is not the correct explanation of (A).
(c) (A) is true, but (R) is false.
(d) (A) is false, but (R) is true.

349. Match List-I with List-II and selected the correct answer from the codes given below:

List-I (Values of R_n Statistics)	***List-II (Pattern of Distribution)***
A. < 0.5	1. Perfect uniform
B. 0.75 – 1.25	2. Tending to uniform
C. 1.75 – 2.00	3. Tending to random
D. 2.15	4. Tending to cluster

Codes:

	A	B	C	D
(a)	2	1	4	3
(b)	1	2	3	4
(c)	4	3	2	1
(d)	3	4	1	2

350. Given below are two statements, one labelled as Assertion (A) and other labelled as Reason (R). Select your answer from the codes given below:

Assertion (A) : Remote sensing is defined as the science and art of acquiring data about earth's objects from a distance without physical contact.

Reason (R) : The collection of data is only conducted by means of remote sensors installed in aircraft and satellite.

Codes:

(a) Both (A) and (R) are true and (R) is the correct explanation of (A).
(b) Both (A) and (R) are true, but (R) is not the correct explanation of (A).
(c) (A) is true, but (R) is false.
(d) (A) is false, but (R) is true.

351. Ria is an example of:

(a) Neutral shore
(b) Compound shore
(c) Emerged upland shore
(d) Submerged upland shore

352. The Indian plateau owes its existence due to:
(a) compressional forces
(b) tensional forces
(c) emergence
(d) subsidence

353. The comprehensive theory of geosyncline was put forward by:
(a) Hall and Dana (b) E. Haug
(c) J.A. Steers (d) J.W. Evans

354. Match List-I with List-II and select the correct answer from the codes given below:

List-I (Shape and Alignment of Dunes)	***List-II (Specific names of Dunes)***
A. Longitudinal	1. Reversing
B. Transverse	2. Coastal
C. Parabolic	3. Seif
D. Complex	4. Barchan

Codes:

	A	B	C	D
(a)	3	4	2	1
(b)	1	2	3	4
(c)	2	1	4	3
(d)	4	3	1	2

355. Match List-I with List-II and select the correct answer from the codes given below:

List-I (Theories of Cavern formation)	***List-II (Scholars)***
A. Two cycle theory	1. Swinnerton
B. Water table theory	2. Gardner
C. Static water zone theory	3. Marott
D. Invasion theory	4. Davis

Codes:

	A	B	C	D
(a)	3	2	1	4
(b)	4	1	2	3
(c)	2	3	1	4
(d)	4	2	3	1

356. Lateral planation theory of pediment formation was proposed by:
(a) McGee (b) Gilbert
(c) Lawson (d) Davis

357. Given below are two statements, one labelled as Assertion (A) and the other labelled as Reason (R). Select your answer from the codes given below:

Assertion (A): Hawaii Island is a region of volcanic activity.

Reason (R) : Convergent plate margins are sites of volcanic eruptions.

Codes:
(a) Both (A) and (R) are correct and (R) is the correct explanation of (A).
(b) Both (A) and (R) are correct, but (R) is not the correct explanation of (A).
(c) (A) is correct, but (R) is false.
(d) (A) is false, but (R) is correct.

358. Which one of the following descriptions is appropriate for the term 'barotropic'?
(a) Isobars and isotherms are parallel.
(b) Isobars and isotherms are not parallel.
(c) Isobars and isohalines are parallel.
(d) Isobars and isohalines are not parallel.

359. Match List-I with List-II and select the correct answer from the codes given below:

List-I (Surface condition)	***List-II (Precipitation Efficiency (P-E) index)***
A. Forest	1. > 127
B. Desert	2. < 16
C. Rain forest	3. 32 – 63
D. Grasslands	4. 64 – 127

Codes:

	A	B	C	D
(a)	3	1	2	4
(b)	3	1	4	2
(c)	4	2	3	1
(d)	4	2	1	3

360. Match List-I with List-II and select the correct answer from the codes given below:

List-I (Component)	***List-II (Volume % in dry air)***
A. Oxygen	1. 0.03
B. Argon	2. 78.08
C. Carbon-dioxide	3. 0.93
D. Nitrogen	4. 20.94

Codes:

	A	B	C	D
(a)	4	2	3	1
(b)	4	3	1	2
(c)	3	4	2	1
(d)	4	3	2	1

361. Given below are two statements, one labelled as Assertion (A) and the other labelled as Reason (R). Select your answer from the codes given below:

Assertion (A) : Tropical climates are of special geographical interest.

Reason (R) : Over 75% of the World's population inhabits between latitudes 30° N and 30° S.

Codes:

(a) Both (A) and (R) are true and (R) is the correct explanation of (A).
(b) Both (A) and (R) are true, but (R) is not the correct explanation of (A).
(c) (A) is true, but (R) is false.
(d) (A) is false, but (R) is true.

362. In Koppen's classification of climate the symbol Aw refers to:
(a) Monsoon climate
(b) Tropical rainforest climate
(c) Steppe climate
(d) Tropical savanna climate

363. Which one of the following is the main energy source for the formation of hurricanes?
(a) Geothermal energy of the Earth
(b) Latent heat derived from condensed water vapour
(c) Large scale fossil fuel burning
(d) Formation of Ozone (O_3) hole

364. Which one of the followings is the correct average air mass density at the surface of the Earth?
(a) 0.9 kg m^{-3} (b) 1.2 kg m^{-3}
(c) 1.5 kg m^{-3} (d) 0.7 kg m^{-3}

365. In which one of the following atmospheric layers the temperature decreases with height at an average rate of about 0.6°C per 100 m?
(a) Troposphere (b) Stratosphere
(c) Thermosphere (d) Ionosphere

366. Match List-I with List-II and select the correct answer from the codes given below:

List-I (Nature of the change)	*List-II (Possible anthropogenic causes)*
A. Desertification in the semi-arid area	1. Effect of groynes up the coast
B. Gully development in a valley bottom	2. Overgrazing
C. Increasing coast erosion	3. Runoff from a new road
D. Greater river-flood intensity	4. Urbanisation

Codes:

	A	B	C	D
(a)	2	3	4	1
(b)	2	3	1	4
(c)	3	2	1	4
(d)	4	3	2	1

367. Which one of the following was first to put forward the concept of 'life form' among plants in 1934?
(a) A.S. Moffat (b) R.H. Whittaker
(c) Christen Raunkiaer (d) E.O. Box

368. Match List-I with List-II and select the correct answer from the codes given below:

List-I (Elements)	*List-II (Density in gm/cm³)*
A. Sea water	1. 2.4
B. Oceanic crust	2. 1.03
C. Continental crust	3. 2.8
D. Continental margin	4. 2.9

Codes:

	A	B	C	D
(a)	4	2	1	3
(b)	2	4	1	3
(c)	2	4	3	1
(d)	3	4	2	1

369. Match List-I with List-II and select the correct answer from the codes given below:

List-I (Sea configuration)	*List-II (Deposits)*
A. Sea bottom	1. Hadalpelagic
B. Surface layer of sea water	2. Pelagic province
C. Deep-sea trenches	3. Benthic province
D. Sea water column	4. Epipelagic zone

Codes:

	A	B	C	D
(a)	3	4	2	1
(b)	3	4	1	2
(c)	4	3	2	1
(d)	1	4	2	3

370. Which one of the following is the correct average slope angle of continental slope?
(a) 2° (b) 4°
(c) 6° (d) 8°

ANSWERS

1. (b)	2. (c)	3. (c)	4. (a)	5. (a)	6. (b)	7. (c)	8. (b)	9. (c)	10. (b)
11. (c)	12. (a)	13. (c)	14. (c)	15. (b)	16. (a)	17. (b)	18. (d)	19. (c)	20. (c)
21. (a)	22. (b)	23. (c)	24. (b)	25. (a)	26. (b)	27. (d)	28. (b)	29. (b)	30. (a)
31. (b)	32. (a)	33. (c)	34. (a)	35. (a)	36. (a)	37. (b)	38. (d)	39. (a)	40. (d)
41. (d)	42. (c)	43. (b)	44. (a)	45. (b)	46. (c)	47. (c)	48. (a)	49. (c)	50. (b)
51. (a)	52. (b)	53. (a)	54. (d)	55. (c)	56. (b)	57. (d)	58. (a)	59. (c)	60. (c)
61. (b)	62. (c)	63. (a)	64. (b)	65. (d)	66. (b)	67. (b)	68. (d)	69. (b)	70. (d)
71. (a)	72. (b)	73. (c)	74. (a)	75. (d)	76. (d)	77. (a)	78. (a)	79. (b)	80. (a)
81. (a)	82. (b)	83. (c)	84. (c)	85. (c)	86. (c)	87. (a)	88. (d)	89. (d)	90. (c)
91. (a)	92. (d)	93. (b)	94. (b)	95. (b)	96. (a)	97. (b)	98. (c)	99. (c)	100. (b)
101. (d)	102. (a)	103. (b)	104. (a)	105. (d)	106. (c)	107. (b)	108. (b)	109. (d)	110. (c)
111. (d)	112. (c)	113. (b)	114. (a)	115. (c)	116. (a)	117. (b)	118. (b)	119. (b)	120. (a)
121. (b)	122. (d)	123. (b)	124. (d)	125. (b)	126. (d)	127. (b)	128. (a)	129. (a)	130. (b)
131. (c)	132. (c)	133. (a)	134. (c)	135. (c)	136. (b)	137. (a)	138. (c)	139. (c)	140. (c)
141. (d)	142. (c)	143. (b)	144. (b)	145. (b)	146. (c)	147. (a)	148. (b)	149. (d)	150. (c)
151. (c)	152. (d)	153. (b)	154. (c)	155. (a)	156. (a)	157. (a)	158. (b)	159. (d)	160. (c)
161. (d)	162. (a)	163. (b)	164. (a)	165. (b)	166. (b)	167. (b)	168. (c)	169. (d)	170. (b)
171. (c)	172. (b)	173. (c)	174. (a)	175. (b)	176. (b)	177. (c)	178. (d)	179. (c)	180. (a)
181. (d)	182. (c)	183. (b)	184. (c)	185. (c)	186. (b)	187. (d)	188. (b)	189. (b)	190. (a)
191. (b)	192. (a)	193. (d)	194. (d)	195. (d)	196. (b)	197. (a)	198. (c)	199. (a)	200. (d)
201. (d)	202. (a)	203. (b)	204. (c)	205. (d)	206. (c)	207. (b)	208. (a)	209. (a)	210. (b)
211. (b)	212. (b)	213. (b)	214. (a)	215. (c)	216. (c)	217. (c)	218. (c)	219. (d)	220. (c)
221. (d)	222. (a)	223. (b)	224. (b)	225. (d)	226. (c)	227. (b)	228. (a)	229. (b)	230. (c)
231. (d)	232. (d)	233. (b)	234. (d)	235. (c)	236. (b)	237. (b)	238. (a)	239. (d)	240. (a)
241. (a)	242. (d)	243. (c)	244. (b)	245. (a)	246. (d)	247. (a)	248. (a)	249. (c)	250. (a)
251. (d)	252. (b)	253. (b)	254. (c)	255. (a)	256. (d)	257. (c)	258. (a)	259. (c)	260. (a)
261. (c)	262. (b)	263. (b)	264. (d)	265. (d)	266. (d)	267. (c)	268. (d)	269. (d)	270. (d)
271. (d)	272. (d)	273. (a)	274. (b)	275. (a)	276. (b)	277. (b)	278. (c)	279. (c)	280. (c)
281. (c)	282. (a)	283. (d)	284. (c)	285. (a)	286. (d)	287. (b)	288. (c)	289. (b)	290. (d)
291. (c)	292. (d)	293. (c)	294. (d)	295. (d)	296. (c)	297. (d)	298. (c)	299. (d)	300. (d)
301. (c)	302. (b)	303. (d)	304. (b)	305. (d)	306. (c)	307. (a)	308. (d)	309. (c)	310. (c)
311. (a)	312. (b)	313. (d)	314. (c)	315. (c)	316. (c)	317. (d)	318. (d)	319. (b)	320. (c)
321. (c)	322. (a)	323. (c)	324. (a)	325. (c)	326. (c)	327. (c)	328. (a)	329. (d)	330. (c)
331. (c)	332. (b)	333. (c)	334. (d)	335. (d)	336. (a)	337. (c)	338. (c)	339. (d)	340. (b)
341. (a)	342. (b)	343. (c)	344. (a)	345. (d)	346. (d)	347. (c)	348. (b)	349. (c)	350. (c)
351. (d)	352. (c)	353. (a)	354. (a)	355. (b)	356. (b)	357. (b)	358. (a)	359. (d)	360. (b)
361. (a)	362. (d)	363. (b)	364. (b)	365. (a)	366. (b)	367. (c)	368. (c)	369. (b)	370. (b)